Accounting
in
Business
Decisions

THIRD EDITION

Accounting in Business Decisions

theory, method, and use

HOMER A. BLACK, Ph.D., C.P.A.
Professor and Chairman of Accounting
Florida State University

JOHN E. CHAMPION, Ph.D., C.P.A.
Professor of Accounting
Florida State University

GIBBES U. MILLER, Ph.D., C.P.A.
Associate Professor of Accounting
Florida State University

Prentice-Hall, Inc.
Englewood Cliffs, New Jersey

10   9   8   7   6   5

ISBN: 0-13-001545-8

Library of Congress Catalog Card No.: 78-39389
Printed in the United States of America

Prentice-Hall International, Inc., London
Prentice-Hall of Australia, Pty. Ltd., Sydney
Prentice-Hall of Canada, Ltd., Toronto
Prentice-Hall of India Private Limited, New Delhi
Prentice-Hall of Japan, Inc., Tokyo

Contents

Depreciation of Tangible Assets.   Adjustments for Amortization of
Intangible Assets.   Step. 5: Reflectiong Adjustments on a Work Sheet.
Summary.

Purpose of Chapter.   Income Distributions.   Retained Income
Statement.   Adjustments for Revenue Earned Currently but Collected
Previously.   Adjustments for Costs Expiring Currently but to Be Paid for
Later.   Adjustments for Revenue Earned Currently but to Be Collected
Later.   Summary of Adjustments.   Reflecting Adjustments on a Work
Sheet.   Financial Statement Classification Work Sheet.   Combined
Adjustment and Classification Work Sheet.   Closing the Periodic
Accounts.   Balancing the Accounts Which Are not Closed—
the After-Closing Trial Balance.   Adjustments for Uncollectible Accounts.
Writing off Uncollectible Accounts.   Summary.

Purpose of Chapter.   Financial Accounting Principles and Conventions.
Basic Standards of Financial Reporting.   The Independent Auditor's
Report.   Supplementary Standards of Financial Reporting.
Inclusiveness, or Adequate Disclosure.   Clarity of Presentation.
Timeliness.   Materiality.   Comparability.

INCOME STATEMENT CLASSIFICATION: Bases of Classifying
Revenue.   Major Types of Revenues and Deductions from Revenue.
Bases of Classifying Expenses and Losses.   Classification of Expenses by
Object.   Classification of Expenses by Function.   Classification of
Expenses by Responsibility Center.   Limitations of Expense Classification.
Reporting the Results of Operations.   Extraordinary Items.   Prior Period
Adjustments.   Outline of the Income Statement.   Earnings per Share.
Illustration of Expanded Income Statement.   Illustration of Expanded
Retained Income Statement.   Summary.

Purpose of Chapter.   Need for Appraising Financial Results—
An Illustrative Case.

BASES AND METHODS OF COMPARISON: The Need for
Comparisons.   Computing Individual Relationships.   The Use of
Averages.   Graphic Comparisons.   Analysis of Composition.   Analysis
of Change.   Comparisons with Predetermined Goals and with Ideals.
Comparisons with Other Businesses.   Limitations of Comparisons.

MEASURES FOR APPRAISING OPERATING RESULTS: Rate
of Income on Stockholders' Equity.   Effect of Income Taxes on Return
on Stockholders' Equity.   Rate of Income on Total Assets.   Components
of Rate of Income as a Basis for Action.   Limitations of the Income
Statement.

TESTS FOR MEASURING LIQUIDITY AND SOLVENCY:
Amount of Net Working Capital. Current Ratio. Quick Ratio.
Composition of Assets and Equities. Turnover Rates of Specific Assets.

MEASURES OF LONG-RANGE SOLVENCY: Importance of
Long-Range Solvency. Earnings Coverage of Debt Service Requirements.
Ratio of Stockholders' Equity to Total Equities. Assumptions and
Limitations of the Financial Position Statement. Summary.

part II PROBLEMS IN MEASURING, PLANNING, AND CONTROLLING ASSETS AND EQUITIES

Purpose of Chapter. Criteria for an Effective Management Information
System. The Business Transaction as a Unit of Information. General
Features of a System of Internal Control. Steps in the Data-Collection
and Summarization Process. Need for Time-Saving Methods. Time
Saving in Preparing Source Documents. Special Journals. Advantages
of Specialized Journals. Special Columns in Journals. Cash Receipts
Journal. Cash Payments Journal. Other Types of Subsidiary Ledgers.
Short-cuts in Journalizing. Ledgerless Bookkeeping.

MACHINE ACCOUNTING: Electromechanical Equipment.
Punched-Card Equipment. Electronic Equipment. Selection of
Accounting Machines. Use of Computers in Improving Management.
Illustration of a Computer Application in Inventory. Summary.

Purpose of Chapter.

MEASURING AND CONTROLLING CASH: Accounting for
Income Versus Accounting for Cash Changes. Importance of Accounting
for Cash. Cash in the Financial Position Statement. Controlling Cash
Receipts. Controlling Cash Disbursements. Petty Cash. Other Cash
Accounts. Reconciling the Bank Accounts. Temporary Investments.

MEASURING AND CONTROLLING RECEIVABLES: General
Nature and Basis of Measurement: Sales Discounts. The Gross Price
Method of Recording Cash Discounts on Sales. The Net Price Method
of Recording Cash Discounts on Sales. Age Distribution of Accounts
Receivable. Estimating Uncollectibles on the Basis of Credit Sales.
Correcting Uncollectible Account Entries. Other Deductions from
Accounts Receivable. Special Problems in Reporting Accounts
Receivable. Internal Control of Accounts Receivable. Accounts
Receivable Turnover Rates. Other Measures of Accounts Receivable
Control. Determining Credit Policy.

MEASURING AND CONTROLLING NOTES RECEIVABLE:
General Basis of Measuring Notes Receivable. Bills of Exchange.

Interest on Notes Receivable.   Accounting for Interest-Bearing Notes
Receivable.   Discount on Notes Receivable.   Accounting for
Non-Interest-Bearing Notes Receivable.   Discounted Notes Receivable.
Endorsement with Recourse.   Internal Control Procedures for Notes.
Summary.

Purpose of Chapter.

MEASURING INVENTORY: Objectives and General Approach for
Financial Reporting.   Components of Inventory Acquisition Cost.
Discounts on Purchases.   The Net Price Method of Accounting for Cash
Discounts on Purchases.   The Gross Price Method of Accounting for Cash
Discounts on Purchases.   Measuring Inventories when Unit Costs
Change.   Basic Illustration for Comparing Inventory Methods.
Specific-Identification Method.   First-In, First-Out (FIFO) Method.
Last-In, First-Out (LIFO) Method.   Weighted-Average Method.
Comparison of the Results of the Cost Methods.   Effect of Inventory
Methods on Decisions.   Recoverable Cost of Inventory.   The
Lower-of-Cost-or-Market Inventory Method.   Special Problems in
Measuring Inventories.   Disclosure of Inventories in Financial Statements.
Methods of Determining Inventory Quantities and Costs.   Purchases
and Related Accounts.

PLANNING AND CONTROLLING INVENTORY: Objective of
Inventory Planning.   Perpetual Inventory Records as a Basis for Control.
Planning Inventories.   Number of Days' Supply in Inventory.   Inventory
Turnover Rate.   Timing Inventory Acquisitions.   Standard Order
Point.   Standard Order Quantity.   Inventory Control when Types of
Items Change.   The Retail Inventory Method.   Internal Control of
Inventories.   The Gross Margin Inventory Method.   Summary.

Purpose of Chapter.

THE ACQUISITION COST OF LONG-LIVED ASSETS: Basic
Components of Acquisition Cost.   Capital and Revenue Expenditures.
Cost Components of Specific Types of Long-Lived Assets.   Interest Cost
on Asset Acquisitions.   Allocations of Cost in Joint Purchase Transactions.

DEPRECIATION: Depreciation Methods and Criteria.   Estimating
Useful Life.   The Straight-Line Method of Depreciation.   Production
Methods of Depreciation.   The Uniform-Rate-on-Declining-Balance
Depreciation Method.   The Sum-Of-the-Year's-Digits Depreciation
Method.   Comparison of Depreciation Methods.   Group Depreciation.
Composite Depreciation.   Depreciation on Historical Versus Current
Costs.

OTHER PROBLEMS OF ACCOUNTING FOR LONG-LIVED
ASSETS: Accounting for Asset Retirements Under Item Depreciation

Method. Accounting for Asset Retirements Under Group Depreciation
Method. Comparison of Item and Group Depreciation. Accounting for
Trades of Plant and Equipment. Accounting for Partial Replacements.
Revision of Depreciation Rates. Depletion of Natural Resources.
Amortization of Goodwill and Other Intangible Assets.

REPORTING AND INTERPRETING LONG-LIVED ASSETS:
General-Purpose Reporting Requirements. Comparison of Depreciation
with Cost. Turnover of Long-Lived Assets. Internal Control.
Summary.

Purpose of Chapter. Characteristics of a Liability. Accrual of
Liabilities. Settlement of Liabilities. Interest on Notes Payable.

ACCOUNTING FOR BONDS PAYABLE: Nature and Statement
Classification. Bond Premiums and Discounts. Recording Authorization
of Bonds Payable. Accounting for Periodic Interest Payments.
Accounting for Bonds Issued at a Discount. Accounting for Bonds
Issued at a Premium. Bond Issue Costs. Retirement of Bonds Payable.
Accounting for Serial Bonds. Accounting for Bond Investments.

ACCOUNTING FOR OTHER LIABILITIES: Liability Under
Warranty. Other Deferred Revenues. Liability Under Pension Plan.
Corporate Income Taxes Payable. Influence of Taxation on Accounting
Methods. Matching Income Tax Expense with Business Income.
Reporting Liabilities Under Long-Term Leases. Contingent Liabilities.
Accounting for Payroll Costs and Liabilities.

PLANNING AND CONTROLLING LIABILITIES: General
Purposes of Planning. Budgeting Borrowings and Repayments.
Controlling Payments: The Voucher System. Analysis of Liability
Balances. Summary.

Purpose of Chapter.

ACCOUNTING FOR CORPORATE OWNERS' EQUITY: Capital
Stock and Its Status. Rights of Stockholders. Composition of Corporate
Owners' Equity. Par, No-Par, and Low-Value Stock. Stated or Legal
Capital.

ACCOUNTING FOR PAID-IN CAPITAL: Issuance of Par-Value
Stock. Issuance of No-Par Stock. Presentation on Financial Position
Statement. Accounting for Stock Issue Costs. Accounting for Stock
Subscriptions. Different Classes of Stock. Cumulative Preferred Stock.
Stock Option Plans. Reacquired Capital Stock (Treasury Stock).
Par-Value Method of Accounting for Treasury Stock. Cost Method of
Accounting for Treasury Stock. Other Paid-in Capital Accounts.

ACCOUNTING FOR RETAINED INCOME: Components of
Retained Income. Restrictions of Retained Income. Stock Dividends.

Stock Splitups. Management Planning for Stockholders' Equity. Management Performance as to Stockholders' Equity.

ACCOUNTING FOR PARTNERSHIP OWNERS' EQUITY: The Partnership as an Accounting Entity. The Partnership Agreement. Factors Relating to Partners' Shares of Income. Examples of Partnership Income-Sharing Plans. Entries to Record Partner's Income Shares. Dissolution of Partnerships. Summary.

Purpose of Chapter.

COMBINATION OF BUSINESS ENTITIES: Purchase Versus Pooling of Interests. Accounting for the Purchase of a Business Entity. Accounting for a Pooling of Interests.

COMBINED FINANCIAL STATEMENTS: Preparation of Combined Financial Statements. Inventory Markups Between Divisions.

CONSOLIDATED FINANCIAL STATEMENTS: Criteria for Preparing Consolidated Statements. Reciprocal Elements of Investment and Stockholders' Equity at Acquisition. Consolidation Procedure After Acquisition. Minority Interest in Consolidated Stockholders' Equity. Nonreciprocal Remainder in Investment and Subsidiary Equity Accounts. Other Types of Eliminating Entries. Computing Consolidated Net Income. Consolidated Financial Statements.

ACCOUNTING FOR FOREIGN BRANCHES AND SUBSIDIARIES: Criteria for Combining or Consolidating Accounts of Foreign Entities. Exchange of Currencies. Translating **Foreign** Accounts into Domestic Currency. Special Problems in Translating Accounts.

FINANCIAL REPORTING FOR DIVERSIFIED COMPANIES: Diversified Companies, or Conglomerates. Two Definitions of Accounting Objectives. Should Segment Reporting Be Required? Summary.

Purpose of Chapter. Impact of Changing Price Levels on the Significance of Accounting Measurements. Specific Price Movements Versus General Price Movements. Operating Versus Holding Gains. Illusory Gains. Should Accounts Reflect the Changing Value of the Dollar? Comprehensive General Price-Level Adjustments. Partial Price Adjustments Within the Historical-Cost Framework. Price Adjustments Which Depart from Historical Costs. Acceptability of Using Current Values in the Accounts. Summary.

Purpose of Chapter. Different Objectives of Business Accounting and Income Taxation. Importance of Income Taxes in Business Decisions.

Effect of Taxation on Business Form.   Tax Saving by Means of Long-Term Capital Gains.   Tax Saving in Choice of Financing Methods.

TAX SAVING BY CHOICE OF ACCOUNTING METHODS: Circumstances in Which Tax Postponement is Desirable.   Cash Versus Accrual Basis of Accounting.   Installment Sales Method. Percentage-of-Completion and Completed-Contract Methods.   Inventory Method.   Depreciation Method.   Other Important Choices of Accounting Method.

OTHER DIFFERENCES BETWEEN FINANCIAL AND TAXABLE INCOME: Nontaxable Exchanges.   Gains on Involuntary Conversions. Percentage Depletion.   Loss Carrybacks and Carryforwards.   Summary.

Elements. Degrees of Controllability. Distinction Between Controllable and Variable Expenses. Allocation of Common Financial Elements to Responsibility Centers.

PREPARATION OF THE BUDGET: The Sales Budget. The Planning Budget and the Flexible Budget. Illustration of Flexible Budget.

MEASURING AND REPORTING PERFORMANCE: Content of Budgetary Reports. Illustration of a Planning Budget. Illustration of a Performance Report. Analysis of Variances from Budget. Summary.

Purpose of Chapter.

FUNDS FLOW ANALYSIS: Working Capital and Its Sources. The Flow of Funds. Importance of Measuring Funds Flows. Funds from Operations. Nonoperating Sources and Uses of Funds. Method of Determining Sources and Uses of Net Working Capital. Summarizing Changes in Working Capital Accounts. Summarizing Changes in Noncurrent Accounts. Reconstructing Entries to Explain Net Working Capital Changes. Statement of Changes in Net Working Capital. Alternative Forms and Titles.

PROJECTING FUTURE CASH FLOWS: The Cash Budget. Forecasting Cash Receipts. Forecasting Cash Disbursements. Controlling Cash Balances. Summary.

Purpose of Chapter. Production Costs and Distribution Costs. Basic Elements of Production Cost. Production Cost Centers. Direct and Indirect Production Costs. The Relationship of Production Cost to Income. Reporting Cost of Goods Sold to a Manufacturer. Periodic and Perpetual Inventory Methods. Systems for Assigning Production Costs to Product Units. Illustration of Job Order Cost Accounting Procedure. Limitations of the Job Order Cost System. Accounts Required in a Process Cost Accounting System. Illustration of Process Cost Accounting Procedure. Summary.

Purpose of Chapter. Manufacturing Cost Behavior. Predetermined Manufacturing Overhead Rate. Bases for Allocating Predetermined Overhead to Products. Factory Overhead Variances. Other Causes of Overhead Variances. Disposing of Overhead Variances.

INCOME MEASUREMENT UNDER DIRECT COSTING: Effects of Full Costing Illustrated. Direct Costing Defined. Income Effects of Direct Costing Illustrated. Management Uses of Direct Costing. Summary.

Illustrations

Preface

During the last decade striking changes have occurred in the way in which enterprises are operated, in the information needs of their managers and others who are vitally concerned with enterprise affairs, and in the technology of meeting those needs. The trend toward career managers, educated in the liberal tradition but with an accent on modern professional concepts and methods and an acute awareness of social goals, has accelerated.

The role of accounting, always at the heart of profit and nonprofit enterprises, has become increasingly significant as economic activity has expanded and become more complex. The critical importance of timely and relevant financial information, soundly grounded in practical economics and responsive to the changing needs of society, has made knowledge of the purposes, concepts, and basic methods of modern accounting imperative for the educated person.

In the first edition of *Accounting in Business Decisions: Theory, Method, and Use* we took a leading role in the growing trend toward teaching the underlying concepts and analytical methodology of business administration, as opposed to merely describing current institutional practices. In the dozen years since then accounting knowledge has expanded vastly, while at the same time the pace of change in its content has quickened. One response to these changes, consistent with our objective of offering a sound foundation in accounting for both those who provide accounting information and those who use it, might be to expand the content of our text. We have chosen instead to accentuate more concisely the fundamental concepts which are the foundation of accounting. In keeping with this objective Chapter 1, "Accounting's Role in Allocating and Using Economic Resources," relates the purpose of accounting to the economic activity of society. In the four chapters following we have tried to present a unified, and pedagogically sound, treatment of the basic concepts and methods of accounting which have been developed to meet users' information needs.

This edition of *Accounting in Business Decisions* reflects recent pronouncements of the major professional bodies in accounting, including the American Institute of Certified Public Accountants and the American Accounting Association. We have removed or simplified the discussion of some of the more complex technical topics which, in addition to being subject to a rather high degree of obsolescence, are better suited to an advanced-level course in accounting.

Accounting educators today are placing greater—and, we think, fully deserved—emphasis on sound educational methodology. To this end we have made a serious effort to focus on the educational objectives in the statement of purpose at the beginning of each chapter, and to identify the purpose of each discussion question, problem, and case. We have tried conscientiously to prune unnecessary verbiage from the chapters and needless busywork from the problem material. Our goal is to challenge the student to apply the ideas to which he is exposed in the text, in order to achieve a higher level of understanding.

The Third Edition of *Accounting in Business Decisions* is a major revision. Ideas for change have come partly from the authors' experience in teaching from the Second Edition, partly from professors at other colleges who have used the text, and partly from our faculty colleagues and graduate assistants at Florida State University. We think the Third Edition is a definite improvement over the first two and hope that our users will share this view.

Some of the noteworthy changes in the Third Edition are

1. The relationship of accounting to basic economic objectives is spelled out more clearly.
2. A new and more sophisticated series of illustrative cases is used to point out the need for accounting information and to explain the meaning of basic accounting terms and methodology.
3. Introduction to the fundamental concepts of accounting is spaced over several chapters, as the need arises, and the relationship of the concepts to the objectives of accounting is emphasized.
4. The text and problems incorporate major provisions of recent pronouncements by the Accounting Principles Board.
5. The text discussion is more concise, with the result that the average chapter length has been reduced from 23 pages to 17 pages.
6. Flexibility in the order in which chapters may be assigned has been retained.
7. The rich variety and ample number of questions, problems, and cases has been retained, while the content of the assignment material has been modernized and streamlined.
8. There have been significant changes in the sequence of chapters and the depth of coverage, as detailed in the later Preface section, "Changes in Structure."

The Third Edition retains a great deal of flexibility, both in the sequence in which some chapters may be assigned and in the possibility of omitting particular chapters. The following chapters are complete units within themselves:

Chapter 8, "Financial Statement Analysis"
Chapter 9, "Accounting Information and Control Systems"
Chapter 15, "Accounting for Entities with Multiple Units"
Chapter 16, "Accounting for the Effects of Changing Prices"
Chapter 17, "Planning and Accounting for Income Taxes"

Those who wish to emphasize managerial accounting early in the course may do so by assigning Chapters 1–7, followed by Chapters 18–26.

Because of the number of optional chapters, this text may be used for a course of either one or two terms. It is suitable both for college accounting courses and for management development programs. While its arrangement is flexible, the book is a unified whole and the discussion flows logically from one chapter to the next.

The strength of the problem material has, in our opinion, been enhanced. Most of the discussion questions, problems, and cases are either new or have been substantially revised. In all types of problem material the emphasis has been placed on accomplishing educational objectives with a minimum of unnecessary detail.

CHANGES IN STRUCTURE

In keeping with the objective of developing a tightly knit, teachable text, a number of significant changes have been made in chapter organization and sequence.

Each chapter begins with a concise statement of purpose, including a brief transition from the preceding chapter, and ends with a summary of major points covered.

Chapter 2 of the preceding edition, "Measuring Business Financial Position," has been replaced by two chapters, 2 and 3, "Business Financial Position: Principles of Valuation" and "Business Financial Position: Accounting Procedure." Likewise, former Chapter 3, "Measuring Business Income," has been replaced by new Chapters 4 and 5, "Measuring Business Income: Basic Concepts" and "Measuring Business Income: Accounting Procedure." The first chapter of each pair deals with basic concepts and the second with accounting methodology. The new chapters are shorter and focus more clearly on unified segments of subject matter. The result should be better understanding by the student.

The material on measuring the flow of working capital and cash has been moved from Chapter 5 to Chapter 21, following the chapters on budgeting. The method of analysis has been changed from a work sheet to a simpler T-account approach.

Problems involved in measuring, planning, and controlling assets and equities have been treated more concisely in this edition.

An entire chapter, 16, is devoted to "Accounting for the Effects of Changing Prices."

The material on planning and accounting for income taxes has been moved from Chapter 23 to Chapter 17.

The coverage of the management accounting topics of budgeting, control, and cost accounting has been significantly expanded, comprising seven chapters in the Third Edition as compared with five chapters in the Second.

As a result of the reorganization, discussion of the classification and measurement of income statement and financial position accounts—the traditional topics of financial accounting—has been completed in Chapter 14 of this edition as compared with Chapter 16 of the preceding edition. The three major parts, Accounting Theory and Methodology; Problems in Measuring, Planning, and Controlling Assets and Equities; and Accounting in Management Planning and Control, are of approximately equal length, and the chapters within each part are closely related to each other.

The purpose of the structural changes has been to provide a more logical flow of subject matter and a more tightly knit text.

ACKNOWLEDGMENTS

In an undertaking of this sort it is impossible to give full credit for all contributions. First of all, we should like to acknowledge a profound debt for the intellectual stimulus and encouragement we have received from Professor William A. Paton, of the University of Michigan, and Professors Harold M. Heckman and the late Professor John F. Burke of the University of Georgia.

We are deeply indebted to our colleagues at the Florida State University, as well as to the many professors at other universities and the numberless students who have given constructive suggestions for the improvement of *Accounting in Business Decisions*. We particularly wish to thank the following for their assistance in this revision:

Professors John F. Bussman, Florida Technological University; Charles H. Calhoun, III, University of South Carolina; W. R. Heck, Florida State University; Rudolph S. Lindbeck, Florida State University; Michael W. Lowrance, University of South Carolina; Edward V. McIntyre, Florida State University; William L. Stephens, University of South Florida, and Messrs. Richard T. Harrison, Stephen A. Hafer, William L. Toonk, William Menke, and Thomas Reilly, Florida State University.

We would also like to thank those who provided further comments and criticism: Professors Russell Bowers, University of Wisconsin; W. Neil Gentry, Georgia State University; C. L. Mitchell, The University of British Columbia; and Paul Richards, Northeastern University. Working with Professor Richards were Messrs. Louis Lanzillotti, Warren Chase, Brian Doherty, Joseph Bylinski, Jerry Leabman, David Brigham, and John Condon.

We are particularly indebted to R. Gene Brown who, while an Associate Professor at Stanford University, was a co-author of the Second Edition. Many of Professor Brown's ideas have been carried forward to the Third Edition.

Special thanks go to Beverly Pitts and Sheila Lutz who did a painstaking job of preparing the manuscript and solutions.

We are deeply indebted to the American Accounting Association, the American Institute of Certified Public Accountants, the National Association Accountants, and to many other publishers and companies for their generous permission to quote from their publications and financial reports.

Most important of all has been the support, patience, and understanding of our wives and children.

HOMER A. BLACK
JOHN E. CHAMPION
GIBBES U. MILLER

Accounting in Business Decisions

part I

ACCOUNTING THEORY
AND
METHODOLOGY

chapter 1

Accounting's Role in Allocating and Using Economic Resources

The Need for Accounting in Business Decisions:
An Illustrative Case

Hamilton Hartman had just been given the greatest challenge of his brief career as a business manager. While serving as president of Hartman Mobile Home Sales, Inc., a family business established by his late father, he had seen its annual sales mushroom from less than $500,000 to more than $1 million in just three years. At the same time the firm's *total assets* had almost doubled, rising from $225,000 to $400,000. There seemed to be no end to the spiraling demand for mobile homes. It was a new way of life for a growing multitude of working people, students, and retirees.

The challenge came in the form of an offer from a manufacturer of mobile homes, MacDonald Mobile Home Builders, to sell its entire business to Mr. Hartman and his associates for $1.5 million. The present owner, John Mac-Donald, had retired from active management and wished to dispose of his ownership interest. Existing management and production personnel wished to continue under the new ownership.

The purchase opportunity appealed to Mr. Hartman for several reasons. It would provide a dependable source of supply to fill the ever-increasing demand for mobile homes. It would offer an excellent potential for increasing the *rate of return* earned on the Hartman family's business investment. It would challenge Hamilton Hartman's managerial skill to a greater extent. Moreover, it would probably allow the Hartman company to sell mobile homes at more competitive prices and render better service to the buying public.

The financial statements of MacDonald Home Builders, an unincorporated business, for the past three years showed a steady increase in sales and profits. In the most recent year total assets averaged $2 million and net income was $240,000, a return of 12 per cent on the total resources used in the business.

Mr. Hartman approached Mr. Curtis, the banker who had long served his firm, to discuss ways of financing the purchase. Early in the discussion Mr. Curtis observed that the financial reports of MacDonald Mobile Home Builders had not been *audited*. He pointed out that, although his bank might be willing to lend some of the funds required to purchase the manufacturing business, it would require that MacDonald's statements be audited by a Certified Public Accountant. He also requested that a *projection* be made of the amounts of cash expected to become available each three months to repay any bank loans.

Mr. MacDonald had expressed his willingness to accept a long-term *promissory note* in payment of about one-third of the purchase price. Mr. Hartman discussed with his family the possibility of raising additional cash to finance the purchase, but found that only about $200,000 would be available from this source. It was clear that additional *stock* would have to be sold to outsiders in order to provide most of the remaining funds required. In discussions with business friends to determine their willingness to make such an investment, Mr. Hartman was told that the best way to secure additional stockholder funds was to provide evidence of greater potential profits than businesses subject to similar risks.

Soon thereafter Mr. Hartman conferred with Mr. Rentz, a partner in the CPA firm which had audited the financial statements and prepared the income tax returns of Hartman's company for many years. After making appropriate arrangements with Mr. MacDonald, Mr. Rentz agreed to audit the accounting records of MacDonald Home Builders. He reminded Mr. Hartman, however, that his *audit report* could only state whether or not the MacDonald financial statements presented the results of operations and financial position fairly in terms of *historical values* based on past events. In estimating the *current value* of a business and in determining what price he would be willing to pay for it, a buyer should consider its prospects for *future profits*. Mr. Rentz agreed to make a *special analysis* for Mr. Hartman's private use in estimating the future profitability of the MacDonald business.

As the audit and analytical work proceeded, Mr. Rentz observed that MacDonald did not use a *cost accounting system*. Without accurate knowledge of the unit costs of manufacturing mobile homes, he stated, it was difficult to measure reliably the cost of manufactured inventory and the firm's periodic net profit. Furthermore, lack of information about the unit costs of different models of mobile homes made it quite difficult to forecast future profits.

Mr. Rentz agreed to make the best estimate he could of the costs of manufacturing the various home models. He urged Mr. Hartman, however, to give serious thought to having a cost accounting system installed if he should decide to buy the MacDonald company. Such a cost system would do more than facilitate the measurement of business *income* and *financial position*. It would provide information on the relative profitability of various models so that pricing and production decisions could be made more intelligently. It would also give information as to *variances* of actual manufacturing costs from *predetermined standard costs* based on the efficient use of productive factors, thus helping production management to control costs.

Mr. Hartman outlined his main decision problems related to the MacDonald offer as follows:

(1) Should his firm buy the manufacturing company, and if so, what maximum price could be justified?

(2) How much of the purchase price could be obtained, and on what terms, from the bank, from Mr. MacDonald and other long-term creditors, and from issuing additional shares of capital stock to the Hartman family and the public?

(3) On what time schedule could any borrowed funds reasonably be repaid?

(4) What additional sales outlets should be developed to market the manufacturing plant's output, and how should these outlets be financed?

(5) Which model lines should be emphasized in production and sales and which, if any, should be discontinued?

(6) How should the firm's financial information system be modified to fill management's needs for future *planning*, for *controlling* operating activity as it took place, and for *reporting* the results achieved to management, creditors, stockholders, and other interested parties?

Mr. Hartman's discussions with the CPA, the banker, and other business friends had led him to believe that accounting information would greatly assist him in solving these problems.

Purpose of the Text and of Chapter 1

The Hamilton Hartman decision situation just described is hypothetical, but it does point to some of the types of real problems which accounting can help solve. The situation has been used to set the stage for this book, whose objectives are to convey to the reader a *knowledge of the purposes of accounting*, an appreciation of the *uses to which accounting information may be put*, and a basic understanding of the *theory and methodology underlying the preparation of accounting reports*. In today's economic environment it is imperative that those who can benefit from accounting information understand its *potential uses* as well as its *limitations*, including the assumptions used in choosing from alternative accounting measurements. This book is designed as a basic text both for those who aspire to a career in accounting and for those who need to use accounting information.

The illustrative case introduces a number of technical terms, concepts, and measurement alternatives which will be carefully explained in later parts of the book.

Chapter 1 shows in broad terms how accounting information may be used effectively by *economic entities*, both those that seek a profit and those that do not. It identifies the major needs of the important classes of accounting information users. It describes and compares the economic and accounting concepts of *profit,* and explains two other fundamental concepts of accounting, *assets* and the *accounting entity.*

The Economic Entity

Economics is the study of the most desirable use of scarce resources, or means, to satisfy human wants, or ends. These resources, in the form of capital, labor, and management ability, are utilized by an organizational unit, the *economic entity,* to produce goods and services. On the basis of important differences in their goals, economic entities may be classified as either *business entities* or *nonprofit entities.*

Broadly defined, a *business entity* is an economic organization which produces goods and services for sale through the exchange economy with the hope of earning a reward, called *profit.* Examples of business entities are manufacturers, wholesalers, retailers, transportation companies, and professional firms such as architects and accountants.

Nonprofit entities take several forms. Charitable organizations, financed by gifts, usually provide free services on the basis of need. Governments, financed principally by taxes, provide such services as general government and police protection without regard to the amount of tax assessed on the party benefited. Some government activities, such as street and sidewalk paving, are financed by charging the cost of the service to the benefited property owners.

Accounting can help an economic entity significantly in accomplishing its goals, whether or not it is profit-oriented.

Major Goals of the Business Entity

A business organization is founded because its owners and managers think that there is an existing *demand*—or a potential demand—*for the goods and services* which it can provide. If there is such a demand, and if the business suceeds in satisfying it effectively, the business will prosper and its owners and managers will be rewarded financially.

To satisfy the demand, the owners and managers must obtain *economic resources*—capital, labor, and management ability—and organize them efficiently. They are induced to do this by the expectation of economic reward for their time, energy, and ability; for the use of their property; and for their assumption of business risks. Noneconomic motives, too, such as a desire to serve others, often greatly influence the conduct of business affairs.

The motives of the individuals who control the business are translated into the *objectives of the business,* which are sometimes stated, sometimes implied. Important business aims are to survive, to earn a profit, to grow in absolute terms, and to grow in relation to other firms—to gain a larger share of the market.

The short-run objectives of a business may differ in some degree from its long-range objectives, but the two should be consistent. Enlightened owners and managers realize that the extent to which they accomplish their goals depends on the actions of their customers, employees, suppliers, and public, who are also motivated by self-interest. To achieve its long-run objectives, the business must attract and retain the patronage of customers on the basis of better quality of goods and services, lower prices, or a similar appeal.

Modern businesses are recognizing to an increasing extent their social responsibility, one aspect of which is the importance of their financial health to employees, customers, and the community. Another is the need to control those types of business activity which pollute the natural environment. To survive and prosper for the long term, a business must attract and keep customers, it must remain financially sound and pay a satisfactory reward to its owners and managers, and it must discharge its social responsibilities acceptably.

Economic and Accounting Concepts of Profit

Up to this point the term "profit" has been used as though it has a widely understood and accepted meaning, but actually it is often misunderstood. To some people "profit" has an evil connotation, implying the unfair extortion of funds from the unprotected customer. In reality profit performs two socially useful functions: (1) It *motivates* business firms to produce the goods and services desired by society, and (2) it *regulates* production at the optimal quantity through the operation of the exchange economy's price system.

Economists define a firm's *profit* for a time period as the remainder after subtracting both the contractual and implicit costs of the period from total revenue from goods and services. *Contractual costs* of productive factors are payments that are definitely fixed in amount before the factor's service is received. *Implicit costs* are not set by contract; they are estimates of what the productive factor would earn if it were employed on a contractual basis.[1] *Revenue* is measured by the selling price of the firm's goods and services.

In a competitive economy a firm's payments to its hired factors of production are based on the estimated additional revenue that these factors will produce for the firm. If actual results are better than expected, the business has an *economic profit*. If they are worse than anticipated, an *economic loss* results.

Example 1   A business was financed by issuing $100,000 of its own bonds paying 8 per cent annual interest and by issuing its own common stock for $100,000. What are the related annual economic costs?

There is a yearly *explicit cost* of $8,000 for the contractual interest on the bonds. There is no contractual payment to common stockholders, but there is an *implicit cost* of using the stockholders' capital. It is equal to the estimated cost of obtaining the stockholders' funds for one year on a fixed basis of compensation.

Economic profits and losses arise because there is *uncertainty* as to the outcome of future events. Owners of productive factors can reduce their uncertainty by contracting to receive their compensation in a fixed amount. Alternatively, they may elect to be paid on the basis of actual business results. In the latter case their reward consists of two parts: a *normal return* for the use of the productive factor, plus a *reward (economic profit)* or minus a *penalty (economic loss)* which reflects the results of risk bearing.

---

[1] See pp. 1–7 of *Business Economics: Principles and Cases,* by M. R. Colberg, D. R. Forbush, and G. R. Whitaker (Homewood, Ill.: Richard D. Irwin, Inc., 1964).

The presence of large and sustained economic profits in a given industry tends to attract additional capital into the industry. At the same time that additional goods and services are being supplied, competitive forces tend to reduce the industry's economic profit. On the other hand, the existence of continued economic losses tends to cause capital to flow out of the unprofitable industry into more attractive fields, thus better serving the needs of the economy.

The *accountant* measures the profit, or *income*, of a business by subtracting only the *explicit costs* of hired factors from total revenue. He does not deduct implicit costs in computing profit. Thus, *accounting income* is influenced by the extent to which productive factors are compensated on a *contractual basis*.[2]

Example 2

The owner-manager of the firm in Example 1 contracted to work for the firm at an annual salary of $12,000 although he could have earned $20,000 in a comparable position for another firm. He wished to leave funds in the business to help finance its growth. It is assumed for simplicity that the $100,000 of funds obtained from stockholders could have been hired at a contractual rate of 8 per cent. In a given year total firm revenues were $100,000 and other explicit costs were $60,000. What were the economic and accounting profits for the year?

Solution

Economic Profit		*Accounting Profit*	
Revenue.........................$100,000		Revenue.........................$100,000	
Deduct explicit and		Deduct explicit	
implicit costs:		costs:	
Management salary.........	$20,000	Management salary.........	$12,000
Bond interest.................	8,000	Bond interest.................	8,000
Implicit cost of			
stockholder funds.........	8,000		
Other.........................	60,000	Other.........................	60,000
Total.....................	$96,000	Total.....................	$80,000
Economic profit..............	$ 4,000	Accounting profit..............	$20,000

Note: The effect of income taxes is ignored in both solutions.

Generally the accounting profit for a given firm is higher than the economic profit because a significant part of the implicit cost of productive factors is not included in the accounting profit computation. Why does the accountant ignore these costs? The reasons are explained partly in the later section of this chapter, "Business Income: The Accounting Concept of Profit," and more fully in later chapters.

Accounting Definition and Objectives

Accounting is a process of *measurement* and *communication* in which the major responsibilities are *recording, analyzing, reporting,* and *interpreting* financial information of an economic entity. *Financial information* refers to the effects of economic transactions and events which can be expressed meaningfully in terms of money.

Accounting is not an end in itself; it is a useful tool. It is a language for

---

[2] There are other important differences between the economic and accounting concepts of profit, but they are beyond the scope of this text.

DECISION MAKING

communicating the financial facts about an economic entity or activity to those who have an interest in *analyzing, interpreting,* and *using* those facts. The objectives of accounting are to provide information for the following purposes:

(1) For making decisions concerning the alternative uses of limited resources. This involves identifying important decision problems and determining goals.

(2) For planning and controlling the effectiveness with which an economic entity's human and material resources are used.

(3) For assisting in, and reporting on, the custodianship of economic resources.

(4) For aiding the accomplishment of social goals through government and other social organizations.[3]

To be most useful accounting information should be adapted to the particular needs of its users. The various groups which rely on accounting information about an organization have different decisions to make; consequently, their information needs often differ. Accounting's effectiveness depends on how well it identifies and communicates the information relevant to important users' requirements.

The Accounting Entity and Legal Forms of Business Organization

The accountant must be careful to report only those economic events which pertain to the *particular entity* if the various parties who have a stake in the entity's affairs are to have clear, meaningful, and reliable information about its finances. Regardless of the *legal form* of the economic entity, accounting treats the entity as an organization apart from its owners, beneficiaries, managers, employees, customers, creditors, and other interested parties. Accounting reflects all the financial dealings of the entity from the *point of view of the organization.*

Nevertheless, the *legal form* in which a business is organized does have an important bearing on the rights of owners, creditors, and others in its resources. Businesses may be classified according to their legal form of organization as *single proprietorships, partnerships,* or *corporations.*

A *single proprietorship* is a business owned by one individual, and not incorporated. The law does not recognize a business conducted as a *single proprietorship* as having a status separate from the personal financial affairs of the owner. A creditor of the *business* may look to the owner's *personal resources* as well as to those committed to the business in seeking satisfaction of his claims. Likewise, a personal creditor of the owner may depend on the resources of the business as well as on the proprietor's personal resources. Unless the owner has special agreements to the contrary with some of his creditors, such as banks, he may withdraw business resources for his personal use as he wishes.

A *partnership* is an association of two or more persons as co-owners to carry on a business for profit. The law does not recognize the partnership as a being apart from its owners; however, the legal relationships between the partners and the partnership creditors, and between one partner and his copartner(s), are

---

[3] Adapted from American Accounting Association, *A Statement of Basic Accounting Theory* (Evanston, Illinois: The Association, 1966), p. 4.

quite complex. The rights and obligations of each partner are spelled out in the partnership agreement and in the law of the state in which the partnership is organized.

Creditors of a partnership, like those of a single proprietorship, are not limited to the resources of the business in having their claims paid. If the business does not have sufficient resources to pay its debts, the personal assets of any *general* partner may be used for this purpose. In *limited* partnerships the personal assets of a limited partner may not be seized by partnership creditors. The loss of such a partner is limited by contract to his investment in the business. All partnerships, however, must have at least one *general* partner who has unlimited liability for the payment of partnership debts.

In the eyes of the law a *corporation* is a separate legal person that can make contracts, own property, owe debts, sue, and be sued. The resources invested in the business belong to the corporation, and the debts it incurs are debts of the corporation as a separate person. Creditors can collect their claims only from the resources of the corporation; when the corporation's assets are exhausted, the creditors have no rights in the personal resources of the corporation owners. As a result of this *limited liability* feature an owner of stock in a corporation can lose only the sum he has invested in the stock. A single proprietor or a general partner has *unlimited liability;* he can lose all his investment in the business and all his personal resources as well.

In exchange for this privilege of limited liability given to corporation stockholders, the law imposes a corresponding responsibility. The *stated capital* of the corporation, a cushion of protection on which creditors rely, may not be voluntarily reduced by stockholder withdrawals of resources.

The boundaries of a *business accounting entity* are governed partly by legal requirements (as in the case of a corporation), but mainly by usefulness to owners, managers, and other important users. It is often useful to treat major activities or organizational subdivisions of a business as separate accounting entities in order to facilitate management control. These smaller entities may then be combined in accounting reports to give a financial picture of the enterprise as a whole. A business should have accounting records separate from those of its owners, even if it is unincorporated and thus has no separate legal being.

The lines of *nonprofit accounting entities* are determined partly by usefulness, but perhaps to a greater extent by legal requirements. If the voters of a community authorize a bond issue to finance a public project, care must be exercised to see that these funds are used strictly as the law anthorizes. A separate accounting entity, called a *bond fund*, is used to account for the receipt and use of the bond proceeds. Another accounting entity, called a *stores fund*, might be established to account for a central supply storeroom which serves all parts of the community government.

The Accounting Concept of Assets

An *economic resource* is a productive factor, and as such it is capable of benefiting the entity in its future economic activities. *Assets*, an accounting term, refers to those economic resources of the entity which can be measured objectively in terms of money.

Example 3   The News Publishing Company bought a printing press for $12,000 cash. The *cash was* an asset of the company because it could benefit future operations by being used to acquire any good or service or to pay any debt. The printing press *is* an asset, *equipment*, because it is expected to benefit future operations by assisting in the publication of newspapers for sale.

Accounting is concerned with providing information about the *forms* which these assets take (such as cash, accounts receivable, merchandise inventory, equipment, and buildings); their *valuations in terms of money;* the *sources* from which the business has acquired them (creditors and owners of the business); and the *changes* in their forms and valuations (for example, merchandise which had cost $40 was sold for $60 cash).

As to form, assets may be classified into the broad groups of *monetary assets* and *nonmonetary assets*. The former group consists of money and claims to specific amounts of money. *Nonmonetary assets* include physical resources, contracts owned for services to be received, and all other resources except money and money claims.

Not all the important economic resources, events, and relationships of an economic entity can be expressed objectively in money terms. Those that cannot may be called *qualitative* factors, to distinguish them from the *quantitative*, or measurable, data reflected in accounting.

Example 4   Employee morale is a very important element in entity activities, but accounting cannot objectively measure in money terms the extent to which morale is good or poor.

Other qualitative factors which must be weighed in making business decisions are relations with customers, the government, and the general public; convenience of the business surroundings; reputation of the business; and many more. Sometimes qualitative considerations are more important than quantitative factors in business decisions.

Business Income: The Accounting Concept of Profit

Earlier a distinction was made between economic profit as the reward for risk taking and accounting profit as the reward of the factors of production which are not hired on a contractual basis. A business is an economic organization whose purpose is to acquire factors of production—*wealth*—and to combine and utilize them in such a way that wealth is increased. The change—increase or decrease—in wealth which results from such business activity is called *income*.

A major concern of accounting is to measure the *income* which results from business activity over time periods of specified length, usually a year. When the accountant seeks to measure periodic income in a particular business, he is soon confronted with difficulties. How does he know that a change in wealth has occurred, or exactly when it takes place, or how large the change is?

The following is an operational definition of *business income*. It takes into account some of the problems which the accountant faces in measuring business income in specific situations.

The income of a business is the change in its net assets which results from (a) the excess or deficiency of revenue over related expired costs and (b) other gains or losses to the business entity from sales, exchanges, involuntary conversions or obsolescence of its assets.[4]

Key words in this definition require further explanation.

Net assets refers to the amount by which total assets exceed total liabilities; thus, *Assets − Liabilities = Net Assets. Liabilities* are the claims of creditors against the entity.

If the net assets of a business increase as a result of its *operations*, the business has earned a *net income.* If they decrease, it has incurred a *net loss. Profit* and *earnings* are widely used synonyms for income.

A business expects to exchange its goods and services for other assets, mostly money and claims to money. The *inflow* of such assets to the business in exchange for its goods and services is called *revenue.* Revenue is *recognized* by accounting when the inflow is assured and when its amount can be measured dependably.

Example 5 A jewelry store sold a watch to a customer for $100 cash. It also repaired a ring on credit for another customer for $10. The store has *sales revenue* of $100 and *service revenue* of $10.

Expired costs, which are deducted in computing income, are of two types: *expenses* and *losses.* The *outflow* of assets—or more literally, the using up of asset service benefits—in connection with earning business revenue is called *expense.* Asset service potentials which expire without benefit to the business are called *losses.* These asset expirations are called *expired costs* because productive assets are measured initially at their acquisition cost to the business.

Example 6 The watch sold in Example 5 had cost the jeweler $55. The salesman who made the sale received a commission of $10. Both of these items are *expenses.*

Example 7 A thief stole $200 cash from the jewelry store. The theft was not covered by insurance and is treated as a *loss* in computing business income.

A *gain* results when an asset that is not held for sale in the ordinary course of business is sold for more than its unexpired cost. If such an asset is sold for less than its unexpired cost, there is a *loss* on its disposal. *Gains are added* in computing business income; *losses are deducted.*

The term *loss* is used in accounting with several different meanings. As the preceding discussion shows, it refers to two types of deductions which are used in computing business income. If the income of the business as a whole is negative, after deducting expenses and losses from the sum of revenue and gains, the business has incurred a *net loss.*

A basic problem in measuring business income is the need to determine how much of the revenue stream is equal to the asset expirations—expenses and losses—which were incurred in seeking income, and how much represents an increase in the firm's net assets. That is, the revenue stream must be separated

---

[4] Adapted from American Accounting Association, Committee on Accounting Concepts and Standards, *Accounting and Reporting Standards for Corporate Financial Statements, 1957 Revision* (Columbus, Ohio: The Association, 1957), p. 5.

into the part which represents a *recovery of the capital* used up and the part which represents *income,* an *increase of capital.*

Money Measurement

Accounting deals with economic events and relationships which can be expressed objectively *in terms of money.* The effects of such events on a given accounting entity should be reported by means of a common denominator. Ordinarily the most useful common denominator is the monetary unit of the country in which the business is located.

Example 8   It is far more useful to report that a business owns cash of $500, merchandise inventory of $50,000, and land of $14,000 than it would be to report that it owned $500 in money, 10,000 units of various classes of merchandise of different value, and two and one-half acres of land.

Exchange Transactions

In a modern economy most business is conducted by exchanging money and claims to money for factors of production which are used in producing goods and services and then exchanging these goods and services for money and claims to money. Businesses do not *consume* goods and services in the sense that individuals do; they use them in their efforts to increase wealth. Wealth is increased if the goods and services produced by the business entity are sold for more than their cost.

As a rule the factors of production used by a business are acquired in a market exchange; the business output is likewise sold in a market exchange. It is logical, therefore, for the success of the business (its *income*) to be measured as the difference between the market prices of output sold and the market prices of factors purchased. These market prices have an additional advantage of being relatively free from the personal bias of one party, since they are usually agreed upon by arm's-length bargaining between the buyer and the seller.

Major Objectives of Users
of Accounting Information

The major user groups to whom accounting must provide information are owners, management, creditors, governmental agencies, and employees. The nature of the needs of these groups for accounting information is elaborated in the following paragraphs.

(1) The *owners* need periodic reports of the *progress* of the business toward its financial objectives, that is, its *income.* They also are interested in frequent reports of the money valuations of business assets and claims against the business. This information is useful to them both as a check on the past performance of the business entity and as a clue to what may happen in the future. Ownership shares of a business are valuable largely because their holders expect to benefit from future income distributions and from increases in the selling price of the shares.

Potential investors and investors' advisory services examine accounting information for the light it will shed on the desirability of investing in the business. Where the ownership and the management of a business are largely vested in different people, as is often true in large corporations whose stock is widely held by the public, owners may use accounting reports to help check on the faithfulness and effectiveness of their hired managers. Important business performance measures for this purpose are the *amount of income* and the *percentage of income to the total assets invested*.

(2) *Management* relies on accounting to aid in planning and controlling the operations of the business. *Controls* are used to determine whether the performance of the business is in line with its objectives and plans. Accounting controls may also be used to help safeguard the business assets, to check the accuracy of its accounting information, and to promote operating efficiency.

Accounting provides a means of evaluating management's performance in carrying out *individual activities*, as well as in operating the business as a whole. Accountants can establish guideposts, or *standards* of performance, to inform management whether an activity is accomplishing the business objectives. Accounting can be used as a guide to future action by forming the basis for financial *plans*, or *budgets*. Accounting information can also be helpful in choosing a course of action from such alternatives as to whether to make a product or buy it already made; whether, and when, to replace a machine; whether to add a new product to the line; whether to install labor-saving machinery; whether to change a pricing policy; and whether to discontinue a product line or activity of the business.

(3) *Creditors* and prospective creditors, such as bankers, bondholders, and suppliers of goods and services, are also interested in accounting information about a business. They investigate its financial standing before deciding whether to extend credit to it at all, what amount to extend, and under what terms. They are primarily interested in *liquidity*, the ability of the business to convert its property into money on short notice without loss, and *solvency*, its ability to pay its debts. They are also interested in the trend of business income over time in estimating its liquidity and solvency at future dates.

(4) State and federal *governments* are concerned with the accounting of a business in various ways—sometimes as taxing bodies, sometimes as customers on cost-plus contracts, and in other cases as regulatory authorities. Accounting records are essential in computing the liability of a business for federal income taxes. Railroads and public utilities must secure the approval of the appropriate regulatory agency for the rates they charge their customers and must make periodic financial reports to these agencies. Many companies are required to submit comprehensive financial reports to the Securities and Exchange Commission before they can offer their capital stock for sale to the public. Organized stock exchanges require listed companies to present financial reports at prescribed intervals. Information agencies of the federal government collect financial data of individual businesses and summarize them to aid government and businesses in planning. Examples of such information are the censuses of business and the national income statistics compiled by the Department of Commerce.

(5) *Employees* have an important stake in the finances of their company. They seek assurance of steady employment by a financially sound employer, and they frequently participate in company bonus, profit-sharing, and pension

plans. Labor unions, when negotiating for increased compensation, often use accounting cost and profit data in an effort to gauge the employer's ability to pay proposed wage or fringe benefit increases.

Other frequent users of accounting information are *trade associations* of the businesses in a given industry. They develop statistics to permit association members to compare their performance with the average results of other firms. *Credit-reporting agencies* collect and summarize accounting information to assist their clients in deciding to whom to extend credit. *Customers, students, and research workers* may study financial statements in connection with various problems they are investigating.

The extent of public interest in the accounting of an entity varies widely from one situation to another. In the smallest business perhaps only the owner-manager and the Director of Internal Revenue are concerned.

Summary   *Accounting* collects and communicates financial information concerning an economic entity, whether it is a business entity organized for profit or a nonprofit entity.

The economist defines *profit* as the remainder after subtracting both contractual and implicit costs of the period from total revenue. The accountant defines profit—*business income*—as the excess of revenue over *explicit costs* only. Moreover, he includes in his business income measurement only those events and transactions which can be measured objectively in terms of money.

Assets are those economic resources of the entity which can be measured objectively in terms of money. Accounting seeks to provide useful information about assets, asset sources, and income for the following purposes:

(1) Making decisions concerning alternative uses of limited resources.
(2) Planning and controlling the effective use of resources.
(3) Reporting on the custodianship of resources.
(4) Aiding in the accomplishment of social goals.

Major users of accounting information about an entity are the owners, management, creditors, state and federal governments, and employees. The accounting information concerning an entity should be carefully distinguished from the affairs of its owners, whether the entity is organized as a single proprietorship, a partnership, or a corporation. To be useful, accounting information should be tailored to the needs of the most important users.

Discussion Questions and Problems

1-1   A university is a nonprofit entity and a retail music store is a business entity.
a. Explain how their financial objectives differ.
b. In what major ways do you think accounting information could be useful to these two entities?

1-2
a. If you were to establish a business and act as its owner and manager, what would be your principal financial objectives? Your principal nonfinancial objectives?

b. In what way will the interests of your customers, employees, suppliers, and the public affect the way in which you pursue your financial objectives?

1-3   An economist and an accountant have reviewed the operations of a business for a year, and each has computed a different amount of profit. Using profit components and amounts of your own choosing, illustrate specifically how their differences in profit measurement might occur.

1-4   A television repair shop is organized as a corporation.

a. Explain how contractual costs might affect its income and give a specific example.
b. How would implicit costs affect its income? Give an example.

1-5

a. Is a business conducted as a single proprietorship a legal entity? An accounting entity? Explain.
b. Why might the owners of a business prefer to incorporate it?
c. Why might the creditors prefer that the business not be incorporated?

1-6   For the third straight year a salesman for a real estate agency received an award for making more than $1 million of sales. At a dinner in her honor the president of the agency said, "Sally, you are a great asset to us." Would an accountant agree? Why?

1-7   In its warehouse a manufacturing business has stored an old machine which is no longer in use. The machine is still in good running condition, but far superior machines are now on the market. It could be sold as scrap for about $25, but it would cost at least that much to move it away. Is this machine an asset? Explain.

1-8   The records of the Atlas Company disclose the following information:

Balance on deposit in the bank	$ 8,800
Amount owed for property taxes	1,000
Cost of merchandise held for sale	18,000
Amount owed to Javes Company for part of the merchandise referred to above	4,000
Land owned for the purpose of erecting a store building in the future	40,000
Mortgage note owed to the insurance company which lent money to buy the land. The note is to be repaid in five years	28,000

Required   a. List the assets of Atlas.
b. List its liabilities.
c. Compute its net assets.

1-9   For each of the following examples state
a. Whether there would be an increase, decrease, or no change in net assets.
b. Whether there would be a revenue, an expense, a gain, a loss, or no change in income.
   (1) Equipment shown on the accounting records at $10,000 is sold for $12,000 cash.
   (2) Merchandise is bought on credit for $13,000.
   (3) Merchandise which cost the company $3,000 is sold to customers for $4,000 cash.
   (4) A part payment of $6,000 is made for the merchandise bought in (2).
   (5) Merchandise which cost $500 is stolen. There is no insurance.
   (6) Vacant land is bought for investment for $5,000 cash.
   (7) The land in (6) is later sold for $4,500 cash.

1-10   The Specialty Shop paid $7,000 for a shipment of merchandise just received from India. The demand for these imports is so great the management of the shop estimates that all can be sold quickly for $20,000. Should revenue be recognized now in the accounting records? What specific factors did you consider in arriving at your answer?

1-11   Suppose that the entire shipment in Question 1-10 was destroyed by fire shortly after it arrived. Only $6,000 is expected to be recovered from insurance. How would this affect the Specialty Shop's income for the year?

1-12   State whether the following items are assets, liabilities, revenues, expenses, or some combination from the point of view of your business:

a. Store building owned by the business.
b. Rent paid on equipment obtained from a rental agency.
c. Merchandise inventory.
d. Note payable to a bank.
e. The cost of merchandise that has been sold during the year.
f. Sums owed for merchandise purchased on credit.
g. Sums due from customers for merchandise sold on credit.
h. Land owned by the business.
i. Sales orders received and not yet filled.
j. An efficient management.
k. Amount of sales for the period.
l. Payment to bank on the loan in item d.
m. Collection from customers on the balance in item g.

1-13   State specifically how each of the following events affects assets, liabilities, revenue, and expense:

a. Merchandise previously bought for $4,000 was returned to the manufacturer and a cash refund was received.
b. Cash of $10,000 was borrowed from the bank.
c. Cash of $5,000 was received for the sale of merchandise which had been bought on credit for $3,000.
d. Merchandise which had been bought on credit for $8,000 was sold to customers on credit for $10,000.
e. One of the customers in event d returned merchandise sold to him for $1,200 (cost to the seller was $800). He had not yet paid his account.
f. The market price of a stock investment held by the company increased to $25,000. The stock had been bought several years ago for $15,000.
g. The bank loan of $10,000 plus interest of $600 was paid before the end of the year.

1-14   During its first year of operations Surefire Corporation reported revenue of $50,000, expense of $35,000, and a loss of $12,000 from damage to its equipment. During the second year revenue was $90,000, expenses were $65,000, and there was a gain of $3,000 from the sale of land held as an investment. Compute the corporation's income for each of the two years.

1-15   A medium-sized toy shop is organized as a corporation. Give an example of a specific decision that might be made by each of the following as a result of accounting information about the toy shop:

a. Owners.
b. Prospective owners.

c. Management.
d. Creditors.
e. The U.S. government.

1-16   For each of the following entities state what groups other than the present owners and management would be interested in its financial reports, and why they would be interested:

a. Gasoline service station.
b. City government.
c. Telephone company.
d. Manufacturing company whose stock is listed on the New York Stock Exchange.
e. A family-owned retail dress shop.

Cases   **1-1   Hartman Mobile Home Sales, Inc. (A).** Review the information presented in the illustrative case at the beginning of Chapter 1.

Required
a. What types of financial information about MacDonald Home Builders does Mr. Hartman need in deciding whether, and under what terms, to buy the business?
b. What alternatives does Mr. Hartman have in selecting the type of legal organization he will use if he buys MacDonald's business?
c. How will the legal form of organization affect the sources by which the purchase of the business may be financed?
d. What choices does Mr. Hartman have with respect to establishing accounting entities if he acquires the business? What major entity or entities would you recommend for accounting purposes? Why?
e. If the MacDonald business is purchased and incorporated, what major groups will be interested in its financial affairs? What types of information will each group be chiefly interested in?

1-2   Kenneth Andre. On June 30, 1973, Kenneth Andre, who was recently awarded a degree in business administration from the state university, received a share of his late father's estate. Included in Kenneth's inheritance was $94,000 in cash and 50 per cent of the outstanding stock of the Superior Furniture Manufacturing Company, a family-owned corporation. Kenneth owned 20 per cent of the outstanding stock previously as a result of a graduation gift, and the remaining 30 per cent is held equally by his mother and sister.

As Kenneth sees it, his alternatives are to sell his shares of the corporation or to continue operating the business. On the advice of the Andre family's attorney Kenneth has engaged you, an independent Certified Public Accountant, to aid him in making his decision.

In your initial inspection of the company's operations and examination of its records, you discover the following facts:

(1) The company occupies two rented buildings, one used for manufacturing operations and the other for a warehouse. The lease agreement, which will expire on September 30, 1973, contains an option to purchase the land and buildings. If the lessee elects to purchase the property, one-fourth of the total rentals already paid may be applied to the $100,000 purchase price if the option is exercised before the expiration date. Property taxes and major repairs are paid by the owner of the property.

(2) Prior to his death, Kenneth's father acted as general manager of the business and personally supervised all advertising and selling.

(3) Operations have been on a two-shift basis, although these shifts have not been working at full capacity. The plant manager stated, "We've got to do something about this old machinery. The maintenance costs and lost time due to breakdowns are exorbitant."

(4) The warehouse contains a considerable amount of shopworn and obsolete furniture.

(5) Manufacturing materials are purchased on a "hand-to-mouth" basis. The materials used in the manufacture of all the company's products are of a similar type.

(6) Although there are no signs of increasing competition in the local area, sales records indicate a slow but consistent decline in the company's sales.

(7) The company has not maintained records of the unit costs of manufacturing its products. The present records consist of a checkbook, a sales record, an expense record, and an itemized list of prices paid for the major tools and equipment used in the business. Kenneth's father used these records as the basis for determining the company's annual net income for tax purposes.

The only other financial records pertain to the payroll. These records show for each pay period the hours worked, wage rate, gross wages earned, deductions for Social Security taxes and federal income tax, and net pay for each employee.

(8) In your examination of the sales invoice file you discover that many of the accounts receivable are between six months and two years past due.

(9) The company's liabilities consist of several small accounts payable arising from the purchases of materials on credit and installment notes payable to the bank for the purchase of the delivery trucks. All payments have been made when due.

(10) One bookkeeper keeps all accounting records and handles all cash receipts and payments. The bookkeeper prepares the weekly payrolls and also checks all incoming shipments of materials against the invoices.

Required

a. What major *business* decisions does Kenneth Andre face?

b. Referring to the problem of the old machinery in item (3) of the case, outline the steps Kenneth should follow in making the decision.

c. What major *accounting* decisions does Kenneth face?

d. How would the information desired by a prospective purchaser of the business differ from that needed by Kenneth?

e. In what general ways might the $94,000 cash bequest be used in the business?

chapter 2

Business Financial Position:
Principles of Valuation

The Need for Reporting Financial Position:
An Illustrative Case

Several weeks after his first discussions of the possible purchase of the MacDonald Mobile Home Builders manufacturing enterprise, Hamilton Hartman received a set of the MacDonald financial statements which had been audited by Heilman and Rentz, CPAs.

Mr. Hartman looked first at the MacDonald financial position statement, which is presented in Illustration 2-1. He knew that financial statements are *historical reports* which show the assets of a business and the claims against it, measured at values based on past exchange transactions of the business. He was aware that *increases in the values* of business assets since they were acquired are *not ordinarily reported* in the historical financial statements. He recognized that while a financial position statement (or balance sheet) shows the *resources* in which a business has invested and the *sources* by which those investments were financed, it does not show the current value of the business as a whole. Still, he thought it would be worthwhile to discuss with Mr. Rentz, the CPA, how the historical information contained in the financial statements might help

Illustration
2-1

MACDONALD MOBILE HOME BUILDERS
Financial Position Statement
December 31, 1972

ASSETS

Current assets:			
Cash		$ 50,000	
Accounts receivable	$255,000		
Less estimated uncollectibles................	5,000		
Estimated collectible accounts..............		250,000	
Materials and supplies inventory..............	70,000		
Work in process inventory	110,000		
Finished product inventory.....................	370,000		
Total inventories		550,000	
Total current assets			$ 850,000
Property, plant, and equipment:			
Land		200,000	
Building...	800,000		
Less accumulated depreciation.............	160,000	640,000	
Equipment	500,000		
Less accumulated depreciation.............	150,000	350,000	
Total property, plant, and equipment			1,190,000
Total assets..................................			$2,040,000

LIABILITIES

Current liabilities:			
Accounts payable.................................		$100,000	
Notes payable to banks..........................		300,000	
Total current liabilities			$ 400,000
Long-term liabilities:			
6% mortgage note payable due 1976–1980			500,000

OWNERS' EQUITY

John MacDonald, capital			1,140,000
Total equities..................................			$2,040,000

(*Note:* Round numbers have been used to simplify the illustration.)

in deciding on a reasonable purchase price for the MacDonald business. Mr. Rentz had made a special analysis to aid Mr. Hartman in estimating the current worth of the business.

Mr. Rentz pointed out that the manufacturing enterprise would have value to the Hartman firm chiefly because of the earnings that could be anticipated in the future from using its existing resources. He had begun his special analysis by estimating the earnings Mr. Hartman could expect each year in the reasonably foreseeable future from the MacDonald business. This estimate was highly subjective, of course, since future events cannot be predicted with certainty.

Mr. Rentz had then translated this projected stream of future earnings into a *present value*, or present worth, of the business by using the mathematical process of *discounting*. The present value of each future year's expected earnings was estimated by using a *discount rate* and the *time* that would elapse from the present until the earnings would be realized. In selecting a discount rate to use in the calculation, Mr. Rentz had tried to reflect the *time value of money* to Hartman's firm—the earnings that would be foregone by investing in the MacDonald enterprise rather than by putting the money to another use. The discount rate also allowed for the *uncertainty* associated with the estimated future earnings—uncertainty both as to how much they will be and how long they will continue. With an estimated earnings stream of a given amount, Mr. Rentz explained, the present value of the business will be lower as the discount rate is increased. Therefore the greater the time value of money in other uses and the greater the uncertainty involved in the investment being evaluated, the higher should be the discount rate used.

Mr. Hartman observed that this approach to estimating the value of a business seemed a little like crystal-ball gazing. "What safeguards are there to avoid serious over- and undervaluations of a business?" he asked.

Mr. Rentz replied that the market prices of individual assets help to set upper and lower limits to the selling price of a business in the following ways:

(1) If the assets of a business can be sold individually, their *total liquidating value sets a lower limit* to the value of the business. If the estimated value of the business in operation is less than its liquidating value, and if this condition seems likely to continue, the owners should seriously consider terminating the business and selling its assets individually.

(2) A buyer should not be willing to pay more for a business than he would have to pay to duplicate its earning power; therefore the current replacement cost of buying the same assets, or the cost of buying assets that will perform the same services, sets the *upper limit* to the value of the assets of the business. Other factors which form a part of the value of a business, though not assets, are sales orders already received, good organization, and good customer relations.

Competition also helps to establish the selling price of a business, Mr. Rentz continued. There may be other would-be purchasers whose bids are considered in determining the exchange price. Both the seller and the buyer can benefit by using the present value approach in estimating the worth of a business. If no buyer offers a price as high as the seller's subjective valuation of the business, he may reject all offers and continue to operate it himself.

Mr. Rentz showed Mr. Hartman the forecasts he had made of the future earnings of MacDonald Mobile Home Builders. He explained his assumptions as to future changes in selling prices and quantities sold and changes in the costs of the various productive factors used. He emphasized that the information contained in this special analysis was for Mr. Hartman's private use, and not for the use of others, as is an audit report.

Mr. Rentz suggested that Mr. Hartman engage an expert appraiser to estimate the current value of the property, the plant, and the equipment to provide a partial check on Mr. Rentz's subjective estimates of the value of the MacDonald business. He reminded Mr. Hartman that the land valuation of $200,000 shown on the financial position statement was the price paid by Mr. MacDonald several years ago, and that real estate values in the area had increased sharply since then because of population growth and inflation. He also pointed out that, because of rapidly increasing construction costs, the current values of the factory building and equipment were probably greater than the values shown in the position statement.

Mr. Hartman agreed that these assets should be appraised. He planned to estimate the current value of the inventories himself because of his experience in the industry.

Mr. Rentz concluded by observing that there was likely to be a range for bargaining between the buyer and seller in setting the final selling price of the business. "If the highest price you are willing to pay is more than the lowest price he is willing to take, you can probably work out a deal even if he rejects your original offer," he said.

Purpose of Chapter

Accounting is concerned with reporting the *form* of the economic resources—the assets—of an entity; the *sources* of financing them, described as *equities;* and some measure of the *economic significance*, or money valuation, of these assets and equities. This chapter deals with three key questions that must be answered in assigning a money valuation to assets and equities:

(1) What resources and equities should be measured?

(2) What is the proper yardstick, or basis of valuation, to be used in making these measurements?

(3) When should the measurements be made?

The chapter presents some basic standards of measurement which have been developed in an effort to make accounting information meaningful and reliable.

It also explains why accounting reports are ordinarily *more concerned with reporting actual past events* than with estimating the results of future events.

The Meaning of Financial Position

Assets were defined in Chapter 1 as the economic resources of an entity which can be measured objectively in terms of money. *Equities* are the sources by which the assets of the entity are financed. These sources are of two types, *liabilities* and *owners' equity*. Together, the assets and equities of an accounting entity reflect its *financial position*, or *status*, at a specific point in time.

Liabilities. A *liability* is a claim against the entity by a creditor, arising from a past transaction and requiring that at some future time the entity pay a sum of money or some other resource, or perform a service. Examples of liabilities are notes payable, accounts payable, and bonds payable.

Example 1   The News Publishing Company bought a lot on which to locate a new plant, signing a promissory note agreeing to pay $3,000 plus interest each year for five years. The company incurs a liability, a *note payable*, in the amount of $15,000 on the day the note is signed. The liability for *interest* on the note will *accrue*, or build up, as time passes under the debt contract.

Example 2   The News Publishing Company made an advance collection of $1,800 for 100 one-year subscriptions at $18 each on January 1,1972. On that date the company has a liability to provide newspaper service to these subscribers for one year. On July 1 the liability is $900, representing the obligation to furnish newspaper service for the remaining half year.

Liabilities usually require the payment of a specific amount of money to a particular party at a definite future time. Sometimes, however, the amount of money to be paid under a liability is indefinite, or the specific identity of the creditor is not yet known, or the exact due date is uncertain. Estimates must be made in order to report such liabilities as accurately as possible.

Example 3 Nouveau Products sold 400,000 of a particular type of household appliance in 1972, with a warranty contract in which it agreed to replace defective parts within one year from date of sale. The estimated cost of replacing the parts in the future is a liability during the life of the warranty, even though the persons for whom the replacements are to be made, the dates, and the exact cost of each replacement are uncertain.

Owners' Equity

Owners' equity is derived from two major sources, *paid-in capital* and *retained income.*

Paid-in capital reflects the *investments of the owners* in the business and the *donations* of resources to the business. It is measured by the market value of the assets invested or donated at the time they are received by the business.

Retained income measures the cumulative results of operating activities since the business was formed, reduced by asset distributions to the owners out of income. Stated differently, retained income is increased by the net incomes of individual profitable years, decreased by the net losses of individual unprofitable years, and decreased by dividends or similar distributions to owners. It is a measure of the *capital accmulated in the business as a result of operations.* Cumulative retained income is positive if the total of net income since the organization of the business exceeds the total of net losses and dividends. It is negative—a *deficit*—if the sum of net losses and dividends exceeds net income.

Example 4 A corporation was formed in 1970, with the owners investing $105,000 for its shares of common stock. It incurred a net loss of $4,000 in 1970 and earned net incomes of $6,000 in 1971 and $10,000 in 1972. Dividends of $7,000 were paid in 1972. What was its owners' equity at the end of 1972?

Solution The owners' equity on December 31, 1972, was $110,000, consisting of $105,000 of paid-in capital and $5,000 of retained income (− $4,000 + $6,000 + $10,000 − $7,000).

Since it is illegal for the stated capital of corporations to be voluntarily reduced by stockholder withdrawals, it is important to maintain the distinction between paid-in capital and retained income in the accounting records. No such legal requirement applies to unincorporated businesses. The owner's investment and retained income of a *single proprietorship* are usually combined under the title *capital,* preceded by the owner's name. In a *partnership* each partner has a capital account.

In contrast to liabilities, which are usually specific claims against the business, owners' equity represents an *indefinite* and *residual* claim. It is *indefinite* in that the owners *hope* to receive distributions of income if the business is successful and to recover their investment if it is terminated; but they are *promised* neither. The owners of a corporation have a specific *right* to receive only the income that is distributed, after the board of directors formally declares a dividend.

Owners' equity is a *residual* (remainder) claim in that when a business is terminated the owners have a right to receive only the assets that remain after all liabilities have been paid.

Example 5   The corporation in Example 3 also owed $100,000 of notes payable bearing interest at 6 per cent a year. The interest of $6,000 a year must be paid whether or not there is a net income. The *dividend* of $7,000 paid in 1972 could be made only out of accumulated earnings, and only if the board of directors decided that a dividend was desirable.

Suppose that on December 31, 1972, financial difficulties forced the corporation to sell its assets for $150,000. The creditors, the holders of the notes payable, would receive $100,000 in full payment of their claims. Only $50,000 of assets would remain to be paid to the stockholders, the residual equityholders.

The Accounting Equation

Assets and equities are, in a sense, two different ways of looking at the same set of financial events which have affected an entity. *Assets* show the *forms* of the entity's economic resources, while *equities* show the *sources* from which they were financed. All assets of an entity were obtained from some source; therefore the following equation must always hold true:

$$\text{Assets} = \text{Equities}.$$

By substituting the two main types of equities for total equities, the expanded equation becomes

$$\text{Assets} = \text{Liabilities} + \text{Owners' equity}.$$

Example 6   Three individuals organize a business and each invests $5,000 cash in it. What is its resulting financial position immediately after the formation of the business?

Solution   The business has an *asset* of $15,000 in the form of cash and *owners' equity* of $15,000, resulting from paid-in capital.

Example 7   Immediately after its organization the business in Example 6 buys equipment on credit for $5,000. What is its financial position then?

Solution   Assets, $20,000, Liabilities, $5,000, + Owners' Equity, $15,000. The assets have been increased by equipment costing $5,000; the liability is an account payable.

In determining an unknown financial amount it is sometimes helpful to remember that any term of an equation may be transferred to the opposite side of the equation if its sign is changed. Thus

$$\text{Assets} - \text{Liabilities} = \text{Owners' equity}$$

and

$$\text{Assets} - \text{Owners' equity} = \text{Liabilities.}$$

Example 8   A business has assets totaling $17,000 and owes debts of $11,000. What is the equity of the owners?

Solution   Assets — liabilities = owners equity: $17,000 — $11,000 = $6,000.

Example 9   The assets of a business have increased to $40,000, although the owners' initial investment was only $6,000 and reinvested earnings have amounted to $12,000. How much does the business owe?

Solution   Assets — owners' equity = liabilities: $40,000 — $18,000 = $22,000.

The term "net assets" refers to the excess of total assets over total liabilities; thus

$$\text{Assets} - \text{Liabilities} = \text{Net assets.}$$

The money valuation of net assets is equal to the money valuation of owners' equity.

Example 10   In Example 8 net assets are $6,000 and are equal to owners' equity of $6,000. In Example 9 net assets are $18,000.

The accounting equation is used as the framework for classifying and measuring the effects of business transactions and events on an entity.

Financial Position Statement Form and Classifications

The *financial position statement* of an entity is a report of its assets and equities at a specific point in time. It reflects the effects of past events and transactions on these assets and equities. The titles of the asset and equity items in the statement describe their specific nature. These asset and equity items are classified into general groups in the financial position statement in order to give readers a broad indication of the nature and liquidity of the resources of the business, as well as of the types and approximate due dates of the claims against it. *Liquidity* refers to the ease with which an asset can be converted into cash without loss. For example, land is usually less liquid than merchandise.

The outline of group headings commonly used in preparing the financial position statements of corporations is presented in Illustration 2-2.

The format in Illustration 2-2 shows the assets on the left side of a page (or on the left of two facing pages) and the equities on the right side. This is called the *account form* of the financial position statement.

Illustration
2-2

FINANCIAL POSITION STATEMENT GROUP HEADINGS

ASSETS		LIABILITIES		
Current assets............................	$ xx	Current liabilities............	$xx	
Investments.............................	xx	Long-term liabilities	xx	
Property, plant, and equipment....	xx	Total liabilities....................		$ xx
Intangible assets........................	xx	STOCKHOLDERS' EQUITY		
Other assets.............................	xx	Capital stock..........	$xx	
		Retained income.....	xx	
		Total stockholders' equity......		$ xx
Total assets	$xxx	Total equities		$xxx

An alternative arrangement is to list the assets at the top of the page and the equities at the bottom. This is the *report form* of the financial position statement, an example of which appears in Illustration 2-1.

Statement users wish to know whether the business has sufficient assets to pay its liabilities as they come due, with enough remaining to meet payrolls, buy supplies, and pay other day-to-day costs of operation. To help provide this information, the financial position statement groups together the *current assets* (those *expected* to be available to pay debts and operating costs in the near future) and the *current liabilities* (debts which will have to be paid in the near future).

Deducting current liabilities from current assets leaves *net working capital*. This is the money valuation of the assets which will be available, after paying current debts, to meet the operating needs of the business in the near future.

Example 11   The net working capital of MacDonald Mobile Home Builders was $450,000 on December 31, 1972. This is the excess of its current assets of $850,000 over its current liabilities of $400,000.

A comparison with the reader's personal affairs may explain the meaning of net working capital better.

Example 12   Suppose that your only means of support is a salary, which you collect once a month. On December 31 your have just received a month's salary of $800 in cash. During December you have made purchases on credit at several stores, resulting in total accounts payable of $250. What is your net working capital, and what does it mean?

Solution

Current assets on December 31..	$800
— Current liabilities on December 31	250
= Net working capital on December 31	$550

You must pay your current liabilities promptly in order to maintain your credit standing. Your net working capital of $550 is the amount of assets available for meeting your January living costs, such as rent, food, and entertainment. Your operating cycle is one month, the time interval between the periodic replenishments of your assets by receipt of your pay checks.

The length of the *operating cycle* of a business is important in deciding what specific assets and liabilities are current. Businesses are engaged in a continuing round of activities, consisting of

(1) Purchasing goods for sale or productive factors for use.
(2) Selling goods or services.
(3) Collecting for the sales.
(4) Paying for the purchases (not necessarily in this sequence).

The operating cycle of a given business is the average period of time which elapses from the beginning to the end of this round of activities. For a retail clothing store it is usually several months; for a tobacco manufacturer, whose product requires a long period of curing, it is several years.

Current assets include cash and other assets which are reasonably expected to be converted into cash, or sold or consumed, during the normal operating cycle of the business.

Current liabilities are liabilities which are expected to be paid from current assets within one operating cycle, or to require the creation of other current liabilities. A business which completes several operating cycles in a year uses *one year* as the dividing line between current and noncurrent assets and liabilities. A business with a longer operating cycle, such as the tobacco manufacturer, would use the *typical length of the operating cycle* as the dividing line.

The *investments* section includes stocks, bonds, and other securities which the business owns and plans to retain for more than a year (or more than an operating cycle, if it is longer than a year).

Property, plant, and equipment are physical assets of relatively long life which the business intends to use in its operations rather than to sell.

Intangible assets have no physical substance; their potential benefit to the business lies in the rights they confer upon it. Examples are organization costs, patents, and goodwill, which are usually classified in a separate section for intangible assets.

The *other assets* section includes receivables which are not current assets, as well as items of plant and equipment which are no longer being used in the business.

Sometimes the *fixed asset* caption is used to refer to property, plant, and equipment as well as to intangibles.

Long-term liabilities are obligations which cannot be classified as current. They fall due beyond the end of the next year or of the next operating cycle (whichever is appropriate for distinguishing between long- and short-term assets and liabilities of the particular business).

Capital stock is the investment of owners in a corporation represented by certificates of ownership.

Retained income has been defined earlier.

All these terms will be explained in greater detail in later chapters.

Adapting Accounting Measurements to the Purpose to Be Served

Chapter 2 has considered the types of business resources and equities which are reported in financial statements. A question that will now be examined is,

What *basis of valuation* should be used in measuring the assets and equities of a business?

The proper basis of valuation to be used depends on the purpose for which the measurements are intended. Three main purposes, which were either stated or implied in the illustrative case at the beginning of this chapter, are

(1) To estimate the total liquidating value of the individual parts of a business.

(2) To estimate the "fair" value of the earning power of the business as an operating unit.

(3) To report on the periodic progress of a business in accomplishing its economic objectives.

To these might be added another purpose:

(4) To determine the income tax liability of a business under income tax laws and regulations. (This is a special purpose which is beyond the scope of this text.)

Asset and equity valuations for the above purposes require different valuation data and different estimation techniques.

If the business is being terminated and the owners are considering piecemeal disposal of the business assets, special accounting reports based on *current market values* would be useful. Such a liquidation would be desirable if the business cannot be operated profitably by the present owners, and if prospective buyers are not willing to pay as much as the sum of the liquidating values of the individual assets. Liquidating values would also be pertinent if the owners are considering a sale of the business as a unit. As Mr. Rentz, the CPA, pointed out in the illustrative case, the minimum price for a business being sold as an operating unit is generally the sum of the current market values of its individual assets. Liquidating values are likewise appropriate when the disposal of a major segment or operating unit of a business is being considered.

Information about the progress and financial standing is needed about businesses which *plan to continue operations indefinitely* more often than it is needed for the purpose of liquidation or sale. For this reason, this book emphasizes the measurement principles which apply to financial statements of the *going concern*, of which the *financial position statement* is of major importance. This statement reports, as of a specific point in time, the assets and equities of the business which have resulted from *past* transactions and events, and which the business will use in the future in reaching its income objectives and in settling its financial obligations. Knowledge of the results of past operations, coupled with knowledge of the business plans and objectives, aids owners, managers, creditors, and others in evaluating the successfulness of current operations and in projecting future accomplishments. *For this purpose, the proper basis for valuing business assets and equities in the financial position statement is historical cost.* Later sections of this chapter examine in detail some operational guides which are used in measuring the historical costs of the assets and equities of a going business.

The illustrative case at the beginning of the chapter outlined an analytical framework that is useful in estimating the value of a business as an *operating unit*.

This approach, a subjective one, involves *discounting estimated future earnings* at a rate that allows for the time value of money and for uncertainty. It is also useful in deciding how much a business is willing to pay for, or ask for, any asset which is being bought or sold because of its earning power.

Value in Use and Value in Exchange

In a modern exchange economy individuals can limit their current consumption, save money, and invest it productively with the expectation of having a greater sum to spend—the original amount saved plus earnings on the investment—at a later time. The fact that economic resources can be invested to increase their amounts over time gives rise to the *time value of money*.

Example 13   Suppose that you have inherited $10,000 cash which you do not need to spend for consumption during the year. You decide to deposit your money in a savings account which pays interest at 5 per cent yearly. What is the time value of money?

Solution   If the outcome is as expected, you will have $10,500 (the original sum plus 5 per cent earnings) available to spend at the end of the year. By making the investment, you have taken advantage of the time value of money and have earned an additional $500 for increased consumption or investment at the end of the year. The time value of money in this case is 5 per cent a year.

The investment in Example 13 is described as a *financial investment* because funds were committed to someone else to use under definite terms as to period of investment and rate of compensation. Most investments made by a business are *real* rather than financial. A *real investment* is a commitment of funds for an indefinite time period to specific productive assets, such as land, buildings, and equipment, instead of savings accounts or securities such as stocks and bonds.

Real investments produce new products and services which are *expected*—but not promised—to bring monetary returns greater in amount than the funds initially invested. The amounts, timing, and degrees of uncertainty associated with the monetary returns which flow from a real investment are relatively indefinite. The time value of money in a real investment is measured by the compound interest rate which will discount the expected future returns to a present value equal to the initial investment.

In deciding whether to invest in assets for a particular use, most businessmen estimate subjectively whether the expected future returns from the use of the asset will justify the cost. If this estimation procedure is carried out formally, it involves estimating the amount of future returns and the time when they will be received. These estimated returns may then be translated into a *present value* by using a compound discount rate (such as the 5 per cent in Example 13). The discount rate should make an appropriate allowance for the time value of money in alternative uses and for the uncertainties involved in the particular investment. In the illustrative case at the beginning of this chapter Mr. Rentz, the CPA, outlined the same procedure for estimating the value of a business as a productive unit.

When there are no competing demands for his funds, a businessman will buy a productive asset if its estimated present (discounted) value is greater than its purchase price.

Example 14   A businessman is considering buying a labor-saving machine which costs $4,000. After estimating the annual savings in supplies and operating costs that will result from the machine, he calculates that the present value of the machine to him is about $5,000. Since the machine's *value in use* seems to him to be *more than its initial cost*, he will buy it unless there is a better alternative use of his money.

Assume that the business in Example 14 did buy the machine for $4,000. What is the proper value of the machine in a financial position statement prepared immediately after the purchase: its cost of $4,000, its discounted subjective value in use of $5,000, or some other figure?

If the purpose is to measure objectively the progress of the business entity toward its economic goals, the asset should be valued in the financial position statement at its acquisition price of $4,000. The financial position statement will then measure objectively the actual cost of the resource which the entity acquired with the *hope* of realizing its expected value through future use. The value in use will not be *realized* until the entity receives the monetary returns from the use of the asset. When these new assets are actually received they can be measured objectively at their market exchange prices in order to determine whether an actual improvement in financial position—an *income*—has been realized from the investment.

As a general rule, the value first assigned to an asset by a business is its *exchange*, or purchase, *price*. This is an objective measure of the resources which the business has committed to this particular asset. Later financial reports can measure business financial progress—*income*—by comparing the *results achieved* (additional resources obtained from selling goods and services) with the *resources used* in producing the goods and services. If the results (*revenues*) exceed the effort expended (*expenses*), there is a *net income*.

Businesses do not ordinarily report increases in asset values derived from using productive assets, such as the machine in Example 14, until both the *fact* that the increase has occurred and its *amount* are supported by *objective evidence*. Usually the evidence required to justify recording an increase in value is the sale of the asset's services, or the sale of the asset itself.

Reliability of Exchange Value

Ordinarily there is much uncertainty involved in the buyer's subjective estimate of an asset's value in use. The market exchange price at which he actually buys the asset is a more reliable indication of its value for several reasons:

(1) It reflects an exchange value agreed upon by two independent parties, the buyer and the seller, in an arm's-length transaction.

(2) In a competitive market the exchange price is also influenced by the values placed on the asset by other buyers and sellers.

To the buyer, the expected value in use of the goods or services acquired is *at least equal to the bargained price*. To the seller, the selling price is at least equal to the value which he thinks he can obtain from alternative uses of the goods or services which he is selling. Both buyer and seller may feel that they are better off as a result of a bargained transaction.

Standards for Accounting Classification and Measurement

Reliability is the major criterion by which the usefulness of accounting information is judged. Economic resources must be capable of being measured dependably in order to be included as assets in a business financial position statement. Value and cost changes must also be capable of being measured dependably if they are to be shown as elements of business income. The following standards are widely used in judging the reliability of accounting measurements:

(1) Relevance.
(2) Objectivity (including verifiability).
(3) Freedom from personal bias.
(4) Consistency.

Relevance. The financial statements of a going business should report facts which pertain to the entity's economic resources, the sources by which they are financed, and progress toward the entity's economic objectives. Information is costly to obtain, however, and only that information which has usefulness greater than the cost of providing it should be reported.

Objectivity. The financial events and transactions which are reflected in an entity's accounting reports should be supported by *adequate evidence*. Only data which can be traced to actual market exchanges and contracts should be used. The evidence should be sufficient in kind and quantity to *verify* the existence of the events and transactions being reported.

Freedom from personal bias. Users of accounting reports rely on the reported facts in making decisions which pertain to their individual interests. To be *fair*, accounting presentations must be free of any tendency to manipulate the decisions of one user group to the benefit of another. The way in which accounting reports an entity's financial events and relationships should not be unduly influenced by the owners, the management, or others who stand to benefit from biased reporting.

Consistency. How useful accounting reports are depends to a great extent on whether they can be *compared* from one time to another. An entity must use consistent standards and methods of classification and measurement. To be compared at different times, asset and equity categories should have unchanged meanings and should be measured in the same manner over time. This does not mean that an entity cannot change its accounting methods, but if a change is made it should be clearly indicated and its effect should be explained.

Application of Standards in Measuring Historical
Exchange Transactions

Monetary assets have been defined as *money* or *claims* to specific amounts of money, called *receivables*. The proper measure of monetary assets is the amount of money which they currently represent, or the amount of money which they are expected to bring in the near future in the normal course of events.

If there is a substantial waiting period before a receivable is to be collected in cash, the debtor and creditor usually agree that interest will be charged at a stated rate.

Monetary assets have a *general potential for providing service*—that is, they are available now, or are expected to be available soon, for their owner to use to pay debts or make purchases.

Nonmonetary assets represent specific types of service potentials. Merchandise is expected to benefit the business by sale, while equipment is expected to benefit it by use. A *nonmonetary asset* should be valued initially at its *historical cost*—the cash or cash equivalent price agreed to be paid for it when it is acquired.

When a business gives something other than money or a promise to pay money in exchange for a nonmonetary asset, it is sometimes difficult to estimate the *cash equivalent price* of the asset received. Evidence of the exchange price in the transaction might be (1) the cash sale price of assets similar to the one given in exchange or (2) the cash sale price of assets similar to the asset received in exchange. The more reliable of these two estimated prices, considering the circumstances of the case, is called the *fair market value*. This is the initial accounting valuation—the *historical cost*—of the asset acquired.

Example 15   A business exchanged merchandise for a plot of land. The merchandise had been acquired several months earlier for $3,000. At the time of the exchange the business could have bought similar merchandise for $2,500 and could have sold it to customers for $3,300. Estimates of the value of the land, based on recent sales of similar tracts, ranged from $2,200 to $3,000. At what valuation should the land be recorded on the books of the business?

Solution   The more reliable evidence of exchange value in this case seems to be the current replacement cost of the merchandise, $2,500. This is the initial valuation that should be assigned to the land on the books of the business.

General Guides for Measuring Liabilities,
Paid-in Capital, and Retained Income

Measuring liabilities. Liabilities usually arise in transactions in which the business receives an asset, or incurs an expense or a loss. Initially the liability should be measured at the same amount as the corresponding asset, expense, or loss. This initial measure is the amount of money that would currently be required to settle the debt. The measurement of changes in liabilities, from interest and other causes, is discussed in a later chapter.

Measuring paid-in capital. If the owners invest money in the business, the amount of their paid-in capital can be determined simply and directly. If the investment is in the form of nonmonetary assets, or if creditors agree to exchange their claims for an ownership interest, the rules for determining the fair market value in a noncash exchange apply. The amount of the paid-in capital is either the value of the consideration given by the business (ownership shares) or the value of the consideration received by the business (an asset or settlement of a liability), whichever is supported by better evidence.

Retained income. The periodic amounts of net income and net loss of a business are measured under principles explained in Chapters 4 and 5 and later chapters. Income distributions to the owners are usually in the form of money. If noncash assets are distributed to owners, the amount of the distribution is measured by using the fair market value rule which applies to noncash exchanges.

Summary   The *financial position* of a business at any given point in time is reflected by its *assets* (economic resources) and its *equities* (sources by which the assets are financed). Equities consist of *liabilities*, the claims of creditors against the entity; *paid-in capital*, the investment of the owners and donations; and *retained income*, resulting from business operations minus distributions to owners. The total assets of an entity are equal to its total equities.

Assets are classified in the financial position statement as current assets; investments; property, plant, and equipment; intangible assets; or other assets. Liabilities are classified as either current or long-term.

The proper basis for valuing the assets and equities of a business depends on the *purpose of the measurement:* whether it is to estimate the liquidating value of the business, to estimate its fair value as an operating unit, or to report on its progress in attaining its economic objectives. Most often accounting reports are needed for the last purpose by businesses which plan to continue in operation indefinitely. *Historical cost* is the proper valuation basis in such circumstances.

The value of a business as an operating unit, as well as the value of any other real investment, is *subjective.* It involves *discounting* the estimated future earnings at a rate that allows for the time value of money and for uncertainty. If the discounted present value is greater than the purchase price, the businessman will make the investment, provided that there are no competing demands for his funds.

Reliability is the major criterion for judging the usefulness of accounting information. Supporting critieria are *relevance, objectivity, freedom from personal bias,* and *consistency.*

Discussion Questions and Problems   **2-1**   The Jiffy Taxi Manufacturing Company sells or leases its product, depending on the customer's preference. It was formed several years ago with capital stock issued for $250,000. It currently owes creditors $30,000 on account and has outstanding notes payable of $100,000.

Jiffy has sold taxis with a two-year warranty against defective major components. It has collected lease rentals of $300,000 during the current year. Of this sum, $220,000 applies to the current year.

a. List the liabilities of Jiffy and their amounts, where sufficient information is given.

b. What other liabilities cannot be measured from the information given? What information do you need to measure them?

2-2 The Jiffy Taxi Manufacturing Company (see Question 2-1) has earned income and paid dividends as follows during its life:

Year	Net Income (or Net Loss)	Dividends
1970	($11,000)	0
1971	20,000	$ 5,000
1972	25,000	10,000

a. What was its retained income at the end of 1972?
b. What was its owners' equity at the end of 1972? What were the major components?

2-3 The financial position statement of Sands Company showed total stockholders' equity of $185,000 on December 31, 1973. Paid-in capital amounted to $50,000. A stockholder who owned 20 per cent of the stock wrote the president of Sands that he was having a personal financial crisis, and requested that the president send him a check for the $37,000 "which belonged to him."

a. How should the president reply to the stockholder?
b. If Sands had liabilities of $40,000, what were its total assets?

2-4 On December 31, 1973, a business owns total assets of $148,000 and owes debts of $82,000.

a. What were the major sources of its assets, and how much was obtained from each source?
b. The owners had organized the business by investing $20,000 of their personal funds on January 1, 1973. What changes have occurred in owners' equity during the year? Give possible reasons for the change.

2-5 On a given date the net assets of a business were $25,000 and its liabilities were $14,000. What was the total of owners' equity? Of assets?

2-6 Hapstone Company began the year with various assets totaling $150,000 and liabilities totaling $60,000. The year-end financial position statement showed assets of $212,000 and liabilities of $122,000.

a. What additional information do you need in order to determine the company's income for the year?
b. Assume whatever facts are necessary in part a. Compute Hapstone's income for the year.

2-7 A business had the following financial position just before deciding to cease operations: assets, $80,000; liabilities, $23,000; and owners' equity, $57,000 (of which $25,000 represented the investment of the owners).
All the assets were sold for $50,000 cash. How should the money be distributed in winding up the business?

2-8 Mr. Hardley presents the following information from his records to show that assets do not always equal equities:

Assets	$28,000
Liabilities	12,000
Owners' equity	15,900

Does this invalidate the accounting equation, Assets = Equities? Explain.

2-9　What is meant by net working capital? How is it computed? Why is it of interest to the management of a business? To its bankers? To its owners?

2-10　Although it is sometimes appropriate for an owner to estimate the value of his business as a whole, it is rarely appropriate for this value to be recorded in his accounting records.

a. When is it appropriate for an owner to estimate the value of his business?
b. How should this value be estimated?
c. Is it possible for the value of the business as a whole to be more or less than the total estimated value of the individual assets? Why?
d. When would it be appropriate to record the increase in the value of a business in its accounting records?

2-11　An expert appraiser estimates that a business is currently worth $75,000. Total owners' equity as shown in the financial position statement of the business is $60,000. How can you account for the difference? What major assumptions are used in making each of the two measurements?

2-12　The Rondon Company's accounts show net assets of $200,000. A would-be buyer of the business makes an offer of $250,000 for the business.

a. Why would the buyer offer more than the value of the net assets as shown on Rondon's books?
b. Why might Rondon decline the offer?
c. If Rondon accepts the offer, will the assets be valued differently on the buyer's books? Explain.
d. If Rondon declines the offer, will the assets be valued differently on its books? Explain.

2-13　Accountants frequently contend that, although the information in the financial position statement is based largely on past events, every single measurement in them depends on some assumption regarding future happenings. Is this true? What are some of these assumptions?

2-14　What basis of valuation would you use in preparing a financial position statement for a company that is planning to cease operations? What specific assets and equities might be valued differently from the amounts shown on the firm's books?

2-15　The City of *H* donated land to its only manufacturer for plant expansion.

a. Should this land be reported as an asset on the firm's books? Explain.
b. Is this donation income to the firm? Explain.

2-16　The time value of money is evident when considering that an investment in a savings account or in a bond earns interest at a stated rate as time passes. It is more difficult to see when estimating the present value of assets that will be used in operating a business.
What factors should be considered in selecting the discount rate to be used in estimating the present value of business assets?

2-17　Alpha Company bought land in 1933 for $10,000, converting it into a parking lot at a cost of $30,000. In 1972 Alpha offered the lot for sale, subjectively estimating that its discounted present value was $150,000. Beta Company, which estimated that the lot was worth $200,000, offered $180,000 for it and the offer was accepted.

At what value should the lot be recorded on Beta's books? What accounting principles govern your answer?

2-18   The financial vice president of Company X instructs his chief accountant to lean in the direction of understating the effect of unfavorable events in the accounting reports and overstating the effects of favorable events. "The president is a confirmed pessimist," he says, "and you will be doing him and everyone else a favor by making an allowance for his pessimism in our financial reports."

a. Will the accountant be doing the president a favor if he complies with the vice president's suggestion? Explain.
b. Will he be doing a disservice to anyone else? Why?
c. What should the chief accountant do?

2-19   The purchasing director of Newton Company ordered $10,000 worth of merchandise from Marvin Company, requesting that credit be extended for 60 days. In reply to a request for financial information concerning Newton Company, the purchasing director replied that the firm had $100,000 of current assets and only owed $20,000 of current liabilities.

a. What additional information does Marvin Company need in order to decide whether to extend credit?
b. If Marvin Company does extend credit and ship the merchandise, how will the assets, equities, and working capital of Newton be affected?

2-20   The BNJ Corporation was organized on January 1, 1973. For each of the following 1973 events, show the effects on the corporation's assets, liabilities, and owners' equity by using the following symbols:

Asset increase	$= A+$	Owners' equity increase	$= OE+$
Asset decrease	$= A-$	Owners' equity decrease	$= OE-$
Liability increase	$= L+$	No effect on total assets,	
Liability decrease	$= L-$	liabilities, or owners' equity $= 0$	

a. Received $100,000 cash from investors in exchange for stock of the corporation.
b. Bought land for $20,000, paying $4,000 down in cash and giving a $16,000 five-year promissory note for the balance.
c. Nicholson, president of the corporation, sold a portion of his stock to Jones, the treasurer, for $12,000 cash. The stock had cost Nicholson $10,000.
d. Purchased merchandise for $7,000 cash.
e. Sold half of the merchandise for $6,000, of which $2,000 was on credit. The remainder was collected in cash.
f. Bought as a temporary investment for $2,000 cash U.S. government securities due in six months.
g. Paid $1,000 cash on the note in part b.
h. Collected $400 from a customer on his account in part e.
i. Sold part of the land for $9,000 cash. One-fourth of the original cost in part b applied to the land sold.
j. Paid salaries and other expenses totaling $8,000, not previously recorded, in cash.

2-21   Refer to the transactions in Problem 2-20. For each item that affects the financial position statement, indicate what type of account is affected, and the amount of the change, by using the following symbols:

Current assets	= CA	Current liabilities	= CL
Investments	= INV	Long-term liabilities	= LL
Property, plant, and equipment	= PPE	Paid-in capital	= PC
Intangible assets	= INT	Retained income	= RI
Other assets	= OA	No account affected	= None

2-22   The Grale Company had the following account balances at the close of business December 31, 1973:

Accounts payable	$ 6,800
Accounts receivable	14,000
Cash	3,000
Goodwill	10,000
Land	12,000
Merchandise inventory	29,000
Notes payable (due in 5 years)	8,000
Notes receivable (due in 6 months)	6,000
Capital stock	40,000
Retained income	18,000
Taxes payable	1,200

Required   Prepare a classified financial position statement.

2-23   The following are the account balances of the Elmo Corporation on December 31, 1973:

Investment in U.S. government bonds (plans are to retain these indefinitely)	$ 4,000
Retained income	9,000
Cash	2,500
Accounts payable	16,000
Land	5,000
Organization cost	500
Capital stock (to be computed)	?
Merchandise inventory	19,000
Notes payable (due in 1976)	15,000
Buildings	29,000

Required   a. Prepare a financial position statement.
b. Compute the net working capital.
c. If retained income was $2,000 on January 1, 1973, and the company paid no dividends during the year, what was its 1973 income?
d. Assume the same facts as in part c, except that dividends of $2,000 were paid in 1973. What was Elmo's 1973 income?

2-24   Rachine and Brombley formed a partnership to operate a business in 1969. The partnership showed the following balances on December 31, 1973:

Accounts payable	$ 3,000	Franchise	$ 6,000
Accounts receivable	5,000	Land	10,000
Rachine, equity (or capital)	25,000	Merchandise inventory	20,000
		Unexpired insurance	1,200
Brombley, equity	15,000	Salaries payable	2,700
Notes payable	8,500	Notes receivable	12,000

Required   a. Prepare the December 31, 1973, financial position statement.

b. If the business had been incorporated, what additional account might have appeared as an asset?

c. If the business had been incorporated, how would the components of owners' equity differ?

d. How would the position of the creditors and owners differ in the corporation as compared with the partnership?

Cases   **2-1**   **Hartman Mobile Home Sales, Inc. (B).** Refer to the illustrative case at the beginning of Chapters 1 and 2.

Required   a. In Illustration 2-1, which assets are monetary and which are nonmonetary? Does this distinction have any bearing on how reliably the two types of assets are measured? Explain.

b. Mr. Rentz, the CPA, made a special analysis to assist Mr. Hartman in deciding whether, and under what terms, to buy the MacDonald business. How does the criterion of *reliability* apply to this analysis, as compared with the MacDonald financial statements based on historical measurements? How does the standard of *relevance* apply to the two types of reports?

c. Suppose that Mr. Rentz used a discount rate of 10 per cent in subjectively estimating the value of the MacDonald business. If Mr. Hartman felt that the uncertainty was greater, would he use a higher or lower discount rate? Would his estimated value of the business be higher or lower than that of Mr. Rentz?

d. How would the following bases of valuation affect Mr. Hartman's decision regarding the MacDonald purchase opportunity?

(1) Value in use.

(2) Value in exchange.

(3) Liquidating value.

e. What do you think would be the best method of estimating the value of each of the following assets to the purchaser of the business?

(1) Accounts receivable.

(2) Work in process inventory.

(3) Land.

(4) Goodwill.

f. It is logical to assume that the purchase of MacDonald Home Builders will cause the sales revenue of Hartman's business interests to increase. How might the expenses be changed if the MacDonald business is purchased? How should these changes be considered in determining the price Hartman is willing to pay?

g. As a potential stockholder in the Hartman enterprise, what information in the audited financial statements of MacDonald Mobile Home Builders would you be most interested in? Why?

chapter 3

Business Financial
Position:
Accounting Procedure

Purpose of Chapter

Chapter 3 explains the double-entry system of accounting, which is used to reflect the effects of financial events on the individual assets and equities of an entity. It shows how a financial position statement is prepared from the underlying accounting records. It defines the major types of assets, liabilities, and stockholders' equity.

Types of Business Transactions

Accounting measures the effects of business activities on assets and equities by breaking these complex activities into identifiable, measurable events, or *transactions*. These transactions are of two chief types: those related to *acquiring and financing* productive resources, and those related to *producing and selling* goods and services.

Transactions related to acquiring and financing resources, which are discussed in the remainder of this chapter, are of the following main types:

(1) Receipt of assets invested in the business by the owners.

(2) Withdrawal of owners' investments.

(3) Purchase of productive facilities and services.

(4) Borrowing of money.

(5) Payment of debts owed to others.

Transactions pertaining to producing and selling goods and services, discussed in Chapters 4 and 5, deal with

(6) Use of facilities and services in production.

(7) Sale of goods and services.

(8) Collection of debts owed by others.

Double-entry Accounting

Each business transaction has dual effects of one of the four following types:

(1) It increases both an asset and an equity.

(2) It decreases both an asset and an equity.

(3) It increases one asset and decreases another asset.

(4) It increases one equity and decreases another equity.

Illustration 3-1

SUMMARY OF EFFECTS OF ACQUIRING AND FINANCING RESOURCES ON THE ACCOUNTING EQUATION

Type of Transaction	Assets	= Liabilities +	Owners' Equity
1. Assets increased and equities increased:			
a. Owners invest cash	+$10,000		+$10,000
b. Merchandise inventory is purchased on credit	+ 8,000	+$8,000	
Subtotals	$18,000 =	$8,000 +	$10,000
2. Assets decreased and equities decreased:			
a. Owners withdraw cash	− 100		− 100
Subtotals.............................	$17,900 =	$8,000 +	$ 9,900
b. A payment is made on account......	− 5,000	− 5,000	
Subtotals.............................	$12,900 =	$3,000 +	$ 9,900
3. Assets increased and assets decreased:			
Land is purchased for cash	− 2,000		
	+ 2,000		
Subtotals.............................	$12,900 =	$3,000 +	$ 9,900
4. Equities increased and equities decreased:			
a. A 6-month note payable is given to satisfy an account payable		− $2,000	
		+ 2,000	
Subtotals.............................	$12,900 =	$3,000 +	$ 9,900
b. A dividend is declared to be paid later......................................		+ 500	− 500
Subtotals.............................	$12,900 =	$3,500 +	$ 9,400
c. A creditor accepts a share of stock in settlement of his claim.............		− 200	+ 200
Totals	$12,900 =	$3,300 +	$ 9,600

Accounting shows both of the effects of every transaction; that is what is meant by *double-entry accounting*. Accounting maintains the equality of total assets and total equities at all times, as demonstrated in Illustration 3-1. The subtotals show that the equality of assets and equities has been preserved after every transaction.

The Account

A record which shows the *changes* and the *balance* of each type of asset and equity about which the business wishes information is called an *account*. The principal types of information in an account are

(1) The *account title*, which describes the asset or equity.

(2) The amount of each *increase* and *decrease*.

(3) The *account balance*—the difference between increases and decreases.

Each business transaction is analyzed to determine the accounts which it affects, whether the change is an increase or a decrease, and the amount. The record of an account distinguishes increases from decreases by recording them in different positions, for example:

Asset, Cash

	Increases			*Decreases*
(1a)	10,000		(2a)	100
			(2b)	5,000
Balance, 2,900			(3)	2,000
				7,100

Liability, Accounts Payable

	Decreases			*Increases*
(2b)	5,000		(1b)	8,000
			Balance, 3,000	

The numbers in parentheses refer to the transactions in Illustration 3-1.

The basic form illustrated above is called a *T-account*, because of its appearance. It is useful for teaching purposes, and is also the skeleton of an account arrangement often used in manually kept accounting records. A more elaborate account form commonly used in practice is shown in Illustration 3-2.

Illustration 3-3 shows how the information in the Cash T-account would appear in an account kept by hand.

A variation of the account form provides for a continuous balance, as shown in Illustration 3-4.

Rule of Debit and Credit

Assets are entity *resources*. They are classified according to type of resource. *Equities* show the *sources* by which the entity's assets are financed. Accounting records show changes in equities in an *opposite* way from changes in assets, as shown

Illustration
3-2

Account Form

ACCOUNT TITLE .... ACCOUNT NO. ....

DATE	EXPLANATION	POSTING REF.	DEBIT AMOUNT	DATE	EXPLANATION	POSTING REF.	CREDIT AMOUNT
MONTH	DAY					MONTH	DAY		

Illustration
3-3

Asset, Cash .... ACCOUNT NO. _1_

DATE	EXPLANATION	P/R	DEBIT	DATE	EXPLANATION	P/R	CREDIT
1972 May 1		J1	10000 —	1972 May 8		J3	100 —
	Bal. 2,900			14		J5	5000 —
				16		J6	2000 —
							7100 —

Illustration
3-4

Asset, Cash .... ACCOUNT NO. _1_

DATE	EXPLANATION	P/R	DEBIT	CREDIT	BALANCE	DR. CR.
1972 May 1		J1	10000 —		10000 —	Dr
8		J3		100 —	9900 —	Dr
14		J5		5000 —	4900 —	Dr
16		J6		2000 —	2900 —	Dr

in the preceding T-accounts for the asset, Cash, and the liability, Accounts Payable.

The rule of opposites is very useful in analyzing the effects of transactions on assets and equities. Total assets equal total equities, and this equality is maintained in recording each transaction.

Increases in assets (such as Cash in Illustrations 3-3 and 3-4) are recorded on the *left-hand side* of asset accounts. *Decreases in assets* are recorded on the *right-hand side*.

Increases in equities (such as Accounts Payable) are recorded on the *right-hand side* of equity accounts, and *decreases in equities* are recorded on the *left-hand side*.

Total changes recorded on the left-hand side of accounts will therefore equal total changes on the right-hand side of accounts. Balances of the left-hand side of accounts—*assets*—will equal balances on the right-hand side of accounts—*equities*.[1]

A change on the *left-hand* side of any account is called a *debit*, and a change on the *right-hand* side of any account is a *credit*. Likewise, balances on the left-hand side of an account are debit balances, and balances on the right-hand side are credit balances. To summarize:

Debits (entries on the left) show:	*Credits (entries on the right) show:*
Increases in assets	Decreases in assets
Decreases in liabilities and owners' equity	Increases in liabilities and owners' equity

Illustration of Debits and Credits in T-accounts

Illustration 3-1 showed the *increases* and *decreases* in assets, liabilities, and owners' equity which result from various types of transactions connected with acquiring and financing business resources. These effects are now shown in terms of *debits* and *credits* in T-accounts for each specific asset and equity. The references are to the transaction numbers on p. 41. The following symbols are used in the account titles to identify the type of account:

A = Asset
L = Liability
OE = Owners' Equity

A, Cash

	Debit			*Credit*
(1a)	10,000	(2a)		100
Balance,		(2b)		5,000
2,900		(3)		2,000
				7,100

L, Accounts Payable

	Debit			*Credit*
(2b)	5,000	(1b)		8,000
(4a)	2,000	Balance,		
(4c)	200	800		
	7,200			

A, Merchandise Inventory

(1b)	8,000		

L, Notes Payable

		(4a)	2,000

A, Land

(3)	2,000		

L, Dividends Payable

		(4b)	500

OE, Owners' Investment

(2a)	100	(1a)	10,000
(4b)	500	(4c)	200
	600		10,200
		Balance,	
		9,600	

---

[1] Some right-hand balances are not equities, but reductions of assets, or *contra-assets*, as explained on p. 51.

The Journal

Recording the effects of transactions in the accounts is not the first step in the accounting process. The *first step* is the preparation of *basic business documents*, such as checks and sales tickets, which serve either to get things done or to report what has been done. The following description of the steps in the accounting process is based on a hand-kept system of records. It is used to help explain the flow of accounting information in an entity, even though many modern accounting systems use short-cuts and high-speed equipment in processing their financial information.

In a manual accounting system the second step is to analyze each transaction to determine its complete debit and credit effect on particular assets and equities. This analysis is entered in a chronological record, called a *journal*. Then at some convenient later time the effect of transactions on each asset or equity, as shown by the *journal entry*, is transferred to the proper accounts. The process of transferring this information from the journal to the accounts is called *posting*.

The essential components of a journal entry are

(1) The name of the account(s) to be debited.
(2) The name of the account(s) to be credited.
(3) Debit and credit amounts.
(4) Descriptive information about the transaction:
   (a) Date.
   (b) Concise explanation.

The simplest form of the journal is shown below.

Example 1   A business was organized and the owners invested $10,000 in cash in exchange for capital stock. Show this in journal form.

Solution

GENERAL JOURNAL

PAGE /

DATE MONTH DAY	DESCRIPTION	POST. REF.	DEBIT	CREDIT
1972 May 1	A, Cash		10000 —	
	OE, Capital Stock			10000 —
	The owner invested cash in the business.			

Note that the name of the account to be credited is slightly indented to the right.

When a business has a large number of transactions of a given type, such as sales on credit, specialized forms of the journal are frequently used. These are illustrated in Chapter 9. The abbreviations "A" for asset, "L" for liability, and "OE" for owners' equity are used in this text as an aid in analyzing transactions. Such notations are not used in practice.

Steps in the Accounting Process

The complete accounting process consists of the following steps:

(1) Preparing basic business documents.
(2) Recording transactions in the journals.
(3) Posting the journal entries to the accounts.
(4) Preparing a trial balance (usually as the first part of a work sheet).
(5) Making any necessary correcting and adjusting entries.
(6) Preparing the financial statements.
(7) Journalizing and posting closing entries.
(8) Preparing an after-closing trial balance.

In this text the information ordinarily contained in basic business documents is given in illustrations and problems, and the first recording step required is journalizing. The following illustrative case explains how steps (2), (3), (4), and (6) are carried out. The remaining steps of the accounting cycle will be explained in Chapters 5 and 6.

ILLUSTRATION OF THE ACCOUNTING PROCESS

After extensive negotiations with John MacDonald and various sources of financing, Hamilton Hartman completed arrangements for his family and business associates to buy Mr. MacDonald's manufacturing business. A new corporation, Hartman Mobile Home Builders, Inc., was formed to acquire the MacDonald firm's assets and to assume its liabilities, effective at the close of business on March 31, 1973.

Journalizing

Hartman Mobile Home Builders, Inc., engaged in the following financing transactions on March 31, 1973.

Entry (3) is a *compound entry*, containing more than one debit and more than one credit. The debits all reflect increases in the assets of the new corporation, Hartman Mobile Home Builders, Inc. Accounts Receivable—Estimated Uncollectibles has a credit balance, but it is not a liability or owners' equity account. Instead, it is a deduction from (*contra-account* to) Accounts Receivable. These two accounts together reflect the estimate of the buyer and seller that only $260,000 will be collected of the many accounts actually owed, which total $266,000. The related accounting procedure will be explained in more detail in a later chapter.

A comparison of the purchase price of various assets, shown in entry (3), with the valuations in the December 31, 1972, financial position statement of MacDonald, shown in Illustration 2-1, shows a number of differences. During the months of January, February, and March the Accounts Receivable balance changed as a result of additional sales and collections. The inventories changed as a result of additional purchases, completion of products, and sales. The net

1973   (*1*)

Mar. 31 A, Cash	600,000	
OE, Capital Stock.................................		600,000

Issued shares of stock to the Hartman family and business associates in exchange for cash.

(2)

31 A, Cash	220,000	
L, Notes Payable to Banks		220,000

Borrowed funds from City National Bank, giving a promissory note in exchange.

(3)

31 A, Accounts Receivable...............................	266,000	
A, Materials and Supplies Inventory	60,000	
A, Work in Process Inventory	90,000	
A, Finished Product Inventory.......................	380,000	
A, Land...	300,000	
A, Building...	700,000	
A, Equipment	370,000	
A, Accounts Receivable—Estimated Uncollectibles		6,000
L, Account Payable to MacDonald		2,160,000

Received the assets of MacDonald Mobile Homes Builders at agreed purchase prices, as listed above. Set up a temporary liability to MacDonald, to be settled in a later entry.

(4)

31 L, Account Payable to MacDonald	890,000	
L, Accounts Payable.............................		90,000
L, Notes Payable to Banks......................		300,000
L, 6% Mortgage Note Payable.................		500,000

Assumed the liabilities of MacDonald Mobile Homes Builders, thus reducing the amount owed MacDonald for the purchase of his business.

(5)

31 L, Account Payable to MacDonald	1,270,000	
A, Cash		800,000
L, Notes Payable to MacDonald, Due 1975–1990		470,000

Gave MacDonald cash and a series of long-term notes in settlement of his equity in the business, at agreed prices.

valuations of Building and Equipment, reflected in the difference between the two asset accounts and their contra-accounts for accumulated depreciation, declined as a result of depreciation for the three months. The precise changes resulting from these events are not shown, in order to simplify the illustration.

Even if the financial position statement of MacDonald as of March 31, 1973, had been presented, there would still be differences between the *book values* of the assets as shown in the statement and the *exchange values* agreed upon by the buyer and seller of the business in their bargaining. It is these exchange values that are shown in entry (3). They are the proper valuations for the new business to use initially in measuring the assets purchased.

Entry (4) shows that the liabilities of the new corporation are increased by assuming the debts of the MacDonald business. The amount owed to Mac-Donald for his business is correspondingly reduced by $890,000. The net amount owed to MacDonald is $1,270,000, the difference between the credit to Account Payable to MacDonald in entry (3) and the debit to that account in entry (4).

Entry (5) shows that cash and long-term promissory notes payable are given to MacDonald as evidence of the amount owed him for his business.

The following transactions occurred immediately after Hartman Mobile Home Builders acquired MacDonald's business.

1973	(6)		
Mar. 31	A, Cash	3,000	
	A, Accounts Receivable..........................		3,000
	Collected amounts owed on account from several MacDonald customers.		

	(7)		
31	L, Accounts Payable..................................	5,000	
	A, Cash		5,000
	Paid several of the accounts owed to suppliers, included in the MacDonald debts assumed.		

Posting

After journalizing transactions it is necessary to *post* their debit and credit effects periodically to the specific asset and equity *accounts* affected. If monthly financial statements are desired, posting must be completed monthly. Each asset and equity account is usually on a separate page. The group of individual accounts is called a *ledger*, which may be in the form of a bound book, a loose-leaf binder, or a file.

T-account forms are used below to represent the ledger accounts of Hartman Mobile Home Builders, Inc. The figures in parentheses in the ledger accounts are cross-references to the corresponding journal entries. The numbers at the top right of each account are *account numbers*, whose purpose is to organize the accounts in some orderly fashion in the ledger.

In posting, the journal debits and credits are also cross-referenced to the ledger account numbers, as follows:

1973	(7)			
			Ref.	
Mar. 31	L, Accounts Payable		21	5,000
	A, Cash..		1	5,000

A, Cash   #1

	(Debits)				(Credits)		
1973				1973			
Mar. 31	(1)	600,000		Mar. 31	(5)	800,000
31	(2)	220,000		31	(7)	5,000
31	(6)	3,000				805,000
		823,000					
Balance, 18,000							

A, Accounts Receivable   #2

1973				1973		
Mar. 31	(3)	266,000		Mar. 31	(6)	3,000
Balance, 263,000						

A, Accounts Receivable—Estimated Uncollectibles   #3

	1973		
	Mar. 31	(3)	6,000

A, Materials and Supplies Inventory   #4

1973		
Mar. 31	(3)	60,000

A, Work in Process Inventory   #5

1973		
Mar. 31	(3)	90,000

A, Finished Product Inventory   #6

1973		
Mar. 31	(3)	380,000

A, Land   #7

1973		
Mar. 31	(3)	300,000

A, Building   #8

1973		
Mar. 31	(3)	700,000

A, Equipment   #10

1973		
Mar. 31	(3)	370,000

			L, Accounts Payable			#21
1973			1973			
Mar. 31	(7)	5,000	Mar. 31	(4)	90,000	
			Balance, 85,000			

			L, Notes Payable to Banks			#22
			1973			
			Mar. 31	(2)	220,000	
			31	(4)	300,000	
					520,000	

			L, 6% Mortgage Note Payable			#23
			1973			
			Mar. 31	(4)	500,000	

			L, Account Payable to MacDonald			#24
1973			1973			
Mar. 31	(4)	890,000	Mar. 31	(3)	2,160,000	
31	(5)	1,270,000	*Balance, 0*			
		2,160,000				

			L, Notes Payable to MacDonald			#25
			1973			
			Mar. 31	(5)	470,000	

			OE, Capital Stock			#31
			1973			
			Mar. 31	(1)	600,000	

Persons studying accounting for the first time often think that the ledger is an unnecessary duplication of the journal—that everything is done twice. It is hard to show in a textbook illustration why this is not true, because the large number of transactions and the timing of the various steps of the accounting process in real life are hard to illustrate. The *journal shows the entire effect of each individual transaction,* but it does not give a picture of asset and equity account balances. The *ledger summarizes the changes and balance of each asset and equity account,* but it does not show the other accounts affected and the explanatory information contained in the journal analysis of each transaction. Both are useful steps in the accounting process.

The Trial Balance

Accounting condenses the results of a multitude of entity transactions so that their effects can be more easily interpreted. Each journal entry is a complete analysis of the financial effects of a transaction. Ledger accounts summarize the effects of transactions according to each type of asset and equity. A list of the asset and equity balances which result from this analysis and summarization is helpful in interpreting the total effects of business events. It is useful as a preliminary step in preparing financial statements. Such a list, illustrated below, is called a *trial balance.*

HARTMAN MOBILE HOME BUILDERS, INC.
Trial Balance
March 31, 1973

	Debits	Credits
A, Cash	$ 18,000	
A, Accounts receivable	263,000	
A, Accounts receivable—estimated uncollectibles		6,000
A, Materials and supplies inventory	60,000	
A, Work in process inventory	90,000	
A, Finished product inventory	380,000	
A, Land	300,000	
A, Building	700,000	
A, Equipment	370,000	
L, Accounts payable		85,000
L, Notes payable to banks		520,000
L, 6% Mortgage notes payable		500,000
L, Notes payable to MacDonald		470,000
OE, Capital stock		600,000
Totals	$2,181,000	$2,181,000

The total of debit balances must always equal the total of credit balances. If it does not, an error has been made in addition, in computing account balances, in listing the balances, in posting from the journal to the ledger, or in journalizing. The fact that the total debits and credits in the trial balance are equal is necessary, but not sufficient, evidence to prove that the accounts are accurate. The trial balance would still balance if entire transactions were omitted, if wrong amounts were used in a journal entry, or if the wrong account were debited or credited.

With a trial balance it is a relatively easy matter to prepare a classified financial position statement, such as that shown in Illustration 3-5 on p. 56.

MAIN TYPES OF ASSET AND EQUITY ACCOUNTS

Asset Accounts

The following are definitions of types of assets that are commonly owned by commercial and industrial concerns. It is not complete, but merely representative. The account titles of specific assets vary to some extent from one business to another.

Assets have debit balances, but the list contains some accounts which have credit balances because they are *contra-asset* accounts—that is, asset-deduction accounts.

Cash, the most liquid of all assets, refers only to those items which are unrestricted as to use and are available readily for the payment of any obligation of the business. Cash includes currency, coin, readily transferable money orders and checks, and demand deposits in bank accounts. Time, or savings, deposits may also be classified as Cash if the bank is not expected to require a waiting period before allowing withdrawals.

Temporary investments are short-term commitments of funds to productive use. They are commonly held in the form of *marketable securities*—the certificates of ownership or indebtedness of other entities which can be sold readily in an established market at a reasonably definite price. They may be promissory notes or bonds owed by corporations or governments, or shares of the capital stock of corporations. The securities which most often meet the test of ready marketability at a reasonably assured price are U.S. government obligations.

Whether investments are classified as temporary or long-term depends on the investor's *intent*. Regardless of the legal life of a security, it is a *temporary investment* if the owner plans to hold it for a short time, and a *long-term investment* if he plans to hold it indefinitely.

Accounts receivable are claims against customers for sales of goods or services in the ordinary course of business. Such sales are usually made on *open account*, which means that cash payment is due according to the seller's customary terms as to time period and rate of cash discount. In the simplest case there may be no document supporting the account except a sales ticket. Although the customer does not sign a written promise to pay at a certain time, the seller has a legally enforceable claim against him. Sometimes accounts resulting from sales are identified as *accounts receivable, trade*.

Notes receivable, or *notes receivable, trade*, are promissory notes owned by a business as a result of sales to its customers. A promissory note is an unconditional written promise to pay a stated amount of money to the person owning the note, either when demanded or at a determinable future time.

Estimated uncollectibles contra-accounts may be established for all receivables combined, or for individual types of receivables. A business which extends credit expects as a matter of course that some of its customers' accounts and notes will not be paid in full. It does not know when credit is granted *which specific accounts* will be uncollectible; if it did, it would not extend credit to those customers. In measuring the amount of collectible accounts or notes receivable at any time when financial statements are being prepared, a business should make an appropriate deduction for the estimated total amount of uncollectibles. This is sometimes called an *allowance for bad debts*.

Accrued receivables are amounts owed to the business on contracts for services extending over a period of time. Examples are *accrued interest receivable* for the use of money and *accrued rent receivable* for the use of property. The account for *accrued interest receivable* should be separate from *notes receivable*, which shows the *face amount* of the promissory note on which the interest has accumulated.

Businesses often own receivables of more unusual types, such as *claims* against insurance companies for losses; claims for tax refunds; *advances* to or *accounts receivable* from officers, employees, stockholders, and affiliated companies; dividends receivable on investments in corporate stock; advance payments to suppliers; and others. A separate account should be kept for each type of receivable which is relatively large in money value.

Inventories are expendable physical articles held for sale, for use in manufacturing a product, or for consumption in carrying on business activity. Examples are:

Merchandise. Goods purchased by the business which are ready for sale.

Finished goods. Goods manufactured by the business which are ready for sale.

Goods in process. Goods being manufactured for sale by the business which are not yet completed.

Materials. Articles such as raw materials, semifinished products, or finished parts, which the business plans to incorporate physically into its finished product.

Supplies. Articles which will be consumed by the business in its operations but will not physically become a part (unless a negligible part) of the product.

Prepaid expenses are contractual services for which the business has paid in advance, or for which it has incurred a liability. Examples are

Unexpired insurance. Insurance protection which has been paid for in advance.

Prepaid rent. Prepayments for the use of land, buildings, or equipment.

Prepaid salaries. Payments to employees in advance of their services.

Property, plant, and equipment are physical assets which are expected to render their services through *use* rather than through consumption over an indefinitely long future time. They also include *natural resources*, whose physical quantity is reduced as the resources are extracted.

Land. A site, or location, not including any structures or improvements.

Buildings. Structures erected on land.

Land improvements. Attachments to land other than buildings, such as streets and sidewalks.

Equipment. A wide variety of physical assets used in business operations, including factory and office machines, automotive equipment, tools, furniture, furnishings, and animals.

Mineral deposits; timber tracts. Natural resources which are extracted for use in production or for sale.

Long-term intangibles consist of long-lived assets without physical substance whose potential benefit to the business lies in the rights they confer upon it.

Patents. Grants by the United States to an inventor giving him the exclusive right to sell or use his invention for 17 years.

Copyrights. Exclusive rights to reproduce or sell a literary or artistic work, granted by the United States for 28 years and renewable at the end of that time.

Trademarks. Distinguishing symbols used by a company to identify its product. If registered, they have an indefinite legal life.

Franchises. Privileges, often exclusive, granted to a business by a government or a manufacturer. Government franchises permit the owner to use public property. Dealer franchises permit the owner to sell the manufacturer's product within a certain territory.

Leaseholds. Long-term contracts for the use of real estate belonging to another.

Leasehold improvements. Improvements made by the tenant on the landlord's property which, as permanent attachments to the land, belong to the landlord. The tenant has the right to use them during the period of the lease.

Goodwill. The excess of the price paid for a business as a whole over the exchange value of its individual identifiable assets. Goodwill is thus the price paid for future service benefits which cannot be classified in customary asset categories. Examples of causes of goodwill are good customer relations, good management, and good employee morale.

Organization costs. All costs reasonably incurred in organizing the business, including legal fees, costs of printing corporate stock certificates, incorporation fees paid to governmental agencies, and fees for the services of the promoters of the business.

Long-term investments resemble temporary investments because they are usually commitments of funds for the purpose of earning a monetary return on financial instruments. A key difference is that the investor intends to hold them for a *long or indefinite time* period, rather than a short one. The purpose of the investing company is usually to earn a return directly in the form of dividends on corporate stocks or interest on corporate or government bonds. However, the investing company may own the stock of another company which is an important customer, or an essential source of supply, in order to ensure good trade relations.

Other types of long-term investments which businesses often own are life insurance policies, usually on the lives of key employees, which name the business as beneficiary; real estate held for rental rather than for use; and accumulations of funds—*sinking funds*—to pay off large amounts of debt.

Liability Accounts

Liabilities which require the payment of money ordinarily include the word "payable" as a part of their title. They may be short-term or long-term, depending on when the payment is due. The following are common types of liabilities payable in money:

Accounts payable, or accounts payable, trade. Balances owed to others for goods and supplies purchased on open account and for services such as utilities.

Notes payable, or notes payable, trade. The unpaid face amount of promissory notes owed to suppliers of goods, services, and equipment.

Notes payable to banks. Promissory notes to banks, generally arising from cash loans.

Other notes payable. Separate accounts are needed for *notes payable to officers, to employees, to affiliated companies,* and to others.

Dividends payable. The amount owed by a corporation to its stockholders as a result of an income distribution formally authorized by the board of directors.

Accrued payables. Liabilities for services received in the past, or taxes relating to past periods, which are to be paid later. Examples are *accrued interest payable, accrued salaries payable,* and *corporate income taxes payable.*

Liabilities as an agent. *Employee income tax withheld, employee social security tax withheld, sales tax payable,* and other items owed in the capacity of a tax-collecting agent for governmental units, together with withholdings for other agencies, such as *union dues withheld* and *insurance premiums withheld.*

Other payables. Loans to a company by its officers, employees, stockholders, and affiliates not evidenced by promissory notes.

Bonds payable. Long-term promissory notes issued by a corporation under a formal legal procedure which permits more than one lender to participate in the loan.

Some liabilities represent claims against the entity which are to be satisfied by delivering goods or rendering service. The following are examples:

Liabilities for future services, such as *liabilities under warranties,* the amount of which must often be estimated.

Advances from customers. Collections already received which apply to future deliveries of goods.

Rents collected in advance and similar advance collections for services.

Stockholders' Equity

Capital stock. Paid-in capital represented by ownership shares in a corporation. If there are two or more classes of stock, they may be distinguished by such titles as *capital stock, preferred* and *capital stock, common.*

Additional paid-in capital. That part of the stockholders' investment in the corporation which is not credited to *capital stock.* If the stock has a par value, the excess may be described as *capital stock—premium.*

Donated capital. An equity equal to assets contributed to the corporation by stockholders or outsiders.

Retained income. Cumulative net income of the corporation, after deductions for net losses and dividends to stockholders.

Illustration of Comprehensive Financial
Position Statement

Illustration 3-5 shows a financial position statement which includes most of the types of assets and equities defined in the preceding pages.

Note that the heading of the financial position statement shows three things:

(1) The name of the business.

(2) The name of the statement.

(3) The *specific date* at which the reported financial position existed. This is the last day of the accounting period.

The money columns of the statement do not represent debits and credits, but rather *details* and *totals,* moving from the left to the right.

**Illustration
3-5**

THE CORNER SHOP, INC.
Financial Position Statement
August 31, 1972

ASSETS

Current assets:

Cash..	$ 3,060	
Temporary investments...	1,000	
Notes receivable, trade	600	
Accounts receivable, trade............................$14,200		
Deduct estimated uncollectibles................ 900		
Estimated collectible accounts	13,300	
Accrued interest receivable.....................................	20	
Advances to employees	200	
Merchandise inventory	17,600	
Prepaid expenses	400	
Total current assets		$36,180
Long-term investments:		
Cash surrender value of life insurance..		800
Property, plant, and equipment:		
Equipment (cost)	$ 6,100	
Deduct accumulated depreciation...........................	500	
Unexpired cost		5,600
Intangible assets:		
Leasehold improvements...............................	$ 1,200	
Organization costs	300	
Total intangible assets.......................................		1,500
Total assets		$44,080

LIABILITIES

Current liabilities:

Notes payable to banks (current maturities)....................	$ 6,000	
Accounts payable, trade	16,700	
Corporate federal income tax payable	209	
Accrued interest payable...	100	
Accrued social security tax payable	350	
Employee social security tax withheld.........................	50	
Employee federal income tax withheld.........................	200	
Total current liabilities		$23,609
Long-term liabilities:		
Notes payable to banks (noncurrent maturities due 1974–1977)......		4,000
Total liabilities		$27,609

STOCKHOLDERS' EQUITY

Capital stock, $10 par, authorized, issued, and outstanding,		
1,500 shares..	$15,000	
Retained income..	1,471	
Total stockholders' equity...................................		$16,471
Total equities		$44,080

Alternative Forms of the Financial
Position Statement

The financial position format of The Corner Shop, Inc., which is shown in Illustration 3-5, is the most commonly used arrangement in the United States. In another popular arrangement current liabilities are deduced from current assets to emphasize the working capital position of the business. Long-term assets are then reported, followed by the sources of net current assets and long-term assets.

Most U.S. public utility companies, as well as many industrial companies in other countries, report long-lived assets before current assets.

Summary

This chapter has shown how the effects of business transactions on specific assets and equities are first analyzed in the *journal*, and then summarized in the *ledger* according to the specific asset and equity accounts affected. From a list of the resulting ledger account balances, called a *trial balance*, financial statements may be prepared.

Definitions of various asset, liability, and stockholders' equity accounts in common use were presented, and the form of a comprehensive financial position statement was illustrated.

Discussion Questions and Problems

3-1   To accounting students it sometimes seems that ledger accounts are an unnecessary repetition of journal entries. Explain the purpose of each.

3-2   The word "charge" is a synonym for "debit." Perhaps every reader has at some time unknowingly given record-keeping instructions to a clerk in a retail store such as "Please charge this to my account" or "Please give me credit for this."

a. What account on the books of the store would be debited, what account would be credited, and what would be the explanation be for the "charge" entry?
b. What would be the accounts debited and credited, and the explanation, in the second situation?

3-3   If the trial balance of a firm shows that the debit account total equals the credit account total, does this mean that all account balances are correct? What does it mean?

Give examples of things that might cause the trial balance to balance, although some of the account balances are incorrect.

3-4   One manufacturer reported all balances due it in one account called Receivables. Why is this objectionable? List several different components of this account which should be reported separately.

3-5   The classification of a given type of resource may change, according to the circumstances. How would you classify *Land* in the financial position statement of each of the following?

a. A manufacturer who uses the land for an employee parking lot.
b. A manufacturer who is holding idle land in the hope that it will increase in value over the next decade or two.

c. A real estate dealer who is selling lots in a highly popular new subdivision.

d. A farmer who grows grain.

3-6   The Haney Medical Center has just purchased several U.S. government securities, which mature in five years, for investment purposes. Under what classifications might these securities appear in Haney's financial position statement? What factor would determine the proper classification?

3-7   A business receives a monthly statement of its checking account from its bank and finds three "debit" slips enclosed.

a. What type of account is debited on the bank's books as a result of these slips?

b. If one slip reports that the bank charged the account $500 for a note of the business which came due during the month, what journal entry should the depositor make?

3-8   State in what way the accounts in each pair are similar to each other and in what way they are different.

a. Capital stock of the company itself and a temporary investment in the stock of another company.

b. Machinery and patents.

c. Rent receivable and rent received in advance.

d. Accounts receivable and accounts receivable—estimated uncollectibles.

e. Inventory of office supplies and unexpired insurance.

f. Accumulated depreciation of equipment and accounts receivable—estimated uncollectibles.

3-9   Prepare the stockholders' equity section of a firm's financial position statement from the following information:

(1) Common stock of $100,000 par was issued for $110,000 cash.

(2) Preferred stock has a par value of $100 per share. Five thousand shares have been issued for $120 cash per share.

(3) Earnings of the company over its entire life have totaled $210,000, and owners have received dividends of $60,000 from the company.

3-10   Refer to Illustration 3-1.

Required a. Set up T-accounts for each account affected, using the symbols "A," "L," and "OE" and an appropriate title for each account. Record the debits and credits which result from each transaction in these accounts. Use the number of each transaction (la, etc.) to identify the parts of each entry.

b. Prepare a trial balance.

3-11   Refer to Illustration 3-1.

Required a. Prepare journal entries for each transaction.

b. Can you prepare a trial balance readily from the journal entries? A financial position statement?

3-12

Required   Journalize the following transactions of the Pearl River Corporation.

(1) The corporation paid $15,000 for stock in a company which supplies it with raw materials.

(2) The corporation paid an income tax liability of $10,000 that was recorded earlier.

(3) The corporation's stockholders invested an additional $60,000 cash in the corporation, in exchange for common stock with a par value of $50,000.

(4) The corporation traded land being held as a future building site, with a cost of $15,000, for machinery of equal value.
(5) The corporation collected $5,000 to apply on the accounts of charge customers.
(6) The corporation paid $7,000 cash on notes payable.
(7) The corporation issued bonds payable in exchange for $100,000 cash.

3-13   Fred Sazio owns the Hamilton Import Corporation, which rents the building and equipment it uses. On December 31, 1972, the corporation had the following account balances:

Cash............................	$ 5,000	Owed to suppliers	$22,000
Due from customers......	18,000	Owed to bank on note...	30,000
Goods held for sale	40,000	Par value of stock issued to Sazio ...	20,000

Required   a. Using appropriate account titles, enter these balances in ledger accounts. What is the most likely title of the missing account? What is its balance?
b. Journalize the following additional transactions for January 1973.
c. Post the transactions to the ledger accounts.
d. Prepare a trial balance at January 31, 1973.

January transactions:
(1) Mr. Fazio invested $15,000 additional cash in exchange for common stock.
(2) He collected $6,000 cash from customers.
(3) He paid $4,000 cash to suppliers.
(4) He paid $5,000 on the note to the bank.
(5) He bought merchandise on account for $7,000.
(6) He bought equipment for the office on account for $1,000.

3-14

Required   Prepare a properly classified financial position statement from the following account balances of the Calhoun Corporation at the end of its accounting period, June 30, 1973.

Mortgage note payable due in 1977	$20,000
Accrued interest payable on mortgage note, due July 1, 1973.....................................	1,200
Building (cost)	30,000
Building—accumulated depreciation...............	8,000
Accounts receivable—estimated uncollectibles...	400
Retained income.......................................	13,800
Land..	12,500
Rent collected in advance............................	800
Patents..	600
Cash..	5,000
Donated capital..	8,000
Merchandise inventory...............................	14,500
Capital stock..	20,000
Accounts payable.......................................	10,400
Accounts receivable....................................	20,000

3-15   The stockholders of the J. A. Rodgers Music Company invested $10,000 cash for their shares of stock on January 2, 1973. On January 3 the management leased a building for one year at a monthly rent of $300, to be paid at the end of the month. Sound and recording equipment costing $12,000 was purchased on January 4 for a 10 per cent cash down payment and a promissory note for the remainder, due in six months.

On January 5 sales supplies and merchandise were purchased on account for $100 and $640, respectively. On January 5, $40 worth of merchandise was returned to the manufacturer for credit.

On January 6 a stockholder returned his stock and received the $1,000 he had paid for it. On January 7 the firm from which the equipment had been purchased accepted the stock as a $1,000 reduction of the balance due on the note.

Required   Journalize the preceding transactions.

3-16   The X-Road Ice Cream Company wished to borrow money from a bank. The owner drew up the following financial statement for this purpose.

1973 FINANCIAL STATEMENT

Supplies	$ 3,000	Mortgage owed (due 1/1/78)	$20,000
Building	38,000	Unpaid salaries	1,500
Equipment	12,000	Owed to suppliers	3,000
Cash	6,000	Payroll taxes due	500
Accounts receivable	2,000	Interest owed	1,000
Land	20,000	Investment and profit	55,000
Total assets	$81,000	Total interests	$81,000

Required   a. List the major weaknesses of this statement.
b. Prepare a statement in proper form. The business was incorporated with capital stock of $40,000.
c. List the accounts whose valuation the banker may question, and state how you would go about obtaining an appropriate valuation for accounting purposes.

3-17   During the month of May 1973, the following transactions took place at the Tots' Toy Company.

(1) On May 1 the business was formed. One owner invested $30,000 cash and the other transferred to the toy company his ownership of land valued at $3,000 and a building valued at $47,000.
(2) On May 2 the business purchased manufacturing equipment for $26,000 cash.
(3) On May 2 tools were bought for $500 on account.
(4) On May 7 materials to be used in the manufacture of toys were purchased on account for $4,000.
(5) The owners decided to offer $1,800 for a lot adjacent to the building, for which the present owner was asking $2,000. The offer was made on May 10, but no reply was received on that date.
(6) Some of the materials received in (4) were defective, and on May 11 they were returned to the supplier for credit. According to the supplier's invoice, the returned material cost $100.
(7) On May 17 a payment of $2,500 was made to the supplier of the materials.
(8) The owners each withdrew $250 cash, a total of $500, for their personal use on May 31.
(9) On May 31 office supplies, which had been ordered on May 30, arrived. Their cost of $280 was to be paid within ten days.
(10) On May 31 the company obtained a $6,000 cash loan from the bank, giving a two-year promissory note secured by a mortgage on the land and building.

Required
    a. Journalize the preceding transactions.
    b. Post the journal entries to ledger accounts.
    c. Prepare a trial balance.
    d. Prepare a financial position statement as of the end of May.

3-18   The T-accounts below show in summary form the transactions of the Rotor Corporation, which was organized in January, 1973.

Required
    a. Place an identifying letter A (Asset), L (Liability), or OE (Owners' Equity), as appropriate, to the left of each account title.
    b. Prepare a statement of financial position.
    c. Identify the debit and credit parts of each entry by letter and explain briefly the nature of the transaction they reflect.

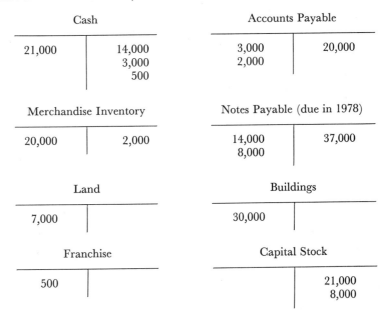

Cash				Accounts Payable	
21,000	14,000			3,000	20,000
	3,000			2,000	
	500				

Merchandise Inventory				Notes Payable (due in 1978)	
20,000	2,000			14,000	37,000
				8,000	

Land				Buildings	
7,000				30,000	

Franchise				Capital Stock	
500					21,000
					8,000

3-19   The Landcraft Realty Corporation was formed on January 1, 1974. All the following transactions took place during January 1974.

(1) Issued capital stock for cash, $50,000.
(2) Issued capital stock of $40,000 in exchange for a tract of real estate valued at $40,000.
(3) Received a corporation charter, and paid the secretary of state $100 and the lawyer who had represented the corporation during its formation $1,000 worth of capital stock.
(4) Erected a small building to serve as a temporary office on the corner of the tract. The total cost of $3,000 was to be paid within 15 days.
(5) Bought office equipment for cash, $400.
(6) Paid $200 for advertising material to be used in publicizing the development.
(7) Paid in cash one-half of the amount owed in (4).
(8) Settled the remainder of the debt in (4) by issuing shares of the company's stock.
(9) A surveyor surveyed the tract so that it could be subdivided into lots. Paid his fee of $600 in cash.

(10) Received grading equipment which had originally cost the owners $10,000 and was now appraised at $5,850, together with cash of $1,650, in exchange for the remaining shares of capital stock.

Required

a. Record the preceding transactions in T-accounts, or

b. Journalize the preceding transactions and post to ledger accounts.

c. Prepare a financial position statement as of January 31, 1974.

3-20 The Lowrance Manufacturing Corporation was organized on April 1, 1973. It issued stock with a par value of $100,000 for $105,000 cash. The City of Watasassa donated land valued at $10,000 to the corporation.

A building costing $50,000 was built on the land. Cash was given for 20 per cent of the cost and a ten-year mortgage note payable was given for the remainder.

Raw materials costing $14,000 were bought on account to permit manufacturing operations to begin. When finished, the goods are expected to sell for $25,000. Machinery costing $20,000 was installed, half being paid in cash and the remainder to be paid within 30 days.

Shortly after the corporation was formed one stockholder asked permission to withdraw and his request was granted. He was given a cash refund of the amount he had paid for a 2 per cent interest in the corporation.

Cash of $4,000 was paid on the mortgage note principal, and $1,000 was paid on the account for raw materials.

Required

a. Journalize the preceding transactions.

b. Post to ledger accounts.

c. Prepare a trial balance.

d. Prepare a financial position statement as of April 30, 1973.

Cases

3-1   Hartman Mobile Home Sales, Inc. (C). Refer to the illustrative case in this chapter.

Required

a. The illustration states, "Even if the financial position statement of MacDonald as of March 31, 1973, had been presented, there would still be differences between the *book values* of the assets as shown in the statement and the *exchange values* agreed upon by the buyer and seller of the business in their bargaining."

Which particular assets do you think would have exchange values significantly different from their book values on MacDonald's books? Why?

b. Assume that MacDonald's asset values have been adjusted to equal the sales values agreed upon. Journalize on MacDonald's books the transfer of the assets to Hartman and the related settlement.

3-2   Kent Lumber and Supply Company. You have just been employed as an accountant by the Kent Lumber and Supply Company, which sells building materials to contractors and homeowners. The business began operations on July 1, 1972, and on June 30, 1973, you proceed to prepare the annual financial statements.

The bank statement as of June 30, 1973, shows a balance of $4,500, which agrees with the balance in the company's checkbook. The office safe contains $300 in cash and $200 in undeposited checks, made payable to the Kent Lumber and Supply Company. Included in the undeposited checks is a check for $50, dated July 10, 1973, which has been credited to a customer's account.

On June 30, 1973, the total of customers' accounts arising from credit sales amounts to $25,000. Also, the company has received sales orders of $7,500 to be shipped within the next few days. Non-interest-bearing promissory notes, signed by customers and made payable to the business, total $1,500. Advances have been made to employees in the amount of $300. These are supported by signed receipts.

The business purchased office supplies costing $950 for cash during the year. It is estimated that the cost of the supplies used was $600. Merchandise was purchased from suppliers at a total cost of $100,000, of which $32,000 is unpaid at the end of the year. The total lumber inventory as of June 30, 1973, is $55,000, and the cost of other building supplies available for sale is $8,000. The June 30, 1973, inventory lists some promotional materials of the type used during the grand-opening celebration. It is estimated that the cost of these unused materials is $200. Suppliers have loaned at no charge demonstration samples, valued at $1,000, for promotional purposes. The company has placed purchase orders for additional lumber and building supplies in the amount of $37,000.

A year ago the company obtained the use of a showroom and warehouses under a ten-year lease agreement at an annual rental of $5,000. Because of its desirable location, the company could easily sublease this property for $8,000 a year. On July 1, 1972, the company paid two years' advance rent to the landlord. The company is also using power saws and other mill equipment, valued at $12,500, for which it pays rent of $1,200 a year. The rental charge for this equipment has been paid through June 30, 1973.

During the year office equipment costing $1,500 was purchased for cash. It is estimated that 10 per cent of its life has expired by year-end. On July 15, 1972, the company rented two heavy-duty delivery trucks for $400 per month. The company paid a month's rent in advance on that date and has maintained this policy consistently. On June 30, 1973, the company purchased for $3,000 cash an automobile to be used by the general manager. The list price of this car was $3,600. The company immediately took out a one-year comprehensive-coverage insurance policy on the automobile, paying a total premium of $150.

Kent Lumber and Supply Company maintains a bulk-storage tank for the gasoline used by its delivery trucks. The 1,000-gallon tank was first filled on August 1, 1972. Refills during the remainder of the year totaled 6,000 gallons. The gasoline is purchased at a contract price of 30 cents per gallon. A meter reading on June 30, 1973, indicated that 6,600 gallons were used during the year.

The CDE Railroad has a railroad siding adjacent to the lumber yard, making it unnecessary for the company to truck the lumber to the main railroad yard. This results in an estimated annual saving of $2,000 in transportation costs.

All employees are paid monthly on the last day of the month. Total monthly salaries are $6,000, all of which have been paid when due.

The telephone company installed a PBX switchboard which cost $1,750. The monthly charge for the use of this equipment, $60, has been paid for every month except June.

The owner of the Kent Lumber and Supply Company originally invested $50,000 cash in the business, and he withdrew $8,000 during the year.

Required   a. Prepare a statement of financial position as of June 30, 1973.
   b. List the items which you did not include in the statement of financial position, and give your reasons for excluding them.
   c. What has been the increase or decrease in owners' equity since July 1, 1972? Prepare a schedule to prove your answer.

chapter 4

Measuring Business Income: Basic Concepts

Purpose of Chapter

The *income* of a business is the excess of the *values realized* from the sale of its products and services over the *costs incurred* in using economic resources to provide those products and services.

This chapter explains some of the basic assumptions and concepts which accountants use in trying to measure business income meaningfully and reliably. It discusses the use of an *accounting period* of definite length in measuring income; the concept of *matching* expired costs with the associated revenue of a given time period; the *going-concern* assumption, which allows the accountant to take a long-run view in measuring business income; and the idea that revenue should not be recognized in measuring business income until it is *realized*.

The income of a business was defined in Chapter 1 as *the change in its net assets which results from (1) the excess or deficiency of revenue over related expired costs and (2) other gains or losses to the business entity from sales, exchanges, involuntary conversions, or obsolescence of its assets.*

The Accounting Period

If the operation of a business consisted of a single brief undertaking, such as buying shares of corporate stock in the hope of making a quick gain on reselling them, it would be rather simple to measure business income. The venture would be so short that there would be little need for financial statements during its life. It would be satisfactory to measure income at the end of the venture. Income would be the difference between the net assets available for distribution to the owners at the end of the venture and the net assets originally invested.

Most modern businesses are not of this temporary, or venture, type, but are formed with the purpose of *operating indefinitely*. It is not usually satisfactory to wait until the business terminates to compute its income.

Even the simplest business is a complex series of overlapping ventures of varying duration. Each venture consists of a cycle of *buying* an asset, *paying* for it, *selling* the product of the business to a customer, *collecting* for the sale, and *buying* another asset (not necessarily in this sequence). The assets during one of these cycles might be shown as follows:

In the cycle just illustrated the growth of assets from $100 to $120 at the time of the sale conforms to the *realization* concept. Income is *realized* and taken into account only when some definite, measurable inflow of assets occurs as a result of the sale of goods or services by the business or the disposal of other business assets.

If it were possible to take a still photograph of business operations, the picture would show many individual cycles in progress. Some would have just been completed; others, just begun. In between these extremes would be numerous cycles of various types and sizes in many different stages of completion.

An example of a *completed cycle* would be a sale just rung up on the cash register. *New cycles* would be illustrated by merchandise just received from the manufacturer and a fire insurance policy just purchased. *Cycles well under way* would be represented by unsold goods on the shelves, accounts receivable not collected, an office desk with one-fourth of its service life gone, and an insurance policy with two-thirds of the protection period expired.

Income information for the typical business must be provided frequently during its life. The stockholder and the banker need quarterly and annual reports of how the business is doing. The income tax collector requires an annual report of income as a basis for collecting tax. The business manager needs monthly, or even more frequent, income information to guide him in the day-to-day operation of the enterprise.

Example 1   At the end of a one-year business undertaking the manager received the following statement:

Net assets available for distribution (= owners'
        equity) at the end of the venture.................... $24,000
Deduct net assets invested by the owners................. 28,000
Net loss .... ($ 4,000)

The manager would be justified in objecting to this belated information. If he had known of such an unprofitable tendency earlier, he could have taken action to correct it, or could even have discontinued operations.

Income and its components, *revenue and expired cost,* which measure the changes in owners' equity resulting from business activity, have meaning only if the *period of time* over which the change occurs is known. To measure their amounts, one must decide how long the time period is to be and how to select the events to be considered during that period.

Income is a *total* change which occurs over a period of time. If too long a period is used, total income does not reveal important changes in income's *rate* and *direction* (whether it is a net income or a net loss).

Example 2   The first information that the owner-manager of a business received about its income was at the end of a year, when he was told that the net income was $24,000. He would have been able to manage the business much more intelligently if he had known monthly income results such as the following:

Month	Income for Month	Annual Rate of Income
January.	$10,000 net income	$120,000 net income
February.	2,000 net income	24,000 net income
March	(1,000) net loss	(12,000) net loss

The annual rate for each month shows what the results for the year would have been if the rate at which income was earned during the month continued for an entire year. If January's results were about normal for a month, receipt of the monthly income reports showing a sharp decline in February would have led the manager to investigate its cause. Perhaps the business would thereafter have earned income more nearly in line with the $120,000 annual rate indicated by January's operations.

Just as each year's income is the result of varying rates of earnings for each of 12 months, so is each month's income composed of weekly, daily, and hourly rates. Frequent measurements, up to a practical limit, give better information about the rate at which income is being earned than do infrequent ones. They also give it in time for appropriate action.

Practically all businesses measure income at least once a year. The calendar year, January 1 through December 31, is the most popular basic accounting period, but many companies have recognized the advantages of using their *natural business year.* This period, which differs from one business to another, begins in the slack season, continues through the activities of the busy season, and ends in the slack season a year later. Its use reduces the margin of error in measuring revenue, expired costs, assets, and equities; however, the resulting balances in the financial position statement may not be representative of the asset and equity balances which prevail during most of the year.

The period for which financial reports are prepared is called the *fiscal period.* An example is the fiscal year beginning June 1, 1972, and ending May 31, 1973. Management usually needs detailed reports of income once a month or oftener. Some banks even compute their income every day. In addition, practically all business managements should receive daily reports on the movements of the important components of income, such as major classes of revenue and expense. The more frequent the income reading, the better is management able to determine the direction and rate of business progress. However, the cost of obtaining frequent reports should not exceed the benefit received from them.

Accrual Accounting

The effects of business events and transactions, some of which are occurring continuously, on the income of a business are identified with specific periods of time by a process called *accrual accounting*. Any time period selected for computing the income of a business is artificial. Business activity does not halt simply because the last day of the accounting period has ended. Instead, there will be quantities of unsold merchandise on hand; shipments in transit to customers and from suppliers; accounts to be collected; bills to be paid; contracts for services, both with customers and with suppliers, in various stages of completion; productive facilities with various fractions of their useful lives expired—in fact, many business activities at many stages of progress.

In the face of this complexity of real business events, accountants have developed the following guides for determining what revenue the business has earned during the accounting period and what costs have expired, as well as what other gains and losses have occurred.

1. The heart of the accrual accounting process consists of *matching revenue with the related expired costs*.

In the process of matching, *revenue* is usually the controlling factor. Revenue is identified with time periods on the occurrence of some critical event or events, which will be described later in this chapter.

A *cost is incurred* when a payment is made or a liability is created for property, for services, or for a loss. *Cost expirations* may be classified as either *expenses* or *losses*.

The costs which have a cause-and-effect relationship with the period's revenue are accrued as *expenses* of the same period. That is, they are *matched* with revenue.

2. Costs which cannot be directly identified with segments of revenue are treated as *expenses* or *losses* of the accounting period in which the business is considered to receive the related service, or when a potential for future service benefit disappears.

3. Other gains and losses, unrelated to the sale of goods and services by the business, are identified with the time period in which the gain or loss is evidenced by sale of an asset or other dependable evidence.

The Going-Concern Assumption

In making accounting measurements, the business enterprise is assumed to have an *indefinite life*, unless there is convincing information to the contrary. Exceptions are a venture which is specifically organized for a limited life and an organization on the verge of terminating its affairs. The assumption of indefinite enterprise life, referred to as the *going-concern concept*, permits accounting measurements to be made on the basis of *long-run considerations*. Thus, in measuring the expired and unexpired cost of long-lived assets such as equipment and buildings, it is assumed that the business will continue to use them for their entire useful lives, rather than sell them earlier.

Another approach would be to try to measure the resources of the business in terms of their current sale or liquidating values (that is, their *short-run values*).

In most cases this information is not relevant to the purposes of the financial statement user. The business does not intend to sell its plant and facilities, but to use them in carrying on its operations of manufacturing and selling goods or of providing services. Businesses are judged by their success in earning a profit by utilizing their assets to create and exchange goods and services. The estimated sales prices of assets that are owned for use in the business rather than for sale are often undependable.

Realized Versus Unrealized Changes in Asset Values

The historical cost of an asset is ordinarily the proper starting point for measuring it in accounting, rather than the asset's subjective present value to the owner or its estimated selling price in the market. (See the section "Value in Use and Value in Exchange" in Chapter 2.) For example, if merchandise on hand originally cost $5,000 but could be sold for $8,000 on the last day of the accounting period, the original cost of $5,000 should ordinarily continue to appear on the accounting records. There are few exceptions to the rule that accounts are kept in terms of past exchange prices.

In recent years an increasing number of accountants and businessmen have urged that accounting reflect changes in asset values in the financial statements when such changes can be identified and measured objectively. They argue that *current values* are much more significant measures of the resources of a business than measures based on *historical values*. Likewise, they contend that a meaningful report of the financial progress of a business must include changes in the values of assets still on hand, such as inventories, plant, and equipment, as well as value changes which have been *realized* through exchange transactions. Because of a conservative bias, accountants already tend to report *declines* in the values of assets whether or not such declines have been realized. The weight of opinion among accountants is that any *unrealized increases* in values, if reported at all, should be in *supplementary* statements or footnotes—not in the primary financial statements.

To include unrealized gains on assets in business income would not be new in accounting. Before World War I business income measurement in the United States centered on comparing the current values of assets owned at the beginning and end of the accounting period. After adjusting the change in net asset value during the period to allow for the owners' additional investments and withdrawals, the resulting figure was reported as *income* for the period.

The shift of the accountant's concept of income from one of *asset valuation* to one of *realization* resulted from several factors. A primary one was the desire to report business income as the difference between *accomplishment*—revenue—and the *effort expended* to achieve that accomplishment—expired cost. Other factors favoring the realization approach were a desire to report income only when the additional assets were in *disposable form* (cash or near cash) and a great concern for *objective measurement* which could be implemented effectively.

Alternative Bases of Recognizing Revenue

The first step in accrual accounting—and a key one—is selecting a type of event which signals that the business should recognize revenue. Events which are sometimes used as the basis of revenue recognition in the accounts are

(1) Sale of the product or service.
(2) Collection of the sales price in cash.
(3) Production of a product or service to be sold later.
(4) Passage of time, where a service is being sold over a stated time period.

(*1*) *Sale of the product or service.* Business progress is measured by the excess of the net assets which it obtains by producing and selling goods and services over the net assets which it expends in their production and sale. The actual *sale* of business output, which is usually the time when legal title passes, is a very critical event. At this point the business parts with a good or service and receives in exchange *a different asset,* which is usually money or a legally enforceable right to collect money in the future. Revenue has been realized—even though the selling price has not been collected in cash—if there is good reason to believe that it *will be collected.* The price of the good or service sold—the amount of the revenue—is objectively determined in a bargained market transaction.

Example 3　　A retail appliance store sells an electric fan for $25 cash. It has a revenue of $25, the source of the new asset, cash. If the sale had been on account to a solvent customer, there would still have been revenue of $25, the source of the new asset, accounts receivable.

Businessmen who are optimistic by nature are sometimes inclined to count on favorable events which they *hope* will happen as though they have already occurred. Occasionally, businessmen tend to be unduly pessimistic. The selection of the *sale as an objective event* which warrants the recognition of revenue in the accounts helps to neutralize the effect of such optimism and pessimism.

Example 4　　A retailer bought a number of men's coats at $25 each, marking them to sell at $40 each. The style proved so popular that the manufacturer raised its price to merchants to $30 a coat. The retailer then marked its selling price up to $50. At the end of its accounting period the retailer has ten unsold coats on hand. How much revenue has been realized on the unsold coats?

Solution　　None. There is no certainty that the coats will be sold at all or, if so, when; what additional effort will be needed to sell them; or what price they will bring. Only when each coat is sold is there objective evidence that there is any revenue and how much there is.

Most businesses which deal in a product or a service which is rendered over a short period of time use the *sale basis* of recognizing revenue.

(*2*) *Collection of the sales price in cash.* In some situations there is a great deal of uncertainty as to whether, when, and to what extent sales on credit will be collected in cash. If the amount to be collected cannot be estimated within a reasonable range of error, periodic revenue should be reported on a *cash basis.* The revenue of an accounting period in such cases is the amount of cash collected for goods delivered or services performed. Matched against this as deductions are the costs related to this revenue, whether or not they have been paid for in cash.

Some types of sales to consumers on a long-term installment basis are subject to great collection risks. Under these circumstances the revenue of each period should be the installments collected during that period.

(*3*) *Production of a product or service to be sold later.* As a general rule, revenue from a product or a service should be taken into income only when the item is *sold*, not when it is produced. In cases where there is a high degree of assurance that the sale will be made, when it will be made, what the sales price will be, and what the related costs will be, it is appropriate to account for revenue at the time production takes place. An example would be the production of gold, which the national government stands ready to buy at a fixed price. Usually the major costs involved are in mining and refining the gold, and transportation costs are negligible. Other examples are agricultural products which have an assured market at a fixed price.

In some cases businesses work on only a few major products during a year. Examples are road contractors and shipbuilders. The periodic income figure derived from reporting only output *sold* as revenue would not be a good measure of business activity. Where reasonably reliable estimates can be made of revenues and remaining costs, it is appropriate to recognize revenue each year in proportion to work done. To illustrate, assume that a road builder has agreed to pave a road for $12 million, and that during 1972 he has incurred paving costs totaling $8 million. Reliable estimates indicate that the cost of completing the project will be $2 million. The contractor is justified in recognizing eight-tenths of the revenue, or $9.6 million, in his accounts because eight-tenths of the work has been done.

(*4*) *Passage of time.* When a business sells a service which, according to contract, is to extend over a definite time period, it is customary to consider that the revenue is realized at an *equal amount per day*.

Example 5   A bank lends money to a customer for 30 days. The service which the customer receives is the use of the bank's money, for which he agrees to pay *interest*. The bank realizes interest revenue of an equal amount each day during the term of the loan if the loan principal remains unchanged.

Other types of revenue which *accrue* in equal daily amounts are rent for the use of property and insurance premiums for protection of the customer against risk.

Criteria for Recognizing Revenue

To justify recognizing revenue in any situation, the following conditions must be met:

(1) The revenue must have been *earned* by transferring a good, rendering a service, or producing a good.

(2) The business must have received another asset in exchange, or have a high degree of assurance that an asset will be received.

(3) The exchange price of the good or service must be measurable with a high degree of dependability.

Collections of cash in *advance* for a good or service to be delivered later *are not revenue.* They are liabilities until the revenue is earned.

Unperformed Contracts

The question sometimes arises as to whether a revenue or a cost should be recorded in the accounts under a contract where neither contracting party has yet performed his contractual obligation.

One such situation occurs when a business has ordered goods from a manufacturer and the order has been accepted but the goods have not been shipped. Because neither party has performed his obligation under the contract, customarily neither party records any changes in assets and equities. This is true even though the contract is legally enforceable. The uncertainties are so great prior to the actual delivery of the goods that it is unwise for the seller to reflect revenue or for the purchaser to reflect an expenditure until the actual exchange occurs.

A similar procedure applies to contracts for rendering service. If the recipient of the service is obligated to make a payment in advance, he should record the right to receive the service as an asset and the obligation to make the payment as a liability (or as a reduction in Cash if the payment has actually been made). But if payment is to be made after the service has been performed and no service has yet been rendered, neither party to the contract should make an entry.

Convenience in Recording Revenue Realization

The *selection* of the types of events which signal that a business should recognize revenue should not be confused with the timing of *recording* the events in the accounting records. The particular time when recording is done is largely a matter of clerical efficiency, but all relevant events must be considered when income is measured for a certain period.

Example 6   A business keeps a soft-drink machine for the use of its employees. A few drinks are sold each day, and the coin box is emptied and the supply of drinks replenished about once a week. When should the sales be recorded?

Solution   It would be extremely inconvenient to record a sale every time an employee buys a drink. The most convenient time for recording the sales would probably be when the machine is refilled. However, an income statement should include the gain from selling drinks for the accounting period.

Revenue from the sale of goods should be recorded as soon after the sale as practical. This is usually accomplished by recording the sale on a cash register or a sales ticket at the time of the transaction, and then entering all sales in the permanent accounting records daily. When an accounting period ends, it is especially important that all the sales of that period be considered in measuring the period's revenue.

Revenue earned with the passage of time, such as the bank's interest on a loan, is considered to *accrue* in equal amounts each day, but for convenience it is usually *recorded* in total when the term of the loan ends. If the accounting period ends before the loan is repaid, revenue must be recorded for the number of days for which the loan has been outstanding during the accounting period. The revenue has been *earned* even though it will not be *collected* until a later period.

Timing of Cost Expiration

Expired costs are of two classes, *expenses* and *losses*. *Expenses* are asset expirations which are associated with the sale of goods and services and with related business activities. Cost expirations which do not benefit the business, such as the damage of uninsured property by fire, are *losses*. Losses also occur when equipment or similar assets, which are held for use, are sold for less than their unexpired cost.

It is easy to recognize when some types of assets render their services to the business. When goods are transferred to a customer at the time of sale, the service potential of an *asset, merchandise,* is used up as far as the business is concerned and becomes an *expense, cost of goods sold.* At the same time, the business realizes revenue in the amount of the sale price. The revenue and expense are associated directly with each other; that is, they are *matched.*

Many other costs which expire during an accounting period cannot be directly associated with particular sales, even though there is strong evidence that they *benefit the operations of the business.* Examples of these expenses are rent, interest for money borrowed, utilities, and insurance. It is customary to associate expenses of this type with accounting periods in proportion to the part of the service contract which expires during each period.

Example 7   A business which uses the calendar year as its accounting period bought a contract for insurance protection for a year beginning October 1, 1972, for a total cost of $240. What was its expense for insurance for the accounting period 1972?

Solution   The 1972 expense is proportionate to the fraction of the contract's life which expired during 1972, $\frac{3}{12}$ of $240, or $60. The remaining $180 of the cost of the insurance policy was an asset at the end of 1972, the cost of a service benefit to be received in future accounting periods.

Losses are measured by the amount needed to reduce assets at the end of the year to that part of their cost which will presumably benefit future business operations.

Example 8   A machine which was carried on the books at its unexpired cost of $2,200 was damaged in an accident. After the accident its usefulness was severely limited, and it was reliably estimated that a machine with equal service potential for the future could be acquired for $400. How should these facts be treated in the accounts?

Solution   The amount of the asset's cost which will not benefit the future, $1,800, is a *loss.* The remaining $400 is an asset.

Convenience in Recording Cost Expiration

Criteria for determining which expired costs should be matched with the revenue of a given accounting period are (1) expiration which is *directly* associated with the revenue-producing activities of the period, and (2) expiration through obsolescence, accident, or a similar cause not directly associated with the revenue-producing activities. The time when the actual record of the cost expiration is made in the accounts, like the time of recording revenue, is largely a matter of record-keeping efficiency. In some cases the exact time when the individual cost expirations occur could be determined, but it is not practical to so do.

Example 9 It would be physically possible to match the cost of wrapping supplies with the revenue from the sale of the articles wrapped, but to do so would require an unreasonable amount of time and effort in proportion to the value of the information obtained.

For convenience, the expired cost of supplies used and small unit costs of merchandise sold are usually not recorded at the time of each sale transaction. Instead, the *total* expired cost of supplies or merchandise is measured *indirectly* at the end of the accounting period by the following formula:

Assets acquired — Assets unexpired at end of period
= Costs expired during period.

Example 10 The *X* Company had selling supplies costing $200 on hand on December 31, 1971. During January, 1972, the company bought additional supplies for $150. It was not practical to record a cost expiration each time supplies were used; therefore, on January 31 an estimate was made which indicated that the supplies still on hand had cost approximately $250. What was the amount of supplies expense for January?

Solution
Cost of supplies on hand at beginning..................................... $200
+ Cost of supplies acquired during period   150
= Total cost of supplies available for use.................................... $350
− Cost of supplies not used (estimated cost at end of period)..........   250
= Expired cost, or expense, of supplies used during the month....... $100

Income Statement Form

Illustration 4-1 shows the major components of an income statement. The heading includes the name of the business and the name of the statement, as well as the *period of time* covered, the year ended December 31, 1972. This is in contrast to the financial position statement, which reports assets and equities as of a *certain day*.

This is a condensed form of income statement. The detailed components of net sales revenue, operating expenses, and extraordinary gains and losses will be explained in later chapters.

Under federal income tax law a *corporation* is subject to corporate income tax

Illustration
4-1

THE ALPHA CORPORATION
Income Statement
For the Year Ended December 31, 1972

Net sales revenue......................................	$500,000
Deduct cost of goods sold expense..................	300,000
Gross margin on sales	200,000
Deduct operating expenses...........................	150,000
Income before income tax............................	50,000
Deduct corporate income tax expense.............	20,000
Income before extraordinary items ($3.00 per share of capital stock)	30,000
Add extraordinary gain:	
Gain on sale of land, $60,000, less applicable income tax, $15,000 ($4.50 per share)...	45,000
Net income ($7.50 per share).......................	75,000

as a separate legal person. Single proprietorships and partnerships are not legal or taxable entities. The income of these unincorporated businesses is taxed to the owners at the *individual* income tax rates which apply to the respective owners. Corporate stockholders are taxed as *individuals only on the dividends* they receive from the corporation.

Stockholders tend to attach great importance to the corporation's income per share of stock. For this reason, *per share* as well as total amounts should be reported for income before extraordinary items, extraordinary gains and losses (less income tax effect), and net income. These per share amounts are computed by dividing the total figure by the average number of shares of stock outstanding.

Cost of goods sold is an expense of a trading enterprise: a manufacturer, wholesaler, or retailer. Service enterprises do not have a comparable deduction in their income statements.

Alternative Titles and Forms of the Income Statement

Accounting terminology is constantly changing as accountants seek to communicate more effectively with financial statement users. The income statement is often called the "Profit and Loss Statement," or the "Earnings Statement," or the "Operating Statement."

The form of Illustration 4-1 up to *Income before extraordinary items* is called the *multiple-step* form of income statement. Cost of goods sold, operating expenses, and income taxes are deducted in sequence, leaving subtotals. An alternative form in wide use is the *single-step* form. All revenues are added together and all expenses are added together. Total expense is then deducted from total revenue.

These alternative *forms* of the income statement have *no effect on the amount of net income* that is reported.

Summary A major objective of accounting is to measure the income of a business over time. *Income* from the accountant's point of view is the change in owners' equity which results during a time period from carrying on business activity. Income does not include the investments and disinvestments of the business owners.

Income is measured for a selected time period by determining what *revenue is realized* within that period, and then deducting the related expired costs. The principal basis for recognizing revenue from products is the *sale*, and the principal basis for recognizing revenue for services contracted for a definite time period is the passage of *time*. Under appropriate circumstances in exceptional cases, revenue may be recognized on the basis of *cash collection* or *production*.

The expiration of entity assets which results from business operations is called *expense*. A *cost is incurred* when a payment is made or a liability is created for property, for services, or for a loss. When a service benefit from such a cost is used during the current period, the cost is said to have expired and to have become an *expense*. A cost which expires without identifiable benefit to the business is called a *loss*.

The process of measuring the income of specific time periods is chiefly one of *matching revenue and the related expired costs*. This process is the heart of *accrual accounting*. The *income statement* reports the revenues recognized during a stated period of time and the costs which expired during that period.

Discussion Questions and Problems

4-1 George and Tom agreed to set up a temporary roadside refreshment stand to serve motorists attending a July 4 music festival. How should they go about measuring their income from this venture? List specific items of revenue and expense that you would expect to find in their income statement.

4-2 George and Tom found their venture so successful that, after winding up the affairs of the temporary refreshment stand, they decided to set up a permanent quick-stop snack shop in the area. They bought a building, equipment, and supplies and paid other necessary costs. How would their problems of measuring periodic income from this business differ from the problem of measuring income in Question 4-1? List specific income statement items which will be more difficult to measure, and explain why.

4-3 Each of the following businesses, now reporting income on a calendar year basis, wishes to use a fiscal year which is best suited to its normal operating cycle. Suggest the ending date for an appropriate accounting period for each business and give the reasons for your recommendation.

a. A large urban department store whose major sales occur during the Christmas season.
b. A midwestern wheat farmer.
c. A winter tourist hotel.
d. A swimsuit manufacturer.
e. An automobile manufacturer.

4-4 A retail establishment had sales revenue of $200,000 during 1973. During the year it bought merchandise costing $160,000 and sold merchandise costing $125,000. It paid building rent for two years in advance in January 1973, a total of $6,000. It paid salaries of $30,000 during the year, and employee salaries of $2,000 for the last part of December were still unpaid at the end of the year. What was the firm's income for the year if there were no other expenses? Explain how you used the matching concept in computing income.

4-5   A wholesaler bought merchandise costing $500,000 from manufacturers in 1973. Merchandise costing $370,000 was sold to customers, and merchandise costing $50,000 was totally destroyed in a fire. The wholesaler carried no property insurance. Explain how the matching concept is used here in computing 1973 income.

4-6   "The accountant is not justified in assuming that the business entity will continue in operation indefinitely. Studies of business mortality rates show that a high percentage of businesses fail during the first year, and that many more fail in the next year or two."

a. What effect does the going-concern assumption have on the measurement of income and financial position? Give specific examples.
b. Is this assumption justified in view of the high failure rate among new businesses? Explain.

4-7   A laundry bought a building for $50,000 in 1973, expecting that it would have a useful life of 20 years. At the end of 1973 market values of real estate had risen and the building could have been sold for $60,000. The laundry planned to continue to use it for the rest of its useful life. Use benefits were expected to be about equal each year. How would these facts affect the laundry's income for 1973? What concepts related to income measurement most directly apply to this situation?

4-8   One approach to measuring business income would be to determine the resale values of the assets at the end of a period, subtract the liabilities owed at the end of the period, and compare the resulting net asset figure with net assets at the beginning of the year.

a. What other factors must be considered in measuring periodic income by this approach?
b. What advantages would this approach to measuring income (as modified by your answer in part a) have over today's dominant concept of measuring income only as *realized*?
c. What are the advantages of the realized income concept?

4-9   Mr. Mueller bought a share of *R* Mfg. Co. stock, which is actively traded on the stock exchange, for $120 on January 17. Every day he followed the stock quotations with great interest. On January 31 the stock's closing price was $139 a share.

a. How much was his income during January?
b. During February a market decline set in, and on February 28 the stock was quoted at $114 a share. How much was Mr. Mueller's income for February?
c. In March the *R* Mfg. Co. paid a cash dividend of $8 a share. Mr. Mueller received the dividend on March 16, and on March 24 he sold the share for $132. What was his income for March?

4-10   A builder formed a construction company in September. After several months' effort, the company completed a residence for a total cost of $18,000 and advertised it for sale. By November 30 the company had received three offers: one of $21,000 cash; one of $22,000 to be paid in monthly installments over 20 years with 6 per cent annual interest; and another of $20,000 cash plus a residential lot worth $3,200. The builder decided to wait for a higher offer, which he seemed certain to get.

a. What basis should the construction company use in recognizing revenue for the year? Why?
b. How much was its revenue for the year under this basis?

c. How much were its expenses?

d. What would its income for the year have been if the third offer had been accepted and the sale closed on December 27?

4-11   Use a letter to show what basis of recognizing revenue you think would be most appropriate for each of the businesses listed below. Explain briefly the reasons for your choice.

Bases of recognizing revenue:

a. Sale of product or service.
b. Collection of the sales price in cash.
c. Passage of time, where a service is being performed over a stated time period.
d. Partial production of a product or service to be sold or delivered later.
e. Completion of production of a product or service to be sold or delivered later.

Type of business:

1. Ladies dress manufacturer.
2. Silver mining company.
3. Small loan company.
4. Large bank making loans primarily to businesses.
5. Contractor building a major dam.
6. A record club which mails its members records if they do not previously state that they do not wish to buy the record. Members have the right to return unwanted records.
7. Concessionaire who sells football programs at the Super Bowl.
8. A life insurance company.
9. An automobile repair shop.
10. An automobile dealer.

4-12   Compute the amount of revenue for the current year in each of the following situations. In each case the calendar year is the accounting period.

a. A monthly magazine began operations on July 1 and collected for 50,000 two-year subscriptions at $12 each during the first few days of the month. An edition was published each month from July through December.

b. A road contractor signed a contract to pave a road for $1 million. By the end of the year actual construction costs of $600,000 had been incurred, and the engineers were in general agreement that the project could be completed in a few months at an additional cost of $200,000.

c. A second-hand furniture dealer sold his merchandise to individuals on credit in a poverty-stricken area. A small down payment was required. Frequent repossessions were necessary. Sales in the current year totaled $50,000. The dealer had paid $20,000 for the furniture sold.

d. An equipment dealer rented an office machine to a business for three months on December 31 of the current year. The rent is to be paid when the machine is returned.

4-13   Richard Drake is a citrus grower in Florida. Although his fruit is picked and sold during only two months of the year, Mr. Drake incurs costs throughout the year for the care and upkeep of the orchards. What problems would Mr. Drake have in measuring monthly net income?

4-14   Necessary preliminary arrangement for the Novelty Shop, prior to its opening for business, included applying for telephone service. The telephone company bills the customer for each month's service at the end of the month. No deposit or installation fee was required.

a. Did the installation of the telephone increase the assets of the Novelty Shop?
b. Did it result in an expense at the time of installation?
c. If the monthly service charge is $30, how would this affect the computation of income for the first two weeks?
d. What would be the effect on assets and income if the service charge for the first month were paid in advance at the beginning of the month?
e. What would be the effect on assets and income if an installation charge of $10 were paid at the beginning of the month?
f. How often do you recommend that telephone expense be recorded? When?

4-15   The Public Loan Company makes many small loans to its customers for terms of one, two, and three months. It takes promissory notes in exchange and collects interest at the end of the loan period, when the principal is collected. The company prepares an income statement once a year. Usually it makes about 2,000 loans a year, of which about 300 will not have matured at the end of the year.

a. State how you would compute Public's interest revenue for a year.
b. Considering clerical efficiency, when do you recommend that Public record the interest revenue on individual loans?

4-16   The Bussman Co. had the following cash transactions in 1973. Explain how each item paid or collected affects 1973 income.

a. Payment for a three-year insurance policy which expires in 1975.
b. Payment for 1973 salaries.
c. Issuance of capital stock for cash.
d. Collection of a customer's account for a sale made in 1973.
e. Payment for salaries for the last week of December 1972.
f. Cash loan received from the bank.
g. Payment for equipment purchased in 1973.
h. Payment of refund to stockholder in exchange for his share of capital stock.
i. Receipt of $6,000 for sale of land which had cost $5,000.
j. Refund received for merchandise returned to the manufacturer.
k. Payment for merchandise bought on credit in 1973.
l. Cash refund to customer who returned merchandise.
m. Collection of rent for a three-year period ending in 1975.

4-17   Karl Clothing Company was organized in November with cash of $5,000. During the month it bought goods on credit for a total cost of $15,000. By November 30 one-third of the goods had been sold on account for sales prices totaling $7,300. Although one-half of the accounts were collected in November, none of the purchases were paid for. Rent of $375 and salaries of $250 for November were paid in cash.

Required   a. How much revenue did the store have in November?
b. What types and amounts of expenses did it incur?
c. What was its income for November?
d. What types and amounts of assets did it have on November 30?
e. Explain specifically why the income for November differs from the change in Cash in November.

4-18   On the first day of December, Karl Clothing Company (see Problem 4-17) closed. All unsold goods were returned to suppliers for full credit. All customers' accounts were collected in full in December, and all debts were paid. Rent of $375 and salaries of $250 were paid for in cash.

Required a. List the store's revenues and expenses and compute its income for December.
b. What were its assets at the conclusion of this series of events?

4-19 On January 1, 1973, John Donaldson paid $4,500 for a three-year fire insurance policy. On December 31, 1974, a question has arisen as to the amount of unexpired insurance that should be shown in the current balance sheet.

One proposal is to show unexpired insurance at $900, which is the amount of the refund which could be received from the insurance policy if the policy were cancelled by the insured on December 31, 1974.

A second proposal is to show unexpired insurance at $1,500, representing one-third of the original premium cost.

A third proposal is to show unexpired insurance at $1,800, which is the one-year premium cost for a policy of the same amount as the policy in force.

Required Discuss each proposal as to its acceptability, as to the general accounting principle underlying it, and as to its effect on reported income. (Adapted from AICPA Examination in Theory of Accounts.)

4-20 The Wright Auto Agency has agreed to trade a new automobile, fully serviced, from its floor for a needed hydraulic lift. The automobile cost Wright $3,600 and is listed to sell at $4,500. In exchange, the lift manufacturer has agreed to install a hydraulic lift in Wright's garage, ready for use. The lift normally sells for $3,400 and costs about $500 to install.

Required a. What effect does this exchange have on Wright's revenues of the current year?
b. What additional information do you need in order to record the trade?
c. Assuming such additional facts as are necessary, how much income does Wright have from this trade in the current year?
d. How will the way in which this event is recorded affect Wright's income in future years?

4-21 The Millvale Company manufactures handbags.

Required Use a letter to indicate whether the following events which affected the company in 1973 would result in (a) revenue, (b) expense, (c) extraordinary gain, (d) extraordinary loss, or (e) none of these.

(1) Paid the cost of organizing the corporation.
(2) Paid the president's salary.
(3) Received cash from a bank loan.
(4) Bought on credit leather to be used in making handbags.
(5) Used the administration building for the year.
(6) Sold handbags on account.
(7) Sold handbags for cash.
(8) Sold an unneeded warehouse for $20,000 more than its unexpired cost.
(9) Used materials in the manufacture of handbags sold.
(10) Bought new machinery.
(11) Collected accounts receivable resulting from sales made earlier.
(12) Paid a stockholder cash in exchange for his stock in the company.

(13) Sold stock held as an investment for $10,000 less than it had cost some years earlier.

(14) Earned interest on a note receivable.

(15) The owners invested additional cash for stock of the company.

(16) Sold handbags in exchange for a note receivable.

(17) The resale value of one of the buildings doubled during the year, as a result of a high demand for commercial property in the area.

(18) Paid income taxes on 1972 income.

(19) Income taxes on 1973 income, computed to be $25,000, were not paid by the end of the year.

(20) Received an order from a mail-order house for 5,000 handbags. This was an unusually large order.

4-22   The following account balances appear in the ledger of the Ripley Hardware Store as of December 31, 1973:

Salaries	$ 24,000
Cash	5,600
Cost of goods sold	120,000
Store rent	7,200
Utilities	1,400
Gain on sale of display counters	3,000
Sales	180,000
Advertising expense	4,200
Prepaid insurance	600
Licenses	200
Merchandise inventory, Dec. 31, 1973	80,000
Accounts payable	5,000
Depreciation of store equipment	1,000
Store equipment—unexpired cost	8,000
Corporate income tax (including $660 on the gain on sale of display counters)	5,500

Required   Prepare a multiple-step income statement in good form.

Required   **4-23**   From the following information, prepare a statement of Mr. Willkins' income from business activities for 1973.

Boyd Willkins, a young attorney, opened an office for the practice of law on January 1, 1973. He paid a year's rent of $1,200 for an office. Early in January he rented law books for one year, paying the annual rental of $300 in advance. He paid $50 for one-year subscriptions to professional journals.

Mr. Willkins billed clients a total of $16,000 as fees for legal services rendered during the year, of which he had collected $12,000 by December 31. He expected that he would be able to collect all of the remainder except $300. During December he received a check for $200 (not included in the preceding collections) as a retainer for services to be performed in January and February 1974.

Early in 1973 Mr. Willkins had much idle time on his hands, which he utilized by acting as rental agent for several individuals who owned real estate. He collected commissions of $900 and incurred advertising costs of $100 in this connection.

Other payments during the year were as follows: secretarial assistance (part-time), $2,400; stationery and postage (of which approximately $20 worth was unused at the end of the year), $260; utilities, $190; professional license for the year, $40; lunches for Mr. Willkins, $305; and payments on his personal income tax for the preceding year, $155.

4-24 Bill James had owned a small unincorporated dry-cleaning establishment for several years, but had kept inadequate financial records until he got into difficulty with the Internal Revenue Service.

Required From the following data relating to his affairs for 1973 prepare an income statement in good form. Show supporting computations.

Cash payments for the year:		Cash collections for the year:	
City business license for 1973 ... $	50	From customers for 1972 services	$ 1,470
Supplies purchased................	1,400	From customers for 1973	
Salaries of employees	11,400	services	18,000
Mr. James' church contribution	300	Refund of 1972 income tax	290
Property taxes for 1972 (1973 taxes were $40 more).......	150		
Claims paid for damaged clothing	310		
Building rent.......................	1,500		
Utilities	830		

On December 31 Mr. James owed $400 for supplies which had been purchased during the year and $60 for December utilities. He had begun the year with supplies costing $300 on hand, and at the end of the year supplies inventory amounted to $150. Charge customers owed the business $2,100, all of which was expected to be collectible.

Required **4-25** From the following trial balance of Zircon Company at the end of its accounting year, December 31, 1973, prepare an income statement and a financial position statement in good form. The Retained Income balance on December 31, 1973, was $21,600.

	Debits	Credits
Accounts payable..		$ 11,000
Accounts receivable	$ 15,200	
Sales revenue		125,000
Prepaid insurance	600	
Notes receivable (due within 12 months)	2,000	
Investment in stock of business affiliate	18,000	
Cost of goods sold	80,000	
Capital stock..		25,000
Merchandise inventory (Dec. 31, 1973)................	22,000	
Bonds payable (due in 1981)		20,000
Patents..	9,000	
Corporate income tax expense	4,400	
Interest expense..	1,000	
Corporate income tax payable		4,400
Notes payable to banks (payable on demand)		8,000
Retained income (Dec. 31, 1972).......................		6,000
Delivery equipment	8,000	
Accumulated depreciation on delivery equipment...		4,000
Depreciation expense on delivery equipment	2,000	
Goodwill..	12,000	
Organization cost..	500	
Land..	6,700	
Salary expense..	22,000	
Totals	$203,400	$203,400

Cases **4-1** **Porter-Sloan Boat Company.** On June 1, 1973, John Sloan and Steve Porter received a franchise from the Plastic Boat Company to retail Cruise River boats.

Their costs associated with obtaining the franchise, $500, were paid in cash, of which each contributed half. Both of the men had other full-time jobs and had entered into this venture to provide additional income. Steve's father, who was in the farm machinery business, agreed to allow them to display their boats free in a showroom in one of his buildings.

John and Steve demonstrated the boats to prospective customers during their off hours. They decided to call their business the Porter-Sloan Boat Company, and on June 5, 1973, they purchased for cash with personal funds one boat, Model X12453, for $900. Each contributed $450. The boat was listed to sell for $1,495. One week later they purchased on account from the Plastic Boat Company another model, LR65712, which was listed to sell for $1,995, for $1,200. On June 16 they sold the Model LR65712 for cash $1,900. On June 25 they had an offer of $1,300 for Model X12453, which they refused.

The two men were quite encouraged when they reviewed their financial situation at the end of the month. Steve stated that they were really doing well because they had $1,900 in cash, $500 more than the amount that they had invested.

Required

a. Comment on Steve's statement.

b. What was the company's net income for the month?

c. Prepare a financial position statement as of June 30, 1973.

d. Is the net income for this company a realistic figure? Explain.

e. What are some of the accounting problems that the company might face in the future even though the situation now seems to be a very simple arrangement?

4-2   Smoky Valley Cafe.[1] On August 12, 1946, three people, who had previously been employed to wait on tables in one of the cafes in Baxter, Oregon, formed a partnership. The eldest of the three was Mrs. Bevan, a middle-aged widow. The other two were Mr. and Mrs. Elmer Maywood. The partnership lasted for slightly more than four months, and in connection with its dissolution the preparation of a balance sheet became necessary.

Each of the partners contributed $2,000 cash, a total of $6,000. On August 12, the partnership purchased the Smoky Valley Cafe for $16,000. The purchase price included land valued at $2,500, improvements to land at $2,000, buildings at $10,500, and cafe equipment at $1,000. The partnership made a down payment of $4,500 (from its $6,000 cash) and signed a mortgage for the balance of the $16,000. The doors of the cafe were opened for business shortly after August 12.

One of the things that made this particular piece of property attractive to them was the fact that the building contained suitable living accommodations. One of these rooms was occupied by Mrs. Bevan, another by the Maywoods.

The Maywoods and Mrs. Bevan agreed on a division of duties and responsibilities which would allow them to keep the cafe open 24 hours a day. They agreed that Mrs. Bevan would operate the kitchen, Mrs. Maywood would have charge of the dining room, and that Mr. Maywood would attend the bar. Mrs. Bevan agreed to keep the accounting records. She was willing to perform this task because she was vitally interested in making the business a success. She had invested the proceeds from the sale of

---

[1] Based on a case argued before the Supreme Court of the State of Oregon, March 28, 1950. See 216 P2d 1005.

Copyright (c) 1956 by the President and Fellows of Harvard College. This case appears in *Management Accounting: Text and Cases* by Robert N. Anthony, 3rd ed. (Homewood, Ill.: Richard D. Irwin, Inc., 1964). (Slightly modified.)

her modest home and from her husband's insurance policy in the venture. If it failed, the major part of her financial resources would be lost.

A beer license was granted by the state authorities. On August 15, the partnership sent a check for $35 to the distributor who supplied beer. This $35 constituted a deposit on bottles and kegs necessary for the operation of the bar and would be returned to the Smoky Valley Cafe after all bottles and kegs had been returned to the beer distributor.

The Smoky Valley Cafe was located on a major highway, and a great deal of business was obtained from truck drivers. One of these truck driver patrons, Fred Mead, became a frequent customer. He soon gained the friendship of Mrs. Maywood.

In October, the partners decided that to continue to offer their patrons quality food, they would have to add to their equipment. This new equipment cost $416, and because the supplier of the equipment was unimpressed with the firm's credit rating, the equipment was paid for in cash.

The month of November did not improve the cash position of the business. In fact, the cash balance became so low that Mrs. Bevan contributed additional cash in the amount of $400 to the business. She had hopes, however, that the future would prove to be more profitable.

On the night of December 12, Fred Mead stopped in the cafe to see Mrs. Maywood. Shortly after he left, Mrs. Maywood retired to her room. A few hours later, Mr. Maywood came in and asked for her, and after a brief search discovered that she had departed through a window. Her absence led him to the conclusion that she had departed with Fred Mead, and he thereupon set out in pursuit of the pair.

On December 16, Mrs. Bevan decided that the partnership was dissolved because she had not heard any word from either of the Maywoods. (The courts subsequently affirmed that the partnership was dissolved as of December 16, 1946.) Although she had no intention of ceasing operations, she realized that an accounting would have to be made as of December 16. She called in Mr. Bailey, a local accountant, for this purpose.

Mrs. Bevan told Mr. Bailey that they had been able to pay $700 on the mortgage while the partnership was operating. Cash on hand amounted to $65, but the bank balance was only $10. Mr. Bailey found bills owed by the cafe totaling $92. Mrs. Bevan said that her best estimate was that there was $100 worth of food on hand.

Mr. Bailey estimated that a reasonable allowance for depreciation on the property, plant, and equipment (combined) was $322.

Required
a. Prepare a financial position statement for the Smoky Valley Cafe as of August 12, 1946.
b. Prepare a financial position statement as of December 16, 1946.
c. Compute the income of the business for the period of its operations.
d. What weaknesses are there in the method of preparing the statements in parts b and c?

chapter 5

Measuring
Business Income:
Accounting Procedure

Purpose of Chapter

Chapter 4 explained the following basic ideas related to measuring business income: the *accounting period* for which income is measured, the *matching* of revenue with the related expired cost to determine a period's income, realization as a requirement for recognizing revenue in the accounts, and the assumption of a *going concern* to permit a long-run view in making accounting measurements.

Chapter 5 shows how revenues and expenses are recorded in the debit-credit framework of accounting. It illustrates how accrual accounting is applied in making *end-of-period adjustments* to separate the costs already incurred into two parts: (1) the part which is an *expense* of the current period and (2) the remaining part which is an *asset* to be carried forward at the end of the period, because it has potential service benefit to the future.

Accounting procedures are shown for separating the following types of cost accounts into their *expired* (expense) and *unexpired* (asset) components:

(1) Prepaid costs of services, such as insurance and rent, are separated into the expense for the current period and the asset balance at the end of the period.

(2) Inventories of merchandise and finished goods are separated into cost of goods sold expense and the ending inventory, an asset balance.

(3) Long-term tangible assets, such as buildings and equipment, are separated into an expired part—*depreciation*—and an unexpired part—the ending asset balance.

(4) Intangible assets are separated into the portion which expired during the current period and the unexpired portion at the end of the period.

Position Accounts and Change Accounts

The accounts used to report the *financial position* of a business at any given time are *assets*, which show the forms of the entity's economic resources, and *equities*, which show the sources by which the assets are financed. Assets, liabilities, paid-in capital, and retained income accounts may therefore be referred to as *position accounts*. Their balances are *cumulative*, showing the effect of all increases and decreases for each type of account since the business was founded.

Income is the *change* in owners' equity which results from the activities of the business, other than owners' investments and disinvestments. Income measurement and reporting are so vital to business that separate accounts are used to record each major type of *revenue* and each type of *expired cost* for every accounting period. Revenue and expense accounts may thus be called *change*, or *periodic*, accounts. Their balances are cumulative only from the beginning of the accounting period. At the end of the period they are transferred to the cumulative owners' equity account, *retained income*.

The accounting equation may be expanded as follows to show the effects of these changes:

$$\text{Assets} = \text{Liabilities} + \overbrace{\text{Owners' equity}}$$
$$\text{Assets} = \text{Liabilities} + \overbrace{\text{Owners' investment} + \overbrace{\text{Income}}}$$
$$\text{Assets} = \text{Liabilities} + \text{Owners' investment} + \overbrace{\text{Revenue} - \text{Expired cost.}}$$

The rules of debit and credit may also be expanded to account for the effects of income transactions. Increases in owners' equity are recorded by credits and decreases by debits; therefore

(1) *Revenue*, which is an *increase in owners' equity*, is recorded by a *credit*.

(2) *Expense*, which is a *decrease in owners' equity*, is recorded by a *debit*.

ILLUSTRATION OF ACCOUNTING FOR INCOME TRANSACTIONS

The transactions of Hartman Mobile Home Sales, Inc., for the month of April 1973 will be used to show how revenues and expenses are recorded in the accounts. The following steps in the accounting process will be illustrated:

Step 1: *Journalizing* April transactions.

Step 2: *Posting* to ledger accounts.

Step 3: Preparing a month-end *trial balance before adjustments*.

Step 4: Journalizing *adjustments* for the expired cost of prepaid services.

Step 5: Preparing a *partial work sheet* reflecting the transactions and adjustments.

The starting point for illustrating the April accounting procedure is the accompanying March 31 trial balance, which contains the account balances at the beginning of April.

HARTMAN MOBILE HOME SALES, INC.
Trial Balance
March 31, 1973

	Debits	*Credits*
A, Cash..	$ 22,000	
A, Accounts receivable........................	10,000	
A, Notes receivable...........................	97,000	
A, Estimated uncollectible accounts and notes receivable		$ 2,000
A, Merchandise inventory.....................	230,000	
A, Unexpired insurance	3,000	
A, Supplies inventory	2,000	
A, Land	40,000	
A, Building	24,000	
A, Building—accumulated depreciation ...		6,000
A, Equipment..................................	15,000	
A, Equipment—accumulated depreciation		6,000
L, Notes payable to banks....................		130,000
L, Accounts payable		60,000
L, Payroll taxes payable		5,000
L, Long-term notes payable		56,000
OE, Capital stock.............................		100,000
OE, Retained income		78,000
Totals	$443,000	$443,000

Step 1: Journalizing April Transactions

The following are *summaries* of the transactions which occurred during April 1973. For example, while there were several individual collections on account from customers, the total collections for the month are recorded in one entry. Individual transactions would be recorded in the same manner as the summary transactions of a given type.

1973   (*1*)

Apr. 1 A, Franchise.. 6,000
                   A, Cash...   6,000
                   Paid cash for an exclusive right to sell Optimobile
                   Homes in the area for ten years.

                                            (*2*)

     30 A, Cash... 10,000
                   OE, Sales Revenue   10,000
                   Sold mobile homes for cash.

1973   *(3)*

Apr. 30   A, Accounts Receivable 90,000
          OE, Sales Revenue   90,000
          Sold mobile homes on credit.

(4)

30   A, Notes Receivable 71,000
    A, Cash 19,000
        A, Accounts Receivable   90,000
        Collected down payments on the homes sold on credit
        and accepted promissory notes for the balance.

(5)

30   A, Cash 4,000
        A, Accounts Receivable   4,000
        Collected on accounts owed from prior months.

(6)

30   A, Cash 70,500
        A, Notes Receivable   70,000
        OE, Interest Revenue   500
        Collected $70,000 on the principal of customers'
        notes due, together with interest of $500 which
        accrued during April.

(7)

30   OE, Advertising and Delivery Expense 4,000
        A, Cash   4,000
        Paid for April expenses.

(8)

30   OE, Officers' Salary Expense 3,500
        L, Payroll Taxes Payable   500
        A, Cash   3,000
        Paid officers' salaries, after deducting employee
        income and social security taxes to be paid to the
        federal government.

(9)

30   A, Supplies Inventory 400
        L, Accounts Payable   400
        Bought supplies on credit.

(10)

30   OE, Administrative Expense 5,500
        L, Accounts Payable   5,500
        Incurred various expenses on credit.

(11)

30   A, Merchandise Inventory 60,000
        L, Accounts Payable   60,000
        Bought on credit mobile homes for resale.

1973   *(12)*

Apr. 30   L, Accounts Payable 50,000
          A, Cash..   50,000
          Made payments to creditors on account.

(13)

30   L, Notes Payable to Banks................................... 30,000
     OE, Interest Expense   600
        A, Cash..   30,600
        Made payments due on the principal of bank loans,
        plus interest which accrued during April.

(14)

30   L, Long-term Notes Payable 10,000
     OE, Interest Expense   300
        A, Cash..   10,300
        Paid an installment on principal, plus interest which
        accrued during April.

(15)

30   L, Payroll Taxes Payable 4,000
        A, Cash..   4,000
        Paid to the government the various employer and
        employee payroll taxes which were due during April.

(16)

30   OE, Dividend 2,000
        A, Cash..   2,000
        Paid a dividend to stockholders.

Transactions which directly affect revenue and expense are shown in entries (2), (3), (6), (7), (8), (10), (13), and (14). End-of-period adjusting entries, to be shown later in this chapter and in Chapter 6, also affect revenue and expense.

Step 2: Posting to Ledger Accounts

The following T-accounts of Hartman Mobile Home Sales, Inc., reflect the March 31 account balances and the posting of the transactions for April 1973:

A, Cash   #1

1973			1973		
Mar. 31	Bal.	22,000	Apr. 30	(1)	6,000
Apr. 30	(2)	10,000	30	(7)	4,000
30	(4)	19,000	30	(8)	3,000
30	(5)	4,000	30	(12)	50,000
30	(6)	70,500	30	(13)	30,600
		125,500	30	(14)	10,300
	Balance 15,600		30	(15)	4,000
			30	(16)	2,000
					109,900

A, Accounts Receivable   #2

1973				1973			
Mar. 31	Bal.	10,000		Apr. 30	(4)	90,000
Apr. 30	(3)	90,000		30	(5)	4,000
		100,000				94,000

Balance 6,000

A, Notes Receivable   #3

1973				1973		
Mar. 31	Bal.	97,000		Apr. 30	(6)	70,000
Apr. 30	(4)	71,000				
		168,000				

Balance 98,000

A, Estimated Uncollectible Accounts and Notes Receivable   #4

				1973		
				Mar. 31	Bal.	2,000

A, Merchandise Inventory   #6

1973		
Mar. 31	Bal.	230,000
Apr. 30	(11)	60,000
		290,000

A, Unexpired Insurance   #7

1973		
Mar. 31	Bal.	3,000

A, Supplies Inventory   #8

1973		
Mar. 31	Bal.	2,000
Apr. 30	(9)	400
		2,400

A, Land   #11

1973		
Mar. 31	Bal.	40,000

A, Building   #12

1973		
Mar. 31	Bal.	24,000

A, Building—Accumulated Depreciation   #13

				1973		
				Mar. 31	Bal.	6,000

A, Equipment   # 14

1973				
Mar. 31	Bal.	15,000		

A, Equipment—Accumulated Depreciation   # 15

	1973		
	Mar. 31	Bal.	6,000

A, Franchise   # 16

1973			
Apr. 1	(1)	6,000	

L, Notes Payable to Banks   # 21

1973			1973		
Apr. 30	(13)	30,000	Mar. 31	Bal.	130,000
				Balance 100,000	

L, Accounts Payable   # 22

1973			1973		
Apr. 30	(12)	50,000	Mar. 31	Bal.	60,000
			Apr. 30	(9)	400
			30	(10)	5,500
			30	(11)	60,000
					125,900
				Balance 75,900	

L, Payroll Taxes Payable   # 23

1973			1973		
Apr. 30	(15)	4,000	Mar. 31	Bal.	5,000
			Apr. 30	(8)	500
					5,500
				Balance 1,500	

L, Long-Term Notes Payable   # 24

1973			1973		
Apr. 30	(14)	10,000	Mar. 31	Bal.	56,000
				Balance 46,000	

OE, Capital Stock   # 31

	1973		
	Mar. 31	Bal.	100,000

OE, *Retained Income* #32

	1973		
	Mar. 31	Bal.	78,000

OE, *Dividends* #34

1973			
Apr. 30	(16)	2,000	

OE, *Sales Revenue* #41

	1973		
	Apr. 30	(2)	10,000
	30	(3)	90,000
			100,000

OE, *Interest Revenue* #42

	1973		
	Apr. 30	(6)	500

OE, *Advertising and Delivery Expense* #51

1973			
Apr. 30	(7)	4,000	

OE, *Officers' Salary Expense* #52

1973			
Apr. 30	(8)	3,500	

OE, *Administrative Expense* #53

1973			
Apr. 30	(10)	5,500	

OE, *Interest Expense* #56

1973			
Apr. 30	(13)	600	
30	(14)	300	
		900	

Step 3: Ending Trial Balance Before Adjustments

The accompanying trial balance at the end of April reflects the combined effect of March 31 balances and April transactions on the accounts of Hartman Mobile Home Sales, Inc.

HARTMAN MOBILE HOME SALES, INC.
Trial Balance
April 30, 1973

	Debits	Credits
A, Cash	$ 15,600	
A, Accounts receivable	6,000	
A, Notes receivable	98,000	
A, Estimated uncollectible accounts and notes receivable		$ 2,000
A, Merchandise inventory	290,000	
A, Unexpired insurance	3,000	
A, Supplies inventory	2,400	
A, Land	40,000	
A, Building	24,000	
A, Building—accumulated depreciation		6,000
A, Equipment	15,000	
A, Equipment—accumulated depreciation		6,000
A, Franchise	6,000	
L, Notes payable to banks		100,000
L, Accounts payable		75,900
L, Payroll taxes payable		1,500
L, Long-term notes payable		46,000
OE, Capital stock		100,000
OE, Retained income		78,000
OE, Dividends	2,000	
OE, Sales revenue		100,000
OE, Interest revenue		500
OE, Advertising and delivery expense	4,000	
OE, Officers' salary expense	3,500	
OE, Administrative expense	5,500	
OE, Interest expense	900	
Totals	$515,900	$515,900

Step 4: Journalizing Adjustments

It is usually most convenient to *record* the *incurrence of a cost* when an economic resource is purchased, either on credit or for cash. Likewise, it is usually most convenient to *record a revenue item* when goods or services are sold, either on credit or for cash. These *transaction entries* are first recorded in the journal and then summarized in the ledger and trial balance.

The firm's income statement and financial position statement must show the results of all revenues and expenses that have *accrued* during the period. The purchase of an economic resource may occur *in advance* of the time the expense resulting from its use accrues, or the resource may be used in one period and the resulting accrued expense may be paid for in a *later period*. Similarly, cash for a revenue item may be *collected before or after the revenue accrues*.

To convert the trial balance accounts to the accrual basis used in preparing financial statements, it is necessary to prepare *adjusting entries* for the types of differences described in the preceding paragraph. Adjusting entries for prepaid expenses, inventories, and long-lived physical and intangible assets are explained in the following sections of this chapter. Other adjusting entries are discussed in Chapter 6.

Adjustments for the Expired Cost
of Prepaid Services

The March 31 trial balance showed $3,000 in the asset account for *unexpired insurance*. This represented the premiums which applied to fire, accident, and other casualty insurance policies for the 12 months beginning March 31, 1973.

Prepaid expenses for services, such as Unexpired Insurance and Prepaid Rent, apply to contracts for a specific period of time. These costs are usually considered to expire in equal amounts each day, but for convenience the cost expiration is recorded as an adjustment at the end of the accounting period.

The *expired cost* for the current period may be computed by multiplying the total contract cost by the fraction of the contract's life which elapsed during the current period. For Hartman Mobile Home Sales, the April expiration is $\frac{1}{12}$ of the total insurance premium of $3,000, or an expense of $250.

It is usually desirable to check this computation of expired cost by computing the *remaining asset* at the end of the period. For insurance policies, this is done by multiplying the total premium of each policy by a fraction, the numerator of which is the number of months of protection remaining after the end of the accounting period, and the denominator of which is the total months of protection under the policy. For Hartman, $\frac{11}{12}$ of $3,000 leaves an asset of $2,750 at the end of April.

If there are several insurance policies with different protection periods, the computations are made separately for each policy. A single adjustment can be made to show the combined expiration of all prepaid insurance premiums.

The effect of the insurance premium expiration for April is shown by the following entry:

1973 (Adjustment A)

Apr. 30   OE, Insurance Expense.................................... 250
            A, Unexpired Insurance   250
               To record expired insurance premiums for April.

After Adjustment A is posted to the accounts affected, there will be an insurance expiration of $250 in Insurance Expense and an asset of $2,750 for Unexpired Insurance (the $3,000 debit balance in the trial balance minus the $250 credit adjustment).

Some types of prepaid expenses for services, such as advances to employees for compensation, do not always expire in direct proportion to the passage of time. It is usually rather easy to determine how much the employee has earned, and at the same time to compute how much of the prepayment—the compensation advance—has become an expense.

Adjustments for the Expired Cost of Inventories

The direct method—perpetual inventories. In some cases it is *possible* to identify the expiration of a given amount of cost with *specific events* which occur during the accounting period, rather than with the passage of time. If these individual cost expirations are relatively large in amount, it may be *practical* to transfer the expired cost from an asset account to an expense account while the period is in progress. In such cases the amount of the expired cost is measured *directly*. The amount of unexpired cost, or asset, at the end of the period is measured *indirectly;* it is the remainder computed by subtracting the expired cost from the acquisition cost of the assets available for use or sale.

The direct method of measuring the cost expiration of inventories is called the *perpetual inventory method*. The asset account for inventory is debited every time there is an addition to inventory, and is credited every time an inventory item is sold or used. The ledger account for inventory should therefore have a balance equal to the cost of inventory actually on hand, when all journal entries have been posted.

Example 1   On April 1, Hartman Mobile Home Sales, Inc., bought three mobile homes for $3,000 cash each. On the next day it sold one of them for $4,000 cash. How would these transactions be recorded under the perpetual inventory method?

Solution

Apr. 1	A, Merchandise Inventory...............		9,000	
	A, Cash................................			9,000
	Bought three homes at $3,000 each.			
2	A, Cash....................................		4,000	
	OE, Sales Revenue..................			4,000
	Sold one home for cash.			
2	OE, Cost of Goods Sold Expense......		3,000	
	A, Merchandise Inventory.........			3,000
	The asset inventory was reduced, and expense was increased, for the cost of the home sold.			

Businesses whose inventories consist of relatively few items, each with a large unit cost, usually find it desirable to keep perpetual inventory records for each class of goods. The accountant can then determine the cost of each unit sold by referring to the records and can make an entry like the second one of April 2.

It would be practical for Hartman to use the perpetual inventory method for mobile homes because of their large unit value. Its expired cost for April would be summarized by the following entry:

1973	(Adjustment B)		
Apr. 30	OE, Cost of Goods Sold Expense..............	82,000	
	A, Merchandise Inventory................		82,000
	To record the cost of homes sold in April.		

Adjustment B is a *summary entry;* the cost of each home sold could be recorded individually at the time of the sale.

The perpetual inventory records should be checked at least once a year by a physical count of the inventory balance on hand. This procedure will help to detect clerical errors, thefts, and other shortages.

The indirect method—periodic inventories. The expired cost of inventory may be measured *indirectly* by determining the unexpired cost of the items on hand at the end of the period, and then subtracting this figure from the total cost of inventory items available during the period. This is called the *periodic inventory method*.

In cases where inventory items are of relatively small cost, it is often impractical and unduly expensive to keep a continuous record of the quantity and cost of each article on hand after each sale. In such situations a physical count of inventory on hand is taken periodically, often once a year, and used to compute the cost of inventory used or sold. The effect is to determine the cost of the *asset ending inventory directly*, and the *expired cost indirectly*.

Example 2   How would the facts of Example 1 be shown under the periodic inventory method?

Solution   The entries for the purchase and the cash sale would be the same. There would be no entry showing the cost of goods sold on April 2. Instead, total cost of goods sold for the month would be recorded in a single sum on April 30. It would be computed by *subtracting the cost of the ending physical inventory* from the *cost of merchandise available* for sale during the period (beginning inventory plus purchases during the period).

Hartman Mobile Home Sales, Inc., uses the periodic inventory method for accounting for its supplies. A physical count on April 30, 1973, showed that supplies costing approximately $1,800 were still on hand. The adjusting entry follows:

1973   (Adjustment C)

Apr. 30   OE, Supplies Expense..................................... 600
             A, Supplies Inventory..............................   600
             To record cost of supplies used during April,
             computed as follows:
               Cost of supplies available (March 31
                 balance plus April purchases)...... $2,400
               Less cost of supplies on hand at
                 month end   1,800
               Cost of supplies used .... $ 600

The perpetual and periodic methods of computing the expired and unexpired costs of inventories may be summarized as follows:

Known Amounts	*Unknown Amount*
Perpetual:	
Acquisition cost — Cost of goods sold	= Asset, ending inventory
Periodic:	
Acquisition cost — Asset, ending inventory	= Cost of goods sold

If there are no record-keeping errors or unauthorized withdrawals of inventory, the perpetual inventory method should give the *same results* for the ending inventory and the cost of goods sold as does the periodic inventory method. The difference between the methods is in the *frequency* with which issues are recorded and remaining asset balances are brought up to date.

Cost Expiration of Long-Lived Assets

The expiration of assets which represent prepaid service contracts can usually be identified with the passage of time. The expiration of inventories can be traced physically as the inventory items are sold or used. In contrast, the useful life of a machine or a patent, acquired for *use* in the business rather than for resale, is generally long but *indefinite*. The length of the useful life of machines depends partly on *physical factors* such as wear and tear from use and corrosion. The useful life of intangible rights such as patents depends partly on the *legal life* of the right or privilege. More often, the useful life of both tangible and intangible long-lived assets ends because of *economic factors*: the asset becomes obsolete because it is inadequate for the purpose for which it is being used or uneconomical to operate as compared with a newer asset.

Two basic accounting concepts are especially important in measuring the expired costs of long-lived assets: *matching* and *going-concern*. The costs of assets are generally considered to expire as the assets render their services. In measuring periodic income, these expired costs must be *matched* against the periodic revenues to which they contribute. In order that a *long-run*, rather than a liquidating, *view* may be taken in measuring periodic income, it is assumed that the business will continue in operation indefinitely, or at least until its existing facilities and long-term contracts have reached the ends of their useful lives.

Example 3   A business bought a building for $40,000. It is expected to have a useful life of 40 years and no salvage value at the end of that time. How does this affect its periodic income?

Solution   The total expired cost from the use of the building for the 40-year span is $40,000. The average expired cost per year is $1,000.

The process of assigning the expired cost of long-lived assets to accounting periods may be referred to by the general term *cost amortization*. It is called by the following specific names in connection with different types of long-lived assets:

(1) The periodic expired cost of physical assets such as buildings and equipment is called *depreciation*.
(2) The expired cost of natural resources is called *depletion*.
(3) The expired cost of intangibles such as patents is called *amortization*.

While the account titles used to describe the cost expiration of long-lived assets vary, the essence of the accounting process is the same: an *asset is reduced by a credit* (either directly to the asset account or to an asset-contra account)[1] and *owners' equity is reduced by a debit* (either to an expense or a loss account).

The total cost amortization during a long-lived asset's life is the difference between its *acquisition cost* and the expected *net proceeds* of its disposal at the end of its useful life. *Net proceeds* is equal to *salvage value* minus the cost of disposing of the asset. Salvage value may be ignored in computing periodic cost amortization if its amount is expected to be negligible, or if the cost of disposing of the asset is expected to approximately equal the proceeds.

---

[1] *Contra-accounts*, sometimes called *valuation accounts*, are used to show reductions in the account to which they are related. They are preferable to direct reductions of the related account when their amounts cannot be measured accurately.

Adjustments for Depreciation of Tangible Assets

Depreciation is the cost of the service benefit received during the accounting period from a long-lived physical asset. A widely used formula for computing periodic depreciation, the *straight-line method*, is

$$D = \frac{C - S}{n},$$

where

D is the amount of depreciation per time period
C is the asset's acquisition cost
S is the asset's net salvage value
n is the expected number of time periods of useful life

The total depreciation on an asset for a given accounting period is computed by multiplying D, the depreciation per time period, by the number of such time periods which elapsed during the accounting period.

The straight-line depreciation method is based on the assumption that equal service benefit is received from an asset during equal time periods of its service life. The method derives its name from the fact that a graph of depreciation by years would form a horizontal straight line. Other depreciation methods are discussed in Chapter 12.

The effect of recording depreciation is similar to the effect of recording expired insurance, which is to *transfer an expired cost from an asset account to an expense account*. Depreciation differs from insurance expense because of the indefinite length of the asset's life. Because of this indefiniteness, the asset reduction is shown in a separate account from that which shows the acquisition cost of depreciable assets in use. The balance of this separate *contra-account* at any time shows cumulative depreciation since the asset was acquired. The unexpired cost of the asset is computed by deducting the accumulated depreciation balance from the acquisition cost of the asset.

The effect of adjusting entries for depreciation for Hartman Mobile Home Sales, Inc., is shown in the following illustrations.

The building of Hartman Mobile Home Sales, Inc., cost $24,000 and is expected to have a useful life of 20 years and a net salvage value of zero. Depreciation per full year is ($24,000 — 0)/20, or $1,200. Depreciation per month is $100, $\frac{1}{12}$ of $1,200. The following entry records depreciation for April:

1973   (Adjustment D)

Apr. 30   OE, Depreciation Expense—Building 100
            A, Building—Accumulated Depreciation...   100
            Depreciation for April.

Hartman's resulting account balances at the end of April are shown in the following T-accounts:

A, Building		#12

1973		
Mar. 31	Bal.	24,000

A, Building—Accumulated Depreciation #13

	1973		
	Mar. 31	Bal.	6,000
	Apr. 30	Adj. D	100
			6,100

OE, Depreciation Expense—Building #54

1973			
Apr. 30	Adj. D	100	

Depreciation Expense—Building of $100 will be shown as a deduction in the income statement for April 1973. The building will be shown as follows in the financial position statement for April 30, 1973:

Building, cost.....................................	$24,000
Less accumulated depreciation................	6,100
Unexpired cost................................	$17,900

The effect of the April adjusting entry for depreciation is to reduce the unexpired cost of the building from $18,000 on March 31 ($24,000 − $6,000) to $17,900 on April 30 ($24,000 − $6,100).

The equipment of Hartman Mobile Home Sales, Inc., originally cost $15,000. It is expected to have a useful life of five years and a salvage value of $3,000. Depreciation per full year is therefore ($15,000 − $3,000)/5, or $2,400, and depreciation per month is $200. The adjusting entry for April follows:

1973   (Adjustment E)

Apr. 30   OE, Depreciation Expense—Equipment 200
            A, Equipment—Accumulated Depreciation...   200
            Depreciation for April.

Depreciation Expense—Equipment of $200 will be shown as a deduction in the April income statement. Equipment will be presented as follows in the April 30, 1973, financial position statement:

Equipment, cost................................	$15,000
Less accumulated depreciation...............	6,200
Unexpired cost	$8,800

Except for the salvage value, the computation of depreciation on the equipment follows the same pattern as building depreciation.

Adjustments for Amortization of Intangible Assets

The *economically* useful life, rather than the legal one, should be used in measuring the expired cost of *patents*, *copyrights*, *trademarks*, and *franchises*. Often an invention is useless long before the period of protection granted by the patent ends. The future time span during which copyrights and trademarks can be expected to benefit the business is frequently short or doubtful.

The complex questions involved in measuring and accounting for *goodwill* are discussed in Chapter 12. Basically, however, goodwill is an intangible asset which expires over the period of expected benefit.

The expired costs of long-lived assets are credited directly to the asset account when the probable useful life of the asset can be estimated with a high degree of certainty. When the useful life is more uncertain an asset-contra account is used.

On April 1, 1973, Hartman Mobile Home Sales, Inc., bought a franchise for the exclusive right to sell Optimobile Homes in its area for ten years. In the absence of definite information that this franchise will not be a valuable right for ten years, the franchise cost should be transferred to expense over the contract period. This is shown in the following adjustment:

1973   (Adjustment F)

Apr. 30   OE, Franchise Expense 50
            A, Franchise................................   50
            The expired franchise cost for April was
            $\frac{1}{12}$ of $\frac{1}{10}$ of \$6,000.

Step 5: Reflecting Adjustments on a Work Sheet

Many businesses use a *work sheet* to show the effect of end-of-period adjustments on the trial balance amounts, as a step to aid in preparing formal financial statements. Work sheet adjustments are recorded later in the permanent accounting records, the journal and the ledger. Statements can be prepared more quickly when a work sheet is used, without waiting for the formal journal adjusting entries to be recorded and posted. The work sheet adjusting entries are tentative; any errors in them can be corrected before the financial statements are prepared and before the formal adjusting entries are recorded in the accounts.

Illustration 5-1 is a partial work sheet for Hartman Mobile Home Sales, Inc., for the month of April 1973. It has pairs of columns—debit and credit— for the *Trial Balance Before Adjustments*, for *Adjustments*, and for the *Trial Balance After Adjustments*. For brevity, only the accounts affected by adjusting entries are shown. A partial work sheet for Hartman for April, containing all accounts and all adjustments, appears in Illustration 6-2 on p. 117.

The procedure for recording adjusting entries in the work sheet is as follows:

     (1) In the Adjustments columns, record the debits and credits of each adjusting entry which is needed at the end of the period.
         (a) Identify the debit and credit parts of each adjusting entry by the same key letter (A, B, C, etc.).
         (b) At the bottom of the work sheet, or on an accompanying sheet, write a brief explanation of each adjusting entry beside the key letter for the entry.
         (c) Add the debit and credit Adjustment columns to be sure that their totals are equal.

(2) Beginning with the first account, compute the adjusted balance of each account and extend it to the appropriate column (debit or credit) of the Trial Balance After Adjustments. These are the balances to be used in preparing financial statements. The totals of the Trial Balance After Adjustments columns should be equal (when all accounts are included).

Illustration 5-1

HARTMAN MOBILE HOME SALES, INC.
Work Sheet (Partial)
For the Month Ended April 30, 1973

Ledger Account Title	Trial Balance Before Adjustments		Adjustments		Trial Balance After Adjustments	
	Debits	Credits	Debits	Credits	Debits	Credits
Merchandise inventory	290,000			B 82,000	208,000	
Unexpired insurance.............	3,000			A 250	2,750	
Supplies inventory	2,400			C 600	1,800	
Building—accumulated depreciation		6,000		D 100		6,100
Equipment—accumulated depreciation		6,000		E 200		6,200
Franchise............................	6,000			F 50	5,950	
Insurance expense.................			A 250		250	
Cost of goods sold expense			B 82,000		82,000	
Supplies expense			C 600		600	
Depreciation expense— building			D 100		100	
Depreciation expense— equipment			E 200		200	
Franchise expense.................			F 50		50	

Explanation of adjusting entries:
  A. Expired insurance for April.
  B. Cost of goods sold.
  C. Supplies used.
  D. Building depreciation.
  E. Equipment depreciation.
  F. Franchise amortization.

Summary   There are two major objectives in accounting for the expiration of the cost of assets:

(1) To show as expense the cost of the benefits which the current period receives from the sale or use of the asset—that is, the expense which *accrues* this period —and

(2) To carry forward as an asset at the end of the current period that part of the asset's acquisition cost which corresponds to service benefits expected in the future.

Accounting for the cost expiration of service contracts for a period of time, for inventories, for long-term tangible assets, and for long-term intangibles follows the same basic pattern. The *expired part is debited to an expense* and the *asset is correspondingly reduced by a credit.* Where the amount is definite the asset account may be credited directly. Where it is uncertain, an asset-contra account may be credited.

The expiration of service contracts can be identified with the passage of time. The expiration of inventories can be traced physically. The expiration of long-lived assets (depreciation, depletion, amortization) depends partly on physical or legal factors, but primarily on economic factors.

Periodic adjusting entries to record the effects of cost expirations may be shown first in work sheet form to facilitate the preparation of financial statements.

Discussion Questions and Problems

5-1

a. How are *position accounts* and *change accounts* shown in the financial statements?

b. Indicate whether the following accounts are normally position accounts or change accounts by using the letters *P* and *C*.

(1) Accounts payable	(11) Gain on sale of equipment
(2) Unexpired insurance	(12) Investment in U.S. bonds
(3) Rent expense	(13) Salary expense
(4) Dividends	(14) Accrued salaries payable
(5) Equipment—accumulated depreciation	(15) Cash
	(16) Cost of goods sold
(6) Interest revenue	(17) Supplies inventory
(7) Capital stock	(18) Dividends payable
(8) Depreciation expense	(19) Retained income
(9) Organization cost	(20) Supplies expense
(10) Sales revenue	

5-2

a. Why are end-of-period adjusting entries needed for inventories, unexpired service contracts purchased, long-lived tangible assets, and long-lived intangible assets?

b. How are the adjustments for the various types of accounts mentioned in part a similar to each other?

c. How are these adjustments different from each other?

5-3

a. Name one long-lived tangible asset that would *not* require end-of-period adjustment.

b. Explain why no adjustment is needed in this case.

5-4

a. What is meant by amortization, depreciation, and depletion?

b. How are these terms similar to each other?

c. How are they different?

5-5

a. Use an illustration to show how the expired cost of a service contract purchased might be computed *directly*.

b. Show how the expired cost might be computed *indirectly*.

c. How do the results of these two methods differ? Which is better? Explain.

5-6

a. Use an illustration to show how the expired cost of inventory might be computed *directly*. What is this method called?

b. Show how the expired cost might be computed *indirectly*. What is this method called?

c. How might the results of these two methods differ?

d. Under what circumstances would you prefer to use the direct method? The indirect method?

5-7   Illustrate how physical factors might affect the useful life of a retail store building. Show how economic factors might affect its life. What would determine the useful life used for accounting purposes in your illustration?

5-8   In each of the following situations state whether you think a *periodic* or a *perpetual* inventory system would be appropriate, and why.

(1) Retail fur salon	(6) Gasoline service station
(2) Flour miller	(7) Variety store
(3) Urban supermarket	(8) Automobile dealer
(4) Fifth Avenue jeweler	(9) University bookstore
(5) Hardware store	(10) Candy wholesaler

5-9   Explain how the following cash payments of 1973 are related to the expired costs of 1973.

a. Payment for a three-year insurance policy which expires in 1975.

b. Payment for 1973 salaries.

c. Payment of cash for land.

d. Payment for equipment purchased in 1973.

e. Payment of annual installment on mortgage note payable issued for a building bought in 1972.

f. Payment of account payable for merchandise bought in December 1972.

5-10   Mrs. Canon owned a retail store. During 1973 the following events occurred.

(1) Sold merchandise on account for $75,000. The merchandise had cost $53,000.

(2) Collected $71,000 from customers, of which $7,000 applied to 1972 sales.

(3) Purchased merchandise on account for resale at a cost of $58,000.

(4) Paid cash of $55,000 for purchases, of which $5,000 applied to 1972 purchases.

(5) Received a cash refund of $600 from a manufacturer for faulty goods returned after they had been paid for.

(6) Paid cash for the following items which applied to 1973: salaries, $13,000; utilities, $600; rent, $2,700; groceries for personal use, $1,100.

(7) At the end of 1973 customers had out on approval goods which had cost $400 and were marked to sell for $600. These goods were not included in the sales figure given above.

(8) During the year merchandise marked to sell for $800, and costing Mrs. Canon $500, was stolen. She recovered $400 from the insurance company.

Required   Record the preceding transactions in journal form.

5-11   On March 1, 1973, Ralph Bryant formed a corporation to operate a retail clothing business. He deposited $6,000 in cash in the corporation's checking account at the First National Bank and received 60 shares of $100-par value capital stock in exchange.

On March 1, Mr. Bryant rented a store, signing a four-year lease which required him to pay $300 rent each month in advance. Mr. Bryant paid the rent for March and April on this date.

On the same day he hired a salesclerk to work at a salary of $100 a week, to be paid at the end of each week.

On March 1, he received merchandise costing $4,000 from the Metro Manufacturing Co., to be paid for at the end of the month.

On March 2, he sold a suit which had cost $50 for $80 cash.

On March 7, he paid the salesclerk's salary, deducting $10 payroll taxes which were to be paid to the federal government at the end of the month.

On March 14, he sold on account for $125 a dress which had cost $70.

Required
a. Record the preceding selected transactions in journal form. Use the perpetual inventory method.
b. What adjustment is needed in connection with rent in order to prepare financial statements for the month of March?

5-12 On May 1, 1973, two individuals formed the Pinnacle Corporation. One invested $7,000 in cash and the other turned over to the company a plot of land worth $10,000. Both received capital stock in exchange.

May 1: Ordered merchandise expected to cost $4,000. Because the firm had not established a credit rating, the manufacturer stated that he would require a promissory note when the merchandise was shipped in a few days.

May 5: Merchandise costing $3,800 was received and a promissory note was given to the manufacturer for this amount. The remaining items were out of stock.

May 6: Hired a salesclerk, agreeing to pay him $320 for the remainder of the month, payment to be made on May 31.

May 7: Paid $300 for a second-hand cash register which was expected to last about three years.

May 8: Sold merchandise on account to various customers for a total of $2,100. Because the items were of small unit value, management decided to take a monthly inventory to determine the amounts to be reported in the financial statements.

May 10: Collected $200 as part payment for some of the sales of May 8.

May 11: Returned unsatisfactory merchandise costing $200 to the manufacturer, who had agreed by telephone to allow full credit on the the balance due on the note.

May 31: Paid the clerk's salary. His total earnings were only $270 because he had been absent for several days. Payroll taxes withheld amounted to $20.

May 31: The clerk carelessly gave three $10 bills for a $20 bill in making change for an unidentified person. The error was not discovered until after the person had left.

May 31: A physical count of the merchandise remaining on hand amounted to $2,200 at cost. Record the expired cost. (*Hint:* Post the transactions related to inventory to a T-account in order to compute the amount for this entry.)

May 31: Received a utility bill of $40 but made no payment.

May 31: Sent the manufacturer a check for $1,025 consisting of payment for all the interest which had accrued to date, $25, and the balance to apply on the principal of the note.

Required Record the preceding transactions in journal form.

5-13 The T-accounts below show in summary form the transactions of the Fashion Shoppe for the year 1973.

Required   a. Place an identifying letter, A (Asset), L (Liability), or OE (Owners' Equity), as appropriate, to the left of each account title.

b. Reconstruct the journal entries which must have resulted in these ledger postings, including a brief but plausible explanation.

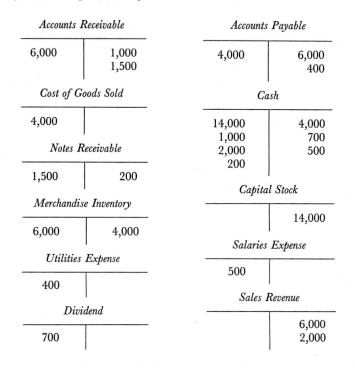

5-14   At the time of taking a trial balance at the end of the accounting year, December 31, 1973, the ledger contained the following accounts:

A, Unexpired Insurance

1973		
Jan. 1	(36 months)	720
Apr. 1	(12 months)	600

A, Equipment

1972	
July 1	8,000
1973	
Apr. 1	4,800

The equipment item bought in 1972 was expected to have a useful life of ten years and a salvage value of $800. The balance of Equipment—Accumulated Depreciation was $360 on December 31, 1972. The equipment bought in 1973 was expected to last four years and have no salvage value.

Required a. Journalize and post to T-accounts the necessary year-end adjusting entries for 1973.
b. How will the resulting account balances be reported in the 1973 financial statements?

5-15 At the end of its accounting year, December 31, 1973, the Olde Tobacco Shoppe's ledger showed the following information:

A, Merchandise Inventory

1973			1973		
Jan. 1	Balance	20,000	May 3	Purchase return	500
Apr. 3	Purchase	10,000			
June 15	Purchase	12,000			
Oct. 10	Purchase	14,000			

A physical inventory taken on December 31 showed that the cost of unsold goods was $23,000.

Required a. Journalize the necessary adjusting entry.
b. If several items had been shoplifted during the year, would the information show up under this inventory system? If not, how could it be detected by the use of accounting records?

5-16 On June 30, 1973, the Ejex Mfg. Co. bought a patent from an inventor for $9,000 cash. At that time 9 years of the patent's original legal life of 17 years remained. Ejex planned to use the patented invention in making a product which was expected to have a life cycle of 5 years.

Required a. What useful life would you use in accounting for the patent? Why?
b. Journalize the December 31, 1973 adjusting entry.
c. Show how the related information would appear in the year-end financial position statement.

5-17 On October 1, 1973, the Boise Corporation paid cash for the following items:

An accounting machine costing $6,000.

A supply of record forms costing $360, which were expected to be sufficient for about 6 months.

A service contract costing $120, which provided for making repairs and maintaining the machine for one year.

The Boise Corporation prepares monthly financial statements.

Required a. Journalize the entries needed on October 1.
b. What information do you need on October 31 to make the necessary adjusting entries, and how would you obtain it?
c. Assuming such facts as are necessary to complete your solution, journalize the adjusting entries.

5-18 The trial balance of the Mosley Corporation as of December 31, 1973, and supplementary information are given below.

Required Prepare a work sheet which shows the necessary adjustments and a trial balance after adjustments. Key the debit and credit parts of each adjusting entry by using letters.

	Debit	Credit
Accounts payable		$ 15,100
Accounts receivable	$ 18,000	
Cash	7,000	
Equipment......................................	50,000	
Equipment—accumulated depreciation...		15,000
Capital stock		16,000
Merchandise inventory........................	49,000	
Patents	6,300	
Rent expense...................................	9,000	
Salary expense..................................	8,500	
Sales revenue...................................		93,000
Retained income (Dec. 31, 1972)		12,100
Unexpired insurance...........................	3,400	
Totals...	$151,200	$151,200

Additional information:

The equipment was bought on January 1, 1970. It is expected to have a useful life of ten years and no salvage value.

Included in Salary Expense is a prepayment of $250 for an employee's salary for January 1974.

The inventory at the end of the year at cost, determined by physical count, was $14,000.

The Unexpired Insurance represents an all-risk policy purchased on November 1, 1972, and expiring October 31, 1975. Its total cost was $3,600.

5-19   The trial balance of Brandt Tire Company as of December 31, 1973, before adjustment, was as follows:

Accounts payable	$12,000
Accounts receivable	14,500
Capital stock	20,000
Cash	4,000
Cost of goods sold expense	60,000
Dividends	1,800
Equipment......................................	6,000
Equipment—accumulated depreciation...	1,800
Franchise.......................................	1,000
Merchandise inventory	22,000
Other expense..................................	1,900
Prepaid rent....................................	3,600
Retained income (Dec. 31, 1972)	2,500
Sales revenue...................................	80,000
Unexpired insurance	1,500

Required   a. Set up a trial balance before adjustments in the first two columns of a six-column work sheet.

b. Using the following information, prepare adjustments.

(1) Brandt uses a perpetual inventory system. A physical inventory taken on December 31, 1973, showed that the actual cost of inventory on hand was $22,300.

(2) The company leases its premises at $300 per month. Rent for the year ending December 31, 1973, was paid on January 31, 1973.

(3) The equipment was three years old at the beginning of the year and has no estimated scrap value. Depreciation has not been recorded for 1973.

(4) The franchise was bought on January 1, 1970, for $2,500. It gives Brandt an exclusive right to market tires in the area for 5 years beginning on that date.

c. Prepare a trial balance after adjustments.

5-20   Walter Borroughs, owner of a meat market, decided to open another market in a different section of town. He started his new business, which he named "Borroughs Suburban Market," on Monday, January 2, 1973. The following are the transactions of this market for January.

(1) On January 2, Mr. Borroughs opened a bank account for the new market by depositing $2,000 of his personal funds.

(2) On January 4, the landlord authorized Mr. Borroughs to make certain repairs and alterations to the building, which he would be permitted to deduct from January's rent due at the end of the month. Mr. Borroughs paid $125 cash for these repairs.

(3) On January 5, Mr. Borroughs purchased from the K & Y Company new equipment costing $1,500, paying $250 down and signing a note agreeing to pay the balance in 30 days.

(4) Purchases of meat from the Lean Meat Company during January cost $3,800, of which $900 was still unpaid at the end of the month.

(5) Employee salaries of $600 were paid for the three weeks ending January 31. Payroll taxes of $60 were withheld.

(6) The market purchased wrapping supplies for $120.

(7) Total sales for the month were $5,200. This amount included $700 of sales on credit, of which $400 had been collected by the end of the month.

(8) Rent of $400 for the month became due on the last day of the month, but was not paid.

Additional information:

(9) It was estimated that the cost of the meat on hand on January 31 was $350.

(10) About one-third of the supplies were used during the month.

(11) The unexpired cost of the equipment on January 31 was $1,475.

Required a. Journalize the transactions of Borroughs Suburban Market as shown in the first 8 items.

b. Post the journal entries to T-accounts.

c. Prepare a trial balance before adjustments on a six-column work sheet.

d. Record adjustments on the work sheet, using the additional information.

e. Prepare a trial balance after adjustments.

f. Prepare a formal income statement and a financial position statement.

Cases **5-1   Worldwide Records, Inc.** Worldwide Records, Inc., recently signed a five-year exclusive contract with a popular singing group. The contract calls for Worldwide to have the sole recording and distributing rights of the group's recordings for five years. On January 3, 1973, the contract was executed with Worldwide paying the group $180,000 cash. In addition, royalties will be paid to the group on record sales in excess of a stated minimum.

The marketing manager of Worldwide thinks that this contract will be highly profitable to the corporation for a long time and thinks that this assumption should be reflected in the company's income statements. The treasurer, however, contends that singing groups often have a short popularity span. He thinks that the group will fade from the scene in 2, or at most 3, years.

a. Discuss the accounting measurement problem involved in this situation.

b. What additional facts would you like to have in making a decision as to how to measure this information in the financial statements? How, if at all, could you obtain it?

c. Assume such facts as could reasonably be obtained in a real-life situation. Make the necessary entry for the payment to the group and the year-end adjustment.

5-2   Random Sample Candy Store. George Random opened the Random Sample Candy Store on March 1, 1973, and engaged in the following transactions during March. The business was not incorporated.

March

1	George Random opened a bank account for the business by depositing $2,800 from his personal funds.
1	Paid $120 for a business license for the remainder of the calendar year.
1	Ordered various candies costing $5,500 from a local wholesaler.
1	Signed a five-year lease calling for rent of $200 a month, to be paid in advance each month. Gave the landlord a check for the first month's rent.
1	Bought display equipment costing $3,000 from the manufacturer. Made a cash down payment of $1,200 and signed a promissory note agreeing to pay the remainder on March 31, together with interest of $12.
1	Bought wrapping supplies for cash, $80.
4	The shipment of candy was received from the wholesaler. The total cost of $5,500 was to be paid on March 31.
1-31	Total cash sales made to customers throughout the month were $1,800.
1-31	Total sales on credit for the month were $925.
1-31	Customers returned merchandise sold to them on account for $200, which had cost the Random Sample Candy Store $120. One-third was spoiled.
1-31	Total collections on the credit sales during March were $150.
31	Sent the candy wholesaler a check for $1,500.
31	Paid the clerk's salary of $180 by check, deducting $15 for candy which the clerk had bought on credit earlier during the month. (The sale had already been recorded.)
1-31	Mr. Random had given candy at various times to prospective customers. He estimated that such gifts had a cost of $60 and a retail value of $100.

Additional data:

(1) It had been impractical to keep a record of the cost of each item of merchandise sold during the month. Mr. Random and his clerk stayed until midnight on March 31 counting the unsold merchandise and multiplying the quantities of each kind of candy by the unit wholesale cost. The next day Mr. Random added the figures on a friend's adding machine and arrived at a total of $3,900. Wrapping supplies estimated to have cost $30 were also on hand.

(2) At a party Mr. Random inquired of an accountant friend how long the display equipment might be expected to last. He was told that 10 years was a reasonable estimate.

a. Journalize the preceding selected transactions for March.

b. Post to T-accounts.

c. Prepare an adjustment and classification work sheet, making adjustments from the transaction data and additional information.
d. Prepare an income statement and a financial position statement for March.
e. Comment on the store's operating results for March and any other matters shown by its financial statements which you think need attention.

chapter 6

Periodic Revenue
and
Expense Accrual

Purpose of Chapter

Chapter 5 showed how revenues and expenses are recorded in the accounts, and how end-of-period adjusting entries are made to separate costs for which payment has already been made into (1) the expense of the current period and (2) the remaining asset, which has a potential benefit to future periods.

Chapter 6 distinguishes *income distributions*, such as dividends, from expenses and losses, which are *deductions in computing the income* available for distribution to owners. It also explains how end-of-period adjusting entries are made in applying accrual accounting to

(1) Revenue collected in an earlier period but earned in the current period.
(2) Service benefits which expire in the current period but are to be paid for in a later period.
(3) Revenue earned in the current period but to be collected in a later period.

In addition, it explains the basic adjustments which are needed to reflect the estimated uncollectible accounts which will result from sales on credit.

Income Distributions

The earning of income by a business causes an inflow of additional net assets, which may either be distributed to the owners or retained for use in the business. Income distributions made by a corporation to its owners are called *dividends*.

Dividends in the form of cash are journalized as follows:

1973

Apr. 30	OE, Dividends...	2,000	
	A, Cash		2,000
	Paid the stockholders a cash dividend.		

If the dividend is in the form of some asset other than cash, the appropriate asset account should be credited. When the board of directors declares a dividend on one date, to be paid on a later date, the entries are

1973

Apr. 30	OE, Dividends	2,000	
	L, Dividends Payable		2,000
	Declared a dividend payable in cash on May 15.		
May 15	L, Dividends Payable	2,000	
	A, Cash		2,000
	Paid the dividend declared on April 30.		

Retained Income Statement

Retained income has a cumulative balance which reflects the periodic net income or net loss of every period since the corporation was formed, reduced by all income distributions to owners. It is customary to prepare a *statement of retained income* (or retained earnings) for each accounting period, in addition to the financial position statement (illustrated in Chapter 2) and the income statement (shown in Chapter 4). This statement shows the following types of information:

Balance of retained income at the beginning of the period...	$xxx
Add net income for the current period (or deduct net loss)...	xxx
Total...	xxx
Deduct dividends	xx
Retained income at the end of the period	$xxx

A retained income statement is shown in Illustration 6-1.

A negative cumulative balance in retained income is called a *deficit*. Illustration 6-1 shows how such a deficit at the beginning of the year is treated in the Retained Income Statement. If a deficit exists at the date a financial position statement is being prepared, it is shown as a *deduction* from paid-in capital in arriving at total stockholders' equity.

Retained income is not a pool of money, nor is it any asset. It merely shows the *source* from which additional assets have come into the business and have

Illustration
6-1

SEASIDE CORPORATION
Retained Income Statement
For the Year Ended December 31, 1973

Retained income, December 31, 1972 (deficit)	($15,000)
Add net income for 1973 (see Income Statement).........	32,000
Total	17,000
Deduct dividends	7,000
Retained income, December 31, 1973....................	$10,000

been retained for use in the business. It is not generally legal for a corporation to declare a dividend unless it has a positive (credit) balance in retained income. In addition, the board of directors must decide that the corporation has the *assets* needed to pay a dividend, and that it is more desirable to distribute these assets to owners than to keep them in the business for its use.

Adjustments for Revenue Earned Currently but Collected Previously

Revenue should be reported in the income statement of the period in which it is *realized*. Revenue is realized in the period in which the following conditions are met:

(1) Revenue is *earned* by transferring or producing a good or by rendering a service.

(2) The business must have received another asset in exchange, or must be assured that an asset will be received.

(3) The exchange price of the good or service must be dependably measurable.

For clerical efficiency, revenue is usually recorded in the accounts when there is a *transaction*, such as delivery of goods to the customer or collection of cash from him. At the end of the period it is necessary to determine whether amounts shown as revenue in such transaction entries correctly show the revenue that *accrued* during the period. If not, adjustments such as those described in this chapter are necessary.

When a business collects in advance for revenue to be earned during more than one future accounting period, it is desirable to credit the *unearned revenue* initially to a *liability* account. The liability shows an obligation to render service or deliver goods in the future, represented by an advance collection. An illustration of such an advance collection is shown in Entry (1).

1973   *(1)*

July 1	A, Cash..	12,000	
	L, Subscriptions Collected in Advance......		12,000
	Collected for 1,000 three-year subscriptions to a monthly magazine at $12 a subscription.		

By the end of the accounting year 1973 the business has earned one-sixth of the amount collected on these subscriptions, or $2,000. It will earn the remaining $10,000 as it issues the magazine to subscribers during the next 30 months. Adjusting Entry (1) must be made to show the $2,000 earned as 1973 revenue and to reduce the year-end liability for unearned revenue to $10,000:

1973   *(Adjustment 1)*

Dec. 31   L, Subscriptions Collected in Advance 2,000
           OE, Subscription Revenue (1973)   2,000
           To transfer the earned part of subscriptions collected from a liability to a revenue account.

The effect of the adjustment is shown in the following T-accounts:

L, Subscriptions Collected in Advance

1973				1973			
Dec. 31	(Adj. 1)	2,000		July 1	(1)	12,000	
				Balance, 10,000			

OE, Subscription Revenue (1973)

		1973		
		Dec. 31	(Adj. 1)	2,000

The $10,000 liability for Subscriptions Collected in Advance would appear in the financial position statement for December 31, 1973. Subscription Revenue of $2,000 would be reported in the 1973 income statement.

Other types of advance collections of revenue for which similar adjustments are needed are Rent Collected in Advance, Service Fees Collected in Advance, and Interest Collected in Advance.

Adjustments for Costs Expiring Currently but To Be Paid for Later

Costs expire, and should be *accrued as expenses or losses*, when the firm receives a current benefit from the cost factor or when the factor loses its potential to provide benefits in future periods. Clerical efficiency may dictate that these cost factors be recorded in the accounts when they are purchased or paid for in cash. At the end of each period it is necessary to make adjusting entries for expired costs in two types of situations:

(1) Costs incurred in earlier periods which expired in the current period. Several illustrations of this type of adjustment appeared in Chapter 5.
(2) Costs which expired in the current period, but will be paid for in a later period. Such adjustments are illustrated in this section.

When a business has received a service during the current period but has not paid for it by the end of the period an adjustment is needed to accrue the expired cost. At the same time a liability is set up for the unpaid sum.

During April 1973, Hartman Mobile Home Sales, Inc., *paid* interest of $900 which accrued on its notes payable during the month. At the end of April an additional $200 of interest had accrued but *had not been paid*. This is recorded in Adjustment G:

1973   (*Adjustment G*)

Apr. 30   OE, Interest Expense............................... 200
                    L, Accrued Interest Payable..................   200
                    To record the expense and the liability for
                    interest on notes payable which accrued but
                    was not paid during April.

(Alternatively, the liability might be called *Interest Payable*.)
The effect of Adjustment G is shown in the following T-accounts:

	L, Accrued Interest Payable	#24
	1973	
	Apr. 30 (Adj. G) 200	

OE, Interest Expense		#56
1973		
Apr. 30 (13) 600		
30 (14) 300		
900		
30 (Adj. G) 200		
Balance 1,100		

Accrued Interest Payable of $200 is shown as a liability in the April 30, 1973, financial position statement. In the income statement Interest Expense is reported as $1,100, the sum of all interest which accrued during April, whether paid or not.

A similar adjustment is necessary for the employ*er's* share of social security taxes which accrued during April. The employ*ees'* share was deducted from their pay and credited to a liability account, Payroll Taxes Payable. The *employer's* share involves a debit to an expense and a credit to a liability, as shown in Adjustment H:

1973   (*Adjustment H*)

Apr. 30   OE, Payroll Tax Expense........................... 250
                    L, Payroll Taxes Payable.....................   250
                    To record employer's share of social security
                    taxes for April.

Payroll Tax Expense of $250 is reported in the April income statement. Payroll Taxes Payable of $1,750, reflecting the balance in the account before adjustment plus the $250 adjustment (see Illustration 6-2 on p. 117), is reported as a liability in the April 30 financial position statement.

Other types of expired costs which require similar adjustments are accrued salaries of employees, accrued property taxes, accrued income taxes, and various types of accruals relating to service contracts for a time period.

Adjustments for Revenue Earned Currently but To Be Collected Later

For convenience, revenue for a service which a firm renders over a period of time is often recorded when it is collected. If an accounting period ends before the earned revenue has been collected, an *asset* for the sum receivable must be *debited* and a *revenue* account must be *credited* to report financial position and income properly.

Hartman Mobile Home Sales, Inc., collected $500 of interest earned on notes receivable during April 1973. By April 30 it had earned, but had not collected, an additional $300 of interest on these notes. This is reflected in Adjustment I:

1973	*(Adjustment I)*		
Apr. 30	A, Accrued Interest Receivable................	300	
	OE, Interest Revenue		300
	To record the revenue and the asset for interest on notes receivable which accrued but was not collected during April.		

(The asset might also be referred to as *Interest Receivable*.)

The effects of Adjustment I are shown in the following T-accounts:

A, Accrued Interest Receivable	#5
1973	
Apr. 30 (Adj. I) 300	

	OE, Interest Revenue	#42
	1973	
	Apr. 30 (6) 500	
	30 (Adj. I) 300	
	Balance 800	

Accrued Interest Receivable of $300 will be reported among the current assets in the April 30 financial position statement. Interest Revenue of $800 will be reported in the April income statement.

Summary of Adjustments

The end-of-period adjusting entries needed to reflect accruals properly are of four general types:

(1) *Debits to record expired costs*, offset by credits to either
  (a) Assets or asset-contras for costs incurred earlier (prepayments), or
  (b) Liabilities for payments to be made later.
(2) *Credits to record realized revenue*, offset by debits to either
  (a) Liabilities for sums previously collected in advance, or
  (b) Assets for sums to be collected later.

Reflecting Adjustments on a Work Sheet (continued)

Illustration 6-2 shows the complete trial balance of Hartman Mobile Home Sales, Inc., for April 30, 1973, together with Adjustments A through I which have been explained in Chapters 5 and 6.

Both journal entries and T-accounts have been used in explaining the effect of adjustments on the accounts. In actual accounting practice adjusting entries are often recorded *only on a work sheet* at the end of each *month*. At the end of the *year* they are also *journalized* and *posted* to the ledger. The debit and credit balances in the Trial Balance After Adjustments are the proper account balances to use in preparing the income statement, the retained income statement, and the financial position statement.

The Financial Statement Classification
Work Sheet

A work sheet may be helpful not only in *showing the effects of accrual adjustments* on the accounts, but also in *classifying account balances* according to the financial statement in which they appear. Illustration 6-3 is a statement classification work sheet. It takes the adjusted account balances and classifies them according to whether they will be used in preparing the income statement, the retained income statement, or the financial position statement.

The work sheet is a means to an end, not an end in itself. It should be prepared only if it will aid the summarization and reporting process. Its design is flexible; it should be arranged so as to group the information needed for the financial statements that are required for the particular business in question.

The following is an outline of the procedure used in preparing a statement classification work sheet.

(1) List the account titles and their debit and credit balances under the Trial Balance After Adjustments.

(2) Label a pair of columns (debit and credit) for each formal financial statement to be prepared. In this case a pair of columns is needed for Income Statement, one for Retained Income Statement, and another for Financial Position Statement.

(3) Starting with the first account, extend each adjusted account balance to the appropriate column (debit or credit) for the financial statement in which that account should appear. (*Example*: Cash, a debit in Trial Balance After Adjustments, is also a debit in the Financial Position Statement columns.)

(4) (a) Compute subtotals of the Income Statement columns. If the credit total is the larger, revenue exceeds expired cost and there is a *net income*. If the debit total is the larger, there is a *net loss*.

(b) Enter the net income in the debit Income Statement column and in the credit Retained Income Statement column. The effect is to *balance* the pair of Income Statement columns and to *transfer* the net income to the Retained Income Statement columns. (If there is a *net loss*, enter its amount as a credit in the Income Statement columns and as a debit in Retained Income.)

(c) Total the Income Statement columns. Total debits must equal total credits.

Illustration
6-2

HARTMAN MOBILE HOME SALES, INC.
Work Sheet (Partial)
For the Month Ended April 30, 1973

Ledger Account Title	Trial Balance Before Adjustments		Adjustments		Trial Balance After Adjustments	
	Debits	*Credits*	*Debits*	*Credits*	*Debits*	*Credits*
Cash	15,600				15,600	
Accounts receivable	6,000				6,000	
Notes receivable	98,000				98,000	
Estimated uncollectible accounts and notes receivable		2,000				2,000
Merchandise inventory	290,000			B 82,000	208,000	
Unexpired insurance	3,000			A 250	2,750	
Supplies inventory	2,400			C 600	1,800	
Land	40,000				40,000	
Building	24,000				24,000	
Building—accumulated depreciation		6,000		D 100		6,100
Equipment	15,000				15,000	
Equipment—accumulated depreciation		6,000		E 200		6,200
Franchise	6,000			F 50	5,950	
Notes payable to banks		100,000				100,000
Accounts payable		75,900				75,900
Payroll taxes payable		1,500		H 250		1,750
Long-term notes payable		46,000				46,000
Capital stock		100,000				100,000
Retained income		78,000				78,000
Dividends	2,000				2,000	
Sales revenue		100,000				100,000
Interest revenue		500		I 300		800
Advertising and delivery expense	4,000				4,000	
Officers' salary expense	3,500				3,500	
Administrative expense	5,500				5,500	
Interest expense	900		G 200		1,100	
Totals	515,900	515,900				
Insurance expense			A 250		250	
Cost of goods sold expense			B 82,000		82,000	
Supplies expense			C 600		600	
Depreciation expense—building			D 100		100	
Depreciation expense—equipment			E 200		200	
Franchise expense			F 50		50	
Accrued interest payable				G 200		200
Payroll tax expense			H 250		250	
Accrued interest receivable			I 300		300	
Totals			83,950	83,950	516,950	516,950

Illustration 6-3

HARTMAN MOBILE HOME SALES, INC.
Statement Classification Work Sheet
For the Month Ended April 30, 1973

Ledger Account Title	Trial Balance After Adjustments		Income Statement		Retained Income Statement		Financial Position Statement	
	Debits	*Credits*	*Debits*	*Credits*	*Debits*	*Credits*	*Debits*	*Credits*
Cash...	15,600						15,600	
Accounts receivable	6,000						6,000	
Notes receivable	98,000						98,000	
Estimated uncollectible accounts and notes receivable.......................		2,000						2,000
Merchandise inventory....................	208,000						208,000	
Unexpired insurance	2,750						2,750	
Supplies inventory	1,800						1,800	
Land	40,000						40,000	
Building	24,000						24,000	
Building—accumulated depreciation		6,100						6,100
Equipment......................................	15,000						15,000	
Equipment—accumulated depreciation.		6,200						6,200
Franchise.......................................	5,950						5,950	
Notes payable to banks		100,000						100,000
Accounts payable............................		75,900						75,900
Payroll taxes payable......................		1,750						1,750
Long-term notes payable		46,000						46,000
Capital stock..................................		100,000						100,000
Retained income.............................		78,000				78,000		

Ledger Account Title	Trial Balance After Adjustments Debits	Trial Balance After Adjustments Credits	Income Statement Debits	Income Statement Credits	Retained Income Statement Debits	Retained Income Statement Credits	Financial Position Statement Debits	Financial Position Statement Credits
Dividends	2,000				2,000			
Sales revenue		100,000		100,000				
Interest revenue		800		800				
Advertising and delivery expense	4,000		4,000					
Officers' salary expense	3,500		3,500					
Administrative expense	5,500		5,500					
Interest expense	1,100		1,100					
Insurance expense	250		250					
Cost of goods sold expense	82,000		82,000					
Supplies expense	600		600					
Depreciation expense—building	100		100					
Depreciation expense—equipment	200		200					
Franchise expense	50		50					
Accrued interest payable		200						200
Payroll tax expense	250		250					
Accrued interest receivable	300						300	
Totals	516,950	516,950	97,550	100,800				
Net income, to retained income			3,250			3,250		
Totals			100,800	100,800	2,000	81,250		
Ending retained income, to financial position					79,250			79,250
Totals					81,250	81,250	417,400	417,400

119

(5) (a) Compute subtotals of the Retained Income Statement columns. If the credit total is larger, retained income is positive at the end of the period. If the debit total is larger, there is a *deficit*.

   (b) Enter the positive balance as a debit in Retained Income to balance the pair of columns, and transfer it as a credit to the Financial Position Statement columns. (If there is a deficit, show its amount as a credit in Retained Income and as a debit in the Financial Position Statement columns.)

   (c) Total the Retained Income columns. Debits must equal credits.

(6) Add the debit and credit Financial Position Statement columns. If their totals are not equal, an error has been made somewhere on the work sheet. Common types of errors are

   (a) Incorrectly computing the adjusted balance of accounts affected by adjustments.

   (b) Failing to extend adjusted debit balances as debits, and adjusted credit balances as credits.

After the statement classification work sheet has been completed and any errors have been corrected, it is ready to be used in preparing the formal financial statements. Each statement is prepared from the items classified in the appropriate pair of columns in the work sheet. Thus *all items* in the Income Statement columns of the work sheet, and *only* those items, are used in preparing the formal Income Statement. Placing a check mark beside each item in the work sheet as it is used in the financial statements helps to prevent omissions and duplications. The formal financial statements are classified and arranged according to the illustrations in Chapters 2, 4, and 6, but their components should be the same as those on the work sheet. For example, Equipment—Accumulated Depreciation is a credit balance in the Financial Position Statement columns of the work sheet, but a *deduction from the related asset* in the formal statement.

Modifications of the columns used in the work sheets may be made to conform to the particular statements which are being prepared. If there are many accounts, extra columns may be used to group together accounts of a single type, which may then be reported in a supporting schedule to one of the primary financial statements.

Combined Adjustment and Classification Work Sheet

Work sheets are generally used to serve two purposes: to summarize the effect of adjustments and to classify the adjusted balances according to the financial statements in which they will be reported. Illustrations 6-2 and 6-3 could be combined to form such a work sheet, with the duplication of the Trial Balance After Adjustments eliminated. In fact, the use of a pair of Trial Balance After Adjustments columns is optional. It is probably unnecessary if there are few adjustments.

Closing the Periodic Accounts

The accounts which show the details of *changes in retained income* for the accounting period—revenues, expired costs, and income distributions—have served their purpose when they have been formally reported in the income statement, the retained income statement, and the financial position statement. Their combined effect is then transferred to the *cumulative* position account, Retained Income, by the process of *closing the books*. At the same time the balances of these accounts which showed the period's changes in retained income are *reduced to zero*, or *closed*. They are then ready to be debited or credited to show the revenues, expired costs, and income distributions of the next accounting period.

The accounts which are *not closed* are those which show the *financial position* of the business at a given point in time: assets, liabilities, paid-in capital, and Retained Income. These account balances are cumulative; they are carried forward to the next accounting period to be increased and decreased by the transactions of that period.

In the closing process the revenue and expired cost accounts for the period are transferred to an *Income Summary* account. This is a temporary account which is used only during the closing process to collect in one place the information pertaining to the period's net income or net loss. The Income Summary and Dividends accounts are then transferred to the cumulative position account, Retained Income. After these transfers the balance in Retained Income is the balance at the end of the period—the same as the final figure in the period's retained income statement.

Closing entries, like all other entries, are first recorded in the journal and are then posted to the ledger. If an account to be closed has a credit balance, it must be *debited* for the amount of its balance. After the closing entry debiting this account has been posted, its total debits will equal its total credits; it will have a *zero balance*. It is then said to be *closed*, and is ready to record changes of a similar type for the next accounting period.

An account with a debit balance is closed by *crediting* it. The other account affected in each closing entry is the account to which the balance of the closed account is to be transferred:

(1) *Income Summary*, for revenues and expired costs, and

(2) *Retained Income*, for the Income Summary and Dividends accounts.

The revenue or expired cost balance to be closed is that *after adjustments*. A convenient place to secure data for closing entries is the work sheet. Balances which appear in the Income Statement columns are all closed. Each may be closed individually, as shown in the following journal entries:

1973

Apr. 30	OE, Sales Revenue	100,000	
	OE, Income Summary........................		100,000
	To close Sales Revenue.		

1973

Apr. 30	OE, Income Summary.................................	82,000	
	OE, Cost of Goods Sold Expense		82,000
	To close Cost of Goods Sold Expense.		

Instead of closing the accounts individually, time may be saved in journalizing and posting by closing all revenue accounts in one compound entry and all expired costs in another compound entry.

Although Hartman Mobile Home Sales, Inc., closes its books only once a year, its income statement data for April are used for the following illustrative closing entries:

1973		(Closing A)		
Apr. 30	OE, Sales Revenue		100,000	
	OE, Interest Revenue.............................		800	
	OE, Income Summary			100,800
	To close the revenue accounts.			

		(Closing B)		
30	OE, Income Summary		97,550	
	OE, Advertising and Delivery Expense.....			4,000
	OE, Officers' Salary Expense.................			3,500
	OE, Administrative Expense			5,500
	OE, Interest Expense			1,100
	OE, Insurance Expense			250
	OE, Cost of Goods Sold Expense			82,000
	OE, Supplies Expense...........................			600
	OE, Depreciation Expense—Building			100
	OE, Depreciation Expense—Equipment ...			200
	OE, Franchise Expense			50
	OE, Payroll Tax Expense			250
	To close the expired cost accounts.			

The effects of these two closing entries on the ledger accounts are illustrated in the following three T-accounts. Only one revenue and one expense account are illustrated; closing entries would affect other accounts in a similar way.

OE, Income Summary #33

1973				1973			
Apr. 30	(Closing B)	97,550		Apr. 30	(Closing A)	100,800	
					Balance 3,250		

OE, Interest Revenue #42

1973				1973			
Apr. 30	(Closing A)	800		Apr. 30	(6)	500	
				30	(Adj. I)	300	
		800				800	

OE, Interest Expense #56

1973							
Apr. 30	(13)	600		Apr. 30	(Closing B)	1,100	
30	(14)	300					
30	(Adj. G)	200					
		1,100				1,100	

After posting the closing entries the revenue and expired cost accounts have zero balances; they are *closed* and ready to show the corresponding changes in owners' equity during the next accounting period. The double rulings beneath the totals of each closed account are a customary method of showing that the account is closed. The Income Summary account now has a credit balance of $3,250, which is the net income for April.

Income Summary is now closed to Retained Income by the following entry:

1973		*(Closing C)*		
Apr. 30	OE, Income Summary		3,250	
	OE, Retained Income....................			3,250
	To close Income Summary.			

The two accounts affected would then appear as follows:

OE, Retained Income   #32

			1973		
			Mar. 31	Bal.	78,000
			Apr. 30	(Closing C)	3,250

OE, Income Summary   #33

1973			1973		
Apr. 30	(Closing B)	97,550	Apr. 30	(Closing A)	100,800
30	(Closing C)	3,250			
		100,800			100,800

The Dividends account is closed to Retained Income by the following entry:

1973		*(Closing D)*		
Apr. 30	OE, Retained Income...........................		2,000	
	OE, Dividends			2,000
	To close Dividends.			

The two accounts affected then appear as follows:

OE, Retained Income   #32

1973			1973		
Apr. 30	(Closing D)	2,000	Mar. 31	Bal.	78,000
			Apr. 30	(Closing C)	3,250
				Balance 79,250	81,250

OE, Dividends   #34

1973			1973		
Apr. 30	(16)	2,000	Apr. 30	(Closing D)	2,000

The credit balance of $79,250 in Retained Income is the *cumulative* amount of income retained in the business from its formation to the end of April 1973.

It is the same as the final amount in the Retained Income Statement for April and as the amount of Retained Income in the April 30, 1973, Financial Position Statement.

The following diagram shows the effects of the closing process on the expanded accounting equation.

Balances Before Closing	Assets = Liabilities + Paid-in capital + Retained income, shown by: Retained income end of last year + Revenue this year − Expired cost this year − Income distributions this year
Balances After Closing	Assets = Liabilities + Paid-in capital + Retained income, end of this ¡year

Many businesses prepare financial statements monthly or quarterly, but as a rule *closing entries are made only once a year.* The balances in the revenue, expired cost, and income distribution accounts at any time represent the changes in retained income which have occurred since the date of the last closing entries. The balance in the Retained Income account is the cumulative amount of earnings reinvested in the business from its formation through the date of last closing.

Example 1   A business which uses the calendar year as its accounting period closes its books once a year but prepares monthly financial statements for the guidance of management. The credit balance in the Sales Revenue account on January 31 was $14,000, and on February 28 it was $26,200. What did each balance represent?

Solution   The balance at the end of January, $14,000, was the total Sales Revenue for the year to date, January 1 through January 31. It was also, of course, the Sales Revenue for the month of January. The balance on February 28 was Sales Revenue for the year to date, January 1 through February 28. Revenue for February alone could be determined by subtracting the balance at the end of the preceding month from the balance at the end of the current month ($26,200 − $14,000 = $12,200).

Balancing the Accounts Which Are Not Closed— the After-Closing Trial Balance

Asset, liability, paid-in capital, and retained income accounts are not closed. Their balances are carried forward to the next accounting period. Computation of balances during the next year may be made easier, however, if these accounts are *balanced*: that is, if their ending balances are carried forward to a new ledger page or a new section of a ledger account. The following illustration shows how the Retained Income account would be balanced:

OE, Retained Income					#32
1973			1973		
Apr. 30	(Closing D)	2,000	Mar. 31	Bal.	78,000
30	Bal. carried forward	79,250	Apr. 30	(Closing C)	3,250
		81,250			*81,250*
			Apr. 30	Bal. brought forward	79,250

Even if the accounts are not balanced, it is usually desirable to prepare a list of account balances which remain open after the adjusting and closing entries have been posted. Such a list, called an *After-Closing Trial Balance*, helps to determine whether adjusting and closing entries have been made correctly. The accounts included—those still open—are assets, liabilities, paid-in capital, and the Retained Income account. Revenues, expired costs, the Income Summary account, and Dividends, which have no balances after the closing process, do not appear in the After-Closing Trial Balance.

Adjustments for Uncollectible Accounts

It is a well-established practice of modern businesses to grant credit to customers. They usually make careful credit investigations before extending credit to individual customers and employ effective collection procedures, including legal action if necessary. Under these circumstances most businesses can reasonably expect that only a very small part of their sales on credit will result in *uncollectible accounts*, or *bad debts*. Even for the relatively small portion of accounts which are likely to prove uncollectible, past experience usually gives information that permits close estimation of total accounts receivable likely to be bad. Businesses should record sales revenue and a corresponding asset for accounts receivable *at the time of sale on credit* if the expected rate of collection of accounts is high, and if the uncollectible total can be estimated within reasonable limits.

The purpose of an *estimated uncollectibles* contra-account, which is deducted from Accounts Receivable in order to compute expected *collectible* accounts, was explained briefly in Chapter 3 on p. 52. The following assumed facts will be used to illustrate the procedure for accounting for uncollectibles:

Accounts receivable balance, Dec. 31, 1972	$ 20,000
Accounts receivable—estimated uncollectibles balance, Dec. 31, 1972	500
Total sales revenue, 1973	130,000
Sales on credit, 1973	100,000
Collections on account, 1973	90,000
Total losses specifically determined for uncollectible accounts for the last five years	4,000
Total sales on account for the last five years	400,000

If there are only a *few* individual customers' accounts receivable, the most satisfactory method of estimating the amount of uncollectibles is usually to analyze the collectibility of each account. This may be done by gathering information on the credit standing of each customer at the date of the estimate and by considering how old the uncollected balances are.

If there are *many* individual accounts receivable, it is usually more practical to use statistics of past loss experience as a basis for estimating what amount of receivables now owned will eventually become uncollectible. A percentage of loss actually experienced is computed by *dividing the actual past losses by the total exposures to losses.* The denominator is the net sales made on credit during a given period of time. The numerator is the amount of the definitely uncollectible accounts which resulted from the net credit sales of the same time period.

From the data given above the *actual past loss percentage* is computed as follows:

Net sales on account, 1968–1972	$400,000
Actual uncollectible accounts from these sales...	4,000
Percentage of loss ($4,000/$400,000)	1%

If there is no significant change in economic conditions or in the credit and collection policy of the business for which the loss estimate is being made, this past loss percentage may be used to estimate the losses from the current year's sales on account. This computation would be as follows:

Net sales on account, 1973..........................	$100,000
Estimated loss from uncollectibles, based on past experience: multiply by 1%	1,000

The adjusting journal entry at the end of 1973 would be as follows:

1973
Dec. 31   OE, Uncollectible Sales Revenue (1973)......... 1,000
        A, Accounts Receivable—Estimated
            Uncollectibles   1,000
        To record estimated uncollectibles at 1% of sales
        on account.

Uncollectible Sales Revenue is a contra-account to Sales Revenue. Accrual accounting, under which sales revenue is recognized in the accounts at the time of a sale on credit, results in an *overstatement* of both revenue and assets to the extent that some of the accounts will not be collected. This overstatement is largely corrected by the adjusting entry for estimated uncollectibles. The estimated overstatement of revenue should be *matched with revenue* in the same period in which revenue is recorded. Thus the contra-account for Uncollectible Sales Revenue is deducted from Sales Revenue in the income statement of the period in which the sale is made. There is usually a time lag after the sale before it can be determined which particular customers' accounts are bad. This may even occur in a later accounting period. For proper matching the revenue deduction should be made in the *period of sale*, however, and not at the later time when it is finally determined that the account cannot be collected.

Sometimes the income statement account debited is called *Bad Debts Expense*, while the asset-contra is often labeled *Allowance for Bad Debts*. These accounts have the same effect on income and asset measurement as the accounts used above.

The effects of the 1973 adjusting entry for estimated uncollectibles are shown in the following T-accounts:

A, Accounts Receivable

1972			1973		
Dec. 31	Balance	20,000	Jan. 1–Dec. 31	Collections on account	90,000
1973					
Jan. 1–Dec. 31	Sales on account	100,000			
		120,000			
	Balance, 30,000				

A, Accounts Receivable—Estimated Uncollectibles

			1972		
			Dec. 31	Balance	500
			1973		
			Dec. 31	Adjustment	1,000
					1,500

OE, Sales Revenue

			1973		
			Jan. 1–Dec. 31	Cash sales	30,000
			Jan. 1–Dec. 31	Sales on account	100,000
					130,000

OE, Uncollectible Sales Revenue

1973			
Dec. 31	Adjustment	1,000	

The income statement presentation for 1973 is

Sales revenue	$130,000	
Deduct uncollectible sales revenue	1,000	
Net sales revenue		$129,000

The related accounts are shown as follows in the financial position statement of December 31, 1973:

ASSETS

Current assets:		
Accounts receivable.................................	$30,000	
Deduct estimated uncollectible accounts	1,500	
Estimated collectible accounts.................		$28,500

One reason for showing the deductions for uncollectibles in separate accounts is that they are *estimates,* while the sales revenue and accounts receivable balances from which they are deducted are definite amounts based on market exchange transactions. The contra to Accounts Receivable is a deduction from the *total accounts* owed to the business. It cannot be deducted from the individual customers' accounts receivable at the time the adjusting entry is made, because it is not yet known just which particular customers will not pay.

Estimates of *uncollectible notes receivable* may be made in the same way as estimated uncollectible accounts. There may be a separate contra-account for notes, or total estimated uncollectible accounts and notes receivable may be combined in a single contra-account.

Writing Off Uncollectible Accounts

Follow-up efforts to collect accounts receivable should be carried out regularly throughout the accounting period. When an account is definitely determined to be uncollectible it should be written off the books promptly. The decision that a particular account is bad may be based on formal legal action, such as a customer's bankruptcy; on his death or disappearance; on the expiration of the statute of limitations (the period in which payment of the debt can legally be enforced); on the existence of disputed items in the account balance; or on the inability of a collection agent to obtain payment.

The following entry shows that a particular account is uncollectible:

1974

Jan. 1   A, Accounts Receivable—Estimated Uncollectibles... 50
                  A, Accounts Receivable   50
                  To write off the uncollectible account of the Exco
                  Corporation resulting from a 1973 sale.

Recognition that a particular account is definitely uncollectible usually occurs in an accounting period later than that of the sale, as in the preceding journal entry. The write-off entry has no effect on the income of 1974, the year of write-off, and no net effect on assets. This is shown in the following comparison:

	Balances Before Write-Off	Balances After Write-Off
Accounts receivable, debit	$30,000	$29,950
Deduct estimated uncollectibles, credit...	1,500	1,450
Estimated collectible accounts	$28,500	$28,500

Income *was affected* in 1973 when the sale was made. The total estimated uncollectible revenue of $1,000, including the $50 sale to Exco Corporation, was deducted from total sales revenue in 1973. This procedure for estimating uncollectibles permits better performance measurement by a proper *matching of cause and effect*. The effect, uncollectible accounts of approximately $1,000, is associated with the cause, selling on credit, in the year in which the cause occurred—1973.

The write-off entry avoids the accumulation of worthless claims in Accounts Receivable. It also permits management to compare the actual uncollectibles (the debits to Accounts Receivable—Estimated Uncollectibles) with the advance estimate (the credits to Accounts Receivable—Estimated Uncollectibles) so that future estimates can be made more accurately.

Summary The *income distributions* of a corporation, called dividends, are reported in a *statement of retained income,* which also shows the retained income at the beginning of the period and the net income or net loss for the current period.

When revenue is collected in a period before it is earned it is normally credited to a liability. An adjusting entry is necessary to reduce the liability and record the revenue earned during the period.

When a service already received has not been paid for, an adjusting entry is needed to debit an expense and credit a liability for the amount owed.

When revenue has been earned but not collected, an adjusting entry is made debiting a receivable (asset) account and crediting revenue.

Expected uncollectible accounts arising from sales on account should be matched with the revenue from the sale in the period in which the sale occurs. To do so, an adjusting entry is made at the end of each period debiting a revenue contra-account and crediting an accounts receivable contra-account. When specific customers' accounts are definitely determined to be bad, they are written off against the accounts receivable contra-account which was previously established for this purpose.

Columnar work sheets are often helpful in showing the effects of adjustments on the trial balance and also in classifying account balances according to the financial statement in which they are to appear.

After the accounts which show the changes in retained income for an accounting period have been reported in the financial statements, their balances are reduced to zero by a process of *closing the books.* Accounts so closed are revenues, expired costs, and income distributions, and their balances are transferred to Retained Income. An Income Summary account is used in the closing process to summarize the effects of revenues and expired costs.

Discussion Questions and Problems

6-1 How are the effects of expenses and income distributions similar? How are they different? How should each be reported in the financial statements?

6-2 The Retained Income Statement has sometimes been described as the "linking" statement. Explain specifically what "linking" this statement accomplishes.

6-3
a. Explain the difference between *revenue* and *cash receipts.*
b. Give examples of items that are revenue of a given period but not receipts of that period, items that are receipts but not revenue, and items that are both revenue and receipts.

6-4
a. Explain the difference between *expense* and *cash disbursements.*
b. Give examples of items that are expense of a given period but not disbursements of that period, items that are disbursements but not expense, and items that are both expense and disbursements.

6-5 As the company accountant, you have just presented financial statements to your president showing a retained income increase of $30,000. "That is impossible!" exclaims the president. "The company has $12,000 less cash than it had last year." What plausible explanations can you offer the president?

6-6 Explain how the following cash payments of 1973 are related to 1973 expired costs:

a. Payment for three-year lease which expires in 1975.
b. Payment for salaries for the last week of December 1972.
c. Payment of a dividend to stockholders declared in 1973.
d. Payment of damages to a customer injured in a fall on the firm's premises.

6-7   Explain how the following cash receipts of 1973 are related to 1973 revenue:
a. Issuance of capital stock for cash.
b. Collection of a customer's account for a sale made in 1972.
c. Collection of rent for a three-year period ending in 1975.
d. Collection of refund for merchandise returned to the manufacturer.

6-8   Clark Corporation's Retained Income balance was $23,000 on January 1, 1972, and $27,000 on December 31, 1972. A dividend of $2,000 was declared in December 1972, to be paid in January 1973.
a. Did the company's net assets increase or decrease during the year? Explain.
b. Prepare a retained income statement.

6-9   The Claussen Company had a credit balance of $11,000 in its Retained Income on December 31, 1972, and total net assets of $55,000 on the same date. On December 31, 1973, total assets were $103,000, total liabilities were $30,000, and capital stock amounted to $50,000. A cash dividend of $6,000 had been paid during the year.

Required a. Determine by computation what other change in owners' equity occurred during the year.
b. Prepare a retained income statement.

6-10   Although the accounting rules for determining what types of events should be shown in the financial statements are carefully defined, the particular time when these events are journalized and posted is to a large extent a matter of clerical efficiency.

Required a. If a business prepares financial statements each month, state when you would record (1) transaction entries and (2) adjusting entries for each of the following events. Books are closed annually on December 31.
b. Show what accounts would be debited and credited in each case.
  (1) Office supplies are bought about once each month and are used constantly in small amounts every day.
  (2) Building rent is paid in advance at the beginning of each month.
  (3) Equipment is rented at a fixed daily rate and rent is paid early in the following month.
  (4) City business license fees for the current calendar year are paid in January.
  (5) Property taxes for the calendar year are paid in October.
  (6) The business has five different insurance policies, the premium on each of which is paid at the beginning of the policy year of each policy. None of the policy years coincides with the calendar year.
  (7) Employees are paid once a week on Thursday for work done through the preceding Saturday.

6-11   Advances by customers, rent collected in advance, and similar items will probably not require future payments. How can you justify classifying them as liabilities? What type of year-end adjustment is needed in each case?

6-12   A weekly newspaper began operations on July 1 and collected for 2,000 one-year subscriptions at $10.40 each during the first three days of the month. Editions were published on July 7, 14, 21, and 28. The newspaper prepares monthly income statements.

Prepare the necessary adjusting entry for July 31.

6-13   The Newman Department Store hired three additional salesclerks on Monday, July 26, 1972, to assist in its two-week Anniversary Sale. The clerks were paid a total of $450 on Saturday, August 7. The store's fiscal year ended on July 31.

Required   a. Prepare entries necessary on July 26, July 31, and August 7.
b. If no entries had been made until August 7, state in detail what the errors would have been on the three principal financial statements for (1) the fiscal year ending July 31, 1972, and (2) the fiscal year ending July 31, 1973.

6-14   You are about to make adjustments on December 31, the end of the accounting period of the Ultra Corp.

Required   Describe a situation and journalize the appropriate entry to illustrate each of the following types of adjustment:

a. An expense is debited and a liability is credited.
b. An expense is debited and an asset-contra account is credited.
c. An asset is debited and revenue is credited.
d. A liability is debited and revenue is credited.

6-15   At the time of taking a trial balance at the end of the accounting year, December 31, 1973, the ledger contained the following accounts:

L, Rent Collected in Advance

1973		
Jan. 1	(6 months)	3,000
May 1	(24 months)	1,200
Oct. 1	(12 months)	2,400

OE, Service Revenue

1973	
Mar. 15	2,400
May 9	800
Nov. 1	1,200

The entries in Service Revenue each represent collections at the end of a two-month service contract period for services which were rendered continuously. An additional contract for two months, at a total fee of $1,000, began on December 16, 1973.

Required   Journalize and post the necessary year-end adjusting entries.

6-16   At the end of the accounting year, December 31, 1973, the ledger contained the following accounts.

	A, Building		*A, Building — Accumulated Depreciation*	
1969			1972	
Jan. 1	60,000		Dec. 31 Balance	6,000

	OE, Executives' Bonus Expense		*OE, Operating Revenue*	
1973			1973	
July 5	7,500		Jan. 1–June 30	250,000
			July 1–Dec. 31	175,000

The building is expected to have no net salvage value.

A contract with the officers provides that the president is to receive a bonus of 2 per cent, and the secretary-treasurer 1 per cent, of the operating revenue. The bonus is to be paid semiannually, not earlier than five days after the end of each six-month period, and not later than 95 days afterward.

Required   a. Journalize and post the necessary year-end adjusting entries.

b. Comment on the provisions of the bonus contract.

6-17   The founding of a business was properly recorded on January 1, 1973. On December 31, 1973, however, the accountant failed to make closing entries.

Required   What would each of the following account balances represent in a trial balance taken on December 31, 1974?

a. Cash	e. Capital Stock
b. Accounts Payable	f. Dividends
c. Salary Expense	g. Equipment
d. Sales Revenue	h. Retained Income

6-18   Estimated uncollectible accounts receivable are recorded in the accounting period in which the sale is made so as to match cause and effect in the income statement of the proper period. This is especially important when a sale on credit is made in one period, and the account receivable is finally determined to be uncollectible in a later period.

Required   a. How can advance estimates of uncollectible accounts be said to match cause and effect?

b. When an account is later determined to be bad and is written off, what is the effect on the estimated collectible amount of accounts receivable? On income? On owners' equity?

6-19   On November 30, 1973, the Coleman Company determined that the $750 account receivable from Jasper Bros. would not be collected. On that date Accounts Receivable totaled $31,500 and Accounts Receivable—Estimated Uncollectibles had a credit balance of $2,000.

Required   Journalize the necessary entry.

6-20   The following is a list of selected account balances of the Millstone Company at the end of the year on December 31, 1972:

Unexpired insurance	$ 150	Dividends	$ 300
Salary expense..............	500	Insurance expense	150
Rent collected in advance	400	Accrued property tax pay-	
Property tax expense	175	able	175
Cash	770	Sales revenue	2,500
Equipment	1,800	Rent revenue	200
Accrued salaries payable...	60	Cost of goods sold	1,500
Depreciation expense.......	300	Loss from theft	120
Accounts receivable.........	6,200	Retained income, January	
Owners' investment.........	5,000	1, 1972	2,600

Required   a. Journalize the necessary closing entries.

b. Prepare a T-account showing the balance of Retained Income at the end of the year.

6-21   The Styx Company, which uses a calendar year accounting period, records adjusting entries prior to taking a trial balance. The accompanying list presents the account balances on December 31, 1973.

Required   a. Prepare an eight-column statement classification work sheet.

b. Prepare an income statement, a retained income statement, and a statement of financial position.

c. Journalize closing entries.

d. Prepare an after-closing trial balance.

	Debit	Credit
Accounts payable..		$ 8,500
Accounts receivable...	$ 24,000	
Accrued salaries payable		200
Cash	2,000	
Cost of goods sold..	45,000	
Depreciation expense	1,000	
Dividends	1,500	
Equipment	10,000	
Equipment—accumulated depreciation		6,000
Insurance expense	500	
Owners' investment...		5,000
Organization cost...	400	
Merchandise inventory	20,000	
Rent expense	1,200	
Salary expense...	10,800	
Sales revenue		75,000
Retained income, Dec. 13, 1972		21,800
Unexpired insurance	100	
Totals	$116,500	$116,500

6-22   The Embry Corporation makes necessary adjustments before taking its trial balance at the close of its fiscal year. The accompanying trial balance was taken from the ledger on September 30, 1972, the end of the year.

Required   a. Prepare a statement classification work sheet.

b. Prepare an income statement, a retained income statement, and a statement of financial position.

Interest expense	$ 3,000
Mortgage note payable	50,000
Repair expense	1,600
Long-term investment in bonds	10,000
Buildings	120,000
Interest revenue	500
Accrued interest payable	500
Accrued interest receivable	250
Buildings—accumulated depreciation	48,000
Depreciation expense	3,000
Property tax expense	1,700
Capital stock	35,000
Insurance expense	2,000
Dividends	3,000
Rent revenue	16,000
Unexpired insurance	500
Salary expense	6,500
Rent collected in advance	1,000
Cash	6,000
Retained income, October 1, 1971	5,150
Accounts payable	1,400

The mortgage note payable is due in five equal annual installments, beginning on June 30, 1973.

6-23

Required   From the following trial balance of the McMurray Co. for the year ended December 31, 1972, and supporting information, prepare

a. An adjustment and classification work sheet.

b. An income statement, a retained income statement, and a statement of financial position.

c. Journalize adjusting and closing entries.

	Debit	Credit
Accounts payable		$ 6,880
Accounts receivable	$ 10,440	
Cash	2,500	
Cost of goods sold expense	55,000	
Equipment	10,000	
Equipment—accumulated depreciation		2,000
Capital stock		45,000
Goodwill	5,000	
Merchandise inventory	25,000	
Maintenance and repair expense	3,500	
Rent expense	2,200	
Sales revenue		95,000
Retained income, December 31, 1971	1,700	
Unexpired insurance	540	
Salary expense	33,000	
Totals	$148,880	$148,880

The equipment was acquired at the beginning of 1971. It is expected to have a total useful life of five years and no salvage value.

Rent of $200 for December has not been paid.

Salaries of $600 for the last week of December have not been paid.

A one-year insurance policy was taken out, effective March 1, 1972.

6-24   The following trial balance and supporting information pertain to the Cunningham Corporation for the year ended December 31, 1973.

Required   a. Prepare a combined adjustment and classification work sheet.

b. Prepare an income statement, a retained income statement, and a financial position statement.

Accounts payable............	$ 15,000	Merchandise inventory	$185,000
Accounts receivable.........	40,000	Retained income	11,700
Cash	6,000	Salaries	25,000
Capital stock.................	30,000	Sales revenue	220,000
Dividends	3,000	Unexpired insurance.......	1,200
Fixtures and equipment ...	20,000	Utility expense..............	500
Fixtures and equipment— accumulated depre- ciation	4,000		

It is the policy of the business to count the inventory on hand at the end of the year. The merchandise on hand on December 31, 1973, had an invoice cost of $25,000 and was marked to sell for $37,000.

The fixtures and equipment were all acquired at one time in a prior year and are expected to have a total useful life of ten years from the date of original acquisition.

The president's salary for December, $1,500, has not been paid. In addition, a salesclerk received a cash advance for $200 of his salary for January, 1974.

All the insurance policies are for a three-year term, and all were effective January 1, 1973.

The utility company required a meter deposit of $40, which was included in the balance of Utility Expense.

6-25   Allcharge, a large credit card company, sends monthly billings to its members for charges incurred by them at participating businesses. Allcharge adds a monthly service charge of $1\frac{1}{2}$ per cent per month, based on the average balance of accounts receivable during the month. Interest revenue is the major source of Allcharge's earnings.

On April 1, Allcharge owned total accounts receivable of $2,100,000. During April it processed additional charges to members of $700,000 and collected payments of $900,000 from them.

Required   Journalize the necessary adjusting entry on April 30.

6-26   The Vincent Gift Shop made sales on credit (after deducting sales returns) of a total of $240,000 during the years 1971–1973. Losses from accounts finally determined to be uncollectible were $7,200, based on these credit sales. Net sales on credit in 1974 were $120,000 and cash sales during the year were $20,000. By the end of 1974 all of the customers' accounts except $22,000 had been collected, and all of these resulted from 1974 sales.

Required   a. Set up in T-accounts the balances which would appear in the December 31, 1974, trial balance.

b. Journalize and post the necessary adjusting entry on December 31, 1974.

c. Show in detail how the information affecting customers' accounts and revenue would appear in the 1974 income and financial position statements.

d. During 1975 the Gift Shop credit manager proceeded to collect, or to write off as uncollectible, all the accounts which resulted from 1974 sales. One account, that of Mrs. J. U. Knopp, $73, was written off as uncollectible on February 17. Journalize the necessary entry.

e. What was the effect on 1974 income of the entry in part d? On 1975 income?

f. What would have been the effect on 1974 income and financial position if no adjusting entry had been made in part b? On 1975 income?

6-27   The Porter Pottery Co. was organized early in 1972. Selected accounts from its ledger on December 31, 1972, appeared as follows:

A, Accounts Receivable

Sales on account	60,000	Collections	45,000

OE, Sales Revenue

		Cash sales	20,000
		Sales on account	60,000

Inquiry discloses that bad debts typically amount to 2 per cent of sales on account for pottery manufacturers with similar credit policies.

During 1973, cash sales are $30,000 and sales on account are $150,000. Collections on account in 1973 are $120,000. Specific customers' accounts arising from 1972 sales are found to be uncollectible in 1973 as follows:

Winston Dept. Store	$215
Cline Novelty Co.	500
R. D. Numan	85

Required   a. Journalize and post the necessary adjusting entry for 1972.

b. Show how the information relating to customers' accounts and sales should appear in the 1972 financial statements.

c. Journalize and post closing entries for 1972.

d. Journalize and post the adjusting entry and write-offs for 1973.

e. Show how the information relating to customers' accounts and sales would appear in the 1973 financial statements.

Cases   **6-1**   **Tom the Tailor.** Tom Gowan, who had opened a tailor shop on July 1, 1973, presented the accompanying income statement to the Merchants Bank in support of a loan application early in July 1974:

TOM THE TAILOR
Profit and Loss Statement
For the Year Ended June 30, 1974

Cash received:		
Investment by owner	$ 2,000	
Cash sales	16,000	
Loan from brother, Jim Gowan	500	
Total cash received		$18,500

Cash expenses:

Equipment...	$ 1,800	
Cloth	6,100	
Supplies	300	
Helper	3,000	
Shop rent	1,500	
Advertising..	200	
Owner's salary	5,000	
Total cash expenses...		17,900
Net profit		$ 600

Further investigation by the bank vice president revealed the following information:

(1) Uncollected customers' accounts for work completed amount to $3,500. All are considered to be good.

(2) The equipment is expected to last a total of five years.

(3) Cloth purchased but not yet paid for amounted to $900 on June 30, 1974.

(4) Cloth on hand on June 30, 1974, had cost $1,300.

(5) The helper's salary for the last week in June, $60, had not been paid.

(6) Advertising space for July and August 1974 had already been paid for at a cost of $100.

(7) On June 16, Tom had inadvertently burned a cigarette hole in a customer's tuxedo which had been brought in for alteration. Tom offered to pay $40 for replacing the burned trousers, but the customer insisted that the replacement would not match the jacket, and demanded $100. This matter had not been settled on June 30.

Required

a. List the major ways in which Tom's Profit and Loss Statement fails to comply with accepted accounting method.

b. Using a work sheet for adjustments and classification, prepare corrected financial statements for presentation to the bank.

c. What major items do you think the banker should discuss with Tom? Why?

chapter 7

Reporting
Business Income

Purpose of Chapter

Earlier chapters have shown how accounting provides information about an economic entity that is of potential use to various parties who have an interest in the entity's affairs: its managers, stockholders, creditors, the government, and others.

Chapter 7 deals primarily with financial reporting for parties *external* to the business, and explores in some detail the major reporting standards which particularly affect these external reports. It also examines the bases of classifying the accounts reported in the Income Statement.

Financial Accounting Principles and Conventions

Financial accounting provides information to *outsiders* such as investors, creditors, and governmental agencies, who make decisions that affect external relationships of the firm. These external financial reports are prepared on the basis of a body of underlying accounting *principles* and *conventions*.

A *principle* may be defined as:

> A proposition asserted to be controlling in a given system or domain of inquiry and having acceptance among members of a professional group deemed to be competent in a society; growing out of observation, reason, or experience, a principle purports to be the best possible guide in the choice of alternatives leading to the qualities desired in an end product.[1]

A *convention* is

> A statement or rule of practice which, by common consent, express or implied, is employed in the solution of a given class of problems or guides behavior in a certain kind of situation. A convention . . . may be said to exist when it is known that an alternative, equally logical rule or procedure is available but is not used because of considerations of habit, cost, time, or convenience.[2]

Many years of practical experience have resulted in the development of a body of general guides to accounting practice, referred to as *generally accepted accounting principles*. As used by the accounting profession, this term includes both principles and conventions (under Kohler's definitions) as well as the accepted *methods* of applying them.

Generally accepted accounting principles have resulted from the gradual widespread acceptance of approaches used by businesses to solve their problems of accounting for new situations. These "principles" have sometimes resulted more from practical expediency than from reasoned logic. As a result individual "principles" are often in conflict with each other, and a great variety of accounting *methods* are generally accepted—methods which sometimes give significantly different results in reporting the same set of facts. Usually, however, there is *one method* which reflects the facts in a given situation or industry *better* than other methods.

Organizations which have a major influence on the development and use of generally accepted accounting principles are

> The *American Institute of Certified Public Accountants* (sometimes referred to as the AICPA), an organization dominated by accountants in independent public practice.

> The *Securities and Exchange Commission (SEC)*, a federal agency which regulates financial reporting for certain companies which offer their securities to the public, as well as financial reporting to the stock exchanges.

> The *American Accounting Association (AAA)*, a body whose most influential members are accounting educators.

In recent years there has been a great effort by individuals and by professional organizations, notably the AICPA and the AAA, to reexamine the basic body of ideas on which accounting is based. Their objectives have been to remove, where possible, the internal conflicts among accounting principles and to narrow the range of accepted methods for reporting a given set of events.

---

[1] Eric L. Kohler, *A Dictionary for Accountants,* 3rd ed. (Englewood Cliffs, N.J.: Prentice-Hall, Inc., 1963), p. 394.
[2] *Ibid.,* p. 136.

Basic Standards of Financial Reporting

The users of general-purpose financial statements need assurance that these reports present *reliable information*. To help provide this assurance, professional accounting organizations and groups which represent important classes of financial statement users have developed *standards* for financial report preparation. The basic standards, already discussed in Chapter 2, are

(1) Relevance.
(2) Objectivity (including verifiability).
(3) Freedom from personal bias.
(4) Consistency.

The Independent Auditor's Report

The *independent auditor* is a professional accountant who reviews the system of internal controls of a business and its accounting records and reports. On the basis of this review, called an *audit*, he expresses a professional *opinion* as to the *fairness of the information* reported in the firm's financial statements. The *audit report*, expressing the auditor's findings, is relied on greatly by the outside users of the firm's financial statements.

The independent auditor is not an employee of the business whose records he audits, but rather is an independent contractor. Although paid by the business for which he performs the audit, he has a high degree of responsibility, both professional and financial, to the public to maintain sound standards of quality in financial reporting. His performance is governed by law and professional ethics.

The auditor's opinion follows a prescribed wording, which is varied to reflect differences in the auditor's findings. The standard short-form audit report used in the United States consists of two main parts: a statement of the *scope of the work performed* and an expression of *opinion as to the fairness of the financial statements*. The standard wording is used in the following two paragraphs.

(Scope)

We have examined the statement of financial position of A Company as of December 31, 19xx, and the related statements of income, retained income, and flow of funds for the year then ended. Our examination was made in accordance with generally accepted auditing standards, and accordingly included such tests of the accounting records and such other auditing procedures as we considered necessary in the circumstances.

(Opinion)

In our opinion, the accompanying statements of financial position, of income, of retained income, and of flow of funds present fairly the financial position of A Company at December 31, 19xx, and the results of its operations for the year then ended, in conformity with generally accepted accounting principles applied on a basis consistent with that of the preceding year.

The independent accountant must give a *qualified opinion*, stating the matters to which he takes exception, if he has not been able to satisfy himself completely as to the fairness of presentation in the statements. An opinion is *qualified* when the terms "except," "exception," or "subject to" are used in stating the opinion. "Subject to" is used when the outcome of a matter is uncertain. Any modifying phrase in the standard short-form opinion has the effect of qualifying the opinion in some way.

If the questionable matters are of such a nature, or are so material, that they would destroy the significance of an opinion on the statements as a whole, the auditor should clearly *deny an opinion.*

The purpose of the *scope* paragraph is to assure the reader of the financial statements that the auditor has observed the *accepted standards of auditing*, and that to the best of his judgment he has followed necessary *auditing procedures* in making his examination.

There are three significant elements in the *opinion* paragraph, indicated by the following key words:

(1) *Present fairly.*

(2) In conformity with *generally accepted accounting principles.*

(3) Applied on a basis *consistent.*

If the statements *present* the financial position and operating results of the business *fairly*, in the auditor's judgment the accounting methods and measurements used are suited to the nature and circumstances of the particular business entity. Businesses have some freedom of choice in selecting their own methods of accounting within rather broad limits.

The broad limits, or guides, which accountants use in determining the acceptability of accounting methods and measurements are called *generally accepted accounting principles*. Accountants do not unanimously agree what these individual principles are. Accounting methods have developed to serve a useful purpose.

The auditor is concerned with the *consistency* with which generally accepted accounting principles are applied in the entity's accounts, so as to assure the user that the accounting information furnished by the company at one time is *comparable* with that furnished at other times. This does not mean that a business cannot change to a better method of accounting, within the limits of generally accepted accounting principles. If it does change, however, it should disclose the *nature of the change* and *its effect* on the financial statements, and should provide sufficient information to permit the reader to compare the affected account balances before and after the change.

Another important purpose of *consistency* in accounting measurements is to prevent manipulation of the results. Shifting from one method to another without restriction would permit a dishonest accountant or manager to change the measurements of income and financial position to suit his own purposes.

Supplementary Standards of Financial Reporting

The following standards of financial reporting, which support and amplify the basic reporting standards discussed earlier, are discussed in the following sections:

(1) Inclusiveness, or adequate disclosure.

(2) Clarity of presentation.

(3) Timeliness.
(4) Materiality.
(5) Comparability.

Inclusiveness, or Adequate Disclosure

Ideally, accounting reports should reflect all significant financial information which pertains to the decisions to be made by a given statement user group.

General-purpose financial reports should include a summary of *all the transactions* of the company for the period for which the statements are prepared. These transactions should be accounted for according to the principles of recognition, classification, and measurement which have been presented in earlier chapters.

General-purpose statements almost always include an income statement, a financial position statement, and a retained income statement. Statements of *funds flows*, to be discussed in Chapter 21, are rapidly becoming one of the primary statements. Other types of reports frequently used are *schedules* of cost of goods sold, receivables, investments, plant assets, liabilities, and changes in invested capital. Not all of these reports are necessary in every case; the accountant must decide which of them will best disclose the information which the user is likely to need.

The *use of any accounting period,* whether the natural business year or the calendar year, is an *arbitrary* way of giving information about where the business stands financially and what its past progress has been. It is arbitrary because few business transactions come sharply to a close at the end of any one accounting period. The period is selected to present a cross section of a continuing stream of events, so that statement users may form their judgments about the effectiveness of past performance and about the probable nature, size, and direction of future business events. Considering these purposes, the accountant should not close his eyes to significant events which occur between the closing date of the accounting period and the actual date when the statements for the period are completed and issued.

Example 1   An accountant is about to release financial statements for the calendar year 1972. Because the work of preparing the statements has been complex, it has taken until January 30, 1973, to complete them. Suddenly, on January 30, a disaster against which the business carries no insurance destroys all of its physical assets. What is the effect of this event on the financial statements for the year 1972?

Solution   Since only *transactions completed* during a period should be reflected in the *accounts,* the accountant would not *record* the loss in 1972. But would statements prepared on such a basis fill the needs of a prospective merchandise creditor or investor in a distant city who examined the statements in February 1973 without first-hand knowledge of the disaster? Obviously not.

Although the disaster should not be formally recorded in the accounts until 1973 when it occurred, it should be reported prominently in a descriptive note which forms an essential part of the 1972 statements.

Footnotes such as that described in Example 1 are integral parts of the financial statements. Examples of other important events occurring after the closing date of the accounting period which should be disclosed in footnotes or elsewhere in the statements are substantial changes in the form of business ownership, mergers, purchase or disposal of major items of property, and adverse decisions of lawsuits which require the company to pay damages.

Often events which occur after the end of a period give definite information about transactions which had been completed at the end of the year, for which some facts were unknown at the time. Such information, if available in time, should be used in the accounts and reports of the year just closed.

Footnotes are also used to disclose events or conditions which have already taken place in the year for which transactions are being reported, but which *cannot yet be recognized as assets or equities* under the accepted principles of accounting. Examples are important purchase contracts and long-term leases which have not yet been performed by either party to the contract, but which will most likely require the payment of substantial sums in the future.

Example 2   The B. F. Goodrich Company Annual Report for 1969 contained the following footnote:

"NOTE E—LEASES

Minimum net annual rentals under leases for certain real properties used primarily in retail and warehouse operations approximate $10,000,000. Terms of the leases, which in most cases contain renewal options, average ten years."

Clarity of Presentation

The *words* used in describing financial information and the *arrangement* of material in the statements must both be *clear*. Extremes of both brevity and elaborateness should be avoided. Often the exact titles of ledger accounts are inappropriate for use in the financial statements because they are too condensed to be informative.

Example 3   The ledger account "Bonds Payable" would be more adequately disclosed in the statement of financial position as "6% First Mortgage Bonds Payable due July 1, 1975."

Ledger account titles which are too technical or cumbersome for the statement user should be simplified, but *simplicity* and *conciseness* of wording should not be carried so far as to sacrifice exactness of meaning.

It is undesirable to combine so many financial elements under one statement item that important information is buried, and just as undesirable to present so many detailed items that the reader "cannot see the forest for the trees."

The classification of similar items into *groups*, the arrangement of items in relation to each other, and the location of *subtotals* and *totals* may also make the statements clearer. Just as the right-hand column is the most prominent one on the front page of a newspaper, a statement containing a number of figures may use several columns, with the more important amounts appearing toward the right. Varying degrees of indentation of descriptive captions are also used to denote relative importance. Such methods of achieving emphasis in arranging statement items allow the busy reader to look at the more significant amounts first. He should then study the details which comprise the totals in order to get the full meaning of the report.

Timeliness

Financial reports should be made available soon enough to be *useful in solving current problems* and in appraising the recent performance of business officials and employees. Although important for all financial reports, timeliness is usually more essential for internal reports for management than for external reports. In fact, incomplete details obtained promptly may be more useful to management than complete information received only after great delay. The qualities of completeness and accuracy are of little comfort if the information is furnished too late to prevent avoidable losses.

Many large companies supplement their comprehensive annual financial reports to stockholders with more condensed quarterly reports. In addition, they should release special bulletins to report major financial events affecting the company. Internal reports to management should be much more frequent. Complete financial reports usually need be prepared no oftener than once a month, but practically every management needs daily *flash reports* which summarize concisely such critically important information as the daily volume of sales, the current backlog of customers' orders, and the day's cash receipts, payments, and ending balance.

A company which cannot complete its reports within a reasonable time is not receiving full value for the cost of operating its accounting system. It should either streamline procedures so that the reporting process can be completed more promptly, or reduce the quantity of information reported to manageable proportions.

Materiality

Materiality is a practical guide which helps the accountant decide *to what extent to follow accounting principles*. Materiality refers to the *relative importance* of an item under the particular circumstances.

Materiality may be *quantitative* or *qualitative*. *Relative size* is more important than absolute size in determining whether an item is quantitatively material.

Example 4   An asset item costing $25 may be immaterial in the financial reports of a company which owns total assets of $1 million, and yet material to a company with total assets of $1,000.

In deciding whether or not the amount of an item is material, it should be compared not only with other similar items but with the total of items of its class (such as total assets) and with net income. A group of items which are immaterial as single units may be material *in the aggregate*.

Example 5   If the million-dollar company in Example 4 owned several hundred similar $25 assets, they would be material when considered together.

Materiality may be *qualitative* rather than quantitative. A transaction small in amount may be important if it is *unexpected or improper*, or if it violates a law or contract. It also may be material because, although small, it indicates the probable course of future events or a significant change in business practice.[3]

Deciding what is material in accounting is a matter of *exercising informed judgment*, not of applying specific rules. The dividing line between what is material and what is not varies according to the company, the circumstances surrounding the transaction, and the use to which the information is likely to be put.

Three different aspects of materiality should be recognized: (1) materiality in setting and carrying out the rules for recording transactions, (2) materiality in preparing financial reports, and (3) materiality from the auditor's point of view in expressing an opinion on the fairness of the financial statements.

Materiality in record-keeping. It is customary to follow accounting principles strictly in journalizing and posting, with a few minor exceptions. Journal entries and ledger accounts are carried out to the nearest cent.

An exception to the strict application of principles is often made for long-lived assets of small unit value, such as pencil sharpeners. Because this item will benefit the operations of the business in future years it should, according to principle, be accounted for as a long-lived asset, Equipment. The clerical cost of keeping records of such assets and recording annual depreciation would undoubtedly outweigh the usefulness of the resulting information. For convenience, most companies would probably debit the cost of such immaterial assets directly to an expense account at the time of purchase.

Materiality in financial reporting. An item in an accounting report is *material* if there is reason to believe that knowledge of it would influence the decisions of an informed user of the report.[4]

Earlier paragraphs have pointed out how some immaterial items may be combined in the financial statements to improve readability.

A common reporting practice which involves both materiality and clarity is that of *rounding amounts* in financial statements to the *nearest dollar*. It is usually easier for the statement reader to grasp the size and relative importance of an amount that has been rounded than of one that is expressed in dollars and cents. In some cases, businesses feel that rounding of amounts to the *nearest thousand dollars* makes financial statements still clearer.

Sometimes amounts in financial statements give a *false appearance of exactness*, while actually they are based upon estimates that are only rough approximations. An example is depreciation, which is measured on the basis of an indefinite future life and an estimated salvage value in the distant future. Of course, some accounts, such as Cash, can be measured accurately to the penny (although even Cash is measured on the assumption that checks received will be paid when presented to the bank upon which they are drawn).

Materiality in auditing. In his examination the auditor may find that his client's system of internal control has some weakness, or that the client has been inconsistent in his reporting practices. Unless the effect on the financial statements is quite significant, however, the auditor will not *take an exception* in his opinion.

---

[3] American Accounting Association, Committee on Concepts and Standards, *Standards of Disclosure for Published Financial Reports,* Supplementary Statement No. 8 (The Association, 1954).

[4] *Idem.*

Comparability

Figures standing alone usually do not mean much. The informed reader of a financial statement is not especially impressed to learn that the company has earned a net income of $10 million. To be meaningful, accounting amounts must be related to appropriate standards of comparison, such as

(1) The same class of information for the company at other dates.
(2) Related classes of information for the company at the same date.
(3) The same class of information for other companies.
(4) Predetermined goals.

If these comparisons are to be valid, accounting data of the same class must have been collected and measured according to uniform standards of quality.

Example 6   In 1972 and prior years a business considered all items of equipment which cost under $10 to be immaterial and debited them to Supplies Expense. If it changed its policy in 1973 so as to treat all items under $25 as immaterial, its financial statements in 1973 would not be comparable with those of earlier years. The account balances affected would be the following:

	Comparison of Amounts Under New Policy with Those Under Old Policy
OE, Supplies expense	Larger
A, Equipment (cost)................................	Smaller
A, Equipment—accumulated depreciation......	Smaller
OE, Depreciation expense...........................	Smaller

Whether or not the policy change in Example 6 is material depends on the relative importance of equipment items purchased in the $10 to $25 cost range.

Example 6 is not intended to imply that a company may never make a desirable change in its accounting policies or procedures. The nature of such a departure from consistency should, however, be disclosed clearly in the financial statements, together with sufficient information to enable the reader to use the same basis of accounting in comparing the amounts before and after the change.

Comparability of financial-statement items among businesses is also desirable from the standpoint of the user of the statements, but there are many limits on such comparability in actual practice. Often a particular asset or equity is measured in different ways by various businesses. Some of these differences in method result from different operating conditions; others, from management preferences. These differences, although they may be necessary, desirable, and acceptable to professional accounting groups, often severely limit the comparability of financial data of separate businesses.

Another limitation on the comparability of financial statements is accounting's implicit *assumption that the monetary unit is a stable common denominator* for expressing the effects of transactions at different times. Costs of assets acquired in different years, for example, are added together and reported in a single balance-sheet account as though dollars of the same purchasing power were used to buy all of them. Changes of individual prices and of general price levels—especially rapid changes—distort the comparability of financial information compiled in this manner.

INCOME STATEMENT CLASSIFICATION

The *income* of a business was defined in Chapter 1 as *the change in its net assets which results from (1) the excess or deficiency of revenue over related expired costs and (2) other gains or losses to the business entity from sales, exchanges, involuntary conversions, or obsolescence of its assets.*

Revenue was defined as *the inflow of assets to the business in exchange for its goods and services.*

Chapter 4 dealt with the basic accounting concepts which apply to measuring business income; Chapter 5, with the basic accounting procedures for measuring and reporting income. This section considers some additional aspects of classifying and reporting revenues and income deductions in the income statement.

Bases of Classifying Revenue

Revenues of a business may be classified into various accounts to enable management and external statement users *to appraise the results of past operations* and *project the results of future operations.* Revenue classification also assists management in *controlling operations* while they are in progress.

Revenues may be classified according to the nature of their source: *sale of products* or *sale of services. Gains* on the disposal of property not held primarily for sale are also reported as additions to income. These major sources may be further subclassified, if management wishes, to show the revenue from each type of product or group of products, from each type of service, and from each type of property on which gains were realized.

Management is usually more interested in a detailed classification of revenues than are other statement users, because it is management which must take the necessary steps to insure that sufficient revenues are earned to achieve the firm's objectives. To help accomplish these objectives, revenues should be classified according to the *lines of responsibility* within the organization, as well as by the nature of the revenue source. The accounts should make it possible to report to each responsible manager how much revenue was realized by his division or department.

The legal form in which a business is organized has no effect on its classification of revenue accounts.

Major Types of Revenues and Deductions
from Revenue

The following main types of revenue accounts are commonly found in various types of businesses.

Sales revenue. The gross proceeds realized by transferring products to customers.

Deductions from sales revenue. Debits made to revenue contra-accounts to give information helpful to management in evaluating and controlling sales performance. The principal types are

Sales returns. Cancellations of the original sales.

Sales allowances. Price reductions after sales have been made, often to compensate for damages to merchandise.

Sales discounts allowed. Price reductions to induce customers to pay promptly. These are referred to as *cash discounts.* *Trade discounts* on sales are reductions from the list price to certain classes of customers, such as dealers, or reductions where the customer buys more than a stated quantity. Trade discounts do not appear separately in the accounts; only the final price they help to determine is recorded.

Uncollectible sales revenue. The amount by which Sales Revenue is estimated to be overstated because some of the sales on credit will never be collected. Many businesses treat such losses as an expense (*Bad Debts Expense*) for which responsibility is assigned to the department head in charge of granting credit and making collections. However, such losses are not expired costs like other expenses, but instead are *unrealized revenue* which was included in the Sales Revenue account.

Service revenue. The gross proceeds realized by rendering services to customers. This classification applies to such businesses as public utilities and banks, which render services rather than sell products. Revenue contra-accounts may also be used by these businesses.

Nonoperating revenue. Revenues from other than the primary revenue sources of the business. Typical examples are[5]

Interest revenue. Revenues from extending credit, earned at a fixed rate per time period.

Rent revenue. Revenues for the use of land, buildings, or equipment, based upon charge per time period.

Royalty revenue. Revenues based upon the income from the use of property.

Bases of Classifying Expenses and Losses

Business managers and outside statement users need information on various types of expenses to aid them in appraising the past performance of the business and in estimating its future results. The management needs detailed information on the amount of each type of expense so that it can (1) measure the performance of the individuals who are responsible for carrying on each phase of business activity, (2) appraise the costs of various segments of enterprise operations, and (3) initiate measures to control these costs.

Business operations consist of combining various productive factors, or *inputs,* in such a way as to produce the entity's *final output,* which may be either a product or a service. There may be many intermediate outputs, called *func-*

---

[5] Interest, rent, and royalty revenues are *operating revenues* if they are from a recurring and significant activity of the business.

tions or *activities*, which result from the productive process. It is useful to classify expenses along the following lines:

(1) The nature of the *input*, or *object* of the expense. Examples are the *salaries* of employees, *supplies* used, and building *rent*. These object expense accounts denote the input factors of labor, materials, and facilities, respectively.

(2) The nature of the *output*, or *function*, which is carried on with the inputs which are used. Examples are *purchasing*, *warehousing*, and *advertising*.

(3) The *responsibility center*, or organizational subdivision within the business, whose manager is responsible for controlling the expense.

As a rule, the expenses of a business are classified along all three of these lines so that useful internal and external reports may be prepared.

Classification of Expenses by Object

Classifying expenses by *object*, or type of input, groups together costs which are acquired in a similar way and are subject to similar measures of control. Management control efforts may be concentrated on the quantity, type, and price of the input acquired, as well as the efficiency with which it is used.

Example 7   In controlling the price of *supplies* used, management may install a central purchasing department manned by people who are trained in buying effectively. In controlling the quantity of supplies used, management may provide physical safeguards over the custody of supplies and over their issuance to the operating departments, together with a limit on the maximum amount of supplies that can be issued to accomplish a given amount of work.

Objects of expense for various companies are basically similar, but object classifications may be condensed into a few accounts or expanded into many. The following object classification, recommended to its members by the National Retail Dry Goods Association, is a typical example:

Cost of Goods Sold	Traveling
Payroll	Communication
Rent	Repairs
Advertising	Insurance
Taxes	Depreciation
Interest	Professional Services
Supplies	Unclassified
Services Purchased	

Many variations of object classifications are used in business practice.

Classification of Expenses by Function

The classification of expenses by object provides important information, but it is of limited value to management in controlling costs. For this purpose attention should be centered on the output—*what has been done* with the inputs used. Expenses classified on this basis are said to be classified according to *function*, or type of activity.

The simplest functional classification of costs includes only *production* and *distribution*. *Production cost*, associated chiefly with manufacturing, consist of costs incurred in getting the product ready for sale. They are identified with the product as it is being transformed, and then the entire product cost is treated as Cost of Goods Sold Expense when the product is sold. *Distribution costs* include all costs incurred by a merchandising company after the goods are purchased and are ready for sale, and by a manufacturer after goods have been produced and are ready for sale.

An expanded functional classification consists of *production*, *selling*, *general administration*, and *financing*. The selling function might be further subclassified into the following functions:

> Inventory control
> Building occupancy (including warehousing)
> Sales promotion
> Direct selling
> Packaging
> Shipping and delivery
> Sales administration

After expired costs have been classified by function (and subclassified by object within each function), it is desirable to try to determine whether the costs of the function for a given time period represent the desired level of efficiency in utilizing resources. To make this appraisal it is necessary to have a *standard of performance* by which the cost actually incurred for each measurable unit of activity is compared with the standard, or desired, cost for each unit of activity.

Example 8   The costs of a retailer's delivery function seemed excessive, both as a percentage of Sales Revenue and as an average cost of delivering one parcel one mile. The manager of the delivery department and the controller began a study to determine what could be done to reduce these unit costs.

To establish a *standard unit cost*, it must be possible to measure the activity in terms of highly similar physical units. This condition is found in standardized manufacturing and other types of repetitive operations more often than in activities which perform an individualized service.

Classification of Expenses by Responsibility Center

Within a well-organized business a single manager has the responsibility for seeing that a given function is performed properly. As a result, if expenses are classified according to function, they are also automatically classified according to *responsibility center*, or organizational unit within the business. One organizational unit may have several functions to carry out, but the responsibility for carrying out a single function should not be divided between the managers of different units.

A combined basis of classifying expenses by functions and by responsible managers is needed to permit appraisal of past performance and to localize the responsibility for future action. Within each function, information about the amount of each object of expense helps the responsible manager to determine what type of action is needed to control expenses.

The following accounts illustrate the combined functional and object bases of classifying expenses:

> Purchasing—Salaries
> Purchasing—Supplies
> Purchasing—Communication

Periodic reports to the manager of the Purchasing Department should list the amount of expense for each object. The total of these expenses represents the cost of performing the purchasing function during the period. An appraisal of performance of the purchasing function can be made by considering the total costs incurred in relation to the quantity and quality of purchasing activity performed.

Limitations on Expense Classification

As the number of accounts in the expense classification increases so does the clerical cost of doing the accounting work. Detailed classification of expenses should not be carried beyond the point where the cost of getting the additional information is greater than its usefulness justifies.

The types of items to be included in each expense account should be defined sharply to facilitate the classification of expense items and to assure the *comparability* of a given expense account from one time to another. A Miscellaneous Expense account may be used to combine dissimilar small items which do not justify separate expense accounts. If its balance becomes large, some of its major components should be classified in separate accounts.

Reporting the Results of Operations

Users of a firm's income statement rely on the information it contains to help them in evaluating the firm's past operating performance and in estimating its future performance. Such evaluations and projections are hindered by the occurrence of unusual events and transactions which affect the income of the business, and by the occasional need to record in the current period a revenue or expense adjustment which actually applies directly to some earlier period(s).

Recognizing this difficulty, the Accounting Principles Board of the American Institute of Certified Public Accountants has established criteria for recognizing *extraordinary items* and *prior period adjustments* in reporting periodic income, and has specified how they should be reported in the financial statements. It is the Board's view that the net income for the current period should reflect *all items of profit and loss recognized during the period, with the sole exception of prior period adjustments.*

Extraordinary Items

Extraordinary items are defined by the Board as

> . . . the effects of events and transactions which have occurred during the current period, which are of an extraordinary nature and whose effects are material . . . . They will be of a character significantly different from the typical or customary business activities of the entity. Accordingly, they will be events and transactions of material effect which would not be expected to recur frequently and which would not be considered as recurring factors in any evaluation of the ordinary operating processes of the business.[6]

Examples of extraordinary items are material gains and losses from

(a) The sale or abandonment of a significant part of the business, such as a plant.

(b) The sale of an investment which was not acquired to be resold.

(c) The write-off of goodwill because of unusual events within the period.

(d) The condemnation or expropriation of properties.

(e) A major devaluation of a foreign currency.[7]

Some types of gains or losses, regardless of size, are not extraordinary items (or prior period adjustments) because by nature they are typical of the entity's *customary business activities*. Examples are

(1) Write-downs of receivables, inventories, and research and development costs.

(2) Adjustments of contract prices already accrued in the accounts.

(3) Gains or losses from fluctuations of foreign exchange.[8]

The effects of items of these types should be shown in *income before extraordinary items*. If they are material, they may be disclosed separately in this part of the income statement.

Prior Period Adjustments

Material adjustments related to prior periods should not affect the measurement of net income of the current period. In statements for a single year they should be shown as additions to, or deductions from, the beginning balance of retained income. Such adjustments must have all four of the following characteristics:

(a) They can be *specifically identified with* and directly related to the business activities of *particular prior periods*.

(b) They are not attributable to economic events which occurred after the date of the financial statements for the prior period.

(c) They depend primarily on determinations by persons other than management.

(d) Their amounts could not be reasonably estimated before such determination.[9]

---

[6] AICPA, *Accounting Principles Board Opinion No. 9,* "Reporting the Results of Operations" (New York: The Institute, 1966), Par. 21.

[7] *Idem.*

[8] *Idem.*

[9] *Ibid.,* Par. 23.

Prior period adjustments are rare. Examples are

   (1) Material, nonrecurring adjustments or settlements of income taxes.

   (2) Settlements of significant amounts resulting from lawsuits or similar claims.[10]

Normal, recurring corrections which are a natural result of using estimates, such as adjustments of depreciation because of a change in estimated useful life, are *not* prior period adjustments.

Outline of the Income Statement

A simplified form of the income statement appeared in Illustration 4-1. This basic outline is expanded in Illustrations 7-1 and 7-2 to include the additional types of accounts introduced in this chapter.

Illustration 7-1 shows a *multiple-step* form of income statement for a trading business. The essential feature of this form is that various types of additions to, or deductions from, income are added or subtracted in succession. The intervening totals (or differences) are usually labeled appropriately.

Illustration 7-1

OUTLINE OF MULTIPLE-STEP INCOME STATEMENT

    Sales revenue
    — Deductions from sales revenue (revenue contra-accounts)
    = *Net sales revenue*
    — Cost of goods sold expense
    = *Gross margin on sales*
    — Operating expense
    = *Income from operations*
    + Nonoperating revenue and gains
    — Nonoperating expenses and losses
    = *Income before income tax and extraordinary items*
    — Corporate income tax expense
    = *Income before extraordinary items*
    + *Extraordinary gains:*
       + Gain (describe nature)
       — Income tax effect of gain
    + Gain after tax effect
    — *Extraordinary losses*
       — Loss (describe nature)
       + Income tax effect of loss
    — Loss after tax effect
    = *Net income* or (*net loss*)

The arrangement used in Illustration 7-2 is the *single-step* income statement. The following organization is used:

   (1) All revenues and additions to income are grouped together and added.

   (2) All revenue contras, expenses, and deductions from income are grouped together and added.

---

[10] *Idem.*

(3) The total of expenses and deductions is then subtracted from the total of revenues and income additions.

Income statements used in this text will ordinarily follow the multiple-step form.

Illustration
7-2

OUTLINE OF SINGLE-STEP INCOME STATEMENT

Sales revenue
+ Nonoperating revenue and gains
= *Total revenue and gains*
Deductions from sales revenue (revenue contra-accounts)
Cost of goods sold expense
Operating expenses
Nonoperating expenses and losses
Corporate income tax expense
− *Total expenses and income deductions*
= *Income before extraordinary items*
+ *Extraordinary gains:*
+ Gain (describe nature)
− Income tax effect of gain
+ Gain after tax effect
− *Extraordinary losses*
− Loss (describe nature)
+ Income tax effect of loss
− Loss after tax effect
= *Net income* or (*net loss*)

Earnings Per Share

The periodic net income or net loss of a business is the most important indicator of its past operating performance *in total*. The income figure alone, however, does not show how much the business earned (or lost) in relationship to the capital invested. One measure that has been widely used to report the earnings in proportion to capital used is the *earnings per share of common stock.* This figure is an important aid to present and potential common stockholders in gauging the past performance of the corporation and in making their projections about its future. Earnings per share has an important influence on the market value of shares of stock.

Earnings per share information has been widely reported in annual corporate financial reports and in financial periodicals for many years. In the past the method of computing earnings per share has sometimes differed from one business to another, resulting in misleading information. To end this abuse the Accounting Principles Board of the AICPA now requires a uniform method of computing and reporting earnings per share information. The following are highlights of the board's requirements for companies with simple capital structures:

(1) Earnings per share, or net loss per share, should be shown on the face of the income statement.

(2) Earnings per share amounts should be reported for (a) income before extraordinary items and (b) net income. It may also be desirable to show the per share amounts of extraordinary items.

(3) The number of shares used in the computation should be the weighted average number of common stock shares outstanding during the period being reported on.

Example 9

The Capital Sales Corporation had 8,000 shares of common stock outstanding on January 1, 1973. On May 1, 1973, 3,000 additional shares were issued. The corporation had a net income before extraordinary items of $90,000 for 1973, and a gain (after income tax) of $4,000 on the sale of some unneeded equipment. What earnings per share information should it report?

Solution

The weighted average number of shares outstanding during the year is computed as follows:

$$8,000 \text{ shares} \times 4 \text{ months} = 32,000$$
$$11,000 \text{ shares} \times 8 \text{ months} = 88,000$$
$$\text{Total} = 120,000 \text{ shares}/12 \text{ months}$$
$$= \text{Average number of shares outstanding, } 10,000$$

Income before extraordinary items	$90,000	$9.00 per share
Extraordinary gain (after income tax)	4,000	0.40 per share
Net income	$94,000	$9.40 per share

The foregoing rules apply to corporations with *simple capital structures*—those having only common stock, or having no other securities that could potentially dilute the amount of earnings per share of common stock. The method of computing earnings per share for companies with complex capital structures is beyond the scope of this text. [The interested reader should refer to *APB Opinion No. 15*, "Earnings Per Share" (New York: AICPA, 1969).]

Illustration of Expanded Income Statement

Illustration 7-3 shows how the additional accounts described in this chapter would appear in an income statement. This is a multiple-step income statement, such as might be used for reporting to outside users. Statements prepared for the internal use of management are more likely to be classified according to organizational units and functions, with object of expense information being given for each unit or function.

Operating expenses include the costs of carrying on the principal activities of the business.

Income from operations is the difference between revenues from the primary sources of the business and the expenses of its main activities.

Nonoperating revenues are *additions* to income from sources other than the principal ones. A common type of nonoperating revenue is the interest revenue of an industrial company.

Nonoperating expenses are *deductions* from income resulting from actitivies other than the principal ones.

Corporate federal income tax is a significant expense of business corporations. It is usually set apart from other expenses in the income statement because of its large amount, which is frequently almost 50 per cent of net income before deducting the income tax, and because separate presentation helps the statement reader to estimate the effect of future income taxes more accurately. Business proprietorships and partnerships are not subject to income tax, but their owners must pay personal income taxes on their shares of business earnings.

Illustration 7-3

CAPITAL SALES CORPORATION
Income Statement
For the Year Ended December 31, 1973

Sales revenue		$950,000	
Deductions from sales revenue:			
Sales returns and allowances	$ 8,000		
Uncollectible sales revenue	12,000	20,000	
Net sales revenue		930,000	
Deduct cost of goods sold expense		510,000	
Gross margin on sales		420,000	
Deduct operating expenses:			
Advertising	20,000		
Depreciation	10,000		
Insurance	6,000		
Rent	30,000		
Repairs	11,000		
Salaries and wages	150,000		
Supplies	12,000		
Taxes (other than income tax)	16,000		
Miscellaneous	5,000		
Total operating expenses		260,000	
Income from operations		160,000	
Add nonoperating revenue:			
Interest revenue		3,000	
		163,000	
Deduct nonoperating expense:			
Discounts lost	1,000		
Interest expense	6,500	7,500	
Income before federal income tax and extraordinary items		155,500	
Corporate federal income tax expense on above		65,500	
Income before extraordinary items		90,000	Per common share $9.00
Add extraordinary gain:			
Gain on sale of equipment	5,333		
Less federal income tax on above	1,333		
Gain on sale of equipment, after income tax effect		4,000	
			Per common share $0.40
Net income		$94,000	Per common share 9.40

Illustration of Expanded Retained Income Statement

Illustration 7-4 shows how *prior period adjustments* are reported in the retained income statement.

**Illustration
7-4**

CAPITAL SALES CORPORATION
Retained Income Statement
For the Year Ended December 31, 1973

Retained income at beginning of year:	
As previously reported......................................	$100,000
Deduct adjustment for additional income taxes applicable to 1972 income	30,000
As restated..	70,000
Add net income for 1973 (see Income Statement)	94,000
Total...	164,000
Deduct cash dividends, at $2.00 per share	20,000
Retained income at end of year............................	144,000

Summary   In his audit report the independent auditor of a business gives an opinion as to the *fairness* with which the financial statements present the affairs of the business, in conformity with *generally accepted accounting principles.* As used here, the term "principle" includes *principles* (under the usual meaning) and *conventions*, as well as the *methods* of applying them.

In addition to the basic standards governing financial reporting—relevance, objectivity, freedom from personal bias, and consistency—it is important to observe the supplementary reporting standards of inclusiveness, clarity, timeliness, materiality, and comparability.

In the income statement revenues are classified according to source. Deductions in computing the income for a period consist of *revenue contra-accounts*, *expenses*, and *losses*. It is ordinarily useful to classify expenses according to function or responsibility center, and then further according to object.

Extraordinary gains and losses are reported as the final additions and deductions before net income, and their income tax effect should be disclosed. Material *adjustments related to prior periods* are shown as additions to, or deductions from, the beginning balance of retained income. The face of the income statement must show amounts per common share outstanding for income before extraordinary items and net income.

**Discussion
Questions
and
Problems**

7-1   Compare the meaning of "generally accepted accounting principles" with the meaning of the "principles of physics." Consider in your answer the differences in the ways the two kinds of principles have been developed.

7-2   State whether you would consider each of the following to be an accounting principle or an accounting convention, and why:

a. The going-concern concept.
b. Materiality.

c. The rule of debit and credit.

d. The accounting entity.

7-3

a. Is it generally desirable to round amounts in journal entries and ledger accounts to the nearest dollar?

b. Is it desirable to round amounts in the financial statements?

c. What accounting principle or convention applies in these situations?

7-4

a. What is the purpose of an independent audit?

b. Does the auditor's opinion tell whether or not the statements are correctly prepared? Explain.

c. Company *A* and Company *B* are in the same industry. Their auditors' opinions state that their financial statements have been prepared in accordance with generally accepted accounting principles. Does that mean that uniform methods of measurement have been used? Explain.

7-5   There are several different methods of measuring the value of the inventory at the end of a period, and at the same time of measuring cost of goods sold for the period. Suppose that a firm has been using one method and decides to change to another.

a. Under what circumstances do you think it would be permitted to do so?

b. If it is allowed to make the change in measurement methods, how should the statement readers be informed of the change?

c. What problems can be created by such changes of measurement methods?

7-6   The general ledger trial balance of a wholesale company consisted of about 100 accounts. The accounting department prepared monthly statements for the use of management, usually issuing them around the 20th of the following month. The accounting department frequently had to spend several days in locating errors so that the trial balance would balance, or in finding the causes of discrepancies in the records.

a. What criticism can you make of this situation?

b. What constructive suggestions can you offer?

7-7   A retail merchant sold a delivery truck for a gain of $1,000. Should this be reported as a part of sales revenue? If not, where should it be reported, and why?

7-8

a. List several examples of expenses classified according to object, function, and responsibility center that might be appropriate for a large automobile dealer.

b. For what purpose might each type of classification of expense be useful?

7-9   Answer Question 7-8 for a large city newspaper.

7-10   Company *C* and Company *D* are similar companies in the same industry. Company *C* computes depreciation on a certain type of equipment over a ten-year life, using the straight-line depreciation method. Company *D* uses an eight-year life for the same type of equipment, and uses a depreciation method which charges more depreciation to earlier years than later years of the equipment's life.

a. Comment on whether these companies have applied generally accepted accounting principles consistently.

b. What problems does the investor face in comparing the performance of Companies *C* and *D*?

c. How would you suggest that the problems in part b be solved?

7-11   The annual report of the S. S. Kresge Company for the year ended January 27, 1971, contained the following item:

Minimum Annual Rents Total $96,455,000: Minimum annual rentals under 1,227 leases for stores occupied at January 27, 1971 aggregated $96,455,000. These leases expire during 10-year periods as follows:

1981	$12,404,000
1991	40,212,000
2001	42,092,000
2002 to 2035	1,747,000
	$96,455,000

Certain leases provide for additional rents based on sales volume in excess of a specified base.

Most leases on K marts and certain leases on Kresge and Jupiter stores are gross leases under which the lessor pays property taxes, insurance and specified building and parking lot maintenance and repair costs.

a. What is the purpose of this note?
b. Would the amounts shown above be reported as liabilities in the January 27, 1971, financial position statement? Explain.
c. What standard of financial reporting caused this note to be included in Kresge's financial statements?

7-12   The Rhyne Co. was established 40 years ago. It has gradually expanded its plant and equipment through the years, although many items have reached the ends of their individual service lives and have been retired. The company has used the straight-line method of depreciation in its general-purpose financial statements throughout its history.

Some of the components of the Property, Plant, and Equipment account were acquired at the time of the company's formation. Others still on hand represent purchases in most of the years of the company's life. During this time there have been a major depression and many recessions, recoveries, and booms, one world war, and several smaller wars.

a. Comment on the comparability of the Depreciation Expense account of the company from year to year.
b. What are the limitations on the comparability of the assets and equities in its balance sheets among various years?

7-13   The Largo Corporation is preparing financial statements for the year ended December 31, 1973. Without considering the following items, its net income was $50,000.

Required   Describe how the following facts should be disclosed in those statements, and give reasons.

a. The company changed its method of computing the cost of its inventory from one generally accepted method to another generally accepted method, effective December 31, 1973. As a result of the change, Cost of Goods Sold for 1973 was increased from $820,000 to $875,000, and the ending inventory of merchandise was decreased from $180,000 to $125,000. How, if at all, should this change be reported in the company's 1973 financial statements?

b. During 1973 the corporation was required to pay additional federal income tax for 1970 because the Internal Revenue Service disallowed deductions of $20,000 that had been used in computing the income subject to tax. The additional tax paid was $10,400, and interest of $1,800 was charged on the late payment.

c. In January 1974, before the financial statements for 1973 had been issued, the company entered into an agreement to sell for $180,000 a building which had an unexpired cost of $160,000. This building housed about 40 per cent of the company's operations. At the same time, the company signed a ten-year lease for a larger building, agreeing to pay annual rentals of $20,000, plus property taxes and insurance.

7-14   The annual report of J. Ray McDermott & Co., Inc. for the year ended March 31, 1969, contained the following item:

> (15) During the year the Company realized a gain of $1,184,363 on the sale of certain oil and gas properties. In addition the Company realized a gain of $1,146,600 from the sale of stock of the Offshore Company and a gain of $528,305 from insurance proceeds on the destruction of a piece of equipment by fire. After income taxes of $885,521, these nonrecurring items resulted in a credit to income of $1,973,747, which is included in the income statement as extraordinary items.

a. What was the purpose of this note?
b. How would this information affect the income statement for the year? The financial position statement at the end of the year?

7-15   The audit report for American Motors Corporation for the year ended September 30, 1968, contained a standard *scope* paragraph. The *opinion* paragraph was as follows:

> In our opinion, subject to the final determination of the loss on sale of the Appliance Division referred to in Note C, the financial statements referred to above present fairly the consolidated financial position of American Motors Corporation and consolidated subsidiaries at September 30, 1968, and the consolidated results of their operations and the sources and applications of working capital for the year then ended, in conformity with generally accepted accounting principles applied on a basis consistent with that of the preceding year.

The following item was included in *Notes to Financial Statements:*

> *Note C: Sale of Appliance Division.* As of July 3, 1968, the Corporation sold certain assets of its Appliance Division, including investments in appliance subsidiaries, for a price which is subject to independent determination. As of September 30, 1968, the final sales prices had not been determined but an amount has been provided for the resulting loss on sale which, in the opinion of management, is considered adequate.
>
> In order to provide meaningful information with respect to the automotive operations, the consolidated statements of net earnings and sources and applications of working capital are presented so as to exclude detailed transactions of the Appliance Division and to report the net loss of the division and its effect on working capital as separate items.

Required
a. What type of audit opinion is this?
b. What is the purpose of the special wording of the opinion?
c. Where would you expect to find the estimated loss on sale of the Appliance Division assets reported in the financial statements? Why?

7-16 The following footnote appeared in the financial statements of Potter Instrument Company, Inc., for the year ended June 29, 1968:

> The balance of retained earnings as of the beginning of the fiscal year ending in 1967 has been restated to reflect a retroactive charge for $49,513 arising out of the payment during 1968 of assessments for additional federal income taxes for the fiscal years ending in 1961 through 1964, and certain state income taxes from 1961 to 1966.

Required
a. Why was this charge made against beginning retained income rather than against income of the current year?
b. Show the journal entry that the company must have made in 1968.

7-17 In 1973 Consolidated Sales, Inc. changed its method of accounting for inventories, with the result of increasing the ending inventory and decreasing the cost of goods sold by $152,000. After this change the financial statements as of December 31, 1973, showed the following selected balances:

Inventories	$ 78,961,000
Cost of goods sold	219,840,000
Net income	47,520,000

Required
a. How should this change be reported in the financial statements?
b. Is the change significant enough to warrant comment in the auditor's opinion? Explain.

7-18
a. State whether each of the following items should be reflected in net income of the current year or shown as an adjustment to retained income as of the beginning of the year. Give reasons to support your choice. Assume that all amounts are material.
b. For items which should be reflected in net income, indicate whether they should be included in *income before extraordinary items* or in *extraordinary items* and why.

 (1) A correction of accumulated depreciation due to a revision in the estimated useful life of certain assets.
 (2) The settlement of a lawsuit for a negligent act of a company employee three years ago. The suit has been in progress for two years, but the company previously expected it to be dismissed.
 (3) Loss from the seizure of a plant by a hostile foreign government.
 (4) A write-up of the estimated uncollectibles because of the financial difficulty recently experienced by a number of large customers.

7-19 The cashier-bookkeeper of the Waine Company carefully completed accurate financial statements for the company as of the end of its year, December 31, 1973, and left them on the president's desk on January 10. Total assets as shown by the balance sheet were $300,000 and net income was $21,000. The bookkeeper-cashier did not report to work on January 11, and an investigation soon disclosed that he had disappeared with $10,000 of the company's cash. He was not bonded. Efforts to trace him were fruitless.

Required a. What consideration, if any, should be given to this situation in the financial reports of 1973?

b. What journal entries should be made in 1973? In 1974?

c. What would be your answer to part a if the amount involved were $1,000? $10?

7-20   The Jones Construction Company had 50,000 shares of common stock outstanding on January 1, 1973. On October 1, 1973, an additional 20,000 shares were issued. The corporation had a net income before extraordinary items of $1,100,000 for the year, and a gain (after deducting the related income tax) of $165,000 on the sale of a plant which had been closed down.

Required Compute earnings per share and show how the results would be presented in the financial statements.

7-21   York Manufacturing Company reported earnings per share of $12 for 1973. On January 1, 1973, there were 60,000 shares of common stock outstanding. On June 1, 1973, an additional 20,000 shares were issued.

Required Compute the net income which York Manufacturing Company reported for 1973.

7-22   The Quasar Corporation had 10,000 shares of common stock outstanding on January 1, 1973. On December 31, 1973, the company acquired 1,000 shares of its own stock, reducing the number outstanding on December 31 to 9,000 shares. On January 2, 1974, the company resold the stock at the same price for which it was purchased. Reported net income for 1973 was $99,950.

Required a. Compute earnings per share based on the number of shares outstanding at December 31, 1973.

b. Compute earnings per share based on the average number of shares outstanding during the year.

c. Which do you think is the more representative figure for earnings per share? Why?

7-23   The following accounts are from the Trial Balance After Adjustments of the Walters Company for the year ended December 31, 1973, together with supplementary information:

Building rent	$ 5,000	Depreciation—office equipment	$	200
Uncollectible sales revenue	400	Dividends received		400
Interest on notes payable	600	Insurance expense		500
Advertising expense	1,100	Payroll taxes		2,100
Sales	195,000	Revenue from various sources		150
Salesclerks' salaries	22,000	Depreciation—delivery trucks		1,000
Federal income taxes	5,797	Gasoline and other delivery ex-		
Gain on sale of office equipment	1,200	pense		1,400
Sales returns and allowances	800	Miscellaneous office expense		1,250
Office salaries	5,000	Miscellaneous selling expense		4,100
Merchandise inventory	80,000	Manager's salary		8,000
Cost of goods sold	116,950	Dividends paid		2,000

Approximately 60 per cent of the building space is used to display merchandise; 30 per cent, as a stock room; and 10 per cent, as an office for the manager and the bookkeeper.

The dividends were received on an investment in the stock of a manufacturer, held to assure a steady source of supply.

Of the payroll taxes, $210 applies to the manager's salary. The rest represents a 7 per cent combined rate on all other salaries.

Assume that a federal tax rate of 22 per cent applies to all income.

Required   Prepare an income statement in multiple-step form. Classify operating expense according to the functions of Selling, Delivery, and General Administration.

7-24

Required   a. Using the information of Problem 7-23, prepare a single-step income statement.
b. Which form of statement do you think is better for external reporting? Why?
c. Which form do you think is better for reporting to the company's management? Why?

7-25   The December 31, 1973, Trial Balance After Adjustments of the Grange Chemical Company is shown below.

Required   a. Prepare a multiple-step income statement. Assume that an income tax rate of 50 per cent applies to all income. The use of a classification work sheet is optional.
b. Prepare a retained income statement.
c. What kind of expense classification did you use in the income statement? What are its advantages and disadvantages in reports to management and outsiders?

GRANGE CHEMICAL COMPANY
Trial Balance
December 31, 1973

	Debits	Credits
Accounts payable		$ 70,000
Accounts receivable	$ 75,000	
Accrued salaries payable		3,000
Accumulated depreciation		60,000
Additional income tax assessment for 1969........	30,000	
Advertising expense	15,000	
Capital stock		100,000
Cash...	20,000	
Cost of goods sold	462,000	
Depreciation...	26,000	
Dividends...	10,000	
Federal income taxes....................................	55,000	
Federal income taxes payable		18,000
Gain on sale of equipment.............................		8,000
Insurance expense	4,000	
Interest expense	6,000	
Interest revenue...		2,000
Merchandise inventory	92,000	
Notes payable...		100,000
Prepaid expenses...	2,000	
Property, plant, and equipment	331,000	
Rent expense	12,000	
Retained income, Jan. 1, 1973........................		154,000
Salaries and wages.......................................	45,000	
Sales...		670,000
Totals	$1,185,000	$1,185,000

7-26 The accompanying trial balance of the Hatchford Appliance Store at the end of its accounting year, December 31, 1973, reflects all needed adjustments.

Required Prepare properly classified general-purpose financial statements, making such changes in terminology as you think appropriate. The use of a statement classification work sheet is optional. Income tax on the store equipment gain is $375.

HATCHFORD APPLIANCE STORE
Trial Balance
December 31, 1973

Prepaid expenses	$ 1,100	
Sublease revenue		$ 2,500
Capital stock—par		110,000
Wages and salaries	47,000	
Amortization of leasehold improvements	4,000	
Cash	28,200	
Equipment	19,000	
Sales		290,000
Premium on capital stock		3,000
Reserve for depreciation		6,800
Refund of prior years' income tax		3,150
Notes payable		5,000
Gain from donation of land (in 1967)		4,000
Miscellaneous operating expense	2,600	
Gain on sale of store equipment		1,500
Loan to president	1,000	
Sales returns and allowances	1,000	
Federal income tax payable		4,000
Merchandise inventory	77,000	
Advertising expense	2,500	
Depreciation	1,900	
Dividends	4,500	
Cost of goods sold	215,000	
Interest revenue		500
Notes receivable	14,000	
Organization cost	2,500	
Maintenance	3,100	
Accrued expenses payable		500
Uncollectible sales revenue	750	
Employee payroll taxes payable		4,000
Federal income tax expense	4,000	
Temporary investments (market value 12/31/73, $15,300)	15,000	
Accounts receivable	39,000	
Leasehold improvements	16,000	
Accounts payable		36,500
Retained income, Dec. 31, 1972		26,600
Accounts receivable—estimated uncollectibles		1,100
Totals	$499,150	$499,150

Cases 7-1 American Machine & Foundry Company. The scope paragraph of the auditor's report for American Machine & Foundry Company for the year ended December 31, 1968, contained standard language. The opinion paragraph was as follows:

In our opinion, the statements mentioned above present fairly the consolidated financial position of American Machine & Foundry Company and subsidiaries at December 31, 1968, and the consolidated results of their operations and the source and use of their consolidated working capital for the year then ended, in conformity with generally accepted accounting principles applied on a basis consistent with that of the preceding year after a restatement to include overseas subsidiaries explained in Note 1 and except for the changes in methods of accounting explained in Notes 2 and 3. We approve both the restatement and the changes.

The following is an excerpt from Note 2:

Bowling receivables at December 31, 1968 amounted to $99,781,000 against which an allowance for possible losses of $54,458,000 (including the unusual provision described below) was available. At December 31, 1967 bowling receivables and related allowance were $120,714,000 and $15,751,000, respectively.

The Company made provisions for possible losses on its bowling business of $9,022,000 in 1967 and $4,928,000 during the nine months ended September 30, 1968 under a policy of providing for such losses in proportion generally to the revenues received and to be received from machines on long-term lease.

An evaluation of matters affecting the worldwide bowling industry, completed during the third quarter of 1968, indicated a need for additional allowance for possible losses. As a result of this evaluation, the Company adopted the policy of expending all possible losses currently. As of September 30, 1968, an unusual provision of $42,600,000 ($21,500,000 after taxes) was added to the cumulative allowance for possible losses. This provision includes $14,000,000 ($6,600,000 after taxes) which was to be provided in 1968 and future years under the previous accounting policy. During the three months ended December 31, 1968, $437,000 was provided out of income for operations.

Note 3 was as follows:

Note 3: Write-Down of Bowling Equipment—During 1968, in connection with its review of bowling receivables, the Company estimated the impact of future repossessions of leased bowling equipment, taking into consideration the current very limited market for such used equipment and related assets. Based on this, the Company, which previously wrote off losses on such equipment as it was re-acquired, has provided for unusual possible losses on future repossessions in the amount of $13,000,000 ($7,400,000 after taxes).

Required   a. What type of audit opinion is this?
 b. What is the general purpose of the unusual language in the audit opinion?
 c. Explain the purpose of the accounting change described in Note 2. What was its effect on income for the current year? Where was the change reported? What was its effect on cumulative retained income?
 d. Explain the purpose of the accounting change described in Note 3. How did it affect current income and cumulative retained income? Where would the unusual possible losses on future repossessions be reported in the financial statements?

7-2   William Schwartz. William Schwartz had been manager of the used car department of a large automobile dealer for several years, and his income from salary and commissions had reached the level of approximately $10,000 a year. Early in 1972 he decided that he could gain greater personal satisfaction and monetary reward by going into business for himself. Disposing of corporate stocks which he had accumulated, partly by savings and mostly by inheritance, he acquired for $57,000 the capital stock of a used car lot, service station, and repair garage on July 1, 1972. In recent years he had been earning about 5 per cent a year on the average market value of his stocks.

The bookkeeper prepared the accompanying financial statements at the end of Schwartz's first year of ownership of the business.

SCHWARTZ AUTO CENTER
Income Statement
For the Year Ended June 30, 1973

Sales revenue		$420,000
Deduct expenses:		
Advertising	$ 1,800	
Bad debts	1,000	
Cost of goods sold	340,000	
Depreciation...................................	3,500	
Insurance	1,500	
Property and payroll taxes.................	6,200	
Salaries	52,000	
Supplies	5,800	
Utilities..	2,200	
Total expenses		414,000
Net income		$ 6,000

SCHWARTZ AUTO CENTER
Financial Position Statement
June 30, 1973

ASSETS

Accounts receivable.............................	$ 18,000	
Buildings	40,000	
Cash..	2,000	
Equipment.......................................	15,000	
Inventories.......................................	52,000	
Land	12,000	
Unexpired insurance............................	1,000	
Total assets		$140,000

LIABILITIES

Accounts payable.................................	$ 12,000	
Accumulated depreciation on buildings	2,000	
Accumulated depreciation on equipment...	1,500	
Bank notes payable	20,000	
Estimated uncollectible accounts	1,000	
Mortgage note payable	40,000	
Payroll taxes payable	500	
Total liabilities.................................		$ 77,000
Capital stock and income		63,000
Total...		$140,000

Schwartz's office and the office of the secretary-bookkeeper were located in a partitioned area off the front of the repair garage.

A major part of the advertising consisted of newspaper advertising and radio announcements, chiefly devoted to the used cars.

The service station, staffed by a manager and three other employees, sold gasoline, oil, tires, and accessories, as well as providing a car wash and tire repair service.

Used car sales were under an assistant manager and two full-time salesmen. Schwartz spent a large part of his time appraising cars for purchase and arranging for the financing of cars sold.

The repair garage had a service manager and three additional employees, one of whom was responsible for issuing repair parts and completing invoices for work done. About one-third of the work consisted of reconditioning used cars bought for resale. The remainder was general repair work for customers.

The original face amount of the mortgage note payable, secured by the land and buildings, was $44,000. On June 30, 1973, Schwartz had paid the annual installment of $4,000 on principal and an additional $3,080, the interest for one year at 7 per cent. The interest had been added to the cost of the building.

The bank notes payable were six-month, 8 per cent notes signed on March 31, 1973, to finance an increase in inventory. No interest had yet been paid or recorded.

The buildings are expected to have a total useful life of 20 years and the equipment, 10 years.

The accounts receivable were for gas, oil, and repair service.

A major part of the land was used for displaying used cars for sale. Most of the building area was devoted to the repair shop. Significant amounts of equipment were used in both the service station and the repair garage.

The inventories consisted of gas, oil, accessories, tires, a large quantity of repair parts, and used cars for resale.

Schwartz had limited his salary to $3,000 for the year.

Corporate federal income tax rates were 22 per cent of the first $25,000 of taxable income and 48 per cent of all income over $25,000.

Required
a. Prepare corrected financial statements. The use of an Adjustment and Classification Work Sheet is recommended.
b. Under previous ownership, operated as an unincorporated business, the firm had earned an annual net income ranging from $15,000 to $20,000 in recent years, excluding the owners' drawings. Evaluate the results under Schwartz's ownership.
c. Schwartz seeks your professional advice as to how to improve the profit picture. Applying the classification principles outlined in Chapter 7, propose a detailed classification of operating accounts for his use.
d. Comment on the major measurement problems the bookkeeper would encounter in applying your account classification, and suggest how she should solve them.

7-3   Paramount Pictures Corporation. The management and the accounting staff of Paramount Pictures Corporation—and those of the entire motion picture industry—have been faced with a number of difficult business and accounting decisions in recent years. Major factors have been the revival of feature films through the sale of rights to the television industry, rapid technological developments in the motion picture industry and closely allied fields, and protracted antitrust and other suits against motion picture companies.

The following discussion is based on excerpts from the annual reports of the Paramount Pictures Corporation, selected because of the interesting application of accounting principles which is required. These situations do not reflect the full range of normal operating activities of the company.

The following excerpts were taken from Paramount's Annual Report for 1959.

CONSOLIDATED BALANCE SHEET[11]

	January 2, 1960	January 3, 1959
	($000 omitted)	
....		
Development costs and other deferred charges, less amortization (see Note D)............	9,966	9,746
....		
(Total assets)	$171,776	$166,671

STATEMENT OF CONSOLIDATED EARNINGS

	Fiscal Year Ended	
	January 2, 1960 (52 Weeks)	January 3, 1959 (53 Weeks)
....		
Amortization of development costs (see Note D)......	1,510	1,917
....		
Earnings for year	$ 7,519	$12,554

Note D—Development Costs:

To the extent that development costs have been claimed for income tax purposes, amounts thereof equivalent to the reduction in Federal income taxes have been amortized by the company. The balance includes $3,991,000 of costs incurred in the development of a color television tube and $4,190,000 of costs incurred in developing television and electronic facilities and equipment. Such costs are being deferred until commercial production becomes significant.

FROM THE PRESIDENT'S LETTER TO STOCKHOLDERS

Chromatic Division

Work is proceeding toward Chromatic's goal of the development of color television tubes and sets of the various sizes now having general public acceptance in black-and-white sets. It is expected that these sets will be useful under the same conditions of surrounding illumination, and within the same space and with the same reliability and ease of operation as present black-and-white sets.

The auditor rendered an unqualified opinion on the 1959 Annual Report.
The following excerpts are from Paramount's Annual Report for 1960:

---

[11] Source: 1959, 1960, 1962, and 1963 Annual Reports of Paramount Pictures Corporation.

CONSOLIDATED BALANCE SHEET

	December 31, 1960	January 2, 1960
	($000 omitted)	
....		
Development costs and other deferred charges, less amortization (see Note D)	10,341	9,966
....		
(Total Assets)	$174,035	$171,776

CONSOLIDATED STATEMENT OF INCOME AND RETAINED EARNINGS

	Fiscal year ended	
	December 31, 1960	January 2, 1960
	($000 omitted)	
....		
Costs and expenses:		
....		
Amortization of development costs (see Note D)......	944	1,510
....		
	124,299	110,806
Income before items below	7,026	4,410
....		

Note B—Inventory:

The company revised its amortization table during the year to reflect current revenue experience and applied the new table to production and domestic print costs of all pictures released in 1960, including those produced by outside producers. The new table amortizes approximately 46 per cent of the costs within 13 weeks after domestic release, 82 per cent within 52 weeks, and all but a small residual value within 104 weeks. Such residual values have been established for all pictures released since January 1, 1953 in partial recognition of the possible future income from television and to bring the accounts into agreement with the position to be taken by the company for income tax purposes. Advertising, foreign prints and other costs relative to distribution of all pictures are charged to expense as incurred. These changes had no material net effect on income for the year.

Note D—Development Costs:

To the extent that development costs have been claimed for income tax purposes, amounts thereof equivalent to the reduction in federal income taxes have been amortized by the company. The balance includes $4,471,000 of costs incurred in the development of a color television tube and $4,423,000 of costs incurred in developing television and electronic facilities and equipment. Such costs are being deferred until production becomes significant.

FROM THE PRESIDENT'S LETTER

International Telemeter Company

This wholly owned Division of our company is engaged in the development and promotion of "Theatre-in-the-Home" or pay television. Apart from its intriguing possibilities for expanding the motion picture market, there is reason to believe that the Telemeter systems, both on cable and over the air, are in the forefront of developments in this field. There is, therefore, a twofold basis for our interest and investment in this new medium. It must be borne in mind, however, that this is a new and unprecedented venture.

FROM THE AUDITORS' OPINION

In our opinion, the accompanying statements present fairly the consolidated financial position of Paramount Pictures Corporation and affiliated companies at December 31, 1960 and the results of their operations for the year, in conformity with generally accepted accounting principles. These principles have been applied on a basis consistent with that of the preceding year, except for the change, which we approve, in the method of amortizing film costs as described in Note B to the financial statements. . . .

The following note appeared in the Annual Report for 1962.

Note E—Research and Development Costs:

Deferred research and development at December 29, 1962 comprises $4,379,000 for a color television tube and $3,728,000 applicable to pay television facilities. Current research and development is charged to expense as incurred and previously deferred balances are being amortized over ten years. The amortization started in 1961 for pay television costs and in 1962 for color tube costs. If the previous policy of deferring color tube expenditures (net of the reduction in taxes resulting from current deduction) had been followed in 1962, the net loss would have been $858,000 less than the reported amount.

Both projects are discussed in the letter to stockholders elsewhere in this report.

FROM THE AUDITORS' OPINION

The company has invested substantial sums in the development of a color television tube and pay-television facilities. Recovery of the unamortized costs is dependent upon successful commercial applications of the two projects.

In our opinion, subject to the ultimate realization of the unamortized costs referred to above, the accompanying statements present fairly the consolidated financial position of Paramount Pictures Corporation and its subsidiary companies at December 29, 1962 and the results of their operations for the year, in conformity with generally accepted accounting principles. These principles have been applied on a basis consistent with that of the preceding year except for the change, which we approve, in the amortization of research and development costs as explained in Note E to the financial statements.

The following information is from the Annual Report for 1963.

Note E—Research and Development Costs:

Events during 1963 and early 1964 have made it apparent that the realization of material revenues from the color television tube and pay-television system is farther in the future than previously contemplated. Because of this fact, the deferred research and development costs of $8,107,000 at December 29, 1962 have been charged to retained earnings. Research and development costs in the 1962 statement of income included $970,000 of amortization of previously deferred amounts.

Both projects are discussed in the letter to stockholders elsewhere in this report.

The auditors' opinion took no exception to the 1963 financial statements as prepared by the corporation.

Required
a. What was the reason for the change in the company's method of amortizing the costs of released productions? In what way did this change affect income of the year of the change? In what way did it affect the financial position statement at the end of the year of the change?

b. Comment on the company's first accounting method with respect to development costs, its effect upon the auditor's opinion, the effect of the change in policy on income in the year of change, and the apparent justification for the change in policy. What will be the effect on matching of revenue and related expired costs if the projects under development prove highly profitable in the future? What was the the effect of the change in policy on assets?

c. To what extent would you say that the financial statements of a company are tentative? Give examples from the current case to illustrate your points.

chapter 8

Financial Statement Analysis

Purpose of Chapter

No matter how adequately the accounting statements summarize the financial affairs of a business, accounting fails to accomplish its purpose unless its information is put to *use*. The use may be in helping management decide on and carry out actions needed to operate the business, or in guiding investors and creditors in deciding whether to invest in, or lend to, the business.

Regardless of how thoroughly the accountant has reported and analyzed the financial information of the business, the statement user must make his own interpretations of the data and form his own conclusions. Interpretations are aided by *comparisons*: comparisons of one financial statement item with another for the same period, comparisons of statement items with the corresponding items of the same firm at earlier periods, and comparisons with the financial results of other firms in the same industry.

This chapter explains some of the more significant types of comparisons which assist the statement user in interpreting the financial results of the firm. The uses and limitations of ratios, averages, and graphic comparisons are discussed. Particular attention is given to several measures which are widely useful in appraising the results of the operations of a business and in evaluating its liquidity and solvency.

Need for Appraising Financial Results—An
Illustrative Case

Sound Center, Inc., retails high-fidelity sets. The capital stock of the company, which has been in operation for a number of years, is owned by the Winkle family, heirs of the deceased former owner-manager. Mr. Farley, who has been the manager of the company for the past two years, does not own any of the company's stock. His compensation consists of an annual salary of $15,000 and a commission of 1 per cent of the sales of the business. The sales-clerks receive a base salary plus a commision of 3 per cent of sales.

The Winkles have become increasingly dissatisfied with the amount of their annual dividends from the company, and have privately discussed the possibility of hiring a new manager to replace Mr. Farley. They are particularly upset because a competitor in the community has been prospering, while the results of Sound Center, Inc., have been poor. As a majority of the board of directors, they have asked Mr. Farley to prepare a thorough analysis of the company's operating results and financial status for discussion at the meeting of the board on January 10, 1974. Mr. Farley requested the company's accountant to prepare statements comparing the financial results of the business for the past two years to aid in this discussion.

The accountant has prepared the accompanying financial statements, which are as follows:

A comparative income statement for the years ended December 31, 1972 and December 31, 1973;

A comparative retained income statement for the two years; and

A comparative financial position statement as of December 31, 1972 and December 31, 1973.

These comparative financial statements will be used in a number of examples in the remainder of this chapter in order to illustrate some commonly used methods of analyzing financial statements.

SOUND CENTER, INC.

Income Statement

	For the Years Ended	
	Dec. 31, 1973	Dec. 31, 1972
Net sales revenue	$300,000	$250,000
Deduct cost of goods sold expense	210,000	170,000
Gross margin on sales	90,000	80,000
Deduct operating expense:		
Advertising	6,000	3,500
Commissions on sales	12,000	10,000
Depreciation	2,500	2,100
Insurance	4,500	4,900
Rent	10,000	10,000
Salary, manager	15,000	15,000
Salaries, other	22,000	20,000
Supplies and miscellaneous	6,800	6,200
Taxes (other than income tax)	3,700	3,300
Total operating expense	82,500	75,000
Income before federal income tax	7,500	5,000
Corporate federal income tax expense	1,650	1,100
Net income (to Retained Income Statement)	5,850	3,900

SOUND CENTER, INC.
Retained Income Statement

	For the Years Ended	
	Dec. 31, 1973	*Dec. 31, 1972*
Retained income at beginning of year	$ 43,700	$ 41,300
Add net income (from Income Statement)	5,850	3,900
	49,550	45,200
Deduct dividends......................................	2,000	1,500
Retained income, end of year (to Financial Position Statement)	47,550	43,700

SOUND CENTER, INC.
Financial Position Statement

	December 31	
ASSETS	*1973*	*1972*
Current assets:		
Cash...	$ 7,000	$ 11,000
Accounts receivable	73,000	70,000
Deduct estimated uncollectibles	(4,000)	(3,000)
Merchandise inventory	92,000	64,400
Prepaid expenses...................................	7,000	5,600
Total current assets	175,000	148,000
Property, plant, and equipment:		
Equipment (cost)	47,500	21,000
Deduct accumulated depreciation	(9,500)	(7,000)
Total property, plant, and equipment......	38,000	14,000
Total assets	213,000	162,000
LIABILITIES		
Current liabilities:		
Notes payable to banks..........................	28,000	18,000
Accounts payable.................................	55,550	41,700
Corporate federal income tax payable	450	300
Total current liabilities.......................	84,000	60,000
Long-term liabilities:		
Long-term notes payable	31,450	8,300
Total liabilities	115,450	68,300
STOCKHOLDERS' EQUITY		
Capital stock, $50 par, 1,000 shares.............	50,000	50,000
Retained income (from Retained Income Statement)	47,550	43,700
Total stockholders' equity......................	97,550	93,700
Total equities	213,000	162,000

Mr. Farley has sensed the growing impatience of the board of directors, but he feels that he has done as well as could be expected in managing the business, considering its neglected state at the time of Mr. George Winkle's death. He hopes to convince the board that his policies are just beginning to bear fruit in increased revenues and profits, and that even better results can be expected in the future. Mr. Farely knows that the two questions uppermost in the minds of the directors on January 10 will be

(1) How well has the business done in comparison with what could be expected of it?
(2) What can be done to improve future performance?

In the days remaining until the board meeting, Mr. Farley busily prepares analyses that will help him answer these questions.

BASES AND METHODS OF COMPARISON

The Need for Comparisons

Account titles and balances alone are usually not sufficient to give a clear understanding of the operating results and financial status of a business. An amount has significance only if it is compared with some other related amount. The statement reader must have some frame of reference, some *standard of comparison*, by which to measure both the overall results and the individual financial elements of the enterprise.

The following types of comparison are often useful in analyzing financial information:

(1) Comparison with another balance of the same company for the same accounting period.
   Example: Comparing net income with sales revenue.
(2) Comparison with the corresponding balance or relationship of the same company for an earlier accounting period.
   Example: Comparing net income for 1973 with net income for 1972.
(3) Comparison of the actual amount of a given financial category with the planned amount.
   Example: Comparing actual sales with budgeted sales for 1973.
(4) Comparison of the actual results with some standard which represents a norm or desirable level of achievement.
   Example: Comparing the actual labor cost of a manufacturing operation with an engineering estimate of what labor costs ought to be.
(5) Comparison with the corresponding balance or relationship of another company for the same accounting period.
   Example: Comparing the sales revenue for Company A with that Company B.

Comparisons of the financial data of a business may be in the form of individual relationships, tables of figures and relationships, or charts and graphs.

Computing Individual Relationships

The relationship between two amounts, such as a and b, which are being compared may be expressed as a *ratio* or as a *percentage*. The ratio of a to b

expresses how many units of *a* there are for each *one* unit of *b*. The percentage of *a* to *b* (%) shows how many units of *a* there are for each *one hundred* units of *b*. The formulas for these computations are

$$\text{Ratio of } a \text{ to } b = \frac{a}{b}$$

$$\text{Percentage of } a \text{ to } b = 100\left(\frac{a}{b}\right).$$

Any ratio may be converted to a percentage by multiplying it by 100; any percentage may be converted to a ratio by dividing it by 100.

Example 1   Cost of goods sold expense of Sound Center, Inc., for 1973 amounted to $210,000 and sales were $300,000. What was the ratio of cost of goods sold to sales? The percentage?

Solution $$\text{Ratio} = \frac{\text{Cost of goods sold}}{\text{Sales}} = \frac{\$210,000}{\$300,000} - 0.70 \quad \text{or} \quad 0.70 \text{ to } 1$$

$$\text{Percentage} = 100(0.70) = 70\%.$$

Cost of goods sold for the year was $0.70 for each dollar of sales, or $70 for each $100 of sales.

The Use of Averages

In comparing the amount of one item with other items of the same class, it is often desirable to select a typical, or *average*, item which is representative of the items in the group. Three common methods of measuring the average item which is to be used as a standard of comparison are the *arithmetic mean*, the *median*, and the *mode*.

The *arithmetic mean* of a group of measurements may be computed by dividing the sum of the measurements by the number of items.

The *median* is the middle value of a series of numbers which have been arrayed in the order of their size.

The *mode* is the value which appears most frequently in a series of numbers.

Example 2   The owner of a restaurant wished to determine the amount of its typical lunch check. He arranged the checks for one day in the order of their size, from smallest to largest, and listed the amounts as follows:

$0.80	$1.30	$1.50
1.00	1.40	1.60
1.00	1.40	1.60
1.10	1.40	1.70
1.20	1.50	1.80
1.50	1.50	2.00
1.30	1.50	2.20

What was the average amount of a lunch check?

Solution   (1) The *arithmetic mean* would be computed by dividing the sum of the amounts, $30.00, by the number of items, 21. The result is approximately $1.4286, or $1.43 if rounded to the nearest cent.

(2) The *median* is the eleventh item in the series, $1.40.

(3) The *mode* is $1.50, which occurs four times.

Choosing the appropriate method for measuring the average number of a particular group depends on the *use* to be made of the results and the *qualities* of the measurements which comprise the class. In drawing conclusions about a class of information on the basis of an average, the analyst must be certain that the average is actually *representative* of that class. For example, the day selected in the preceding example may not be a typical day for the restaurant. Each type of average has some disadvantages.

Averages based on accounting information usually have to be computed in special analysis. Debits and credits in journal entries and ledger accounts are often totals of classes of information. The sales of the restaurant in Example 2 would probably be recorded in the journal in one item which represented the total sales for the day, not the price of each meal sold.

Graphic Comparisons

Often it is desirable to present financial information in a summary form which is easy to interpret and which emphasizes changes over time. Visual aids, such as the *line graph* (Illustration 8-1), the *bar chart* (Illustration 8-2), and the *pictogram* (Illustration 8-3), convey quickly information about business relationships which would require the use of long and complex tables or descriptions.

Illustration 8-1 Line graph

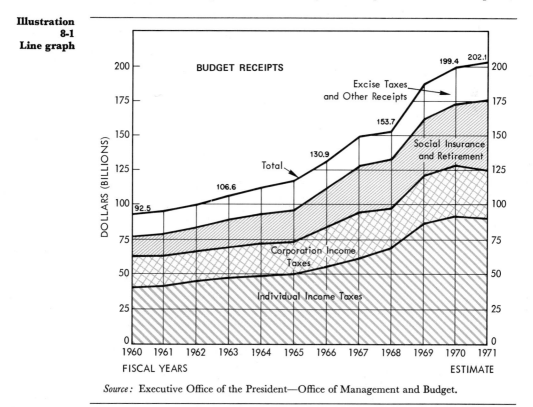

Source: Executive Office of the President—Office of Management and Budget.

**Illustration
8-2
Bar Chart**

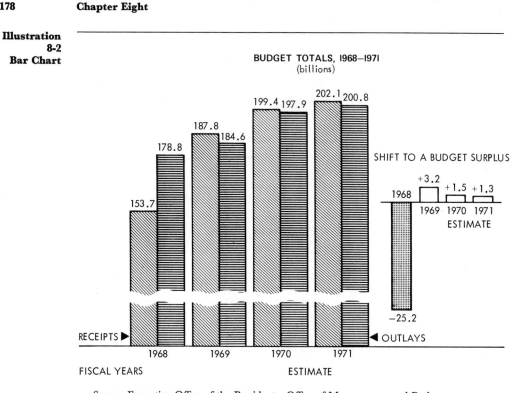

BUDGET TOTALS, 1968–1971
(billions)

SHIFT TO A BUDGET SURPLUS

Source: Executive Office of the President—Office of Management and Budget.

Analysis of Composition

Ratios and percentages may be used to compare the size of the *components* of an accounting category with the *total* of that category. One common comparison of this type is to determine the percentage of each principal expense and of net income to *net sales.* The same procedure would be used as in Example 1, which showed the calculation of the percentage of cost of goods sold to net sales. The total percentages of each of the components of the net sales dollar would add up to 100 per cent. The individual percentages are often shown in a separate column beside the corresponding amounts in the financial statements to aid the reader's interpretation. The pictogram in Illustration 8-3 is another way of showing the analysis of composition.

Composition percentages help the statement analyst judge the size of each of the components relative to their total and to each other. A comparison with the percentages for similar items for the preceding year shows changes in the composition of the total from one year to the next.

When there is a cause-and-effect relationship between the individual components and their total, analysis of composition is often meaningful and useful. An outstanding example of such an analysis is computing the relationship of *variable expenses to sales,* which will be discussed in detail in a later chapter. However, percentages of composition are quite often misinterpreted, and for that reason they should be used with caution. The following example shows how percentages of composition might lead to an incorrect interpretation.

**Illustration
8-3
Pictogram**

THE BUDGET DOLLAR

FISCAL YEAR 1971 ESTIMATE

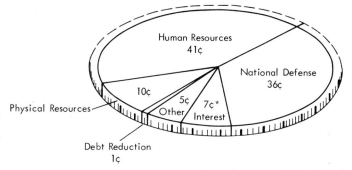

Where it comes from. . .

Other

5¢

Corporation Income Taxes 17¢

Individual Income Taxes 45¢

9¢ Excise Taxes

24¢

Social Insurance Taxes and Contributions

Where it goes. . .

Human Resources 41¢

National Defense 36¢

Physical Resources

10¢

5¢ Other

7¢* Interest

Debt Reduction 1¢

*Excludes Interest Paid to Trust Funds

Source: Executive Office of the President—Office of Management and Budget.

Example 3

	1973		1972	
	Amount	Per Cent of Net Sales	Amount	Per Cent of Net Sales
Net sales for the year.........	$100,000	100%	$ 50,000	100%
Advertising expense	$ 5,000	5	$ 5,000	10
All other expenses	80,000	80	44,000	88
Total expenses	$ 85,000	85	$ 49,000	98
Net income.....................	$ 15,000	15%	$ 1,000	2%

Noting that advertising expense was 5 per cent of sales in 1973 compared with 10 per cent in 1972, the reader might think that there has been a change in the *amount* of advertising expense. Actually, the percentage is smaller only because the amount of sales, on which the percentage of advertising expense is based, has doubled. The amount of advertising expense has not changed at all.

Analysis of Change

Comparisons of the financial results of one period with those of the same company for an *earlier* period are often made by computing the amounts of change and entering them in a column of the financial statements beside the amounts which are being compared.

Example 4   Sales of Sound Center, Inc., as shown by its comparative Income Statement, were $250,000 in 1972 and $300,000 in 1973, an increase of $50,000.

Such comparisons are often of limited value, because they do not show how large the change is *relative* to the amounts being compared. A more meaningful comparison is a *percentage of change* or a *ratio* of one amount to the other. The proper *base year* to use in making such comparisons is the *earlier year* in both cases. The appropriate formulas are

$$\text{Percentage of change} = 100\left(\frac{\text{Amount of change}}{\text{Base-year amount}}\right)$$

$$\text{Ratio of later year to earlier} = \left(\frac{\text{Amount for later year}}{\text{Base-year amount}}\right).$$

Example 5   The *percentage* of increase in sales of Sound Center, Inc., from 1972 to 1973 is computed as follows:

$$100\left(\frac{\text{Amount of change}}{\text{Base-year amount}}\right) = 100\left(\frac{+\$50,000}{\$250,000}\right) = 100(+0.20) = +20\%.$$

The *ratio* of Sound Center's 1973 sales to those of 1972 is computed as follows:

$$\frac{\text{Amount for later year}}{\text{Base-year amount}} = \frac{\$300,000}{\$250,000} = 1.20$$

Sometimes percentages of change cannot be computed, as when the item amounted to zero in the base year. In other cases percentages are difficult to interpret because they are so large.

Example 6   The net income of Company *C* increased from $10 in 1973 to $4,000 in 1974. The percentage of increase is 39,900 per cent. In such a case it would be easier to interpret a ratio showing that the *increase* was 399 times as much as the income of the base year, or that the *amount* of the income for the second year was 400 times as great as that of the first year.

Percentages of change and ratios for a series of successive years are much more useful than for a single year in making comparisons over time. These methods of comparison are intended to give the reader an idea of the *direction* in which the company's financial results are changing and the *rate of change*. Estimates of future results on the basis of such past comparisons must be made very cautiously, however, because the factors which have resulted in the past relationships may not continue to operate in the same way. To interpret the figures about a business meaningfully, the individual must be familiar with the operating conditions which lie behind them, and with the plans of management and the changed conditions which are likely to exist in the future.

It is often just as difficult to interpret percentages, without absolute amounts, as it is to understand the significance of amounts without relating them to a standard of comparison. It means little to determine that net income in 1973 is 10 per cent larger than in 1972 if the net income is totally inadequate in both years in comparison with the total assets invested in the business. As someone has aptly remarked, "It is *money*, not percentages, that you deposit in the bank."

When an analyst compares the operating results or financial position of a business with its own financial data for an *earlier period*, he assumes that the data have been compiled in a comparable manner by means of accounting, and that the economic influences at work on the two dates are reasonably similar. In interpreting the meaning of changes, the analyst must make proper allowances for factors which have actually changed.

Example 7   Gross margin on sales of $90,000 of Sound Center, Inc., for 1973 might not be better than the 1972 gross margin of $80,000 if the firm's accounting methods changed, or if external economic factors which affect the firm changed materially during the year. A major increase in the general price level, or a change in the firm's method of accounting for cost of goods sold, might mean that the gross margin increase was not as favorable as it would seem at first glance.

Comparisons with Predetermined Goals and with Ideals

One basis of comparison that is very useful to management in appraising actual financial results is the *goal*, or *planned achievement* of the business for the period. Later chapters explain how information on departures of actual results from the plan can be used by management in deciding on future action.

The often limited validity of comparisons of current financial results with those of the same company at other times, with those of other companies at the same time, and with planned results has led management and other interested groups to try to develop standards of comparison which express *what the company should have done under the circumstances*. Such standards are usually based on the *normal* conditions which the company faces. Standards of this type are highly developed in many manufacturing companies. They receive detailed attention in Chapter 24, "Standard Costing for Production Control."

Comparisons with Other Businesses

People who analyze the results or prospects of a business often compare selected items from its financial statements with those of similar companies. They make an effort to select for comparison a *typical*, or average, *business* whose results are representative of the firms in the industry.

Industry averages are often very useful in evaluating the financial status or operating performance of a given company, but the user must be fully aware of their limitations. The company being analyzed may not be similar to the group in size, geographical location, nature of products or services, or other important characteristics. A further limitation of comparability results from differences in accounting methods between companies.

Limitations of Comparisons

The variety of comparisons which could be made for any company is almost endless, but there are practical limitations on the number which *should be* made in any given case. The following are some of the main requirements and limitations of comparisons.

(1) Each comparison should be *meaningful*. The amounts compared should represent events, economic factors, or conditions which are *related to each other*. The figures alone do not tell the whole story, and the person who analyzes and interprets them must be familiar with the actual physical operating conditions of the company if his interpretations are to be valid.

(2) Each comparison should be *useful* and its proper use should be understood by the user. The time spent in making comparisons is wasted unless these are actually employed in interpreting the affairs of the business. If they are potentially useful but are not being used, management and others should be educated to their value.

(3) The data being compared should be *comparable*, both as to method of collection and as to the conditions in effect.

(4) The figures selected for comparison should be *representative*.

(5) The *cost* of making the analyses *should not exceed the benefit* to be gained from them. If they are of little significance, they might well be omitted. The number of comparisons is not the important thing; a few comparisons analyzed thoroughly are of much greater value than a large number merely glanced at superficially.

(6) The comparisons should be used as a *basis for decisions and actions*. Mathematical analysis of financial data does not solve business problems. The analysis may indicate that some trouble exists or even help to pinpoint its cause, but the remedy can come only through appropriate management action.

MEASURES FOR APPRAISING OPERATING RESULTS

Rate of Income on Stockholders' Equity

Because of the dominance of the income objective in business, a widely used measure of business operating performance is the *rate* (or percentage) *of income as compared with stockholders' equity*. This is one of a number of useful comparisons which compute a *rate of change*. The general formula is

$$\text{Rate of change} = \frac{\text{Amount of change during period}}{\text{Weighted-average balance during period}}.^{1}$$

The specific formula for the present comparison is

$$\frac{\text{Rate of income on}}{\text{stockholders' equity}} = \frac{\text{Net income for the period}}{\text{Weighted-average balance of stockholders' equity}}.$$

Example 8 What was the rate of income on stockholders' equity of Sound Center, Inc., for 1973?

Solution
$$\frac{\text{Net income}}{\text{Average stockholders' equity}} = \frac{\$\ 5,850}{\$95,625} = 0.61 \qquad \text{or} \qquad 6.1\%.$$

The average used was the simple average of the beginning and ending totals of stockholders' equity: $\frac{1}{2}(\$93,700 + \$97,550)$. The dates when the change in balance took place are unknown in this illustration; therefore a simple average of the beginning and ending balances is used.

The *rate of return*, or *income*, on stockholders' equity measures the profitability with which management has used the capital invested by stockholders and retained income. It may be compared with the rate of return of the same company for earlier periods, with that of similar companies, and with the planned rate. Due attention should be given to the limitations on comparability. The rate of return is computed from the point of view of the *corporation* as a business organization, not from the point of view of the stockholders as individuals. Rarely, and only by coincidence, does the total sum which stockholders have paid for their shares equal the total stockholders' equity on the books of the corporation.

Extraordinary gains and losses cannot be expected to recur with the same degree of certainty as operating revenues and expenses. The statement user should therefore give them a different weight in making his evaluations. This is made easier by computing a *rate of income before extraordinary items* on stockholders' equity, in addition to computing the rate of *net income* on stockholders' equity.

Chapter 7 dealt with the approved method for reporting *earnings per share* of common stock.

Effect of Income Taxes on Return on Stockholders' Equity

Corporate income tax reduces income and the rate of return on stockholders' equity. Often, because of the different objectives and concepts of income as

---

[1] The weighted-average balance is found by multiplying the individual balances in the account during the period by the length of time the amounts remained unchanged, then dividing the total of the resulting products by the total length of time. For example, if stockholders' equity were $20,000 for the first three months of the year and $60,000 for the remaining nine months, the weighted-average equity would be $50,000, computed as follows: [3($20,000) + 9($60,000)]/2 = [$60,000 + $540,000]/12 = $50,000. When the balance of an account does not change significantly during the period, a simple average of beginning and ending balances is sufficiently accurate for computational purposes.

shown on the income statement and of taxable income as shown on the income tax return, the amount of income tax to be paid does not seem to be consistent with the income before tax which is shown on the financial statements. This occurs because the amounts of revenues and expenses reported in the income statement differ from those shown in the tax return. Moreover, different tax rates may apply to some of the components of taxable income.

For these reasons, comparisons of the rate of *net income after tax* for a company from period to period are sometimes of limited value. The same problems may exist when comparing one company with another at the same time. When there are significant differences between the income before tax shown on the income statement and taxable income, it is useful to compute the rate of income by using *income before income taxes are deducted*.

Example 9   The income statements for two similar companies, A and B, appeared as follows:

	Company A	Company B
Sales	$100,000	$ 80,000
Cost of goods sold.................	70,000	40,000
Gross margin........................	$ 30,000	$ 40,000
Operating expenses...............	20,000	20,000
Income before income tax	$ 10,000	$ 20,000
Income tax paid for year	6,000	4,000
Net income	$ 4,000	$ 16,000

Problem   Is income before or after income tax a more useful figure for comparison purposes? How can you account for the fact that the rate of income taxes paid was 60 per cent of business income before tax for Company A and only 20 per cent for Company B?

Solution   In this case income before tax is probably the more useful comparison. Many different items could account for the differences in the tax rate of the two companies. One would be the use of different methods of computing depreciation on fixed assets for tax purposes by the two companies. Another might be the use of different methods of reporting revenues for tax purposes.

A logical extension of accrual accounting requires that the tax effect be matched with *business income before tax* in the period in which the business income accrues. This matter is discussed in Chapter 13.

Rate of Income on Total Assets

Comparisons of various measures of the income of a business with its stockholders' equity have one important weakness in common: they do not show the efficiency with which management has employed the *assets* of the business, without regard to their source. A measure designed to give this information is the *percentage of income before deducting interest and income tax to total assets* (or, what amounts to the same thing, the percentage as compared to total equities). The formula is

Percentage of income before interest and tax to total assets

$$= \frac{\text{Income before interest and tax}}{\text{Weighted-average total assets}} = \frac{I}{A}.$$

Interest is added back to income so that businesses which borrow extensively can be compared in operating efficiency with businesses which do not borrow as much.

Example 10   The computation for Sound Center, Inc., for 1973 is made as follows:

$$\frac{I}{A} = \frac{\$7,500}{\$187,500} = 4\%.$$

The asset figure used here is the simple average of the beginning asset total of $162,000 and the ending total of $213,000. No interest expense has been added back to net income because none is shown in the income statement.

This percentage alone does not show fully the performance of the firm's management. It should be supplemented by the *percentage of net income to stockholders' equity*, to show how effectively the business has been financed and has managed its income tax matters.

There are many possible combinations of changes in amounts which would increase the rate of return of a business.

Example 11   Some of the possible combinations of changes in amounts which would double the rate of return (before interest and taxes) of Sound Center, Inc. from 4 per cent to 8 per cent are

(a) Increase the *amount* of income while using the same average total assets:

$$\frac{I}{A} = \frac{\$15,000}{\$187,500} = 8\% \text{ return.}$$

Changes in the amount of income may, of course, require changes in total assets.

(b) *Reduce* total assets employed while continuing to earn the same dollar income:

$$\frac{I}{A} = \frac{\$7,500}{\$93,750} = 8\% \text{ return.}$$

There would be an additional problem of finding a profitable investment for the assets released from the business.

(c) Increase the amount of income in relation to the amount of assets used, while both are changing:

$$\frac{I}{A} = \frac{\$20,000}{\$250,000} = 8\% \text{ return.}$$

Components of Rate of Income as a Basis for Action

The rate of return on assets helps to show whether the performance of the business as a whole is up to expectations, but it does not pinpoint the trouble spots or indicate what type of corrective managerial action is needed. Further investigation is required to determine which specific revenues, expenses, assets, and equities need attention.

Top management can evaluate the performance of its individual department or division managers by using the rate of return on assets of each such internal unit. This is done by dividing the income of each unit by the assets which it used in earning the income.

In planning specific management action to increase the rate of return it is useful, as a starting point, to break the rate-of-return formula into its two principal components:

(1) Percentage of income before interest and income tax to revenue.

(2) The number of times the assets are turned over.

The *percentage of income before interest and income tax to revenue* shows how well the managers of each department have performed in earning revenues greater than the expenses incurred in generating the revenues.

The *asset turnover* shows how hard the assets, on the average, have been worked. Generally, the *higher* the percentage of income before interest and income tax to revenue and the *larger* the turnover, the *more profitable* the business is. Asset turnover can be computed for the total assets of the firm, for the assets of any department, or for specific assets, such as inventory and accounts receivable.

The formula for computing *percentage of income before interest and income tax to revenue* is

$$\frac{\text{Income before interest and income tax}}{\text{Net revenue}} = \frac{I}{R}.$$

The formula for computing the *asset turnover* is

$$\frac{\text{Net revenue}}{\text{Weighted-average total assets}} = \frac{R}{A}.$$

Example 12   (a) The income before interest and income tax as a percentage of revenue of Sound Center, Inc., for 1973 was

$$\frac{I}{R} = \frac{\$7,500}{\$300,000} = 2.5\%.$$

(b) The number of asset turnovers was

$$\frac{R}{A} = \frac{\$300,000}{\$187,500} = 1.6 \text{ asset turnovers.}$$

(c) The product resulting from multiplying these two results by each other (percentage of income to revenue and number of asset turnovers) is the rate of return (before interest and income tax) on total assets. Thus

$$\frac{I}{R} \times \frac{R}{A} = 2.5\% \times 1.6 = 4\% \text{ rate of return.}$$

A business may earn a satisfactory rate of return on its total assets even though its income before interest and tax is a small percentage of revenue, if it has a *high enough rate of turnover*. Food retailers usually operate under such conditions. On the other hand, an adequate rate of return may result from a combination of high margin and low turnover, illustrated by the typical operations of a jewelry or furniture store.

Example 13	*Grocery Store*	*Jewelry Store*
Financial statement data:		
Sales revenue...	$500,000	$100,000
Income before interest and income tax.....................	5,000	5,000
Average total assets	50,000	50,000
Comparisons:		
Rate of return on total assets	10%	10%
Income before interest and income tax as a percentage of revenue	1%	5%
Number of asset turnovers	10	2

An increase in the rate of return on assets may result from an increase in the percentage of income before interest and tax to revenue, an increase in the number of turnovers, or a favorable combination of changes in both.

Further analysis of these two components of the rate of return is needed to give management useful guides in deciding on future courses of action. Income is not the result of a single, homogeneous set of factors, but the *difference* between two types of flows which have opposite effects: *revenue*, which tends to increase income, and *expense*, which tends to reduce it. The behavior of the amounts of various classes of revenue and expense is influenced by many complex causes, and separate types of action on each class are often needed to improve operating results. Likewise, the amounts of each type of asset used in carrying on business operations respond to many complex influences. Later chapters show how management can plan for an increased rate of return in view of these many complications.

Limitations of the Income Statement

The income statement is useful for many purposes, but its user should be fully aware of its limitations. One limitation, just pointed out, is that the behavior of major income components can be quite different. Another limitation has to do with the assumptions and conventions on which accounting is based. These assumptions and conventions are somewhat arbitrary and may significantly limit the reliability of the resulting financial statements, even though the rules of accounting measurement and recording are followed accurately.

The principal assumptions and their limitations are

(1) That the business is an *entity* apart from its owners. In reality, however, the dividing line between the financial affairs of the business owners and those of the business itself is often indistinct.

(2) That the *monetary unit* is a suitable common denominator for measuring business activities. Many factors which are important to the success of a business cannot be measured in terms of money, however, and the monetary unit's value often changes so rapidly and extensively that it is far from being a stable yardstick.

(3) That accounting measurements should be based primarily on *exchange transactions*. But the significance of internal events, such as production, and of future events to the success of the business may far outweigh that of exchange transactions which have been completed or are in progress.

(4) That for purposes of accounting measurement, *continuity* of the business for the indefinite future, rather than liquidation, is the better assumption. Many businesses do have short and unsuccessful lives, however. Income cannot be measured precisely for a business that is likely to continue in operation indefinitely.

(5) That revenue and expired costs can be identified with, and therefore accrued in, specific *time periods*. In trying to do so, accountants allocate revenues and costs to time periods largely on the basis of assumed relationships and estimates of future events which may not be justified. For example, the periodic amount of depreciation expense and the unexpired cost of the depreciable asset carried forward to future periods are both based on estimates of useful economic life which are subject to substantial margins of error.

(6) That revenue should be based on *realization*, or the performance by the firm of the principal activities necessary to transfer a good or render a service to a customer, in exchange for another asset which can be measured reliably. A limitation of the realization concept is that *unrealized changes* in the value of assets are often of *major importance* to financial statement users. These are not shown in financial statements which are based on historical exchange prices.

Despite the imperfections of accounting's underlying assumptions, the income statement serves many useful purposes. It gives the user a foundation on which to base his own judgmental estimates about the future. The user who has studied accounting knows the general nature—and the limitations—of the assumptions which have influenced the measurements reported in financial statements.

TESTS FOR MEASURING LIQUIDITY AND SOLVENCY

Creditors and potential creditors of a business are chiefly interested in the answer to the question

Will the business be able to pay its liabilities as they come due, both in the near and distant future, and will it have enough working capital and facilities left to carry on normal operations?

This question deals with the *solvency* of the business, also often called *liquidity* when referring to the ability of a business to meet its obligations in the *near future*. The *liquidity* of the business can be determined to a large extent by the soundness of the items which appear as *current assets* in its statement of financial position on a given date, and the rapidity of their probable conversion into cash. Liquidity is more complex than that, however, even when used to measure the ability to pay a short-term debt. The soundness of the assets may change quickly, or other requirements for their use may intervene before the due date of the liability. More important, most creditors anticipate a continuing relationship with a customer. It is true that the given extension of credit may be merely for 30 or 60 days, but when the current claim is settled the customer will probably soon apply for additional credit.

The continuing liquidity of a business, or its *long-range solvency* from the point of view of a long-term creditor or investor, depends on the soundness of the *financial structure* of the business and its *profitability*. A sound financial structure is one which has a proper balance between various types of long- and short-term liabilities and owners' equity. The requirements for paying principal and periodic interest to creditors and dividends to stockholders should be well within the ability of the business.

Profitability, the income-earning ability of a business, is also important to creditors. Although creditors' claims are usually fixed in amount, a healthy margin of income over and above debt service requirements helps to assure creditors that their payments of interest and principal will be made when due.

The *liquidity*, or short-range solvency, of a business cannot be determined without giving some consideration to its *long-range solvency*. The ability of the business to earn income has an important influence on both. In addition to the measures of profitability such as the percentage of net income to revenue, rate of return on stockholders' equity, and rate of return on assets, there are some special quantitative measures designed to indicate the ability of the business to meet its obligations. Important ones are the amount of *net working capital*, the *current ratio*, the *quick ratio*, the *composition of total assets*, and *asset turnover rates*.

These tests are merely *indications of solvency and profitability*. The actual solvency and profitability of a firm depend on *future events*.

Amount of Net Working Capital

Net working capital is the margin of current assets remaining after deducting the sum required to pay liabilities which come due during the next year or next operating cycle (whichever is longer). The formula is

$$\text{Net working capital} = \text{Current assets} - \text{Current liabilities.}$$

Example 14 At the meeting of the owners and management of Sound Center, Inc., it was decided to expand the business. This expansion would require additional investment in cash, receivables, and inventories, so Mr. Farley approached the First City Bank for a short-term loan. Mr. Keyes, the vice president of the bank, made some calculations concerning the liquidity and solvency of the business prior to taking action on the loan request.

One of Mr. Keyes' computations was of the amount of net working capital, which he computed for the two years as follows:

	December 31, 1973	December 31, 1972
Total current assets	$175,000	$148,000
Deduct total current liabilities......	84,000	60,000
Net working capital.................	$ 91,000	$ 88,000

The net working capital is the amount of current assets that would remain for making additional payments, assuming the payment of existing current liabilities.

Mr. Keyes did not use the totals of current assets and current liabilities presented by the company without further study. Being interested in the bank's *margin of safety* if it made the loan, he had to be sure that the net working capital was not *overstated* by an *overstatement* of current assets of an *understatement* of current liabilities. He scanned the items in each category to determine whether their classification as current, and their amounts, seemed to be proper.

Mr. Keyes concluded that the working capital had increased only slightly, by $3,000, but at this point he could not judge whether the change was favorable or unfavorable. It was quite possible that Sound Center needed an additional margin of safety of current assets over current liabilities. It was also possible that the existing margin was too great—that is, that too much was invested in inventories or receivables or too much unproductive cash was being kept on hand. To make this decision, Mr. Keyes needed a standard for comparing the Sound Center's liquidity with that of similar businesses. This standard might take many forms, but it is usually expressed in terms of a ratio or percentage, such as the *current ratio*.

Current Ratio

The *amount* of net working capital is less helpful in measuring the liquidity of a business than the *relationship* of total working capital to the amount required. A measure of this relationship is the *current ratio*, which is computed as follows:

$$\text{Current ratio} = \frac{\text{Current assets}}{\text{Current liabilities}}.$$

Example 15   Continuing his calculations, Mr. Keyes determined the current ratio for Sound Center, Inc., for the two years:

	December 31, 1973	*December 31, 1972*
Total current assets	$175,000	$148,000
Divided by total current liabilities	84,000	60,000
Equals the current ratio	2.08	2.47

There was a significant *decrease* in the current ratio, but whether this represented a worsening in liquidity depended on several things:

(1) Whether Sound Center has been able to pay its debts at maturity in the past under similar current ratios.

(3) Whether the existing ratio is in line with the current ratios of the better managed businesses in the same field.

(3) Whether the turnover of the important assets of the business is changing.

Creditors usually consider a decrease in the current ratio to be undesirable if no significant improvement has occurred in asset turnover or composition. If the firm can still meet its debts when they come due without financial strain, a decrease in the current ratio should not cause alarm. A decrease in the current ratio may even mean that the business is using is assets more efficiently than previously. A change in the current ratio must therefore be interpreted along with data of similar firms and with other factors which affect the firm's financial position and income potential.

The current ratio is used in an effort to predict whether resources will be on hand in the *near future* in sufficient quantities and at the right time to pay liabilities as they mature. It gives only an approximation, and is subject to a margin of error to the extent that the assets will be collected, or the liabilities will mature, at irregular intervals.

The amounts of current assets and current liabilities in the statement of financial position may not reflect their typical amounts during the next accounting period. In fact, if the business is using a *natural year* as its accounting period, the balances of current assets and current liabilities at the end of the year are probably *not typical* of the balances which exist during most of the year.

Even if these difficulties can be overcome, the current ratio must be supported by additional analysis in determining short-term solvency. Arbitrary ratios are far inferior to a cash budget for estimating the needs of the business for the coming period, and even the cash budget is imperfect. Exercise of judgment cannot be avoided in deciding whether the firm's current position is sound, for there is no standard current ratio which is satisfactory in all circumstances.

Quick Ratio

Most retail businesses complete several operating cycles within a year, which means that the dividing line between their current and noncurrent assets and liabilities is twelve months. Although they may expect to collect enough assets during the next year to pay current debts, irregularity in the rate of either collections or payments may cause temporary financial embarrassment. Thus, even if the current ratio is satisfactory, the *degree of liquidity* of assets may not be.

Example 16   In the following illustration, business *ABC* has a higher current ratio than business *XYZ* but slow-moving inventory forms a large part of its current assets. Although *ABC* is probably in a sound current condition now, it may run into temporary difficulty in meeting its debts during the year. Inventory cannot be used for paying rent or salaries. *XYZ* is in a more liquid position.

	ABC	*XYZ*
Cash	$ 5,000	$18,000
Accounts receivable	10,000	12,000
Merchandise inventory	25,000	10,000
Total current assets	$40,000	$40,000
Total current liabilities	$15,000	$20,000
Current ratio.....................................	2.67	2.00

For the reason illustrated, it is usually desirable to supplement the current ratio with a computation of the *quick*, or *acid-test*, *ratio*. This ratio shows the relationship to current liabilities of the assets which will quickly be converted into cash. Its formula is

$$\text{Quick ratio} = \frac{\text{Cash} + \text{Short-term receivables} + \text{Temporary investments}}{\text{Total current liabilities}}$$

The *quick assets* consist of *cash, receivables,* and *temporary investments.* Inventories are excluded, because they must first be sold and then the resulting accounts receivable must be collected before cash is available for making payments. Prepaid expenses are also omitted from quick assets, as are any receivables which the business does not expect to collect in the very near future.

Example 17   The quick ratio of Sound Center, Inc., for the two years is computed as follows:

	December 31, 1973	December 31, 1972
Cash	$ 7,000	$11,000
Plus estimated collectible accounts receivable...	69,000	67,000
Total quick assets	76,000	78,000
Divided by total current liabilities	84,000	60,000
Equals quick ratio	0.90	1.30

The quick ratio of Sound Center, Inc., is significantly lower than it was at the end of 1972. One year ago the firm had $1.30 of liquid assets for each dollar of liabilities to be paid during the next year. Now the liquid assets are only 90 cents for each dollar of current liabilities. The firm may have difficulty meeting its debts as they come due because of its weakened liquidity.

Mr. Keyes, the banker, must judge whether Sound Center's liquidity is now, and is likely to continue to be, sound enough to warrant his making the requested loan. He can obtain further information on this point by looking at the details of the asset and equity structure of the firm. An indicator of these structures is the *percentage composition* of assets and equities.

Composition of Assets and Equities

Working capital may appear to be adequate in amount and sufficiently liquid on the basis of the three preceding computations, but it may still lack the proper *balance* between components. One way of attempting to judge whether the balance is proper is to determine the *percentage of each asset to total assets.* This measure of asset composition is then compared with that of the same company at earlier dates and with that of similar companies at the same date.

Example 18   The percentage composition of the assets of Sound Center, Inc., was as follows:

	December 31, 1973		December 31, 1972	
	Amount	*Per Cent*	*Amount*	*Per Cent*
Current assets:				
Cash.....................................	$ 7,000	3.3%	$ 11,000	6.8%
Accounts receivable, net	69,000	32.4	67,000	41.4
Merchandise inventory	92,000	43.2	64,400	39.7
Prepaid expense	7,000	3.3	5,600	3.5
Total current assets	175,000	82.2	148,000	91.4
Property, plant, and equipment:				
Equipment (unexpired cost)......	38,000	17.8	14,000	8.6
Total assets........................	213,000	100.0	162,000	100.0

The most striking changes in the asset composition of Sound Center are

(1) The decline of cash from 6.8 per cent to 3.3 per cent of total assets.
(2) The decline of accounts receivable from 41.4 per cent to 32.4 per cent.
(3) The decline of current assets from 91.4 per cent to 82.2 per cent.
(4) The increase of equipment from 8.6 per cent to 17.8 per cent of total assets.

Measures of composition should be used with caution. One asset, such as cash, may appear to be the proper percentage of total assets, while in truth both cash and total assets are too small or too large by the same proportion. The ratio of one asset to the total may falsely appear to be satisfactory because of an opposite effect of another asset on total assets.

A similar analysis of composition is often made for equities, in order to detect significant changes in debt and ownership structures.

Turnover Rates of Specific Assets

A most important influence upon the liquidity and solvency of the firm is the rate at which accounts receivable, inventory, and other important current assets are "turned over" during a period of time. Such *turnover rates* for individual assets are computed by *dividing the total change* in the asset over a given time period by *the weighted-average balance* of the asset during that same time period. More detailed consideration is given to turnover rates in later chapters.

Mr. Keyes, the bank vice president, postponed a decision on the loan application of Sound Center, Inc., until he could analyze the turnover of accounts receivable, inventories, and accounts payable, and until Mr. Farley furnished a *statement of funds flows* for the business.

MEASURES OF LONG-RANGE SOLVENCY

Importance of Long-Range Solvency

Prospective short-term creditors of a business are interested in its current position *now* and its probable current position in the future when payments on the debt come due. If the time to maturity is short, a satisfactory current position at the date of the statement of financial position is usually sufficient indication that the firm will be able to pay the loan when it is due, unless the business is incurring substantial losses. However, banks and suppliers are normally interested in maintaining a *continuing relationship* with a healthy customer. Both are concerned with whether the trend of income and other financial factors of the customer are such that its financial health will last.

Even more directly concerned with the *long-range solvency* of the enterprise are its long-term creditors, such as holders of installment notes on equipment, mortgage notes, or bonds. A satisfactory current position of the borrower today may assure the lender that he will receive his interest payments promptly for a short while. This is of little comfort, however, if the downward trend of the debtor's income and the deterioration of his current position cast doubt on his ability to pay the principal or interest several years from now.

Stockholders, too, study the factors which point to the long-range solvency of the company in deciding whether to change their stockholdings. If creditors cannot be paid, stockholders are unlikely to receive dividends. Moreover, they may suffer substantial losses in a forced closing or a reorganization of the business.

Earnings Coverage of Debt Service Requirements

A business usually expects to pay the interest on loans, and often the principal as well, by using funds derived from operations. The number of *times* the borrower has *earned debt service requirements* in the past, and is likely to earn them in the future, is an indication of the margin of safety of the long-term creditors.

The following condensed financial summaries of the Borrower Company for the year ended December 31, 1974, are used as the basis for later analysis:

BORROWER COMPANY
Income Statement
For the Year Ended December 31, 1974

Revenue..	$800,000
Deduct operating expense	768,750
Income from operations	$ 31,250
Deduct bond interest expense.......................................	6,250
Income before federal income tax................................	$ 25,000
Deduct corporate federal income tax expense....................	7,500
Net income	$ 17,500

BORROWER COMPANY
Statement of Financial Position
December 31, 1974

ASSETS

Current assets	$150,000	
Noncurrent assets..	250,000	
Total assets		$400,000

LIABILITIES

Current liabilities	$ 50,000	
5% Bonds payable due Dec. 31, 1984	125,000	
Total liabilities.......................................		$175,000

STOCKHOLDERS' EQUITY

Capital stock..	$100,000	
Retained income	125,000	
Total stockholders' equity		225,000
Total equities		$400,000

The number of times debt service requirements are earned is computed as follows:

$$\frac{\text{Income before interest and income taxes}}{\text{Periodic interest}} = \frac{\text{Number of times debt}}{\text{service requirements earned}}$$

$$\frac{\$31,250}{\$\ 6,250} = 5 \text{ times}$$

At present the amount of earnings available for the payment of interest is five times as large as the amount required to pay interest. Earnings available for the payment of interest could decline 80 per cent, to one-fifth of their present amount, and still barely provide enough for the payment of interest.

Income tax is not deducted in computing the earnings available for the payment of interest. In planning income taxes may be considered as a *contingent expense*; there will be no income tax unless there is a net income subject to tax, after deducting interest and all other expenses.

The analyst wishes to estimate the margin of safety with which the *future earnings* of the business will cover its *future debt service requirements*. After analyzing the past coverage as a point of departure, he should project what the coverage will be in the future, allowing for his proposed loan's effect on both earnings and interest requirements.

Ratio of Stockholders' Equity to Total Equities

Another important relationship bearing on the long-range solvency of a business is the *proportion of its total equity which is furnished by stockholders*.

Most lenders hope to collect their interest and principal from a solvent business which continues in operation. However, it is a well-known fact that businesses sometimes *do fail*. When a business liquidates, the creditors' claims must be paid first; then the remaining assets, if any, are distributed to the stockholders. Stockholders are thus the final, or *residual*, claimants of both the income of a living business and the assets of a dying one. Any loss which occurs in disposing of the assets reduces the stockholders' equity first.

The ratio of stockholders' equity to the total equities (which equal the total assets) of the business shows the relative size of the margin of safety. For Borrower Company, the ratio is computed as follows:

$$\frac{\text{Stockholders' equity}}{\text{Total equities}} = \frac{\$225,000}{\$400,000} = 0.5625 = 56.25.$$

This means that the total assets of the company could shrink 56.25 per cent before there would be any loss to the creditors in liquidation. A major shrinkage might result from continued operating losses or from losses on the disposal of important assets, such as investments or buildings.

The greater the risk of decline in the assets of a business, the greater is the margin of protection which creditors need. This required margin is indirectly a protective feature for the stockholders, too, because usually no equity holder gains by a forced liquidation of a business.

If other factors remain constant, there is usually a greater risk of shrinkage in assets the longer the time period involved. Creditors stand more chance of losing on a loan due two years from now than on one due next year, and still more chance of losing on a ten-year loan. The range of periodic fluctuation in the income of the business also affects the safety of the loan. Electric utilities have fairly stable income because the demand for their service usually changes little in good times or bad, and substantial loans to them for long periods are considered quite safe. On the other hand, manufacturers of factory machinery often suffer wide swings in periodic income and frequent losses; consequently, long-term loans to them are made more cautiously.

As in practically every other case involving analysis of the long-term solvency of a business, the analyst is trying to *predict* what the margin of safety will be in the future. In his analysis of the ratio of stockholders' equity to total equities, therefore, he should take into consideration *expected future changes* in liabilities and equities.

Assumptions and Limitations of the Financial Position Statement

Users of the statement of financial position are interested primarily in forming *judgments as to the probable course of future events*. The nature of the company's assets and the contractual terms of its liabilities and owners' equities will have a very important influence on its course of business operations, its income, and its financial status in the future.

The financial position statement results from the same assumptions and conventions that are used in preparing the income statement. These assumptions and their limitations were discussed earlier in this chapter. The financial position statement is *not* intended to show what the business is *worth* at the date of the statement. The value of any asset, or of a business as a whole, is largely subjective. It depends on projections of future prospects by the persons who are estimating its worth. The expectations of each person who makes such an evaluation usually differ from those of others, and the value estimates of a single person frequently change from time to time.

The values in the statement of financial position are measurements resulting from *exchange transactions of the* past. Most of the individual assets of the typical business are stated at their *unexpired cost*—that part of their original cost which represents the proportion of the asset's service benefits expected to be received by the business in the future. The statement of financial position does, of course, show the amount of cash which the business expects to collect for its *monetary assets*. Unless the business intends to cease operations in the near future, a major consideration in the measurement of its assets is their effect upon the *future earning power* of the business as a going concern.

The historical statement of financial position provides a useful *starting point* for subjective estimates about the future. There is continuity between the past and the future. Many of the resources, contracts, relationships, policies, and people that have shaped past results will continue to influence the firm's affairs in the future.

Summary   Appraisal of the past results of a business is designed to answer two principal questions:

(1) How well has the business done in comparison with what could be expected of it?

(2) What can be done to improve future performance?

Comparisons of several types help to provide answers to these questions: comparisons with other items in the financial statements of the company at the same time, comparisons with the corresponding results of the company at earlier periods, comparisons of actual results with planned results, comparison of actual results with a desired standard of performance, and comparisons with the corresponding results of other similar companies.

Comparisons alone do not tell the whole story, and they are but a prelude to management action. Comparisons should be meaningful, useful, and reliable, and the cost of making and using them should not exceed the resulting benefit.

One useful measure of *past operating performance* is the rate of income on stockholders' equity. Perhaps even more useful is the *rate of income before interest and income tax to all assets*, and its components, (1) the percentage of income before interest and income tax to revenues and (2) the number of asset turnovers. These measures indicate management's efficiency in the administration of assets, regardless of source, and they give valuable clues as to where and how managerial action can be taken to improve future results.

Measures of financial position are often concerned with determining the *liquidity* and *solvency* of the firm. The current and quick ratios relate the amount of liquid assets on hand to the amount of maturing debts in an effort to show whether the firm will be able to meet its obligations in the near future. The amount of working capital and the composition of the current assets and liabilities also give some indication of the firm's debt-paying ability. Important in measuring the liquidity and solvency of the firm from a going-concern viewpoint are the turnover rates of current accounts such as inventories, receivables, and accounts payable. Useful measures of the long-range solvency of a business are the adequacy of earnings to cover debt service requirements, and the margin of safety provided to creditors by the equity of the stockholders.

The foregoing caluclations concerning the financial results of the business deal with *historical data*, but they are a necessary *basis for projecting probable future conditions*. They facilitate decisions by management concerning future actions, stockholder decisions about investing or disinvesting in the firm's shares, and creditor decisions relating to present and future loans to the business.

Discussion Questions and Problems

8-1   On a given day, the stock of the Superior Oil Company of California sold on the New York Stock Exchange for $1,588, while Standard Oil of California was selling for $66.

a. How can you account for the fact that Superior Oil was selling for a much greater price? What can you conclude about the relative profitability of the two companies?

b. On the previous day, Superior Oil stock had sold for $1,566, while Standard Oil sold for $64. Which stock had the greater price rise?

c. If you had purchased Standard Oil at $64 and sold it the next day for $66, what effect would this have on the accounting records of the company?

8-2   Percentages and ratios are often used in analyzing financial statements.

a. What are two specific advantages of using ratios and percentages?
b. What are two specific disadvantages?

8-3   The local owner of a hardware store would like to know the amount of his "average" sale and has asked your help. A section of the cash register tape which he considers to represent a typical day shows the following sales:

$ 2.30	$22.10	$15.40	$13.40
9.80	.90	4.48	17.30
12.65	15.10	1.13	21.13
1.15	3.33	.87	14.50
4.92	6.94	9.86	4.98

a. Compute the arithmetic mean, the median, and the mode.
b. Of the three calculations, which do you feel is the most useful? How can it be used?

8-4   In many companies it is important to know the ratio or percentage of cost of goods sold to sales. The Eazy Sales Company has experienced the following in this regard:

	Cost of Sales	Sales
1971....................................	$100,000	$150,000
1972....................................	112,000	165,000
1973....................................	99,000	145,000

a. Why is the percentage of cost of sales to sales revenue important?
b. Does the trend for the Eazy Sales Company seem favorable?
c. What conclusions can you reach by knowing the percentages that you cannot reach by examining the absolute amounts? What conclusions can you reach by knowing the amounts but not the percentages?

8-5   It is often difficult to evaluate the profitability of single proprietorships, partnerships, and family corporations because the dividing line between reward for management services and return on capital is not distinct.

a. Why is this statement true?
b. How is it possible to analyze and compare the financial statements of two businesses of this type if one deducts management salaries and one does not?

8-6   The percentage of net income to total assets for your company for 1973 was the highest in the industry.

a. Does this mean that operating performance was satisfactory?
b. Does this mean that your company was the most successful in the industry?
c. What other ratios or percentages would assist you in answering the questions asked above?

8-7   Company *Y*'s net income was 10 per cent of sales in 1973, while Company *Z*'s was 5 per cent.

a. Did Company *Y* perform better during 1973 than Company *Z*?
b. Under what specific circumstances can you say that Company *Z* outperformed Company *Y*?

8-8   William Foster sold 500 shares of *S* Company capital stock, for which he had paid a total of $5,000, to George Hanson for $6,000.

a. What factors should George Hanson have considered before he decided to buy the stock?

b. Why did he probably decide to pay $6,000 for it?

c. Why was Foster willing to sell if for $6,000?

d. When stock changes hands at a price different from that received by the corporation when the stock was issued, is there any direct effect on the corporation's accounts?

8-9   Paul Pierre owns 100 shares of the Marietta Corporation. He read in the newspaper that the return on stockholders' equity for the past year for Marietta was 23 per cent. Paul was disturbed at this, for he had just received the annual report of the corporation and calculated the return on his investment, based on earnings per share, to be 16 per cent.

a. How can both percentages be correct?

b. If Paul had received a dividend on his stock which represented 4 per cent return based on his purchase price, how could he compute a return of 16 per cent?

8-10   Some businesses like to measure the operating performance of their subdivisions, such as divisions and departments. In doing so, which do you think would be more suitable: rate of income before tax on the assets of each division, or rate of income after tax on stockholders' equity? Why?

8-11   "It is impossible to measure income exactly for any business which plans to continue in operation."

a. Do you agree with this statement? Why?

b. List income statement items which can be measured with a high degree of accuracy.

c. List income statement items for which there is a relatively large margin of error in measurement.

8-12   The Able Company's current ratio has dropped during the last three years from 3.8 to 1 to a new low of 1.6 to 1.

a. What does this tell you about the liquidity of the company?

b. If the turnover of inventories had been increasing over the three years, could you make a better judgment about the firm's liquidity?

c. If the quick ratio had remained constant at 0.8 to 1, what would you know about the composition of the current assets of the company?

d. How would knowledge of the absolute amounts of the current assets and liabilities help you in making a judgment about Able's liquidity?

8-13   "The statement of financial position is not intended to show what the business is *worth* at the date of the statement."

a. What *does* the statement of financial position show?

b. List the items in a statement of financial position which are usually stated at approximately their current values.

c. List the items in a statement of financial position which usually do not reflect approximate current values.

d. Should the assets which are not now reported at their current values be so reported? Explain.

8-14   "The accountant is not justified in assuming that the business entity will continue in operation indefinitely. Studies of business mortality rates show that a high percentage of businesses fail during the first year, and that many more fail in the next year or two."

a. What effect does the assumption of continuity have on the measurement of income and financial position? Give specific examples.
b. Is this assumption justified in view of the high failure rate among new businesses? Explain.

8-15   The Rich Corporation's statement of financial position as of the end of the year shows common stock outstanding of $15 million and retained earnings of $30 million.

a. Does this information tell you anything about the success of the company in the past?
b. How could you use this information to project future income?
c. Could the Rich Corporation pay a cash dividend of $30 million? A cash dividend of $40 million?

8-16   The comparative income statements of the SureRoll Tire Company (rounded to the nearest thousand dollars) for 1973 and 1972 are presented below.

Required   a. Compare the percentages of each income statement item to sales for the two years. Include a column for per cent of increase or decrease of 1973 amounts as compared with 1972. Round to the nearest tenth of 1 per cent.
b. Based on these comparisons, what areas should be a matter of concern to the company's management?

	1973	1972	
	Amounts	*Amounts*	*Per Cent*
	(in thousands)		*of Sales*
Net sales...............................	$360	$300	100.0%
Cost of goods sold	299	260	86.7
Gross margin on sales	61	40	13.3
Operating expenses	54	30	10.0
Income before income tax	7	10	3.3
Corporate federal income tax ...	1.75	2.5	.8
Net income	5.25	7.5	2.5

8-17   The following information, rounded to the nearest thousand dollars, was taken from the Royal Company's financial statements:

	1973	1972	1971
Assets at end of year....................	$100	$ 80	$40
Liabilities at end of year..............	50	36	20
Revenue for year	300	200	
Expense for year	290	190	

Required   a. Compute the amount of owners' equity at the end of each year and the percentage of change from 1972 to 1973.
b. Compute the percentage of total stockholders' equity to total equities at the ends of 1972 and 1973. How can you account for the increase in stockholders' equity from 1971 to 1972?
c. Compute the rate of return (before interest and tax) on average total assets, the the percentage of net income to revenue, and the number of asset turnovers for 1972 and 1973.

d. In general, how would you rate the performance of the Royal Company in 1973 as compared with 1972?

8-18   The following information relates to the operating results of the Ace Sales Company for 1973:

Net sales	$1,000,000
Percentage of income before interest and tax to total assets...	10%
Percentage of income before interest and tax to net sales......	2%

Required   a. Compute the asset turnover rate for 1973.

b. Compute average total assets for 1973.

8-19   The Thromb Company is considering issuing $1,000,000 of 8 per cent, ten-year bonds payable. Its operating revenues and expenses are not expected to change materially in the near future, and the income tax rate is expected to continue at 50 per cent of taxable income. The company's condensed income data for the last three years were as follows (in thousands of dollars):

	1973	1972	1971
Sales revenue	$5,000	$4,500	$4,800
Operating expenses	4,600	4,300	4,500
Income before income tax...............	$ 400	$ 200	$ 300
Federal income tax	200	100	150
Net income	$ 200	$ 100	$ 150

Required   a. Using past experience as a guide, compute the maximum and minimum number of times debt service requirements may be expected to be earned in the future.

b. Does the bond issue seem sound in view of the coverage of its service requirements by earnings? Explain.

8-20   The following data pertain to the Melodrome Company. All amounts are rounded to the nearest thousand dollars.

	1973	1972	1971
Assets..............................	$680	$550	$400
Capital stock	250	250	200
Retained income	90	120	80

Required   a. Compute the ratio of average stockholders' equity to average total equities for 1971, 1972, and 1973. Total assets and total equities were unchanged in 1971.

b. Is the margin of safety of creditors relatively more or less in 1973 than it was in 1972 and 1971?

8-21   The G Company had the following unrelated transactions in 1973:

(1) Accounts payable of $10,000 were paid in cash.

(2) The company purchased long-term investments for cash, $5,000.

(3) Sold a vacant lot that had not been used in the business for cash, $20,000.

(4) Determined that $3,000 of accounts receivable were uncollectible.

(5) Declared a $4,000 cash dividend to be paid during the first week of the next accounting period.

(6) Inventory which had cost $400 was considered obsolete when the physical inventory was taken.

(7) The company borrowed $2,000 from the bank and gave a 90-day, 6 per cent promissory note.

(8) Purchased a three-year insurance policy for $1,800.

(9) The bank notified the company that a customer's check for $150 had been returned marked "insufficient funds."

(10) The owners of the company made an additional cash investment of $10,000.

Required   Considering the above transactions separately, how would each affect the company's

a. Current ratio?

b. Quick ratio?

c. Net working capital?

8-22   State whether each of the following transactions would increase, decrease, or have no effect on (1) the amount of net working capital and (2) the current ratio:

a. Sale of merchandise on account.

b. Sale of merchandise for cash.

c. Borrowing cash on a short-term note payable.

d. Collection of accounts receivable.

e. Purchase of merchandise on account.

f. Purchase of equipment on account.

g. Purchase of equipment in exchange for long-term notes payable.

h. Declaration of dividend payable in cash.

i. Payment of dividend declared earlier.

j. Payment of accounts payable.

k. Return of merchandise to supplier for credit.

l. Issuance of capital stock for cash.

m. Recording periodic depreciation.

n. Sale of used equipment for cash.

8-23   The incomplete financial position statement of Delta Company is shown below.

DELTA COMPANY

Financial Position Statement

December 31, 1973

ASSETS

Current assets:			
Cash		$ 25,000	
Accounts receivable		?	
Inventories		?	
Total current assets			?
Property, plant, and equipment:		$400,000	
Less accumulated depreciation		?	
Unexpired cost			?
Total assets			?

LIABILITIES AND STOCKHOLDERS' EQUITY

Current liabilities:			
Accounts payable		?	
Accrued liabilities		$ 40,000	
Total current liabilities			$100,000
8% bonds payable, due 12/31/83			?
Capital stock			?
Retained income			?
Total liabilities and stockholders' equity			?

Required Use the following information as of December 31, 1973 to complete Delta Company's financial position statement.

(1) Delta's quick ratio is 1:1.

(2) The amount of working capital is $100,000.

(3) There are 10,000 shares of common stock outstanding with a par value of $10 per share and a market value of $15 per share.

(4) Net income before interest and income tax was $64,000, which provided a "number of times debt service requirements were earned" ratio of 8. The amount of bonds outstanding did not change during the year.

(5) The ratio of stockholders' equity to total assets is 0.60:1.

8-24 The following data relate to the Messiqua Company for 1973. All amounts are rounded to the nearest thousand dollars.

Sales revenue.....................................	$900,000
Average total assets	300,000
Average stockholders' equity	210,000
Income before income tax	45,000

Required   a. Compute the rate of return before tax on average stockholders' equity.

b. Calculate the rate of return before tax on average total assets.

c. Determine the percentage of income before tax to revenue.

d. Calculate the number of times the assets were turned over in 1973.

e. Compute the following for 1974, assuming no change in any factor other than that described:

(1) Income before tax if it is 12 per cent of revenue.

(2) Average total assets if the number of asset turnovers is four.

(3) Sales revenue if the number of asset turnovers is 2.5.

(4) Rate of return before tax on stockholders' equity if the percentage of income to revenue is 3 per cent.

(5) Sales revenue if average total assets increase by $50,000 and the number of turnovers during 1974 doubles over 1973.

(6) Rate of return before tax on stockholders' equity if owners' equity increases by $20,000.

f. For each of the changes in part e indicate whether or not the expected results are favorable from the stockholders' viewpoint.

8-25 The accompanying trial balances are those of the Nolo Corporation. Additional stock was issued on August 31, 1973, and the dividends were paid on December 30 of each year.

	Trial Balance		
	December 31, 1973	December 31, 1972	% of Total Assets, 1972
Accounts payable	$ 2,000	$ 5,000	12.8%
Accounts receivable	8,000	10,000	25.6
Capital stock, $100 par	20,000	16,000	41.0
Cash...	7,000	9,000	23.1
Dividends	5,000	4,000	—
Equipment.......................................	10,000	8,000	20.5
Equipment—accumulated depreciation......	4,000	3,000	7.7
Federal income tax expense....................	3,300	2,200	—
Federal income tax payable....................	3,300	2,200	5.7
Merchandise inventory..........................	26,800	15,000	38.5
Operating expenses	70,000	90,000	—
Retained earnings, Jan. 1.......................	?	12,000	40.5
Sales...	85,000	100,000	—

Required a. Prepare comparative statements of income, retained income, and financial position for the two years.

      b. Using net income *after tax*, compute the following for 1973 (1972 figures are shown in parentheses):

        (1) The rate of return on simple average stockholders' equity (1972: 26.1%).

        (2) Net income as a percentage of revenue (1972: 7.8%).

        (3) Net earnings per share of capital stock outstanding at year end (1972: $48.75).

        (4) Net earnings per simple average share of capital stock outstanding during the year. Comment on the difference between this calculation and the one made in b(3) (1972: $48.75).

      c. Using income before income tax and interest, compute the following for 1973:

        (1) Rate of return on simple average total assets (1972: 27.0%).

        (2) Percentage of net income before interest and tax to revenue (1972: 10.0%).

        (3) The number of turnovers of simple average total assets (1972: 2.7).

      d. Compute the following for 1973:

        (1) Current ratio (1972: 4.7 to 1).

        (2) Amount of net working capital (1972: $26,800).

        (3) Quick ratio (1972: 2.6 to 1).

        (4) The percentage composition of total assets, rounded to the nearest tenth of 1 per cent (1972 percentages are shown above).

        (5) The percentage composition of total equities, rounded to the nearest tenth of 1 per cent (1972 percentages are shown above).

      e. Comment on any differences between the two years which seem significant to you.

      8-26   The accompanying condensed financial statements are those of the Arabic Co.

Required a. Is the Arabic Co. more or less liquid at the end of 1973 than it was at the end of 1972? Present the following comparisons to support your conclusion (amounts for 1972 are shown in parentheses):

        (1) Amounts of net working capital (1972: $62,100).

        (2) Current ratios (1972: 5.1 to 1).

        (3) Quick ratios (1972: 3.5 to 1).

        (4) Composition of assets (1972: Cash, 16.2%; Accounts Receivable (net), 23.8%; Inventories, 19.2%; Plant and Equipment (net), 40.8%).

      b. Is the company more or less solvent from a long-range point of view? Present the following comparisons:

        (1) Earnings coverage of debt service requirements (1972: 3.8).

        (2) Ratio of stockholders' equity to total equites (1972: 0.385).

ARABIC CO.
Income Statement
For the Years Ended December 31, 1973, and December 31, 1972

	Dec. 31, 1973	Dec. 31, 1972
Sales	$400,000	$360,000
Operating expenses	380,000	345,000
	$ 20,000	$ 15,000
Bond interest expense	3,600	3,900
Income before income tax	$ 16,400	$ 11,100
Income tax expense	3,700	2,500
Net income	$ 12,700	$ 8,600

ARABIC CO.
Statement of Financial Position

	Dec. 31, 1973	Dec. 31 1972,
ASSETS		
Cash.............	$ 10,000	$ 21,100
Accounts receivable (net)	23,000	31,000
Inventories	52,000	25,000
Plant and equipment..................	100,000	80,000
Plant and equipment—accumulated depreciation...	(35,000)	(27,000)
Total assets	$150,000	$130,100
LIABILITIES		
Accounts payable	$ 30,000	$ 12,500
Income tax payable	3,700	2,500
6% bonds payable due 12/31/83	60,000	65,000
Total liabilities	$ 93,700	$ 80,000
STOCKHOLDERS' EQUITY		
Capital stock	$ 35,000	$ 31,500
Retained income................	21,300	18,600
Total stockholders' equity............	$ 56,300	$ 50,100
Total equities	$150,000	$130,100

ARABIC CO.
Statement of Retained Income
For the Years Ended December 31, 1973, and December 31, 1972

	Dec. 31, 1973	Dec. 31, 1972
Retained income, beginning of year..............	$ 18,600	$ 20,000
Net income for the year	12,700	8,600
	$ 31,300	$ 28,600
Dividends	10,000	10,000
Retained income, end of year............	$ 21,300	$ 18,600

Cases **8-1** **The Novelty Store.** Shortly after the close of their second year in business, the three directors and stockholders of The Novelty Store met to discuss the results of the year's operations, to take action in connection with a dividend to stockholders, and to make plans for the year which was just beginning. Each had just received a copy of financial statements which the accountant had prepared, showing in adjacent columns the income, retained income, and financial position of the store for the years ended June 30, 1973, and 1972. These statements are illustrated as Exhibits A, B, and C, respectively.

Calvin Borman, who served as President and General Manager of the store, owned 30 per cent of the company's stock, for which he had paid $6,000 at the time of organization. William Dalton, the Vice President, had acquired 40 per cent of the stock for $8,000. His only participation in the business was in the role of a member of the board of directors. John Farnham, whose stock ownership was identical with that of Borman, acted as Secretary-Treasurer and Assistant General Manager of the corporation.

Mr. Borman called the meeting to order and asked if there were any comments on the financial statements.

Mr. Dalton, quickly making calculations on the back of one of the statements, exclaimed, "The business has really done well. Last year earnings per share were $46.40 and this year they are $58.50. That is an increase of approximately 26 per cent over last year. You can say all you like, but that is *the figure* that counts in my book."

Mr. Farnham frowned slightly and said, "I disagree with you, Bill. Earnings per share have increased, but our return on our total equity is not very good."

"Both of you gentlemen are talking about our improvement. It looks to me as though we are worse off this year than at the same time last year. Our cash in the bank was over $5,000 then, and now we only have $1,800," remarked Mr. Borman. He continued, "It just doesn't make sense to me that our sales went up last year and our cash went down! And if you calculate net income as a percentage of sales, it is 4.1 per cent this year compared with 4.6 per cent for last year—$85,000 more in dollars of sales, yet decline in the percentage of profit."

"I'm convinced of one thing already," said Mr. Farnham. "You can't analyze the results of a company by trying to summarize everything through the use of one or two ratios. We had better examine these three statements separately and review their individual components so that we can see what we have done, and what plans we wish to make for next year."

THE NOVELTY STORE
Income Statement
EXHIBIT A

	For the Year Ended	
	June 30, 1973	June 30, 1972
Credits:		
Sales	$285,000	$200,000
Interest received	0	300
Gain on sale of U.S. bonds	0	5,180
Total credits	$285,000	$205,480
Deduct debits:		
Advertising	$ 10,000	$ 7,000
Cost of goods sold	173,900	123,000
Depreciation	2,000	1,500
Insurance	2,200	1,880
Interest paid	1,300	900
Uncollectible sales revenue	5,100	2,800
Miscellaneous expense	6,000	3,000
Payroll	46,500	35,000
Rent	12,000	11,000
Sales returns and allowances	11,000	7,500
Taxes, income	3,300	2,620
Total debits	$273,300	$196,200
Net income	$11,700	$ 9,280

THE NOVELTY STORE
Statement of Retained Income
EXHIBIT B

	For the Year Ended	
	June 30, 1973	June 30, 1972
Credits:		
Beginning balance	$ 9,280	$ 0
Net income	$ 11,700	9,280
Total credits	$ 20,980	$ 9,280
Deduct debits: Dividends	8,610	0
Ending balance	$ 12,370	$ 9,280

"I guess you're right, John," replied Mr. Dalton. "I was all set to move that we declare a big dividend on the basis of my calculated earnings per share, but Calvin has made me realize that we don't have any cash for paying a dividend, even though we had a nice income this year. I'm puzzled myself about this cash business. Not only did our net income and sales increase, but you remember that we sold government bonds at a profit last year. Perhaps we made a mistake in a paying such a large portion of our net income in dividends this year."

The three men sat quietly for a few minutes and finally Mr. Borman spoke. "You know, boys, we have all of the company's financial statements right before us; yet it is amazing how our interpretations have differed. I think we've all been working conscientiously, but we have not used our financial information effectively. We need to have an expert help us analyze our performance for the last two years, and I'm certain that it would help us to understand future financial reports as well as help in planning future action. What do you think?"

There was unanimous agreement that Mr. Borman's suggestion should be followed through.

THE NOVELTY STORE
Statement of Financial Position
EXHIBIT C

	June 30, 1973	June 30, 1972
DEBITS		
Accounts receivable	$31,690	$17,550
Cash	1,800	5,150
Equipment	20,000	20,000
Merchandise inventory	27,100	28,550
Unexpired insurance	900	700
U.S. bonds due in 1977	0	5,000
Total debits	$81,490	$76,950
CREDITS		
Accounts payable	$15,580	$24,650
Accrued expenses payable	5,640	1,900
Accumulated depreciation	3,500	1,500
Capital stock, $100 par	20,000	20,000
Corporate federal income tax payable	3,300	2,620
Estimated uncollectible accounts	5,100	2,000
Notes payable to bank, due in six months	16,000	15,000
Retained income	12,370	9,280
Total credits	$81,490	$76,950

Required   a. Prepare an income statement and statement of financial position in classified form, suitable for managerial analysis. The income tax rate is 22 per cent.

b. Compute several appropriate ratios or other statistics concerning the operating performance of the Novelty Store. Do you feel that 1973 was an improvement over 1972? In what areas might performance be improved?

c. Assume that you were approached by Mr. Borman with a request to borrow $10,000 on a 30-day note and an additional $10,000 on a one-year renewable note. Would you approve either or both loans? Support your answer with appropriate measures of the liquidity and solvency of the Novelty Store.

Note: Total assets were $73,450 shortly after the business was formed on July 1, 1971.

8-2   **National Cash Register Company.** The accompanying financial statements are those of the National Cash Register Company for the years ended December 31, 1969 and 1968. You are asked to make the following analyses of the company's liquidity, solvency, and profitability. *Round all amounts to the nearest million dollars* before making any calculations.

Required   a. Prepare the following analyses of the company's liquidity and solvency at the ends of 1969 and 1968:
   (1) Amount of working capital.
   (2) Current ratio.
   (3) Quick ratio.
   (4) Composition of assets by major types.
   (5) Composition of equities by major types.
b. Prepare the following analyses of the company's operations:
   (1) Rate of return after income tax on simple average stockholders' equity. Stockholders' equity at December 31, 1967, was $423,500,000.
   (2) Rate of return before income tax on simple average total assets. Total assets on December 31, 1967, were $1,072,106,000.
   (3) Turnover rate for total assets.
   (4) Percentage of net income before tax to sales revenue.
   (5) Number of times interest requirements were earned.
c. Comment on any significant changes in the company's liquidity, solvency, and profitability.

Results of Operations

Income:	1969	1968
Income from sales, services and equipment rentals	$1,254,641,000	$1,127,150,000
Other income	20,946,000	20,216,000
	1,275,587,000	1,147,366,000
Costs and expenses:		
Manufacturing	736,083,000	667,235,000
Selling, general and administrative	429,581,000	385,724,000
Interest	26,241,000	21,776,000
Minority interest in net earnings of subsidiaries	3,367,000	3,080,000
Unites States and Foreign income taxes (including deferred tax of $7,012,000 in 1969 and $8,058,000 in 1968)	36,200,000	31,967,000
	1,231,472,000	1,109,782,000
Net income for the year:	$ 44,115,000	$ 37,584,000
Primary earnings per share	$4.12	$3.78
Fully diluted earnings per share	$4.11	$3.67

Earnings Retained for Use in the Business

Balance January 1,	1969	1968
The National Cash Register Company............	$230,683,000	$206,145,000
Combined Paper Mills, Inc.	18,067,000	16,553,000
	248,750,000	222,698,000
Add—Net income for the year	44,115,000	37,584,000
Deduct—Cash dividends:		
The National Cash Register Company—$1.20 per share...	12,625,000	11,145,000
Pooled companies prior to acquisition	40,000	387,000
Balance December 31	$280,200,000	$248,750,000

The 1968 financial statements have been restated to include CPM, Inc.
See Financial Review on pages 6 through 8 for additional infomation.

Financial Position

	December 31	
	1969	1968
ASSETS		
Current assets:		
Cash	$ 39,692,000	$ 31,697,000
Marketable securities at cost (approximate market)	4,413,000	728,000
Receivables		
Current accounts......................................	268,286,000	212,542,000
Installment accounts	97,583,000	92,531,000
Balance due from issue of securities	16,060,000	18,000,000
	381,929,000	323,073,000
Less—provision for doubtful accounts	8,265,000	7,419,000
	373,664,000	315,654,000
Inventories at lower of cost or market*		
Raw stock and production supplies	70,964,000	53,530,000
Work in process	166,493,000	131,055,000
Finished goods..	231,437,000	184,572,000
	468,894,000	369,157,000
Prepaid expenses	21,271,000	17,003,000
Total current assets....................................	907,934,000	734,239,000
Property, plant and equipment:		
Land	12,413,000	11,341,000
Buildings	136,622,000	125,434,000
Machinery and equipment...........................	404,379,000	351,948,000
	553,414,000	488,723,000
Less: Accumulated depreciation......................	259,966,000	232,675,000
	293,448,000	256,048,000
Rental equipment...	407,127,000	306,117,000
Less: Accumulated depreciation	189,486,000	147,620,000
	217,641,000	158,497,000
Other assets	25,505,000	11,653,000
Total assets	$1,444,528,000	$1,160,437,000

*U.S. inventories are principally on a LIFO basis and international on a cost basis.

	December 31	
	1969	*1968*
LIABILITIES AND STOCKHOLDER'S EQUITY		
Current liabilities:		
Notes payable	$ 176,875,000	$ 91,635,000
Accounts payable	43,066,000	44,510,000
Accrued taxes	44,040,000	34,703,000
Accrued payroll	42,502,000	44,352,000
Other accrued liabilities	87,506,000	68,486,000
Customers' deposits and service prepayments	66,239,000	59,076,000
Total current liabilities	460,228,000	342,762,000
Long-term debt (exclusive of installments due in one year)	351,441,000	231,837,000
Lease purchase obligations................................	1,900,000	2,000,000
Deferred income tax..	11,007,000	2,365,000
International employees' pension and indemnity reserves	19,072,000	18,747,000
International operations reserve..........................	8,609,000	8,091,000
Minority interests	16,161,000	14,270,000
Stockholders' equity:		
Preferred stock—cumulative, 2,000,000 shares authorized and unissued, $5 par value.........		
Common stock, represented in 1969 by 10,701,821 shares (10,604,550 in 1968) of a total of 14,000,000 authorized shares, $5 par value...	295,910,000	291,615,000
Earnings retained for use in the business	280,200,000	248,750,000
	576,110,000	540,365,000
Total liabilities and stockholders' equity	$1,444,528,000	$1,160,437,000

part II

PROBLEMS IN
MEASURING, PLANNING, AND
CONTROLLING
ASSETS AND EQUITIES

chapter 9

Accounting Information and Control Systems

Purpose of Chapter

Earlier chapters have shown how accounting provides financial information to management, stockholders, creditors, and others to aid them in making their decisions concerning a business. *External users*, such as stockholders and creditors, use this information in evaluating the firm's profitability and financial soundness, as a first step in deciding whether to continue, expand, or reduce their financial commitments to the firm. *Management* uses this information in *planning* business activities and in *controlling* them—that is, in keeping the business moving toward its objectives at the desired rate. Part III of this text deals in considerable detail with the role of accounting in management planning and control.

To provide a sound basis for effective decision making and control, the information prepared for these user groups must be *timely, accurate, concise,* and yet *complete*. Chapter 9 deals with some of the guidelines for an effective information system and with some of the methods which have been developed for processing information efficiently and reliably.

Criteria for an Effective Management Information System

The accounting information system must provide timely, relevant, and reliable information to aid decision making at all levels of management, in addition to meeting the needs of outsiders. Firmin lists the following objectives for the management information system[1]:

(1) Management's objectives must be defined clearly.

(2) The system must yield information that will permit management to evaluate the firm's position in comparison with its goals.

(3) The evaluation must be sufficiently timely to allow adaptations in the firm's operations or its objectives.

(4) The system must aid in the evaluation of alternative choices of action.

(5) The cost and value of the information must be measurable.

(6) The system must recognize functional and personal relationships within the firm.

(7) It must have the flexibility to provide a variety of information for many users, internal and external, with diverse objectives.

The accounting system is the heart of the firm's management information system. The information needed for management decisions is much broader than historical financial data, however. The system must also furnish information on such matters as production and sales orders, which normally are not included in the financial reports. It must make available information dealing with future prospects and with environmental factors affecting the firm, in addition to data relating to past events.

The Business Transaction as a Unit of Information

Accounting measures the financial progress and position of the organizational units of the business, and of the business as a whole, by breaking the complex business activities into identifiable, measurable financial *transactions*. Accounting analyzes, records, summarizes, and reports a multitude of transactions in such a way that those who are concerned with the affairs of the entity can more readily understand their significance.

This chapter deals with some of the general methods used in collecting, condensing, and summarizing the many details of transactions. These methods are essentially ways of grouping the transaction data according to the accounts which they affect, beginning with the raw data of the underlying business papers and ending with the reporting of financial facts under appropriate account titles in the financial statements. These methods, like other details of the accounting system, should be tailored to the requirements of the particular business.

While the accounting system is collecting financial information to be reported to user groups it can also provide safeguards in the administration of the business

---

[1] Peter A. Firmin, "The Potential of Accounting as a Management Information System," *Management International Review*, 2 (1966), pp. 45–46.

assets. The next section deals with the design of this aspect of accounting, called the system of *internal control*.

General Features of a System of Internal Control

A system of internal control consists of all measures employed by a business to (1) safeguard its resources against waste, fraud, and inefficiency; (2) promote accuracy and reliability in accounting and operating data; (3) encourage and measure compliance with company policy; and (4) judge the efficiency of operations of the responsibility centers of the business.

The value of a good system of internal control in *deterring* errors, fraud, and waste is undoubtedly greater than its value in *detecting* them. One of its basic objectives is to remove the opportunity to commit irregularities or to use assets in a manner contrary to the objectives of the business. How well it can accomplish this is a practical matter. Rarely is a system designed so perfectly that it will foil all fraudulent schemes. Sometimes the cost of a complete cure is greater than the probable cost of the disease, and management may elect to take a calculated risk by not incurring the extra cost of a foolproof system.

Many accounting procedures are designed so that *errors* will be detected automatically as a part of routine proofs of clerical work. The detection and prevention of *wasteful use* of assets is a much more difficult, although a no less important, matter. Constant vigilance by management is needed to help ensure that cash and other assets are employed efficiency and profitably. The various means of comparing the actual performance of the business with the planned performance, described in later chapters, are very effective in promoting the profitable use of assets.

Internal control procedures are tailored to the particular business entity more than perhaps any other feature of the accounting system. They depend on the size and type of the business; the physical location of its parts; the number, ability, and character of its employees; and the wishes of management. However, the following rules, which have been developed from the experience of many businesses, apply to most businesses and to most types of assets.

(1) Duties should be so assigned that no one individual has complete control over a phase of *business operations* and also over the *accounting* for those operations, or over the custody of a business asset and the related accounting.

Example 1 No one employee should be solely responsible for making sales, collecting for them, and recording them in the journals and ledgers. In such a case it would be too easy for him to misappropriate cash or merchandise and falsify the records to conceal the shortage. Errors and waste, likewise, would often go undetected.

Example 2 No one employee should be responsible for collecting cash, paying it out, and having custody of the cash balance. Such combined duties would enable him to take cash receipts and cover the shortage by reporting fictitious cash payments. Independent verification of his work by another would make it easier to discover errors and inefficiency.

(2) Duties should be organized so that one employee, acting independently, *verifies* the work of another while carrying the necessary work forward.

This does not mean that the second employee duplicates the work of the first, but rather that *checks and balances* which promote honesty and accuracy are built into their work procedures.

Example 3   The following organization of duties is designed to prevent or detect errors, fraud, and waste in handling the mail cash receipts of a medium-sized or large organization:

The *mail clerk* opens the mail and lists cash remittances in triplicate, giving the names and amounts. His total of receipts is the amount for which employees subsequently handling the money or records are *accountable*.

The *accounts receivable bookkeeper* receives a copy of the remittance list from the mail clerk and posts credits in the individual customers' ledger accounts. The total of credits posted must equal total remittances.

The *cash receipts bookkeeper* receives a copy of the remittance list and makes cash journal entries debiting Cash and crediting Accounts Receivable. The total of these entries must agree with total remittances.

The *cashier* receives the money from the mail clerk and returns a signed copy of the remittance list to him as a receipt. The cashier prepares a deposit slip in duplicate and takes it and the money to the bank. The total of the deposit must agree with total remittances.

The *treasurer*, an officer who supervises the work of handling the money of the business, compares the duplicate deposit slip, receipted by the bank, with the total remittances listed by the mail clerk to be sure that all money has found its way into the bank.

The mail clerk has an opportunity to take money, but *he cannot conceal the shortage* because he has no access to the accounting records. If he fails to list a customer's payment, ultimately the customer's complaint is likely to lead to his detection. The accounts receivable and cash receipts bookkeepers can falsify records, but they have *no access to money*. The cashier can take money, but the shortage will be obvious when the treasurer compares the duplicate deposit slip with the mail clerk's remittance list.

Smaller businesses cannot make such an elaborate division of duties, but they can use many of the features described above even if only two employees handle cash and cash records. In both cases, two or more employees conspiring together can defeat the scheme of internal control. It is difficult to devise a system which cannot be defeated by such *collusion* of employees. Fortunately, most would-be embezzlers are reluctant to take someone else into their confidence.

(3) *Physical safeguards* should be used where they are justified to verify business activities and to protect business assets. Adding machines, cash registers, and other forms of mechanical equipment help to improve the efficiency as well as the accuracy with which records are kept. Safes and locked cages help to protect cash and other assets from unauthorized use. *Forms* used for authorizing or recording transactions of a given type, such as sales tickets or checks, should be *serially numbered* by the printer and all numbers should be accounted for. The purpose is to prevent the falsification of records of sales, payments, and other types of transactions.

The preceding paragraphs have presented some representative features of a system of internal control, although by no means all possible features. The designer of the accounting system must decide what events are to be recorded; when, by whom, and how they are to be recorded; and what the flow of work and division of duties within the organization are to be. Internal control is built of the raw materials of the accounting system—the *forms* (basic documents, journals, ledgers, and reports); the *procedures* carried out by people in preparing the forms; and *mechanical devices*. Larger organizations formally set forth their systems in *manuals*, which are useful in instructing new employees and in settling questions of procedure.

The system that is best on paper may fail in practice. Constant supervision is needed to ensure that each system operates according to plan. Some supervision comes about routinely through the operation of the automatic checks, but more is needed. Many businesses have an *internal auditing* department whose duty it is to see that the accounting system operates accurately to carry out the plans and policies of management. In addition, most businesses have a periodic *independent audit* made by a public accounting firm. One of the primary obligations of the auditor is to satisfy himself that the company's *system of internal control is adequate*, both in design and in practice.

The auditor or systems man should also be constantly alert for ways of improving the system of internal control by increasing its efficiency, incorporating better methods and equipment, and solving new problems as they arise.

Steps in the Data-Collection and Summarization Process

The following are usually the chief stages of the process of collecting and summarizing financial data:

(1) Preparation of *source documents*, the underlying business papers which initiate business transactions and which also serve as the first report of them after they have occurred.

(2) Preparation of *journal entries*, which analyze each transaction in terms of its debit and credit effect on the assets and equities of the enterprise.

(3) Posting the debit and credit parts of the journal entries to a *ledger*, which contains a separate *account* of the debits and credits to each type of asset and equity.

(4) Preparation of a *trial balance*, which lists the balances of all of the accounts at the end of the accounting period, and perhaps of a *work sheet*, which aids in the preparation of formal financial statements by providing for adjustments and by grouping together the account balances which are to be used in each statement.

(5) Preparation of formal *financial statements*, such as the income statement, the retained income statement, the financial position statement, the funds flow statement, and various special types of reports for internal and external use.

During an accounting period even a moderate-sized business may have *thousands* of individual sales, purchases, receipts, payments, and other transactions. By means of the accounting process, these may be condensed into *hundreds* of journal entries, which are then further condensed into *tens* of ledger account balances and financial statement items. In this final stage of condensation and orderly arrangement, the summarized information about business transactions is more meaningful to the reader of the financial statements.

Need for Time-Saving Methods

This book makes extensive use of the *general journal entry*, such as the following, in analyzing and explaining how various types of business events affect the firm's assets and equities:

> *1973*
>
> Mar. 1   A, Accounts Receivable................................. 190
>   OE, Sales Revenue.................................   190
>   Sold merchandise on account to Alfred Adams.

This form is a useful teaching device, but it is cumbersome in actual business practice when the *number* of transactions of a given type is very great. Even the smallest business makes thousands of individual sales on account during an accounting period and also completes thousands of several other common types of transactions. If each transaction were recorded in the manner illustrated above, journalizing would consume a great deal of time. Then if each of the thousands of debits and credits were transferred separately to the ledger accounts, a vast amount of time would also be required for posting. There would be many opportunities for errors in posting individual amounts.

Obviously more efficient methods of journalizing and posting are needed for practically any business. The remainder of this chapter describes some of the general features of these methods, as well as of means of preparing source documents and financial statements more efficiently. Some of these time-saving methods are *manual*, while others involve the use of *machines*.

Time Saving in Preparing Source Documents

The first record of a business transaction is usually contained in a *source document*, such as a sales invoice, purchase invoice, check, or receipt. When much descriptive information is needed about each event, the source document often consists of a standardized form on which the particular information about each transaction is written at the time the transaction occurs. Frequently several copies of the source document are prepared to furnish information about the transaction to the individuals inside and outside of the business who are principally concerned.

Example 4   At the time of a sale on account, the customer's name, address, the date, the quantity and description of the articles sold, the unit prices, and the total amount of the sale are usually written on a printed sales invoice form. The original may go to the customer, a copy to the accounts receivable bookkeeper, and a copy to the bookkeeper who records sales revenue.

The following are some examples of time-saving methods which may be used in the preparation of source documents:

(1) Use of *billing machines* which can compute the *extension* (price multiplied by quantity) for each item sold, and the *footing* (total of the extensions).

(2) Use of sales invoices *preprinted with quantities and prices* for goods which are frequently sold in standard amounts. If, for example, customers frequently order a gross of Item *K* at a time, a supply of invoices containing the description, quantity, and extension can be printed in advance. At the time of sale only the customer's name and address and the date need be recorded.

(3) Use of *mechanical registers*, such as the cash register. The only record at the time of each cash sale transaction is made when the cashier depresses the keys which indicate the amount, and sometimes the nature, of the sale. The machine lists the amount of each individual sale on a tape, which is locked within the machine, and at the same time accumulates a total of all cash sales. Usually the single figure representing the total cash sales for the day, perhaps from thousands of transactions, is recorded as *one journal entry*.

(4) Use of the *same form in two or more stages* of a complex transaction, or use of equipment which permits the preparation of the source document, journal entry, ledger record, and perhaps other records in a single writing. For example, the employee's paycheck, a payroll journal, and an entry in the individual employee's continuous earnings record can be prepared in one writing.

Special Journals

When a particular type of transaction recurs frequently, its details can usually be recorded and the combined effect of all such transactions can be transferred to the appropriate ledger accounts more efficiently by means of a *special journal*. A special journal is used to record transactions of only one type. For example, many businesses find that their numerous sales on account justify the use of a special *Sales Journal*, such as that shown in Illustration 9-1.

Illustration 9-1

SALES JOURNAL — Page 7

Date	Inv. no.	Customer's Name	Posted	Dr. Accts. Rec., Cr. Sales Rev.
1973				
Jan. 1	115	Adams, Alfred	✓	19
1	116	Warren, James............	✓	12
1	117	Carver, W. J.	✓	112
1	118	McIntosh, O. R.	✓	5
2	119	Mathis Company.........	✓	94
2	120	Barker, Carolyn	✓	10
2	121	Davis, John W.	✓	47
3	122	Adams, Alfred	✓	33
31	206	Madison Mfg. Co.	✓	215
31	207	Ehrlich, J. K.	✓	7
31	208	Magnuson, Alice	✓	80
31		Monthly total.............	3/70	8,450

The numerals "3" and "70" in the "Posted" column opposite the monthly total of $8,450 indicate that this amount has been posted as a *debit* to general ledger account number 3, Accounts Receivable, and also as a *credit* to general ledger account number 70, Sales Revenue. The general ledger accounts would then appear as follows:

A, Accounts Receivable   *(Account #3)*

1973		Ref.	Debit	Credit	Balance
Jan. 1	Balance brought forward		10,200		10,200
31		S7	8,450		18,650 Dr.

OE, Sales Revenue   *(Account #70)*

1973		Ref.	Debit	Credit	Balance
Jan. 31		S7		8,450	8,450 Cr.

The notation "S7" in the posting reference collumns of the general ledger accounts is an abbreviation for "Sales Journal, page 7."

A separate account must be maintained for each customer, showing the transactions with the customer—sales, sales returns, and collections—and the balance he owes the business. These individual customers' accounts are kept in the *Accounts Receivable subsidiary ledger*, a separate group of accounts whose total balances must equal the balance in Accounts Receivable, the *general ledger controlling account*. The check marks in the "Posted" column of the Sales Journal denote that the amounts have been recorded in the individual customers' accounts. Posting to the subsidiary ledger should be done frequently—perhaps daily—so that the customers' account balances will be current. Frequent posting also reduces the peak work load, which usually occurs at the end of the month.

Advantages of Specialized Journals

The following are advantages of using specialized journals, rather than using the general journal as the only book of original entry for transactions:

(1) They *save time in recording journal entries*. In the illustrated Sales Journal, the act of writing an amount in the money column indicates that Accounts Receivable is to be debited and Sales Revenue is to be credited. The names of these accounts to be debited and credited need not be written for each entry, since they are already printed at the top of the column. It is also unnecessary to write the amount of each transaction twice, because it is understood that the amount to be debited and the amount to be credited are the same.

(2) They *save time in posting* to the ledger. In the illustration there were 94 sales on account during the month. Posting only the column total as a debit to Accounts Receivable and as a credit to Sales Revenue requires 93 fewer debit postings and 93 fewer credit postings than would be required if each debit and credit were posted individually. No saving is made in this illustration in posting to the subsidiary accounts receivable ledger.

(3) *Duties* of keeping special journals may be *divided* among several employees, each of whom is a specialist in recording one type of transaction.

(4) A relatively *unskilled employee* may be used to keep each special journal.

A business may use a special journal for any type of transaction which occurs frequently. The particular journals which are used in a given business depend chiefly on the nature of its transactions and their frequency, and on the number of classifications needed in the accounts and reports. Types of special journals which are often found in practice are

Cash Receipts Journals
Cash Payments Journals
Sales Journals
Purchases Journals
Sales Returns and Allowances Journals
Purchase Returns and Allowances Journals
Notes Receivable Registers
Notes Payable Registers

No matter how many specialized journals a business uses, there are almost always unusual transactions which cannot be recorded in any of them. Every business should therefore have a *General Journal* in addition to the special journals. It is ordinarily used to record adjusting and closing entries, corrections, and unusual or complex transactions which affect many accounts or require an extended explanation.

Special Columns in Journals

A *special column* in a journal is one which is used to collect all the debits, or all the credits, to a particular account. The total of each column is then posted periodically—usually once a month—as a single debit or credit to the appropriate account.

The single money column in the illustrated Sales Journal is a special column whose amounts always represent debits to Accounts Receivable and credits to Sales Revenue. Several special columns may be used in a given special journal, and special columns are often appropriate in a general journal. They should be used whenever the transactions recorded in a particular journal involve frequent debits or credits to a given account.

Cash Receipts Journal

A *Cash Receipts Journal* is a specialized journal which usually has more than one special column. By definition, each cash receipts transaction involves a *debit to Cash*; therefore, a special column for *Cash, Debit* is needed. Other special columns are needed for accounts which are often debited or credited in cash receipts transactions. It is also usually desirable to provide a *Miscellaneous Debit* and a *Miscellaneous Credit* column to record debits and credits to accounts which are infrequently affected in cash receipts transactions.

Illustration 9-2 shows how transactions are journalized in a Cash Receipts Journal. When there are special columns for both the account debited and the account credited in a transaction, the bookkeeper does not have to write the name of either account in journalizing. No individual posting to the general ledger is needed for transaction amounts in these special columns. Examples of such transactions are the *cash sales* on the first line and the *collection on account*

Illustration
9-2

CASH RECEIPTS JOURNAL

| Date | Explanation | MISCELLANEOUS ACCOUNTS | | | | ACCTS. RECEIVABLE | | Sales | Cash |
		Title	LF	Debit	Credit	✓	Credit	Credit	Debit
1973									
Jan. 1	Cash sales							680	680
1	Burke, Marshall					✓	55		55
1	Edison, Miriam					✓	20		20
2	Mathis Company					✓	200		200
2	Tollman, Augustus					✓	27		27
2	Issuance of stock	Capital Stock	60		5,000				5,000
2	Collection of note and interest	Notes Receivable	4		1,000 }				1,020
		Interest Revenue	75		20 }				
2	Cash sales							900	900
3	Magnuson, Alice					✓	8		8
3	Property tax refund	Property Taxes	93		50				50
3	Borrowed on note	Notes Payable	41		3,000 }				2,970
		Notes Payable—Discount	42	30					
3	Cash sales							550	550
31	Evander, Mary					✓	70		70
31	Capitol Sales Co.					✓	300		300
31	Cash sales							1,300	1,300
	Monthly totals			830	11,500		7,100	27,430	45,200
				(×)	(×)		(3)	(70)	(1)

Total debits

Total debits		
	830	
	45,200	
	46,030	

Summary:
Debits:
Miscellaneous 830
Cash 45,200
Total debits 46,030

Credits:
Miscellaneous 11,500
Accounts Receivable 7,100
Sales 27,430
Total credits 46,030

(×)—*Miscellaneous Accounts columns are not posted in total. Each account debit or credit in these columns is posted individually.*

from Marshall Burke on the second line. A credit to the individual customer's account in the Accounts Receivable *subsidiary ledger* must be posted for each transaction of the latter type.

When accounts for which there are no special columns are debited or credited, the name of the account affected and the amount are recorded in the "Miscellaneous Accounts" section. Each such amount must be posted individually to the general ledger, and the number of the appropriate ledger account should be written in the "LF" (ledger folio) column to show that this has been done.

At the end of the month, all columns should be totaled and a summary should be prepared to prove the equality of debit and credit column totals. No totals should be posted until this proof has been completed; otherwise, errors might be carried forward into the ledger, where they would be difficult to locate. The totals of the special columns—Cash Debit, Accounts Receivable Credit, and Sales Credit—are then posted to the respective general ledger accounts and the account numbers are written below the column totals. "(×)" under each of the Miscellaneous column totals indicates that the totals are not to be posted; their component amounts must be posted individually.

After this additional posting, the Accounts Receivable and Sales Revenue accounts would appear as follows:

A, Accounts Receivable   *(Account #3)*

1973		Ref.	Debit	Credit	Balance
Jan. 1	Balance brought forward		10,200		10,200
31		S7	8,450		18,650 Dr.
31		CR5		7,100	11,550 Dr.

OE, Sales Revenue   *(Account #70)*

1973		Ref.	Debit	Credit	Balance
Jan. 31		S7		8,450	8,450 Cr.
31		CR5		27,430	35,880 br.

Cash Payments Journal

Just as the number and types of special journals differ from one business to another, so do the number and variety of special columns used in a given type of journal.

Another common type of multiple-column special journal is the Cash Payments Journal, shown in Illustration 9-3. The posting routine from this journal, which parallels that of the Cash Receipts Journal, may be summarized as follows:

(1) Post the individual debits to creditors' accounts in the Accounts Payable subsidiary ledger currently, and indicate by a check mark that this has been done.

(2) Post the individual debits and credits in the Miscellaneous Accounts columns individually, and show by writing the general ledger account number in the "LF" column that this has been done.

Illustration 9-3

CASH PAYMENTS JOURNAL

Date	Ck. No.	Explanation	Title	LF	Debit (Misc)	Credit (Misc)	✓ (A/P)	Debit (A/P)	Discounts Lost Debit	Cash Credit
1973										
Jan. 1	1	City license	Prepaid Licenses	9	120					120
1	2	Dunn Mfg. Co.					✓	392		392
1	3	Ware, Inc.					✓	980	20	1,000
2	4	Payroll	Accrued Wages Payable	43	2,110					2,110
2	5	Cash refund	Returned Sales	71	50					50
2	6	Refund of overpayment	Accts. Rec./Mathis Co.	3/✓	20					20
3	7	Delaware Co.					✓	693		693
3	8	Payroll taxes for December	{ Employees' Income Tax Withheld	44	300					
			Employees' S. S. Tax Withheld	45	60					
			S. S. Tax Payable	46	60					420
31	91	Kay Distributors					✓	1,210		1,210
31	92	Valley Ry. Co.	Merchandise Inventory	8	40					40
		Monthly totals			22,650	50		20,820	180	43,600
					(×)	(×)		(40)	(91)	(1)

Summary:

Debits:
- Miscellaneous ... 22,650
- Accounts Payable ... 20,820
- Discounts Lost ... 180
- Total debits ... 43,650

Credits:
- Miscellaneous ... 50
- Cash ... 43,600
- Total credits ... 43,650

(3) Total the columns at the end of the month, prove the equality of debits and credits, and post the totals of the special columns as debits or credits to the appropriate accounts in general ledger. Write below the total the number of the account to which the column total has been posted.

The entry for the payment of Check No. 6 on January 2 needs further comment. This payment was to the Mathis Co., a customer, to refund an overpayment of their account. The Mathis Co.'s account is in the Accounts *Receivable* subsidiary ledger, and prior to this entry it would have a *credit* balance —an abnormal balance for a customer's account. Because cash payments to customers by this company are rare, no special column is maintained in the Cash Payments Journal for debits to the Accounts Receivable controlling account. The $20 debit must, therefore, be posted individually to Accounts Receivable in the general ledger. To correct the customer's account balance and to maintain agreement between the controlling account and the subsidiary ledger, it must also be posted to the subsidiary account for Mathis Co. This double-posting is indicated by the numeral "3" and the check mark in the "LF" column.

Check No. 8 on January 3 is in payment of three general ledger liability accounts, all to the same payee. It requires debits to three accounts in the Miscellaneous Accounts debit column and a single combined credit to Cash. This illustrates the fact that an entry in a multicolumnar special journal may be recorded on more than one line if necessary.

Other Types of Subsidiary Ledgers

In addition to subsidiary ledgers for Accounts Receivable and Accounts Payable, the total of whose individual account balances must equal the balance of the corresponding controlling account in the general ledger, businesses often maintain subsidiary ledgers for other accounts. The number of accounts of a single type needed to justify the use of a subsidiary ledger is a matter of judgment. A few individual accounts receivable could be treated as general ledger accounts; but when they reach 10 or 12 in number, it is usually advantageous to open a special ledger for them.

Short-cuts in Journalizing

When subsidiary accounts are affected frequently by a single type of transaction, clerical work can often be reduced by journalizing only the *total of a batch* of source documents. For example, assume that a business makes hundreds of sales on account daily. For purposes of management control and reporting, it needs to know (1) the additions to and the balance of the Accounts Receivable controlling account; (2) the amount of Sales Revenue for each time period, such as a day; and (3) the changes in and the balance of each customer's account. The first two types of information can be determined by adding the individual sales invoices for the day and recording only their total in the Sales Journal. This is much quicker than listing in the Sales Journal the date, customer's name, amount, and other data for each sale. *Debits to individual customers' accounts* in the subsidiary ledger can be *posted directly* from copies of the sales invoices.

Work can be reduced in a similar fashion in journalizing cash receipts from customers. This is done by recording in the Cash Receipts Journal as debits to Cash and credits to Accounts Receivable only the *daily totals of collections* on account. *Individual credits* to customers' accounts in the subsidiary ledger are *posted directly* from duplicate copies of the receipts or from other source documents which report the collections.

Ledgerless Bookkeeping

One method of saving time in posting is *ledgerless bookkeeping*, which means *not posting* to the ledger at all. Instead, copies of basic source documents related to each account are filed together, and the information in the open items in the file can be used at any time to determine the account balance.

Example 5   A certain company which has thousands of individual customers does not post to individual ledger accounts for them, but instead maintains a file of the unpaid invoices owed by each. Its procedure consists of the following steps:

(a) Making *one entry* in the *sales journal* each day to debit Accounts Receivable and credit Sales Revenue for the total of the day's sales on account, usually recorded on several hundred invoices.

(b) *Filing two copies of each unpaid invoice* in a separate section for each customer. If a customer has an unpaid balance at the beginning of the month, there would already be a ticket for that amount in his file.

(c) Making *one entry* in the *cash receipts journal* each day to debit Cash and credit Accounts Receivable for the total of cash remittances.

(d) Matching copies of the cash remittance ticket for each customer with the appropriate invoice or invoices in his file, marking the invoices "Paid," and transferring them to a *paid invoice file*. When the amount of a remittance is not exactly equal to the amount of the invoice, the remittance ticket is filed in the customer's unpaid invoice file.

(e) Once a month the *balance owed* by each customer is determined by adding the debit items (beginning balance and unpaid invoices of the current month) and subtracting the credit items (partial cash payments on account). A statement is mailed to the customer showing his balance at the end of the month, supported by copies of the unpaid invoices. A copy of the statement is filed in the open invoice file to show the account balance at the end of the period.

(f) A *total of the unpaid customers' balances* is obtained and compared with the balance in the Accounts Receivable controlling account in the general ledger.

The preceding illustration merely describes the general features of ledgerless bookkeeping, not all possible variations.

Although ledgerless bookkeeping saves time, it is not without disadvantages. If source documents are lost, the accounts will be out of balance and the error will be difficult to discover. Also, it is practically impossible to tell at a later date, when the documents have been transferred to another file (such as the "Paid" file in Example 5), what changes occurred in an account during a given period. For these reasons, ledgerless bookkeeping is rarely used for the general ledger. Its use is ordinarily restricted to classes of accounts which have many individual subsidiary units, such as accounts receivable and accounts payable.

MACHINE ACCOUNTING

Three general types of machines are available for collecting and summarizing accounting information: *electromechanical equipment*, *punched-card equipment*, and *electronic equipment*. There are many makes and models of these machines, ranging from the relatively small, simple, and inexpensive to the large, complex, and costly. Technological changes in these types of machines have been particularly rapid in recent years. The following discussion describes only in a general way the accounting functions which may be performed by each type of machine.

Electromechanical Equipment

Two basic operations are involved in collecting information about business transactions and recording it in the appropriate accounts:

(1) *Listing*, or writing the descriptive information such as the date, a reference to the source document, and the amount.
(2) *Adding or subtracting* the amounts.

The simplest type of accounting equipment has only *one register;* that is, it is capable of accumulating only one total at a time. Such a machine is suitable for relatively simple bookkeeping operations.

Example 6　A bookkeeping machine with a single *vertical* register may be used for recording transactions in the sales journal illustrated earlier in this chapter. The process would consist of recording a date, brief descriptive information or reference, and an amount for each sale. At the end of a "run," or continuous series of entries journalized at one time, the machine provides a total which can be recorded in the journal, avoiding the necessity of adding the transaction amounts in a separate operation.

Accounting equipment which has *two or more registers* can be used to accumulate the totals of several columns at a time. Several registers which accumulate *vertical* totals would be appropriate for recording entries in a multi-columnar journal.

A machine which has a *horizontal register* (a "crossfooter") may be used to compute the difference between debits and credits on a single line. Such a machine is especially useful in posting items to an account and at the same time computing the new balance of the account.

Example 7　A machine with a crossfooter can be used to post debits for sales on account to each customer's account in the Accounts Receivable subsidiary ledger. The previous balance is recorded in the machine, the debit for the current transaction is recorded, and the machine then computes the ending balance. A similar approach can be used for posting credits.

A machine with a crossfooter is especially useful to banks, which need current balances of their depositors' accounts.

Machines with several registers can be used to post transactions and compute account balances, at the same time accumulating the total debits and total credits to several different accounts.

Some types of electromechanical accounting equipment are *semiautomatic,* being designed to print a total when the operator presses the proper key. Still others print totals or move from one stage of operation to the next *automatically* on the basis of instructions built into the machine or its attachments.

Electromechanical machines increase the accuracy and legibility of accounting records, as well as the speed with which the work is done. They facilitate *proofs* of the accuracy of journalizing and posting. They also can perform several stages of accounting work with one writing, such as the preparation of an original source document, journal, and ledger.

Punched-Card Equipment

Recording the details of accounting transactions in the appropriate accounts and reports consists of three basic stages:

(1) *Recording* transaction information on a source document.
(2) *Classifying* the information on the source document according to the accounts affected.
(3) *Summarizing* the resulting account balances.

Punched-card equipment completes these stages accurately, automatically, and at high speed. It is also useful for recording, classifying, and summarizing statistical data other than accounting data.

(1) *Recording information.* Transaction information is *recorded* on a *punched card* of standardized size and shape, like that illustrated in Illustration 9-4. Instead of being written or printed, alphabetical and numerical information is shown on the card by means of *punched holes*. Each card has from 80 to 90

Illustration 9-4

columns in which information can be punched. One or more columns is used to record each class of information. For example, the first 12 columns might be used to record the *customer's name* and the next 6, to record the *amount of a sale*. A number is recorded by a single punch in a column; a letter is recorded by a combination of two punches. The machine "reads" the data punched on the card by means of impulses which the card causes as it passes through the machine. Cards can be handled at a rate of from hundreds to thousands per minute.

The *punched card* may be the *original source document* of a transaction. A common example is the use of punched cards for *payment by check*. In other cases the information on various sizes and shapes of source documents, such as *purchase invoices*, is *transferred* to punched cards. Such a procedure is followed when a business uses a *bank service center* or other data-processing center to process the information needed in preparing reports and other records.

Several punched cards may be needed to record the information contained on a single source document. For example, a separate card may be required for *each account* to be debited for the purchase, and another card may be required for the total credit to Accounts Payable.

The machine used to punch the cards is operated by a keyboard similar to that of a typewriter. Cards can also be punched automatically as copies of other cards, or as by-products of other machine operations.

(2) *Classifying information.* To obtain totals of the effects of transactions, the information contained on the punched cards is classified according to the individual accounts affected. The purpose is the same as that of *journal entries* in a manual record-keeping system. To simplify or speed processing, the unit records are grouped in like transactions by passing them through a *sorter*. This has the effect of grouping transactions in the same way journal entries are grouped in special journals.

(3) *Summarizing information.* The information on the punched cards, classified by accounts affected, can be summarized by passing the cards through a *tabulator*. An electrically wired control panel gives the tabulator a variety of instructions, such as to *list* items, to *select* items of a given type, to *add*, and to *subtract*. The usual accounting records and reports can be prepared by the tabulator as follows:

(a) A *journal*, such as a sales journal, is printed by passing all the punched cards for the sales of a period through the tabulator, which lists each item and obtains a total. Sometimes the machine is instructed to accumulate details but to *print only totals*.

(b) An *accounts receivable subsidiary ledger* can be printed by passing the punched cards for sales and those for cash collections on account, sorted by customer, through the tabulator. The tabulator can print a ledger account and a customer's statement in the same operation.

(c) *General ledger accounts* can be posted by passing *summary cards*, containing the total debits and credits for each batch of sales, collections, and other transactions, through the tabulator.

(d) A general ledger trial balance and financial statements can be printed by passing *balance cards* for each account, obtained in step (c), through the tabulator.

The information on a single set of punched cards can be used to accumulate several different types of records. In the preceding outline, cards for each sale were used on successive runs through the sorting and tabulating equipment to prepare the *sales journal* and the *accounts receivable ledger*. If they were punched to provide information as to *salesman* and *geographical area*, successive runs could also summarize sales by salesman and by region.

Electronic Equipment

Electronic computers are designed to receive a mass of *input* data, store it for future use, perform arithmetic operations upon it, make logical decisions regarding it, and supply the information, or *output*, which results from these operations, all at a very high rate of speed. Thus, there are four major elements of an electronic data-processing system: (1) *input*, (2) *information storage*, (3) *processing*, and (4) *output*.

The *input* to the system is composed of the same type of information that provides the basic transaction data for a manual bookkeeping system, but much more detail is usually fed into the computer. This is possible because of the enormous information storage capacity of the electronic system. Data must be fed into the processing operation at high speed in order to use the computer's capability efficiently. *Punched cards*, which must be moved through the equipment physically, slow down the processing operation. Far superior as an input medium is plastic *tape*, which contains the data as magnetic impulses.

Recently great progress has taken place in using the basic document itself as the input. This is made possible by having the basic document prepunched on an input card, or by using *magnetic printing* which permits the computer to "read" the necessary information. Examples of the use of magnetic printing are found on gasoline station charge slips for credit card sales and on special numbers printed on the checks and deposit slips used by some banks.

Great strides are also being made in the use of *optical scanners* which can read printed and handwritten numbers and letters and create the input without requiring the preparation of an intermediate punched card or input tape. Further refinement of these scanners will decrease bookkeeping effort and increase data-processing possibilities for many medium-sized and large businesses. Already some of the scanners are being used in the transportation industry to provide the "direct input" into the accounting system.

A recent development in the recording of transactions is described in the following quotation from the May 1971 issue of *Fortune*:

> A cash register with a brain, the NCR 280 data terminal rings up sales, keeps inventory totals current, and checks on customers' credit. National Cash Register's is one of several such systems now on the market. Price tags on merchandise are electronically coded, and when a pen-sized device is waved over the tag and a button on the 280 punched, the machine records the transaction, totals it, even computes the sales tax. If it is a charge sale, the clerk holds the same device over the credit card, which is also coded; the 280 verifies the customer's credit before recording the charge.

Once accounting data have been introduced into the computer, they are *stored* until needed for the preparation of financial statements or for processing.

Information storage is often called the *"memory"* element of the data-processing system. It is physically accomplished by recording the information on magnetic tapes, drums, or discs similar to oversized phonograph records. Literally millions of bits of information can be stored in the memory of the system.

Example 8   At Norton Air Force Base, San Bernardino, California, there are more than 15,000 magnetic tapes in a tape "library" which contains stored information. As each 2,400-foot tape has a storage capacity of 800 characters per inch, there are theoretically more than 3.4 billion pieces of information available to management for information and decision-making purposes.

The arithmetical and logical operations of the computer are performed in the *processing* element of the system. The processing which takes place is determined by a set of instructions called a *program*, which is fed into the machine by the operator. The equipment will perform all the necessary processing steps as called for by the program, *selecting the data* from storage, *adjusting the data* when necessary, and either *returning the new information into storage* or *creating a report* based on the processed information. This processing takes place at extremely high speeds, often in excess of several thousand computations per second. The efficiency and quality of the processing operation are largely determined by the program of instructions, which is fed into the equipment either directly through a keyboard or through tape or punched cards. Programs which are to be used frequently are stored in the computer's memory for recall when needed.

Underlying most computer programs is the preparation of a *flow chart* or block diagram, which permits the person creating the program to break down the operation into simple and logical steps. An example of a flow chart for processing information on inventory is shown in Illustration 9-5 on p. 235.

The output of the electronic data-processing system is usually in the form of a printed report, a bill to send to customers, a check, a new journal, or some other form needed by the business. High-speed printers can print out in excess of 1,000 lines per minute.

The advantages of using electronic data-processing equipment are not gained without sustaining some disadvantages. Most electronic equipment is very costly, and rapid advances in technology create a high rate of obsolescence. The speeds and capacities of computers have been increasing at a geometric rate for a number of years, for little increase in the costs of equipment. To assist in combating the rapid obsolescence, many businesses lease equipment rather than purchase it. Problems sometimes arise in the installation and use of the equipment, either because of poor planning or because the personnel and the structure of the business are not readily adaptable to the new processing facilities. To solve this problem, many managers contract with independent businesses whose sole purpose is to provide processing facilities to others. These businesses, called *"service centers,"* charge for their processing services on the basis of actual time spent. These services are particularly useful for small and medium-sized businesses.

A problem also arises with regard to *internal control*. Electronic data-processing equipment has made internal control more complex, yet more important than ever. This happens because the data-processing department comprises in one section of the organization the accounting functions which were formerly divided among many employees. For example, the same person might run the programs for posting to the general ledger and for writing checks; thus collusion would not be necessary in order to defraud the company. Auditors have been quite concerned because of this lack of separation of duties. They have also been concerned because the direct input of financial data into a computer, without the creation of an intervening visible record of the transaction, makes verification of reported financial information more difficult.

These problems of internal control have been largely solved through (1) the use of programs with built-in cross checks, (2) the use of control or "dummy" transactions or programs, and (3) increased attention to the proper segregation of duties among employees. Separation of responsibility for writing programs, running them, and storing them is an important internal control procedure. In addition, the employees responsible for the data-processing function are usually removed from the actual authorizing or originating of transactions, so that a built-in control exists.

Selection of Accounting Machines

As might be expected, the cost of accounting machines increases somewhat in proportion to the increase in the complexity of the information which they can process and the efficiency with which they can process it.

The selection of accounting machines, like that of all other parts of the accounting system, must be made by *balancing* two opposing factors: (1) the *effectiveness* of the machine in doing the particular job and (2) the *cost* of getting the job done. Although the most advanced designs of electronic computers can usually accomplish a given task more quickly than can other types of equipment, they are not appropriate except for handling a relatively large volume of data.

At the other end of the scale, some businesses may not need any accounting equipment at all, although usually they can appropriately use some of the time-saving methods of keeping manual records.

Other factors which should be considered in selecting particular accounting methods, in addition to the quantity of source data and the cost of processing the information, are the nature of the information needed, the safeguards and proofs which are needed, and the quality of the personnel who are available to do the work.

Use of Computers in Improving Management

In the early years of the computer most companies used it to improve the quality and reduce the cost of *clerical work*. Now that many firms have achieved this goal, they are giving greater attention to utilizing the computer in *improving managerial effectiveness*. Toan[2] advances the idea that

> . . . *with a satisfactory degree of effectiveness in straight data processing, it should be possible to improve the effectiveness with which corporate resources are employed. It should be*

---

[2] Arthur B. Toan, Jr., "Current Concepts in the Uses of Computers," *Price Waterhouse Review*, Vol. XII, No. 1, Spring, 1967, p. 43.

possible with better, faster, more accurate working documents and information to carry out basic policies and more routine day-to-day operations with increased efficiency, greater profits and a greater volume of business per dollar of assets employed. With faster, more complete, more accurate information, it should be possible:

(1) to handle a given volume of sales with a lower inventory and a shorter production/delivery cycle;

(2) to attain a higher percentage of on-time deliveries;

(3) to reduce interruption, expediting, short-run and other emergency costs;

(4) to schedule men and machines to a higher percent of their productive capacity;

(5) to decrease losses from obsolescence or from the unsaleability of products;

(6) to improve product quality, reduce manufacturing defects, etc.

He observes that many firms in the United States have obtained these objectives, at least in part, by having more accurate and more complete information available more rapidly.

The most recent and most highly developed computer systems are the *real-time systems*, where there is an instantaneous response in the communication network to any physical transaction at the time when it occurs. This approach is used in the more advanced airline reservation systems, as well as in the control of missiles and in space exploration.

Illustration of a Computer Application in Inventory[3]

Colorama Electronics Corp., Inc., produces various types of electronic assemblies in a single factory. The firm's inventories of $3.6 million at year end represent 67 per cent of total assets. Raw materials and supplies consist of about 20,000 different components. At present a manual perpetual inventory record-keeping system is in use, but the tremendous volume of clerical work has caused the company to consider installing a computer.

The volume of activity in the Raw Materials and Supplies Inventory system alone consists of the following:

	Volume (average)
Inputs:	
Purchase orders	450 line items daily
Material received reports	450 line items daily
Vendors' invoices.............................	450 line items daily
Issued requisitions	3,500 daily (single item)
Master files, requiring updating:	
Inventory master file..........................	20,000 items
Open-order master file	1,000 orders
	3,000 items

---

[3] Adapted by permission of the American Institute of Certified Public Accountants and Lybrand, Ross Bros. & Montgomery.

Outputs:
Daily:
   (1) Open-order variance report
      (a) Quantity variances on material
          received reports ....   30 items
      (b) Price and quantity variances on
          vendors' invoices ....   20 items
   (2) Shortage report (new purchase
          order requests, etc.)...............   800 items
   (3) Priced issues report....................   750 items
Weekly:
   (1) Report of
      (a) Lead time variances
      (b) Overdue deliveries...............   1,300 items (total)
   (2) Complete inventory status report...   20,000 items

Illustration 9-5 is a *flow chart* showing how the daily output of the Raw Materials and Supplies Inventory system might be accomplished on a computer. An explanation of the daily processing steps follows.

Run 1 reads the input cards and writes the data on tape.

Run 2 sorts the data according to transaction code number, inventory item number, and order number.

Run 3 updates the *Open-Order Master File* as follows:

(1) Purchase orders create a new record for each order.

(2) Quantity of goods received is compared with quantity ordered and an *exception report* is printed if the two quantities differ by more than 10 per cent. An *exception variance report* is also printed out if the goods have been previously received. The open-order record in the Master File is updated to show the receipt of goods.

(3) Prices and quantities on the supplier's invoices are compared with master file data and discrepancies are printed out on the exception report.

Run 4 sorts the transaction tape into transaction code sequence within each inventory item number.

Run 5 updates the Inventory Master File as to *on hand, on order,* and *available balances,* as to *issues* for the quarter to date, and as to *average unit price.* The on-hand and on-order status are examined to determine whether a replenishment purchase order is needed. If so, information for this order is printed on the *Shortage Report,* together with data for all items which have fallen below the safety level.

Run 6 reads the priced issues tape and sorts it into numerical sequence for Production Orders or Research Projects. On the final pass, the high-speed printer produces the *Priced Issues Report.*

Summary   The accounting information system must provide timely, relevant, and reliable information to aid decision making at all levels of management, in addition to meeting the needs of outsiders.

Accounting is a process of *condensing* and *summarizing* numerous enterprise transactions and presenting the results in such a way that they can be under-

**Illustration
9-5**

COLORAMA ELECTRONICS CORP., INC.
Flow Chart of Inventory System

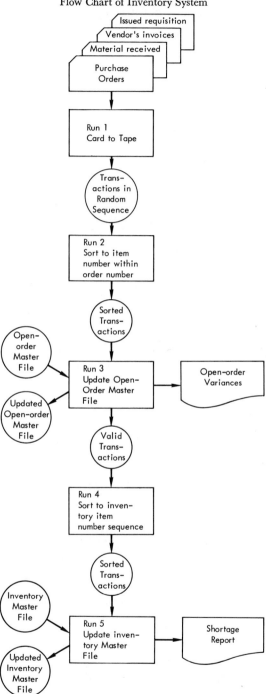

Adapted by permission of the American Institute of Certified Public Accountants and Lybrand, Ross Bros. & Montgomery.

stood and used by those who are concerned with enterprise affairs. The steps in the condensation and summarization process, referred to as the *accounting cycle*, are preparation of source documents, recording journal entries, posting to ledger accounts, and preparation of a trial balance, a work sheet, and financial statements.

The transactions of each business usually are of relatively few types, some of which recur with high frequency. Manual as well as machine methods are available for saving time and increasing accuracy in each step of accounting.

Some of the manual methods consist of preparing several records at a single writing, using special journals for transactions of a given type, using special columns for accounts which are frequently debited or credited, summarizing information according to batches and journalizing the batch total, and omitting journals or ledgers altogether.

Types of machines available range from the electromechanical bookkeeping machine with a single register to multiple-register machines, punched-card equipment, and, ultimately, electronic equipment.

The methods and machines appropriate in a given case depend on the nature of the information required, the volume of raw data to be processed, the controls needed by management, the ability of the accounting personnel, and the cost of obtaining the information by the particular method or machine.

Discussion Questions and Problems

9-1   One of the first steps of an audit engagement is an extensive review of the adequacy of the client's system of internal control. To a large degree, the extent to which the auditor makes a detailed examination of the client's record of transactions is based on his findings regarding internal control. Why is so much emphasis placed on this facet of a business?

9-2   One of the most dramatic purposes of an internal control system is in making fraud harder to commit and easier to detect. Other important functions are often overlooked.

a. What other purposes does a system of internal control have? Give specific illustrations of how each of these purposes might be accomplished.
b. Does internal control apply to assets other than cash? To liabilities? Explain.

9-3   After recommending that his client install a cash register, an auditor was aghast to see several employees ringing up sales on it. "Why, you might as well use a cigar box!" he exclaimed.

a. Why did the auditor object?
b. What division of duties would you recommend to overcome his objection?
c. In buying a cash register how should the client have planned if several employees were required to ring up sales on it?

9-4   The town of Millvale erected a toll bridge across a river which passed through the town. Because of the small amount of revenue expected from tolls, one councilman argued that the town could only afford to have one employee at a time collecting them.

a. What weaknesses are there in this arrangement?
b. From the standpoint of internal control, what would be the advantages of having two employees?
c. How might mechanical devices help solve this problem?

9-5   Large businesses often have elaborate systems of internal control, internal auditing departments, and annual audits by Certified Public Accountants.

a. Are these measures sufficient to prevent error, fraud, and waste in the use of business resources? Explain.
b. Describe some practical, inexpensive methods by which the owner of a small business which has four employees can secure effective control over receipts and payments of cash and over receipts and issues of inventory items.

9-6   In Example 3 of this chapter it was stated, "The mail clerk has an opportunity to take money, but he cannot conceal the shortage because he has no access to the accounting records."

a. Under what circumstances could he take money without being detected?
b. How would you prevent it?

9-7

a. What is the purpose of having the cash register tape locked in the register?
b. Why do cafeterias often have one employee at the end of the serving line to prepare a charge ticket, and another at the exit to collect money? Are any purposes other than prevention of dishonesty involved in this practice?
c. Why should the auditor or chief accountant be concerned if one of the following numbered forms is missing?

   (1) Check.
   (2) Cash receipt.
   (3) Sales invoice.
   (4) Receiving report for incoming merchandise.

9-8   Special journals and accounting machines are important in condensing and summarizing financial data. How can these methods also be used to improve the system of safeguarding and efficiently managing the firm's assets?

9-9

a. Explain the difference between a *special* journal and a *general* journal.
b. What is meant by a *controlling* account? Give an example and explain how it operates.
c. How does a business decide what special journals to use? What special columns in these journals?

9-10   It was suggested in this chapter that before posting to the general ledger the equality of the debit and credit column totals in a multicolumnar journal should be proved. Suppose that this was not done, and that the total of a column in the Cash Receipts Journal was incorrectly added by $100.

a. How would this error first be discovered?
b. What steps would normally be followed to find the cause of the error?
c. Would there be any way that the error would be discovered through the operation of the routine system of internal control if the incorrect total was in the Cash Debit column? In the Accounts Receivable Credit column? In the Sales Revenue Credit column? In the Miscellaneous Accounts columns? Explain.

9-11   The management of the Dill Company, a large hardware store, wishes to know the amount of gross margin on the firm's three classes of merchandise. The goods, designated as class 1, 2, and 3, are sold for cash and are supplied by a large number of manufacturers and distributors. The company keeps its accounting records by hand.

a. What special journals would you recommend for Dill?

b. Explain specifically how the need for gross-margin information would affect your design of the company's classification of accounts and its journals.

9-12   A retail automobile dealer sold new and used cars and also did motor and body repair work. The dealer sold about 30 cars a month and received in exchange installment notes receivable with terms ranging from 3 to 36 months. As a rule there were also about 20 repair orders a day, of which about one-fourth were for cash. The dealer's bookkeeper opened a ledger page for each automobile purchaser and repair customer. She copied information from the invoices in the customers' ledger accounts and also sent each repair customer an itemized monthly statement.

a. What controlling and subsidiary accounts seem to be appropriate in this situation?

b. What special journals, and with what columns, would you recommend?

c. Other than the purchase of a bookkeeping machine, what time-saving procedures would you suggest?

9-13   A wholesaler uses the following books of original entry:

Cash Receipts Journal   Sales Journal
Cash Payments Journal   Sales Returns and Allowances Journal
Purchases Journal   General Journal

List the types of entries that you would expect to find in its General Journal.

9-14   A retail business has used a single-column sales journal, kept manually, to record sales on account. The number of sales has increased to such an extent that this procedure has become cumbersome, yet the company does not feel that it can afford a machine. Describe two ways in which this company can save time in collecting information about sales and accounts receivable.

9-15   The Carol Company uses, among other journals, a single-column Purchases Journal and a single-column Purchase Returns and Allowances Journal, as well as a Cash Payments Journal with a special column for Accounts Payable, Debit. It occasionally gives promissory notes to creditors for past-due accounts.

a. Describe in detail the procedure for posting to the Accounts Payable controlling account and subsidiary ledger.

b. If the list of subsidiary ledger account balances at the end of the month does not agree with the controlling account balance, what steps would you take to look for the error?

c. Why might it be desirable to add the totals of the single-column journals twice (or to check the adding machine tapes carefully)?

9-16

a. Describe the procedure for posting the following General Journal entry of a business which uses an Accounts Receivable controlling account and an Accounts Receivable subsidiary ledger.

1973

Apr. 22   A, Notes Receivable 300
               A, Accounts Receivable/Smith Co. ...   300
           Received a promissory note from the
           Smith Co. for their past-due account.

b. Suggest two ways the journals might be effectively redesigned if there were many such transactions.

c. What type of subsidiary record would you recommend for the promissory notes if they required (1) only one payment of principal and interest, or (2) many installment payments?

9-17   The National Company is a large wholesaler of flowers and candies, dealing with about 500 customers and 75 suppliers. It makes extensive use of special journals, including the following:

> Purchases Journal with one money column
> Sales Journal with one money column
> Cash Receipts Journal with four money columns
> Cash Disbursements Journal with four money columns
> Sales Returns and Allowances Journal with one money column

For each journal specify the most likely use of the special columns, naming the account(s) affected and indicating whether debit or credit.

9-18   The Wilson Department Store makes sales on account and for cash, sales being divided about equally between the two. Cash sales are recorded on cash registers, while charge slips are prepared for sales on account.

Four journals are used besides the General Journal. Both the Sales and the Purchases Journal have one column. The Cash Receipts Journal has the following columns:

> Accounts Receivable, Credit
> Cash, Debit
> Miscellaneous Debit and Credit

The Cash Payments Journal has the following columns:

> Accounts Payable, Debit
> Cash, Credit
> Miscellaneous Debit and Credit

Required   State in which journal (if any) each of the following transactions would be recorded.

(1) Capital stock is issued for $100,000 cash.
(2) An account receivable of $25 is collected.
(3) Goods are bought on credit for $1,000.
(4) Defective goods costing $100 are returned to the supplier for credit.
(5) Cash sales for the day total $500.
(6) A sale of $50 is made on account.
(7) Wrapping supplies are purchased for $100 cash.
(8) The utility bill for the month, $125, arrives.
(9) A $15 cash refund is given to a customer for merchandise returned by him.
(10) A $200 promissory note is received from a customer who owes a past-due account.
(11) A $25 account receivable is written off as uncollectible.
(12) A customer is allowed full credit, $40, for returned merchandise previously sold to him on account.
(13) Paid $800 cash for merchandise previously bought on account.

9-19   A business with 500 active charge accounts now keeps its Accounts Receivable subsidiary ledger in pen and ink. It is considering the purchase of a bookkeeping machine.

a. Will the machine improve the accuracy of posting? Explain.
b. What other advantages is the machine likely to provide?

9-20   By preparing several accounting records at one writing the bookkeeper can save time while minimizing errors in recording.

a. How can this be done in connection with the accounts receivable of a small firm which does not own an accounting machine?
b. Explain how errors can be reduced for the accounts receivable records of a medium-sized company which owns electromechanical equipment.
c. How can it be done for the accounts receivable of a large company owning punched-card equipment?

9-21   A medium-sized hospital employs a chief accountant and four office clerks, one of whom devotes full time to maintaining patients' accounts receivable records by hand and to typing periodic statements of account for the patient or his insurance company. This work is especially time-consuming because charges to patients are of 16 different types, some of which are made several times during a single illness. The accounts receivable subsidiary ledger is rarely in agreement with the controlling account, and the bookkeeper often spends hours looking for errors.

Required a. Outline some of the advantages that this hospital could expect from the use of an electronic bookkeeping machine.
b. What are some of the problems that could be anticipated in installing such a machine?
c. What types of cost would be reduced and what types would be increased if the machine were installed?

9-22   A manufacturer of children's toys is considering installing an electronic data-processing system to perform the accounting and inventory control procedures he feels necessary. Several of the companies which sell and lease computers have discussed the matter with him and recommended a "feasibility study."

a. As president, what would you expect a "feasibility study" to accomplish?
b. What factors should you consider in choosing one of the various computer systems?
c. What are the advantages of leasing equipment instead of purchasing it? What are the advantages of purchasing?

9-23   "Punched-card and electronic equipment not only make it possible to do the routine accounting work more rapidly; they also permit a business to gather useful information which it might not be feasible to collect by manual methods." Give an example of one type of such information and explain how it would be used.

9-24   It has been pointed out that internal control becomes more complex and important when an electronic data-processing system is installed.

a. Which elements of an internal control system are strengthened when an EDP system is installed? Which are weakened?
b. How can a computer program be adjusted or constructed in such a manner as to provide built-in controls?
c. What new problems arise for auditors in evaluating an EDP system?

9-25   This chapter has pointed out that the four major elements of an electronic data-processing system are input, information storage, processing, and output.

a. What are the equivalent elements of a manual accounting system?
b. What is a "program" and how does it enter into the data-processing system?

9-26   The Winfred Company does not keep a general ledger record or subsidiary accounts for accounts payable during the accounting period. Instead, when an invoice is received it is filed according to due date, which is usually within ten days. When an invoice is paid during the same month, the company debits the appropriate asset or expense account and credits Cash. At the end of each accounting period unpaid invoices are recorded in the general journal, summarized according to accounts debited, and credited to Accounts Payable.

a. How does this differ from the procedure under a manual accounting system? Be specific.
b. What advantages and weaknesses does Winfred's method have?
c. If the typical payment were made 30 days rather than 10 days after receipt of the invoice, would the method be equally desirable? Explain.

9-27   The Marginal Company keeps a pen-and-ink Sales Journal with the following money columns: Accounts Receivable Debit, Sales Department A Credit, Sales Department B Credit, and Sales Tax Payable Credit. The company makes about 100 sales on account each month.

Required a. Record the sales transactions as though they were all the sales on account of the company during the month of November 1973.

Invoice #1105	Nov. 1, 1973
Sold to: J. E. Dawson	
Items: Dept. A	$200.00
Dept. B	20.00
Sales tax	6.60
Total	$226.60

Invoice #1106	Nov. 1, 1973
Sold to: N. K. Barnes Co.	
Items: Dept. A	$600.00
Sales tax	18.00
Total	$618.00

Invoice #1107	Nov. 1, 1973
Sold to: Magic Motors	
Items: Dept. A	$150.00
Dept. B	300.00
Sales tax	13.50
Total	$463.50

Invoice #1108	Nov. 2, 1973
Sold to: Monroe, Inc.	
Items: Dept. A	$900.00
Dept. B	50.00
Sales tax	28.50
Total	$978.50

Invoice #1109	Nov. 2, 1973
Sold to: Adams Mfg. Co.	
Items: Dept. B	$800.00
Sales tax	24.00
Total	$824.00

Invoice #1110	Nov. 2, 1973
Sold to: City of Wilkes	
Items: Dept. A	$500.00
(Tax-exempt)	

b. Describe the posting procedure that is necessary for individual items.
c. Total the journal, and describe the necessary end-of-month posting procedure.
d. The company's policy has been to absorb the cost of freight on shipments. What account should be charged? If it changes this policy to one of charging transportation cost to the customer, what modifications would you recommend in the Sales Journal?
e. What manual bookkeeping methods would you suggest if the sales invoices numbered 500 a month?

9-28   The Akins Co. maintains the following books of original entry (among others which are not relevant to this problem):

(1) *Purchases Journal* with a single column. (Only merchandise purchased on account is recorded in this journal.)

(2) *Cash Payments Journal* with money columns for Miscellaneous Accounts, Debit and Credit; Accounts Payable Debit; Accrued Wages Payable Debit; and Cash Credit.

(3) *General Journal* with one debit column and one credit column.

After closing entries for the fiscal year ended April 30, 1973, were made, the credit balance in the Accounts Payable controlling account was $9,000. The subsidiary ledger contained a separate ledger page showing the date, posting reference, debit amounts, credit amounts, and balance of each creditor's account. The balances on April 30, 1973, were as follows:

	Debit	Credit
Barker Co..		$1,500
Darron Sales Corp................................		400
Fryer, M. J..	$ 200	
N-T Products.....................................		2,500
Odell, James......................................		4,000
Warren, M. E.....................................		800
Totals..	$ 200	$9,200

Required

a. Enter the April 30 balances of the controlling and subsidiary ledger accounts in ledger account forms. Also record a beginning balance of $14,000 in Cash, $5,900 in Capital Stock, and $900 in Accounts Receivable.

b. Journalize the transactions listed below in the appropriate journals.

c. Post to the appropriate general ledger and subsidiary ledger accounts.

d. Prepare a trial balance of the resulting general ledger accounts and a schedule of Accounts Payable subsidiary ledger balances.

e. If transactions of the types illustrated were five times as frequent during a month, what modifications of these journals would you recommend?

Transactions:

May   1—Paid the Barker Co. balance in cash.

1—Gave James Odell a 30-day, 6 per cent promissory note for the balance owed him.

2—Returned to N-T Products unsatisfactory merchandise billed at $800. Paid freight of $40 on the return shipment. The Akins Co. mailed N-T Products a debit memorandum for $840 for the two items described.

3—Purchased merchandise costing $2,000 from the Barker Co.

4—Received merchandise from M. J. Fryer listed at $700.

7—Received a credit memorandum of $840 from N-T Products for the items returned on May 2.

8—Purchased delivery equipment on account from the Mansfield Equipment Co., $800. Payment is due in 30 days.

9—M. E. Warren owed the Akins Co. $900 for merchandise which had been sold to him and properly recorded in April. Both agreed to apply Mr. Warren's account against the balance owed by the Akins Co., and Mr. Warren mailed a check for the difference.

11—Paid the Barker Co. invoice of May 3 in full.

12—Purchased merchandise of a list price of $500 from Darron Sales Corp.

18—Purchased merchandise of a list price of $400 from M. E. Warren; terms, net 30 days, f.o.b. destination. Paid transportation charges of $10 by check.

20—Returned unsatisfactory merchandise having a list price of $200, received on May 12, to Darron Sales Corp.

31—Paid the note due Odell.

31—The monthly payroll consisted of gross salaries of $1,200. Deductions were $125 for employees' payroll taxes.

The company follows the practice of recording the accrual of the payroll in the General Journal. It draws one check for the net amount to be paid the employees, fills pay envelopes, and records the payment in the Cash Payments Journal.

9-29 The Jarrett Corporation uses the following books of original entry, among others:

(1) *Sales Journal* with a single money column.

(2) *Cash Receipts Journal* with money columns for Miscellaneous Accounts, Debit and Credit; Accounts Receivable Credit; Sales Credit; and Cash Debit.

(3) *General Journal* with two columns.

At the beginning of the year, on January 1, 1973, the general ledger contained the following balances:

Cash	$9,000	Accounts payable................	$ 4,500
Accounts receivable...............	7,500	Capital stock	12,200
Accounts receivable—		Retained income.................	600
estimated uncollectibles	400	Merchandise inventory..........	1,200

The balances in the Accounts Receivable subsidiary ledger were

	Debit	Credit
Adams, R. J...	$ 500	
Canling Co.	500	
Foster Mfg. Co.....................................		$ 50
Luttrell Distributors.............................	3,000	
Makin, Inc.	2,500	
Zamar Sales Corp.	1,050	

Required a. Enter the January 1 balances of the general and subsidiary ledgers in ledger-account forms. Use three-column accounts for the subsidiary ledger.

b. Journalize the transactions listed below in the appropriate journals.

c. Post to the appropriate general ledger and subsidary ledger accounts.

d. Prepare a trial balance of the resulting general ledger and a schedule of the Accounts Receivable subsidiary ledger balances.

e. If transactions of the types illustrated were five times as frequent during a month, what modifications of these journals would you recommend?

Transactions:

Jan. 2—Collected the balance due from R. J. Adams.

3—Makin, Inc. returned unsatisfactory merchandise which had been billed to them at $400 and sent a check for $1,000 to apply on their account.

4—Cash sales totaled $2,700.

5—Received a 20-day, 6 per cent promissory note from Luttrell Distributors for the full amount of their balance.

Jan. 6—Sold merchandise on account to Makin, Inc.; list price, $2,000. Cash sales for the day totaled $1,825.

7—Sold merchandise on account to Dale Co., $575.

8—Sold merchandise on account to Foster Mfg. Co., $895. Sold merchandise on account to Luttrell Distributors for $400.

9—Cash sales totaled $1,050.

10—Received a check for $100 from a manufacturer to help defray the cost of advertising his product locally.

11—Issued additional capital stock of $1,000 par value for $1,200 cash.

12—The collection agent who had been engaged to collect the balance due from the Canling Co. reported that he had collected $250 from them, and that the remainder was uncollectible. He sent a check for $225, the sum collected minus his fee.

16—Collected the full amount due from Makin, Inc., for the sale of January 6.

17—Collected the amount due from Foster Mfg. Co., after deducting the amount of their overpayment shown by the January 1 balance.

18—Cash sales totaled $1,675.

19—Received a refund check of $200 from the Shoal Mfg. Co. for merchandise returned to them for credit. No entry had been made at the time the merchandise was returned.

25—Collected the note of January 5 from Luttrell Distributors, including $10 interest.

26—Sold merchandise on account to Luttrell Distributors for $500. Sold merchandise on account to Makin, Inc. for $650.

31—Collected the full amount due from Dale Co.

9-30   Gail's DoNut Shop made all its sales and purchases for cash. The following journals were used:

(1) *Cash Receipts Journal*, with columns for Miscellaneous Accounts, Debit and Credit; Sales Credit; and Cash Debit.

(2) *Cash Payments Journal*, with columns for Miscellaneous Accounts, Debit and Credit; Materials and Supplies Debit; Salaries Debit; Payroll Taxes Payable Credit; and Cash Credit.

(3) *General Journal* with two money columns.

Required   a. Journalize the following selected transactions for July 1973.

b. Total and summarize the journals and describe the posting procedure in detail.

Transactions:

July 1—Collected $140 for cash sales.

2—Paid $150 for food materials to be used in making doughnuts.

5—Received a refund of $300 for income taxes erroneously assessed against the corporation in 1970.

6—Cash collections for sales were $220.

7—Bought a new piece of kitchen equipment on credit for $600. Made a cash down payment of $100.

8—The cash register tape showed sales of $80, but the cash in the register totaled only $77.

9—Paid $60 for food materials and $20 for paper supplies sufficient to last about a week.

12—Threw away spoiled food materials which had cost about $20. A periodic inventory is taken at the end of the month, when the inventory account is adjusted to show the actual cost of materials on hand.

July 13—Gave a check for $25 for an advertisement in the high school newspaper.

19—Paid cash of $104 for food materials.

21—Paid property taxes for the calendar year, $120.

22—Cash sales totaled $150.

24—Paid $180 for food materials.

27—Returned spoiled food for credit, $30. No refund was received at this time.

28—Paid rent for the month of July, $120.

29—Paid $50 for repairs to the parking lot pavement.

30—Sold additional capital stock for $1,050 cash. Its par value was $1,000.

31—Paid a cash dividend of $250.

31—Depreciation on equipment for the month was $50.

31—A physical inventory showed that unused food materials costing $54 were on hand.

31—Paid salaries of $2,000 earned by employees for the month. From this $200 was deducted for payroll taxes.

Adjustments are journalized monthly. You may ignore adjustments other than those specifically mentioned.

Cases

9-1   Dimple Department Store. The Dimple Department Store, located in a four-story building, had 23 sales departments. Its accounting work was done by the chief accountant, the accounts receivable bookkeeper, the accounts payable bookkeeper, and the cashier, all of whom were located in the accounting office on the second floor.

Through a pneumatic-tube system, the cashier received the duplicates of the cash sales tickets, together with the money. She returned any necessary change to the salesclerk through the tube system. She also received duplicate copies of charge sales tickets through the tube system. During lulls in activity she ran adding-machine lists of cash sales and charge sales, in total and by departments. This information was then given to the chief accountant, who recorded the total sales for the day in the Sales Journal and the Cash Receipts Journal. The former journal contained the following columns: Cash Debit, Accounts Receivable Debit, Sales Credit, and a departmental Sales Credit column for each of the 23 departments. The Cash Debit column was not posted, because it duplicated information contained in the Cash Receipts Journal. Among other columns, the Cash Receipts Journal contained columns for Cash Debit, Accounts Receivable Credit, and Sales Credit. The use of the memorandum Cash Debit column in the Sales Journal permitted the entire analysis of sales by departments to be summarized in that journal.

The accounts receivable bookkeeper received the daily batch of duplicate charge sales tickets, together with the total as determined by the tube cashier. Then she posted the charges to the subsidiary accounts of the approximately 5,000 charge customers by using a bookkeeping machine. Her machine accumulated the total of postings to the debit side of individual customers' accounts; it was necessary for this figure to agree with the adding-machine total of daily charge slips. Posting of all types required about six hours a day of the accounts receivable bookkeeper's time.

The accounts payable bookkeeper received the original purchase invoices from the receiving departments, which had verified the type, quantity, and quality of incoming goods. The bookkeeper then prepared an adding-machine list of the day's invoices, using the total as a proof figure to verify the accuracy of posting to the accounts payable subsidiary ledger. She also listed each invoice in a columnar pen-and-ink Purchases Journal, with columns for purchases of each of the 23 departments and a total column. The chief accountant posted this journal to the general ledger monthly. The accounts payable bookkeeper then posted credits by machine to the individual creditors' accounts, which were kept on separate sheets in a tray. Her regular work usually required about five hours a day.

The chief accountant journalized the Cash Receipts, Cash Payments, and General Journals, and did all posting to the general ledger. He prepared financial statements monthly, prepared the store's tax returns, supervised the work of the accounting office, and handled special problems.

Mail remittances from charge customers were given to the accounts receivable bookkeeper, who totaled them daily and posted them to the accounts receivable subsidiary ledger. The total formed the basis for an entry in the Cash Receipts Journal by the chief accountant.

Many charge customers paid their bills by check or in cash at the office window. The accounts payable bookkeeper usually received the money, writing duplicate receipts in a standard, unnumbered receipt book. The original receipt was given to the customer and the duplicate to the accounts receivable bookkeeper. The accounts receivable bookkeeper tended the window while the accounts payable bookkeeper was at lunch, and often when the latter had a peak workload. Sometimes the chief accountant also helped at the window when the two bookkeepers were busy.

All cash receipts were deposited in the bank daily, and all payments were made by prenumbered check. The chief accountant made the daily deposit.

Duplicate copies of the machine-posted accounts receivable subsidiary ledger accounts were mailed once a month to charge customers. Most suppliers submitted monthly statements of account. The bank sent a monthly statement of the deposit account to the chief accountant.

Because most telephone calls were from customers inquiring about their accounts, the accounts receivable bookkeeper usually answered the telephone. She made memoranda about errors in the customers' statements, complaints concerning unsatisfactory merchandise, and similar matters. The chief accountant authorized individual customers' accounts to be written off as uncollectible.

Required

   a. Comment specifically on weaknesses of the system described as to (1) possibility of error, (2) possibility of fraud, and (3) efficiency.

   b. Outline the ways in which you would recommend that these weaknesses be overcome, with due consideration to the cost of your protective measures.

   c. Who should be responsible for preparing the monthly list of accounts receivable subsidiary account balances? Of accounts payable?

   d. Who should check the following against the Dimple Department Store's records: (1) suppliers' monthly statements of account, (2) the monthly bank statement, (3) customers' inquiries about their balances and customers' complaints?

9-2   Harrison Oil Distributing Company Computerized Practice Case. The computerized practice case for the Harrison Oil Distributing Company, information and forms for which are separately bound, is designed to introduce the student to the computer as an aid in accounting. In this application the student is concerned only with analyzing and journalizing transactions for the month of November. From these analyses the student prepares punched cards for the transactions; the computer prints out the trial balance, income statement, and financial position statement that result from the transactions.

This case emphasizes the computer's capability to serve as an *aid to learning*, rather than its ability to *compile and print data*. This feature is more fully explained in the separately bound practice case prepared for use with this text. The estimated time to work the computerized case ranges from three to five hours, depending on the student's proficiency with the key-punching machine and on his understanding of the accounting principles presented up to this point in the text.

(*Note to instructor:* The computerized and the manual practice case are designed to be assigned separately or in combination. If both are assigned, the authors think that the student's learning experience will be most beneficial if the computerized case is assigned first.)

9-3 Harrison Oil Distributing Company Manual Practice Case. The manual practice case for the Harrison Oil Distributing Company, information and forms for which are separately bound, is designed to provide a comprehensive review of the accounting cycle under manual accounting procedures. The student completes journalizing in special journals and posting for the month of December. Transactions for most of December have already been journalized in the preprinted information. The student prepares financial statements for the entire year.

Repetitive work is kept to a minimum. The estimated time to complete the entire case ranges from six to ten hours, depending on which requirements the instructor specifies and on the individual student's proficiency.

The necessary transaction information and forms for journals, ledger accounts, work sheets, and statements appear in the separately bound practice case prepared for use with this text.

(See the note to instructor for Case 9-2.)

chapter 10

Measuring
and Controlling
Monetary Assets

Purpose of Chapter

Monetary assets were defined in Chapter 2 as "*money* or *claims* to specific amounts of money, called *receivables*." Monetary assets are measured at the amount of money which they currently represent, or the amount of money which they are expected to bring in the near future in the normal course of events.

The following common types of monetary assets were defined in the section "Monetary Assets" of Chapter 3: cash, temporary investments, accounts receivable, notes receivable, the contra-account for estimated uncollectible receivables, accrued receivables, claims, and advances.

This chapter deals in greater depth with the problems of measuring monetary assets and reporting them in financial statements, as well as with some management problems involved in controlling monetary assets.

MEASURING AND CONTROLLING CASH

Cash includes only those items which are unrestricted as to use and are available readily for paying any obligations of the business. Usually it consists of cash on hand and bank deposits which are not designated for a particular long-term use.

Accounting for Income Versus Accounting for Cash Changes

Chapters 4, 5, and 6 outlined the general principles and methods by which *income,* the basic objective of business activity, is measured. It is the difference between *revenue,* the inflow of assets in exchange for the products or services of the business entity, and *expense,* the outflow or expiration of business assets associated with making such sales. The inflow and outflow of cash, matters of central interest in this chapter, are called *receipts* and *disbursements,* respectively.

There is *no direct relationship* between the amount of periodic *income,* or net change in owners' equity which results from operations, and the *net change in cash.* A business may find its cash decreasing even though operations are very profitable, and a cash increase may accompany a net loss. This is true because under the *accrual basis* of accounting, *revenue* is ordinarily taken into account when the business has performed the principal activities necessary to transfer a good to a customer or render a service to him, and when it has acquired in exchange another asset which can be measured reliably. Under the accrual basis revenue is recognized when it has been earned and when it can be dependably measured. The costs associated with this revenue are *matched* with it in the time period in which it is reflected in the accounts.

An *expired cost* (*expense* or *loss*) is recognized in the accounts (1) when an expenditure results in a current service benefit to the revenue-producing activities of the business, (2) when an expenditure is made which does not contribute to current or future revenues, or (3) when a measurable decline occurs in the potential of an asset to yield benefits in future periods.

In contrast to the accrual basis is the *cash basis for measuring income* (not to be confused with a record of cash receipts and cash payments). Many persons use the cash basis for measuring income in their income tax returns, but only rarely does it give an adequate measure of the financial progress of a business toward its income objective. (See the section "Alternative Bases of Recognizing Revenue" in Chapter 4.) Under the cash basis, revenue is recognized in the accounts only when collected, and costs are recognized only when paid for.

In most situations the accrual basis of accounting for income is preferable to the cash basis because it gives management, owners, and outsiders a better estimate of the performance of a business. This point is emphasized in the following examples.

Example 1   During 1973, its first year of operations, a business bought merchandise on account for $10,000, to be paid for in 1974, and sold all of it for $15,000 cash in the first year. What was its income for 1973?

Solution	CASH BASIS		ACCRUAL BASIS	
	Receipts for sales	$15,000	Sales revenue	$15,000
	Deduct payments for		Deduct expired cost	10,000
	expenses............	0		
	Gain on a cash basis......	$15,000	Net income.................	$ 5,000

The net income as determined by the accrual basis is a much better indicator of business performance during the year. The cash basis does not reflect any expense for the cost of goods sold in this case. It would permit the net income to be influenced arbitrarily by management, simply by postponing or speeding up payments.

Example 2   During 1973, its first year of operations, a business bought merchandise for $20,000 cash and sold all of it for $30,000 on account. None of the accounts had been collected by the end of the year, but all were owed by reliable people. What was the income for the year?

Solution

CASH BASIS			ACCRUAL BASIS	
Receipts for sales	$	0	Sales revenue	$30,000
Deduct payments for			Deduct expired cost......	20,000
expenses		20,000	Net income.................	$10,000
Loss on a cash basis......	($20,000)			

Here, again, the accrual basis gives the better measure of business performance.

The actual *receipt* of money for a sale may take place in an earlier period than the *accrual* of revenue, or in the same period, or in a later period.

Example 3(a)   In 1973 a business receives an advance cash deposit of $500 on merchandise which is to be shipped in 1974. This is a cash receipt of 1973, but revenue is realized in 1974 when title to the goods passes to the customer.

Example 3(b)   In 1974 a business sells merchandise on credit for $400 and collects the account before the end of the year. This is both a cash receipt and a revenue of 1974.

Example 3(c)   A business sells merchandise on account for $300 in 1974 but does not collect the account until 1975. This is a revenue of 1974 but a cash receipt of 1975.

The actual *payment* of money for service benefits received by the business may also take place in the same period as the *cost expiration*, or in an earlier or later period.

Example 4(a)   On October 1, 1973, a business paid $1,200 for a one-year insurance policy. Cost expiration for 1974 is $900, proportionate to the protection received for nine months in 1974. The cash payment for this cost was made in the preceding year.

Example 4(b)   In 1974 a business paid $700 for gasoline, all of which was used in making deliveries during the year. The cash payment and the cost expiration both occurred in 1974.

Example 4(c)   In December, 1974, a business hired an employee at a pay rate of $20 a day. He worked ten days in December, but was first paid on January 5, 1975. A cost of $200 expired in 1974, but the related cash payment was not made until the next year.

Cash receipts include many items that will *never become revenue* in any accounting period. Cash received from the owners as investment is *never earned* by the entity. Cash borrowed is a receipt but not a revenue, because the business has an obligation to repay it. Collections of loans previously made to others are not revenue, but the interest is revenue of the periods in which it is earned.

Many *cash disbursements* are for items that will *never become expired costs*. Money paid to owners either as a dividend out of income or as a return of capital invested does not represent a cost. A cash repayment of a loan from another is not a cost (although the interest is). Cash paid out as a loan is likewise not a cost.

Importance of Accounting for Cash

The reader should not assume from the distinctions just made that accounting for cash is unimportant. Although income and cash change, or *cash flow*, are not the same, control of both is vital. Management must be able to *plan cash receipts* so that money will be available in the quantities and at the times needed for making payments. There must be reliable estimates of the amounts of cash that will be available from time to time for making discretionary payments, such as purchasing new plant facilities, making short-term investments, and paying dividends. The method of cash flow analysis shown in Chapter 21 is useful for these purposes.

Accounting records of actual cash receipts, payments, and balances contain essential information about the liquid resources owned by the company and their changes over time. Equally important, the accounting system can provide reasonable *safeguards* to ensure that business cash is used for proper business purposes and is not wasted, misused, or stolen. Although there should be similar accounting measures to protect other assets, accounting control of cash is of critical importance. Money is universally attractive; it can easily be transported, concealed, and put to improper use.

Cash in the Financial Position Statement

Cash includes currency, coin, readily transferable money orders and checks, demand deposits in banks, and time (or savings) deposits if the bank is not expected to require a waiting period before permitting withdrawals.

Cash does not include unused postage; bank accounts required to be used for a particular purpose, either by legal contract or by management policy; and deposits in banks which have failed.

Bank accounts limited to special uses are called *funds*. A *sinking fund* being accumulated to pay off the principal of Bonds Payable at maturity is an example of a special fund that is often required by contract. Usually such a fund is kept by a trustee and is not available to the business for making general payments. Other special funds are sometimes set aside voluntarily for such purposes as constructing plant additions and paying off debts, even though a fund is not required by contract. Management policy requires that these bank accounts be separated from general cash and that they be devoted only to the purposes for which they were established.

Bank accounts which can be used only for the purchase of long-term assets or for the payment of long-term debts are not Cash, nor are they even current assets. Their account titles should indicate that they are specially earmarked funds and should identify their purpose, and they should be classified under Investments in the financial position statement. Bank accounts set aside for the payment of current liabilities, such as Dividends Payable and Wages Payable, are current assets.

Some funds, particularly those designated for long-term uses, may contain stocks, bonds, and other securities in addition to bank accounts. The measurement principles for long-term investments apply to these securities.

An *overdrawn bank account* is not an asset, but a *liability*. It represents a claim against the business.

For convenience a business usually keeps separate *ledger accounts* for Cash on Hand, Petty Cash (explained later), and Cash in Bank, and also for each bank account. In *financial reports* these accounts may be lumped together as *Cash* if they meet the definition of cash.

Controlling Cash Receipts

The objectives and general procedures of a system of *internal control* outlined in Chapter 9 apply with special force to Cash. Some additional procedures which are generally useful in controlling cash are described below.

The basic objective of *cash receipts procedures* and records is to make certain that all money actually collected for the business finds its way into the business treasury, and that the facts of collection are recorded accurately and promptly. It is essential that collections be recorded immediately after receipt. This may be done either on a cash register or on some type of receipt-writing device which locks information as to the amounts of collections securely in the machine. Cash registers in common use print a receipt for the customer and also print, classify, and total information about collections on a tape which is locked in the machine.

The cash collections of each day should be deposited in the bank in total at the end of the day; no payments should be made from them before the deposit. Prompt deposits reduce the risk of theft. By segregating the receipts by days, they discourage temporary "borrowing" by the cashier and make it easier to detect. Distinct separation of the duties of cash receiving and paying helps to ensure that all payments are authorized by a responsible person and that fictitious payments are not used to conceal stolen receipts.

Each individual who handles cash receipts should have a specific *accountability* for them. If two or more persons jointly operate a cash register and the cash on hand at the end of the day is less than the recorded receipts, it is difficult, if not impossible, to pinpoint responsibility for the shortage. Each individual should have sole control over a cash register or of a locked drawer within a register.

In most businesses, mail remittances and cash sales account for the great bulk of cash receipts transactions. The need for controlling them is obvious. Often the following receipts are more susceptible to mishandling because they occur infrequently: collections on notes, borrowings on bank loans, proceeds of the issuance of capital stock and bonds, collections of dividends and interest on investments, and receipts of proceeds of the sale of investments and other business assets not normally intended for sale.

Using a specialized *Cash Receipts Journal* (described in Chapter 9) for recording every collection of money provides internal control by assigning responsibility for journalizing cash collections to one person, who does not handle cash physically.

Controlling Cash Disbursements

Accounting procedures for cash payments are intended to ensure that business cash is disbursed only by a responsible person. Cash is paid only after another responsible person has assured him, on the basis of documentary evidence, that the payment is a proper one for goods or services which the business has received.

All cash payments except the very smallest should be made by check. Check payments are safer than payments in currency and coin because the payee can be named specifically and the payor need not keep large sums of currency on hand for making payments. The business can thereby restrict authority for making payments to one or a very few officers or employees. Checks show specifically how much was paid and to whom, and the endorsements on cancelled checks are evidence that the payee received payment.

Often businesses safeguard their payments by requiring that *two* responsible persons sign each check. The *controller*, or chief accounting officer, signs to certify that the payment is proper. The *treasurer*, after determining that money is available to make the payment, then signs to direct the bank to pay out the company's money to the payee named in the check.

Many businesses have enough cash payment transactions to warrant the use of a special *Cash Payments Journal*, in which only checks issued are recorded. This journal provides internal control by permitting division of work with only one person responsible for recording cash payments.

The treasurer or other company official who is responsible for having sufficient cash available should receive a daily report of the cash balance at the beginning of the day, a summary of cash receipts and payments during the day, and the balance at the end of the day. In addition to a cash forecast for the next month, he usually needs daily totals of payments to be made in the near future.

Petty Cash

Paying by check helps to ensure that all business disbursements are proper. However, the procedure for substantiating, approving, issuing, and recording check payments is rather costly and time-consuming. Many small payments, such as those for carfare of employees and postage due on incoming mail, are hardly worth the effort required to pay by check. For making such payments, businesses customarily set aside a fixed sum of currency and coin, called a *Petty Cash fund*. Payments are not made out of Petty Cash without proper approval, but they are handled by a simplified procedure.

One individual should have sole responsibility for each petty cash fund.

Such a fund can be established by issuing a business check payable to "Petty Cash" in an amount sufficient to make minor payments for a week or two. The effect on the accounts is

(1)

A, Petty Cash 50
　　A, Cash (or A, Cash in Bank) ....　　　　50
　　Established a petty cash fund of fixed amount for
　　making small payments.

The custodian of the fund cashes the check and obtains $50 in currency and coin, which he should keep in a locked box or drawer. He should keep supporting evidence for each payment from the fund. At any time the petty cash drawer should contain money plus paid tickets equal to its fixed balance.

The petty cash payment system involves a *delay in journalizing payments*. Journal entries to record payments out of Petty Cash are made when the fund is replenished, not when the payments are made (although a memorandum record of petty cash payments may be kept). Ordinarily the fund is reimbursed for its payments when its money balance is low, but it should be reimbursed at the end of each accounting period regardless of the remaining amount of currency and coin. The accounts to be debited for the payments are incomplete until the entry for replenishment of the fund is recorded.

The custodian summarizes the payment tickets according to the accounts debited. A reimbursement check is then prepared and recorded in the following manner:

(2)

OE, Communications Expense 8
OE, Payroll Expense 17
OE, Office Supplies Expense................................... 12
A, Merchandise Inventory...................................... 9
OE, Cash Short and Over....................................... 1
　　A, Cash in Bank ....　　　　47
　　Reimbursed the petty cash fund, which had a balance
　　of $3 on hand.

The petty cash tickets and memoranda should be marked "Paid" to prevent their reuse.

In the preceding entry, the *debit* to Cash Short and Over indicates that the currency and coin in the petty cash fund, plus paid tickets, totaled only $49. The shortage may have been due to an error in making change. An overage would be shown by a *credit* to Cash Short and Over. This account is an expense or a revenue, depending on whether it has a debit or credit balance.

The $50 balance in the Petty Cash ledger account is permanent. It is not reduced when cash is paid out of the petty cash fund, nor is it increased when the fund is replenished. It is debited only when the fund is established or increased, and credited when the fund is decreased or discontinued.

Other Cash Accounts

Often payments of a particular type are so numerous that it is desirable to establish a checking account apart from the general bank account. Payroll and dividend payments are common examples. Such special accounts permit the treasurer to delegate authority for signing one type of check to an assistant, while limiting the amount of payments that the assistant can make. Usually the treasurer transfers to the special account only enough to meet a single payroll or dividend payment.

Reconciling the Bank Accounts

Many of the provisions of the system of internal control are carried out as one employee of the business verifies the work of another. The accuracy and honesty with which business records are kept can also be partially determined by making comparisons with records prepared by persons outside of the firm. An example of such a verification is the *reconciliation* of the balance on deposit as shown by the depositor's books with that shown by the bank's satement of the depositor's account. *Reconciling* means explaining differences.

The relationship of the bank to the business is that of *debtor* to a creditor. The bank's record of its dealings with each depositor is a *liability* account, which normally has a credit balance. The bank satisfies this liability by paying money to persons whom the depositor designates. Checks are *orders* to the bank to make such payments.

The depositor keeps a record of his dealings with the bank in an asset account, usually called Cash in Bank. This is merely a special type of account receivable, but it merits a special designation because it represents a resource immediately available for making payments.

If there were no time lags between the collection of money by the customer and its deposit in the bank, or between the issuance of checks and their final payment by the bank, the customer's and bank's accounts of their mutual dealings would have balances *equal in amount* but of an *opposite nature*. That is, they would be *reciprocal* accounts. To illustrate:

Customer's Books
A, Cash in Bank

1974			1974		
July 1	Receipts..................	4,000	July 2	Check #1 issued	300
	Balance, 3,200		3	Check #2 issued	500

Bank's Books
L, Customers Demand Deposit

1974			1974		
July 2	Check #1 paid.........	300	July 1	Deposit	4,000
3	Check #2 paid.........	500		*Balance, 3,200*	

The ideal condition illustrated rarely exists in practice. There are usually *time lags*, and there are occasional *errors* in both the customer's and the bank's accounting records. When the depositor receives the bank's monthly statement of the account, he should compare it with his own records to determine what errors or omissions he has made, what errors or omissions the bank has made, and *what balance was actually on deposit* in the bank subject to check at the end of the month. A summary which itemizes the results of this comparison is called a *bank reconciliation*.

The bank reconciliation should be prepared by an employee of the business who does not handle money or keep cash records, so that irregularities will be discovered.

An example of a completed bank reconciliation summary appears in Illustration 10-1. It consists of two main parts, one for the Cash ledger account and one for the bank's Depositor account. On each of these parts there are additions and deductions which are needed to arrive at the *correct balance of cash available in the bank* account at the end of the period.

The reconciliation may be made in the following steps:

Illustration 10-1

THE NOVELTY COMPANY
Bank Reconciliation
March 31, 1973

CASH LEDGER ACCOUNT

Debit balance, March 31, 1973		$1,610
Additions (debits for items as to which the Cash records are incorrect or incomplete):		
Note receivable collected by bank on March 31, face......	$ 500	
Interest collected on note	5	
Total additions		505
Total debits		$2,115
Deductions (credits for items as to which the Cash records are incorrect or incomplete):		
Bank service charge	$ 2	
Insufficient funds check of customer, returned by bank ...	50	
Interest on note payable owed to bank, paid March 30...	10	
Total deductions		62
True debit balance of Cash in Bank, March 31..............................		$2,053

BANK DEPOSITOR ACCOUNT

Credit balance, March 31, 1973...		$2,708
Additions (credits for items as to which the bank records are incorrect or incomplete):		
March 29 deposit of The Novelty Company credited by bank to Newel Co.'s account	$ 450	
Check of Novel Mfg. Company debited by bank to The Novelty Company's account	750	
Deposit of March 31 in transit to bank........................	180	
Total additions		1,380
Total credits		$4,088
Deductions (debits for items as to which the bank records are incorrect or incomplete):		
Outstanding checks:		
No. 505	$ 200	
508	1,585	
509	225	
510	25	
Total outstanding checks...		2,035
True credit balance of Depositor account, March 31		$2,053

(1) *Compare payments made by the bank with payments shown in the cash disbursements journal.* Amounts and names of payees on the cancelled checks should agree with the company's disbursement record, and the checks should be endorsed by the payees. Discrepancies should be reported to the person who supervises cash record keeping. Check marks in the cash disbursements journal opposite each paid item show that this comparison has been made. Unchecked items are checks issued by the business but not paid by the bank. They are still in the hands of payees or in banking channels—that is, they are *outstanding checks*. They may be presented to the bank for payment at any time; therefore, in the reconciliation they should be deducted from the *bank's* ending balance to compute true available cash.

Later bank statements should be examined to determine if these checks have been paid and if they were recorded properly in the company's cash records.

Other differences often shown by this comparison are payments which the bank has made from the depositor's account but which have not been recorded on the depositor's books. If these payments are correct, they must be deducted from the Cash ledger account part of the reconciliation. Examples are the bank's service charge for handling the account, notes payable and interest owed by the depositor to the bank which were deducted from the deposit account when due, and "insufficient funds" checks which were credited to the depositor's account when they were originally deposited.

An "insufficient funds" check requires corrections of the prior deposit entries made by the bank and the depositor. Most depositors treat incoming checks as Cash until they are proved otherwise. Banks accept such checks for deposit and credit the customer's deposit account, subject to their collection when presented to the payor's bank. If they are not paid when presented to the bank upon which they are drawn, both the depositor and his bank must make correcting entries.

If a deduction from the bank account is incorrect, the amount of the error should be shown on the bank's Depositor account part of the reconciliation. Depending on the circumstances, the correction may require either an addition to or a deduction from the Depositor account part of the reconciliation.

(2) *Compare deposits reported by the bank with receipts shown in the cash receipts journal.* Normally, a deposit should appear on the bank statement the day following collection, but there are exceptions for weekends and for special types of payments. Check marks should be made beside Cash debit and bank credit entries that are in agreement.

Unchecked items in the cash receipts journal may result from *errors* made either by the depositor or by the bank, or may be *deposits in transit* at the end of the period. Errors should be corrected on the part of the bank reconciliation which applies to the incorrect account. Deposits in transit are added to the balance according to the bank on the assumption that the deposit will be completed promptly. The person who makes the reconciliation should follow up to be sure that the money actually does find its way to the bank promptly.

Unchecked items in the credit column of the bank's Depositor account may represent *collections* received by the bank which the depositor has not recorded. Examples are sums borrowed from the bank and added to the deposit account, and the proceeds of customers' notes receivable which the business has left with the bank for it to collect as an agent. Such unchecked items may also be *errors*.

(3) *List the points of difference brought to light by the foregoing in a summary,* such as that in Illustration 10-1.

(4) *Make journal entries on the depositor's books to correct the Cash balance on the books to the "true cash" figure.* All additions and deductions on the Cash ledger account part of the reconciliation require correcting entries. Illustration 10-1 requires the following corrections:

(3)

OE, Miscellaneous Financial Expense	2	
A, Accounts Receivable	50	
OE, Interest Expense	10	
A, Cash		62

    To record payments made by the bank in March, not previously recorded on the books.

(4)

A, Cash	505	
A, Notes Receivable		500
OE, Interest Revenue		5

    To record collections made by the bank in March, not previously recorded on the books.

The second debit in entry (3) assumes that the customer's account is still collectible. If it is not, it should be written off. The third debit reflects an expense of the current month.

The first credit in entry (4) shows that the face amount of the note receivable has been collected. The second credit records the interest revenue on the note.

(5) *Notify the bank of any corrections which it should make.* Information of this sort is found in the additions and deductions on the *bank Depositor* account part of the reconciliation. No action is needed for deposits in transit and outstanding checks; presumably they will arrive at the bank soon.

The person who prepares the April bank reconciliation should first determine that the proper disposition has been made of the reconciling items from March. If not, they should again appear in the April bank reconciliation. Sometimes checks remain outstanding for several months. Follow-up is needed to issue duplicates, where necessary, for such "stale" checks.

Temporary Investments

Temporary investments were defined in Chapter 3 as short-term commitments of funds to productive use, commonly held in the form of marketable securities.

Temporary investments should be *measured* at their *acquisition cost*, which includes not only the quoted purchase price of the security but also other costs directly associated with the purchase. If the transaction is handled by a broker, his commission and any postage, insurance, and transfer taxes applicable to the purchase are a part of the cost of the investment.

The accounting entry for the acquisition of a U.S. government bond having a face amount of $1,000 at a price of 98 (98 per cent of its face amount, or *par*), plus the broker's charge of $9 for commission and postage, would be

(5)

A, Temporary Investments	989	
A, Cash		989

    Paid $980 plus $9 commission and postage for a U.S. bond for short-term investment.

Normally temporary investments are shown in the accounts at cost until they are sold. If the bond issuer in the preceding illustration paid interest quarterly at a rate of 4 per cent per year, the entry to record the first interest collection would be

(6)

A, Cash	10	
OE, Interest Revenue		10
Collected quarterly interest on $1,000 U.S. bond.		

Because the objective in measuring temporary investments is to show what they are expected to bring in cash, current market price quotations must be considered in reporting their amounts in the Statement of Financial Position. Usually it is sufficient to show the market value parenthetically:

ASSETS

Temporary investments (market value, $975), at cost.........   989

If the market value is substantially less than cost and the condition causing the decline seems to be permanent, Temporary Investments should be reported in the Statement of Financial Position at market value. The accountant should preserve the record of cost in the ledger account so that he can compute actual gain or loss when the securities are sold.

Separate general ledger accounts may be used for major types of temporary investments, such as U.S. bonds, corporate bonds, and corporate stocks. Detailed supporting records should be kept of each block of securities acquired.

MEASURING AND CONTROLLING RECEIVABLES

General Nature and Basis of Measurement

Accounts Receivable are the claims of a business against customers for sales of goods and services in the ordinary course of operations. *Notes Receivable* are formal written documents signed by customers which contain an unconditional written promise to pay to the business a stated amount of money, either on demand or at a determinable future time. Other classes of receivables frequently owned by businesses are *accrued receivables, claims receivable, dividends receivable,* and *advances* (to officers, employees, and other companies).

The present chapter deals with (1) some of the more complex problems of measuring receivables and (2) some methods by which business management can plan and control the amount of business capital invested in receivables and the efficiency with which it is utilized.

The proper measure of Accounts Receivable is the amount *estimated to be collectible in the near future* through ordinary business operations. Usually the terms of sale specify no interest for accounts which run for a very short term. Any implied interest for the brief waiting period is usually so small that no attempt is made to estimate it.

Trade accounts receivable become assets when *revenue is realized* because of transferring legal title to goods or rendering service to a customer. Each sum legally receivable should be recorded as an asset when a claim arises, to facilitate proper measurement of the firm's assets and revenue and timely collection efforts.

In measuring accounts receivable at their cash value and assigning the proper amount of revenue to each time period, the total of receivables legally owned should be *reduced by adjustments* for uncollectible accounts, returns, allowances, discounts, and reimbursable shipping charges. These adjustments avoid overstating Sales Revenue and Accounts Receivable.

While the amounts of these adjustments cannot be known exactly in advance, reasonable estimates can be made from the seller's past experience, together with known changes in factors which affect allowances, returns, and losses. These estimates are debited to an appropriately named *revenue deduction account* and credited to an *asset valuation account*—a deduction from Accounts Receivable.

Sales Discounts

Sales discounts are price concessions made to customers to induce them to pay promptly. Because such discounts are usually equivalent to a high annual rate of interest, a well-managed business will normally take advantage of them. The *normal price* of a sale to a business customer is therefore the *net price* which is required to settle the claim within the discount period. On the other hand, some businesses may find that most of their customers fail to take advantage of the cash discount. In such cases the *gross price method* of recording sales may be used. The essential features of both methods are discussed in the following sections.

The Gross Price Method of Recording Cash Discounts on Sales

The following facts are assumed to illustrate the accounting procedures for sales discounts:

Sales for the month of December 1973 were $100,000, all subject to credit terms of 2/10 E.O.M., n/60. (If the customer pays within 10 days of the end of the month of purchase, he is allowed a cash discount of 2 per cent. Otherwise, the account is due without discount at the end of 60 days.)

None of the accounts had been collected by December 31, the last day of the accounting period.

In the past the company has collected about 80 per cent of sales within the discount period.

Under the *gross price method*, the receivable and the revenue are recorded at the gross sales price at the time of sale. The *discount actually taken* by the customer is recorded as a *deduction from sales revenue* when the customer pays his account. The appropriate entries are

(1a)

A, Accounts Receivable	100,000	
OE, Sales Revenue (1973)		100,000

To record total credit sales for December at the gross sales price.

An adjusting entry must be made on December 31 to avoid *overstating* accounts receivable and revenue by the amount the business will not collect—the $1,600 discount which customers are expected to deduct in January. This entry is

(2a)

OE, Sales Discounts Allowed (1973) 1,600
    A, Accounts Receivable—Estimated Discounts Allowed   1,600
    To record the cash discounts expected to be taken in the
    future at 2% of the $80,000 of accounts which are expected
    to be settled within the discount period.

The balance of Accounts Receivable—Estimated Discounts Allowed is a *deduction* from Accounts Receivable.

The relevant accounts would appear thus in the 1973 financial statements:

Partial Statement of Financial Position, December 31, 1973

Current assets:
    Accounts receivable (gross) $100,000
    Deduct estimated discounts allowed....................... 1,600
        Estimated collectible amount............................. $98,400

Partial Income Statement for Year Ended December 31, 1973

Sales revenue (gross)... $100,000
Deduct sales discounts allowed................................ 1,600
    Net sales $98,400

It is to be expected that the actual amount of discounts taken in the following year may often differ from the estimated amount reflected in the year-end adjusting entry. Unless such corrections are major, they can be absorbed in the Sales Discounts Allowed account for the following year.

The Net Price Method of Recording Cash Discounts on Sales

The assumed facts for illustrating the *net price method* for recording sales discounts are the same as those used in the preceding section for the gross price method.

If customers normally take advantage of the cash discounts offered, both sales and accounts receivable are measured initially at *sales price minus available discount*, as follows:

(1b)

A, Accounts Receivable 98,000
    OE, Sales Revenue (1973)......................................   98,000
    To record credit sales for December at the sales price
    minus available discount.

If no additional entry were made in 1973, Accounts Receivable would be reported at $98,000 in the year-end financial position statement and Sales

Revenue would be shown as $98,000 in the Income Statement. However, because customers' past behavior indicates that $98,400 will be collected on the accounts receivable the firm owns at December 31, 1973, the following adjusting entry should be made:

(2b)

A, Accounts Receivable—Estimated Discounts Disallowed...   400
  OE, Revenue from Sales Discounts Disallowed (1973)...   400
  To record the estimated amount of sales discounts which
  will be disallowed on customers' accounts receivable out-
  standing on December 31, 1973.

The debit in this entry is an *addition* to the Accounts Receivable controlling account. It cannot be posted to the individual customers' accounts, because it is not known on December 31 which customers will fail to take the discount.

The effects of the net price method on the *financial statements* are shown in the following excerpts:

Partial Statement of Financial Position, December 31, 1973

Current assets:
Accounts receivable (net) $98,000
Add estimated discounts disallowed 400
Estimated collectible amount $98,400

Partial Income Statement for Year Ended December 31, 1973

Sales revenue (net) $98,000

Nonoperating revenue:
Sales discounts disallowed 400

Variations of the principal sales discounts methods illustrated in this chapter are in use, but the *total reported assets and periodic income should be the same* under all methods.

Age Distribution of Accounts Receivable

In addition to knowing the *amounts* of accounts receivable which are legally owned to a business, management and others wish information on the *quality* of the accounts: how much will eventually be collected on them, and how promptly it will be collected. Two general analyses used in appraising the quality of accounts receivable are the *age distribution* of the accounts and the *provision for estimated uncollectible accounts*.

An analysis of accounts receivable according to the length of time each invoice has been owed is useful in estimating the amount of uncollectible accounts, as well as in evaluating the effectiveness of management's credit and collection policies and procedures. The following is a summary of such an analysis:

MADISON CORPORATION
Accounts Receivable Age Distribution
December 31, 1973

Age in Months	Total Amount	Per Cent of Accounts
0–1......................	$38,000	76%
1–2......................	7,000	14
2–3......................	3,000	6
3–6	500	1
Over 6....................	1,500	3
Totals..................	$50,000	100%

It is useful to compare such summaries with age distributions of earlier periods. Usually increases in the percentage of accounts in the lower age classifications reflect an *improvement* in the quality of accounts receivable and in credit and collection administration. Percentage increases in the older classes are generally *unfavorable*. An analysis of customers' accounts according to the time when credit was first extended to them helps the firm tell the good customers' accounts from the bad.

The age distribution may be used in estimating the uncollectible portion of current accounts receivable. The following illustration estimates the losses from bad accounts from statistics of past experience, which compare the amounts of actual uncollectible accounts with total accounts receivable in each age group:

MADISON CORPORATION
Estimated Losses from Uncollectible Accounts
December 31, 1973

Age in Months	Accounts Receivable	Per Cent of Expected Loss	Amount of Expected Loss
0–1	$38,000	0.2%	$ 76
1–2	7,000	1.0	70
2–3	3,000	5.0	150
3–6	500	25.0	125
Over 6	1,500	50.0	750
Totals	$50,000		$1,171

This estimate indicates that $1,171 of the accounts receivable now on the books—regardless of when they originated—will become uncollectible. This is the correct balance of the Accounts Receivable—Estimated Uncollectibles account after making the period-end adjusting entry. If this account's credit balance before the adjusting entry were $300 (a provision remaining from earlier periods), the appropriate entry would be

(3a)

OE, Uncollectible Sales Revenue (1973) 871
    A, Accounts Receivable—Estimated Uncollectibles 871
    To increase estimated uncollectibles to $1,171, the total of
    estimated uncollectible accounts.

Collection efforts can be improved by placing delinquent accounts in a separate ledger for special attention, or by marking them with a distinctive signal. The aging process can also help in collection efforts.

Estimating Uncollectibles on the Basis of Credit Sales

The section "Adjustments for Uncollectible Accounts" in Chapter 6 described how to estimate the uncollectible accounts which will result from the current year's sales on account. This is done by using the average percentage of actual uncollectible accounts to the credit sales of the year in which the sales were made. The estimated loss on the current year's sales determined by using this percentage is then *added to the balance* already in Accounts Receivable—Estimated Uncollectibles. The previous balance may apply to the uncollected accounts of prior years which are still carried in Accounts Receivable, or it may include a cumulative error which has not been corrected.

To illustrate, assume that the Madison Corporation's sales on account for the current year were $100,000 and its past actual losses from uncollectibles had averaged 1 per cent of sales on account. The entry would be

(3b)

OE, Uncollectible Sales Revenue (1973) 1,000
    A, Accounts Receivable—Estimated Uncollectibles.........   1,000
    To add the expected loss on the current year's credit sales to
    the balance in Estimated Uncollectibles.

The balance in the account would then be

A, Accounts Receivable—Estimated Uncollectibles

(Balance from prior year) ...	300
(Addition for this year) (3b)	1,000
Balance at end of year	*1,300*

The percentage-of-credit-sales method is widely used in practice, but the cumulative balance tends to become excessive or deficient after several years unless periodic efforts are made to keep it reasonably related to the amount of uncollected accounts still on the books.

Correcting Uncollectible Account Entries

The section "Writing Off Uncollectible Accounts" in Chapter 6 explained the following type of entry, made for writing off an account actually determined to be uncollectible in a later year:

1974   (4)
Jan. 30   A, Accounts Receivable—Estimated Uncollectibles ... 120
         A, Accounts Receivable   120
        To write off Amco Corporation's uncollectible
        account.

After other write-offs in 1974 of specific accounts arising from 1973 sales, the account would appear thus:

A, Accounts Receivable—Estimated Uncollectibles

(Actual)			(Estimate)		
1974			1973		
Jan. 30		120	Dec. 31	Balance	1,300
Feb. 7		200			
Dec. 11		80		*Balance, 0*	
18		900			
		1,300			

If all the accounts from sales of 1973 and prior years had been collected or written off, or were expected to be fully collectible at the end of 1974, the 1973 estimate in the illustration was perfect. This would be unusual in actual practice, although reasonably accurate estimates are common.

The collection of an account previously written off as uncollectible would be recorded as follows:

1975	(5)		
Feb. 7	A, Accounts Receivable....................................	120	
	A, Accounts Receivable—Estimated Uncollectibles		120
	To reverse the entry of Jan. 30, 1974, writing off the Amco account.		

	(6)		
7	A, Cash	120	
	A, Accounts Receivable		120
	To record the collection of the Amco Corporation account.		

This seemingly roundabout procedure shows, for credit reference purposes, that the customer finally did pay his account.

Other Deductions from Accounts Receivable

Sales revenue and accounts receivable are reduced by sales returns and allowances. During the accounting period *actual returns and allowances* are debited to a separate *revenue contra-account*. When goods are returned, their unexpired cost should be debited to Merchandise Inventory and credited to Cost of Goods Sold Expense.

Proper matching of periodic revenues and expenses and proper measurement of the ending balance of Accounts Receivable require a year-end estimate of the current year's sales which are likely to be returned in the following year. The entry for the expected returns, based on past experience, should allow for probable damages to goods to be returned and transportation charges which the seller is likely to have to pay.

For convenience, immaterial amounts of estimated revenue-contras may be combined in a single year-end adjusting entry.

Special Problems in Reporting Accounts Receivable

Balances receivable on *installment accounts* should be stated separately according to the year of maturity. Such accounts are current assets if they conform to customary trade practices in the industry.

Businesses frequently sell, or *assign*, accounts receivable to financial institutions in exchange for their present value in cash. If the assignment is made *without recourse*, the purchaser of the accounts bears losses from uncollectibles. The seller records the receipt of cash, the applicable interest expense, and the reduction of accounts receivable owned.

If the assignment is *with recourse*, the seller has a potential, or *contingent*, *liability* to the financial institution. He must pay the account to the latter if the customer does not. A statement of financial position prepared while the company is still contingently liable should report the amount of the contingent liability.

Example 5   Balances of accounts, Dec. 31, 1973:

	Debit	*Credit*
Accounts receivable......................................	50,000	
Accounts receivable assigned		5,000

The December 31, 1973, Financial Position Statement would show these facts as follows:

Current assets:
Accounts receivable (See Note A).................................... $45,000

Current liabilities:
Contingent liabilities (See Note A).................................   —
Note A: The company was contingently liable for $5,000 for accounts receivable assigned with recourse. The expected loss is zero.

Accounts receivable may also be *pledged* as collateral for loans. The pledgor is obliged to collect the accounts and either to pay their proceeds to the lender or to substitute new collateral for them. The pledging company should transfer the accounts to a special ledger so that the proceeds of their collection may be accounted for properly. It should show the face amount of pledged accounts in a footnote to its statement of financial position.

Internal Control of Accounts Receivable

The general objective of internal control procedures for accounts receivable is to ensure that the business *collects* amounts owed by its customers *promptly* and *fully*, and that the collections are properly paid into the company's treasury. This requires measures to prevent *fraud*, *errors*, and *inefficiency* in debiting charge sales to customers' accounts and in recording subsequent deductions for collections, returns, allowances, and write-offs.

Detailed procedures for handling receivables are tailored to suit the individual business. If possible, however, separate employees should approve credit, ship the goods, bill the customers, receive cash, keep the customers' detailed accounts, and maintain the accounts receivable controlling account.

Responsibility for approving credit should be specifically assigned to one employee or department. The procedures should ensure that credit is granted according to the company's policy, and only after proper investigation of the applicant's credit record.

Procedures for shipping goods and preparing sales invoices should provide the accounts receivable bookkeeper a prompt and accurate record of all sales. An individual other than the one who prepares the invoices should check the accuracy of the quantities, prices, computations, discounts, and shipping terms. Copies of sales invoices and collection memoranda should be routed to the *accounts receivable subsidiary ledger bookkeeper* for posting to the individual customers' accounts. The system of cross-checks is strengthened if information as to the total debits and credits for these transactions goes independently to the *general ledger bookkeeper* for posting to the accounts receivable *controlling account*.

Credits to customers' accounts for returns, allowances, and write-offs should be approved by an appropriate executive after he has determined that they are proper. An accounts receivable bookkeeper who has access to cash collections might otherwise pocket them and cover up by falsely recording returns or similar credits in the customers' accounts.

Accounts Receivable Turnover Rates

The accounts receivable *turnover rate* is a measure of the rate of change in accounts receivable over a period of time. The formula for computing it is

$$\frac{\text{Net credit sales for the period}}{\text{Average accounts receivable balance}} = \text{Number of turnovers.}$$

Example 6 From the following condensed ledger account, compute the number of accounts receivable turnovers during 1973.

A, Accounts Receivable

1973			1973		
Jan. 1	Balance	45,000	Various		
Various			dates	Collections on	
dates	Sales on account	200,000		account	190,000
			Dec. 31	*Balance, 55,000*	

Solution
$$\frac{\text{Sales, \$200,000}}{\text{Average balance, \$50,000}} = 4 \text{ turnovers.}$$

The average balance used here is the arithmetic mean of the January 1 balance of $45,000 and the December 31 balance of $55,000.

More representative averages of Accounts Receivable are based on monthly, weekly, or even daily balances of Accounts Receivable. Better still would be a turnover rate for each month, computed by dividing credit sales for the month by the average balance of Accounts Receivable during the month. These 12 monthly rates would reveal important seasonal variations in the rate of turnover and, in comparison with the rates of prior years, would show important trends.

Rapid changes in the balance of Accounts Receivable tend to distort the reliability of the turnover rate. So does the inclusion of accounts arising from several different classes of credit terms in one turnover computation. It would be meaningless, for example, to compute the average turnover of accounts receivable resulting partly from sales on 30-day open account and partly from installment sales on terms ranging up to 24 months. Separate turnover calculations should be made for each such class of receivables.

Actual past accounts receivable turnover rates may be used to *evaluate* the firm's effectiveness in managing its investment in accounts receivable, which depends on the functions of extending credit and collecting from the customers. Turnover rates also aid in *planning* for the future. Given a reliable estimate of sales on account and the expected accounts receivable turnover rate, the cash collections of the forthcoming period and the ending accounts receivable balances can be estimated.

A standard of comparison is needed to determine whether the turnover rate of 4, computed in Example 6, is *good* or *bad*. One such standard is the *rate for the preceding year*. If in this example the prior year's turnover rate had been 3.74, the current year's results would indicate an improvement.

Another standard of comparison is the *planned*, or desired, *turnover rate*. If this had been six turnovers a year in Example 6, additional improvement is still needed. Action to improve turnover can be centered on the *debit changes* (sales on account), on the *credit changes* (collections), or on both. Such action might consist of the following:

(1) Changes in credit terms. Shorter terms result in a proportionately higher turnover rate.

(2) Changes in credit-granting policies. Less liberal extension of credit tends to result in a higher turnover rate.

(3) Action to improve customers' paying habits, to counteract such factors as economic downswings.

(4) Changes in effectiveness of collection efforts. Better follow-up efforts tend to cause a higher turnover rate.

Other Measures of Accounts Receivable Control

A variation of the accounts receivable turnover rate which is sometimes used is the *average collection period* of accounts receivable. It is the reciprocal of (1 divided by) the number of turnovers.

Example 7   What is the average collection period in Example 6?

Solution (a) $$\text{Average collection period} = \frac{1}{\text{Number of turnovers}} = \frac{1}{4} \text{ year.}$$

Expressed in terms of days rather than years, this average collection period is one-fourth of 365 days, or approximately 91 days.

Solution (b)   The average collection period in years can also be computed thus:

$$\frac{\text{Average balance of accounts receivable}}{\text{Credit sales}} = \frac{\$50,000}{\$200,000} = \frac{1}{4} \text{ year.}$$

The *average collection period* is often compared with the company's normal credit period. If the company's normal credit terms are *net 30 days,* an average collection period of 91 days indicates that, on the average, customers are taking about three times as long to pay their accounts as credit terms permit. It is also useful to compare one company's average collection period with that of others in the same industry.

Determining Credit Policy

Management needs data on the *cost of extending credit* as a guide in tightening or relaxing the credit it grants, in increasing or decreasing the service charges made for the extension of credit, and in improving the effectiveness of collections.

If a business liberalizes its credit policy, it should try to match the resulting increased sales revenue with the applicable costs of granting credit. Credit liberalization is undesirable unless it results in a satisfactory rate of income on the assets used by the business. On the other hand, a business should not tighten its credit terms to such an extent that its rate of net income is unsatisfactory.

MEASURING AND CONTROLLING NOTES RECEIVABLE

General Basis of Measuring Notes Receivable

Notes receivable are promissory notes *owned* by a business, containing an unconditional written promise to pay a stated sum of money on demand or at a determinable future time.

Notes receivable usually specify that the maker must pay *interest* at a stated rate for the term of the note. Even if no interest is mentioned, it is often implicitly included in the maturity amount of the note.

Initially, notes receivable should be measured at their *cash equivalent* at the time of receipt. This is the *face amount* of interest-bearing notes, unless there is good evidence that the interest rate specified in the note is not realistic.

The cash equivalent of *non-interest-bearing notes* is their discounted present value at the time of receipt. *Immaterial amounts* of discount which apply to non-interest-bearing notes are usually *ignored* in the measurement process. *Material amounts* of discount, which are included in the face of such notes, are accounted for by using two accounts:

(1) Notes Receivable, which is debited for the face of the note.
(2) Notes Receivable—Unearned Discount, a contra-account which is credited for the discount.

Bills of Exchange

Bills of exchange, or *drafts,* are formal written documents which are often used in settling accounts or loans. A draft is an *order* to pay, whereas a note is a *promise* to pay. The *drawer* of a draft, usually a creditor, orders the *drawee*, usually a customer, to pay a certain sum at a certain time. *Sight drafts* are often used to secure collection from a customer in another city before the goods are delivered to him. They are payable on presentation, and the drawee must honor them by paying them before getting the *bill of lading*, which permits him to obtain the goods. The seller records the shipment as a sale on account and the collection of the sight draft as a credit to the customer's account.

At other times, the terms of sale require that the purchaser *accept*, or agree to pay, a *time draft* due at a specific future time. He does this by writing the word "Accepted," the date, and his signature on the face of the draft. Thereafter the effect of the accepted draft in the hands of the seller of goods is the same as that of a note receivable, and it may be recorded as a debit to the asset, Notes Receivable. A *trade acceptance*, evidencing the purchase and sale of goods, is generally easier for the owner to discount than is an ordinary note.

Interest on Notes Receivable

Credit grantors often provide for compensation for the use of their resources by accepting *interest-bearing promissory notes*, which require the payment of the *face* amount of the note at its *maturity*, or due date, plus *interest* at a specified percentage of the face. Interest accrues in proportion to the length of time the note is owed. Interest on notes of short duration is usually paid at maturity For long-term notes, interest may be due annually, semiannually, or quarterly.

The *interest expense* of the borrower is the difference between the sum he initially receives and the sum he pays back. The same amount is the *interest revenue* of the lender.

Simple interest, or interest based on the unpaid part of the face amount, may be computed by the formula

$$I = S(i)(n),$$

where I is the amount of interest
S is the initial sum borrowed, or principal
i is the interest rate per time period
n is the number of time periods

Example 8   A company borrows $1,000 from a bank for one year and gives in exchange an interest-bearing promissory note for $1,000, providing for the payment of interest at the rate of 6 per cent of the face amount per year. What is the interest cost?

Solution $$I = S(i)(n) = \$1,000(0.06)(1) = \$60.$$

If the term of a note bearing simple interest is less than one year, the appropriate fraction of a year must be substituted for n in the formula for computing interest cost.

Example 9   What is the interest cost of an interest-bearing note of $500 for three months at 6 per cent per year?

Solution $$I = S(i)(n) = \$500(0.06)(\tfrac{1}{4}) = \$500(0.015) = \$7.50.$$

Certain combinations of interest rates and time periods lend themselves readily to mental computations of interest. Unless there is a statement to the contrary, interest for a specified number of days is computed as though there were 360 days in the year. Loans for 60 days are quite common, and so is an interest rate of 6 per cent per year. Since 60 days is one-sixth of a year ($\frac{60}{360} = \frac{1}{6}$), the interest cost for 60 days at 6 per cent is 1 per cent ($\frac{1}{6}$ of 6 per cent) of the principal sum. Interest at 1 per cent may be computed by multiplying the principal by 0.01 (or by moving the decimal point two places to the left).

Example 10 What is the interest cost on an interest-bearing note of $662 for 60 days at 6 per cent per year?

Short-cut Solution Move the decimal point of the principal, $662, two places to the left. The interest cost is $6.62.

Proof $$I = S(i)(n) = \$662(0.06)(\tfrac{60}{360}) = \$662(0.06)(\tfrac{1}{6}) = \$662(0.01) = \$6.62.$$

This short-cut method may also be applied to the computation of interest on loans for terms which are convenient multiples of 60 days (30 days is one-half as much, 90 days is one and one-half times as much, and 120 days is twice as much).

Accounting for Interest-Bearing Notes Receivable

The facts of Example 8 would be journalized as follows:

```
1973                              (1)
Oct.  1    A, Cash...................................................1,000
                L, Notes Payable to Banks.....................          1,000
                Borrowed $1,000 on a one-year, 6% note.

                                  (2)
Dec. 31    OE, Interest Expense ...............................   15
                L, Accrued Interest Payable .................           15
                To record the interest expense for the last
                three months of 1973 and the corresponding
                liability at the end of the year.
```

In the income statement for 1973, Interest Expense would be reported as $15. In the December 31, 1973, financial position statement, the facts would be shown as follows:

LIABILITIES

Current liabilities:
  Notes payable to banks $1,000
  Accrued interest payable..   15

The payment of the note and interest in 1974 would be recorded as follows (assuming that adjusting entries are journalized only at the end of the year):

(3)

1974

Sept. 30   L, Notes Payable to Banks............................ 1,000
           L, Accrued Interest Payable   15
           OE, Interest Expense   45
               A, Cash..   1,060
           Paid the $1,000 note and $60 interest due
           today, including $45 interest which accrued
           in 1974.

The 1974 income statement will include interest expense of $45, the cost of borrowing funds for the first nine months of that year.

Discount on Notes Receivable

As an alternative to an interest-bearing note, credit grantors sometimes accept *non-interest-bearing notes*, whose face amount includes the lender's compensation for waiting. Each payment of a part of the face amount of the note includes a payment for interest. This method of allowing interest is referred to as *discounting* a note. Two common variations of computing the amount of the discount (or interest) are

(1) The *true discount method*, in which the discount is the specified percentage of the *sum originally advanced*

(2) The *bank discount* method, in which the discount is the specified percentage of the *maturity*, or face, value of the note, which includes both the sum originally advanced by the lender and interest (or discount) for the waiting period. The part of the of the maturity value which represents interest may be explicitly stated or the interest may be implicit.

Accounting for Non-Interest-Bearing Notes Receivable

The receipt of a non-interest-bearing note is recorded as follows:

(1)

A, Notes Receivable... 100
    A, Accounts Receivable   100
Received a 30-day non-interest-bearing note on account.

The proper entry for receipt of a note such as that in Example 8, but including interest in its face, is

(2)

A, Notes Receivable (Face)..................................... 1,060
    A, Notes, Receivable—Unearned Discount   60
    A, Accounts Receivable   1,000
Received on account a non-interest-bearing note due
in one year.

In a statement of financial position prepared immediately after receipt of the note, the facts would appear thus:

Current assets:
Notes receivable, face amount $1,060
Deduct unearned discount 60
$1,000

A common illustration of this situation is the practice of including interest and service charges in the face amount of installment notes receivable.

The discount is earned in proportion to the passage of time. If the accounting period ends nine months after receipt of the note, the following entry should be made:

(3)
A, Notes Receivable—Unearned Discount 45
   OE, Interest Revenue 45
To record the accrual of 9 months' interest on $1,000 at 6%.

Treatment in the statement of financial position at that time would be

Notes receivable, face $1,060
Deduct unearned discount 15
$1,045

If the note were a 6 per cent interest-bearing note, the proper entries would be

(4)
A, Notes Receivable 1,000
   A, Accounts Receivable 1,000
Received on account a 6% note due in one year.

(5)
A, Accrued Interest Receivable............................... 45
   OE, Interest Revenue 45
To record the accrual of 9 months' interest on $1,000 at 6%.

The statement presentation would be as follows:

Notes receivable.. $1,000
Accrued interest receivable...................................... 45
$1,045

Note that the total sum receivable, $1,045, is the same whether or not interest is explicitly stated.

Discounted Notes Receivable

Most promissory notes are *negotiable*; that is, they may be transferred to another owner in exchange for cash or in settlement of a debt. The original *payee* of the note transfers legal title by endorsing the note (signing his name on the back). The *maker* of the note must then pay its face amount plus any interest specified to the *endorsee* when the latter presents the note for payment on its due date.

If the endorsement is *without recourse*, the endorser is not held responsible for paying the note if the maker fails to pay the final endorsee on the maturity date. A business which transfers a note without recourse records the transaction as an outright *sale* of the note. The journal entry for sale involves a debit to Cash for the amount received and a credit to Notes Receivable for the face of the note. A debit difference between these two sums is Interest Expense, while a credit difference is Interest Revenue.

Endorsement with Recourse

If a note is transferred *with recourse*, the endorser is responsible for paying the note to the final endorsee at maturity if the maker fails to do so on proper presentation. Even though the endorser has sold the note, he has a *contingent*, or potential, *liability* for paying it which he must show in his accounts and financial statements until the maturity of the note. At that time the contingent liability ceases to exist for one of the following reasons:

(1) The maker of the note pays the full amount owed to the final endorsee, and the endorser has *no further liability*.

(2) The maker of the note fails to pay the amount owed to the final endorsee, and the endorser has an *actual liability* to pay the full amount owed on the note.

Contingent assets and *contingent liabilities* should not be presented in the statement of financial position in the same way as actual assets and liabilities because of the great uncertainty associated with them. Nevertheless, adequate disclosure to the reader of the financial statements requires that the amount of such contingencies be shown. The most common method is to omit both the contingent asset and the contingent liability amounts from the body of the statement, but to refer in the body of the statement to a footnote describing them.

Example 11   The Elson Co. received a $1,000 60-day, 6 per cent note from Marks Co. on March 1 in exchange for merchandise. On the same date the Elson Co. discounted the Marks Co. note with the bank *with recourse*. How should these facts be shown in Elson's financial statements on March 31?

Solution   LIABILITIES

Current liabilities:

....

Contingent liabilities (See Note A) ....   —

    Total liabilities.. $15,500

....

    Total equities $41,700

Note A. The company was contingently liable on March 31 for notes receivable discounted amounting to $1,000. No loss is expected as a result of this contingency.

Internal Control Procedures for Notes

The procedures for handling and recording notes receivable should ensure that the business has an accurate account of notes received, that it uses adequate methods for safeguarding and collecting notes and interest, and that it authorizes and records properly the disposition of notes by sale or collection. Duties of employees should be so divided that each of the functions of recording, keeping custody of, and collecting or discounting notes is performed by a different individual.

A business which has frequent notes receivable transactions should establish a subsidiary notes receivable record to support the Notes Receivable general ledger controlling account. This detailed ledger may consist of a line on a columnar page for each note, with columns for information about the note. An alternative is to use a ledger sheet for each note.

Summary Earning an income is the most important objective of business, but cash is the lifeblood of business. *Cash flow* during a given period *differs from income* because of differences of timing, but it also differs because some types of cash receipts and payments never affect income in any period.

Internal control measures for protecting cash are based on a *division of duties* such that one employee independently verifies the accuracy of the work of another. Cash receipts procedures are intended to ensure that all money collected for the business actually finds its way into the business bank account. Cash payment safeguards are designed to permit payments only after a responsible person has determined from sufficient evidence that the payment is proper. An important step in the control of cash is the preparation of the periodic bank reconciliation.

Account classifications used for money and bank accounts should indicate the extent to which there are restrictions on the use of these resources. Such accounts are ordinarily stated at their face amount. The proper measure of both Accounts Receivable and Notes Receivable is their *current cash equivalent*.

Estimates of future sales returns, allowances, discounts, and uncollectibles should be recorded as contra-accounts to Sales Revenue and Accounts Receivable. The deduction from revenue is necessary for a *proper matching* in income measurement, while the deduction from Accounts Receivable is necessary in measuring the asset. An age distribution of accounts receivable is useful in evaluating the quality of accounts receivable, in estimating the amount of uncollectible accounts, and in expediting collections.

Analytical reports showing the *turnover rate* of accounts receivable, as well as related measures, are useful to management in appraising the past performance of the business in extending credit and making collections. They are also an aid in forecasting the amounts of cash collections and of accounts receivable balances in the future.

Discussion Questions and Problems

10-1 As the company accountant, you have just presented financial statements to your president showing a net income of $50,000. "That can't be right!" exclaims the president, "The company has less cash than it had last year." He points to the following figures in the statement of financial position to support his contention: Cash, December 31, 1972, $32,000; Cash, December 31, 1973, $26,000.

What plausible explanations can you offer to the president?

10-2   Give an example of each of the following:

(1) Receipt   (4) Expense
(2) Disbursement   (5) Gain
(3) Revenue   (6) Loss

10-3   Company *A* has its headquarters in the United States and has an important branch in Mexico. The accounts show that a balance of $2,500,000 is on deposit in checking accounts in domestic banks and a balance of 3 million pesos is on deposit in checking accounts in Mexico. How should these facts be shown in Company *A*'s financial position statement?

10-4   In a small business one employee sometimes handles cash collections from customers and also posts to the Accounts Receivable subsidiary ledger.

a. How could this employee alter the books to conceal a cash shortage?
b. What routine procedure would you suggest that the business follow (other than denying him access to the books) in order to detect alterations of this type?

10-5   A large retailing corporation reported the following as *other assets*:

Customers' notes—deferred maturities.....................		$ 51,675
Cash value of life insurance policies		
(maturity value, $900,000)..........................		136,688
Pension fund:		
Cash	$ 8,966	
U.S. and State of Virginia bonds	49,591	
Corporate securities and real estate		
mortgages................................	287,122	345,679

Required   a. Explain the meaning of each of the accounts named and explain why it is included under noncurrent assets.
b. Why are the cash value of life insurance policies and the cash in the pension fund not included with cash and classified as current assets?
c. Is it ever proper to show corporate securities as a current asset?

10-6   The Barbo Company has four separate bank accounts with the North Bank. The bank accounts include a general checking account, a payroll account, time deposits to be used for replacing special equipment at a later date, and a special bond sinking fund required by legal contract. The Barbo Company has agreed to deposit certain amounts in this fund periodically. In addition the company has funds invested in 12-month certificates of deposit. Mr. Amos Barbo and his wife have a personal joint checking account in the bank.

a. Which of the above accounts should be included as *cash* on the company's financial position statement?
b. How would each of the above items that is not classified as cash be reported on the financial position statement?
c. Outline the steps that should be taken to maintain proper internal control over these accounts.

10-7   The Jackson Company received its bank statement on March 31, 1973, and observed that the statement showed a balance of $128,752.17. The cash account in the ledger showed a balance of $153,413.25 on that date.

a. Which, if any, of the above figures is the "true cash balance"?

b. What steps would management of the company follow in determining the balance to report on the Statement of Financial Position on March 31?

c. As a stockholder in the company, why would you be interested in the "true cash balance"?

d. As a creditor of the company, why would you be interested in the "true cash balance"?

10-8 Credle Company maintains four bank checking accounts, one with each of the banks in the city. On December 31, 1973, the adjusted balances in the banks were as follows:

> Bank #1: $6,540
> Bank #2: An overdraft of $3,200
> Bank #3: $9,180
> Bank #4: An overdraft of $124

a. How would the preceding information be presented in the financial position statement?

b. Why might there be a debit balance in the Cash in Bank account on the depositor's books and an overdraft as shown by the bank's books?

c. Why might there be an overdraft as shown by the depositor's books and a credit balance as shown by the bank statement?

10-9 Two owner-managers of small service businesses were discussing the accounting records kept in their businesses. The manager of one stated, "I recognize revenue in the accounts only when it is collected, and I recognize expenses only when they are paid for. After all, that is how I measure my income for income tax purposes."

The manager of the other concern said, "You should use the accrual basis for measuring your income because it is a much better indicator of business performance during the year."

The owner of the first business replied, "It really doesn't make any difference which method you use, because over a period of years the total income will be the same anyway."

Required Comment on the validity of the statements made by the two owners.

10-10

a. Explain how the following can contribute to the internal control of cash.

b. What essential safeguards must be observed in order for each of these internal control features to be effective?

(1) Cash registers which print receipts.
(2) Printed, prenumbered slips for recording cash sales.
(3) A petty cash system.
(4) Requirement of two signatures on checks.
(5) A separate payroll bank account.
(6) A bank reconciliation.
(7) A regular vacation for the cashier.

10-11

a. How can an employee who writes checks and keeps the Cash Payments Journal embezzle money and conceal the shortage?

b. How can an employee who handles cash collections and posts to the Accounts Receivable subsidiary ledger embezzle money and conceal the shortage?

c. What internal control procedures would ordinarily prevent the irregularities described in parts a and b?

10-12   The manager of a business established a petty cash fund of $50 for making small payments. Several people within the organization were permitted to make payments from the fund, and little effort was made to collect substantiating documents for payments. From time to time when the money in the fund was low, the contents of the coin box in the office soft-drink machine were placed in the petty cash fund. When criticized by the auditor for loose control over the fund, the manager shrugged and replied, "After all, our losses are limited to $50."
Comment on this situation.

10-13   The custodian of a $50 petty cash fund neglected to have it replenished at the end of the accounting period, December 31, 1973, because there was still currency and coin totaling $19 in the fund on that date. Most of the expenditures from the fund had been for postage and wrapping supplies, all of which had been used immediately. The fund was next replenished on January 10, 1974, when total payments amounted to $48.

a. What errors, if any, were there in the 1973 financial statements?
b. What errors, if any, would there be in the 1974 financial statements if the January 10 replenishment is recorded in the usual way?

10-14

a. If a business is using the *gross price* method of recording sales discounts, state how the following would be reported in its financial statements:
(1) Trade discounts on goods sold on account.
(2) Cash discounts on goods sold on account.
(3) Trade discounts when goods sold on account earlier are paid for.
(4) Cash discounts when payments for goods sold on account earlier is made within the discount period.
(5) Cash discounts related to goods paid for after the expiration of the discount period.
b. How would each of the items in part a be reported by a business which uses the *net price* method of recording sales discounts?

10-15   The Atlas Mfg. Co. analyzes the balances of its accounts receivable at the end of each year, using the following age categories: 0–1 month, 1–2 months, 2–3 months, 3–6 months, and over 6 months. Its credit terms are 2/10, n/30. Atlas Mfg. Co.'s fiscal year ends on August 31.

Wilkard Sales Co.

1973			1973		
Apr. 9	Sale	2,000	Apr. 19	Collection	500
Aug. 20	Sale	1,200	May 12	Collection	1,000
			Aug. 22	Return	100
			Aug. 31	Collection	300

a. In what age category or categories should the above account be reported?
b. Assume that the total accounts in each age classification listed above were $90,000, $24,000, $8,000, $10,000, and $16,000, respectively. Show how you would use this information in estimating the amount of uncollectibles.
c. For what other purpose does a company use an age distribution schedule?

10-16   During 1973 the Citon Company had sales of $300,000, of which 70 per cent were sold on credit. Past experience of the company shows that 2 per cent of the credit sales prove uncollectible. The accountant uses the percentage of sales method of estimating losses from uncollectibles at the end of the year.

The balance in Accounts Receivable—Estimated Uncollectibles on January 1, 1973, was $800. Accounts Receivable totaling $1,600 were written off as uncollectible during the year.

a. What was the balance in Accounts Receivable—Estimated Uncollectibles on December 31, 1973, before the adjusting entry for the year was made? What does this balance mean?

b. What adjusting entry would you recommend at the end of 1973? Why?

10-17   Refer to Problem 10-16. The accountant prepared a schedule of the accounts receivable, classified according to age, as follows:

Age in Months	Total Amount	Per Cent of Expected Loss
0–1	$90,000	1%
1–2	18,000	3
2–4	10,000	10
4–6	2,500	20
Over 6	1,400	50

Required a. Considering the schedule above in addition to the information given in Problem 10-16, prepare the appropriate adjusting entry on December 31 to provide for estimated uncollectibles.

b. Compare the two methods used for estimating uncollectibles. Why do they differ? What are the advantages of each method?

10-18   A department manager of the company for which you are the accountant noted that you were preparing an adjusting entry for losses from uncollectibles and asked why you were recording a loss when you had no proof that the accounts would go bad. He suggested that a more appropriate method would be to wait until the account proved to be uncollectible before recording the amount. How would you reply to him?

10-19   On December 31, 1973, the ledger of Company XYZ showed a debit balance in Accounts Receivable—Estimated Uncollectibles.

a. How could this happen?

b. What course of action, if any, would you recommend to correct this situation?

10-20   "Accounting is based on definite events which can be objectively measured. Recording a loss for accounts receivable which are *expected* to become bad in the future, or a revenue deduction for sales returns which are *expected* to occur in the future, violates this principle."

How can you defend the practice of recording expected losses and returns in the face of this argument?

10-21   Answer the following questions, using appropriate illustrations:

a. What effect does the write-off of a definitely uncollectible account arising from a sale in a prior year have on the income of the year of write-off? On total assets?

b. What effect does the collection of an account which was written off as uncollectible in a prior year have on the income of the year of collection? On total assets?

c. What effect does recording the adjusting entry for estimated uncollectibles have on income in the year in which the estimate is made? On total assets?

10-22   Each of the following opinions is held by some accountants as to the proper location of Losses from Uncollectibles in the income statement:

(1) It is a deduction from sales revenue, representing revenue never realized.
(2) It is selling expense, associated with selling goods on credit.
(3) It is an administrative expense, because the credit manager approves the granting of credit.
(4) It is a financial expense, representing the cost of extending credit.

Evaluate each of these opinions and state under what conditions, if any, you would consider each location proper.

10-23   A company which has been in business for several years has never made any adjusting entries to record the estimated cash discounts, returns, and allowances which apply to the year-end balances of accounts receivable. "It would be a waste of time," says the head accountant. "Net income will be the same for each year whether we make these adjustments or not. The charges to revenue deduction accounts which we make in the current year apply to the preceding year's sales, it is true. But their effect on current year's income will be offset by the estimated charges which apply to current year's sales, for which we make no adjustment at the end of the year."

a. What weaknesses are there in this argument?
b. Illustrate the effect of ignoring estimated discounts, returns, and allowances on (1) the income statement and (2) the statement of financial position prepared at the end of 1973. Use figures of your own choice.

10-24   An analysis of the account Investment in Marketable Securities of the Albet Company on December 31, 1973, disclosed the following:

	Cost	Market
U.S. Government bonds	$40,000	$39,800
Braxson Company bonds.....................	20,000	19,700
Crandon Company bonds...................	30,000	30,800
Total	90,000	90,300

a. How should Albet Company report this information on its statement of financial position?
b. What entries affecting the income statement or the financial position statement are necessary on December 31?

10-25   For a number of years the Flawmite Company has been using a petty cash fund of $50 to handle small payments. On January 2, 1973, the fund was increased to $100. The custodian of the fund was instructed that individual payments were to be limited to $5.00. During the month of January the following transactions occurred which affected the Petty Cash fund. The fund had been replenished to $50 on December 31, 1972.

Transactions:

Jan.   3—Paid for light bulbs, $3.00.
         4—Paid for postage on outgoing packages to customers, $4.00.
         6—Changed a $20 bill for a customer.
         7—Purchased a typewriter ribbon, $1.40.
         9—Lent an employee $5.00.

14—Paid freight on incoming merchandise, $3.80.

17—Contributed $3.00 to the Salvation Army.

20—Advanced an employee $3.50 bus fare for making several trips on company business.

28—Paid $5.00 for minor items of merchandise for resale.

31—Paid $5.00 for postage for office use.

The Flawmite Company replenishes the Petty Cash fund at the end of each month.

a. Considering the above information, draft any journal entries necessary.

b. How much cash should be on hand in the Petty Cash box on January 1? On January 31?

c. If a count of the cash in the Petty Cash box revealed that cash was short by $0.80, how should this be reported on the books?

d. If January is a typical month, was there a need for replenishing the fund at the end of each month? If not, when would you suggest that the fund be replenished, and why?

10-26 How would each of the following accounts be classified on the financial statements?

(1) Petty Cash fund

(2) Accounts Receivable—Estimated Discounts Allowed

(3) Uncollectible Sales Revenue

(4) Notes Receivable—Unearned Discount

(5) Installment Accounts Receivable

(6) Unused Postage

(7) Deposits in a foreign bank

(8) Notes Receivable Discounted

(9) Sales Discounts Allowed

(10) Accrued Interest Payable

(11) Credit Balances in Accounts Receivable

(12) An overdrawn bank account

(13) Accounts Receivable—Estimated Uncollectibles

(14) Accrued Interest Receivable

(15) Sales Discounts Disallowed

(16) Debit Balances in Accounts Payable

(17) Accounts Receivable Assigned

(18) Sales Returns and Allowances

(19) A U.S. Government bond being held until March 15 of the current year when the income tax of the company will be paid

(20) Dividends Receivable

10-27 The Caplinger Co. maintains a checking account in the State Bank and prepares a monthly bank reconciliation in two parts, the final figure of which is the correct balance available for spending.

Required Indicate by a letter how each of the numbered items below would be handled in the bank reconciliation for June 30, 1973. Use the following code:

(a) Added to the depositor's Cash balance.

(b) Deducted from the depositor's Cash balance.

(c) Added to the bank's account with the depositor.

(d) Deducted from the bank's account with the depositor.

(e) Not used in the reconciliation.

(1) Deposit mailed to bank on the last day of May and recorded by the bank on June 2.

(2) Deposit mailed to bank on the last day of June.

(3) Check collected on a customer's account and deposited on June 28, but returned by the bank on June 29 marked "insufficient funds."

(4) Check in payment of account payable recorded on the depositor's books at its correct amount of $159, but paid by the bank at $195.

(5) Receipt and deposit from a customer on June 9 recorded on the depositor's books at $100, but recorded by the bank at its correct amount of $110.

(6) Checks written by the depositor in May but paid by the bank in June.

(7) Checks written by the depositor in May but not yet paid by the bank.

(8) Bank service charges for May, recorded by the bank in June, and not recorded on the books.

(9) A note owed to the bank, face amount $1,000 and interest $30, which was charged to the depositor's account by the bank on June 30 and not recorded on the books. The note's maturity date was June 30.

(10) A credit of $50 on the June bank statement made as a result of an error of the same amount discovered on the bank's May statement.

10-28

Required a. Prepare a bank reconciliation for the Darlee Corporation on January 31, 1973, at the end of its first month of operations.

b. Show in general journal form the entries that are necessary to correct the corporation's books.

CASH RECEIPTS JOURNAL, Page 1

1973	Account Credited	Amount
Jan. 2	Capital Stock	20,000
4	Sales	1,000
8	Accounts Receivable	1,600
12	Sales	4,000
20	Notes Payable	10,000
28	Sales	3,120
31	Accounts Receivable	4,200
	Total	43,920

CASH DISBURSEMENTS JOURNAL, Page 1

1973	Check No.	Account Debited	Amount
Jan. 3	1	Equipment	12,000
5	2	Rent Expense	800
7	3	Merchandise Inventory	6,000
9	4	Prepaid Insurance	1,000
12	5	Prepaid Taxes	600
15	6	Merchandise Inventory	10,000
21	7	Organization Cost	2,400
30	8	Utilities Expense	1,400
31	9	Salary Expense	4,000
		Total	38,200

NEIGHBORHOOD BANK
Account of Darlee Corporation

Debits		Credits	Date (1973)	Balance
		20,000	1/2	20,000
12,000			1/4	8,000
20		1,000	1/5	8,980
800			1/7	8,180
		1,600	1/9	9,780
6,000			1/12	3,780
		4,000	1/13	7,780
600,	1,000		1/16	6,180
160,	10,000	9,900	1/20	5,920
2,400			1/25	3,520
		3,210	1/29	6,730
10			1/31	6,720

Enclosed with the bank statement were debit memoranda as follows:

1/5	$ 20	Printing checks
1/20	160	Insufficient funds check of P. T. Brayer included in deposit of 1/9
1/31	10	Service charge for handling account

There were credit memoranda for the following two items:

1/20	$9,900	Proceeds of $10,000, 60-day note to bank, less discount at 6 per cent
1/29	90	Deposit slip improperly added

10-29

Required   a. Prepare a bank reconciliation for the Dalent Company for October 1973.

b. Show in journal form the entries needed to adjust the company's books at the end of October.

The Dalent Company prepared the following bank reconciliation on September 30, 1973:

Balance of Cash ledger account, 9/30.......................		$1,786
Add: Face, $4,000, and interest, $20, of customer's		
note collected by bank		4,020
		5,806
Deduct: Bank service charges for September		6
Correct balance on deposit September 30		$5,800
Balance of deposit account on bank statement, September 30		$6,080
Add: Deposit of 9/30 in transit		800
		6,880
Deduct outstanding checks;		
#117..	$180	
#121..	300	
#122..	600	1,080
Correct balance on deposit, September 30...............		$5,800

The following information was taken from the books of the Dalent Company at the end of October. The company's trial balance was out of balance.

Cash in Bank

1973				1973			
Oct. 1	Bal.		5,800	Oct. 31		CD5	38,600
31		CR3	38,400				

CASH RECEIPTS JOURNAL, Page 3 (condensed)

1973

Oct. 5	Cash sales...	6,000
12	Cash sales...	8,000
19	Collections on account	3,600
26	Cash sales...	14,000
31	Collections on account	7,800
	Total...	38,400

CASH DISBURSEMENTS JOURNAL, Page 5 (condensed)

1973   Ck. No.

Oct. 5	123	....	2,000
10	124	....	4,000
15	125	....	9,000
20	126	....	7,600
25	127	....	6,000
30	128	....	10,000
		Total...	38,600

All check entries were matched by debits to Accounts Payable.

NEW NATIONAL BANK
Statement of Account with Dalent Company

Debits		Credits	Date (1973)	Balance
			9/30	6,080
		800	10/1	6,880
600			10/2	6,280
		6,000	10/6	12,280
2,000			10/8	10,280
4,000,	300	8,000	10/13	13,980
1,040,	9,000	3,600	10/20	7,540
		14,100	10/27	21,640
480			10/29	21,160
10,000			10/31	11,160

A bank debit memorandum dated October 20 was for the principal, $1,000, and interest of a note owed it by the Dalent Company. The latter had authorized the bank to charge its account at the note's maturity. Also included was a memo for $480, dated October 29, for an insufficient funds check included in the October 27 deposit. The company incorrectly added the items composing the cash sales of October 26.

10-30   The Cash in Bank account in the Grambler Corp.'s ledger had a debit balance of $11,250 on November 30, 1973. The Eastern State Bank's statement of account on the same date showed a credit balance of $18,454. A comparison of the book receipts and payments with the bank's deposits and charges disclosed the differences listed below.

(1) The total of cash collections of November 3, all from charge customers, was

recorded on the books as $560. The bank statement showed the correct total, $650.

(2) Deposits in transit of $623 on October 31, as shown by the October bank reconciliation, were credited to the deposit account by the bank in November.

(3) The Grambler Corp. followed the practice of placing its daily collections in a night deposit window after bank closing hours of the corresponding day, and then having its cashier go to the bank on the next business day to claim the night deposit bag and have the deposit recorded by the bank. Collections of November 30 handled in this manner totaled $600.

(4) The Grambler Corp. shipped goods to a new customer in a distant city on November 17; terms, sight draft attached to the bill of lading. The bank, which had been asked to handle the draft, reported a collection on November 30 in the amount of $2,500. The bank charged the Grambler Corp. $5 for the collection service.

(5) Two debit memoranda included with the bank statement were for insufficient funds checks. One, in the amount of $200, was from Otis Hines, a customer, who explained that he had made an error in keeping his check stub balance and would pay the amount due within a week. The other, for $50, turned out to have been a check from a cash customer whose address was fictitious.

(6) The deposit of November 22, $380, did not appear on the bank statement. Investigation revealed that it had been credited to the Grambling Moving Co.

(7) The bank charged a check signed by the Grambling Moving Co. in the amount of $80 to the Grambler Corp.'s account on November 16.

(8) Check No. 1053 was issued to a salesman in payment of his commission. It was recorded in the Cash Disbursement Journal as $283, but was actually drawn for $238 and was paid by the bank at this amount.

(9) The bank enclosed a debit memorandum of $25 for the cost of printing checks, which were expected to be sufficient for about a year's use.

(10) A deposit of $3,100 appeared on the bank statement under the date of November 12. Investigation disclosed that the deposit had been made by the Granville Mfg. Co.

(11) Check No. 1214 appeared on the bank statement as $178. Its correct amount, for the payment of advertising, was $187.

(12) Checks issued by the Grambler Corp. but not yet paid by the bank totaled $2,800. Of this amount, $216 had been issued in October and $50 in September.

Required a. Prepare a bank reconciliation for the Grambler Corp. as of November 30, 1973.

b. Journalize the entries necessary to correct the corporation's books on that date.

10-31 During 1973 the Alpine Company had total sales of $700,000, of which $340,000 were for cash and $360,000 were on account. The Accounts Receivable balance on January 1, 1973, was $30,000 and on December 31, 1973, it was $50,000.

Required a. Compute the number of accounts receivable turnovers for 1973.

b. What was the average collection period?

c. The company's normal credit terms are net 30 days. How could the information computed above be useful to management? With what information should it be compared? What are its limitations?

10-32 The Felton Mfg. Co.'s total sales for 1973, all on account, were $300,000 before deducting cash discounts. Sales terms were 2/10, n/30 to all customers, and the company used the gross price method of recording sales discounts. By December 31, 1973, total cash collections on account amounted to $245,000, after discounts of $4,000 had been deducted. Sales returns and allowances totaled $5,000. At the end of the year accounts billed at $40,000 were still eligible for the cash discount, and it was estimated that discounts would be taken on 80 per cent of these balances. In the past, uncollectible accounts receivable have averaged $\frac{1}{2}$ per cent of gross sales on account minus returns and allowances. This loss ratio is expected to continue.

Required
a. Journalize the foregoing facts.
b. Show how the appropriate items would appear in the December 31 financial position statement.
c. Show how the appropriate items would appear in the 1973 income statement.

10-33   Refer to the facts in Problem 10-32.

Required
How would your answer be changed if the company used the net price method of recording sales discounts?

10-34   The Graham Co. was organized in 1973. At the end of the year its trial balance contained the following balances:

Accounts receivable...	$ 45,000
Sales revenue...	220,000
Uncollectible sales revenue..	2,700
Accounts receivable—estimated uncollectibles.....................	2,700

Of the year's sales, $40,000 were for cash.

The following transactions occurred in 1974:
(1) Sold additional merchandise for cash, $50,000, and on account, $210,000.
(2) Collected accounts totaling $190,000.
(3) Allowed credit of $5,000 for returned sales.
(4) Wrote off as definitely uncollectible specific 1973 accounts totaling $1,400, including T. M. Romont's account of $150.
(5) Several months later, collected Romont's account in full.
(6) At the end of 1974, estimated that the remaining provision for uncollectible 1973 accounts still on the books was correct. Also forecast that the loss percentage based on 1974 net sales would be the same.

Required
a. Journalize the relevant closing entries for 1973.
b. Post the ending 1973 balances after closing to T-accounts.
c. Journalize and post the entries for 1974.
d. Show how the facts relevant to account receivable would be reported in the December 31, 1974, financial position statement.
e. Show how sales revenue and deductions would appear in the 1974 income statement.
f. Explain carefully what the balance in Accounts Receivable—Estimated Uncollectibles at the end of 1974 means.
g. Explain why the balances in Uncollectible Sales Revenue and Accounts Receivable—Estimated Uncollectibles were the same amounts at the end of 1973 but different at the end of 1974.
h. Would the Graham Co.'s income measurement be more accurate if it waited until accounts prove definitely uncollectible before recording any loss? Explain.

Required   **10-35**   Compute the following:
a. Interest to maturity on a 90-day, 6 per cent note for $800.
b. The maturity value of a 30-day, 8 per cent note for $2,000.
c. Interest to maturity on a 45-day, 7 per cent note for $1,000.

Required **10-36**

    a. Journalize the following transactions of the Balkin Co.

    b. Books are closed annually on April 30. Journalize adjusting and closing entries related to notes and interest.

Transactions.

Apr. 1—Received a 6 per cent, 90-day note for $2,500 from the Toper Corp. for a sale made today.

      2—The Danton Mfg. Co. owed the Balkin Co. an account of $1,200. Balkin agreed to accept a 60-day, $800 note of the Roper Co. owed to the Danton Mfg. Co., together with accrued interest, in partial settlement of the account. The Danton note was dated March 3 and carried interest at 6 per cent. The Danton Mfg. Co. transferred ownership of the note to the Balkin Co. by endorsing the note.

      3—Received a 6 per cent, 60-day note for $1,500 from the Nemo Co. to apply on their account.

    30—Adjusting and closing entries for the month were made.

May 2—Collected the Roper note in full.

June 2—The Nemo Co. made the required payment on the April 3 note.

      3—Sold merchandise to Holton Co. for $6,000; terms, net 30 days. The shipment terms were f.o.b. destination, but for convenience the Holton Co. agreed to pay the freight and deduct it when paying for the merchandise.

July 3—Received a 60-day, 6 per cent note dated today for the balance due from the Holton Co., which deducted $150 freight.

10-37 Mr. Baxter, president of Downtown Dept. Store, was disturbed when his chief accountant reported that the accounts receivable turnover rate was 2.55 in 1973. The turnover rate in 1972 had been 3.00. The president immediately asked the chief accountant, the credit manager, and the sales manager to investigate the causes of the lower turnover rate and to initiate whatever corrective action was necessary.

    The accountant submitted the following detailed figures the next day:

	1973		1972	
Accounts receivable, Jan. 1:				
30-day charge accounts	$ 500,000		$ 700,000	
Installment accounts	1,000,000		300,000	
Total		$1,500,000		$1,000,000
Net sales on account:				
30-day charge accounts	2,400,000		$3,000,000	
Installment sales	1,550,000		750,000	
Total		3,950,000		3,750,000
Accounts receivable, Dec. 31:				
30-day charge accounts	400,000		500,000	
Installment accounts	1,200,000		1,000,000	
Total		1,600,000		1,500,000

The installment accounts ranged in terms from 12 to 18 months.

Required a. Summarize briefly the reports that you think should have been made by each manager in response to the president's request.

    b. Make any computations that are necessary to explain the change in conditions from 1972 to 1973, and explain the meaning of your results.

Cases   10-1   Wren Products, Inc. Wren Products, Inc., was organized in 1973. Its credit sales for the year totaled $200,000, and on December 31, 1973, its uncollected accounts receivable totaled $35,000. Income before tax was $10,000, without considering uncollectibles. Credit sales for 1974 were $200,000 and accounts receivable on December 31, 1974, were $42,000, all from 1974 sales. Income before tax in 1974 was $28,000. Losses from uncollectible accounts were typically 1 per cent of net credit sales in the industry. During 1974 Wren Products determined that the following accounts resulting from 1973 sales were definitely uncollectible:

Lemming Co., $500; Martin Sales Corp., $240; Oriole Mfg. Co., $700.

Just before preparing the financial statements at the end of 1973, the accountant informed the president that federal income tax rules permit taxpayers to use one of two methods for determining the deduction for uncollectible accounts:

(1) Deduct only accounts that have definitely been determined to be uncollectible. Make no estimate of future uncollectibles.

(2) Estimate uncollectibles that will result from past sales on the basis of business or industry experience in the past, and record the estimate as a tax deduction and as a contra to accounts receivable.

The president asked the accountant for a careful analysis of the advantages and disadvantages of each method from the standpoint of both the income tax returns and the financial statements. He estimated that sales and income before tax would increase about 20 per cent in 1975 and about 10 per cent annually thereafter. No change in the existing credit policy was contemplated.

Required   a. Record in general journal form the entries that Wren Products, Inc., would make in 1973 and 1974 under method (1).

b. Record the entries that would be needed under method (2).

c. What differences would there be in the income statements for both years under the two methods? In the financial position statements?

d. What are the advantages and disadvantages of each method for financial statement purposes?

e. What are the advantages and disadvantages of each method for income tax purposes?

10-2   Suburban Department Store. The Suburban Department Store, which had previously sold only for cash, opened charge account privileges to selected customers early in 1973. At the end of the year the store management wishes to appraise the results of the change in policy as a basis for deciding whether to continue credit under approximately the same terms, to relax credit terms, to tighten them, or perhaps even to return to the strictly cash sales basis. Also under consideration is a plan to charge each customer a monthly percentage of the unpaid balance beginning the second month after a sale is made. Several other retailers in the city have recently begun such a policy.

The Suburban Department Store's customers are chiefly of modest means. The store, located in a well-established neighborhood, has been in business for 12 years. There were no significant changes in policies or operating relationships, other than the credit policy, during 1973.

Required   a. As president of Suburban Department Store, what types of income statement and financial position data would you ask the accountant to furnish to assist you in deciding on future credit policy?

b. Assuming that the data you requested in part a are available, what analyses would you make in arriving at a decision?

c. What are the chief limitations of the results in parts a and b likely to be?

d. What intangible factors have a bearing on the decision? Explain how they should be considered.

10-3   Riverbend Mfg. Corp. The Riverbend Mfg. Corp. was organized in 1946. All its sales are on credit to wholesalers, retailers, and other manufacturers on payment terms of n/30. The company's income has taken a downward turn in 1973 and 1974, and management is exerting every effort to reduce costs while maintaining or increasing revenue, and to improve the efficiency with which assets are utilized. One sector of the business which is currently under examination is its credit and collection management.

The corporation's accounting department staff compiled the following data for the last two years. Accounts Receivable totaled $500,000 on Dec. 31, 1972.

Quarter Ending	Net Sales on Account		Accounts Receivable Ending Balances	
	1974	1973	1974	1973
Mar. 31	$ 760,000	$ 830,000	$460,000	$520,000
Jun. 30	860,000	900,000	600,000	500,000
Sept. 30	1,070,000	1,020,000	880,000	720,000
Dec. 31	580,000	550,000	460,000	360,000
Totals.................	$3,270,000	$3,300,000		

	Age of Accounts Receivable Balances		Per Cent
	December 31, 1974	December 31, 1973	Loss Expected
0–1 month	$270,000	$241,000	1
1–2 months.........	110,000	71,000	3
2–3 months.........	40,000	22,000	5
3–6 months.........	22,000	11,000	10
6–12 months.........	18,000	15,000	20
Totals..............	$460,000	$360,000	

The column "Per Cent Loss Expected" refers to the estimated loss from uncollectibles which are still on the books on December 31, 1974. The percentages were determined after a thorough analysis of actual loss experience for the past ten years.

The general ledger account Accounts Receivable—Estimated Uncollectibles already reflects the write-offs made during 1974 and an adjustment for estimated uncollectibles based on $\frac{3}{10}$ of 1 per cent (0.3%) of the year's sales on account. Uncollectible account losses have been provided for in this manner in past years. The account appears as follows:

A, Accounts Receivable—Estimated Uncollectibles

1974			1973		
Jan.–Dec.	Write-offs	9,500	Dec. 31	Balance	7,000
			1974		
			Dec. 31	Adjustment	9,810

It is the corporation's regular practice to write off all accounts receivable which have not been collected within 12 months from the date of sale.

The corporation's president has asked you to prepare a thorough report analyzing the company's accounts receivable. He wishes this not only as an aid in deciding on corrective action for the current condition, but also as a means of deciding what types of accounts receivable analysis should be regularly reported in the future.

Required a. Prepare an analytical report to the president, consisting of the following parts:
   (1) Accounts receivable turnover rates for the two years, using the arithmetic mean of year-beginning and year-ending balances. Round the turnover rate to the nearest hundredth. What does this analysis indicate?
   (2) Accounts receivable turnover rates for the two years, using the arithmetic mean of year-beginning and quarter-ending balances. What does this analysis indicate?
   (3) Percentage age distribution of accounts receivable balances at the ends of 1973 and 1974. Round to the nearest whole per cent. What does this indicate?
   (4) The number of days' sales represented by the December 31 balances in accounts receivable, computed for the year as a whole. Use a 360-day year and round to the nearest full day.
   (5) The expected loss from uncollectible accounts on the books on December 31, 1974.
   (6) A summary statement evaluating the company's credit and collection performance, based on the available information.
   b. What measures of accounts receivable performance do you think should be reported regularly in the future? Why?
   c. Make any journal entries that are necessary as a result of your analysis.

chapter 11

Measuring, Planning, and Controlling Inventories

Purpose of Chapter

The term *inventory* refers to items of tangible property which are being held for sale in the ordinary course of business, are being produced for sale, or are to be consumed in the near future in producing goods or services for sale.

Classes of goods for sale, defined in Chapter 3, include the *merchandise inventory* of a trading concern and the *finished goods inventory* of a manufacturer. Goods being produced are the *goods in process inventory* of a manufacturer, and consumable items include *materials* and *supplies inventories.*

The objectives of inventory accounting are to help measure the *periodic income* of a business, to help ascertain its *financial position,* and to assist in *managing its assets* efficiently and profitably.

This chapter explains some of the problems associated with measuring, planning, and controlling the investment in inventories and suggests approaches to solving them. It outlines some widely accepted methods of setting standards of performance for controlling inventory and of appraising actual performance.

MEASURING INVENTORY

Objectives and General Approach for Financial Reporting

In *measuring income* the *expired costs* of inventory items should be matched with the realized sales revenues which they helped create. A major class of expired inventory cost is Cost of Goods Sold Expense. The *unexpired* costs of inventory items—those which are expected to benefit the operations of future periods—are reported as *assets* in the financial position statement at the end of the period.

The principal steps involved in inventory accounting are

(1) Measuring and recording the acquisition costs of inventories.

(2) Tracing their movement through the business, with appropriate reclassifications of cost because of changes in form.

(3) Matching the costs of inventories with revenues in the period in which the revenues related to the inventories are realized.

The matching process is facilitated by tracing costs to the *physical* items of inventory. Initially such costs are debited to asset accounts as *product costs*, to be transferred ultimately to expense in the period in which the goods are sold.

The chief questions in measuring inventories are:

(1) *What types of expenditures* are included in the acquisition cost of inventories?

(2) When units of the same type of inventory item are acquired at different costs during a period, *which unit costs* apply to the goods sold and which costs apply to the goods on hand in the ending inventory?

(3) *What measurement procedure* applies when the current value of an inventory item on hand is no longer equal to its acquisition cost?

(4) How are the *quantities and costs* of inventories on hand at the end of a period determined?

The following sections are devoted to answering these questions.

Components of Inventory Acquisition Cost

The *acquisition cost* of an inventory item includes all expenditures reasonably incurred in bringing it to its existing condition and location. In addition to the *net invoice cost* (the amount of the invoice less discounts), inventory properly includes transportation and insurance charges incurred in getting the article to the owner's place of business. Added components of cost are excise and sales taxes and import duties which are not included in the invoice cost. It is also proper, but often impractical, to include in inventory the cost of purchasing, handling, and storing the item until it is ready for sale or for use.

In some cases freight, express, postage, and other transportation charges can be traced to specific articles, but in other cases it is difficult or impossible to trace them. A retailer rarely includes purchasing and handling costs as components of the asset, Merchandise Inventory, because it is usually *impractical* to trace such costs to individual units of merchandise. In such cases it may be acceptable to add transportation cost to individual items of inventory on the basis of an *average relationship*, such as the average percentage of transportation cost on purchases for an accounting period to the net invoice cost of all items bought during the period.

Discounts on Purchases

In arriving at the net invoice cost of an asset the purchaser must deduct *trade discounts* and *cash discounts*. *Trade discounts* are a formula for setting the price to a customer. *Cash discounts* are an inducement to the customer to pay promptly.

Many sellers use a series of trade discounts from a list price to establish the price to a *particular type of customer*, such as a retailer or wholesaler. The first discount may be allowed to all dealers, regardless of how many items they buy and when they pay for them. An additional discount is often allowed if *large quantities* are purchased.

Example 1   The Home Stove Works sells stoves which have a suggested retail price of $150 to the final purchaser. The manufacturer allows a discount of 20 per cent of list price to all retail dealers, and an additional discount of $16\frac{2}{3}$ per cent to dealers who buy ten or more stoves. On May 1 the Hardy Furniture Store bought ten stoves for resale. What was the net invoice cost?

Solution

Suggested retail price of each stove..	$ 150
Deduct dealer discount, 20%	30
Price to any dealer buying one stove	$ 120
Deduct quantity discount to dealers buying 10 or more, $16\frac{2}{3}$%......	20
Price per stove to dealer buying 10 or more	$ 100
Multiply by number of stoves bought....................................	× 10
Total invoice cost of 10 stoves	$1,000

If no cash discount is offered, that is, if payment terms are "net 30 days,"[1] the Hardy Furniture Store is supposed to pay $1,000 within 30 days from the date of the invoice. The price is $100 per stove whether the store pays early, on time, or late.

Cash discounts are allowed only if the purchaser pays within the cash discount period. His total payment will be one amount if he qualifies for the discount, and a higher amount if he pays late.

Common cash discount terms are expressed as "2/10, n/30," or "3/10, E.O.M." The percentage of the deduction and the time period during which it is available vary from company to company. The payment terms in the first illustration mean that the purchaser will be allowed a reduction of 2 per cent from the price stated on the invoice if he pays within 10 days; otherwise, he must pay the amount of the invoice without cash discount at the end of 30 days. The second illustration means that the purchaser may deduct 3 per cent from

---

[1] The term *net* 30 days is a widely used misnomer. Actually, it should be interpreted as *none*, meaning that the purchaser is allowed no discount.

the invoice price if he pays by the tenth of the month following the date of the invoice. For a purchase made on May 3 under these terms, the discount would be available until June 10.

Discounts are deducted from the list price in the sequence in which they are stated: trade discounts first, then cash discounts.

The Net Price Method of Accounting for Cash Discounts on Purchases

Under the *net price method* of accounting for purchase discounts, the acquisition cost of an inventory item is considered to be the amount of money that would be needed to pay for it at the time of purchase. Any additional payment for *discount lost* is a *penalty*, or loss, not a valid addition to an asset. The normal expectation in business operations is that discounts will be taken; therefore the *net price is the normal price* of the items purchased.

Example 2   Assume that the Home Stove Works in Example 1 allows its customers a cash discount under terms of 2/10, n/30. On June 1 the Hardy Furniture Store buys ten stoves under the same terms as in Example 1, except that a cash discount is available. The sum of money needed to pay for the merchandise at once would be $980 ($1,000 − 2% of $1,000), and this is the acquisition cost of the asset. How would the purchase be recorded?

Solution   *1973*

June 1	A, Merchandise Inventory	980	
	L, Accounts Payable		980
	Purchased 10 stoves, terms 2/10, n/30.		

If the retailer in Example 2 pays within the discount period (any time through June 11), he should record a cash payment of a liability for $980. What entry should he make if he fails to take advantage of the discount and pays on July 1?

The amount of cash discounts available on assets purchased may be large in comparison with net income. For this reason, management and outsiders are interested in the amount of discounts the business fails to take, whether owing to lack of money or to slowness in processing the paper work needed before payment. This information is provided in the following entry for paying after the expiration of the discount period:

1973

July 1	L, Accounts Payable	980	
	OE, Purchase Discounts Lost	20	
	A, Cash		1,000
	Paid the Home Stove Works invoice after the expiration of the discount period.		

Because a discount of 2 per cent for paying 20 days early is equivalent to an annual rate of interest of about 36 per cent, firms with sufficient credit standing will usually borrow to take the cash discount. Creditors consider a customer's failure to take advantage of available discounts as a sign of financial weakness, and may use it as a reason for discontinuing credit to the customer.

The Gross Price Method of Accounting for
Cash Discounts on Purchases

Some businesses record inventory purchased at its *gross invoice cost* and treat discounts actually taken as nonoperating revenue. The Hardy Furniture Store transactions in Example 2 would be recorded as follows under the gross price method:

1973				
June 1	A, Merchandise Inventory............................	1,000		
	L, Accounts Payable.............................		1,000	
	Purchased 10 stoves from Home Stove Works, terms 2/10, n/30.			
June 11	L, Accounts Payable	1,000		
	A, Cash		980	
	OE, Purchase Discount Revenue		20	
	Paid invoice of June 1 less 2% discount.			
or				
July 1	L, Accounts Payable.................................	1,000		
	A, Cash		1,000	
	Paid the Home Stove Works invoice of June 1 after the expiration of the discount period.			

The effects of the two methods on the financial statements may be contrasted as follows:

	Net Price Method	*Gross Price Method*
Asset, inventory......................................	Lower	Higher
Cumulative retained income	Lower	Higher
Expired cost of each item cost of goods sold...	Lower	Higher
Loss from discounts not taken.....................	Shown	Not shown
Revenue from discounts taken....................	Not shown	Shown

The gross price method is subject to the criticism that it records revenue when an asset is *paid for* rather than when it is *sold*. Even if the stoves in the June 11 transaction had not been sold at the end of the accounting period, $20 of revenue on them would be reported in the income statement as Purchase Discount Revenue. Revenue is *realized* when goods are sold, however, not when the seller pays their purchase price.

The gross price method of recording purchase discounts is sometimes defended on the ground that it is more practical than the net price method. It may be necessary to extend unit costs of inventory items to several decimal places under the net price method.

Measuring Inventories When Unit Costs Change

After the problem of how to trace components of inventory cost to the physical items has been settled, it still must be determined which units have been sold when similar units have been acquired at different times and at different costs. This involves selecting an orderly method of assigning *expired* inventory costs to the current period as expense, and treating *unexpired* inventory costs as assets, which are potential expenses of future accounting periods.

Management often uses accounting information in deciding what course of action to follow with regard to inventory. The following criteria help show which method of measuring inventory in the accounts provides the most useful information for decision making in a given case:

(1) The method should help to provide a *useful measure of income for the current period* as a basis for appraising performance. It should match expired inventory costs with the revenues to which those costs are related.

(2) It should help to provide a *useful measure of financial status* at the end of the current period. The unexpired cost of inventory at any date is an asset, which is used in measuring the financial position of the business.

(3) It should help to provide a *useful measure of the income of future accounting periods*. The amount of inventory cost which is treated as an asset at the end of the current accounting period is available for use and is therefore a potential expense of future periods.

(4) It should furnish information useful to management in *planning* future operations. Important aspects of this requirement are its usefulness in measuring the past turnover rates of inventories, the rate of return on assets, and similar comparisons used in appraising past results and in planning for the future.

(5) It should be useful in *promoting effective use* and protection of the economic values represented by the inventory.

(6) It should be *objective, orderly*, and not subject to manipulation for the purpose of influencing the reported results artificially.

(7) The time or difficulty involved in making inventory calculations should not outweigh the usefulness of the resulting information.

The important matter of choosing an inventory method in determining taxable income is discussed in Chapter 17.

No method of measuring inventory fully achieves all the objectives listed. The method that is appropriate in a given setting depends on the nature of the business, the nature of the inventories, the relationships of acquisition cost and selling price, economic conditions and the extent of changes in them, the ability of the personnel who deal with inventory measurement, and the use to which the resulting information is to be put by management and others.

The following are the commonly used basic methods of allocating inventory acquisition costs to cost of goods sold and ending inventory when the unit acquisition costs of a given type of inventory item change:

(1) Specific-identification.

(2) First-in, first-out (FIFO).

(3) Last-in, first-out (LIFO).

(4) Weighted-average.

The importance of the effect of the choice of inventory methods on the financial statements increases as the following increase:

(1) The balance of ending inventory in relation to the cost of goods bought during the period.

(2) The balance of the asset, ending inventory, in relation to the balances of other assets.

(3) The rate of fluctuations in the purchase prices of the inventory item.

Basic Illustration for Comparing Inventory Methods

The following data from the records of Emco Stores in 1973 are used as the basis for illustrating the four methods of assigning unit costs to inventory:

1973	*Units*	*Unit Cost*	*Total Cost*
Jan. 1 Inventory.............................	100	$5.00	$ 500
Purchases:			
Mar. 17......................................	50	$5.30	$ 265
May 25......................................	100	6.00	600
Jul. 10......................................	100	6.50	650
Oct. 1......................................	50	6.60	330
Dec. 7......................................	50	7.00	350
Total purchases........................	350		$2,195
Goods available for sale....................	450		$2,695

During 1973, 300 units were sold at various dates for total sales revenue of $2,400, and there were 150 unsold units in the final inventory.

It is assumed for simplicity that all purchases in 1972, the first year of operations, were made at a unit cost of $5; therefore the cost of the beginning inventory under any of the four methods was $500. Because the *cost of purchases* during a period is the same regardless of the method of deciding which units have been sold, the total cost of goods available for sale in 1973 (beginning inventory plus purchases) *in this illustration* is the same under all four methods, $2,695. The problem is to determine (1) *how much* of the cost of goods available for sale in 1973 *expired* and became cost of goods sold expense, and (2) *how much* of it was *unexpired* at the end of 1973, representing the cost of the asset, inventory.

Specific-Identification Method

One way to determine the cost of items in the ending inventory is to mark each article with its *specific* cost, usually in code. Determining the cost of the ending inventory then consists of adding up the marked costs of the specific unsold items.

Another method which produces similar results is to keep detailed cost records which specifically associate acquisition costs with particular units by using a serial number or some other means of identification. Under either procedure the ending inventory might be

Dec. 31, 1973, Inventory

	Units	Unit Cost	Total Cost
....	10	$5.00	$ 50
....	10	5.30	53
....	5	6.00	30
....	40	6.50	260
....	40	6.60	264
....	45	7.00	315
Total......................................	150		$972

The cost of goods sold is computed by subtracting the cost of the ending inventory from the cost of goods available for sale. The applicable part of the 1973 income statement under the specific-identification method is as follows:

	Units	Amounts	
Sales revenue	300		$2,400
Deduct cost of goods sold:			
Beginning inventory.....................	100	$ 500	
Add purchases	350	2,195	
Goods available for sale	450	$2,695	
Deduct ending inventory...............	150	972	
Cost of goods sold	300		1,723
Gross margin			$ 677

It might seem at first that the specific-identification method matches the expired cost of inventory items with revenue in a convincing way. Accounting seeks to match with revenues the costs which are *economically* related to them, however, and *physical relationships may be misleading*. If a unit of inventory bought at one date has the same economic service potential as one bought at another date, the items might be considered to be identical for purposes of measuring expired and unexpired costs, even though the acquisition costs physically associated with each unit differ. The selection of the specific items which are sold, and consequently of the specific items which remain in the ending inventory, may be purely accidental.

The measurements produced by the specific-identification method may be *erratic* rather than orderly. The method permits management to *influence arbitrarily* the amount of its income and its assets by selecting an item, otherwise identical with its group, for sale purely on the basis of its specific cost. The resulting income and asset measurements may be misleading in *appraising* past performance and present status, and in *planning* for the future.

The specific-identification method is simple to apply and is practical when there are relatively few inventory items. However, it requires much detailed work when the items in inventory are numerous and of small unit value.

The specific-identification method is best suited where differences other than cost, such as color, age, and condition, influence the selection of the particular item sold. When the units of a class are identical with each other, except for acquisition cost, a logical *assumed economic flow* of costs from asset to expense may be more objective and useful than an *identified physical flow*.

First-In, First-Out (FIFO) Method

One type of *assumed cost flow* used as a basis for inventory measurement is the *first-in, first-out (FIFO)* method. It assumes that the first units acquired are the first units disposed of. Consequently, the units on hand in the ending inventory are assumed to be from the most recent purchases.

The Emco Stores' inventory on December 31, 1973, under the first-in, first-out assumption is composed of the last 150 units bought, costed as follows (refer to basic data on p. 297):

Date of Acquisition	Units	Unit Cost	Total Cost
Dec. 7	50	$7.00	$ 350
Oct. 1	50	6.60	330
Jul. 10	50	6.50	325
Dec. 31 Inventory	150		$1,005

Cost of goods sold expense for 1973 is computed by subtracting the unexpired cost in the ending inventory, $1,005, from the cost of goods available for sale, $2,695. Its cost, $1,690, applies to the 300 units bought *earliest*:

Date of Acquisition	Units	Unit Cost	Total Cost
Jan. 1 Inventory	100	$5.00	$ 500
Mar. 17	50	5.30	265
May 25	100	6.00	600
Jul. 10	50	6.50	325
Goods sold	300		$1,690

The FIFO method is often criticized for *failing to match current acquisition costs of inventory with current revenues*. In the illustration, acquisition costs were rising during 1973, and undoubtedly Emco Stores' selling prices were also increasing. Sales revenue of 1973 reflects any higher resale prices in effect during the latter part of the year, but under FIFO the cost of goods sold expense does not include the corresponding higher purchase costs. The higher acquisition costs of the latter part of 1973 will be matched against the revenues of the early part of 1974 because of FIFO's *time lag* in charging incurred costs to expense.

Opponents of FIFO point out that, in comparison with results obtained by matching with sales revenues the acquisition costs prevailing at the time of the sale, FIFO produces the following distortions:

(1) When acquisition costs are *rising*, it *understates* cost of goods sold expense and *overstates* income, the ending inventory asset balance, and retained income.

(2) When acquisition costs are *falling*, it *overstates* cost of goods sold expense and *understates* income, the ending inventory asset balance, and retained income.

The FIFO method generally reports an ending inventory asset balance more closely in line with current acquisition costs than do the other cost methods.

It tends to *promote stewardship* of the current economic values of the inventory if plans for the future, such as setting sales prices, are based on the reported balance of the asset inventory.

FIFO is *objective* because it results in an orderly chronological flow of costs in which the oldest invariably expire first. It is largely free from manipulation to give a desired income figure. The method is reasonably simple to apply, but becomes cumbersome if the balance of a type of inventory represents many different acquisition costs at a given time.

FIFO is suitable for measuring cost of goods sold expense when the turnover of goods is rapid. In such cases there is a minimum time lag before acquisition costs are charged to expense. When management's policy is to set selling prices on the basis of FIFO cost, the method results in accurate matching of costs and revenues.

Last-In, First-Out (LIFO) Method

Another assumed cost flow used in accounting for inventory costs is *last-in, first-out* (*LIFO*), which treats the *last* units acquired as being the first units disposed of. The *ending inventory* is therefore composed of units from the *earliest acquisitions*—the beginning inventory, plus the earliest purchases in the current year if the inventory quantity increased during the year.

The ending inventory of Emco Stores for 1973 under the last-in, first-out method is (see basic data on p. 297):

Date of Acquisition	Units	Unit Cost	Total Cost
Jan. 1 Inventory............................	100	$5.00	$500
Mar. 17	50	5.30	265
Dec. 31 Inventory............................	150		$765

Cost of goods sold expense is determined by subtracting the cost of the ending inventory, $765, from the cost goods available for sale, $2,695. Its amount, $1,930, consists of the 300 units bought *last*:

Date of Acquisition	Units	Unit Cost	Total Cost
Dec. 7..	50	$7.00	$ 350
Oct. 1..	50	6.60	330
Jul. 10..	100	6.50	650
May 25...	100	6.00	600
Goods sold.....................................	300		$1,930

The principal argument for LIFO is that it does a *better job of matching current purchase costs against current sales revenues* than do the other methods of allocating costs. However, the costs which it treats as expired are not those current at the time of the sale, but the latest costs actually incurred. There may still be some time lag in matching costs with revenues unless purchases occur frequently.

LIFO may result in an *asset balance* substantially out of line with current costs if the *quantity* in the inventory *remains stable* or *increases* irregularly over the years. If, for example, Emco Stores has an inventory balance of 150 units of Article

A 30 years later when current purchase costs are $20 a unit, the LIFO ending inventory would still be $765, based on the unit costs of $5.00 and $5.30 incurred in 1972 and 1973. Use of this figure in making business decisions about the inventory would be misleading, because the current cost of 150 units of Article A would be four times as large.

Under LIFO the cost assigned to the asset, inventory, is unreliable to a varying extent. The greater the price changes that occur while the LIFO method is in use, the greater is the difference between the inventory asset cost computed under LIFO and current costs. When there have been significant price changes, use of the LIFO asset amount distorts the rate of inventory turnover, the rate of return on assets, and other ratios resulting from the comparison of assets with each other or with equities.

If the quantity in inventory decreases after remaining stable or increasing for a long period, LIFO may result in a *poorer matching* of costs and revenues than other cost methods. This is true because the costs of inventory items acquired many years earlier will be treated as a *part* of the cost of goods sold in the current period.

LIFO also permits manipulation of reported profit figures. Suppose that a company using LIFO finds early in December that its net income for the year to date is greater than it wishes to report. If prices are rising, the company can purchase some items at the current higher prices and charge them, by the LIFO method, to cost of goods sold expense for the year, even though not a one of them has physically been sold. Conversely, a similar purchase at lower current prices can be used to bolster a sagging net income figure.

LIFO is probably no more difficult to apply in its basic form than is FIFO, although some very complex variations of LIFO are in use.

When prices are rising and inventory quantities are stable or increasing, LIFO results in a lower taxable net income for the current period than do other cost methods. The advantages and limitations of this effect are discussed in Chapter 17.

A condition favoring the use of LIFO is a slow inventory turnover. Under such circumstances the effect of the time lag in matching acquisition costs with revenues would be significant under other inventory costing methods. Another factor favoring LIFO is a product that is relatively free from changes in nature or style. Still another is a situation in which changes in acquisition costs are followed promptly by changes in selling prices.

LIFO tends to be undesirable when there are relatively large fluctuations in the quantity of inventory on hand.

Weighted-Average Method

A third type of assumed inventory cost flow is the basis for the *weighted-average* method. Under this method the costs of units acquired are assumed to flow into a pool, where the cost of one unit cannot be distinguished from that of another. Items withdrawn from stock for sale or use have a unit cost which is an *average* of the cost of all acquisitions, weighted by the quantity acquired at each acquisition cost.

Many variations of the weighted-average inventory method are in use.

The variations differ chiefly in the frequency with which new averages are computed and the extent to which old balances are used in computing the average unit cost. Some common variations in the basic method require that weighted averages be recomputed each time there is an acquisition at a unit cost different from the previous average cost, once a month, or once a year. The costs averaged, under the variation used, may be only those of the purchases for a given period of time, or they may include the beginning inventory balance as well as purchases.

In the following illustration a weighted-average cost is computed at the end of the year from the *combined cost of the beginning inventory and purchases*. It is used as the unit cost of items in the ending inventory and cost of goods sold expense. (See basic data on p. 297.)

Date of Acquisition	Units	Unit Cost	Total Cost
Jan. 1 Inventory	100	$5.00	$ 500
Mar. 17	50	5.30	265
May 25	100	6.00	600
Jul. 10	100	6.50	650
Oct. 1	50	6.60	330
Dec. 7	50	7.00	350
Total available	450		$2,695

$$\text{Weighted-average unit cost} = \frac{\text{Total cost}}{\text{Number of units}} = \frac{\$2,695}{450} = \$5.989.$$

The cost of the ending inventory on December 31, 1973, is $898.35, determined by multiplying the number of units in the ending inventory, 150, by the weighted-average unit cost, $5.989.

The cost of goods sold for 1973 is $1,796.65. It is computed by subtracting the ending inventory, $898.35, from the cost of goods available for sale, $2,695.00. Approximately the same result could be obtained by multiplying the number of units sold, 300, by the average cost per unit, $5.989.

The weighted-average method tends to give an inventory cost *between* those resulting from FIFO and LIFO. It may have more or less of a time lag in matching current costs with current revenues than does FIFO, depending on the length of the inventory turnover period in relation to the frequency with which new averages are computed. Its expired costs tend to be less current than those computed under LIFO.

Over a series of periods in which there are both price rises and price declines, the weighted-average method tends to produce smaller fluctuations in periodic income than FIFO, but larger fluctuations than LIFO.

The effect of the weighted-average method on turnover rates and rates of return, as compared with other inventory methods, depends largely on how frequently new average unit costs are computed and how large current acquisitions are in relation to the beginning balance.

The weighted-average method is generally *objective*, orderly, and free from manipulation. When there are many types of articles in the inventory, or when acquisition costs change frequently, the method requires *many computations*. Sometimes unit costs must be carried to three or four decimal places to yield the necessary degree of accuracy in computing totals. The method is perhaps best suited to situations where inventory is composed of a large number of low-cost units which are replaced infrequently.

The weighted-average method is often criticized because, if it is applied as illustrated above, the average unit costs are influenced to some extent by all costs previously experienced. An unusually large purchase at an abnormal price will have a lasting effect on future calculations of inventory and cost of goods sold. To combat this objection and to give a more current measure of costs, the *moving-average* method may be used.

Under one variation of the moving-average method, a weighted unit cost of all purchases during the preceding 12 months is computed. This unit cost is used during a month to compute the cost of goods sold during that month. At the end of the month a new average unit cost is computed, using the purchases of the most recent 12 months. At the end of January, 1973, for example, January purchases would be substituted in the average calculation for those of January, 1972.

A strong point of both the weighted- and moving-average methods is that they assign equal costs to items in the ending inventory which presumably have equal economic significance. Specific-identification, FIFO, and LIFO do not usually do this.

Comparison of the Results of the Cost Methods

The following are the results produced for Emco Stores in 1973 by the four inventory cost methods just described:

	Specific Identification	FIFO	LIFO	Weighted Average
Sales revenue	$2,400	$2,400	$2,400	$2,400.00
Cost of goods sold expense	1,723	1,690	1,930	1,796.65
Gross margin	$ 677	$ 710	$ 470	$ 603.35
Asset, ending inventory..............	$ 972	$1,005	$ 765	$ 898.35

In later years the beginning inventories will not be the same under the various methods, because the ending inventory of the preceding year depends on the inventory method used. Whether one particular cost method will give a higher or lower gross margin than another depends on the direction of price movements and the increase or decrease in the physical quantity in inventory during the year. The comparative results of methods also depend on the relative amounts of price changes during a period and the relative size of the change in the inventory balance.

Once the beginning and ending inventories have been computed under various inventory methods, their combined effect on the net income of the period can be compared as in Illustration 11-1. The *beginning inventory* is an addition (debit) to cost of goods sold expense, and is therefore a *deduction from net income*. The *ending inventory* is a deduction (credit) from cost of goods sold expense, and is therefore an *addition in computing net income*.

Illustration
11-1

COMPARATIVE EFFECTS OF INVENTORY
METHODS ON INCOME

	Method 1	Method 2
Beginning inventory (*debit* to cost of goods sold expense)	$5,000	$6,500
Purchases ....(Same under both methods)		
Ending inventory (*credit* to cost of goods sold expense).....................................	8,200	8,600
Net *credit* to cost of goods sold expense	$3,200	$2,100
Excess of method 1 net credit over method 2: net *credit*......................................	1,100	

Conclusion   The inventory change of method 1 results in a net credit to cost of goods sold expense which is $1,100 more than that under method 2; therefore, net income for the period is $1,100 more under method 1.

Effect of Inventory Methods on Decisions

In the preceding illustrations it has been assumed that the only financial elements changed by the selection of the inventory costing method are those affected by the *allocation of a given amount of acquisition costs* between accounting periods. The affected elements are

(1) Cost of goods sold expense of the current period.

(2) Asset inventory at the end of the current period.

(3) Cost of goods sold and asset inventory in the future.

Actually, other elements may change as a result of choosing a particular inventory costing method. Management may use the income and asset information, which has been influenced by the inventory method, to decide what quantity of goods to buy, when to buy them, how much to pay for them, and what prices to sell them for. To the extent that the inventory costing method is unrealistic, it can lead management to unwise decisions in these matters.

The choice of an inventory costing method may also affect the rate and amount of *cash flow* into and out of the business through its effects on purchase and sales decisions and on the amount of income tax to be paid. The inventory costing method used in the financial statements need not be the same as that used in the income tax returns, however, unless LIFO is used in the tax returns.

Recoverable Cost of Inventory

A third major problem in measuring inventories relates to the accounting procedures to be applied when the *current value* of an inventory item on hand is *no longer equal to its acquisition cost*. This section deals with situations when the current value is *less* than the acquisition cost.

The justification for carrying *any* amount of inventory cost forward as an asset is the expectation that the business will receive a *future service benefit from it at least equal to its cost.* Often a business cannot reasonably anticipate such future benefit.

Example 3   In 1973 a business purchased two identical units for $6 each. Unit 1 was sold for $10 in 1973 and Unit 2 is in the inventory, unsold, at the end of the year. The $6 cost of the unit sold is an expense which should be matched against the $10 revenue from its sale in 1973. If it is expected that Unit 2 can be sold in 1974 for $10 or more, its full original cost of $6 may appropriately be shown in the 1973 ending inventory as an asset. Unit 2 should not be stated in the inventory at more than $6, because to do so would be to count revenue that has not yet been realized by sale.

Example 4   If Unit 2 had been *damaged* prior to December 31, 1973, and its expected resale price in 1974 is less than $6, would it be proper to carry the original cost of $6 forward as an asset in the ending inventory?

Solution   The unsold unit has lost part of its economic significance and should be valued at less than $6 in the ending inventory.

In Example 4 the accounting concept of *recoverable cost* applies. This means that the unexpired cost carried forward in ending inventory *should not exceed* that part of the acquisition cost expected to be *recovered by future revenues* when the inventory item is sold or used.

The Lower-of-Cost-or-Market Inventory Method

Writing down the ending inventory to recoverable cost is accomplished by the lower-of-cost-or-market inventory method under the following circumstances:

> *Where there is evidence that the utility of goods, in their disposal in the ordinary course of business, will be less than cost, whether due to physical deterioration, obsolescence, changes in price levels, or other causes, the difference should be recognized as a loss of the current period. This is generally accomplished by stating such goods at a lower level commonly designated as market.*[2]

This principle of measurement is carried out by using the *lower-of-cost-or-market* (L/CM) method to determine the amount of the ending inventory. *Market* as used here basically refers to the amount that it would cost at the end of the period to *replace* the inventory item, either by purchase or by manufacture. It relates to prices in the market in which the business *buys*, rather than in the market in which it sells. In determining the market replacement cost of purchased items, it is appropriate to use unit market prices quoted at the date of the inventory by the company's customary sources of supply, for the quantities it usually buys. If the market replacement cost of an item is *less* than its original cost, this is *tentative* evidence that the original cost of the item cannot be recovered. If market is *higher* than cost, the original cost is recoverable and

---

[2] American Institute of Certified Public Accountants, *APB Accounting Principles, Current Text as of February 1, 1971*, Paragraph 5121.07.

should be used in valuing the item in the ending inventory. To use a market higher than cost in measuring the asset would be to record revenue that has not yet been realized.

The fact that the market replacement cost of the item is less than cost is only *tentative* evidence that cost cannot be recovered. To make a *final* decision as to whether cost can be recovered, *upper and lower limits* are applied to the market value, which is then *compared with cost*.

The *highest amount* which may be used as the market value of an inventory item is its *net realizable value*. This is its estimated resale price in the ordinary course of business, less reasonably predictable costs of completing and selling it. If the inventory item were carried over to the following period as an asset of a higher amount, the result would be to *postpone* until the following accounting period the *recognition of a loss* on sale which can reasonably be predicted now.

The *lowest amount* which may be used as the market value of an inventory item is *net realizable value, reduced by a normal profit margin* on the item. To measure an item in the inventory at a replacement cost lower than this figure would be to record a *loss* in the period in which the replacement cost declined and a *greater income than normal* in the following period when the item was sold.

Example 5   A company has one of each of the following items in its ending inventory on December 31, 1973. At what amount should each be stated under the lower-of-cost-or-market method?

Item	Original Cost	Replacement Cost December 31, 1973	Net Realizable Value	Normal Profit Margin
A	$60	$54	$70	$10
B	60	54	60	9
C	60	54	50	8
D	60	54	80	11

COMPUTATION OF INVENTORY AT THE LOWER OF COST OR MARKET

	Item A	Item B	Item C	Item D
Computation of market:				
Market is tentatively replacement cost...	$54	$54	$54	$54
But it may not be more than net realizable value	70	60	50	80
Nor less than net realizable value, reduced by a normal profit margin	60	51	42	69
Therefore market is.........................	$60	$54	$50	$69
Original cost.....................................	60	60	60	60
Ending inventory valuation, the lower of cost or market...........................	$60	$54	$50	$60

Market is the *middle figure* of replacement cost, net realizable value, and net realizable value minus a normal profit margin.

The "original cost" of inventory items which is compared with "market" in the lower-of-cost-or-market method may be determined by the specific-identification, FIFO, or weighted-average method. The resulting inventory measurement might more appropriately be called "the lower of cost or remaining useful cost."

The comparison of original cost and market may be made for individual items in the inventory, for classes of items, or for the inventory as a whole, depending on which seems more appropriate for the particular business.

An analysis of the effects of the inventory valuations of Item C and Item D in the preceding illustration reveals a weakness of the lower-of-cost-or-market method. For Item C, the method shows a *loss* of $10 resulting from a price decline in the *year prior to sale*. For Item D, the additional *gain* from increased selling prices is *not recognized* in the accounts until the period of actual sale. Critics of L/CM argue that it is *inconsistent* thus to record unrealized losses but not to record unrealized gains.

A further charge of inconsistency of L/CM is based on the argument that often in the inventory at a particular date some items are measured at market while others are stated at cost.

When it is necessary to write down the value of the asset, inventory, from original cost to market, the account debited should ordinarily be Cost of Goods Sold Expense.

In recent years there has been growing support for measuring inventories at their *current service value*, whether it is *higher or lower* than historical cost. The great majority of the accounting profession, however, still adheres to historical cost, or *recoverable historical cost*, as the accepted basis for measuring inventories.

Special Problems in Measuring Inventories

Net realizable value. In certain unusual situations it is proper to measure inventories at a figure *higher* than cost. For precious metals, such as gold and silver, the government has established a fixed market price at which it stands ready to accept any quantity offered. The certainty of the sale and of the selling price meet the test of realization. The producer may therefore measure metals on hand in a refined state at their selling price, less the expected cost of marketing them. This valuation method, referred to as *net realizable value*, applies only if the item meets all the following tests:

(1) Its cost cannot be determined.

(2) It can be sold immediately at a quoted market price with only minor additional costs.

(3) Any unit of it is interchangeable with any other unit.

Inventory cutoff problems. It is sometimes difficult to determine just what items should be included in the ending inventory. Use of the exact quantity of goods *on hand* is not always proper, because the legal title to some of them may have already passed to the customer. In addition, incoming items in transit at the end of the period should be included in ending inventory if title to them has already passed to the business. Careful attention is needed at the end of the accounting period and for a short time thereafter to ensure that all the inventory items which the business owns, and only those items, are included in its ending inventory.

Inventory on consignment. Goods which one business (the *consignee*) holds on consignment to be sold for another business (the *consignor*) should be included in the ending inventory of the *owner*. The *owner is the consignor*, although the goods are in the possession of the consignee. Memorandum records of goods on both incoming and outgoing consignments are needed in determining just what items should, and what items should not, be included in the firm's inventory.

Disclosure of Inventories in Financial Statements

It is essential that financial statements disclose clearly what method the particular firm is using for measuring the asset inventory (and the related expired cost). This may be done parenthetically beside the item in the body of the statements, or in a footnote to the statements, by a phrase such as

Inventories, at lower of FIFO cost or market.........$1,635,000

A business using LIFO can assist the statement reader in making more realistic analyses involving the inventory figure by disclosing the approximate inventory cost current at the date of the financial position statement.

Methods of Determining Inventory Quantities and Costs

A fourth major question relating to inventory accounting is *how to determine the quantities and costs of inventories* on hand at the end of the period, and how to match the expired inventory costs with revenues.

The section "Adjustments for the Expired Cost of Inventories," on pp. 93–95 of Chapter 5, discussed the *direct* (*perpetual inventory*) and *indirect* (*periodic inventory*) methods of measuring the expiration of inventory costs, pointing out the circumstances under which each method is desirable. Some additional advantages of the *perpetual inventory method* as a device for *controlling* inventory are presented later in this chapter.

Purchases and Related Accounts

Often businesses which use the *periodic* inventory method keep general ledger accounts for the major types of changes in inventory, such as

Purchases—debited for the invoice cost of inventory acquired.

Transportation In—debited for freight and similar costs on inventory purchases.

Purchase Returns and Allowances—credited for the invoice cost of goods returned to the supplier, or price reductions received on goods bought.

Under this accounting procedure the balance in the Merchandise Inventory account before closing entries are made represents the inventory balance at the *beginning* of the period.

These account balances may be used in a *cost of goods sold schedule*, as in Illustration 11-2. Instead, the same information may be included in the income statement.

Illustration
11-2

THE CORNER SHOP, INC.
Cost of Goods Sold Schedule
Year Ended August 31, 1973

Additions to merchandise inventory during the year:		
Invoice cost of purchases..................................	$74,100	
Transportation in..	3,100	
Total cost of purchases..		$77,200
Deductions:		
Purchase returns and allowances.................................		2,600
Net cost of purchases..		$74,600
Add merchandise inventory, beginning of year....................		14,500
Cost of goods available for sale.......................................		$89,100
Deduct merchandise inventory, end of year........................		17,600
Cost of goods sold (to Income Statement)..........................		$71,500

The individual accounts used to show changes in Merchandise Inventory are closed to Cost of Goods Sold Expense at the end of the year. The cost of the *ending* inventory is set up as an asset by debiting Merchandise Inventory and crediting Cost of Goods Sold Expense. The balance in Cost of Goods Sold Expense is then closed to Income Summary.

PLANNING AND CONTROLLING INVENTORY

Because of the diverse physical and economic characteristics of inventories, the appropriate methods of planning and controlling them may also be quite different. The general methods of planning and controlling inventories which are outlined in the rest of this chapter are often useful.

Objective of Inventory Planning

The objective of *inventory planning* is to try to maintain the investment in inventories at the *lowest amount* which is sufficient to meet the production, sales, and financial requirements of the enterprise. The inventory must be adequate to maintain an efficient level of operations and to meet, within reason, the needs of customers. However, it must not be greater than is necessary to meet these requirements because of

(1) The interest cost, and sometimes the unavailability of capital for investment in inventory.

(2) The cost of handling and storing excessive quantities of inventory.

(3) The dangers of adverse price changes and obsolescence.

(4) The increased exposure to physical deterioration.

The loss from a combination of the causes listed, and often from a single one of them alone, may far exceed losses to the business as a result of fraud.

Example 6   A business with total assets of $100,000 had an average inventory balance of $40,000. A careful study revealed methods of reducing this inventory to $20,000 while continuing to serve the customers' needs adequately. The company was able to reduce its annual interest cost for borrowing money to finance the inventory balance by $1,400. The savings in reduced handling and storage costs and reduced exposure to damage, obsolescence, and price declines were much greater.

The inventory balances of a business must not be *less* than the amount needed to maintain—and, where profitable opportunities are available, to expand—the level of business sales and services to its customers.

Perpetual Inventory Records as a Basis for Control

To promote efficiency in planning, purchasing, and controlling the size of inventory balances, many businesses find it desirable to keep detailed *perpetual inventory* records of each item or major class of items. Such records provide current information about the receipts, issues, and balances on hand of each inventory class.

Some of the advantages of perpetual inventory records are

(1) They provide current information about *quantities on hand,* so that orders can be placed at appropriate times.

(2) They provide a starting point in *planning* the size and timing of *future orders* by furnishing a record of the number of units of each inventory item actually issued during a past period.

(3) They give information needed in *preparing financial statements quickly,* without the necessity of taking a physical inventory.

(4) They furnish for control purposes a record of the inventory *quantities that should be on hand.* The subsidiary inventory ledger balances, when compared with the results of a periodic physical count, reveal the extent of inventory shortages, overages, and clerical errors in the procedures of receiving and issuing inventory items and of keeping records.

The simplest perpetual inventory subsidiary accounts are kept in terms of *quantities only.* Such records have the advantage of relatively low clerical cost. Because the quantities of different types of articles are not stated in the common denominator of money cost, however, the balances of the various subsidiary inventory accounts cannot be combined. It is therefore difficult to report the *investment* in major classes of inventory. It is also impossible to prove the equality of the balances of the detailed quantity records with the general ledger controlling account, inventory, which is stated in terms of money.

Subsidiary inventory accounts expressed in both *money cost* and quantities are useful in *planning* the financial requirements of the inventory, *appraising* overall performance in managing inventories, and *checking on the accuracy* of inventory accounting. Such records are more complex than records of quantities only. They are practical only if the quantities of individual items handled, or their unit costs, are large enough to justify the additional clerical cost.

The basic types of information shown in Illustration 11-3 are usually found in subsidiary inventory cards which reflect costs. In addition, it is sometimes

Illustration
11-3

PERPETUAL INVENTORY (Quantities and costs)

Description of item   Part Y   Standard order quantity   <u>144</u>

Location   Aisle 4, Shelves 9–12   Order point   <u>96</u>

Unit of measure   Number

		RECEIPTS		ISSUES		BALANCE ON HAND		
Date	*Ref.*	*Quantity*	*Total Cost*	*Quantity*	*Total Cost*	*Quantity*	*Total Cost*	*Unit Cost*
1973								
1/1						160	800.00	5.00
1/9	M831			10	50.00	150	750.00	5.00
1/30	M882			70	350.00	80	400.00	5.00
2/8	P 26	144	720.00			224	1,120.00	5.00

useful to record on the detailed inventory records information on *quantities ordered*, *quantities reserved* for special use so that they will be available when needed, and *customary sources of supply*.

Planning Inventories

Standards for judging the efficiency of a firm in managing its inventory may be expressed in several forms:

(1) *Planned inventory balance* at a certain future date, usually the end of the budget period. The balance may be in terms of *quantities* of each type of inventory, *costs* of inventory classes, or *number of days' supply* represented by the balance. The desired future balance should be based on the requirements of later periods and on a consideration of the costs of acquiring and maintaining inventory.

(2) *Planned average inventory balance during the planning period*. This is generally expressed as an average quantity or an average cost.

(3) *Planned inventory turnover rate*. This is an application of the general formula for computing the turnover of an asset. The formula is

$$\frac{\text{Change in inventory during period}}{\text{Average inventory balance}} = \text{Number of turnovers.}$$

The change and balance may both be expressed in terms of *physical quantities* or *money costs*. The quantity or cost of inventory *issued* is used as a measure of the *change* during the period.

Regardless of what standard of efficiency management selects in controlling its investment in inventory, the *starting point* for inventory planning is the *budgeted sales or issues* of the inventory item for the coming period.

Planning the needed *additions* to inventory by purchase or manufacture, setting the proper levels for *inventory balances*, and planning *issues or sales* of inventory items should ordinarily be done first in terms of *physical quantities* of each inventory class. The expected quantities required and the necessary acquisitions of each class may be computed as follows:

	Units
Planned inventory at the end of the current period......................	100
Add expected sales (or issues) during the period........................	50
Total units required..	150
Deduct units in beginning inventory......................................	55
Total *units to be acquired* during the period.............................	95

If there is a substantial time lag between the placing and filling of orders, or between the beginning and end of the manufacturing process, acquisitions must be carefully planned well in advance so that they will arrive when needed. It is essential that a business have an accurate memorandum record of outstanding orders by classes of inventory to aid in proper scheduling of future orders and deliveries and to avoid duplicate orders.

The physical quantities of inventory items to be purchased or produced should be converted into the common denominator of *money costs* to facilitate planning how to finance them. The cost of planned inventory items is an important part of the cash budget.

Number of Days' Supply in Inventory

One way of judging the adequacy of an inventory balance at a given time is to compare it with *expected future needs*.

Example 7   The balance of Item V on hand on January 1, 1973, was 330 pounds. Issues in the future are expected to average 90 pounds a month, or 3 pounds a day. The inventory balance represents 110 days' supply (330 pounds on hand ÷ 3 pounds needed a day).

The desirable standard in terms of *days' supply* should be set by considering the expected future issues of the particular inventory, the reliability of the sources of supply, and the time required to secure replacement. The actual balance at a given time should be compared with the standard, and appropriate corrective action should be taken.

Inventory Turnover Rate

Comparison of the *actual inventory turnover rate* with a desired turnover rate set in advance gives valuable clues as to whether the quantity of the item on hand is satisfactory and whether the item is moving at a satisfactory rate.

Cost of Goods Sold (which is equal to the reduction of inventory) is used as a measure of the *inventory change* during the period. This is divided by the average inventory balance, which should be measured on a comparable cost basis.

The numerator and denominator are *comparable* when both are stated in terms of physical quantities, when both are stated at current cost, or when both are stated at current selling price. Dollar costs, rather than physical quantities, should be used in determining *how effectively the business has employed its investment in inventories*. Inventory turnover rates are also more useful when computed separately for each of various classes of inventory items which are different in behavior.

Illustration 11-4 shows how *annual inventory turnover rates* can be computed by using the arithmetic mean of the inventory balances at the beginning and end of the year, or by using the arithmetic mean of the quarterly balances. It also shows how *quarterly inventory turnover rates* can be computed.

Illustration
11-4

COMPUTATION OF ANNUAL INVENTORY TURNOVER RATES

Date	Balance	Computation of Average of Year-End Balances	Computation of Average of Quarter-End Balances
1973			
Jan 1	$3,400	$ 3,400	$ 3,400
Mar. 31	3,900		3,900
June 30	3,800		3,800
Sept. 30	2,900		2,900
Dec. 31	2,200	2,200	2,200
Totals		$ 5,600	$16,200
Divided by number of items..............		2	5
Equals average balance....................		$ 2,800	$ 3,240
Cost of issues during year		$13,200	$13,200
Divided by average balance..............		2,800	3,240
Equals number of turnovers per year ...4.71 times			4.07 times

COMPUTATION OF QUARTERLY INVENTORY TURNOVER RATES

Quarter	Average Balance for Quarter	Cost of Inventory Issued	Number of Quarterly Turnovers	Equivalent Annual Turnover Rate
1973				
First................	$3,650	$2,500	0.68	2.74
Second.............	3,850	3,100	0.81	3.22
Third...............	3,350	3,900	1.16	4.63
Fourth.............	2,550	3,700	1.45	5.80
Total		$13,200		

The annual turnover rate computed by using the mean of the quarterly balances is more reliable than the rate using the mean of the annual balances, because it is more representative of the conditions which prevailed throughout the year. Separate turnover rates for each quarter indicate still better the changes in the rate of movement which occurred during the year.

In Illustration 11-4 the quarterly rates indicate that the rapidity of inventory turnover has increased substantially each quarter. If an investigation shows that the causes of the increase in the quarterly turnover rate are not seasonal, and if an out-of-stock situation rarely occurs, it may be concluded that there has been a definite improvement in the efficiency of inventory management during the the year.

It is often difficult to determine the *amount* of a desirable standard. How many turnovers should there be during a year, or how many days' supply should be on hand at the end of the year? The results actually achieved in the *past* are often used as a *standard* against which to compare future results. Past standards may represent inefficient performance, however; standards based on *efficient conditions* are preferable.

Timing Inventory Acquisitions

The *right quantities* of inventory must be on hand at the *right time*. There must be a delicate balance between too little and too much.

If the quantities on hand are *insufficient*, there may be costly delays or shutdowns while the company is waiting for an emergency order to be filled. Placing special orders for merchandise or raw material often entails excessive cost. Special runs of items which the company manufactures may require costly setup time, uneconomical production runs, and overtime premiums for employees. Sales orders may be lost because a particular item desired by a customer is not in stock and cannot be obtained soon enough to fill his need.

At the other extreme, inventory can become *too large*. A policy of having everything in stock that might ever possibly be needed, or of having excessive quantities on reserve, ties up capital needlessly and causes unnecessary costs associated with storage and handling, warehouse space, insurance, deterioration of inventory, risk of price fluctuations, and interest on the investment in inventory.

Management action to control the balance of inventory on hand may consist either of measures to control the *withdrawals* from stock or measures to control inventory *additions*. One method of controlling withdrawals consists of special promotions to stimulate sales in what would otherwise be a slack season. Another consists of efforts to stabilize the level of production. In addition to its many other cost advantages, a stable rate of production eliminates sharp seasonal peaks and dips in the quantities of materials used.

Measures to control inventory additions are chiefly directed toward more *efficient timing of purchases*. Two guides which are often useful in improving the timing of purchases are the *standard order point* and the *standard order quantity*.

Standard Order Point

The *standard order point* is the *minimum level* which the balance of an inventory item should be allowed to reach before a replenishing order is placed. The order point should be set at a balance which will be sufficient, with a *margin of safety*, to meet expected requirements for withdrawal from inventory until the ordered items arrive.

The order point should be determined by estimating how much of the inventory item will be used after the order is placed and before it is filled. The time required to fill the order depends on the time necessary to place the order and the time the supplier needs to fill and ship it. The dependability of the sources of supply and variations in the rate of usage from time to time determine what margin of safety should be included in the minimum balance.

Example 8   The normal usage of Material X is 900 pounds a month. The time needed to place an order and to have it filled by the supplier is ordinarily 10 days, although occasionally the required time has been as much as 12 days. What should the order point be?

Solution   Management feels that a margin of safety of 5 days' supply is needed, and therefore sets the order point at 15 days' supply, or 450 pounds. If a replenishing order is placed when the quantity on hand reaches this point, if the order requires 10 days to be filled, and if the rate of usage is normal, there will be 150 pounds (the margin of safety) on hand when the items arrive.

Balance when order was placed....................................	450 pounds
Deduct usage during 10 days ($\frac{1}{3}$ of 900 pounds)................	300 pounds
Balance when order is filled..	150 pounds

Order points should be reviewed frequently and should be revised if significant changes occur in the rate of usage, the time required to fill an order, or other relevant factors.

Standard Order Quantity

A *standard order quantity* is ordinarily useful in controlling types of inventory items in which the investment is significant, and for which the rate of usage is reasonably predictable. The standard order quantity is set so as to *minimize the total* of two types of costs which move in opposite directions as the size of the uniform order changes:

(1) *Cost of maintaining an inventory balance.*

(2) *Cost of ordering.*

The *cost of maintaining an inventory balance* consists chiefly of storage, insurance, deterioration, obsolescence, loss from price fluctuations, and interest on the investment in inventory. These costs are approximately the *same for each unit* carried in inventory. They increase in total as the average number of units in inventory increases. The larger the number of orders placed to fill the inventory needs of a given period, the smaller is the quantity in each order. The maximum number of units on hand at any time is also smaller, and so is the average number of units in inventory during the period.

The *cost of ordering* includes clerical costs, postage, and telephone; the cost of being out of stock, including the lost income on lost sales and the extra transportation costs involved in placing rush orders; the loss of quantity discounts which are available on larger orders; and the extra costs of making small, uneconomical production runs. These costs are approximately the *same for each order* placed. They increase in total as the number of orders placed to obtain a given quantity increases. The fewer orders placed to obtain a given quantity, the less is the total ordering cost.

The behavior of these two types of costs is shown in tabular form in Illustration 11-5 and in graphic form in Illustration 11-6.

Data for illustrations. Both illustrations pertain to Item W, whose expected rate of usage is 100 pounds a month (1,200 pounds a year), spaced evenly throughout the year. *Costs of maintaining inventory* are expected to amount to $0.10 per pound of Item W carried in inventory per year. *Costs of ordering* are expected to be $5 per order. No quantity discounts are available.

Note that only those costs that will be *different* for the various order sizes are considered in the computation of total cost in Illustration 11-5.

Illustration 11-5

COMPARATIVE COSTS OF VARIOUS
STANDARD ORDER QUANTITIES OF ITEM W

Number of Orders Per Year	Size of Each Order (Pounds)	Average Inventory Balance (Pounds)	Cost of Maintaining Inventory ($0.10 Per Pound Per Year)	Cost of Ordering ($5 Per Order)	Total Cost
1	1,200	600	$60	$ 5	$65
2	600	300	30	10	40
3	400	200	20	15	35
4	300	150	15	20	35
5	240	120	12	25	37
6	200	100	10	30	40
12	100	50	5	60	65

The invoice cost of inventory purchased, for example, will be the same total for the year regardless of how many units are ordered at a time (unless there is a quantity discount).

The average inventory balance throughout the year is computed as follows for any frequency of orders:

$$\frac{\text{Minimum balance} + \text{Maximum balance}}{2} = \text{Average balance.}$$

The *minimum* balance should be reached just before the replenishing order arrives, and the *maximum* balance should be attained just after it arrives. The planned minimum balance is the *margin of safety*. Because it *does not differ* for any standard order quantity policy, it is considered to be zero in the calculations.

Illustration 11-5 shows that the combined costs of ordering and carrying an inventory balance are at their lowest point, $35, when the requirements for the year are met by placing three orders of 400 pounds each, or four orders of 300 pounds each. This $35 is not the total cost of maintaining and ordering inventory under these ordering policies, but rather the total of costs *that differ* for different standard order quantities.

Illustration 11-6 shows graphically how inventory ordering and maintenance costs change with the number of orders placed. The optimum frequency of orders is that at which the *total* of these two types of costs *is at a minimum*. This is where the two cost lines intersect, between three and four orders a year in the illustration.

Actual computations of standard order quantities must take into account many complex factors. The costs of ordering and carrying inventory, for example, are estimates. So are the costs associated with being out of stock and with setting up productive facilities.

A common *formula* used for establishing the optimum order size is

$$L = \sqrt{\frac{2QP}{S}},$$

where L is the lot or order size, Q is the annual usage in units, P is the costs

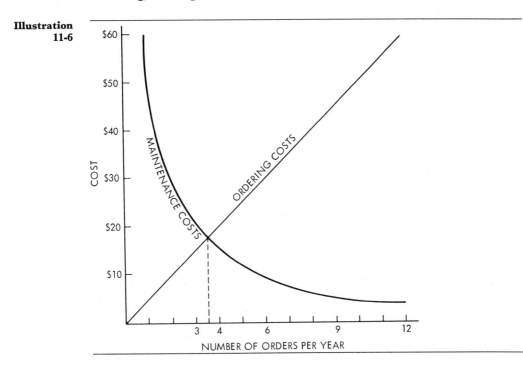

Illustration
11-6

NUMBER OF ORDERS PER YEAR

which vary with the number of orders placed, and S is the cost of maintaining one unit in inventory for one year.

Using this formula, the optimum order quantity for Item W in Illustration 11-5 is

$$\sqrt{\frac{2(1,200)(\$5)}{\$0.10}} = \sqrt{120,000} = 346.$$

Like order points, standard order quantities become outdated. Upward or downward trends in usage, changes in costs, and changes in supply conditions should be taken into consideration in applying them. Both control measures should be used as guides only, and not as complete substitutes for good judgment.

Inventory Control When Types of Items Change

The illustrated methods of controlling the investment in inventories by establishing optimum inventory balances and order quantities are suitable for inventories of *staple* items. It is possible to predict the future requirements for such items with some assurance. These standards are of little use, however, where the types of articles handled change rapidly. This condition affects many items stocked by the typical variety or department store. Control is often exercised in such cases by placing a monetary limit on the total of the investment in inventory and purchase orders which the departmental buyer may have outstanding at any time.

The Retail Inventory Method

A method frequently used by department stores and others for determining how the persons responsible for inventory have discharged their accountability is the *retail inventory method*. It is a means of *measuring* and *controlling* the investment in inventory at any given time. It is based on the following general formula:

(A) Beginning inventory, stated at selling price............... xxx
    Plus purchases during the period, at selling price......... xxx
       Equals total goods to be accounted for......................... xxxx
(B) Sales... xxx
    Plus ending inventory, stated at selling price xxx
       Equals total goods accounted for................................ xxxx

The total goods accounted for in part (B) must equal the accountability established in part (A).

The retail inventory principle for *establishing accountability* for merchandise and collections from sales can be applied to individual employees, departments, branches, and divisions of a company.

The retail inventory method provides a quick way to convert the ending inventory, measured at retail selling price, to its *cost* for use in preparing financial statements. The conversion is based on the assumption that the percentage of cost to retail in the ending inventory is the same as the percentage of cost to retail for the goods available for sale (beginning inventory plus purchases during the period). The detailed procedures for applying this method are beyond the scope of this text.

Internal Control of Inventories

One of the principal means of preventing errors, fraud, and waste in handling inventories is assigning to different individuals the responsibilities for ordering, receiving, testing, paying for, keeping custody of, issuing, and maintaining records of inventory. Internal-control procedures for handling inventories should be designed to ensure

(1) That the business *receives* the proper kinds and quality of goods in the right quantity at the right time and at the best price.

(2) That the goods are *stored* with due attention to protection from obsolecence, damage, and theft, as well as to accessibility and ease of handling for later use.

(3) That cash *payment* is made for purchases only on sufficient evidence that the goods were properly ordered and received and that the amount of the payment is correct.

(4) That there is no *waste or fraud* in the *use* or *sale* of the inventory items.

The system of internal control for inventories should provide a method of charging each individual who receives goods with *accountability* for them. Each individual who releases goods on proper authority should have a receipt discharging his accountability. The system should be completed by determining that the goods in the custody of the responsible individual are equal to the remainder of his accountability.

Additions to accountability may be evidenced by *purchase invoices* and *receiving reports*. Issues may be substantiated by *requisitions*. Balances on hand may be recorded in individual *subsidiary accounts*. Periodically, perhaps once a month, the agreement of the total of the subsidiary account balances with the general ledger inventory account should be proved. At least once a year the accuracy of the individual perpetual inventory records should be determined by taking a physical count of the inventory.

The Gross Margin Inventory Method

Another method frequently used to estimate the cost of the ending inventory and to determine how responsible persons have discharged their accountability for inventory is the *gross margin method*, outlined in Illustration 11-7. It is simpler to apply than the retail method, but sometimes less accurate. Given the sales revenue, the cost of the beginning inventory and inventory additions for the current period, and the percentage of gross margin to sales, the ending inventory at cost can be estimated.

Illustration 11-7

GROSS MARGIN INVENTORY METHOD

		Amounts	Per Cent of Sales
Sales, 1973..		$50,000	100
Deduct cost goods sold:			
Beginning inventory...................	$10,000		
Purchases................................	38,000		
Cost of goods available................	$48,000		
Deduct ending inventory............	?		
Cost of goods sold..............................		?	?
Gross margin...		?	30

If the gross margin applicable to 1973 sales is 30 per cent of sales in Illustration 11-7, it is $15,000. Cost of goods sold is therefore 70 per cent of sales, or $35,000. To complete the calculation:

Cost of goods available for sale..	$48,000
Deduct estimated cost of goods sold (70% of $50,000 sales)......	35,000
Estimated cost of ending inventory......................................	$13,000

The estimated rate of gross margin is usually based on the company's past experience. Changed relationships of costs and selling prices of each class of merchandise, or changes in sales mix during the current period, distort the validity of the inventory calculation. Similarly, errors in sales, beginning inventory, or purchases cause the computed ending inventory to be unreliable.

It can be used to give a quick approximation of what the ending inventory *should be* if a physical inventory is not possible or desirable, or if the reported ending inventory is thought to be inaccurate.

Summary   Inventory should be *measured* at its *unexpired cost*—the amount which is expected to be *recoverable* in future operations. Inventory costs properly include all expenditures reasonably required on the item up to the point when it is ready for sale or use.

When various lots of inventoriable items of a single type have been acquired at different unit costs, there is a problem of deciding which costs apply to the units on hand in the ending inventory. This problem may be resolved by *specifically identifying* costs with units on hand, or by using such assumed flows of cost as *first-in, first-out (FIFO)*, *weighted average*, or *last-in, first-out (LIFO)*. If there has been a decline in the *recoverable cost* of some of the items in the inventory, the decline can be measured by the use of the *lower-of-cost-or-market method*. The inventory method selected should be the one which is best adapted to the circumstances of the case. Each method can be evaluated by the specific criteria listed in this chapter and also by the following general criteria:

(1) Will it give useful information about income and financial position?
(2) Will it permit a proper appraisal of management performance?
(3) Will it help lead to the right action?

The *objective of inventory planning and control* is to maintain the investment in inventories at the lowest amount which is consistent with the available capital of the business and its requirements for future issues. The use of standard order quantities and order points aids in timing the acquisitions of inventory items to achieve this result. Comparison of actual inventory balances and inventory turnover rates with *predetermined standards* and necessary action to correct any deviations help to keep the investment in inventory at an efficient level.

The retail inventory method, the gross margin method, and subsidiary inventory ledgers are all means of improving the *control* exercised over inventories.

Discussion Questions and Problems

11-1   "As a general rule, costs necessary to *prepare an inventory item for sale* are treated as product costs, while those necessary *to make the sale* . . . are treated as expenses of the period in which they are incurred."

a. How are product costs related to the measurement of income? What is the justification for this treatment of such costs?
b. Give three examples of types of cost which could be included in the inventory of a retailer under the quoted rule.
c. Give three examples of costs of making sales which should not be included in the asset, inventory.
d. Explain how the concept of recoverable cost of inventory is related to the term "costs necessary to prepare" in the quoted rule.

11-2   The Manitou Company, organized in 1972 to sell a single product, is attempting to decide which of the following elements of cost to include in inventory and which to treat as period costs.

(1) Invoice cost of purchases (recorded under the net price method.)
(2) Freight, express, and postage on incoming shipments.
(3) Invoice cost of purchases returned for credit.
(4) Transportation charges on returned purchases.
(5) Transportation charges on sales.

(6) Cost of operating the receiving department.
(7) Cost of operating the stores department.
(8) Cost of operating the shipping department.
(9) Advertising.
(10) Sales commissions (paid when goods are shipped).
(11) General administration.
(12) Discounts lost on purchases.
(13) Interest on money borrowed to buy inventory.

Required   a. State which of the cost elements should ideally be treated as parts of inventory cost.
b. Describe the chief practical difficulties involved in following this theoretical treatment for particular items.
c. Compare the effects on 1972 income if all costs you listed in part a, as opposed to only the net invoice cost, are treated as product costs.
d. Compare the effects on 1973 income of treating all costs you listed in part a, as opposed to only the net invoice cost, as product costs. What other information do you need in order to give a complete answer?
e. Assume that the inventory on December 31, 1972, including all cost components, was $50,000 and that it was $40,000 including only net invoice cost. Also assume that the inventory figures for December 31, 1973, were $80,000 and $65,000, respectively. Under which method would higher income be reported for 1973?

11-3   At the end of the first year of operations, the president of a business is discussing the selection of an inventory method with the accountant. "We are free to choose any one of the many inventory methods you boys have dreamed up," says the president.

a. Is the president right? Explain.
b. Outline the answer that the accountant should give, including the considerations that govern the selection of an inventory method.

11-4   The purchasing agent of your company contracted to buy some goods, which were delivered in December at a contract price of $10,000. Soon afterward, and before goods were sold, he discovered that by shopping around he could have obtained goods of identical quality from another supplier for $9,000. Discuss the proper accounting treatment of this situation.

11-5   Effective January 1, 1973, the Potter Corporation, which uses a calendar year accounting period, changed its method of determining inventory. In the 1972 statements ending inventory was costed under the FIFO method, while the December 31, 1973, inventory was costed under LIFO.

a. Discuss the implications of this change with respect to persons who read the corporation's 1973 financial statements.
b. What items in the 1973 financial statements would be affected by the change?
c. Using figures of your own choice, show exactly how you would explain the effect of the change to the reader of the financial statements.

11-6   List the available methods for determining the following:

a. The quantity of ending inventory.
b. The cost of each unit in inventory (assuming that acquisition costs have changed during the period).
c. The extent to which the expected future benefits from an asset do not exceed its cost.

11-7   Some companies keep perpetual inventory records in terms of quantities only; others keep them in terms of quantities and costs; and still others do not keep perpetual inventory records at all.

a. What are the main reasons for maintaining perpetual inventories in terms of quantities only?
b. What are the weaknesses of such a system?
c. What additional benefits result from using perpetual inventory costs as well as quantities?
d. Describe some of the disadvantages of the method in part c.
e. Outline the general conditions under which you would recommend that a business (1) keep perpetual quantity inventory records only, (2) keep perpetual quantity and cost records, or (3) keep no perpetual inventory records.

11-8   "By keeping perpetual inventory records we avoid disrupting our work and spending countless hours taking physical inventory at the end of the year."

a. How, if at all, does a perpetual inventory system lessen the hours involved in taking physical inventory?
b. How can it be used to avoid disrupting work?
c. What purposes other than determining the cost of goods on hand does the process of taking a physical inventory serve?

11-9   It has been suggested that the the perpetual inventory balances be proved with the general ledger controlling account frequently, and that a physical check of the inventory records be made at least once a year.

a. What could cause the balance of the inventory controlling account to be larger than the sum of the balances in the subsidiary ledger? Smaller?
b. How would you handle the differences in part a?
c. What could cause the balance of a perpetual inventory card to be larger than the quantity shown by a physical inventory? Smaller?
d. How would you dispose of the differences in part c?

11-10   Specific identification is sometimes said to be the ideal method for assigning costs to inventory and to cost of goods sold. List arguments for and against the above statement.

11-11   In January 1973 Coe's Hat Shoppe bought a large shipment of summer hats for a cost of $18 each. On December 31 the physical inventory disclosed that 20 of these hats were still on hand. The department manager estimated that they could be sold for about $10 apiece, since they were somewhat shopworn and out of style.

a. At what amount should the unsold hats be stated in the 1973 ending inventory?
b. Does your answer in part a result in good matching of revenue and expense? Explain.

11-12   A computation at the end of the first year of operations shows that LIFO will result in a higher valuation for the ending inventory than will FIFO.

a. Have purchase prices increased or decreased during the year?
b. In this situation, which method will produce a higher cost of goods sold? Which will produce a higher net income for the year?

11-13   It has been said that FIFO and LIFO should be referred to as "cost of goods sold methods" rather than as "inventory methods."

a. Explain what is meant by this distinction.

b. Do you agree? Why?

11-14 Evaluate each of the following statements in terms of how soundly they apply accepted principles of inventory measurement:

a. "I know exactly the cost of my ending inventory," says a retailer, "because I have the original cost of each item marked on it in code."
b. "FIFO is the only method we can use to determine inventory cost," says the retail grocer. "We must move our old stock first, or our loss from deterioration would be exorbitant."
c. "Average cost is the only inventory method open to us," argues the grain elevator operator. "After we have stored the grain, it is impossible to distinguish one shipment from another."
d. "Cost of goods sold should be charged with the replacement cost of each item sold. You haven't made a profit until you have replaced the inventory item. LIFO is the only acceptable method, because it charges replacement costs to cost of goods sold."

11-15 Determining what the proper level of inventory should be at a given time is likely to involve a conflict of the objectives of the sales manager and production manager on the one hand with those of the treasurer on the other.

a. Explain what the principal objectives of each officer are with respect to inventory, and why there is likely to be a conflict.
b. To what general extent should the objectives of each be considered in setting company policies regarding inventory levels?
c. Explain some methods that might result in coordination of effort and agreement by these three managers as to the level of inventory needed.

11-16 The standard order quantity is the order size which is expected to minimize the combined cost of ordering and maintaining an inventory balance.

a. List several types of costs which vary closely with the frequency of orders placed during a period.
b. List several types of costs which tend to vary in total with the average inventory balance.

11-17 The Utah Mfg. Co. had an inventory of 400 units of Material No. 145, each of which had cost $12, in its inventory of December 31, 1972, the end of the first year of operations. During 1973 the company made the following purchases:

Mar. 19	200 units	@ $10
May 24	100 units	@ $ 8
Aug. 14	100 units	@ $ 7.50
Oct. 5	300 units	@ $ 7
Dec. 9	300 units	@ $ 6

According to a physical count, there were 500 units on hand on December 31, 1973.

Required a. Compute the 1973 cost of materials used by FIFO.
b. Compute the 1973 cost of materials used by LIFO.
c. Compute the 1973 cost of materials used by weighted average.

11-18 In 1973 the Sturdy Mfg. Co. shipped goods on consignment to Springfield Distributing Co., to be sold by Springfield. Sturdy Mfg. Co. recorded the shipment as a sale at the planned retail price to the final consumer. By December 31 three-fourths of the consigned goods had been sold by Springfield.

a. How will the unsold goods held on consignment by Springfield affect the income and financial position statements of Sturdy for 1973?

b. If no entry is made to show the unsold goods at the end of the year, what will be the errors in Sturdy's income and financial position statements?

11-19   Standard Stores has a small retail branch in a remote mining community. It is impractical for the company's internal auditors to reach the branch often. In the past year they discovered that the former manager failed to report the full amount of goods sold, pocketing the amount of the understatement. Most of the merchandise which is sold by the branch consists of items of low unit value, and it is shipped from one of Standards Stores' regional warehouses.

a. How can the gross margin inventory method be used to estimate the loss in this situation? To help improve internal control in the future?

b. What are the weaknesses of the gross margin method that might prevent its giving an accurate measure of the loss in this case?

c. Would a perpetual inventory system be appropriate? Why?

11-20   The Baronet Co. is trying to decide whether to treat inward transportation and receiving costs on its purchases as *product* or *period* costs. The following account balances relate to the current year:

Sales....................................	$350,000
Purchases (invoice cost)............	190,000
Transportation on purchases......	18,000
Transportation on sales.............	5,000
Advertising...........................	8,000
Receiving..............................	14,000
Sales commissions...................	17,500
Order filling and packaging......	3,500

Three-fourths of the goods purchased were sold. There was no beginning inventory.

Required   a. Compare the effects on income for the current year under the two methods of accounting for these costs.

b. Compare the effects of the two methods on the year-end financial position statement.

c. Which accounting treatment do you recommend? Why?

11-21   Your retail store received 50 sweaters from a foreign manufacturer. The invoice contained the following information: List price, $30 each; discount to dealers, 30 per cent; additional discount for purchases of 10 or more, 10 per cent; import duty, $2 per sweater; terms, net 30 days, payment to be made in U.S. funds. Your firm paid transportation charges of $15 upon receipt of the shipment, as well as $5 for repairing a hole in one of the sweaters.

Required   a. Compute the acquisition cost of the inventory, showing all details.

b. For items which you do not consider to be a part of inventory cost, explain what accounting treatment you would use.

11-22   On March 3 the Smart Shop purchased 10 dresses, Style 105, from Metro Mfg. Corp. Each dress had a list price of $25, and the shipment was subject to a quantity discount of 10 per cent. Payment terms were 3/10, n/30. The merchandise was so popular that the Smart Shop submitted an identical second order on March 12, together with a check for the full amount owed on the first invoice. The second shipment was received on March 15 and was paid for on March 31. The Smart Shop records cost of goods sold at the end of the month.

Required a. Journalize entries relating to the purchase and payment under the *net price* method.
b. Journalize entries relating to the purchase and payment under the *gross price* method.

11-23 The Wilson Company, which recently completed its second year of operations, now uses the FIFO inventory method. The management wishes to see what effect other inventory methods would have had on income and financial position, because another inventory method may be used in the future.

The controller has presented the following information:

	1973	1972
Sales	$1,200,000	$800,000
Purchases	675,000	515,000
Ending inventory:		
FIFO	187,000	200,000
LIFO	168,000	208,000

Required a. Which method will result in higher income for 1972? What will be the difference in income?
b. Which method will result in higher income for 1973? Explain.
c. Which method will result in higher net income for 1972 and 1973 combined? Explain.
d. Which method will result in higher total assets at the end of 1973? Higher total equities? Explain.

11-24 The following situations deal with the choice of an appropriate inventory measurement method.

Required For each situation, state (1) on the basis of the data given, what method you would use for measuring ending inventory, and why; and (2) what additional information you would need before arriving at a final conclusion as to the appropriate method.

a. A grocer has annual sales of about $1,000,000. His average inventory is usually about $80,000, his total current assets are about $120,000, and his total assets are about $140,000. His net income for the past few years has ranged from $8,000 to $13,000. During recent years, purchase prices have risen about 1 per cent a year on the average, and sale prices have followed suit promptly.
b. A ladies' dress shop has annual sales of about $100,000. Its average inventory is usually about $15,000, its total current assets are about $40,000, and its total assets are about $55,000. Its net income during the past few years has ranged from $2,500 to $5,000. Frequent markdowns are necessary because of style changes and shopwear.
c. A public accounting firm finds it necessary to keep a variety of stationery and forms on hand. The gross revenue of the firm is usually about $100,000. The principal expense is salaries, which average about $40,000. Office supplies used during a year usually amount to about $2,000. At any given time, the amount of supplies on hand is about one-fourth of the annual usage. The total net income of the partners of the firm is usually about $45,000. Total assets average about $10,000, of which about half is composed of receivables from clients.

11-25 The Loess Company, which uses the LIFO inventory method, began 1973 with 2,500 units of inventory, each of which had cost $3.00. During 1973 the following purchases were made:

	Units	Cost Per Unit
January 15...............................	1,500	$4.00
March 3..................................	1,800	4.25
May 9....................................	2,000	3.50
July 13...................................	1,000	3.75
October 9................................	3,000	3.50
December 21.............................	2,000	4.20

Total sales for 1973 were $48,000 and 4,000 units were in the inventory on December 31, 1973.

Required   a. Using the LIFO method, compute the ending inventory, cost of goods sold, and gross margin.

b. Compute ending inventory, cost of goods sold, and gross margin by the FIFO method.

11-26   The Small Company had an inventory of Product D on December 31, 1972, consisting of 22,000 units with a total cost of $4,400. Purchases during 1973 were

	Quantity	Total Cost
January......................................	8,000	$1,280
March	15,000	1,800
May...	10,000	1,300
July	5,000	800
August......................................	10,000	1,600
October	8,000	1,440
November...................................	10,000	1,800

A physical inventory taken on December 31, 1973, showed that 18,000 units were still on hand.

Required   a. Compute the December 31, 1973, inventory using FIFO.

b. Compute the December 31, 1973, inventory using a weighted average of the cost of the beginning inventory and 1973 purchases. Round unit costs to the nearest tenth of a cent.

11-27   The Cycle Company computed its inventory for December 31, 1973, as follows:

Cost	$72,000
Lower of cost or market..............	63,000

Included in the latter figure were goods which had cost $15,000, but because of sudden and unexpected obsolescence these goods had a current market value of only $7,000. The remainder of the difference between cost and the lower-of-cost-or-market valuation resulted from normal shopwear. Sales for 1973 were $140,000. Beginning inventory (at cost) was $90,000 and purchases totaled $80,000. Operating expenses were $30,000.

Required   Prepare an income statement for 1973 adequately disclosing the preceding data.

11-28   The Bruce Corp. presents the following data:

Units of Article L on hand, December 31, 1972...................	100
Unit cost.......	$24
Customary selling price....................................	$42
Unit replacement cost, December 31, 1972.........................	$21
Expected selling price in 1973..	$35
Expected direct costs of sale in 1973.................................	$ 9

The customary income margin is 10 per cent of selling price.

Required
a. Compute the proper amount to include in the December 31, 1972, inventory for Article L under the lower-of-cost-or-market method.
b. If the expected results materialize in 1973, how would they be shown in condensed income statement form?
c. Is the use of L/CM justified in this situation? Explain.
d. What would be the ending inventory under lower of cost or market if the expected selling price in 1973 is $30 and all other facts are unchanged?
e. Assuming that the inventory was determined periodically, make the necessary journal entry for part d.

11-29   The Manatee Company uses the lower of FIFO cost or market in measuring its ending inventory.

Required
a. From the following data, compute its ending inventory for December 31, 1973.
b. Record the necessary journal entry under the periodic inventory method.

Inventory, Dec. 31, 1972............... 1,000 units @ $22
1973 purchases:

Jan. 18	500 units	@ $24
Mar. 20	500 units	@ $25
July 1	500 units	@ $26
Sept. 5	500 units	@ $26
Dec. 19	500 units	@ $28

During 1973 a total of 2,400 units were sold for $96,000 cash. A physical inventory taken on December 31, 1973, revealed that 1,050 units were on hand. The manufacturer from whom the Manatee Company usually made its purchases quoted a price of $28 in lots of 500 units on December 31. Expected resale price in 1974 was $38 a unit; expected cost of selling, $10 a unit; and normal income margin, $4 a unit.

11-30   In an effort to simplify inventory control the Clarke Company switched in 1973 to a quantity-only perpetual inventory system. The inventory records were kept in terms of quantities only during the year, and at the end of the year they were converted to a cost basis. The inventory balance at the beginning of 1973 consisted of 400 units.

The following information taken from the inventory record for Material MQ for 1973 is considered to be typical of conditions expected for the next few years. All figures represent quantities.

Month	Purchases	Issues	Month	Purchases	Issues
January	300	100	July....................	280	200
February.............		120	August................		200
March................	380	140	September...........	160	160
April..................		160	October		120
May...................	400	180	November	260	80
June..................		200	December...........		180

Required
a. Set up a perpetual inventory card showing purchases, issues, and ending balance for each month.
b. Compute the inventory turnover rate for the year as a whole.
c. How many days' supply are on hand on December 31, 1973?
d. What are the limitations of the computations in parts b and c, and how would you overcome them?

11-31   The following inventory information was taken from the records of the Dun Company:

	Units	Unit Cost
Inventory, Jan. 1, 1973............................	2,000	$4.00
Purchases in 1973:		
Feb. 6..	2,000	3.50
Mar. 9..	3,000	3.40
Jun. 16..	1,000	3.30
Oct. 27..	1,000	3.20
Inventory, Dec. 31, 1973	3,000	?

Required   a. Compute the 1973 inventory turnover rate using (1) quantities only, (2) FIFO cost, (3) LIFO cost.
b. For what purposes may these turnover rates be used?
c. Which method do you think best serves these purposes in this situation? Why?

11-32   Thurston Products, Inc., is now earning income (before income tax) of 20 per cent of its average total assets. Of the total assets of $150,000, 40 per cent consists of inventory. The president has asked the controller to develop a plan for controlling the inventory balance more profitably.
The inventory includes the following:

Class	Balance, December, 31, 1972	Expected 1973 Cost of Sales
1	$20,000	$30,000
2	30,000	40,000
3	10,000	20,000

After a careful survey the controller estimates that the annual inventory turnover rates for these classes should be as follows:

Class 1......... 2.0   Class 2......... 2.5   Class 3......... 3.0

Required   a. How many months' supply of inventory is represented by the balance of each class of goods on hand on December 31, 1972?
b. What average inventory balances should be maintained to achieve the standard turnover rates?
c. Judged by the standards in part b, what is the excess investment in inventory on December 31?
d. If the costs associated with maintaining an inventory balance, other than return on investment, are 10 per cent of the inventory cost, how much could be saved a year by maintaining inventories at the standard level?
e. What would be the rate of return before tax on assets if the standard turnover rates were maintained for an entire year?

11-33   Inini Co.'s December 31, 1972, inventory consisted of 400 identical units which had cost $95 a unit. A summary of its 1973 inventory changes was as follows:

	Purchases		Sales	
First quarter.......................	300 units	@ $85	250 units	@ $120
Second quarter..................	200 units	@ $80	200 units	@ $110
Third quarter....................	300 units	@ $75	320 units	@ $105
Fourth quarter..................	400 units	@ $78	380 units	@ $105

Required a. Compute the 1973 annual inventory turnover rate by using the mean of year-beginning and year-ending balances under the FIFO inventory method.

b. Compute the 1973 annual inventory turnover rate by using FIFO cost for the mean of the quarterly inventory balances.

c. Compute a quarterly inventory turnover rate for each quarter using FIFO cost.

d. Which is the best method for computing turnover in this case? Why?

11-34 The production manager estimates that 3,000 pounds of Material X will be needed each month for the next year or so. Usage is expected to be spread evenly throughout each month. The time needed to place an order and have it filled is normally 8 days. The production manager feels that a 3-day supply should be on hand at all times as a margin of safety.

Compute the standard order point. Assume a 30-day month.

Required **11-35** The Walde Co. uses about 20,000 units of a material called Perma every year. A cost study reveals that the costs which vary with the number of orders placed during a year are $15, while the cost of carrying one unit of Perma in the inventory for one year is $0.20.

Required a. Prepare a table to compute the standard order quantity for Perma.

b. Compute the standard order quantity by formula.

11-36 Grissom Co. uses about 500 pounds of Material V in its manufacturing process each month. The supplier of V usually fills orders within two weeks from the date they are placed. Grissom Co. likes to keep a minimum of one month's supply of V on hand at all times in case orders require longer to be filled, and its balance has reached that minimum at the beginning of the current year.

The costs which tend to vary in total with the number of orders placed during a year, including such items as labor, supplies, and postage, total $20 per order. Insurance premiums are 1 per cent per year of the cost of the average inventory balance, and storage costs are approximately $0.06 per pound per year. Loss from obsolescence in recent years has been about 3 per cent of the average inventory balance. The invoice cost of Material V is $3 per pound.

Required a. Determine the standard order point for Material V.

b. Prepare a table to establish the standard order quantity.

c. Compute the standard order quantity by formula.

d. What are the principal limitations of using standard order quantities?

11-37 On May 1, 1973, the entire inventory of the Mooney Company burned up in a fire which destroyed the building. Luckily, the following information was retrieved from a safe where the books were kept. All the information was for the period January 1 through April 30.

Sales	$65,000
Purchases	43,000
Manager's salary.......................................	4,000
Clerks' salaries...	6,000
Sales returns and allowances.........................	3,000
Merchandise inventory, December 31, 1972......	32,000
Purchase returns and allowances....................	1,000

The typical gross margin of the firm is 40 per cent of net sales.

Required   a. Estimate the cost of the merchandise that was burned.

b. Record the loss in journal form, assuming that three-fourths of the loss can be recovered from the insurance company.

11-38   The Peterson Company uses the retail inventory method as a part of its system of internal control over inventories. The beginning inventory for 1973, which had cost $80,000, was priced to sell at $128,000. During the first six months of 1973 goods costing $70,000 were bought and marked to sell at $105,000. During a special sale goods which had been marked to sell for $25,000 were marked down to $15,000. Total sales for the six months were $140,000, and sales returns amounted to $5,000.

Required   a. What should the selling price of the inventory be on June 30, 1973?

b. If the actual inventory on June 30 had a total selling price of $80,000, how might the discrepancy be explained?

11-39   Department J of a small department store had an inventory of $10,000 at retail selling price on January 1, 1973. During 1973 the department purchased merchandise for $30,000 and marked it to sell for $55,000.

During 1973 prices of goods which had originally been marked to sell for $10,000 were increased to $13,000. Other goods which had been priced at $8,000 were reduced to $3,000. Merchandise which had cost $1,300 and which was priced to sell at $2,000 was transferred from Department K to Department J, on authority of the store manager.

Department J's total sales during 1973 were $50,000 and sales returns were $2,000. A physical count of the inventory taken on December 31, 1967, showed goods on hand at retail amounting to $11,000.

Required   a. Compute what the ending inventory should have been at retail.

b. Explain how any discrepancy in the ending inventory probably originated. What corrective action would you recommend?

11-40   The Naive Distributing Company president has been very disappointed with the profit reported by the company's Beach Branch for the first six months of 1973. All merchandise which the branch sells is received from the central warehouse, and records of shipments are kept in the Naive Distributing Company's main accounting office. The salaries of the branch manager and of all branch employees are paid by check from the main office. All branch expenses are likewise paid centrally by check. The branch sells merchandise entirely for cash, and it is the branch manager's responsibility to deposit all collections in a checking account, to be withdrawn only on the signature of the company treasurer.

The selling prices of branch merchandise are set by the central sales department. Markups and markdowns are rare and are not permitted without clearance by the central sales manager. A representative of the central sales department has reported that frequent spot-checks at the Beach Branch show that this policy is being followed.

Condensed income statement data of the branch for the two preceding full years and for the first six months of 1973 are presented in the accompanying tabulation:

	1/1–6/30/1973	1972	1971
Sales...	$120,000	$200,000	$170,000
Purchases from main office, at cost.....	102,000	153,000	136,000
Beginning inventory (cost)..............	65,000	50,000	40,000
Ending inventory (cost)..................	70,000	65,000	50,000
Operating expenses.......................	26,000	39,000	36,000

There have been no significant changes in the percentage of markup from cost to selling price of merchandise as established by the main office. Salary increases at the branch have been negligible. A new branch manager was appointed on December 31, 1972, at the same salary as that of the former manager.

Required a. Make an analysis of the data presented in order to determine the probable cause of the decrease in the income of the Beach Branch.

b. Prepare a report of your findings to the president, together with your suggestions for remedial action.

Cases **11-1 Magnolia Company.** The Magnolia Company, which distributes one type of product, has been using the LIFO inventory method since 1940. Its inventory on December 31, 1972, was as follows:

Year Layer Acquired	Number of Units	Unit Cost	Total Cost
1940............................	8,000	$ 5.00	$ 40,000
1941............................	3,000	5.50	16,500
1948............................	5,000	9.00	45,000
1953............................	4,000	13.00	52,000
1967............................	2,000	20.00	40,000
Totals	22,000		$193,500

In 1973 the employees of the company's principal supplier engaged in a prolonged strike. Sales of 25,000 units for a total of $1,200,000 were filled partly from current purchases of 10,000 units in 1973 at $30 a unit, and partly by reducing the ending inventory below the normal balance. A partial income statement for 1972 showed

Sales (30,000 units)	$1,300,000
Deduct cost of goods sold.................	900,000
Gross margin.................................	$ 400,000
Deduct operating expenses...............	250,000
Income before income tax................	$ 150,000

Required a. How would you suggest that the company report the 1973 events described above in its financial statements?

b. What does your suggestion in part a imply for the financial statements of future years?

c. Comment on the desirability of LIFO in such cases. How could it be modified to present more reasonable results?

11-2 Monongahela Appliance Center. The Monongahela Appliance Center is a retailer of small and medium-sized household appliances. It does about one-fourth of its business for cash and the remainder on account, chiefly on terms of from three to six months. The Center markets about 50 different types of appliances. There are six principal merchandise classes, within which products are similar as to percentage of gross margin to sales. The Center makes about 100 to 150 sales on a typical business day. A recent analysis showed that most of its purchases are made from 30 manufacturers, and that there are typically about 300 purchase invoices during a month. Dollar sales volume ranges between $40,000 and $110,000 per month, averaging about $75,000. The inventory balance at cost ranges from a low of about $70,000 to a high of $130,000.

The management of the Monongahela Appliance Center is seeking a plan of inventory accounting that will provide prompt information for monthly financial statements. It also needs current information in connection with insurance on the inventory, for placing orders, and for evaluating the efficiency with which the investment in inventory is controlled. You are asked to suggest procedures that are suitable in view of the company's operating characteristics. Sales volume fluctuates significantly from year to year, and the company deals in many products whose total market life is less than three years. On the other hand, many of its products are stable in terms of annual and seasonal demand. The unit cost and selling prices of much of the merchandise change frequently.

Required
a. Discuss the advantages and disadvantages of perpetual and periodic inventory systems from the standpoint of the Monongahela Center. On the basis of the information given, which do you think would be more suitable? Why? If you recommend a perpetual inventory system, should it be for quantities only, or for quantities and unit costs?

b. Does specific-identification, FIFO, LIFO, or average cost seem best suited for the Center's inventory? Why?

c. Do you think that the company should establish standard order points and standard order quantities? Why?

d. Would the computation of turnover rates for some or all classes of inventory be useful? If so, how and when would you suggest that they be computed?

e. Could the company use the gross margin inventory method? For what purposes?

chapter 12

Accounting for Long-Lived Assets

Purpose of Chapter

Long-lived assets consist of the following major classes:

(1) *Property, plant, and equipment—physical assets* (such as land, buildings, land improvements, and equipment), which are expected to render their services through *use* rather than consumption over an indefinitely long future time; and *natural resources* (such as mineral deposits and timber tracts), whose physical quantity is reduced as they are extracted.

(2) *Long-term intangibles*—long-lived assets without physical substance whose potential benefit to the business lies in the rights they confer upon it. Examples are patents, copyrights, trademarks, franchises, leaseholds, leasehold improvements, goodwill, and organization costs.

(3) *Long-term investments*, which have some of the features of monetary assets and some of the features of nonmonetary assets.

This chapter explores some of the more complex problems of determining the *acquisition costs* of long-lived assets, the procedures and merits of alternative methods of measuring their *cost expiration*, the methods of accounting for their *sale or exchange*, and special problems of *reporting* and interpreting them in the financial statements. Because many of the problems of accounting for long-term investments are similar to those of long-term liabilities, both are discussed in Chapter 13. Chapter 26 considers some methods of planning and controlling long-lived asset additions.

THE ACQUISITION COST OF LONG-LIVED ASSETS

Basic Components of Acquisition Cost

When first acquired a long-lived nonmonetary asset should be measured at the amount paid for it at the time of acquisition, or to be paid later, in *cash or cash equivalent*. If a consideration other than cash is given to acquire the asset, the current fair market value of this consideration is its *cash equivalent*. Both *trade discounts* and *cash discounts* should be deducted in arriving at the acquisition cost of an asset.

Expenditures other than the purchase price of a long-lived asset should be added to its cost if they are reasonably necessary to prepare the asset for use and can be expected to result in future service benefit to the business.

Capital and Revenue Expenditures

A fundamental problem in accounting for long-term unexpired costs is that of distinguishing between *capital expenditures* and *revenue expenditures*. An *expenditure* consists of making a payment, or incurring a liability to make a payment, for an asset or an expense.

Costs which are incurred with the expectation that they will benefit business operations in future accounting periods as well as in the current period are called *capital expenditures*. They are debited initially to asset accounts and are later allocated to the accounting periods which they benefit.

Costs incurred for the benefit of the current period only are called *revenue expenditures*. They are debited directly to expense accounts and are therefore matched against the revenue of the period in which they are incurred.

A business should make a careful distinction between capital and revenue expenditures. If a revenue charge is improperly treated as a capital expenditure, the result is to *understate expense* (and overstate income) of the period in which it is incurred and to *overstate the assets* at the end of that period. The same error also *overstates expense*, with a consequent understatement of income, in the *future* accounting periods to which the cost is allocated. Debiting a capital expenditure incorrectly to current-period expense creates errors of the opposite nature.

Types of expenditures that are considered to be capital in nature are *additions, improvements,* and *replacements*. An *addition* increases the *quantity* of long-lived assets, illustrated by adding an attachment to a machine. An *improvement* enhances the *quality* of an existing long-lived asset by increasing its probable useful life, capacity, efficiency, operating economy, or the quality of its output beyond that originally anticipated. A *replacement* involves a substitution of a new asset or asset component for part or all of an existing asset.

Ordinary *maintenance and repair* expenditures, made to keep the asset operating as originally planned, are treated as revenue expenditures.

Often it is hard to determine whether a particular expenditure will benefit future periods. The business should follow a *consistent policy* in classifying each type of expenditure. *Materiality* also has an important bearing on the capital-revenue classification. For practical purposes, most companies establish a minimum cost below which expenditure items are charged to current expense regardless of the length of their expected useful lives.

Example 1   A company followed a policy of treating all individual expenditures costing less than $10 as expense, even though the resulting benefit was expected to last for several years. The officers felt that the clerical cost of accounting for such items as long-term assets would be excessive.

Methods of accounting for long-lived assets obtained under long-term lease are discussed in Chapter 13.

Cost Components of Specific Types of Long-Lived Assets

Land. The cost of land includes all the outlays necessary to obtain legal title to it and prepare it for use as a location. In addition to the purchase price agreed on with the seller, land cost includes legal fees, real estate broker's commissions, cost of title search and title insurance, and fees for recording ownership in legal records. If a business acquires land containing structures with the plan of tearing them down, the net cost of razing them is a part of the land's acquisition cost.

Example 2   A company purchased a lot containing an old building for a total cost of $15,000, planning to tear down the old building immediately and replace it with a new one. The cost of demolishing the old building was $3,000, exclusive of scrap, which was sold for $2,000. What was the acquisition cost of the land?

Solution

Contract price...	$15,000
Add cost of demolition...	3,000
	$18,000
Deduct proceeds of scrap	2,000
Net acquisition cost of land.................................	$16,000

Buildings and equipment. The acquisition cost of a tangible asset which is expected to yield service benefits for a long time includes all costs reasonably incurred in purchasing it, transporting it, installing it, testing it, and preparing it for use in the business.

Expenditures made to rehabilitate assets acquired in a run-down condition are a part of the assets' initial cost. A careful distinction should be made, however, between the cost of preparing such assets for initial business use and expenditures made later to keep them in operating condition.

Example 3   A used machine purchased for $600 was reconditioned prior to use at a cost of $400. Its acquisition cost was $1,000, the total expenditure necessary to prepare it for use.

Example 4   If the $400 reconditioning cost were incurred after the machine had been used a year, it would not be a part of the acquisition cost of the asset. It would be an expense unless it was expected to extend the machine's useful life beyond that originally anticipated or to increase its service benefits substantially, as by providing greater capacity.

Natural resources. The acquisition cost of a natural resource includes its purchase cost plus the cost of development incurred until the asset is ready to begin producing.

Patents, copyrights, trademarks, and franchises. The acquisition cost of patents, copyrights, and trademarks is either the cash equivalent paid to purchase them or the cost incurred in developing them. The acquisition cost of franchises includes the amounts paid to the grantor of the franchise, together with any legal and similar fees incurred in establishing the right to operate under the franchise.

Leaseholds and leasehold improvements. The acquisition cost of leaseholds is the amount of rent paid in advance or of costs incurred directly in obtaining the lease. The cost of leasehold improvements includes outlays for purchasing or constructing improvements to the landlord's property which are expected to benefit future periods.

Goodwill. Goodwill should be recorded as an asset *only when it is purchased as a part of the assets of a going business*, or when there is a purchase of a substantial part of the ownership of a business. Like other assets, its acquisition cost is the amount of cash or the cash equivalent of any other consideration which is given in exchange for it. If the total purchase price of the business, or major business interest, which has been acquired exceeds the total acquisition cost which can be attributed to specific assets, the remainder represents goodwill.

Organization costs. These are measured initially at the amount of outlay which can be specifically identified with getting the business organized and legally empowered to carry on its activities.

Interest Cost on Asset Acquisitions

If a significant time elapses after an asset is bought and before it is paid for, the seller usually specifies a rate of interest to be paid for the waiting period. Even if no interest is specified, it is usually reasonable to assume that the payment includes implied interest. Interest should not be included as a part of the asset's cost, but as a cost of credit (that is, as *interest expense*) for the period during which credit was extended.

When the period of construction or installation of an asset is long, some accounting authorities would permit the interest cost on funds borrowed for the construction period to be treated as a part of the acquisition cost of the asset. This is the customary practice in regulated utility companies, where the prices charged by the companies are limited to those needed to permit a fair return on the investment in assets. No return can be earned while the assets are being constructed; therefore interest during the construction period is added to the asset base on which the allowable return is computed. A business whose prices are not regulated does not have a corresponding reason for treating interest during construction as a part of the asset's acquisition cost.

Allocations of Cost in Joint Purchase Transactions

When several assets of different types are acquired in a single purchase, a portion of the common cost should be allocated to each asset to facilitate later accounting. Cost is usually allocated to the individual assets in the proportion that the market value of *each* asset bears to the *total* market value of the assets. To state it differently, it is assumed that the ratio of cost to market value of each asset is the same.

Example 5   A business acquired land, a building, and merchandise inventory in a lump-sum purchase for $80,000. An appraiser estimated the market values of the assets as follows:

Land	$ 20,000
Building.......................................	70,000
Merchandise..................................	10,000
Total market value	$100,000

There is no evidence of the exchange price of the individual assets. How should the cost of each asset be determined?

Solution   The total cost should be allocated to the three assets on the basis of their relative market values at the time of purchase. It appears from the appraised value of $100,000 that the firm made a good buy, but the accounts must show only the total cost of $80,000. Cost may be apportioned to each asset as follows:

	Appraised Value	Per Cent of Total Appraised Value	Total Cost	Allocated Cost
Land......................	$ 20,000	20%	× $80,000	$16,000
Building..................	70,000	70%	× 80,000	56,000
Merchandise............	10,000	10%	× 80,000	8,000
Totals................	$100,000	100%		$80,000

DEPRECIATION

The section "Cost Expiration of Long-Lived Assets" in Chapter 5 (see p. 95) dealt with the general principles which govern accounting for the expiration of these assets. The two following sections explained the basic procedures of accounting for the *depreciation* of long-lived physical assets and for the *amortization* of intangible assets.

Depreciation Methods and Criteria

Accounting for depreciation consists of two main steps:

(1) Determining the total asset cost that is expected to expire over the asset's useful life.

(2) Assigning the total estimated expired cost fairly to each of the accounting periods during which the asset renders service.

The total expired cost over an asset's useful life is computed by subtracting from the *acquisition cost* the *net salvage* value expected to be obtained from the asset at the end of its useful life. Net salvage value is computed by subtracting the expected dismantling and removal costs from the gross salvage value estimated to be received.

The four principal depreciation methods are

(a) Straight-line.

(b) Production.

(c) Uniform-rate-on-declining-balance.

(d) Sum-of-the-years'-digits.

The business must decide whether to compute depreciation separately for *each item* or for *groups of assets*.

The depreciation method chosen should meet the general criteria of *objectivity, usefulness,* and *feasibility*. Sometimes the method that would provide the most useful information is not sufficiently objective, or is impractical to apply.

More specific tests for evaluating alternative depreciation methods are

(1) The method should help provide a useful measure of *income for the current period*. It should match the long-term asset costs which expire during the period with the periodic revenue to which those costs are related.

(2) It should help to provide a useful measure of *financial status* at the end of accounting period. The unexpired cost of plant and equipment, used in measuring financial position, is the difference between original cost and total accumulated depreciation on the asset. Plant and equipment are acquired for *long-term use* rather than for *sale;* therefore, the prices for which they could be sold at various dates during their useful lives are not relevant to measuring the asset balances which relate to their future service benefits.

(3) The method should contribute to a useful measure of the *income of future accounting periods*. The unexpired cost of a depreciable asset at the end of the current accounting period is carried forward to future periods, when it will expire.

(4) It should furnish information useful to management in *planning* future operations. Depreciation often has a significant effect on the past rate and the planned future rate of return on assets. It has a dual impact on this measure. Depreciation for the current period is deducted in computing the *numerator, income*. The undepreciated asset balance is a part of the *denominator,* the *total assets* upon which the rate of return is computed.

(5) It should be useful in promoting *effective use* and protection of the economic values represented by the depreciable asset.

(6) It should be *objective*, orderly, and not subject to manipulation for the purpose of influencing reported results artificially.

The effect of the depreciation method on periodic income tax expense, a critically important matter, is discussed in Chapter 17. It is not unusual for a business to use one method of depreciation in computing its taxable income and another in measuring its business income.

The depreciation method that is most appropriate in a given situation depends on the characteristics of the depreciable assets, such as their potential economic life and pattern of usefulness by time periods; the policies of the firm as to rate of utilization of the assets, adequacy of maintenance, and timing of their retirement from service; and the use to which the resulting information is to be put.

The *total* depreciation assigned to the useful life of a long-lived asset tends to be the same under all the historical-cost methods. Total income over the asset's life might differ under the methods because of the effect of depreciation on income tax expense. In addition, the various historical-cost methods of depreciation may cause quite important differences in the *pattern* of income which a business reports over a series of years. Their differences in the unexpired asset balance at various points in time may also be significant. Such differences are likely to affect the interpretations of those who use the firm's financial statements to form a judgment as to the trend of its income—both in absolute amount and in relation to assets invested—over a series of years.

The smaller the amount of periodic depreciation in relation to other expenses and to revenue, the less is the relative difference in periodic income resulting from alternative depreciation methods. The smaller the total cost of long-lived assets in comparison with other assets, the less is the relative difference in financial position caused by choice of depreciation methods.

While merchandise inventory can be *physically identified* with a single sale, it is difficult—if not impossible—to match the cost of a depreciable asset's service with the resulting revenue. Each item of plant and equipment usually represents a bundle of services of *unknown* number and unknown individual value. These services are available for *use* rather than for direct sale, and are expected to be used for a long and indefinite future time. Since the precise cause (depreciation) and effect (revenue) cannot be directly linked, the depreciation method chosen is one which is *assumed* to reflect the pattern of relationship between expiring assets and the related revenue.

Estimating Useful Life

Depreciation methods differ principally as to (1) the units in which they express the estimated useful life of the asset and (2) the manner in which they determine what fraction of the useful life expires during each accounting period. Under each method, the formula for determining the periodic depreciation for the entire life of the asset is set up in advance. The factors used in computing annual depreciation (D) are cost (C), net salvage value (S), and units of estimated life (n).

The units in which the length of an asset's life is expressed may be time, units of service or output, or a combination of the two.

The amount of the depreciable cost of a long-lived asset to be allocated to any accounting period is proportionate to the fraction of the asset's useful life which expires during that accounting period.

The useful lives of depreciable assets end because of *ordinary wear and tear, inadequacy, obsolescence,* and *casualties.* In estimating the *total useful life* of an asset, it is well to consider how these factors will operate to end the usefulness of *that particular asset*.

Ordinary wear and tear results from actual use of the asset and from the action of the elements over time. The effect of wear and tear on the length of an asset's useful life depends on the intensity of use, the extent of exposure to the elements, and the company's maintenance policy. In some cases idleness of an asset hastens its economic death.

Long before an asset is physically worn out, its useful life may end because it is *inadequate* to fill the company's needs. Inadequacy may result from the *gradual* growth of the business or from changes in management's plans. On the other hand, it may be caused by *sudden changes* in conditions in the company or in the industry.

Obsolescence is the effect of technological progress on existing assets. *Normal obsolescence* usually occurs slowly and is predictable with some accuracy, whereas *extraordinary obsolescence* is caused by unexpected changes or radical innovations.

Casualties result from sudden and unexpected natural phenomena, or from accidents. The effect of gross misuse on an asset is similar to that of a casualty.

Estimating an asset's useful life to a particular business requires a prediction of the wear and tear which will occur under actual use conditions, a projection of the future rate of technological improvements, an estimate of the future adequacy of the owner's repair and replacement policies, and a forecast of his decision as to when to discard or replace the old asset. The effects of *ordinary* wear and tear, *predictable* inadequacy, and *normal* obsolescence can be considered in the estimate. The effects of *unpredictable factors*—extraordinary inadequacy, extraordinary obsolescence, and casualties—should be accounted for *when they actually occur*.

Sudden changes in operating conditions or in the economic environment may dictate that a part of the cost of an asset be shown as a loss in the period of the change.

Example 6   A machine with an original cost of $10,000, an estimated life of 10 years, and no estimated scrap value is being depreciated at the annual rate of $1,000. Its sudden obsolescence in the sixth year of its life might require the recognition of a loss of $4,000 of its potential benefit to future years, in addition to the $1,000 normal depreciation for the current year.

A business may be able to estimate the life of its depreciable assets partially on the basis of its own past experience or that of firms which use assets under similar conditions. The firm must be careful to consider its *own future* operating conditions and policies as they will affect the asset, however.

The conditions which cause each asset's useful life to end, together with the pattern of expected service benefits from the asset by time periods, should be evaluated in estimating how much of the asset's life expires in each period.

The Straight-Line Method of Depreciation

The simplest, and probably the most widely used, method of computing periodic depreciation in financial statements is the *straight-line method*. This method expresses the estimated life of the asset in *years of service* and assigns an equal amount of depreciation to each *full year* of service. A part of the service life of the asset may continue to expire during periods of idleness.

Most businesses apply simplifying rules in computing depreciation for fractions of a service year when assets are acquired or disposed of at a date other than the beginning or end of an accounting period. One common rule treats all changes in the asset account as though they occurred at the *middle* of the accounting period.

Example 7 On April 17, 1973, a business acquired a delivery truck with a cost of $3,200, an estimated useful life of five years, and an estimated salvage value of $200. Applying straight-line depreciation and the midyear rule, the business would charge $300 (one-half of a year's depreciation) to 1973 expense.

Example 8 If the same truck were sold on November 3, 1975, the midyear rule would result in assigning $300, half a year's depreciation, to 1975, the year of disposal.

A similar rule assumes that all changes occur at the *middle of the month*. Other methods compute depreciation to the *nearest full month* or *full year* of use. The rule chosen should be applied consistently. If asset acquisitions and disposals are spaced fairly evenly over time, the results of these conventions will be reasonably accurate.

The *annual rate of depreciation* under the straight-line method is determined by the formula

$$\frac{\text{Annual depreciation}}{\text{Original cost}} = \text{Annual rate of depreciation.}$$

Example 9 The annual depreciation rate of the delivery truck in Example 7 is $600/$3,200, or 18.75 per cent of the original cost.

The straight-line depreciation method results in charging each full year of the asset's life with an equal amount of expired cost, regardless of the amount of service actually rendered by the asset during each year.

The straight-line method is appropriate when the service benefits received from an asset are approximately equal during each year of its life. This is true of some assets which continue to be used approximately the same amount each year without notable changes in operating efficiency. It is also true when the most important service of an asset is its *availability*, not its *use*. Availability may be the most important measure of the service of a standby machine. A strong case may also be made for the straight-line method when the length of an asset's useful life depends more on obsolescence than on physical use.

An asset's service benefits to each accounting period of its life may be viewed as *units of physical use*, such as number of miles driven or number of running hours, rather than as availability for use. The service benefits may also be thought of as *contributions to revenue*, or *cost reductions* resulting from the asset, although such benefits are usually difficult or impossible to trace. By these standards the use of the straight-line method, which assigns equal depreciation to equal time periods, is improper for many common types of assets whose operating efficiency declines and whose operating costs increase with age.

Production Methods of Depreciation

Because of the limitations of the straight-line method, in which depreciation is considered to depend solely on the passage of time, several depreciation methods attempt to charge expired cost to accounting periods in proportion to the *use* of long-lived assets. These methods are called *production methods* of depreciation.

One common production method of depreciation expresses an asset's useful life in units of *operating activity*, such as the number of hours a machine is operated or the number of miles a truck is driven.

Example 10   The delivery truck in Example 7 is expected to have a useful operating life of 50,000 miles. Its depreciation per mile is computed as follows:

$$d = \frac{C - S}{n} = \frac{\$3,200 - \$200}{50,000 \text{ miles}} = \$0.06 \text{ per mile.}$$

If the truck was driven 15,000 miles in 1973, depreciation expense for 1973 would be \$900 (\$0.06 × 15,000). Depreciation in 1974 would be \$600 if mileage driven in that year was 10,000.

Production methods are feasible when an asset's expiration depends almost entirely on use, and when both the total useful life and the part of life expiring each year can be measured in terms of a standard unit of activity. Other forms of the production method state useful life in terms of *units of product* made by the asset, or in *revenue dollars* resulting from the product. It is usually difficult to estimate accurately the output of a long-lived asset in terms of units of product or revenue. Furthermore, *all* productive factors of a business, not just fixed assets, contribute to the earning of revenue, and the individual contribution of each factor usually cannot be identified.

Aside from the difficulties described, production methods are relatively simple and objective. They are appropriate for assets whose length of useful life depends largely on physical use, and whose units of activity have approximately equal economic significance.

The Uniform-Rate-on-Declining-Balance Depreciation Method

The *annual service benefits* derived from many types of long-lived assets *decline* as the assets become older. Moreover, the extent of the usefulness of an asset can be predicted more accurately for its earlier years than for its later years. For these reasons, many businesses use methods which allocate greater amounts of depreciation expense to the earlier periods of an asset's life than to the later periods. Some of these methods, referred to as "*accelerated depreciation*" methods, are arbitrary ways of computing declining annual depreciation charges for assets whose use presumably results in declining annual benefits. One method of depreciation which results in a declining annual charge, the *uniform-rate-on-declining-balance method*, is described in this section. Another, the *sum-of-the-years'-digits method*, is discussed in the following section.

The uniform-rate-on-declining-balance method (also referred to as the "declining-balance method") results in an annual depreciation charge that is a constant percentage of the *unexpired cost* (not of the acquisition cost except for the first year) of the asset at the beginning of the year.

A depreciation rate which will reduce the unexpired cost of an asset (its original cost minus accumulated depreciation) to salvage value during its expected life can be computed by a complex formula. A simpler and more widely used expedient is to use a uniform percentage which is *double the reciprocal of the estimated life*:

$$\text{Uniform rate} = 2\left(\frac{1}{\text{Estimated life}}\right)$$

Example 11 For the delivery truck in Example 7, whose estimated life is five years, the uniform annual depreciation rate is computed as follows:

$$2(\tfrac{1}{5}) = 40 \text{ per cent.}$$

The resulting balances for each year of the truck's useful life would be

End of Year	Year's Depreciation	Accumulated Depreciation	Original Cost	Unexpired Cost
0			$3,200.00	$3,200.00
1	$1,280.00	$1,280.00		1,920.00
2	768.00	2,048.00		1,152.00
3	460.80	2,508.80		691.20
4	276.48	2,785.28		414.72
5	165.89	2,951.17		248.83*

*Income tax rules, on which this application of the method is based, permit depreciating the asset to its salvage value ($200) by the end of its estimated life.

Salvage value is not deducted from cost in computing the uniform depreciation rate.

In some cases unmodified use of the uniform-rate method will leave an unexpired cost *greater* or *less* than the expected salvage value at the end of an asset's estimated life. In such a case depreciation should be taken in an amount sufficient to reduce the unexpired cost to the salvage value. Income tax rules permit the taxpayer to change from the uniform-rate method to the straight-line method at any time, to avoid leaving an undepreciated balance at the end of an asset's life.

The Sum-of-the-Year's-Digits Depreciation Method

Unlike the declining-balance methods, whose periodic charges to depreciation decrease by *decreasing* annual amounts, the *sum-of-the-years'-digits method* (also called the "SYD method") results in depreciation charges that decrease by a *constant* amount each year. It assigns depreciation to each service year of the asset's life in proportion to the number of years of life which remain at the beginning of the current year. The formula is

$$\text{Year's depreciation} = \frac{\text{Number of years remaining at beginning of current year}}{\text{Total of digits of years of life}}\,(\text{Cost–salvage}).$$

Example 12 For the delivery truck in Example 7, the first year's depreciation is computed as follows:

$$\frac{5}{(1+2+3+4+5)}(\$3,200 - \$200) = \frac{5}{15}(\$3,000) = \$1,000.$$

In succeeding years the numerator of the fraction is 4, 3, 2, and 1, respectively.

The resulting balance for each year of the delivery truck's useful life would be

End of Year	Year's Depreciation	Accumulated Depreciation	Original Cost	Unexpired Cost
0			$3,200	$3,200
1	$1,000	$1,000		2,200
2	800	1,800		1,400
3	600	2,400		800
4	400	2,800		400
5	200	3,000		200

When an asset is acquired in the middle of an *accounting year*, proper application of the SYD depreciation method requires that depreciation be recorded for only the appropriate fraction of the depreciation for the first *service year*. During the second year and thereafter, the depreciation of an accounting period is the sum of fractions of the annual depreciation rates for two different service years. For example, if the delivery truck had been acquired on July 1, 1973, depreciation for calendar year 1974 would be

$$\frac{1}{2} \text{ of } \tfrac{5}{15} \text{ of } \$3,000 = \$500$$
$$+\frac{1}{2} \text{ of } \tfrac{4}{15} \text{ of } \$3,000 = \underline{400}$$
$$\text{Total 1974 depreciation} = \$900$$

The uniform-rate-on-declining-balance method and the sum-of-the-years'-digits method are most appropriate for long-lived assets whose annual service benefits decline with age. Whether the rate of decline is more like that produced by the declining-balance method or the SYD method, or whether it resembles neither, depends on the characteristics of the particular asset in question and the circumstances under which it is being used.

Both methods are widely used for income tax purposes, for reasons explained in Chapter 17.

Comparison of Depreciation Methods

The following table summarizes the results of the four depreciation methods as applied to the delivery truck with a cost of $3,200, an estimated useful life of five years, and an estimated salvage value of $200. For simplicity it is assumed that the truck was acquired at the beginning of year 1.

	Year 1	Year 2	Year 3	Year 4	Year 5	Total
Annual depreciation:						
Straight-line............	$ 600	$ 600	$ 600	$ 600	$ 600	$3,000
Production (mileage)	900	600	750	400	350	3,000
Declining-balance....	1,280	768	460.80	276.48	165.89	2,951.17
Sum-of-the-years'-digits..............	1,000	800	600	400	200	3,000
Percentage of annual depreciation to original cost:						
Straight-line............	18.75%	18.75%	18.75%	18.75%	18.75%	
Production (mileage)	28.12	18.75	23.44	12.50	10.94	
Declining-balance....	40.00	24.00	14.40	8.64	5.18	
Sum-of-the-years'-digits...........	31.25	25.00	18.75	12.50	6.25	

The differences in the results of these methods will not be the same when applied in other situations, depending on the length of life, the salvage value of the asset, and the number of service units produced in each period. The general results of the methods may be summarized as follows:

(1) The *straight-line* method produces a *constant amount* of annual depreciation, which is a constant percentage of the asset's original cost.

(2) The *production* method results in an annual depreciation charge which fluctuates with changes in the volume of services produced by the asset. The annual fluctuations follow no set pattern.

(3) The *uniform-rate-declining-balance* method yields a declining annual amount of depreciation, decreasing more sharply the shorter the estimated life. The percentage of depreciation to the original cost declines each year.

(4) The *sum-of-the-years'-digits* method yields an annual depreciation charge which is a declining percentage of the original cost, the rate of decline being greater for short-lived assets.

Group Depreciation

Many records of depreciable assets are kept in terms of *individual items*. A detailed record shows for each item the original cost, later additions to cost, estimated life, estimated salvage value, depreciation for each period, and accumulated depreciation. Earlier illustrations have shown how to account for such individual depreciable units.

A depreciation rate applied to a group of depreciable assets that are similar in *form*, such as a number of identical machines, is called a *group depreciation rate*. All the units are considered together for purposes of computing depreciation. The estimated life of the group is stated in terms of *total service years*. Depreciation per service year is computed as follows:

$$\text{Depreciation per service year} = \frac{\text{Total cost}-\text{Total salvage value}}{\text{Total service years}}.$$

Example 13   In 1973 a business bought 100 identical machines, each with a cost of $60 and an estimated salvage value of zero. Past experience indicates that the useful lives of the individual machines will range from one to five years, as shown by the following table:

Years of Useful Life	Number of Units with Each Life Length	Number of Service-Years
(A)	(B)	(A × B)
1	4	4
2	25	50
3	41	123
4	27	108
5	3	15
Totals	100	300

What is the depreciation rate?

Solution   The total depreciation on the group of assets will be $6,000. Dividing this by the estimated life, 300 *service years*, yields a depreciation rate of $20 per service year.

Example 14   The actual results were that 5 of the machines in Example 13 were retired at the end of year 1, without salvage value, and 23 were retired at the end of year 2. What was the deprecation expense for each year?

Solution   Depreciation for year 1 was $2,000, computed by multiplying the 100 years of service actually received by $20, the depreciation rate per year of service.

    Depreciation for year 2 was $1,900, determined by multiplying the 95 years of service from the remaining units by the depreciation rate of $20 per service year.

Composite Depreciation

A group of assets which are *dissimiliar in form but related in function* may be accounted for by using a *composite depreciation rate*. An example would be using a single depreciation rate for a building. The roof, floors, heating plant, and lighting equipment are likely to have different useful lives, and one or more of them will probably have to be replaced before the useful life of the building as a whole ends. An alternative method is to keep *separate records* of the cost and estimated lives of each of the major segments of such a composite asset and to depreciate each segment separately.

Unless careful revisions are made, group and composite depreciation methods can lead to large errors when the proportion of some items to the total changes, when costs of replacement components change radically, and when errors are made in the estimated lives of the components in computing the depreciation rate.

Depreciation on Historical Versus Current Costs

In recent years there has been a growing body of opinion in favor of recognizing in the accounts significant changes in the current values of long-lived assets. This is not now generally accepted accounting practice, however. All the depreciation methods described in this chapter are *historical-cost methods*— that is, they allocate the original cost of the long-lived asset, minus its net salvage value, to the time periods which are benefited by its services. The effects of all such historical-cost methods on the income of different periods and on the financial position at any given time may be quite different from periodic depreciation charges and remaining asset balances computed on the basis of the *current costs* of the asset services. Differences between historical-cost fixed asset and depreciation measurements and current-cost measurements tend to be more significant:

(1) The greater the depreciable assets are in absolute dollar amount and in relation to total assets,

(2) The longer their useful lives are, and

(3) The more extensive the price changes are that occur during their lives.

Attention is given in Chapter 16 to the effects of general price-level changes on the measurement of long-lived assets and depreciation.

OTHER PROBLEMS OF ACCOUNTING FOR LONG-LIVED ASSETS

Accounting for Asset Retirements Under Item Depreciation Method

When a depreciable asset is disposed of, two accounting entries are needed:

(1) To record depreciation expense for the time since the last adjusting entry was made.

(2) To remove from the records the asset's acquisition cost and accumulated depreciation up to the date of disposal.

Example 15   A piece of equipment acquired at the beginning of 1973 for $1,000, with an original estimated life of five years and an estimated net salvage value of zero, was sold for $240 cash on April 1, 1976. Depreciation had last been recorded on December 31, 1975. The relevant account balances just before recording the sale were

A, Equipment		A, Equipment—Accumulated Depreciation	
1/1/1973 1,000		12/31/1973	200
		12/31/1974	200
		12/31/1975	200
		Balance,	
		600	

What entries were needed at the time of sale?

Solution   The entry to record depreciation for the period from January 1 to April 1, 1976, would be

(a)

OE, Depreciation Expense (1976)....................................	50	
A, Equipment—Accumulated Depreciation..................		50

Depreciation for $\frac{1}{4}$ year.

After posting this entry, the accounts would show the unexpired cost of the equipment on April 1 as $350 ($1,000 original cost minus $650 accumulated depreciation). The equipment was sold for a loss of $110 (sales price, $240, minus unexpired cost, $350). The entry for sale would be

(b)

A, Cash..	240	
A, Equipment—Accumulated Depreciation...................	650	
OE, Loss on Disposal of Equipment...........................	110	
A, Equipment..		1,000

Sold equipment having an unexpired cost of $350 for $240 cash.

If the sales price exceeds the unexpired cost of the asset sold, there should be a credit to Gain on Disposal of Equipment. Any costs incurred in removing retired depreciable assets reduce the gain (or increase the loss) resulting from the sale.

Accounting for Asset Retirements Under Group Depreciation Method

Under the group method of depreciation, when an asset that is part of the group is retired it is considered to be *fully depreciated*—even if it is retired before the end of the estimated average life of the group.

The retirement of *one* of the five machines in Example 13 at the end of year 1 would be recorded as follows:

A, Machinery—Accumulated Depreciation	60	
A, Machinery...		60

To remove the cost and accumulated depreciation of a retired machine from the records.

Comparison of Item and Group Depreciation

The *group method* of depreciation may be simpler to apply than the *item method*, especially for assets of relatively small individual cost. Under the group method no gains and losses are recorded when the individual components of a group are retired, unless it becomes clear that the predicted life of the group as a whole is incorrect.

The group method tends to *match* expired costs with revenues better than the unit method does, because it assigns depreciation to periods *in proportion to the service units* (service years) *received during each period.*

Accounting for Trades of Plant and Equipment

The acquisition of a new asset by trading an old asset, or an old asset plus cash, consists of two distinct elements: a *retirement of the old asset* and an *acquisition of the new*. There may be a gain or loss on the retirement of the old asset. However, the trade-in allowance given on the old asset is not necessarily a good measure of the value received for the old asset, because stated trade-in allowances and list prices are sometimes unrealistic.

The value received for the old asset is either (1) its own *fair market value* at the time of the trade or (2) the excess of the fair market value of the new asset over the cash paid and to be paid, whichever can be determined more dependably. If neither fair market value can be determined reliably, the trade-in allowance may be the best evidence of the value received for the old asset.

Example 16   A business traded equipment with an original cost of $2,000 and accumulated depreciation of $1,600 for other equipment with a list price of $3,000. Payment for the new equipment consisted of a trade-in allowance of $700 on the old equipment plus $2,300 cash. The old equipment could have been sold for $500 cash. What are the proper entries to record the exchange?

Solution   The business received an *overallowance* of $200 on the old equipment, in effect reducing the price of the new equipment to $2,800. Both the trade-in allowance and the unexpired cost of the old asset are irrelevant in determining the acquisition cost of the new. The entry is

A, Equipment (new)	2,800	
A, Equipment—Accumulated Depreciation (old).........	1,600	
A, Equipment (old)...		2,000
OE, Gain on Disposal of Equipment		100
A, Cash		2,300

To record acquisition of new equipment for $2,300 cash plus old equipment with a current market value of $500; to remove the original cost and accumulated depreciation on the old equipment from the books; and to reflect a gain of $100, the difference between the amount realized on the old equipment, $500, and its unexpired cost, $400.

Accounting for Partial Replacements

Replacing a part of an asset rather than the whole often gives rise to difficult accounting problems. Usually the accounting treatment is governed by the *materiality* of the replacement. If it is of *low cost* and of a type which is likely to recur frequently during the life of the asset, the cost of the replacement is treated as an expense. A case in point is the replacement of a spark plug in a motor.

If the replacement is a *major* one which increases the service benefits expected from the asset beyond those originally anticipated, the accounting treatment should reflect the *retirement of the old asset* component and the *acquisition of the new one*. An example is the replacement of a truck motor by a more durable one that extends the estimated useful life of the truck as a whole beyond the life originally expected. The cost and accumulated depreciation of the part being replaced should be estimated and removed from the accounts, and the cost of the new part should be debited to the asset account.

Revision of Depreciation Rates

The estimated remaining useful lives of depreciable assets should be reviewed frequently in order to make appropriate revisions. If it is necessary to revise a depreciation rate, the remaining unexpired cost of the asset should be assigned to the periods of the asset's estimated life, as revised. Any additional depreciation should be charged to the current and future periods, and not treated as a retroactive correction of retained income.

Depletion of Natural Resources

Natural resources include physical assets such as mineral deposits, oil and gas resources, and timber, which yield their service benefits by use or sale after being extracted from the basic deposit or tract. A *physical reduction* in the quantity of the deposit occurs as the resource is exploited, although in some cases the reduction is offset by growth (*accretion*) or development of additional deposits.

The extracted resources are accounted for in a manner similar to that of the inventory of a manufacturer. Costs of extraction, including an appropriate share of the cost of the natural resource, labor, and overhead costs, should be accumulated in an account for *inventory of extracted resources*. When these resources are sold, their costs should be transferred to Cost of Goods Sold Expense.

The acquisition cost of a natural resource includes its purchase cost plus the cost of development incurred until the asset begins producing. Development costs can easily be excessive; in fact, unproductive explorations such as dry wells are a common feature of extractive industries. Such costs should be accumulated as an asset until the production stage is reached or until it becomes clear that the asset will not be productive. In the first case, the asset cost is then systematically *amortized* over its expected useful life; in the second, it is charged promptly to a *loss* account.

The periodic amortization of the cost of a natural resource is called *depletion*. The *unit of production* method is appropriate because of the nature of the operation. Depletion for each unit extracted is determined as follows:

$$\text{Depletion per unit } (d) = \frac{\text{Acquisition cost } (C) - \text{Residual value } (S)}{\text{Estimated life in production units } (n)}.$$

Facts for Basic Illustration

Early in 1973 the Valley Lumber Company acquired a timber tract for $105,000 and incurred costs of $5,000 in developing it. The tract was estimated to contain 5 million (5,000 M) board feet of timber, and it was expected that the cut-over land could be sold for $10,000 after the timber had been cut. During 1973 the lumber cut totaled 1,000 M board feet, of which 800 M were sold for $60,000. Other costs incurred were as follows:

Lumber mill: Direct labor.	$10,000
Depreciation of machinery	5,000
Plant maintenance.	15,000
Selling and administrative costs.	8,000
Corporate federal income tax.	2,640

(1) How should these facts be recorded in the long-lived asset accounts?
(2) What disposition should be made of the cost of depletion during 1973?

Solution

A long-lived asset, Timber Tract, should be debited for the $105,000 acquisition cost and the $5,000 development cost.

Depletion for the year, based on the *timber cut*, is computed as follows:

$$D = \frac{C(\$105,000 + \$5,000) - S(\$10,000)}{n(5,000 \text{ M feet})} = \frac{\$100,000}{5,000} = \$20 \text{ per M feet}$$

1,000 M feet cut × $20 per M depletion rate = $20,000 depletion.

Depletion should be recorded by the following entry:
A, Lumber Inventory.................................... 20,000
    A, Timber Tract—Accumulated Depletion... 20,000

The valuation of the timber tract is reduced by the $20,000 depletion credited to its contra-account.

Cost of Goods Sold Expense should be debited, and Lumber Inventory should be credited, for the cost of the 800 M feet of lumber *sold*. This would include

800/1,000 of the direct labor, depreciation, maintenance, and depletion. The remaining 200/1,000 of these costs incurred during 1973 would remain in the asset account, Lumber Inventory, awaiting sale in future years.

Amortization of Goodwill and Other Intangible Assets

Goodwill is that part of the purchase price of a going business which *cannot be assigned to specific assets*. It may result from good customer relations, good sources of supply, good organization, good management, and a host of similar causes.

Often when new owners buy a business or a substantial equity in it, the buyers and sellers mutually agree on the price of goodwill. But sometimes in lump-sum purchases of businesses no price is specified for goodwill or for any other individual asset. The buyer may then assign a cost to each asset equal to its estimated, or appraised, value. If the sum of the appraised values of the identifiable assets is *less* than the total cost of the business, the difference may be treated as the cost of goodwill. If the appraised values of the identifiable assets *exceed the total cost* of the business, presumably there is no goodwill, and the total cost of the business should be allocated to the identifiable assets.

In some cases where a going business is acquired there is evidence that the goodwill purchased will have a limited life. In other cases there is no evidence of such limited duration. If the factors which are thought to contribute to the value of goodwill are expected to have a limited life, a portion of the cost of goodwill should be transferred each period to the expired cost account, *Amortization of Goodwill*.

Even if the factors contributing to goodwill are expected to last indefinitely, the Accounting Principles Board requires that goodwill be amortized over a period of 40 years.[1] Amortization should be under the straight-line method unless the facts indicate that another method is appropriate.

Other intangible assets whose useful life may be limited by law, regulation, or contract or by their very nature are patents, copyrights, leaseholds, licenses, and franchises for a fixed term. The cost of such intangible assets should be amortized over their useful lives.

Types of intangible assets whose useful lives may be unlimited are trade names, secret processes, subscription lists, perpetual franchises, and organization costs. These intangibles should be amortized over no more than forty years.

REPORTING AND INTERPRETING LONG-LIVED ASSETS

Knowledge of how much of the cost of long-lived assets has expired during the current and past accounting periods and how much applies to the future is useful to management and outsiders in appraising the past performance of

---

[1] American Institute of Certified Public Accounts, *APB Accounting Principles, Current Text as of February 1, 1971,* Paragraphs 5141.29–.30.

the business and its future prospects. The internal control procedures and detailed records used in accounting for long-lived assets help to increase the accuracy of this information and to promote the safety and proper use of the assets. Accounting data are also often useful as a starting point for management decisions relating to the *retention or replacement* of long-lived assets.

The remainder of this chapter deals with *reporting, analysis,* and *internal control* of long-lived assets.

General-Purpose Reporting Requirements

Financial position statements prepared for general use should classify long-lived assets according to their major types. Accumulated amortization should be reported separately for each major type of asset.

Construction work in progress and other property not being used in operations, such as *idle plant* or *plant held for future development,* should also be disclosed as separate amounts. These accounts represent sums invested in assets but not now producing revenue. The statement analyst is interested in knowing what part of the total assets are not in use, and he wishes to compare revenues and income with only the assets which were used in producing them.

The amount of *fully depreciated assets which are still in use,* if material in amount, should also be reported separately. An asset is fully depreciated for accounting purposes when its cost minus accumulated depreciation is equal to its estimated salvage value. For example,

Machine—cost	$5,000
Deduct accumulated depreciation	5,000
Unexpired cost	$ 0

The asset may have an additional useful life; if so, depreciation expense of past periods has been overstated. No further depreciation may be recorded in future periods, however. As a result, the expense of future periods in which the fully depreciated asset is used will be understated. Knowledge of the cost of fully depreciated assets still in use helps the statement reader judge the propriety of the depreciation rates used.

The financial statements should also report the *basis of measuring* long-lived assets. Usually this is *cost,* although in rare instances *appraised values* are used. Interpretation of the data is further aided by a statement of the depreciation method used and the policy followed in distinguishing between capital and revenue expenditures. The amounts of any significant liens, such as mortgages against the property, should be disclosed.

Supporting schedules which show for a series of years the amounts of additions, deductions, and balances of the major types of long-lived assets and their related accumulated amortization accounts are desirable.

Comparison of Depreciation with Cost

The information about long-term assets presented in the typical general-purpose report is often difficult to interpret because the long-lived assets have been acquired over a long period of time at different price levels. Subject to this limitation, the following comparisons dealing with long-lived asset balances are often worthwhile.

The percentage of *accumulated depreciation to cost* gives some indication of the age of the plant. Assume the following balances:

	Company A		Company B	
Plant and equipment—cost...............	$100,000	100%	$100,000	100%
Accumulated depreciation................	20,000	20%	70,000	70%
Unexpired cost.............................	$ 80,000	80%	$ 30,000	30%

If the companies have used reasonable estimated lives and the same depreciation method, the higher percentage of accumulated depreciation to cost indicates that the plant of Company B is much older. In the not-too-distant future, substantial outlays will probably be needed for replacements. Furthermore, the operating expenses for repairs and maintenance of Company B during the next few years are likely to be greater than those of Company A because of the age of the plant.

A comparison of the percentage of *annual depreciation expense to the cost of assets* with the corresponding percentages of similar companies provides clues as to whether the company's periodic charges are reasonable. Of course, due allowance should be made for intercompany differences of depreciation methods and differences in average asset age.

Turnover of Long-Lived Assets

The plant and equipment turnover rate (sales revenue divided by average balance of plant and equipment) is an indication of how intensively plant and equipment were worked during the period. This comparison is of greatest importance for businesses, such as public utilities, which derive most of their revenue from the use of their plant and equipment. The turnover rate for a telephone company might be computed as follows:

$$\text{Operating revenues.}\ldots\ldots\ldots\ldots = \frac{\$30,000,000}{\$100,000,000} = 0.3 \text{ turnover}$$
$$\text{Telephone plant cost}\ldots\ldots\ldots$$

As in the case of other asset turnovers, action to improve the turnover rate may be directed toward increasing revenue or toward reducing the asset balance in relation to the amount of revenue. Usually it takes longer to effect changes of the latter type for long-lived assets than for such short-lived assets as receivables and inventories.

Internal Control

The objectives of internal control procedures for long-lived assets are to ensure that such assets are acquired, used, and disposed of according to company policy. The company's policy for distinguishing capital from revenue expenditures and its procedures for initiating and approving requests for asset additions and disposals should be spelled out in a manual. Responsibility for approving asset changes and for keeping custody of the assets should be assigned to specific individuals. The records and reports of long-lived assets should show how the responsibility was discharged.

Individuals should not establish their own accountability for assets. A person other than the one who has physical custody of long-lived assets should keep accounting records of the asset changes and balances. Detailed records of long-lived assets are essential to

(1) Assist in preparing financial statements by giving information on periodic depreciation expense, cost of assets in use, and accumulated depreciation.

(2) Promote accuracy in estimating future useful lives of assets on the basis of an analysis of past histories of similar assets.

(3) Provide information regarding the operating performance of various types of individual assets. This information is useful to management in evaluating the desirability of replacing assets and in selecting particular types of assets for additions and replacements.

At regular intervals the physical assets themselves should be compared with the records by someone other than the custodian. The aim of this comparison is *more* than to determine that all assets which should be on hand are accounted for. It also ensures a regular examination of the *physical condition* of each asset. Periodically, too, the totals of the subsidiary records should be compared with the three general ledger accounts for which they provide detailed information: Plant and Equipment (cost), Plant and Equipment—Accumulated Depreciation, and Depreciation Expense.

Summary

Capital expenditures, which are expected to benefit the business in more than one accounting period, are debited to asset accounts and are amortized systematically over the useful lives of the assets. The cost which expires each period is called *depreciation* when applied to plant and equipment, *depletion* for natural resources, and *amortization* for intangible assets.

Various alternative methods have been developed for assigning to accounting periods the cost of the benefits received from capital expenditures. The *straight-line* method allocates expired cost to periods in proportion to the lapse of time; the *production* methods allocate expired cost in proportion to some unit of activity; and the *accelerated depreciation* methods charge a decreasing amount of depreciation to each succeeding accounting period. In selecting an appropriate amortization method, the business should consider the extent to which the method properly reflects the service benefits received from the asset in each accounting period.

Financial reports should disclose the amounts of each significant class of long-lived asset, the basis of measurement, the principal changes during the period, and the method and amount of amortization.

The internal control procedures and subsidiary records should be designed to insure that the acquisition, use, and disposal of long-lived assets are in accordance with the best interests of the business. Detailed records may be used to collect information that is helpful in controlling assets and in evaluating alternative assets which are being considered as additions or replacements.

Discussion Questions and Problems

12-1 Define "long-lived nonmonetary assets," and give an example of three different types of such assets.

12-2 State the basic accounting principle for measuring the acquisition cost of a long-lived nonmonetary asset. How should this principle be applied when consideration other than cash is given to acquire the asset?

12-3 Distinguish between a *capital expenditure* and a *revenue expenditure*. How would you differentiate between asset improvements and maintenance expenditures? How should each be treated in the accounting records?

12-4 Your business acquired a used delivery truck on January 6, 1973. Classify each of the following expenditures on the truck as capital or revenue expenditures, and give the reason for each answer:

a. Invoice cost of truck.
b. License for calendar year 1973.
c. Liability insurance premium for 1973.
d. Replacing old motor with a similar new motor at time of purchase.
e. Replacing spark plugs in June 1973.
f. Replacing battery in August 1973.
g. Monthly cost of washing.
h. Gasoline.
i. Repainting in December 1973.
j. Repairing dented fender resulting from accident in July 1973.
k. Painting owners' name on side.
l. Installing heater (not a replacement) in November 1973.

12-5 "The acquisition cost of a long-lived asset includes all costs reasonably incurred in purchasing it and in transporting, installing, renovating, developing, testing, or otherwise preparing it for its initial use in the business." Explain how this statement would apply in determining the acquisition cost of each of the following:

a. The site of an old factory purchased for conversion into a modern shopping center.
b. Patent rights purchased from the inventor of a new toy who will receive a 10 per cent royalty on all sales of the toy.
c. The trademark applied for by a company on its major product which was developed and defended in court by the company.
d. A new machine purchased in Germany by a New York manufacturer for installation in its plant in Orlando, Florida.
e. Land purchased on a mountainside to be used in the stripmining of coal.
f. An old residence obtained under a ten-year lease and remodeled for use as an office suite for the top executives of a business corporation.

12-6 On January 1, a manufacturer purchased machinery having a cash price of $60,000. The purchase contract provided for an immediate cash payment of $20,000 and additional payments of $25,000 each at the end of each year for two years. The machinery was delivered in April. Installation was completed on June 30 at a cost of $3,000, and production began on July 1. How should these transactions be recorded in the accounts of the manufacturer?

12-7 A "market basket" purchase occurs when several assets are acquired in a combined lump-sum purchase. Explain how the acquisition costs of the separate assets are determined in such purchases.

12-8   "Since cause and effect between depreciation and revenue cannot be precisely traced, the depreciation method chosen is one which is *assumed* to reflect a *reasonable* relationship between an expiring asset and resulting revenues." Explain how this statement is applied, and identify the major criteria used in selecting a depreciation method.

12-9   Sometimes in past decades business managements would prepare income statements showing "net income before depreciation," and then subtract depreciation as a final figure. Often the amount charged to depreciation depended on whether the year was a good or a bad one in terms of profits. The latter policy was justified on the ground that the good years were able to bear a larger amount of depreciation expense than the bad ones.

Comment carefully on the implications of the statement presentation and depreciation policy described above.

12-10   The chief engineer of a manufacturing firm suggested in a conference of the company's executives that the accountants should speed up depreciation on the machinery in Department 3 because "improvements are making those machines obsolete very rapidly, and we want to have a depreciation fund big enough to cover their replacement."

Discuss fully the accounting concept of depreciation and the effect on a business concern of the depreciation recorded for fixed assets, paying particular attention to the issues raised by the chief engineer. (Adapted from AICPA Examination in Theory of Accounts.)

12-11   The president and the production manager of a manufacturing company were discussing the recently completed financial statements with the accountant. The president pointed to the following item:

Machinery and equipment.........................	$210,000	
Deduct accumulated depreciation...............	100,000	
Unexpired cost...		$110,000

"I am quite sure that we could not get more than $75,000 on the market for all of our machinery and equipment," said the president. "Accumulated depreciation should be much higher."

"I don't agree," countered the production manager. "The machinery and equipment are as efficient as they ever were. They haven't depreciated at all."

a. Explain the weaknesses of the arguments of the president and production manager.
b. To what extent should market values be considered in accounting for depreciation?
c. To what extent should declines in efficiency be considered in accounting for depreciation?

12-12

a. Explain the difference between a *group depreciation rate* and a *composite depreciation rate*.
b. Explain the difference between *group* depreciation and *item* depreciation.

12-13   Two building construction firms have just bought identical pickup trucks (except for exterior painting) for general use. The purchases were made on the same day.

a. Will the estimated lives of both trucks be the same?
b. What information will the firms need in order to determine the estimated lives of their trucks?
c. Should the firms use the same depreciation method? Explain.

12-14   Under what circumstances would each of the following methods of depreciation be most appropriate for a factory machine?

a. Straight-line.
b. Working hours.
c. Uniform percentage of unexpired cost.

12-15   A manufacturing company uses several hundred identical machines, each of which costs approximately $300. The company's policy is to use each machine as long as it maintains a prescribed minimum level of operating efficiency. For a few machines this minimum is reached within one or two years after original acquisition, but some machines last as long as ten years. Most of the machines—approximately 70 per cent— have operating lives of from four to six years. Each year many new machines are acquired, in the form of both additions and replacements. You are asked to recommend one of the following methods of accounting for these machines:

a. Charge their cost to expense when they are acquired. This policy will not distort periodic income, it is argued, because the cost of acquisitions is fairly constant from year to year.
b. Charge their cost to expense when they are retired from service. This policy is defended on the grounds that each machine meets acceptable standards of efficiency until it is retired.
c. Maintain a detailed record of the cost of each machine, and compute depreciation separately for each on the basis of its estimated life.
d. Consider the machines acquired in each year as a group for depreciation purposes, and compute depreciation on the estimated total service life of each group.

Discuss the advantages and disadvantages, both theoretical and practical, of each procedure. Which do you recommend? Why?

12-16   The financial position statement of Central City Corporation contained the following information:

Property, plant, and equipment, at cost:

Land...	$ 5,256
Buildings on owned and leased land........................	33,688
Leaseholds and leasehold improvements...................	15,482
Machinery, fixtures, and equipment........................	56,881
	$111,307
Less reserves for depreciation and amortization..........	$ 72,059
Net property, plant, and equipment.....................	$ 39,248

a. What differences, if any, should there be in the methods of accounting for the acquisition and the cost expiration of buildings on owned land as compared with those on leased land?
b. What is meant by a leasehold? Give an example of a situation which requires recording the acquisition of a leasehold. How should a leasehold be accounted for after its acquisition?
c. What is meant by leasehold improvements? Give an example. Explain how both the acquisition and the expiration of leasehold improvements should be accounted for.

12-17   Aimes, Inc. purchased a highly specialized machine for $40,000. The expected life was 13 years with a net salvage value of $1,000. Three years later a new machine was invented which would reduce operating costs by 50 per cent. As a result Aimes,

Inc. could profitably use its existing machine for only four more years, at which time the net salvage value would be $1,000.

How would this event be reflected in the accounting records of Aimes, Inc.?

12-18   Early in 1973 your company developed patents on two articles which it expects to manufacture, and a third patent on an improved production process. Patent A, costing $48,000, is associated with making a novelty item which is expected to be in demand a few months or a year. Patent B, costing $85,000, is on a staple product which is expected to be in demand indefinitely. Patent C, costing $20,400, is on a process that is expected to be beneficial for several years. However, the rate of technological progress is irregular in the field, and a further improvement may be developed which will make the new process obsolete. Each patent has a legal life of 17 years from the beginning of 1973.

a. Make the entries necessary to reflect these facts on December 31, 1973. Explain your reasoning in determining each amount.
b. State how the relevant accounts should appear in the December 31, 1973, financial position statement.

12-19   The statement of financial position of Pure Products, Inc., on December 31, 1972, contained the following information:

Buildings, cost...	$150,000	
Deduct accumulated depreciation...............	50,000	
Unexpired cost..		$100,000
Equipment, cost	$ 82,500	
Deduct accumulated depreciation...............	28,500	
Unexpired cost...		$ 54,000

A footnote states that the straight-line method of depreciation is being used for the buildings, with an estimated life of 30 years, and that the equipment is being depreciated over 10 years by the sum-of-the-years'-digits method.

a. Assuming that the buildings were all acquired at one time and that they have no salvage value, how old are they?
b. Assuming that the equipment was all acquired at one time and that it has no salvage value, how old is it?
c. What circumstances would justify the use of these different depreciation methods for the buildings and equipment?

12-20   The Pago Mfg. Co. is considering which depreciation method to use for a new machine which has an acquisition cost of $128,000. The machine is expected to last five years and have a net salvage value of $8,000. Annual production is expected as follows:

Year..................	1973	1974	1975	1976	1977	Total
Production units...	20,000	40,000	56,000	64,000	70,000	250,000

Required   a. Prepare a table comparing annual depreciation charges for the machine's life under the following methods: (1) straight-line, (2) production, (3) declining balance, and (4) sum-of-the-years'-digits.
b. Which method is most appropriate for this machine? List the most important assumptions required to answer this question.

12-21   Gebhart & Sons, Inc., purchased land, together with a building standing on it, as the site for an additional plant. The corporation obtained bids from several contractors for demolition of the old building and construction of the new building, but finally rejected all bids and undertook the construction using company labor, facilities, and equipment. Construction was almost completed by the close of the year.

All transactions relating to these properties were charged or credited to an account titled "Real Estate." The various items in that account are summarized below. You decide that separate Land and Buildings accounts should be set up and that all of the items in the Real Estate account should be reclassified.

Indicate the disposition of each numbered item by *printing* beside the item number the *capital letter* which identifies your answer. If you recommend a reclassification involving two or more of the following accounts, list the appropriate capital letters.

Although there may be other appropriate items not listed, you need give them no attention for purposes of this question and should consider only the following four possibilities:

A. Transfer to Buildings account.
B. Transfer to Land account.
C. Transfer to an expense (or loss) account.
D. Transfer to a revenue (or gain) account.

ITEMS CHARGED OR CREDITED TO "REAL ESTATE"

1. Contract price of "package" purchase (land and old building).
2. Legal fees relating to transfer of title.
3. Invoice cost of materials and supplies used in construction.
4. Direct costs arising from demolition of old building.
5. Discounts earned for early payment of item 3.
6. Total depreciation on equipment used during construction period partially for construction of building and the remainder of the time for regular operations.
7. Total cost of excavation.
8. Proceeds of sale of materials salvaged from razing of old building.
9. Cost of building permits and licenses.
10. Architects' fees.
11. Payment of property taxes on land and old building, owed by the former owner and assumed by the client.
12. Special municipal assessments for sidewalk and street pavings necessitated by the altered use of the site.
13. Premiums for insurance against natural hazards during construction.
14. Premium rebates for certain of the above policies surrendered before completion of construction.
15. Uninsured claims paid for injuries sustained during construction (aggregate amount, $3,000).
16. Installation costs for newly acquired machinery installed in completed wings of the building.
17. Estimated profit on construction of new building to date (computed as follows: Lowest contractor's bid × % of building completion to 12/31 less new building construction costs to date).

(Adapted from AICPA Examination in Theory of Accounts.)

12-22

Required Using letters to indicate your answers, classify the numbered expenditure items below as one of the following:

(a) Buildings
(b) Equipment
(c) Land
(d) Repairs and maintenance expense
(e) None of these (Describe the nature of the accounts affected.)

(1) A lot with a small house on it was purchased for $30,000. The intention was to use the house as a construction office during the construction of an office building on the lot. The construction period was expected to last about one year. Comparable construction offices could be rented for $100 a month.
(2) Legal fees of $300 in connection with acquiring the lot and house were paid.
(3) An office building was completed on the lot at a cost of $60,000 excluding items listed below. Its estimated useful life was 20 years and its estimated salvage value, $2,000.
(4) Cost of cleaning the building prior to use, $200, was paid.
(5) After two years' use, the exterior of the building was cleaned for $500.
(6) During the construction period a night watchman was hired for $3,000 to protect the building against theft and vandalism. He was retained as a permanent night watchman after construction was completed.
(7) At the end of the construction period, whose length was approximately as anticipated, the construction office was demolished. The cost of labor was $400, and the scrap materials were sold for $250.
(8) Insurance of $600 was paid for the construction period.
(9) Insurance of $800 was paid for the first year after construction.
(10) During construction it was necessary to tear out a defective wall. The original cost was estimated at $700, and the cost of replacing it was $900.
(11) Property taxes of $500 were paid for the first year of occupancy.
(12) The cost of electricity during the construction period was $550.

12-23   On January 2, 1973, Tower Co. acquired an automobile which had a list price of $4,900. Tower Co. made a down payment of $1,700 and gave an installment promissory note due over a period of 16 months for the balance. Each monthly payment was to consist of $200 principal plus interest at 1 per cent a month on the unpaid balance at the beginning of the month. The estimated life of the automobile was five years and the estimated salvage value was $400. Also, on January 2, Tower Co. paid $30 for a 1973 state automobile license, $6 for gasoline, and $78 for a six-month maintenance service contract.

Required   Journalize entries for

a. Acquisition of the automobile and related payments on January 2.
b. Depreciation for 1973 and 1974 under the declining-balance method at double the reciprocal of the estimated life.
c. Payment of the first monthly installment on the note.
d. Any related expired costs of the first month not already recorded.

12-24   The owner of a machine wishes to compare the results of alternative depreciation methods before deciding which method to adopt. The machine had an installed cost of $21,000 on January 7, 1973, and actual operations began on January 12. The company has followed the policy of considering that all depreciable acquisitions before the sixteenth of any month were made on the first of the month, and that all additions acquired from the sixteenth through the last of the month were acquired on the first of the following month.

Technological changes in machines of this type have been gradual in the past and

are expected to continue to be so in the future. It is estimated that the useful life of the machine will be eight years, after which it will have a net scrap value of $1,000.

Required
a. Prepare a table showing the depreciation for each year of the machine's life, and its unexpired cost at the end of each year, using the following methods:

(1) Straight-line.
(2) Uniform-rate-on-declining-balance at double the reciprocal of the estimated life.
(3) Sum-of-the-years'-digits.

b. What other factors should the owner consider in selecting a depreciation method, and how would they affect his decision?

c. If the owner wished to consider the production method, what additional information would he need, and how should it be used in making the decision?

12-25   The All-City Co. purchased a machine on December 31, 1972, trading in an old machine of a similar type. The old machine had been acquired on July 1, 1960, at a cost of $80,000. Both old and new machines had an estimated 20-year life and no net salvage value.

The terms of the purchase provided for a trade-in allowance of $25,000 and called for a cash payment of $135,000, or 12 monthly payments of $12,000 each. The All-City Co. chose the latter alternative. The trade-in allowance was the same as a cash sale price which had been offered by another machinery dealer.

Other costs of $5,000 were paid to install the new machine.

Required
a. Journalize entries to reflect the exchange on the books of the All-City Co.

b. Compute depreciation on the new machine for 1973 and 1974 under the declining-balance method at twice the reciprocal of the estimated life. Show all computations clearly labeled.

(Adapted from AICPA Examination in Accounting Practice.)

12-26   The Mathis Corp. bought a machine on April 17, 1973, paying $2,800 in cash and giving a 6 per cent promissory note due in one year for the unpaid balance of $8,000. The machine had an estimated life of eight years and an estimated salvage value of zero. The Mathis Corp. uses the calendar year as its accounting period, and treats all acquisitions and disposals as though they occurred at midyear.

On July 27, 1976, the Mathis Corp. sold the machine for $4,900 cash.

Required
a. Journalize entries to record depreciation for 1973, 1974, and 1975 under the sum-of-the-years'-digits method.

b. Present T-accounts to show the unexpired cost of the old machine at the end of 1975.

c. Journalize all relevant entries in 1976.

12-27   The Quanta Corp. acquired 50 identical motors early in January 1973 at a cost of $300 per motor. Past experience indicates that the total life of the group of motors should be about 250 service-years, and that the net salvage value will be zero. At the end of 1973 an examination of the condition of the motors on hand resulted in scrapping one of them.

Required
a. Record depreciation for 1973 and 1974 under the group method of depreciation.

b. Journalize the entry for scrapping the motor at the end of 1973 under the group method.

c. Journalize the entry for scrapping the motor if the item method of depreciation had been used.

d. Explain the reasoning underlying the differences in accounting under the two methods.

12-28   Range Corporation uses a large number of units of a small type of equipment, and for a number of years it has kept careful records of the service life of each item. The summary of this past experience per hundred units is as follows:

Years of Useful Life	Number of Units with Each Life Length	Number of Service-Years
1	5	5
2	10	20
3	40	120
4	25	100
5	15	75
6	5	30
Totals	100	350

Early in January 1973 Range Corporation acquired 100 units at a cost of $70 each. The actual retirements of these units by years were as follows:

1973...............	6 units	1976...............	20 units
1974...............	10 units	1977...............	15 units
1975...............	38 units	1978...............	11 units

For simplicity, you may assume that retirements occurred at the end of the year, and that no unit had any salvage value.

Required   a. Journalize the entries for 1973 and 1978 using the group method of depreciation on a straight-line basis.
b. Journalize the entries for 1973 and 1978 using the item method of depreciation on a straight-line basis. The average life of each unit is 3.5 years.
c. Explain the differences which result between the two methods in parts a and b.
d. Compute the actual average life of this group of assets.
e. Aside from the error in estimating the average useful life of the group of units, which method—item or group—results in better matching in the periodic income statements? Why?

12-29   Your company acquired a tractor for $8,000 at the beginning of 1973. Depreciation has been recorded under the straight-line method on the basis of an estimated life of four years and estimated salvage value of zero. Just prior to making the annual depreciation entry for 1975, it becomes evident that the tractor will last until the end of 1980.

Required   a. Journalize the entries to reflect these facts in 1975.
b. What are the weaknesses of the method used in part a?

12-30   On July 1, 1973, Sam Co. acquired a new executive automobile for an $8,000 list price. The company gave in exchange $4,000 cash and an old automobile which had been acquired on October 1, 1970, for $6,800. The old automobile had been depreciated under the straight-line method to the nearest full month by using an estimated life of four years and estimated salvage value of $2,000.

Required   a. Journalize the entry for the trade. Show supporting computations in detail.

b. What is the acquisition cost of the new automobile? Defend your answer.

c. Record depreciation on the new automobile on December 31, 1973.

12-31   The Siena Company acquired a factory machine on July 1, 1971, at a cost of $30,000. The company estimated that the machine would have a useful life of 15,000 running hours and no net salvage value. Depreciation has been charged in proportion to actual running hours as follows:

1971............1,000 hours   1972............2,500 hours   1973............2,100 hours

On December 31, 1974, the factory superintendent estimates that because of obsolescence the machine can be used for only 2,400 more hours. Depreciation for the 1,600 hours used in 1974 has not been recorded.

Required   Journalize all necessary entries in 1974.

12-32   The Stark Company reported income for the past three years as follows:

1971......... $70,000   1972......... $18,000   1973......... $39,000

In reviewing the accounts, the auditor finds that in 1971 the company charged an expenditure of $20,000 to Building Maintenance Expense. The expenditure was for an addition to the existing building, which is being depreciated under the straight-line method at 4 per cent a year.

Required   a. Show in detail the changes necessary to reflect each year's income correctly.

b. What accounts in the December 31, 1973, financial position statement should be corrected, and by what amounts?

12-33   The Luce Mining Company acquired a site early in 1973 which it estimates contains 30,000 tons of ore. The site cost $168,000, and it is estimated that the property can be sold for $10,000 after mining is completed. The cost of removing the overburden prior to beginning actual extraction of ore was $17,000. Cost of mining shafts was $5,000.

During 1973 the company mined 4,000 tons and sold 2,500 of them for $45,000 cash. Mining labor amounted to $14,000; repairs, maintenance, and other mining overhead, $8,000; selling costs, $3,000; and general costs of administration, $7,200.

Required   a. Record the foregoing transactions in journal form. Use an account for Mined Ore Inventory and include all relevant costs in it.

b. Prepare an income statement for 1973.

c. Show how the unmined deposit and the unsold but mined ore would be presented in the financial position statement for December 31, 1973.

12-34   Early in 1973 the Certified Lumber Co. was investigating the possibility of buying a tract of standing timber. The company paid a forester $200 for a cruise of the tract, and on the basis of his report of the quantity of salable timber, decided to purchase the tract for $50,000. Legal fees of $100 were paid in connection with the purchase. However, on the forester's advice, Certified Lumber Company waited for a year before beginning to cut the timber in order to allow further growth.

During 1973 the company paid property taxes of $400 on the tract and also paid a fee of $200 for fire protection service. Logging operations were begun in the early spring of 1974, at which time the tract was estimated to contain 2,250,000 board feet of timber. It was felt that the land could be sold for $6,200, minus a commission of $300, at the conclusion of operations.

The total number of board feet sawed into rough lumber in 1973 was 800,000. Of this quantity, 600,000 board feet were sold to a planing mill for $20,000. Costs incurred during the year 1974 were as follows:

Labor	$4,900
Transportation of rough lumber to planing mill	500
Sawmill depreciation	300
Maintenance and repairs	800
Supervision	1,500

Required
a. Show how the relevant facts would appear in the financial position statement of the Certified Lumber Co. on December 31, 1973.
b. Journalize all entries required for the events of 1974.
c. Prepare an income statement for 1974.
d. Show how the information relating to the timber tract and the unsold lumber would appear in the December 31, 1974, statement of financial position.

12-35   On January 3, 1973, a group of individuals formed a corporation to acquire the business of J. E. O'Quin. The organizers of the corporation paid $150,000 in cash, which was equal to the par value of the capital stock of the corporation which they received. The corporation paid O'Quin $140,000 for his business.

O'Quin's business was purchased on January 5, 1973, on the following basis:

	Amounts on O'Quin's Books	Agreed Sale Price
Cash	$ 4,000	$ 4,000
Accounts receivable	14,000	13,200
Merchandise inventory	21,000	23,000
Equipment (10-year remaining life)	90,000	55,000
—Accumulated depreciation	(30,000)	
Supplies	2,000	1,600
Franchise	5,000	12,000
Totals	$106,000	$108,800

The purchasers felt that some of O'Quin's customers' accounts would be uncollectible. The exclusive-dealer franchise, which had been acquired by O'Quin in 1968, had five more years to run. The manufacturer had assured the new owners that they would have the first chance at renewing the franchise when it expired. The price paid for the business in excess of the values of the specific assets was in recognition of the superior earning power of the business, which was expected to last for about ten more years if existing conditions continued.

Required
a. Record journal entries for the formation of the corporation, the acquisition of O'Quin's business, and amortization at the end of 1973.
b. On January 7, 1973, the corporation signed a ten-year lease on a building, promising to pay an annual rental of $4,000 in advance. Rent was paid when due. On July 2 the corporation, with the permission of the landlord, completed remodeling of a showroom at a cost of $2,280. It was estimated that remodeling would not be required again for 15 years. Record the necessary entries on July 2 and December 31, 1973.
c. Show how the facts relating to the long-lived assets would appear in the financial position statement of the corporation on December 31, 1973.

12-36   The Meachum Company acquired a building for $140,000 on January 3, 1963. It has been recording depreciation on the basis of an estimated life of 35 years and an estimated salvage value of zero, under the straight-line method. Depreciation has been computed to the nearest half-year. On January 2, 1974, the Meachum Company completed the installation of a new heating and air-conditioning system at a cost of $28,000. This system replaced the original heating system, which had been expected to serve the entire life of the building. The estimated original cost of the system replaced was $14,000. It was sold for a net salvage value of $1,000.

Required   a. Journalize the entries necessary to record the retirement of the old heating system and the installation of the new heating-cooling system.

b. Journalize the entries necessary on December 31, 1974, if the total estimated life of the building is unchanged.

12-37   The Maple City Manufacturing Co. bought some property containing a warehouse, equipment, and raw materials. The seller offered the entire property for a cash price of $120,000, but agreed as an alternative to accept a down payment of $10,500 and 11 monthly installments of $10,500 each. The Maple City Manufacturing Co. elected the latter plan and signed a purchase contract on January 3, 1973. In deciding whether or not to purchase the property, Maple had engaged the services of an independent appraiser, who had estimated the fair market values of the various components as follows:

Land...	$16,000
Warehouse.................................	80,000
Railroad siding	8,000
Driveways	4,000
Equipment	40,000
Raw materials, Group 1	1,600
Raw materials, Group 2	10,400

Maple planned to use the second group of materials in its manufacturing operations, and to sell the first group in bulk. On January 15 it received $1,200 in cash for the Group 1 materials.

The driveways were repaired for $1,100 and the equipment for $2,600. Both were ready for use on January 21. On June 23 a machine which had been assigned a total cost of $2,000 broke down but was repaired for $300.

Required   Present a properly classified list of the assets acquired by Maple City and the acquisition cost of each.

Cases   **12-1   Amerada Petroleum Corporation.** The 1968 Annual Report of the Amerada Petroleum Corporation contained the following Synopsis of Accounting Practices:

> All intangible drilling and development costs incurred are charged against income each year through a 100% reserve, except those applicable to productive wells in the Kingdom of Libya and the North Sea. The intangible drilling and development costs of productive wells in the Kingdom of Libya are amortized through charges against income under the straight-line method and similar costs with respect to the North Sea will also be amortized on the straight-line method commencing with the first year in which production and income are obtained from such wells.

All geological and geophysical expenses are charged against income as incurred. Lease rentals generally are charged off in full when paid.

Nearly all the Corporation's production is obtained from properties acquired prior to the discovery of oil or gas thereon. Properties that become productive are carried in the accounts at cost, less depletion, and consequently the increase in value resulting from the discovery of oil or gas is not reflected in the Consolidated Balance Sheet. The cost of each producing property is amortized by annual charges for depletion in the proportion which the production for the year bears to the estimated recovery of oil or gas, calculated separately for each property, except for costs applicable to producing fields in Libya which are amortized through charges against income under the straight-line method.

Undeveloped properties are carried in the accounts at cost, which cost is written off in full when properties are surrendered or otherwise disposed of, except in certain cases where properties are written off prior to formal relinquishment. . . .

These accounting practices are followed with respect to both domestic and international operations except where noted above.

The corporation's Consolidated Balance Sheet for December 31, 1968, contained the following information:

PROPERTIES, PLANT AND EQUIPMENT: (in $ thousands)

Lands, wells, and equipment—at cost:	
Developed and undeveloped lands, including intangible drilling and development costs	$502,444
Crude oil and natural gas production equipment	216,073
	718,517
Other property, plant, and equipment—at cost	52,868
	771,385
Less reserves for intangible drilling and development costs, depreciation, and depletion	504,705
Properties, plant, and equipment, net	$266,680

The corporation's Consolidated Statement of Income for the year ended December 31, 1968, is presented in the accompanying illustration.

AMERADA PETROLEUM CORPORATION AND SUBSIDIARIES

Consolidated Statement of Income for
the Year Ended December 31, 1968 (in $ thousands)

Income:	
Oil and gas sales and other operating income	$256,466
Dividends, interest, and other income	8,134
	$264,600
Costs and expenses:	
Operating, exploration, and administrative expenses; taxes other than income taxes; etc.	99,294
Intangible drilling and development costs	24,867
Depreciation, depletion, and leases abandoned and expired	18,982
Provision for income taxes	55,891
	199,034
Net income	65,566

Required   a. How can you justify charging intangible drilling and development costs and geological and geophysical expenses against income each year? How can you explain the appearance of intangible drilling and development costs in Properties, Plant, and Equipment in view of the corporation's accounting policy?

b. What conditions would justify the use of a different method of accounting for drilling and development costs in Libya and the North Sea as compared with the method used elsewhere?

c. Should the increase in value resulting from the discovery of oil or gas be reflected in the balance sheet? If so, how?

d. Comment on the difference in methods of amortizing the cost of producing property in Libya and elsewhere. How do you explain the difference?

e. What circumstances do you think would justify writing off properties prior to formal relinquishment? What type of account should be debited for such write-offs?

12-2   International Paper Company. The Consolidated Financial Position Statement of International Paper Company for December 31, 1970, contained the following long-lived assets (in $ million):

Plants and properties (Note 4)	2,132.1
Less: Reserves for depreciation (Note 4)	1,072.4
Net plants and properties	1,059.7
Woodlands—net (Note 5)	171.2
Investments and advances (Note 6)	87.0
	1,317.9

The Consolidated Earnings Statement for the Year Ended December 31, 1970, appeared as follows (in $ million):

Income:	
Net sales	$1,840.8
Profit on foreign exchange	6.3
Other income—net	11.5
	1,858.6
Costs and expenses:	
Cost of goods sold exclusive of items listed below	1,323.2
Freight and delivery expense	139.3
Selling, general, and administrative expenses.	138.7
Depreciation and depletion	99.1
Interest	38.5
Income taxes—U.S. and foreign (Note 4)	37.3
	1,776.1
Earnings before extraordinary items	82.5
Extraordinary items, net of applicable income tax of $38,400,000 (Note 2)	(39.6)
Net earnings	$ 42.9

Notes accompanying the consolidated financial statements read:

Note 2

A reserve of $78,000,000 before taxes ($39,600,000 after tax effect) was provided in 1970 for estimated extraordinary losses to be incurred in connection with the anticipated abandonment of facilities which are unprofitable, obsolete or unusable and which cannot, in the opinion of management, be made profitable by economically justifiable expenditures and of facilities which do not meet environmental standards and which, in the opinion of management, cannot be brought into compliance for similar economic reasons.

Note 4

Plants and properties at December 31, 1970, were as follows (in $ million):

	Cost	Reserves for Depreciation	Net
Paper and pulp mills......................	$1,559.0	$ 812.7	$ 746.3
Paper-converting plants..................	271.3	118.5	152.7
Sawmills, plywood, and lumber product plants..........................	111.2	57.8	53.5
Woods plant and equipment............	98.0	56.6	41.4
Other properties..........................	92.7	26.0	65.9
Total.....................................	$2,132.2	$1,072.4	$1,059.8

The companies compute depreciation principally on a straight-line method for financial reporting purposes and for tax purposes the companies use accelerated methods. The use of accelerated depreciation for tax purposes results in tax deferrals which are included in deferred income taxes. The net tax deferrals (arising principally from the use of accelerated depreciation methods) included in the provision for income taxes before extraordinary items amounted to $21,286,000 for 1970 and $23,098,000 for 1969.

Taxes on income have been reduced by investment tax credits of $7,423,000 in 1970 and $4,704,000 in 1969.

Note 5

Woodlands at December 31, 1970, were as follows:

	Acres* (in thousands)	Amounts† (in $ million)
United States:		
Owned in fee......................................	6,613	$146.7
Held under lease or contract rights.........	367	12.6
Total—United States........................	6,980	159.3
Canada:		
Owned in fee......................................	1,357	$ 7.2
Held under Government license.	15,140	4.7
Total—Canada................................	16,497	11.9
Total......................................	23,477	$171.2

*As reported by the Companies.
†Stated at cost less depletion.

Note 6

Investments and advances at December 31, 1970 were as follows (in $ million):

Securities of and advances to nonconsolidated affiliated companies, at cost	$48.1
U.S. Government and municipal securities, at cost which approximates market......................................	1.5
Other securities, at cost which approximates market.........	37.3
Total	$87.0

Required   a. How can you justify using accelerated depreciation in computing taxable income and straight-line depreciation in computing income for purposes of general financial reporting?

b. Do you suppose that the cost basis of the woodlands is "realistic"? Explain, indicating changes in accounting treatment that might be more appropriate.

c. What circumstances would justify excluding the securities investments referred to in Note 6 from current assets and net working capital?

d. How can you justify the $78 million provision for estimated extraordinary losses? What external circumstances probably led management to recognize these losses in 1970?

12-3   TKO Computer Company. The TKO Computer Company manufactures computers for sale or rent. On January 2, 1973, the company completed the manufacture of a computer for a total cost of $80,000. The company immediately leased the machine to a customer for a five-year period at a monthly rental of $2,300. Because of rapid technological progress in the field, there is a great probability that the computer will be practically obsolete shortly after the termination of the lease. If it is, it can be sold for $5,000. If it is not obsolete, it is estimated that the computer can be sold as second-hand equipment for $20,000.

On the basis of past experience the TKO Computer Company estimates that its expenses for each year of the lease will be approximately as follows:

	Property Taxes and Insurance	Repairs and Maintenance
First year	$2,000	$1,000
Second year	1,700	2,000
Third year	1,400	3,000
Fourth year	1,100	4,000
Fifth year	800	5,000

These expenses should be considered to occur evenly throughout the year.

Required   a. What estimated life and salvage value do you recommend that the TKO Computer Company use for the computer? Why?

b. Prepare a table showing for each year of the lease the revenue, expenses, income before income tax, the average balance of the machine's unexpired cost during the year, and the per cent of income before tax to the average balance of the machine's unexpired cost under each of the following depreciation methods:

(1) Straight-line.

(2) Declining-balance at double the reciprocal of the estimated life.

c. What conclusions can you draw about the suitableness of each depreciation method in this instance?

d. What further information would you wish before recommending a depreciation method to the management of the TKO Computer Company?

chapter 13

Accounting for

Liabilities

Purpose of Chapter

A *liability,* as defined in Chapter 2, represents a claim against the entity by a creditor, arising from a past transaction. Chapter 3 explained that liabilities which require the future payment of money are called *monetary liabilities,* while claims which are to be satisfied by delivering goods or rendering service are *nonmonetary liabilities.*

The following types of monetary liabilities were defined in Chapter 3: Accounts Payable, Notes Payable, Dividends Payable, Accrued Payables, Liabilities as an agent, Loans Payable, and Bonds Payable. Examples of nonmonetary liabilities defined in Chapter 3 were Liabilities Under Warranty, Advances from Customers, and Rents Collected in Advance.

When a liability is first incurred it should be measured at the amount of money or money equivalent that would currently be required to settle the obligation. If there is a substantial waiting period before a liability is to be paid, the appropriate measure of the debt is its *maturity value, minus interest* for the time remaining until maturity. In such a case an additional liability for *interest accrues* as time passes.

This chapter explores in more detail the characteristics which determine whether a particular item is a liability, some special problems in measuring and reporting liabilities, and some methods useful to management in controlling the amounts of liabilities and in scheduling their payment.

Characteristics of a Liability

In the past there was a tendency to think of an *accounting liability* as a *legal debt*—an enforceable obligation to pay a *certain sum* of money at a fixed or determinable future time.

In recent years, increasing emphasis on the proper measurement of *periodic income* has resulted in a broader definition of liabilities. Today some items which do not strictly fit the legal definition of *enforceable claims* are included in liabilities. An example is the *liability under warranty* contract which is recorded under a common accounting method. Many businesses sell products under a warranty agreement, whereby they promise to make any necessary repairs at no additional charge to the customer during a specified time period. In a strict legal sense there is not yet an enforceable claim against the business. There will be no *legal claim* until specific products sold are found to be defective and the specific customers who bought them request repairs under the warranty agreement.

Under a widely used method of accounting, past experience is used to estimate the costs of servicing products sold in the current period under warranties which expire after the end of the current period. The debit to expense *matches* servicing *costs* associated with products sold during the current period with the sales *revenue* from those products. The credit is to Liability Under Warranty. An alternative method of accounting for warranties is discussed on p. 382.

Accrual of Liabilities

Liabilities may arise at the *moment of an exchange* transaction, such as the borrowing of money or the purchase of productive facilities, goods, or services, all of which are received at the time of purchase.

An entity may receive a service continuously over time, as when it uses someone else's money or property for a period of time, in exchange for a promise to pay interest or rent. Such services are presumably received in equal daily parts, unless there is adequate evidence to the contrary.

Liabilities may also result from the receipt of money or other assets from a customer in exchange for facilities, goods, or services which the entity is to provide later. The entity does not expect to have to pay the liability in cash, but instead to provide goods or services in the future. Such liabilities are for *revenues collected in advance*. They may represent a product or a single *indivisible service*, such as a repair, which the entity is to deliver, or they may represent all or part of a *continuous service* which the entity is to perform over time.

Settlement of Liabilities

Liabilities may be *satisfied* by the *payment* of cash; by the *delivery* of facilities, goods, or services; by *offset* against a claim owed by the creditor *to* the entity; or by *conversion* into another form of liability or an ownership interest. Not all of these alternatives are available in a given case; the method of settlement depends on the particular circumstances.

The consideration given to settle a liability, measured in money or money equivalent, may differ from the amount of the debt which is being settled, even if the debt has been properly accounted for. If the consideration paid is less than the liability there is a *gain*, which increases income. If the consideration is greater than the liability the settlement results in a *loss* and a reduction of income. Such gains and losses often result from the retirement of bonds before their maturity date.

Interest on Notes Payable

Interest on notes payable is computed in the same manner as interest on notes receivable. (Refer to the section "Interest on Notes Receivable" on pp. 270–271 of Chapter 10.) From the point of view of the debtor, the interest on a note which accrues during an accounting period should be *debited to the Interest Expense* of that period. Unpaid interest on notes payable at any date should be reported as a liability for *Accrued Interest Payable*, or *Interest Payable*.

If a non-interest-bearing note payable is given to a creditor before its maturity, the liability at the date of issuance should be measured at the face of the note, minus interest at the current rate which applies to notes of *similar terms and risk*.

Example 1   A company borrows money from a bank for one year and gives in exchange a non-interest-bearing promissory note for $1,060, which includes principal plus *true discount* at the rate of 6 per cent of the initial amount per year. (a) What is the sum borrowed? (b) What is the interest cost?

Solution   (a) $S = S_n - S(i)(n)$,

where S = the initial sum borrowed, or principal
  S_n = the maturity value, including interest
  i = the interest (or *true discount*) rate per time period
  n = the number of time periods
  $S = \$1,060 - S(0.06)(1)$
  $S = \$1,060 - 0.06S$
  $1.06S = \$1,060$
  $S = \$1,060/1.06 = \$1,000$, the sum borrowed

(b) $I = S_n - S$
  $I = \$1,060 - \$1,000 = \$60$, the interest cost.

The following entries show how the facts of Example 1 would be recorded:

		1973	(1)		
Oct.	1	A, Cash..		1,000	
		L, Notes Payable—Discount..................		60	
		L, Notes Payable to Bank—Face......			1,060

Borrowed money on a one-year, non-interest-bearing note. The amount borrowed was computed by using a true discount rate of 6%.

The account L, Notes Payable—Discount, is a deduction from (*contra* to) the liability for the face amount of the note. Together these accounts show the actual amount owed on the note, including accrued interest, at any time. If a statement of financial position were prepared on October 1, the facts would be shown as follows:

LIABILITIES

Current liabilities:		
Notes payable to banks—face.............................	$1,060	
Deduct discount not yet accrued.........................	60	
Total liability on notes..............................		$1,000

The following entry would be necessary at the end of the year:

1973	(2)		
Dec. 31	OE, Interest Expense.........................	15	
	L, Notes Payable—Discount...........		15
	To record the interest expense applicable to three months of 1973 and to increase liabilities by the same amount.		

In the 1973 income statement Interest Expense would be $15. The presentation in the December 31 statement of financial position would be

LIABILITIES

Current liabilities:		
Notes payable to banks—face............................	$1,060	
Deduct discount not yet accrued........................	45	
Total liability on notes.................................		$1,015

The total liability was increased by *reducing* the liability *contra-account*, L, Notes Payable—Discount.

The total of the liabilities for the face amount of the note and accrued interest at any date under the *true discount* method should be the same as for an interest-bearing note which carries the same rate. It is equal to the sum borrowed, $1,000, plus interest that has accrued for the three months to date, $15.

ACCOUNTING FOR BONDS PAYABLE

Nature and Statement Classification

Bonds are similar to promissory notes in that they are formal written promises to pay a certain sum of money, which is the *par* or *face* amount, at a specified due date, the *maturity*. As a rule, bonds also include a promise to make periodic interest payments at a specified percentage of the face amount of the bonds at stated time intervals.

Example 2   A 6 per cent bond for $1,000, maturity date January 1, 1982, requires the payment of the $1,000 face amount on January 1, 1982, and the semiannual payment of $30 interest each January 1 and July 1 until maturity.

A contract, called a *bond indenture*, between the borrowing corporation and the group of lenders sets forth the terms with which the debtor is to comply. A *trustee* is appointed as an intermediary between the borrower and the lenders to assure that the borrower complies with the provisions of the bond indenture.

Bonds payable are ordinarily *long-term liabilities*. If they are to be paid in installments, the installments due within the next year (or operating cycle, if longer than a year) are *current liabilities*.

The descriptive caption used for bonds payable in the financial position statement should disclose the general nature of the security on which they rest. If specific assets are pledged to secure a liability, both the asset and liability captions should reveal this fact in the financial position statement. The interest rate and the maturity date should also be reported.

Example 3   The following title indicates that payment of the bonds is secured by a pledge of property:

5% First mortgage bonds due in 1980............................ $1,000,000

Example 4   The following title shows that the bonds are *unsecured* (they depend on the general credit of the company); that, in the event of *liquidation* of the business, they would rank after claims of other creditors in priority of payment; and that they are due *serially* over several years:

6% Subordinated debentures due in 1975–1978................. $3,000,000

A footnote to the statement of financial position, or a supporting schedule, should report how much of the face amount becomes due each year.

Other important terms of the bonds which might influence the decision of a financial statement reader should also be disclosed. For example, bond agreements often restrict the borrower's payment of dividends during the life of the bond issue to the amount of income earned after the bonds were issued, or permit dividends only if the amount of net working capital exceeds a specified amount. These restrictions are ordinarily reported in *footnotes*.

In addition, the financial position statement should disclose the face amount of bonds which the company has been authorized to issue but has *not issued* at the date of the statement. Such bonds represent an important *potential additional liability* of the company, as well as a potential source of additional funds.

Bond Premiums and Discounts

The *contract interest rate* (or *nominal interest rate*) on bonds is the percentage of the face amount of the bonds which will be paid periodically to the lenders as compensation for the use of their funds over time. This rate is set in the bond contract at a *fixed percentage of the face amount* per time period, and governs the amount of each periodic payment.

The interest rates at which lenders are willing to lend, however, are *flexible*. They change continually, sometimes daily, in response to changing conditions in the market. The supply of and demand for funds for long-term loan determines the *market bond interest rate* at a given time. Moreover, lenders may place a higher or lower evaluation on the risk of lending to the particular corporation than is reflected in the rate of interest specified by the contract.

It is not usually possible for a bond issuer to predict exactly what interest rate the market will charge on its bonds when they are issued. Because the amounts to be paid as interest and as the face amount are fixed by the terms of the bond contract, while the rate of interest charged currently in the market is flexible, lenders will vary the amount they will lend on existing bonds so as to yield them the *current market rate of interest* on bonds of similar terms and risk. The amount they lend is represented by the *market price* of the bonds. The market price adjusts the *true interest yield* on bonds as follows:

(1) If the market interest rate is *higher* than the rate specified in the bond contract, the company borrowing on bonds will receive less than their face amount; that is, the bonds will sell at a *discount*.

(2) If the market interest rate is *lower* than the rate specified in the contract, the bond issuer will receive more than the face amount of the bonds; that is, the bonds will sell at a *premium*.

(3) If the market interest rate and the contract interest rate are equal, the bond issuer will receive the face amount of the bonds; that is, the bonds will sell at *par*.

Recording Authorization of Bonds Payable

The fact that a corporation has complied with the necessary legal requirements for issuing bonds payable, including authorization by the stockholders, may be shown by a memorandum such as the following:

L, 6% Bonds Payable Due January 1, 1983

(Issuance of face amount of	$100,000 authorized Jan. 1, 1973)

The amount of bonds authorized but not yet issued should be reported as descriptive information in the Bonds Payable section of the financial position statement.

Accounting for Periodic Interest Payments

Bonds may be in *registered* form or *coupon* form as to the payment of the periodic nominal interest which is specified in the bond contract. If they are *registered*, interest checks are mailed periodically to those who are shown on the records to be the owners of the bonds. *Coupon* bonds have attached to them a certificate, or coupon, for each periodic interest payment over the life of the bonds. The owner of the bond collects his interest by clipping the coupon and presenting it for payment through banking channels.

Corporate bonds usually provide for semiannual payment of interest. The interest payment dates are often referred to by the first letter of the month in which they fall due. For example, January 1 and July 1 are *J* and *J*, and April 1 and October 1 are *A* and *O*.

For convenience, the bond issuer usually pays a full six months' interest to the bond owner on each interest payment date. If bonds change hands between interest dates, the seller collects from the buyer at the time of sale for the amount of interest he has earned since the last interest payment date.

Example 5   Ten-year, 6 per cent bonds payable were authorized to be issued on January 1, 1973, with interest payments *J* and *J*. Bonds of a face amount of $30,000 were issued on March 1, 1973, at par and accrued interest. The accounting entries should be

1973   (1)

Mar. 1   A, Cash.. 30,300
                OE, Bond Interest Expense.............   300
                L, 6% Bonds Payable in 1983.........   30,000
                Issued bonds of a face amount of $30,000
                at par plus accrued interest for 2 months
                at 6%.

The $300 which the issuer collects for interest is to reimburse him for interest which the buyer will collect on the next semiannual interest payment date but *will not have earned*. The *credit* to Bond Interest Expense in the preceding entry will be *offset* against (deducted from) the debit to the account for the semiannual interest paid, as follows:

OE, Bond Interest Expense

1973			1973		
July 1	(6 months' interest paid on $30,000 par).......900		Mar. 1	(Reimbursement of 2 months' interest).....300	
	Balance, 600				

The $600 balance in the account represents the interest expense which accrued on the $30,000 of bonds payable during the four months they were actually outstanding.

An acceptable alternative method of recording the facts of Example 5 would have been to credit Accrued Interest Payable for $300 on March 1, 1973. The payment of semiannual interest on July 1 would then be recorded by a debit of $300 to Accrued Interest Payable and a debit to Bond Interest Expense for $600. The net effect of both methods is the same.

Accounting for Bonds Issued at a Discount

Bonds sell at a *discount* below their face amount when their *nominal interest rate is lower than the market rate* for other bonds of similar terms and risk. The *true interest cost* for the term of the bonds is computed by subtracting the sum received when the bonds were issued from the total payments made by the borrower over the life of the bonds.

Example 6   On December 31, 1973, a firm issued 6 per cent, three-year bonds of $100,000 par at a price of 97 per cent of par. The proceeds of the issue were $97,000. Interest was payable annually on December 31. What was the total interest cost for the life of the bonds, and what was the average annual interest cost?

Solution
Total payments over life of bonds:

Nominal annual "interest" payments, $3 \times \$6,000$.	....	\$ 18,000
Face amount paid at maturity	....	100,000
Total payments.	....	\$118,000
Deduct proceeds of issue.	....	97,000
Total *effective* interest cost for 3 years.	....	\$ 21,000
Average effective annual interest cost, \$21,000/3	....	7,000

The journal entry to record *any* issuance of bonds involves a *debit to Cash for the proceeds* and a *credit to Bonds Payable for the face* amount of the bonds. If the proceeds are less than the face, as in Example 6, an additional debit to Bonds Payable—Discount is needed. The facts of Example 6 are recorded as follows:

1973

Dec. 31	A, Cash	97,000	
	L, Bonds Payable—Discount	3,000	
	L, Bonds Payable—Face		100,000
	Issued bonds at a discount.		

The *initial* amount of the *liability* under bonds is equal to the amount of *cash* actually borrowed, whether this is greater or less than the face amount of the bonds. This liability is shown in two accounts: Bonds Payable—Face and an account for *premium* or *discount*. A bond discount is a *liability contra-account*, to be deducted from the face amount of the bonds in computing the amount of the bond liability at any time.

The initial liability in Example 6 is \$97,000, as shown by the following excerpt from the financial position statement.

LIABILITIES

Long-term liabilities:		
6% bonds payable due Dec. 31, 1976—Face	\$100,000	
Deduct discount on bonds payable	3,000	
Liability on bonds		\$97,000

Discount on bonds represents *additional interest expense* (above the contractual or nominal interest paid) which applies to the entire life of the bonds. Discount on bonds is *amortized* over the life of the bonds by equal periodic debits to Interest Expense and credits to Bonds Payable—Discount. At the same time Cash is credited for the *contractual* interest paid, which is computed by multiplying the nominal annual interest rate by the fraction of a year involved and by the face of the bonds.

The entry to record the first full year's interest on the three-year bonds issued at a discount in Example 6 would be

1974

Dec. 31	OE, Interest Expense.	7,000	
	A, Cash		6,000
	L, Bonds Payable—Discount.		1,000

The credit to Cash is the 6 per cent nominal interest rate multiplied by the

$100,000 face amount for one year. The credit to Bonds Payable—Discount is one-third of the three-year discount of $3,000. The debit to Interest Expense is the sum of the cash paid and the discount amortization.

The liability contra-account, Bonds Payable—Discount, becomes smaller and the net amount at which the bond liability is shown on the financial position statement becomes larger as the maturity date approaches. For example, the bond liability will be $98,000 (Bonds Payable—Face of $100,000 minus Bonds Payable—Discount of $2,000) at the end of 1974. On the *maturity date* of the bonds the liability must be equal to their face amount.

The method of financial position statement presentation just described shows the liability on a *going-concern* basis of measurement at the date of the statement. The amount to be paid eventually is the face amount of the liability, but that amount is not the proper total of the liability on December 31, 1974, because the face amount is due two years in the future.

It is sometimes contended that the balance of Bonds Payable—Discount is an asset, to be classified as a Deferred Charge to Income. It seems more logical to treat it as a *liability valuation account*, because, although it does have a debit balance, it does not represent a prepayment for future service benefits.

Accounting for Bonds Issued at a Premium

Bonds sell at a *premium* above their face amount when their *nominal interest rate is higher than the market rate* for other bonds of similar terms and risk.

Example 7   On December 31, 1973, a firm issued 8 per cent, three-year bonds of $100,000 par at a price of 103 per cent of par. The proceeds of the issue were $103,000. Interest was payable annually on December 31. What was the total interest cost for the life of the bonds, and what was the average annual interest cost?

Solution   Total payments over life of bonds:

Nominal annual "interest" payments, 3 × $8,000..............	$ 24,000
Face amount paid at maturity......................................	100,000
Total payments..	$124,000
Deduct proceeds of issue..	103,000
Total *effective* interest cost for 3 years..............................	$ 21,000
Average effective annual interest cost, $21,000/3................	7,000

A bond *premium* is shown as an *additional liability* account, to be added to the face amount of the bonds in computing the amount of the bond liability at any time.

The facts of Example 7 are recorded as follows:

1973

Dec. 31	A, Cash	103,000	
	L, Bonds Payable—Face.............		100,000
	L, Bonds Payable—Premium.......		3,000
	Issued bonds at a premium.		

Note that Cash is again debited for the proceeds of the bond issuance and Bonds Payable is credited for the face. An additional credit to Bonds Payable—Premium is needed because the *proceeds are more* than the face of the bonds.

The liability on the date of issuance is equal to the amount borrowed, $103,000, as shown by the following excerpt from the financial position statement:

LIABILITIES

Long-term liabilities:
8% Bonds payable due Dec. 31, 1976—Face... $100,000
Add premium on bonds payable.................. 3,000
Liability on bonds................................ $103,000

Premium on bonds represents a *reduction of interest expense* (below the contractual or nominal interest paid) which applies to the entire life of the bonds. Premium on bonds is *amortized* over the life of the bonds by equal periodic debits to Bonds Payable—Premium. The true periodic interest expense is *less* than the periodic nominal payment for interest.

The entry to record the first full year's interest on the three-year bonds issued at a premium in Example 7 would be

1974

Dec. 31	OE, Interest Expense............................	7,000	
	L, Bonds Payable—Premium	1,000	
	A, Cash		8,000

The credit to Cash is the 8 per cent nominal interest rate multiplied by the $100,000 face amount for one year. The debit to Bonds Payable—Premium is one-third of the three-year premium of $3,000. The debit to Interest Expense is the cash paid, *minus* the premium amortization.

The liability *adjunct-account*, Bonds Payable—Premium, becomes smaller as the maturity date approaches, and so does the total amount of the bond liability. The financial position statement at the end of 1974 will show a bond liability of $102,000 (Bonds Payable—Face of $100,000 plus Bonds Payable—Premium of $2,000). On the maturity date the total bond liability must be equal to the face of the bonds.

Bond Issue Costs

Costs of issuing bonds are incurred for printing the certificates, securing necessary legal and financial advice, and marketing the bonds to prospective lenders. They are long-term unexpired costs similar to organization costs, except that the period of benefit—the life of the bond issue—is reasonably definite.

Bond issue costs should be assigned to periodic expense in the same way as bond discount and may for simplicity be charged to the same account.

Retirement of Bonds Payable

Entries at the *maturity date* to record the retirement of bonds payable are the same whether the bonds were originally issued at par, at a premium, or at a discount: debit the liability, Bonds Payable—Face, for the par of the bonds, and credit Cash for the same amount. At maturity the entire issuance premium or discount will have been assigned to the interest expense of past periods.

The issuer of bonds sometimes retires them *earlier* than their maturity date, either by purchasing them in the market or by redeeming them at a price stated in the contract. When bonds are retired before maturity there may be a *gain* or *loss* on retirement, measured by the difference between the consideration paid to retire the bonds and the value at which the bond liability is currently carried on the books. If the consideration paid is *greater than the book value* of the liability, there is a *loss;* if the consideration is *less than book value*, there is a *gain.*

Example 8   On January 1, 1973, a company issued five-year bonds payable of $100,000 par value for $102,000. What would be the gain or loss on retirement if the issuer repurchased the bonds and cancelled them on December 31, 1975, paying (a) par, (b) 103 per cent of par, (c) 99 per cent of par?

Solution

		(a)	(b)	(c)
Repurchase price..		$100,000	$103,000	$ 99,000
Deduct book value:				
Par...	$100,000			
Add unamortized premium...........	800			
Total book value..................................		100,800	100,800	100,800
Gain on retirement......................................		$ 800		$ 1,800
Loss on retirement.......................................			($ 2,200)	

Entries needed to reflect the retirement of bonds before maturity are

(1) Record the amortization of premium or discount up to date of retirement, thus bringing interest expense up to date.

(2) Remove the two accounts showing the current amount of the liability—face and premium or discount—from the books; record the payment of cash; and record the gain or loss.

The following entry reflects the facts of Example 8(b), assuming that the $400 premium amortization for the third year has already been recorded:

1975

Dec. 31	L, Bonds Payable Due in 1978—Face..................	100,000	
	L, Bonds Payable—Premium............................	800	
	OE, Loss on Retirement of Bonds.......................	2,200	
	A, Cash..		103,000
	To record the retirement of bonds which were carried on the books at $100,800 for $103,000.		

Material losses and gains on bond retirements should be reported as *extraordinary items* in the income statement.

Accounting for Serial Bonds

The preceding illustrations have dealt with *term* bonds, which mature at a single future date. The same general principles of accounting apply to *serial* bonds, portions of whose face amounts fall due at more than one date. When an issue of serial bonds is sold at a single lump-sum price, the premium or discount on the entire issue is allocated to each accounting period in proportion to the face amount of bonds which are outstanding during that period.

Example 9   A company issued bonds of $500,000 par on January 1, 1973, to be paid in three series: $200,000 on December 31, 1974; $100,000 on December 31, 1975; and $200,000 on December 31, 1976. The total issue price was $515,000. How much of the premium applied to each year?

Solution

Year	Par of Bonds Outstanding During Year	Fraction of Total Outstanding	Amortization of Bond Premium
1973	$ 500,000	5/15	$ 5,000
1974	500,000	5/15	5,000
1975	300,000	3/15	3,000
1976	200,000	2/15	2,000
Totals	$1,500,000	15/15	$15,000

The total face amount of bonds outstanding for all or part of the four years is equivalent to $1,500,000 outstanding for one year. During 1973, $500,000, or one-third of this amount, is outstanding; therefore one-third of the total bond premium on the issue should be assigned to 1973. Bond premium is an *adjustment of interest*, and interest accrues in proportion to the amount of the debt owed during a period.

Accounting for Bond Investments

Bonds held as *temporary investments*, as pointed out in Chapter 10, are accounted for on the basis of *cost*, except that they are reduced to market if a decline in their market value below historical cost seems to be permanent.

Initially, *long-term investments* are measured at their *acquisition cost*. Bonds held as long-term investments are measured at their *amortized cost*. Premiums paid when the bonds are bought are treated as *periodic reductions of interest revenue* over the term of the investment, and *discounts* are treated as *additional interest revenue*. The investor's entries to account for long-term bond investments and the related interest parallel the bond issuer's entries to account for his liability. There is one difference: It is customary for the investor to record his investment in a single account, including face plus the unamortized premium which applies to future periods, or face minus the unamortized discount.

Example 10   An investor who uses the calendar year accounting period purchased bonds of $10,000 par, issued in Example 7, on the date of issuance. What would the investor's entries be for 1973 and 1974?

Solution   *1973*

Dec. 31	A, Bond Investment	10,300	
	A, Cash		10,300
	Bought $10,000 face amount of 3-year, 8% bonds.		

1974

Dec. 31   A, Cash..   800
    A, Bond Investment......................   100
    OE, Interest Revenue....................   700
    Interest revenue was the nominal inter-
    est collected, minus $\frac{1}{3}$ of the bond
    premium.

In the long period during which long-term investments are owned there will undoubtedly be fluctuations in their market selling prices, reflecting the effect of changing economic conditions and investor preferences on current rates of interest. These fluctuations in market prices should be ignored in the accounting records unless a *decline* in the market value of an investment appears to be *permanent*, perhaps because the security issuer's credit rating is weakened. If the decline seems to be permanent, the investor should recognize a probable *loss* on the asset at the time when the decline occurs. In other cases it is desirable to report the market value of investments parenthetically in the financial position statement.

ACCOUNTING FOR OTHER LIABILITIES

Liability Under Warranty

Often when products are sold under warranty there is no way of telling how much of the selling price relates to the warranty and how much to the product. Usually the entire selling price is credited to Sales Revenue in the year of sale. Proper matching of revenue and expense requires that all costs, whether incurred in the period of sale or to be incurred in later periods, be matched against this revenue. This leads to the accounting procedure, discussed on p. 371, of debiting Warranty Expense and crediting Liability Under Warranty, in the period of sale, for the entire estimated cost of fulfilling the warranty. When specific services are later rendered under the warranty contract their cost is debited to Liability Under Warranty.

An alternative accounting method divides the selling price into two parts: the selling price of the product and the selling price of the warranty. Sometimes this is done by offering a service contract for a stated period of time at a separate price. In this type of case the following entry should be made in the year of sale:

1973

Dec. 31   A, Cash (or Accounts Receivable)............   7,000
    OE, Sales Revenue   6,000
    L, Deferred Service Revenue   1,000
    Sold equipment for $6,000, together with
    a 2-year service contract for $1,000.

Assuming that the actual servicing costs in the next year were $400, the following entries should be made:

1974

Dec. 31	L, Deferred Service Revenue	500	
	OE, Service Revenue		500
31	OE, Service Expense............................	400	
	A, Cash		400

Under the first method all income from the combined sale of the product and the warranty is recorded in the year of sale. Under the second method income from the service contract is recognized in the future periods to which the contract relates. Ordinarily the second method should result in better matching of revenue and expense.

Liability Under Warranty and Deferred Service Revenue are *current liabilities* if the remaining term of the agreement does not exceed a year or an operating cycle. Otherwise, the appropriate part of the liability should be classified as a *long-term liability*.

Other Deferred Revenues

Other examples of liability accounts for goods or services to be delivered in the future are Customers' Deposits, Rent Collected in Advance, Unearned Subscriptions, and Unearned Service Fees. Such accounts should be classified as *Current* or *Long-Term Liabilities*, depending on when they will probably be earned. When the event occurs which justifies the recognition of revenue, the following type of entry should be made:

L, Unearned Subscriptions.....................................	5,000	
OE, Subscription Revenue..............................		5,000
Earned revenue by delivering magazines under subscription contracts sold in earlier periods.		

Liabilities such as those listed above, which are expected to be settled by delivering goods or rendering services rather than by paying money, are sometimes called *deferred revenues*.

Liability Under Pension Plan

A pension plan is a method adopted by an employer to compensate retired or disabled employees.

From the standpoint of the employer, the simplest type of pension plan to account for is one which requires the employer only to make a certain periodic payment to a pension trust fund. The employer's responsibility for pensions ends there; the rules of the pension trust and the availability of resources in the trust fund will determine the amounts of benefits to be paid to retired employees. The employer's *pension expense* for any accounting period is the amount which it is obligated to pay into the trust fund as a result of the activities of that period. The *liability under the pension plan* on any date is the amount owed but not yet paid to the pension trust fund.

Often pension plans state the *benefits* which are to be paid to retiring employees, rather than how much the employer must pay into a pension fund each period. The *estimated cost* to the employer under such pension requirements should be accrued as *additional cost of employee compensation* during the time the employee is earning a right to the pension. The *payment* of this compensation is *deferred* until after the employees have retired and begin collecting their pensions.

The employer may pay over to an outside agency, such as an insurance company, assets which will be accumulated to pay pension benefits when they become due. A pension plan is said to be *funded* to the extent that resources have been accumulated, or an outside agency has taken over the firm's liability, to make pension payments.

The following entry shows the accrual of employee compensation for a given period, including the cost of pensions:

1973

Dec. 31	OE, Wages and Salaries Expense...........	50,000	
	OE, Pension Expense.........................	10,000	
	L, Accrued Payroll......................		50,000
	L, Liability for Pensions................		10,000

Accrual of employees' compensation, consisting of $50,000 to be paid them currently and the $10,000 cost of pensions to be paid them in the future.

If the pension plan is being funded with an outside agency, the necessary payment is recorded by debiting Liability for Pensions and crediting Cash. If the pension plan is not funded, the Liability for Pensions continues to accumulate on the books of the company. It is debited for specific pension payments to employees who have retired.

The income statement should report the total current expense under pension plans, and the financial position statement should report the related assets and liabilities. In addition, important features of pension plans, including financing and accounting methods, should be disclosed by supplementary notes to the financial statements.

Corporate Income Taxes Payable

Taxes payable on the income of a corporation, as computed in the income tax return of the current year or a past year, should be classified as a *current liability*. In some cases the amount of the income tax liability cannot be determined precisely because (1) the exact meaning of certain tax rules has not yet been established, or (2) the extent to which the taxing authorities will allow borderline deductions or fail to tax borderline revenue items is not known. Using the best information available, the business should estimate the income tax liability and expense which result from the operations of the current period.

If in a later year the business is entitled to an *income tax refund* on the income of an earlier year, an asset should be recorded for Income Tax Refund Receivable. The corresponding credit is to Adjustments of Prior Years' Income Taxes, which is reported in the Retained Income Statement as an addition to the retained income balance at the beginning of the current period.

An *additional tax* assessed in a later year on the income of an earlier year should be credited to Corporate Income Tax Payable. The related debit is to Adjustments of Prior Years' Income Taxes, a deduction in the Retained Income Statement.

Influence of Taxation on Accounting Methods

The objectives of financial reporting and income tax reporting are similar in some respects, but quite different in others. The nature of these differences is discussed more fully in Chapter 17. Regardless of differences in reporting methods, income tax is a significant business expense which must be considered in planning the form of the business, the nature and timing of its transactions, and the method of accounting for those transactions.

Differences between financial and income tax reporting may be *permanent* differences or *timing* differences.

Permanent differences are caused by the fact that some items of business revenue are never subject to income tax, or that some items of business expense are never deductible in the tax return.

Example 11 Interest on the bonds of state and municipal governments is not subject to federal income tax, although a business which earns such interest includes it in measuring business income. This is a *permanent* difference.

Differences of *timing* result from tax provisions which require, or permit, a business to report a revenue or expense item for tax purposes earlier or later than is required by sound accounting principles.

Example 12 When a business collects rent for several years in advance it is ordinarily required to report the entire amount collected as *taxable income* in the year of collection. In the business income statements this rent is accrued as revenue when it is *earned*. This is a difference of *timing*.

A business is not permitted under the tax law to use the LIFO inventory method in its tax return unless it uses LIFO in its financial statements. In many other cases the differences between the amounts of income reported for tax and financial accounting purposes are *immaterial*, and the tax method is used for both purposes in order to avoid extra accounting work.

Often, however, the method which it is desirable for a business to use in its tax return does not properly reflect the income which management, stockholders, creditors, and others use as a measure of the firm's financial progress. If the differences involved are material, the business may be justified in using one reporting method in its income tax return and a different method for reflecting the same facts in its business income statement.

Matching Income Tax Expense with Business Income

Income tax expense should be *matched* in the periodic income statements with the revenue and expense items which affect income tax payments.

The amount to be reported as the *income tax expense* for a given period is the *complete income tax effect* of the taxable income reported in the income statement of that period. This is true even if some of the resulting tax has been paid in the *past*, or is likely to be paid in the *future*, on the business income which accrues in the current period. The income tax expense reported in the income statement may *differ* from the amount of income tax to be paid on the current year's *taxable income* for the following reasons:

(1) Income tax has been *postponed* by
    (a) Reporting *revenue in the financial statements earlier* than in the tax return, or
    (b) Reporting a *deduction in the financial statements later* than in the tax return.

(2) Income tax has been *prepaid* by
    (a) Reporting *revenue in the income tax return earlier* than in the financial statements, or
    (b) Reporting a *deduction in the income tax return later* than in the financial statements.

When timing differences result in *postponing* the payment of income taxes, the postponement should be shown by crediting a liability, Deferred Credit for Income Taxes. This is a current liability if it pertains to an item which will be taxed in the following year or operating cycle.

When timing differences cause income tax to be *prepaid*, the prepayment should be debited to an asset, Deferred Charge for Income Taxes. This is a current asset if it relates to business income of the following year or operating cycle.

The following illustration shows how to account for a tax postponement which results from using different depreciation methods in the income statement and the income tax return.

Example 13   In 1973 Company *T* bought for $90,000 a machine with an expected useful life of three years and an estimated salvage value of zero. The company has elected to use the *sum-of-the-years'-digits* depreciation method in its income tax return, but feels that *straight-line* depreciation is more appropriate in its financial statements because the asset's services will be equal in each year. Total revenue is expected to be $100,000 and expenses other than depreciation are expected to be $20,000 for each of the three years.

	Comparison of Income Tax Returns		
	1973	*1974*	*1975*
Revenue	$100,000	$100,000	$100,000
Deduct expenses:			
SYD depreciation	$ 45,000	$ 30,000	$ 15,000
Other expenses	20,000	20,000	20,000
Total expenses........................	$ 65,000	$ 50,000	$ 35,000
Taxable income............................	$ 35,000	$ 50,000	$ 65,000
Computation of income tax payment:			
22% of $25,000.........................	$ 5,500	$ 5,500	$ 5,500
48% of remainder	4,800	12,000	19,200
Total income tax.....................	$ 10,300	$ 17,500	$ 24,700

The income tax payable each year if Company *T* used straight-line depreciation for tax purposes would be $17,500. The sum-of-the-years'-digits method postpones the payment of $7,200 of income tax from the first year to the third. The tax payable in the second year would be the same under either depreciation method in this illustration.

The accrual of 1973 income tax in Example 13 should be recorded as follows:

OE, Income Tax Expense (1973)............................	17,500	
L, Corporate Federal Income Tax Payable		10,300
L, Deferred Credit for Income Tax..................		7,200
To match income tax expense with the income reported in the 1973 income statement, and to record liabilities for income tax payable currently and in future years.		

Deferred Credit for Income Tax is classified in this case as a long-term liability at the end of 1973.

In 1975, the year in which the timing difference caused by the use of different depreciation methods *reverses*, the following entry is needed:

OE, Income Tax Expense (1975)..	17,500	
L, Deferred Credit for Income Tax........................	7,200	
L, Corporate Federal Income Tax Payable........		24,700
To record the liability for income tax payable currently, including that postponed from 1973.		

Other matters dealing with differences between financial and income tax reporting are discussed in Chapter 17.

Reporting Liabilities Under Long-Term Leases

Traditional long-term lease contracts provide that the owner (*lessor*) of property (such as real estate or equipment) grants to a tenant (*lessee*) the right to use the property, in exchange for a promise by the tenant to pay periodic rent of specified or determinable amounts. The *lessor retains legal ownership* of the property and ordinarily performs such acts as the owner of property is expected to perform. Examples are paying for property taxes, repairs, maintenance, and insurance on the property.

Many lease contracts currently in effect are of the type just described. The lessee accounts for them by debiting Rent Expense and crediting Rent Payable in proportion to the lapse of time under the lease contract. When the accrued rent is paid there is a credit to Cash. If rent is paid in advance, an asset for Prepaid Rent Expense is debited.

Under the traditional type of lease the lessee does not record an asset and liability, except for short-term prepayments and accruals of rent. The contract is wholly *executory* from the standpoint of both the lessor and the lessee; that is, it is to be performed in the future by both parties. The lessor will grant the use of the property and will provide the related services of repair, maintenance, and insurance. In return the lessee will pay periodic rent.

When such wholly executory contracts are material and not subject to cancellation, the lessee should report sufficient information in its financial statements to enable the reader to judge the effect of leases on the lessee's financial position and operations, both present and future. Important provisions of the lease should be reported, including the minimum annual rentals, the period for which they are to be paid, obligations assumed, and restrictions on the lessee's dividend payments and further borrowing and leasing.

Increasingly prevalent in recent years have been cases in which one business acquires property under a lease contract which requires the *lessee* to perform most of the functions that the lessor performs under the traditional executory lease contract. For example, the lessee may be required to pay taxes, repairs, maintenance, and insurance. A study of the circumstances of such a "lease" may indicate that it is really an *installment purchase of the property* by the "lessee." A lease is considered to be in substance a purchase of property if its terms create a *material equity* in the property for the lessee.

For leases which are in substance a purchase of property, the lessee should record an *asset* (or assets) equal to the implied exchange price of the property, and a corresponding *liability* for payment for the property. The periodic payments under the lease must then be divided into parts representing the payment of *interest* and *principal* of the lease obligation. The lessee should record the related interest expense and depreciation (rather than rent expense) on the property which was purchased under the so-called long-term lease.

Contingent Liabilities

A *contingent liability* is an obligation *related to a past event or condition* that *may arise* as a result of a *future event that may occur* (but is not expected to occur). If an event has already occurred to establish the existence of the obligation but not its amount, there is an *estimated liability*. The possibility that a *future loss may occur* without any relation to a past event (such as a fire or storm loss) does *not* result in a contingent liability.

The following are sources of contingent liabilities:

(1) A lawsuit resulting from breach of contract, patent infringement, personal or property damages, or antitrust-law violation.

(2) A commitment to buy goods when prices are fluctuating, that may have to be settled without delivery of the goods.

(3) A guaranty of securities or other obligations. Examples are *notes receivable discounted* and *accounts receivable assigned.*

(4) Product guaranties where experience is not available to permit a reasonable estimate.

(5) Proposed additional income tax assessments for past periods which the taxpayer has not agreed to.

(6) Possible additional compensation to employees in connection with a labor dispute.[1]

Contingent liabilities are not entered in the accounts, except occasionally in memorandum form, unless there is a high probability that a future payment will be necessary. If the probability of payment is low, the financial position

---

[1] Eric L. Kohler, *A Dictionary for Accountants,* 4th ed. (Englewood Cliffs, N.J.: Prentice-Hall, Inc., 1970), pp. 107–108.

statement usually contains a footnote decribing the general nature of the contingency. It is desirable to give an appraisal of the outlook with respect to the contingency, reporting the monetary amount if possible.

Accounting for Payroll Costs and Liabilities

Payroll cost includes salaries, wages, and fringe benefits such as paid vacations and the cost of pension plans. The proper measure of payroll cost during a period is the amount *earned* by the employee during that period, whether or not it has been paid in cash, plus the cost of related fringe benefits.

Payroll accounting is often complicated by the fact that the business must serve as an agent for collecting many types of items, which it withholds from the employees' pay and later pays to the proper organizations. Examples are income taxes, Social Security taxes, union dues, and hospitalization insurance premiums which are assessed on the employee but collected by the business. Although the types of such deductions are numerous, in principle accounting for them is simple. *Credits* should be made to appropriately labeled *liability accounts* when sums are *withheld* from the employees' pay, and *debits* should be made to the same liability accounts when the withholdings are *paid* to the proper organizations.

The following entry illustrates three types of withholdings:

1973

Dec. 31	OE, Salary Expense	10,000	
	L, Employees' Federal Income Tax Withheld		1,000
	L, Employees' Social Security Tax Withheld		500
	L, Employees' Union Dues Withheld...		100
	A, Cash		8,400

Employees earned salaries of $10,000 for December. Made the required deductions as a collecting agent, and paid the remainder to the employees in cash.

Federal Income Tax Withheld is not an expense of the business, but the total amount of wages earned by the employees is. The employer in the illustration pays $8,400 of the employees' earnings directly *to the workers.* He pays the remaining $1,600 of their earnings, *on behalf of the workers,* to the various organizations to which they are indebted.

The amount of employee income taxes withheld must be determined separately for each employee, based on the length of the pay period, the amount of his earnings, the number of personal exemptions to which he is entitled, and the applicable tax rates. Printed tables provide this information readily.

Taxes for old-age, survivor, and disability insurance, referred to here as *Social Security Taxes,* are assessed in equal amounts upon both the employer and the employee. The types of employment and the maximum amount of compensation which are subject to the taxes, as well as the applicable rates, change frequently. In the preceding entry it was assumed for simplicity that the Social Security Tax rate is 5 per cent on both employee and employer. It was also assumed that all the employees' gross earnings for December were subject to Social Security Tax. It is quite likely, however, that the earnings of some employees will exceed the amount subject to these taxes.

The firm would record its share of Social Security Taxes as follows:

1973

Dec. 31   OE, Payroll Tax Expense...................   500
               L, Employer's Social Security Tax
                   Payable.........................   500
               To record accrual of a business tax ex-
               pense at 5% of employees' taxable wages.

Many businesses are also subject to an *Unemployment Compensation Tax*, part of which is payable to the state and part to the federal government. Types of covered employment and tax rates are both subject to change from time to time. The following entry illustrates the accounts affected:

1973

Dec. 31   OE, Payroll Tax Expense...................   300
               L, Federal Unemployment Compensa-
                   tion Tax Payable.................   30
               L, State Unemployment Compensation
                   Tax Payable......................   270
               To record the accrual of a business expense
               for unemployment compensation tax,
               payable to the state at 2.7% of taxable
               wages and to the federal government at
               0.3%.

The details of the expense accounts and liability accounts which are used to record payroll taxes may be varied to suit the needs of the particular business. For example, a *different object* account could be used for each type of payroll tax, or a payroll tax object account could be used for each functional classification of expenses, such as *selling*, *manufacturing*, or *administrative*.

Payment of some of these liabilities might be recorded as follows:

1974

Jan. 10   L, Employees' Federal Income Tax With-
                   held.........................   1,000
           L, Employees' Social Security Tax With-
                   held.........................   500
           L, Employer's Social Security Tax Pay-
                   able.........................   500
               A, Cash......................   2,000
               Paid the liability for the preceding
               month's Social Security Taxes and
               employee income tax withheld.

For convenience, the three liabilities affected in the preceding entry might all be combined in a single account, Payroll Taxes Payable.

Businesses must keep detailed records for each employee, showing the amount of gross earnings and the various withholdings for income taxes, Social Security Taxes, and other purposes.

PLANNING AND CONTROLLING LIABILITIES

General Purposes of Planning

Every business is faced with the problem of obtaining the assets which are necessary for carrying on its operations. *Liabilities* are an important *source* of these business assets.

Some of the important factors which management must consider in planning the liabilities of the business are

(1) The *availability* of different types of credit, including *whether* credit is available at all, *when* it will be available, and the *amount*.

(2) The *terms* under which credit may be obtained, including such factors as *interest cost*, the *length of time* for which the credit is to be granted, the *amounts and timing of periodic repayments*, the nature of the *security* required, and the *restrictions* on the management of the borrower.

(3) The *suitability* of the particular type of credit to the borrower, including the costs and the risks to which it will subject him.

(4) The *sources of repayment*, including the nature of the sources and the amounts that will become available at different times.

Selecting the particular types of credit instruments and tailoring their provisions to the needs of the business are problems of *financial management*. The following sections suggest ways in which accounting information can help solve these problems.

Budgeting Borrowings and Repayments

Management is aided in scheduling future payments of existing liabilities by knowledge of the expected cash inflows from future operations, as well as the expected excess of these cash inflows over cash payments. A prospective *deficiency* of cash available in comparison with required payments signals that management must obtain additional funds from some source, perhaps borrowing. These matters of financial planning are discussed in Chapter 21.

Management can use an *operating budget* and a *cash budget* to estimate how much must be paid on liabilities in the coming period, and when. These budgets can also be used to *plan the timing of maturities under new liability contracts*, such as seasonal loans for working capital.

As a source of long-lived assets, liabilities are an important part of *capital budgeting*, which is explained in more detail in Chapter 26. For both long- and short-term financing by liabilities, it is helpful to use cash budgets to *plan liability payments* when funds are expected to become available.

Illustration 13-1 is a schedule of estimated annual debt-service requirements, which has been prepared to aid management in planning the maturities of debt payments.

**Illustration
13-1**

BETA PRODUCTS CORP.
Schedule of Debt-Service Requirements
For the Years 1973–1976

Description:	1973	1974	1975	1976
Principal maturities (all Dec. 31):				
6% Serial bonds of 1973–1975............	$100,000	$100,000	$100,000	
5% Term bonds of 1974..................		400,000		
6% Mortgage note of 1976..............				$200,000
6% Serial bonds of 1975–1976..........			150,000	100,000
Total principal requirements	$100,000	$500,000	$250,000	$300,000
Interest maturities:				
6% Serial bonds of 1973–1975	$ 18,000	$ 12,000	$ 6,000	
5% Term bonds of 1974	20,000	20,000		
6% Mortgage note of 1976...............	12,000	12,000	12,000	$ 12,000
6% Serial bonds of 1975–1976..........	15,000	15,000	15,000	6,000
Total interest requirements.............	$ 65,000	$ 59,000	$ 33,000	$ 18,000
Total debt-service requirements.............	$165,000	$559,000	$283,000	$318,000

Comparison of the yearly debt-service requirements with expected receipts in Illustration 13-1 may suggest that no additional maturities of principal should be scheduled for 1974, and that slightly more might be scheduled for payment in 1975 than in 1976.

An aid to efficient management of the *payment* of liabilities, particularly current liabilities, is the maintenance of a *tickler file*. In this file invoices, notes, and other evidences of liabilities are filed according to *due date*. The treasurer can determine from the file how much is to be paid on any given date, and can make arrangements to have the necessary cash available then for payment. Such files also aid in making payments on time, thus avoiding penalties and lost discounts.

Controlling Payments: The Voucher System

Medium-sized and large businesses usually find it necessary to install formal procedures for providing *internal control* in paying their liabilities. A system designed to permit payments only on proper authorization is called a *payment voucher system.*

Besides helping to ensure that only proper payments are made, a well-designed voucher system has the following advantages:

(1) It facilitates record keeping for incurring and paying liabilities.
(2) It facilitates prompt payment of liabilities.
(3) It provides information on the amounts and due dates of liabilities.
(4) It accumulates detailed evidence in support of payments.

Under the voucher system *all payments* are made by *check*, but only after an approved *voucher* has been prepared as evidence that the payment is proper. Often the check is a copy of, or an attachment to, the voucher which *authorizes* the payment.

Responsibilities for particular stages of the approval and payment process are assigned to many different individuals. At the end of the process the *treasurer*, after receiving a voucher signed by the *controller* certifying that the payment is justified, signs a check ordering the bank to make the payment. Many supporting documents, each prepared and approved by a different responsible employee, usually accompany the voucher. Some of these documents and their functions are

(1) A *purchase requisition*, prepared by a production or stores department, indicates that the ordered items were needed.

(2) A *purchase order*, prepared by the purchasing department, requests that the supplier ship the goods under specified terms.

(3) A *receiving report* shows how many items were received and in what condition.

(4) A seller's *invoice*, verified as to terms and computations, shows prices and quantities of the items purchased.

The individual vouchers, serially numbered, are often journalized in a *voucher register*. This is a special journal with money columns for Accounts Payable, Credit, and for debits to accounts which are frequently debited. The individual vouchers are then filed according to due date until time for payment, when they are presented to the person who signs checks. They are then transferred to a paid-voucher file.

Analysis of Liability Balances

Management, stockholders, and creditors are interested in the present and continuing ability of the company to pay its liabilities as they come due. A *cash budget* is an exellent means of estimating the amount of money which will be available to meet debt requirements in the future.

Substitute measures which statement readers other than management may use to analyze the liabilities of the firm are the *number of times earnings cover debt-service requirements* and the *ratio of liabilities to total equities*. The former was discussed in Chapter 8. The ratio of stockholders' equity to total equities, which is closely related to the ratio of liabilities to total equities, was discussed in the same chapter.

A firm's prospective future earnings should be enough to provide for paying interest charges on its liabilities in good years as well as bad, with an ample margin of safety. Earnings must also usually provide the funds for repaying principal. A *stable* ratio of income to debt-service requirements is more desirable than a fluctuating ratio of the same size, because it denotes more dependable earnings.

A *lower ratio of liabilities* to total equities is *safer* than a higher ratio. The ratio can be too low, however, resulting in a loss of potential earnings to owners.

Summary *Liabilities* require future payments of fairly definite amounts of money, or the future delivery of goods or services, as a result of past transactions with outside entities.

A major problem in accounting for Bonds Payable is that of assigning appropriate parts of the issuance premium or discount to each period as adjustments of interest expense. The balance of the *premium* which applies to future periods should be *added* to the face amount of the bonds owed to reflect the total bond liability. The balance of the unamortized *discount* should be *deducted* from the face amount of the bonds owed.

Liabilities under Warranty, Liability for Pensions, Corporation Income Tax Payable, and similar liabilities usually cannot be estimated as precisely as can other common types of liabilities. Nevertheless, proper matching of revenue and expense requires that careful estimates of their amount be made and recorded in the accounts.

Contracts that are nominally *long-term leases* may, in effect, be installment purchases of property. If so, the lessee should record the property as an asset and should record the related liability. The lessee should disclose the principal features of obligations under leases which have a material financial effect on the business.

Cash budgets for the coming period and capital budgets for the long-range future are useful in estimating the sums that the business will need to borrow in future periods and the times at which they can be repaid. Schedules of debt-service requirements are also helpful in this regard.

A *voucher system* is a useful means of controlling the payment of liabilities, of estimating the cash needs of the future, and of facilitating the recording of liability transactions.

Discussion Questions and Problems

13-1   Some items which are now considered to be accounting liabilities do not fit into the strict legal definition of a liability as an enforceable *debt* to a specific party. Give two examples of this type of liability and explain why they should be considered as liabilities.

13-2   "Whether or not a particular item is accounted for as a liability depends on whether it involves a *likely*, rather than a *possible*, future payment."

a. Is this statement correct? Explain.
b. Give an example of a situation that is likely (but not certain) to require a future payment, and show how you would account for it.
c. Give an example of an item that will *possibly*, but is not likely to, involve a future payment. How should it be reported?

13-3

a. Give an example of a short-term and a long-term monetary liability.
b. Give an example of a short-term and a long-term nonmonetary liability.
c. Show in journal form how a monetary liability will be settled.
d. Show in journal form how a nonmonetary liability will be settled.

13-4   Your business has just borrowed $10,000 on a two-year term loan and has signed a promissory note for $10,000 plus interest at 5 per cent, to be paid at the end of each year. There is a strong probability that the interest will have to be paid. Should a liability for interest be recorded on the date of the loan? Explain.

13-5   Advances received from customers for products to be shipped later, rent collected in advance, and bonds which may be converted into common stock will probably not require future payments. How can you justify accounting for them as liabilities?

13-6   In purchasing equipment from a dealer you were offered a cash price of $960, and the alternative of signing a note for 12 monthly payments of $90.

a. If you chose the latter alternative, how would you account for the purchase?
b. How would you account for each monthly payment?

13-7   A business wishes to borrow exactly $6,000 for one year.

Required   a. Compare the true interest cost to the borrower if the lender's compensation is in the form of (1) interest; (2) true discount. In each form the rate is 6 per cent.
b. For each method of compensation in part a, prepare the following from the point of view of the borrower:
(1) Journal entry at date of loan.
(2) Adjusting entry at end of accounting period nine months later.
(3) Appropriate sections of financial statements at end of accounting period.
(4) Entry for payment of note one year later.

13-8   "A bond which sells at a premium is a better bond than one which sells at a discount."

a. Comment on the validity of this statement, including a careful explanation of the nature of bond premium and bond discount.
b. Is the interest cost per dollar borrowed higher on the bond which sold at a premium than on the one which sold at a discount? Explain.

13-9   Explain what is meant by the following terms:

a. Nominal interest rate
b. Effective (market) interest rate
c. Registered bonds

d. Coupon bonds
e. Term bonds
f. Serial bonds

13-10   On January 1, 1973, a corporation issued $100,000 face amount of bonds payable, with interest at 6 per cent per year to be paid each January 1 and July 1. Investor B bought a $1,000 bond from Investor A on March 23, 1973, at 105 and accrued interest. A had bought the bond at the time of its original issuance, paying face amount.

a. Why was B willing to pay 105 for the bond?
b. Why did B pay A for the accrued interest? Why did the borrowing company not pay A for the interest he earned?

13-11

a. When bonds payable are retired before their maturity, under what circumstances does a gain arise? A loss?
b. How should such gains and losses be reported in the financial statements?
c. Using assumed facts, journalize the entry to retire bonds payable at a loss. State your assumed facts.

13-12

a. How does the statement classification of a bond owned as a temporary investment differ from the classification of a bond held as a long-term investment? How do the methods of measuring them at dates after purchase differ?

b. How does the measurement of a bond held as a long-term investment differ from that of a bond payable?

c. How do the accounts used for bonds held as a long-term investment differ from those used for bonds payable?

13-13   During the current year a business has sold many units of a product under a three-year warranty, whereby defective parts will be replaced during that period at no additional cost to the purchaser.

a. Outline two methods of accounting which might be used for this warranty. Using figures of your own choice, show the entries for one unit under each method (1) in the year of sale and (2) in a later year when a specific customer's product is repaired.

b. How would you label and classify the resulting financial position statement accounts under each method?

c. Outline the theoretical and practical advantages of each method.

13-14

a. A pension plan is said to be *deferred compensation* to employees. Explain.

b. What is meant by *funding* a pension plan?

c. An employee covered by a pension plan works for the same company for 20 years, collecting each month his salary less Social Security and federal income tax with-holdings. After retirement he lives ten years and draws his pension. During what time period(s) should the employer accrue the cost of the pension? What accounts would be affected if the pension plan is not funded with an outside agency?

13-15

a. List two situations in which the income (before income tax) reported in the income statement of a business will not be the same as the taxable income for the same period reported in its tax return.

b. If a difference between business income before tax and taxable income is *permanent*, how will this be reported in the financial statements?

c. How is a difference of *timing* between the business income statement and the income tax return accounted for?

d. Under what circumstances will a business have a *deferred charge* for income taxes? How is this reported in the financial statements of the year in which it first occurs?

e. Under what circumstances will a business have a *deferred credit* for income taxes? How is this reported in the year in which it originates?

13-16   Your firm signs a five-year lease on January 1, 1973, whereby it will be permitted to use equipment for an annual rental of $10,000, to be paid each December 31.

a. Assume that the terms of the lease are such that it is a traditional lease.
   (1) How will it be accounted for on January 1, 1973?
   (2) How will it be reported in the financial statements for 1973?

b. Assume that the lease is really an installment purchase of the property.
   (1) How will it be accounted for on January 1, 1973? (Assume such additional facts as you need, and state your assumptions.)
   (2) How will it be reported in the financial statements for 1973?

c. What key factors would cause you to determine that the lease in this case is really an installment purchase, rather than an executory contract to use someone else's property?

13-17 The owner-manager of a small business which employs a bookkeeper-cashier and three salesclerks is visiting the business of a friend, whose firm has ten times as many employees. He is especially impressed with the safeguards provided by the latter's payment voucher system and wonders if he should install such a system.

a. What would be the specific advantages of a payment voucher system to such a small business?

b. What would be its disadvantages?

c. What features of a payment voucher system might he effectively adopt?

13-18 The Porpi Corporation signed a note promising to pay a local financial institution $11,800 at the end of two years. The corporation received $10,000 cash at the time of the signing, October 1, 1973.

Required
a. How should Porpi record the note on October 1?

b. What adjusting entry is needed on December 31, 1973?

c. Show how the relevant facts would appear in a partial financial position statement on December 31, 1973.

13-19 Stevens Company owed a supplier a $1,000, 8 per cent note dated April 1, 1973. On September 30 the supplier agreed to accept a piece of land owned by Stevens in settlement of the debt. The land was recorded on Stevens' books at $900.

Required
a. Was there a gain or loss to Stevens? If so, how much?

b. Record the April 1 and September 30 transactions on Stevens' books.

13-20 The Lindley Company issued at par five-year bonds with a face value of $500,000 and a nominal interest rate of 8 per cent. The bonds were issued on July 1, 1974, and pay interest annually on June 30.

Required
a. Show the resulting section of the financial position statement immediately after the bonds were issued.

b. Journalize the necessary adjusting entry at the end of its accounting period, December 31, 1974.

c. Show the resulting accounts in the liability section of the financial position statement at December 31, 1974.

13-21 The J. M. Massey Company issues $500,000 of ten-year, 6 per cent bonds on January 1, 1973. The company uses a calendar year accounting period.

Required
a. If comparable bonds are being offered in the market at effective interest rates of 7 to 8 per cent, will the Massey bonds likely sell at par, a discount, or a premium? Explain.

b. Assume that the bonds were actually sold for 90 per cent of face. Record the sale.

c. Compute the total interest cost for the life of the bonds and the annual interest cost.

d. How much cash is paid for nominal interest each year?

e. Record the interest payment on December 31, 1973.

f. Show in detail how these facts would appear in the liability section of the December 31, 1973, financial position statement.

13-22 On April 1, 1973, the Stroud Corporation issued ten-year, $4\frac{1}{2}$ per cent bonds in the face amount of $200,000. The issuing price was 98 per cent of face. Interest is paid semiannually on October 1 and April 1. Stroud Corporation closes its books on March 31 each year.

Required   a. Set up T-accounts to show all the accounts affected by the preceding information through March 31, 1974.

b. Stroud finds itself with extra funds available on April 1, 1974, and purchases the bonds at par and retires them. Journalize the necessary entry.

13-23   On January 1, 1973, the B. A. Nicholson Pharmaceutical Company issued $400,000 of five-year, 9 per cent bonds at 105 per cent of face. The bonds pay interest semiannually on June 30 and December 31.

Required   a. Record the issuance of the bonds.

b. How much is Nicholson's total and annual interest expense?

c. How much cash must Nicholson pay to bondholders semiannually?

d. What will be the balances of the accounts related to bonds on June 30, 1974?

13-24   The Schenck Company was authorized on January 1, 1973, to issue $1,000,000 face amount of 6 per cent, four-year bonds. Interest is paid by coupons, which mature annually on December 31. Because of an unsettled market the bonds were not issued until July 1, 1973, when they were sold at 107 plus accrued interest.

Required   a. Compute the following:

(1) Total interest cost over the life of the bonds.

(2) Interest cost per full year.

(3) Interest cost for 1973.

b. Record the entries necessary on July 1 and December 31, 1973. The company uses a calendar year accounting period.

13-25   On June 30, 1974, the Gavalas Corporation was authorized to issue $800,000 of ten-year, 8 per cent bonds payable. Interest was payable semiannually on each June 30 and December 31. The corporation uses a calendar year accounting period.

Required   a. Journalize the following 1974 transactions:

(1) Authorization of the bonds.

(2) Issuance of $600,000 of the bonds at 103 on June 30, 1974.

(3) Accrual and payment of interest for 1974.

b. Show how the accounts relating to bonds and interest would appear in the financial position statements:

(1) At December 31, 1974.

(2) At December 31, 1975.

13-26   The J.S. Corporation sold $500,000 of five-year, 6 per cent bonds dated January 1, 1975, to the Whitaker Investment Co. on April 1, 1975, for $505,700 plus accrued interest. Both firms use a calendar year accounting period. Interest is payable semiannually on June 30 and December 31.

Required   a. Record the sale of the bonds on J.S.'s books.

b. Record the purchase on Whitaker's books. Whitaker intends to hold the bonds for 9 to 12 months.

c. Record interest on the books of both parties on June 30, 1975.

d. Show how the bonds would be reported on the financial position statements of both parties on December 31, 1975.

13-27   The Griffin Company received approval on December 20, 1973, to issue debenture bonds payable of a face amount of $1,000,000, due five years from the date of issuance. Annual interest of 7 per cent was to be paid each December 31. On January 1, 1974, the entire authorized amount was issued for cash at 95 per cent of par. On the same day the Flanigan Company acquired Griffin bonds of a face amount of $50,000. Both companies use the calendar year as their accounting period.

Required

  a. Journalize all entries on the books of the Griffin Company for 1974 and show how the relevant facts would appear in its December 31, 1974, financial position statement.

  b. Journalize all entries for 1974 on the books of the Flanigan Company and show how the relevant facts would appear in its December 31, 1974, financial position statement. The Flanigan Company plans to hold the bonds indefinitely.

  c. Show the entries on the books of both companies for the repurchase and retirement of $10,000 of the bonds held by the Flanigan Company on January 1, 1975. The repurchase price was 98 per cent of face amount.

13-28   Heck Cola Company issued $400,000 face amount of ten-year bonds at par on January 1, 1969, to finance needed capital improvements. Because of limited availability of funds the nominal interest rate was 8 per cent. On December 31, 1973, the current market interest rate on similar bonds is 6 per cent. A provision in the old bond contract permits the Heck Cola Company to repurchase the bonds at 104 and retire them after five years.

Required

  a. Assume that $400,000 of five-year, 6 per cent bonds can be issued on January 1, 1974, at par. Compute the saving to Heck if the old bonds are retired and new bonds are issued. Should the bonds be refinanced?

  b. Record the repurchase and retirement of the old bonds on January 1, 1974.

  c. Explain the reason for the inconsistency between the answers in part a and part b.

13-29   On January 1, 1973, the White Tractor Corporation issued $600,000 face amount of serial bonds at par. The bonds paid annual interest at 8 per cent and matured in installments of $200,000 on December 31, 1975, and each of the succeeding two years.

Required

  a. Journalize entries for the issuance of the bonds and for all other events in 1973 and 1974.

  b. Prepare a schedule of debt-service requirements for the entire life of the bonds.

13-30   On July 1, 1974, the Bower Corporation issued $850,000 of bonds payable to finance the construction of a plant. Construction of the plant was expected to require slightly more than a year, and the corporation estimated that it would require some time thereafter for the plant to get into full production. Accordingly, the corporation arranged to issue serial bonds bearing interest at 7 per cent, to be retired on June 30 of each year as follows:

1975..................	0	1978.................$250,000	
1976.................$100,000		1979................. 300,000	
1977................. 200,000			

The corporation's fiscal year ends on June 30. The bonds were issued on July 1, 1974, at a discount of $16,500.

Required

  a. Prepare a schedule showing the cash payments required to service the debt for each of the years ending June 30, 1975, through June 30, 1979.

  b. Prepare a schedule showing the interest expense of each year.

13-31   The Harver Corporation sold home appliances with a two-year warranty contract whereby the corporation agreed to replace defective parts and provide necessary labor. The appliances sold for $400 each and the warranty contract was priced separately at $60. During 1973 the corporation sold 100 appliances and 100 warranty contracts for cash. Past experience, revised to reflect current conditions, indicates that warranty costs per unit per year will be $8 for parts and $16 for labor.

Required   a. Journalize all related 1973 entries, assuming for simplicity that all sales occurred on December 31.
b. How should the accounts related to warranties appear in the 1973 financial statements?
c. The actual costs incurred for warranty service in 1974 were $1,000 for parts and $2,500 for labor. The total estimates for the two-year period are still expected to be correct. Journalize the necessary entries.

13-32   The facts are the same as in Problem 13-31, except that the selling price of the product with warranty is $460 per unit. The warranty contract price is not quoted separately.

Required   a. Complete requirements a, b, and c of Problem 13-31 under these different circumstances.
b. What chief differences are there between the method of accounting in this problem and that in the preceding problem?

13-33   The Kachmar Realty Corporation made the following investments in bonds in 1973:

Date	Face Value	Interest Rate	Purchase Price	Maturity
1/1/73	$100,000	6%	$99,000	12/31/77
3/1/73	80,000	9	81,000	12/31/75
4/1/73	20,000	8	20,000	9/30/73

The March purchase was with temporarily idle funds that will be used to buy an apartment complex in October 1973.

Required   a. Record each purchase.
b. The accounting period ends on June 30. Record the accrual of interest (no cash is received).
c. How would these investments be reported in the financial position statement at June 30, 1973? Assume any additional facts that you need.

13-34   The Sporting Life Magazine Company sold subscriptions to its monthly magazine late in December 1973 to become effective with the January issue. Cash was received for 100,000 subscriptions at $12 each per year. It costs the company about $10 per year to produce and distribute the magazine to each subscriber.

Required   a. Does Sporting Life have a valid liability on January 1, before publishing the first issue? If so, what is its nature and what is its amount?
b. Magazines are distributed to all subscribers in January and February. On March 1 refunds are made to 1,000 subscribers for the remainder of their subscriptions. Record the refund.
c. What is Sporting Life's remaining liability after this refund?

13-35   The following was a footnote to the financial statements of Swift and Company for the year ended October 31, 1970.

> *9. Pensions, deferred compensation and management incentive*
> The Company has pension plans covering substantially all employes. At October 31, 1970, all vested benefits of pensioners and present and former employes not yet retired were fully funded. The excess of accrued pension and deferred compensation expenses over contributions to the pension trusts and other payments is shown as a noncurrent liability in the balance sheet. Changes in the noncurrent liability are summarized as follows:

	1970	1969
Balance at beginning of year....................................	$16,111,000	$ 7,334,000
Charged to costs and expenses:		
Pensions (includes amortization of prior service costs under certain plans over periods of 40 years or less)...	14,651,000	14,889,000
Deferred compensation and incentive....................	738,000	179,000
	15,389,000	15,068,000
Less: Contributions to pension trusts and payments of other pension costs..................................	10,186,000	6,170,000
Deferred compensation and incentive payments........	156,000	121,000
	10,342,000	6,291,000
Balance at end of year...	$21,158,000	$16,111,000

> Under the Company's management incentive plan, $1,089,000 (1969-$1,481,000) was accrued for payment to participating officers and employes, a portion of which is deferred.

Required   a. Was the liability for pensions fully funded? Explain.

b. Prepare the journal entry that might have been used to record the changes in the noncurrent liability for pensions during fiscal 1970.

13-36   The Turin Corp. paid $75,000 cash for a new machine at the beginning of 1973. The machine was expected to have a useful life of five years and no salvage value. The corporation's management felt that the machine would provide equal service benefits each year, but elected to use the sum-of-the-years'-digits method of depreciation in its income tax return. Business and taxable income, without deducting depreciation and income tax, were as follows:

1973.........$30,000	1975.........$50,000	1977.........$60,000
1974......... 30,000	1976......... 50,000	

Applicable income tax rates were 22 per cent of the first $25,000 of taxable income and 48 per cent of the remainder.

Required   a. Record all entries related to depreciation and income tax for 1973, paying careful attention to matching.

b. Show how the related items would appear in the 1973 financial statements.

c. Record the relevant entries for 1977.

d. In retrospect, was the Turin Corp.'s choice of income tax method a wise one? Explain.

13-37   On January 1, 1973, Charybdis Corporation leased some property for four years beginning on that date and collected the rent of $80,000 for the entire period. All the rent collection was taxed in 1973. Income tax on other income was $50,000 for each of the four years. Tax rates were 48 per cent of taxable income over $25,000.

Required   a. Record all entries related to rent and income tax for 1973, paying careful attention to matching revenue and expense.
b. Show how the relevant items would appear in the 1973 classified financial statements.
c. Record all related entries for 1974.

13-38   The Kyle Company, Inc., is contemplating changing its method of computing depreciation for federal income tax purposes for the calendar year 1973 from the straight-line method to the sum-of-the-years'-digits method. However, the company has not decided whether it will record on the books the increased depreciation provision. The company provides you with the following data:

Net taxable income before provision for depreciation........... $1,000,000
Provision for depreciation:
 Straight-line method... 150,000
 Sum-of-the-years'-digits method................................. 250,000

The applicable income tax rate is 48 per cent.

Required   a. If the sum-of-the-years'-digits method of computing depreciation is used for federal income tax purposes, but straight-line depreciation has been recorded and will remain unchanged on the books:
(1) Give the journal entries, if any, relating to income taxes which should be recorded on the books.
(2) Prepare the notes to financial statements, if any, which would be needed.
b. What circumstances would justify Kyle's recording the increased depreciation provision on its books?
(Adapted from AICPA Examination in Auditing.)

13-39   The Flyright Aircraft Company has developed a plan to divert on-line production aircraft to small air-freight companies which need aircraft but are unable to buy them because of limited capital. Flyright sells the aircraft for $2.5 million to the Coast State Bank. The bank then leases the plane back to Flyright, who subleases it to Yukon Air Freight Corporation. The lease and sublease are for the life of the aircraft and Yukon is required to pay all taxes, maintenance, and other expenses on the aircraft.

Required   a. What company should report ownership of the aircraft for accounting purposes?
b. If Flyright pays Coast State $330,000 a year for ten years and Yukon pays Flyright $340,000 a year for ten years, what entries should Yukon make at the date of the sublease signing and on making its first payment of $340,000 at the beginning of the first year?

13-40   The Newham Company signs a five-year lease on January 1, 1973, permitting it to use equipment for an annual rental of $100,000 payable January 1, 1973, and each December 31 thereafter for four years. Newham is to pay for repairs, property taxes, and other expenses of maintaining the equipment. The lease gives Newham an option to buy the equipment for $1 at the end of five years.

The equipment is expected to have a useful life of ten years and to have no salvage value at the end of that time. An outright purchase could now be made for $417,000, and it is estimated that the fair value of the equipment will be $208,500 at the end of five years.

The interest rate currently being charged on loans to buy similar equipment is 10 per cent a year.

Required
a. How should Newham record the signing of the lease?
b. Journalize the entry for the payment on January 1, 1973.
c. Record the payment on December 31, 1973, and any other entries that are required by the information given.
d. How should Newham report the resulting balances in its financial statements at the end of 1973?

13-41   State whether the following items should be reported in the financial statements of the Paradox Corporation for the year ended December 31, 1973, and if so, how.

a. The corporation has outstanding purchase orders for merchandise in the amount of $100,000. This is not an unusual situation.
b. The corporation has a number of claims pending against it, all of which result from ordinary business operations. The ultimate outcome in these matters is uncertain.
c. Effective January 1, 1973, the corporation adopted a profit-sharing retirement plan for the benefit of its employees. The plan requires the corporation to pay an amount equal to 10 per cent of net income before income taxes, and before considering the provisions of the profit-sharing plan. The contributions may not exceed 15 per cent of total wages and salaries paid to the participating employees during the year. The corporation has paid the required contribution of $440,000 for 1973.
d. The corporation borrowed $300,000 on January 1, 1973, on five-year, 6 per cent notes payable. While these notes are outstanding Paradox is required to maintain a current ratio of at least 2.5 to 1, and is permitted to pay cash dividends only to the extent that retained income has increased since the notes were issued.

The following balances appeared in the corporation's 1973 financial statements:

Current assets...	$600,000
Current liabilities....................................	220,000
Retained income, Dec. 31, 1973..................	120,000
Dividends paid, 1973...............................	40,000
Net income for 1973...............................	50,000

13-42   The Quentin Company is subject to the following employment taxes:
(1) Employee Social Security Tax at 5 per cent.
(2) Employer Social Security Tax at 5 per cent.
(3) Federal Unemployment Compensation Tax at 0.3 per cent.
(4) State Unemployment Compensation Tax at 2.7 per cent.

Social Security taxes and employee income taxes withheld by Quentin must be paid to an approved bank by the tenth of the following month, for further transfer to the Director of Internal Revenue.

The Federal and State Unemployment Compensation Taxes must be paid quarterly.

The following are selected account balances from the December 31, 1973, trial balance:

	Credit
Employees' Federal Income Tax Withheld......................	$400
Employees' Social Security Tax Withheld.......................	100
Employers' Social Security Tax Payable.........................	100
Hospitalization Insurance Premiums Withheld.................	50
Federal Unemployment Compensation Tax Payable..........	80
State Unemployment Compensation Tax Payable.............	250

It may be assumed that these balances are correct.

Required
a. Journalize the entry for the employer's share of payroll taxes, using a single object account for the debit.

b. Record the January 9, 1974, payment of the income taxes withheld and the Social Security Taxes to an approved depository.

c. Record the January 15 payment of the premiums withheld to the Health Insurance Co.

d. Record the payment of the December 31 balances of unemployment compensation tax liabilities.

e. How would you recommend that the liabilities be reported in Quentin's December 31, 1973, financial position statement?

Cases   **13-1   American Bakeries Company.** The annual report of American Bakeries Company for the year ended December 28, 1968, contained the following footnote:

Note 1: Long-term Debt—Long-term debt at December 28, 1968, was as follows:

$5\frac{1}{4}$% term loan payable $1,400,000 annually from 1970–1974	$ 7,000,000
$5\frac{1}{4}$% notes payable $280,000 annually from 1969–1971 and $320,000 in 1972..	1,160,000
$4\frac{3}{4}$% note payable $490,000 in 1969 and $240,000 in 1970....	730,000
$4\frac{3}{4}$% notes payable, due in 1969...................................	179,380
$5\frac{7}{8}$% note payable $75,000 annually from 1969–1970, $90,000 from 1971–1973, $100,000 from 1974–1975, and $125,000 in 1976......................................	745,000
5% to $6\frac{1}{2}$% notes payable, due in varying amounts through 1979...	123,838
Non-interest-bearing note, payable $74,687 annually from 1969–1972...	298,750
Liability under employment contract settlements..............	547,997
	$10,784,965
Less—Current maturities...	1,284,158
	$ 9,500,807

Under the terms of the $5\frac{1}{4}$% and $5\frac{7}{8}$% notes payable, the Company, among other things, is required to limit cash dividends and purchases of its stock to an amount not to exceed $5,000,000 plus consolidated net income, as defined, subsequent to December 28, 1963. As of December 28, 1968, retained earnings of $30,200,000 were not available for cash dividends, etc., under this provision of the loan agreements.

The agreements also provide that the company must maintain consolidated net working capital of not less than $10,000,000; consolidated net working capital was $8,342,071 at December 28, 1968. Waivers on the working capital requirement have been obtained from all applicable noteholders for the period December 28, 1968, to and including April 18, 1969.

Required   a. For what purpose is the detailed information given on the required annual payments on notes?

b. Explain how you would compute debt service requirements for 1969 and 1970 from the information given. For what purpose can this information on debt service requirements be used?

c. How can the lenders be benefited by the limitations on dividends and purchases of stock imposed by the terms of the $5\frac{1}{4}\%$ and $5\frac{7}{8}\%$ notes?

d. How can the limitation on the minimum amount of working capital benefit the lenders? How might the present situation affect the American Bakeries Company and the lenders?

13-2   Century Electric Company. The following excerpts are from the financial statements of Century Electric Company for 1968:

ASSETS

Property, plant, and equipment:
    Property rights under leases—Note B............................ $5,145,128

LIABILITIES

Long-Term Debt—less portion classified as current liability:
    Capitalized lease obligations—Note B........................... $4,514,333

Note B read as follows:

Note B: Capitalization of Leases—The capitalized lease obligations relate to land, buildings, machinery and equipment leased from municipalities. Capitalized lease obligations at December 31, 1968 are as follows:

	Facilities Leased from		
	City of Lexington, Tennessee	County of Alcorn (Corinth), Mississippi	Total
Capitalized lease obligations..................	$1,534,833	$3,145,000	$4,679,833
Less portion classified as a current liability	55,500	110,000	165,500
	$1,479,333	$3,035,000	$4,514,333

The Lexington facilities were financed by sale of Lexington, Tennessee Industrial Revenue Bonds. The original issue bears interest of 6.0% to 4.1% per annum and matures serially in progressive annual amounts ranging from $55,500 in 1969 to $113,000 in 1985. The supplemental issue bears interest of 4.75% and matures in 1986 and 1987 in the amount of $100,000 in each of those years. The payments to be made by the Company are in an amount equal to principal and interest payments due on the bonds through 1987.

The construction of the Corinth facilities and the acquisition of machinery and equipment for the plant were financed by sale of Alcorn County, Mississippi Industrial Revenue Bonds in the amount of $3,300,000. The issues bear interest of 5.75% to 6.00% and mature serially in progressive annual amounts ranging from $110,000 in 1969 to $230,000 in 1986 with a final payment of $100,000 in 1987.

The property rights under the lease as shown at December 31, 1968 include

$300,631 of unexpended funds held in escrow by the trustee of the bond issues for purchase of additional machinery to complete the plant facility.

Note E read as follows:

Note E: Commitments and Contingencies—The Company is leasing plant facilities at McMinnville and Humboldt, Tennessee under twenty-two and twenty-six year agreements effective September 1, 1969, and April 1, 1961, respectively. The leases provide for rental payments of $144,500 for thirteen years and $36,000 thereafter, plus taxes, insurance and maintenance costs.

The approximate aggregate average annual rentals payable (excluding capitalized lease obligations—see Note B) under long-term leases are summarized as follows:

1969–1971	$180,000
1972–1981	156,000
1982–1987	47,000

Required

a. In what way were the amounts of Property Rights Under Leases and Capitalized Lease Obligations determined? Why are the amounts different?

b. Comment on the account titles used to reflect this situation.

c. How does the information in Note E affect the year-end financial position statement? Why is it presented?

d. What key factors would justify the different accounting treatment of the leases described in Note B and those described in Note E?

e. Outline the journal entries that will be required under the capitalized leases during the next year. Explain how the amounts for these entries would be determined.

chapter 14

Accounting for Owners' Equity

Purpose of Chapter

The two main sources of owners' equity in any business are the *capital invested (contributed)* by the owners and the *income of the business* that is not paid out to the owners. Chapter 1 pointed out that variations in owners' equity accounts as between individual businesses are caused mainly by differences in the form of business organization—*proprietorship*, *partnership*, or *corporation*. These variations arise because the owners' equity contracts of specific businesses often have different features, and because the states in which the businesses are organized often have different legal requirements.

The major part of this chapter is devoted to owners' equity accounting for corporations, which is generally more complex than accounting for proprietorships and partnerships. The main features of corporate capital stock are discussed, with particular attention to how they affect accounting. The basic components of corporate owners' equity—paid-in capital and retained income—are treated in some detail. Attention is given to accounting for the repurchase of its own stock by a corporation, and to various types of distributions to stockholders.

The chapter concludes with a brief consideration of accounting for the owners' equity of partnerships.

ACCOUNTING FOR CORPORATE OWNERS' EQUITY

Capital Stock and Its Status

A *corporation* is a legal entity whose *owners' equity* is represented by shares of *capital stock*. In exchange for his investment, each owner receives a *share* or *shares of capital stock* as evidence of his ownership interest. The percentage of the total owners' equity which is owned by a given individual may be computed by dividing the number of shares he owns by the number of shares owned by all stockholders.

In determining the number of ownership shares of a corporation for various purposes, it is necessary to know the number of shares in each status: *authorized, unissued, issued,* in the *treasury,* and *outstanding.*

(1) *Authorized* capital stock is the total number of shares, or the total money amount of stock, which the corporation's articles of incorporation permit it to issue. It is common for the number of shares authorized to be substantially larger than the number needed initially, to facilitate later expansion.

(2) *Unissued* capital stock is that part which has not yet been issued.

(3) *Issued* capital stock is that part of the stock which the corporation has given to owners in exchange for money, claims to money, or some other consideration.

(4) *Treasury* stock is stock which has once been issued in exchange for full payment but which the issuing corporation has reacquired. It is available to be reissued or canceled.

(5) *Outstanding* capital stock is that part of the stock which is owned by the public. Unissued or treasury shares held by the corporation itself are not outstanding.

The relationship of these terms to each other is illustrated in the following example.

Example 1   When a corporation was organized, it was authorized to issue 10,000 shares of a single class of capital stock. During the past few years it has issued 6,000 shares but has later reacquired 1,000 of them, which it hopes to reissue at a later date. The status of its capital stock is as follows:

Authorized	10,000 shares
− Unissued	4,000 shares
= Issued	6,000 shares
− In treasury	1,000 shares
= Outstanding	5,000 shares

An individual stockholder who owns 50 shares owns 1 per cent (50/5,000) of the total owners' equity in the corporation.

Rights of Stockholders

The principal rights of the stockholders of a corporation are

(1) To *manage* the corporation. They do so by electing a board of directors, which in turn elects officers of the corporation.

(2) To share in *distributions of assets* by the corporation *out of income* when the board of directors declares such a distribution, or *out of capital* when the corporation is partially or completely liquidated.

(3) To *approve or prevent changes* in the charter and bylaws of the corporation and changes in the rights associated with the existing property of the corporation. One principal right of this type is the *preemptive right*, which permits the stockholder to acquire shares of new issues of stock in proportion to his present ownership interest in the corporation. The purpose of this right is to permit him to maintain his proportionate ownership interest when the owners' equity of the corporation is to be increased by additional issues of stock.

If there is but *one class* of capital stock, *each share carries equal rights.* When a corporation has more than one class of stock, the stockholders of one or more classes often waive some of their rights by contract. For example, one class of stockholders may surrender its right to manage the corporation in exchange for a right to receive greater assurance of income distributions than another class of stock has. This is usually true of *preferred stock.*

Composition of Corporate Owners' Equity

The owners' equity of a corporation has two major classifications: (1) *paid-in*, or contributed, *capital*, and (2) *retained income.* The distinction between these two sources of equity capital is made to show how much of its net assets the business has derived from *contributions*, either from owners or others, and how much it has *earned.*

Paid-in capital is measured by the cash or fair market value of the assets or services contributed permanently to the corporation, chiefly by stockholders, in connection with the following types of events:

(1) Original *investment*, in exchange for stock certificates.

(2) Additional *assessments* on outstanding shares.

(3) Differences between the price paid by the corporation to reacquire its own outstanding shares (*treasury stock*) and the price received if they are later reissued.

(4) Forfeiture of partial payments on *stock subscriptions.*

(5) *Conversion* of liabilities into stockholders' equity.

(6) *Donations* by stockholders.

The only other significant source of corporate paid-in capital is the donation of long-lived property by individuals and institutions other than stockholders.

Retained income measures the earnings of the business that have accumulated from past periods and have not been distributed as dividends or for other purposes. Retained income is derived primarily from operations of the business and includes extraordinary gains and losses.

Par, No-Par, and Low-Par Value Stock

In the early history of U.S. corporations all shares of capital stock were assigned a *par*, or *face* value, frequently of $100 per share, which was printed on the stock certificate. Often the state law required that the issue price of a share of stock be at least par. Creditors of the corporation were thus assured that the corporation had received an amount at least equal to the par value as consideration for the stock. This amount would serve as a cushion of residual equity to absorb losses and help protect the interests of creditors.

Many people misunderstood the significance of the par value, and assumed that the *worth* of a share of stock on the market was always at least its par value. This, of course, was not true; the market value of a share of stock at any time depends on how traders and investors evaluate the *future prospects* of earnings and dividends. Furthermore, stock was often *watered;* that is, noncash property and services received in exchange for capital stock were often recorded in the corporation's accounts at the par value of the stock, which was sometimes far in excess of the value of the consideration received.

These abuses led to the popularity of *no-par* stock, which was not assigned any face amount. One purpose of no-par stock was to emphasize that the nature of a share of stock was an *interest in an indefinite equity*, whatever that might be worth, and *not a claim to a specific amount of money*. The absence of a face amount for the stock was intended to put the would-be purchaser on guard to estimate its worth on the basis of the rights which its ownership conveyed. But state taxes, particularly taxes on the transfer of stock, became excessively burdensome for no-par shares with low market value.

In recent years many corporations have shifted to the use of *low-par* stock—stock which has a nominal par value far below its market value. It is quite common, for example, for a share of stock of $1 par to sell on the market for many times this amount.

Stated or Legal Capital

State laws differ as to how much of the proceeds of capital stock represents a permanent part of the corporation's *capital*. In some jurisdictions this is determined by law, and in others by a resolution of the corporation's board of directors. The minimum amount which must remain invested as a cushion of protection for creditors is called the *stated* or *legal capital*. For stock which has a par value, the stated or legal capital is equal to its par value. The stated value of no-par stock is usually declared by the directors. Some states provide a legal *minimum stated capital* below which shares cannot be issued.

ACCOUNTING FOR PAID-IN CAPITAL

Issuance of Par-Value Stock

It is usually satisfactory to record the *authorization* of an issue of capital stock by a memorandum notation in the capital stock account.

There is no difficulty in recording the *issuance* of stock if the consideration received by the corporation is exactly equal to the par value of the stock. In such a case assets (or sometimes liabilities or expense) are debited and Capital Stock is credited for the amount of the consideration. When the consideration exceeds the par value of the stock, the excess is credited to a *premium* account.

Example 2   A corporation issued 1,000 shares of its $100-par value stock for $105 a share. The appropriate accounting entry is

A, Cash..	105,000	
OE, Capital Stock—Par.............................		100,000
OE, Capital Stock—Premium......................		5,000

Sometimes an account called "Paid-in Capital in Excess of Par" is credited for the premium on capital stock.

Laws of most states forbid the issuance of par-value stock at a *discount*, or for less than par. With the use of low-par-value stock there is little financial reason to issue stock at a discount. Consequently, the issuance of capital stock for cash at a discount is rare.

When stock is issued by a corporation at a discount, it is considered to be *not fully paid*. If the corporation is unable to pay its debts in full, individuals who purchased stock from the corporation at a discount may be required to pay in the amount of the discount. Because of this contingency, Capital Stock—Discount should be carried as a permanent account on the corporation's records.

An *implicit stock discount* occurs when property other than cash is received for stock, if the par value of the stock issued is greater than the fair value of the property.

Example 3   A corporation issued 1,000 shares of $100-par value stock in exchange for patents having a fair market value of $90,000. The accounting entry is

A, Patents..	90,000	
OE, Capital Stock—Discount.............................	10,000	
OE, Capital Stock—Par.............................		100,000

The titles used to record issuance of *low-par* stock are the same as for par stock, but the portion of the proceeds credited to Capital Stock may be small. The statement presentation may be misleading if, as was formerly the custom, proceeds in excess of the nominal par value are described as "Capital Surplus," rather than as "*Paid-in Capital in Excess of Par.*"

Issuance of No-Par Stock

If the *stated value* of no-par stock is equal to the entire proceeds, Capital Stock is credited for the proceeds. When the consideration received exceeds the stated value of the stock, the excess is credited to *paid-in capital in excess of stated value*.

The account "Paid-in Capital in Excess of Stated Value" is similar in nature to Capital Stock—Premium, although by definition "premium" applies only to par value stock.

Example 4   Assume that the stock issued in Example 2 had no par value, that the minimum legal capital was $20 a share, and that the board of directors declared this to be the stated value. The accounting entry is

A, Cash	105,000	
OE, Capital Stock—Stated Value..................		20,000
OE, Paid-in Capital in Excess of Stated Value...		85,000

Example 5   Assume that the stock issued in Example 3 was no-par with a stated capital of $20 a share. The accounting entry is

A, Patents.. 90,000		
OE, Capital Stock—Stated Value....................		20,000
OE, Paid-in Capital in Excess of Stated Value		70,000

Presentation on Financial Position Statement

Results of the capital stock transactions described in Examples 2 and 3, together with other assumed facts, would be presented in a financial position statement as follows:

STOCKHOLDERS' EQUITY

Capital stock, $100 par value per share:		
Authorized, 4,000 shares; issued and outstanding, 2,000 shares.............................	$200,000	
Add premium on capital stock........................	5,000	
	$205,000	
Deduct discount on capital stock....................	(10,000)	
Total paid-in capital................................		$195,000
Retained income...		71,400
Total stockholders' equity............................		$266,400

In comparison, the facts in Examples 4 and 5 would be shown as follows:

STOCKHOLDERS' EQUITY

Capital stock, no-par value, stated value $20 per share:		
Authorized, 4,000 shares; issued and outstanding, 2,000 shares	$ 40,000	
Add paid-in capital in excess of stated value	155,000	
Total paid-in capital................................		$195,000
Retained income...		71,400
Total stockholders' equity............................		$266,400

Note that *total paid-in capital is the same* whether the stock is par or no-par; only the components differ.

Adequate disclosure requires showing the nature of each class of capital stock; the amount of its par value (or the fact that it has no par value); its principal features; and the number of shares authorized, issued, in the treasury, and outstanding. It is recommended that the *total amount paid in* by the stockholders be shown.

Accounting for Stock Issue Costs

The costs of issuing capital stock, both when the business is organized and later when it is expanded, should be debited to an intangible asset, *Organization Cost*. Components of this account are the costs of printing the certificates and related papers, clerical costs, stamp taxes, fees paid to the appropriate state and federal agencies which authorize the issue, and the professional fees of accountants, lawyers, and others whose services are directly related to the stock issues.

Organization Cost benefits the corporation for its entire life, which is an indefinite time. This cost should be amortized over the expected life of the corporation, but not more than forty years.

Accounting for Stock Subscriptions

If the individuals who buy a corporation's stock pay for it immediately upon subscription, the appropriate entries would be like those illustrated in Examples 2 and 3 or Examples 4 and 5. If, however, there is a *contract to purchase stock* and payments are to be made by the subscriber over a period of time, the rights associated with capital stock ownership are often withheld until the stock is paid for. Under such circumstances a *Capital Stock Subscribed* account, rather than Capital Stock, is credited for the *par or stated value* of the shares subscribed for. A *Subscriptions Receivable* account is debited for the *unpaid amount* of the subscription price. Other accounts are debited or credited as usual.

Example 6   An individual subscribed for 100 shares of $100-par value stock at $102 a share. The accounting entry is as follows:

A, Subscriptions Receivable................................	10,200	
OE, Capital Stock Subscribed........................		10,000
OE, Capital Stock—Premium........................		200

The following entries account for the collection of the stock subscription in full and the issuance of the shares:

A, Cash...	10,200	
A, Subscriptions Receivable...........................		10,200
Collected the balance due on the subscription.		
OE, Capital Stock Subscribed.............................	10,000	
OE, Capital Stock—Par...............................		10,000
Issued shares of stock to the subscriber.		

A financial position statement prepared before the subscriptions were collected would show Subscriptions Receivable under either Current Assets or Other Assets, depending on whether they are expected to be collected in the near or distant future. Capital Stock Subscribed, with a notation of the number of shares involved, is shown as a component of capital stock immediately below the amount representing capital stock issued.

Different Classes of Stock

Corporations often have two or more classes of capital stock, each with different rights as to participation in management, participation in distributions from income or capital, and as to other matters. Generally, one of these classes of stock is called *preferred* stock and the other, *common* stock.

The owners of preferred shares receive rights which are superior in some respects to those of the common stockholders, usually in exchange for relinquishing other rights. If preferred stock is *preferred as to dividends*, the rate of the priority which attaches to each share must be stated. The dividend preference of par-value stock is often stated as a *per cent of par*, for example:

STOCKHOLDERS' EQUITY

6% preferred stock, $10 par value per share:		
Authorized, issued, and outstanding, 1,000 shares......	$10,000	
Premium on preferred stock...................................	500	
Total paid-in capital, preferred....................................		$ 10,500
Common stock, no-par value, stated value $1 per share:		
Authorized, 50,000 shares; issued and outstanding, 12,000 shares..		86,300
Total paid-in capital		$ 96,800
Retained income		11,100
Total stockholders' equity...		$107,900

In a given year, each holder of one preferred share in the illustration must receive a dividend of $0.60 a share (6 per cent of $10)—a total of $600 for preferred stockholders as a class—before the common stockholders may receive any dividend. This does not mean that the preferred dividend *must* be paid, however. Any class of stockholders has a right to receive a dividend only if it is *declared* by the board of directors. The board will declare a dividend only if it is legal, feasible, and desirable to do so. If no dividend is declared on the preferred stock in a given year, however, no dividend can be paid to the common stockholders in that year.

The dividend preference rate of *no-par preferred stock* is expressed in terms of dollars of dividends per share, such as "$3.50 preferred stock, no-par value."

If preferred stock is *preferred as to assets in liquidation*, the preferred stockholders must receive the stated amount on termination of the business before the common stockholders receive anything. Sometimes the preference per share upon liquidation is based on the price at which the preferred stock was originally issued.

Cumulative Preferred Stock

Preferred dividend rights may be *noncumulative*, in which case a dividend not declared in a given year is not carried forward to future years as a prior claim. They may be *cumulative*, meaning that a dividend not declared in one year is carried forward as an additional priority of preferred stockholders in future income distributions.

Example 7   A corporation had outstanding 1,000 shares of 6 per cent cumulative preferred stock of $100-par value and 3,000 shares of $100-par value common stock. In its first year, 1972, it did not declare a dividend. In 1973 it wishes to distribute a total of $27,000 in dividends. How much must be distributed to a holder of one share of each class of stock, and how much to each class in total?

Solution	*Order of Priority*	*Total*	*Per Share*
	Preferred stock (1,000 shares, $100,000 par):		
	6% dividend in arrears....................................	$ 6,000	$ 6
	6% current preference....................................	6,000	6
	Total..	$12,000	$12
	Common stock (3,000 shares, $300,000 par):		
	Remainder..	15,000	5
	Total distributed..	$27,000	

Preferred stock dividend rights are sometimes *cumulative only to the extent earned* during a given year.

Occasionally preferred stock has a right to *participate* with the common stock in additional dividends beyond the preference rate. The participation may be limited or unlimited.

A separate set of accounts, such as the following, is needed for each class of stock:

Capital Stock, Preferred—Par	Capital Stock, Common—Par
Capital Stock, Preferred—Premium	Capital Stock, Common—Premium
Capital Stock, Preferred—Discount	Capital Stock, Common—Discount
Subscriptions Receivable—Preferred	Subscriptions Receivable—Common
Capital Stock Subscribed—Preferred	Capital Stock Subscribed—Common

Stock Option Plans

Corporations often grant their officers and other employees *options to buy* shares of the corporation's capital stock.

The financial statements should disclose at the end of each period the number of shares under option, the option price, and the number of shares as to which options might currently be exercised. They should also report the number of shares of stock involved and the option price for any options *exercised* during the period. This information may be shown parenthetically or in a footnote to the financial position statement.

Reacquired Capital Stock (Treasury Stock)

Capital stock is a means by which a corporation obtains *permanent capital*. Most state laws limit the extent to which a corporation can reacquire its own shares from its stockholders, frequently providing that only net assets (equaling owners' equity) in excess of *legal capital* are available for this purpose. In the absence of such a restriction, a corporation in financial difficulty, with insufficient assets to pay its creditors' claims and its stockholders' original investments in full, might give preference to selected stockholders by reacquiring some of their stock before the corporation was liquidated.

Two of the main purposes for which a corporation is permitted to reacquire its own shares are for use in employee stock-purchase plans and in settlement of claims which might otherwise result in a loss. It is also usually permissible for stockholders to *donate* some or all of their shares to the corporation, for this does not reduce the corporation's assets.

When *treasury stock* (reacquired stock that was fully paid when originally issued) is purchased, an asset such as Cash is credited. The account debited is not an asset, but a *reduction of owners' equity*. The transaction represents a *disinvestment* in the business, causing a reduction in the assets of the business.

There are two widely accepted methods of accounting for treasury stock: (1) the *par-value method*, and (2) the *cost method*.

The following condensed information of Pace, Inc., will be used in Examples 8 through 11 to illustrate these two methods.

STOCKHOLDERS' EQUITY (BEFORE REACQUISITION OF STOCK)

Capital stock, $100 par value per share:

Authorized, issued, and outstanding, 1,000 shares	$100,000
Add premium on stock	5,000
Total paid-in capital	105,000
Retained income	20,000
Total stockholders' equity	125,000

Par-Value Method of Accounting for Treasury Stock

The theory underlying the *par-value method* of accounting for treasury stock is that the reacquisition of its shares by a corporation has *terminated the contract* between the corporation and the stockholder. All paid-in capital balances pertaining to these shares should be eliminated when the contract is terminated, and any adjustment between the shareholders whose equity is retired and the remaining shareholders should be made at the same time.

Under the par-value method, the amount paid by a corporation for its own capital stock is treated as a *reduction of paid-in capital* up to the amount per share represented by the reacquired shares, whether or not they are likely to be reissued. If the payment for the reacquired shares exceeds the appropriate reduction of paid-in capital, the excess is treated as a *distribution of retained income*.

Example 8   Pace, Inc. (see data above) reacquired ten shares of its $100-par value stock to be reissued later under an employee stock-purchase plan, paying $112 a share. Early in the next accounting period these shares were reissued to employees for $108 a share. The accounting entry to record the reacquisition under the *par-value* method would be

OE, Treasury Stock—Par	1,000	
OE, Treasury Stock—Premium	50	
OE, Retained Income	70	
A, Cash		1,120

Reacquired 10 shares of the corporation's own stock for $112 a share. Reduced paid-in capital (consisting of the par and premium originally received for the stock) by $105 a share, and treated $7 a share as a distribution of retained income.

The stockholders' equity of Pace, Inc. would appear as follows after the reacquisition of stock shown in Example 8.

STOCKHODLERS' EQUITY (AFTER REACQUISITION OF STOCK)

Capital stock, $100 par value per share:
Authorized and issued, 1,000 shares............ $100,000
   Deduct in treasury,   10 shares............   1,000
   Outstanding,   990 shares......................... $ 99,000
   Add premium on capital stock.................. $ 5,000
   Less amount applicable to treasury stock...   50
     Premium applicable to outstanding shares...............   4,950
      Total paid-in capital on outstanding stock $103,950
Retained income   19,930
      Total stockholders' equity................................ $123,880

The accounting for the *reissuance* of treasury stock under the *par-value method* is similar to that for stock issued for the first time.

Example 9   Pace, Inc. resissued the shares reacquired in Example 8. The accounting entry under the par-value method would be

A, Cash.. 1,080
   OE, Treasury Stock—Par................................   1,000
   OE, Treasury Stock—Premium.........................   50
   OE, Capital Stock—Premium...........................   30
To record reissuance of shares for $108 a share, removal of applicable amounts representing a reduction of original paid-in capital (par and original premium), and receipt of additional premium of $3 a share.

The Stockholders' Equity section of Pace's financial position statement after the entry in Example 9 will be the same as before the stock was reacquired, except that Premium on Stock will be $5,030 ($30 more) and Retained Income will be $19,930 ($70 less).

When stock is reacquired and formally retired, the various paid-in capital accounts should be debited for the average amount paid in on the number of shares retired. If the *paid-in value* of the shares retired *exceeds the cost* of reacquisition, the difference is *credited to Paid-in Capital* from Retirement of Stock. If the *cost exceeds* the *paid-in value*, there should be a *debit to Retained Income*, identified as a *distribution of retained income* on the retirement of stock.

Cost Method of Accounting for Treasury Stock

The *cost method* of accounting for treasury stock treats the reacquisition of stock as an *incomplete transaction*, awaiting later reissuance of the stock. When the stock is reacquired, Treasury Stock is debited for its *cost*. In the financial position statement this cost is shown as a *deduction from total stockholders' equity*, without allocation to par, premium, and retained income.

Example 10   Under the *cost method*, the reacquisition of shares described in Example 8 would be recorded and reported as follows:

OE, Treasury Stock (cost)...................................... 1,120
    A, Cash..   1,120
    Reacquired 10 shares of the corporation's own stock
    for $112 a share.

STOCKHOLDERS' EQUITY (AFTER REACQUISITION OF STOCK)

Capital stock, $100 par value per share:
    Authorized and issued, 1,000 shares............................... $100,000
        (of these, 10 shares are in the treasury and 990 are
        outstanding)
    Add premium on capital stock... 5,000
        Total paid-in capital on issued stock........................... $105,000
    Retained income... 20,000
        Total stockholders' equity on issued stock..................... $125,000
    Deduct cost of 10 shares of treasury stock.......................... 1,120
        Total stockholders' equity on outstanding stock.............. $123,880

Note in Example 10 that the *total* stockholders' equity under the *cost method* of accounting for treasury stock is the same as under the *par-value method*, but that the details are different.

When treasury stock is reissued, the cost method records any *excess of the cost* of reacquisition over the proceeds of reissuance as a *distribution of retained income*. In this situation, all items of stockholders' equity except Retained Income will be shown at the same amounts after the stock is reissued as before it was reacquired.

Example 11   The reissuance of the Pace, Inc. treasury stock under the *cost method* would be recorded as follows:

A, Cash... 1,080
OE, Retained Income... 40
    OE, Treasury Stock (cost)   1,120
    To record the proceeds of reissuing 10 shares of treasury
    stock for $108 a share, and to show the excess of cost
    of reacquisition over the proceeds of reissuance ($112—
    $108 per share, a total of $40) as a distribution of
    retained income.

When treasury stock is reissued at a price that is greater than the cost of the treasury shares, the excess is credited to OE, Paid-in Capital on Reissuance of Treasury Stock. In such cases, all items of stockholders' equity except the paid-in capital account will be shown at the same amounts after the reissuance as before the shares were reacquired.

Other Paid-in Capital Accounts

In addition to the accounts described in detail in earlier sections, other important sources of paid-in capital should be designated by account titles such as "Paid-in Capital—Stock Assessment," "Paid-in Capital—Land Donation," and "Paid-in Capital—Forfeited Stock Subscriptions."

ACCOUNTING FOR RETAINED INCOME

Components of Retained Income

The principal sources of additions to Retained Income are the operating activities of the business and extraordinary gains and losses. Chapter 7 pointed out that *extraordinary items* are reported as components of periodic net income, while *prior period adjustments* are treated as additions to, or deductions from, the balance of retained income at the beginning of the period. Criteria for identifying these items are listed on p. 152.

A corporation does not realize income by issuing, reacquiring, or reissuing its own capital stock, although occasionally such transactions result in *distributions of income*. Income distributions are reported in the Retained Income Statement.

Restrictions of Retained Income

Retained income is not money; it represents a *source* of a part of a firm's total assets, but not of any specific assets. It also sometimes represents (with many important exceptions) the amount *legally available for dividends*.

Restrictions are sometimes placed on the use of retained income as a basis for declaring dividends. These restrictions may result from legal requirements, contractual obligations, or management policy.

A common legal restriction provides that total *distributions to stockholders* (acquisitions of treasury stock plus dividends paid out of income) cannot exceed retained income.

Loan and bond contracts sometimes limit the dividends that a borrower may pay during the existence of the debt. The purpose of this restriction is to help ensure that the borrower will retain in the business assets equal to the restriction, for the purpose of making payments on the debt. (See Case 13-1 for an example.)

Restrictions, also called *appropriations* or *reserves*, of retained income are also used to help explain management's reasons for reinvesting the related assets in the business.

Usually it is satisfactory to report restrictions on retained income parenthetically in the body of the financial position statement, or in a footnote. If the contract requires a formal entry it may be recorded thus:

```
OE, Retained Income..........................................  50,000
        OE, Retained Income Restricted for
             Bond Retirement. ......................              50,000
        To show a restriction of Retained Income
        equal to bonded indebtedness, as required
        by the debt contract.
```

An entry such as the following would record the reduction or removal of the restriction:

```
OE, Retained Income Restricted for Bond
     Retirement..............................  50,000
     OE, Retained Income ....................          50,000
To remove the restriction when the debt
is repaid.
```

Footnotes in the financial statements and Comments in the president's letter to stockholders are probably better means than retained income restrictions for explaining management's earnings retention policy.

Neither the establishment nor the removal of a restriction on retained income affects the amount of income. Neither has any effect on the combined *total* of retained income, restricted and unrestricted, shown in the financial position statement.

Stock Dividends

The board of directors' declaration of a *dividend payable in cash or other property* reduces the amount of retained income (and of total stockholders' equity) immediately and increases the liability, Dividends Payable. The later payment of such a dividend reduces the liability and reduces Cash or some other asset. The final result is an equal decrease in the corporation's assets and its stockholders' equity. The individual stockholders receive a valuable asset from the corporation.

A *stock dividend*, while similar in name to an *asset dividend*, serves a quite different purpose. It is a distribution of stock which has *no effect on the assets* of the corporation. A stock dividend denotes that past asset increases resulting from retained income have been *permanently reinvested* in the business and will not be available for cash dividends. The stock dividend merely changes the *composition* (but not the total) *of stockholders' equity*, by reducing Retained Income and increasing Capital Stock (and perhaps other paid-in capital accounts).

If the corporation which issues the stock dividend is closely held, or if it is publicly held and the number of dividend shares is large in relation to the number of shares previously outstanding (more than 20 to 25 per cent), the amount transferred from Retained Income to paid-in capital for each dividend share should be the amount necessary to meet *legal requirements*.

Example 12 Assume that Pace, Inc., described in Examples 8–11, issued 100 shares of capital stock as a dividend after it had reissued the treasury stock, and that the law requires the amount capitalized per dividend share to be the same as that paid in on each previously outstanding share. What entry is required to record the effect of the stock dividend?

Solution
```
OE, Stock Dividend...................................  10,500
     OE, Capital Stock—Par.........................          10,000
     OE, Capital Stock—Premium.................             500
To record issuance of a 10% stock dividend
and transfer of $105 a share from Retained
Income to paid-in capital accounts.
```

In Example 12 a stockholder will receive one additional stock share as a

dividend for each ten shares that he previously owned. The effect on Stockholder *A*, who owned ten shares before the stock distribution, is as follows:

	Before Stock Dividend	After Stock Dividend
Total stockholders' equity:		
Capital stock—par..............	$100,000	$110,000
Capital stock—premium.......	5,000	5,500
Total paid-in capital.........	$105,000	$115,500
Retained income................	19,960	9,460
Total stockholders' equity...	$124,960	$124,960
Divide by number of shares outstanding...........................	1,000	1,100
Stockholders' equity per share...	$ 124.96	$ 113.60
Multiply by number of shares owned by *A*.................	× 10	× 11
Equity of Stockholder *A*..........	$ 1,249.60	$ 1,249.60

The total equity of each stockholder is *no greater* after a stock dividend than
before; the same equity is merely represented by more shares of stock.

For small stock dividends issued by publicly held corporations the amount
transferred from Retained Income to paid-in capital should be the *fair value*
of the dividend shares.

The reasoning behind this rule is that many who receive stock dividends
think of them as *distribution of corporate income* in an amount equal to the fair value
of the additional shares received as a dividend. However, dividend shares *are
not income* to the recipient, because they do not increase his share of the
unchanged total stockholders' equity.

Issuance of a stock dividend sometimes implies that management plans to
increase the *total cash dividend* paid by the corporation to stockholders in the future. If the previous cash dividend rate were $10 a share for each of the 1,000
shares, the total annual dividend payment amounted to $10,000, of which
Stockholder *A* received $100. Continuation of this same dividend rate per share
in the future would require the company to pay a total dividend of $11,000
($10 times 1,100 shares), of which Stockholder *A* would receive $110 ($10
times 11 shares). If such an increased total dividend is anticipated, the market
value of the stock in total will probably rise. One of the most important determinants of the market value of a share of stock is the amount of its expected
future dividends.

In deciding whether or not to issue a stock dividend, management should
consider its implied promise of higher total cash dividends in the future, and
decide whether or not it wishes to undertake to pay them.

Stock Splitups

The increased marketability of a corporation's stock is desirable to management because it tends to spread the ownership among more people and to
improve the corporation's sources of capital. A *stock splitup*—the issuance of
more than one new share to *replace* one old share—accomplishes this purpose
without requiring a transfer from Retained Income to paid-in capital.

Example 13   A corporation had 1,000 shares of $100-par value stock outstanding in the hands of 50 owners. The current market value of the stock was about $160 a share. Wishing to broaden its ownership, the corporation declared a two-for-one stock splitup, issuing 2,000 shares of $50-par value stock to replace the $100-par value stock. The immediate effect should be to reduce the market value of a new share to about $80, but the ultimate effect should probably be to increase the marketability of the stock and to increase the number of individual stockholders.

The entry for the stock splitup would be

```
OE, Capital Stock—$100 Par...........................  100,000
     OE, Capital Stock—$50 par ........................            100,000
     To record the issuance of 2,000 shares of $50 par
     to replace 1,000 shares of $100 par.
```

Management Planning for Stockholders' Equity

Tailoring the detailed provisions of capital stock contracts to the needs and circumstances of the particular business is one of the major problems of financial administration.

In deciding on particular features of various classes of stocks and bonds, corporate management should project the financial requirements which the security will place on the business. Management should then compare these requirements with the funds which are expected to be available to meet them.

Example 14   A corporation is planning to issue 1,000 shares of $100-par value 6 per cent preferred stock. It is contemplating a provision requiring the retirement of 10 per cent of the stock each year, starting with the third year. Management should compare the total annual requirements for dividends and stock retirement with the sums which will probably become available for those purposes. Although preferred dividends are not a fixed obligation *legally*, financially there is strong pressure on the company to pay them regularly. If it does not do so, its future attempts to secure capital will be severely handicapped.

The restrictions of security contracts on management action should not be so narrow as to hamper effective business operations. Contracts should provide means for modifying their terms in case of hardship.

Management Performance as to Stockholders' Equity

The corporation's board of directors and officers are responsible to the stockholders for their performance in managing the business. The basic purpose of the corporation is to maximize the long-range return to the stockholders. If there is more than one class of stock management is usually elected by, and is primarily responsive to the wishes of, the residual stockholders. The better the terms that financial management can obtain from preferred stockholders and creditors, the greater is the advantage which accrues to common stockholders.

Each share of common stock outstanding at a given time has the same rights as each other share; therefore management has an equal responsibility to each owner of one share. From time to time, however, the corporation finds it necessary to issue additional shares of stock in order to obtain capital. Management has an obligation to the present generation of stockholders to protect their interests when issuing additional stock.

One of the most useful methods of appraising management's stewardship of the corporate assets, analysis of the *rate of return* and its various components, was discussed in Chapter 8. Rates of return computed on stockholders' equity should include *all* components of such equity: capital stock, other paid-in capital items, and both restricted and unrestricted retained income. It is just as important for management to administer soundly and use profitably the assets derived from income as the assets obtained from the direct investment of stockholders.

ACCOUNTING FOR PARTNERSHIP OWNERS' EQUITY

The Partnership as an Accounting Entity

Chapter 1 defined a *partnership* as an association of two or more persons as co-owners to carry on a business for profit. Accounting recognizes a partnership as a *distinct economic* or *business entity*, and separates the affairs of the partnership from the personal affairs of the partners. The respective interests of each partner in the net assets of the entity and in its operating results are accounted for in the *owners' equity accounts* of the partnership.

The owners' equity accounts of a partnership usually include a *capital* account and a *drawing* account for each partner. The capital account represents the amount of the partner's *direct investment* in the business plus his share of the *retained income*. The drawing account represents the reduction of the partner's equity in the business from *withdrawals* during the current accounting period. At the end of each period, each partner's drawing account is closed to his capital account to reflect his net equity in the partnership enterprise.

The law does not recognize an individual's interests in a partnership and his personal affairs as separate entities. Rather, the law holds partners both jointly and individually responsible for the liabilities of the partnership, and subjects the partnership assets to the personal liabilities of the partners. However, if a partner is required, in paying partnership creditors, to bear more than his appropriate share of partnership losses, he has a legal claim against his fellow partners for the excess.

The Partnership Agreement

Partners should specify their respective rights and duties in a *partnership agreement*. This agreement is the main basis for determining how to account for the partnership owners' equity.

A partnership may be formed by an oral agreement between the partners, or even by an implied agreement; but a carefully drawn *written* agreement is highly desirable. The following are some of the principal points which should be covered in the agreement:

(1) The name, location, and nature of the business.
(2) The effective date of the agreement and its duration.
(3) The amount of capital to be contributed by each partner, the time of contribution, and the method of measuring noncash investments.
(4) The rights and obligations of each partner.
(5) The method for determining the compensation of each partner.
(6) The amounts, timing, and limitations on partners' drawings.
(7) Provisions for determining the amount of a partner's equity and for settling it in the event of his death.
(8) Provisions for voluntary withdrawal of a partner.
(9) Method of settling disputes among the partners.

The advice of a competent lawyer and of a competent accountant is needed in drawing up the details of a partnership agreement. Care should be taken to assure that provisions of the agreement do not hinder effective management. To avoid confusion and indecisiveness, authority and responsibility for management functions should be specifically assigned to individual partners. A managing partner, with final executive authority, should be designated.

Factors Relating to Partners' Shares of Income

Individual partners usually contribute one or more of the following to the partnership:

(1) *Capital*, in the form of cash or other property.
(2) *Labor*, including time spent in performing management functions and other duties.
(3) *Risk bearing*, including the possibility of incurring a loss greater than the capital invested. Often some of the partners have their risk of loss *limited* to their investment in the partnership; however, there must be at least one *general* partner who has unlimited liability to the creditors of the partnership. The public must be informed that it is a limited partnership.

Sometimes a partner lends money to the partnership. The *partner's loan* account is not a part of Capital, but a *liability*. This distinction is made clear if the partner requires the partnership to give him a promissory note as evidence of the loan.

In the absence of a specific agreement, the law provides that both profits and losses of the partnership will be shared equally by the partners. If they intend to share income other than equally, the partners should state in the partnership agreement the method by which each partner is to be compensated for his capital, his labor, and his assumption of risk. The compensation for capital may be in the form of a specified rate of *interest* on the amounts invested. The compensation for labor, perhaps as a *salary allowance*, should be in proportion to the amount of time devoted to the business by the partner as well as his ability. The

compensation for risk should be in proportion to the relative risk borne by each partner.

The formula agreed on for dividing net income also applies to net losses unless the partners specify to the contrary. Before making an income-sharing arrangement, the partners should compute the shares that each would receive under the contemplated method of division at various levels of net income and net loss. They may wish to provide for *one method* of sharing income if there is a *net income*—or a net income above a certain minimum—and *another method* if there is a *net loss* or a small net income.

Examples of Partnership Income-Sharing Plans

In accounting for shares of partnership income there are two general problems: (1) computing the amount of each partner's share and (2) recording and reporting the division of income.

The following are basic types of plans which are used for sharing partnership income. The possible variations and combinations of provisions are almost endless.

Basic data for illustrations. Varn and Weldon, partners, had the following balances in their accounts on December 31, 1973, after closing all revenue and expense accounts to Income Summary:

Varn, Capital

1973			1973		
July 1		2,000	Jan. 1	Balance	12,000

Weldon, Capital

			1973		
			Jan. 1	Balance	4,000
			Oct. 1		2,000

Income Summary (1973)

		1973	
		Dec. 31	8,000

Salaries allowed to partners. The partnership agreement provided that Varn, who spent half of his time in the business, would receive a salary allowance of $2,500, and Weldon, who spent full time, would receive a salary of $5,000. The remainder of income after allowing salaries was to be divided equally. The division for 1973 would be as follows:

	Income Shares of Varn	Weldon	Total Available
Partnership net income........................			$8,000
Salaries to partners............................	$2,500	$5,000	(7,500)
Remainder.....................................			$ 500
Equal shares to partners.......................	250	250	(500)
Income of each partner........................	$2,750	$5,250	

If there were a net loss of $2,000 before distribution to partners, the same partnership agreement would result in the following division:

	Income Shares of Varn	Weldon	Total Available
Partnership net loss..............................			($2,000)
Salaries to partners.............................	$2,500	$5,000	(7,500)
Remainder.......................................			($9,500)
Equal shares to partners........................	(4,750)	(4,750)	9,500
Income (loss) of each partner.................	($2,250)	$ 250	

Interest allowed on partners' capitals. If the partnership agreement of Varn and Weldon allowed each partner interest at 6 per cent of his invested capital, with the remainder to be divided equally, it should specify *how to determine the invested capital.* If there are substantial changes in a partner's capital balance during the year, it would not be fair to compute interest on either the capital balance at the beginning or at the end of the year. Instead, interest should be computed on each partner's balance *for the time it was invested,* as follows:

	Capital Balance	Term (Fraction of Year)	Annual Rate	Interest Allowance
Varn:				
1/1 to 6/30........................	$12,000	1/2	0.06	$360
7/1 to 12/31......................	10,000	1/2	0.06	300
Total...........................				$660
Weldon:				
1/1 to 9/30........................	$ 4,000	3/4	0.06	$180
10/1 to 12/31	6,000	1/4	0.06	90
				$270

If income were $8,000 before allowing partners' interest, the distribution to partners would be:

	Income Shares of Varn	Weldon	Total Available
Partnership net income...........................			$8,000
Interest to partners..............................	$ 660	$ 270	(930)
Remainder...			$7,070
Equal shares to partners........................	3,535	3,535	(7,070)
Income of each partner...........................	$4,195	$3,805	

Entries to Record Partner's Income Shares

The total income share of each partner can be recorded by the following type of entry:

```
OE, Income Summary (1973)....................8,000
        OE, Varn, Capital....................................    4,195
        OE, Weldon, Capital..............................    3,805
    To record the total share of income credited to
    each partner.
```

The income of a partnership results from the combined *capital, labor,* and *risk-bearing* interests of the partners. Therefore, no separate compensation for these components is usually deducted in computing partnership income. Instead, each partner's share of the total earnings of the partnership is considered to be a *distribution of income.*

In spite of this, the partners and others who read the partnership's financial statements may be able to appraise the business results more effectively, and make more valid comparisons with other businesses, if the allowances for partners' services are shown in the operating statement. If this type of presentation is desired a separate account may be used to report each component of the partners' income shares. These accounts are closed to Income Summary.

Dissolution of Partnerships

The assets and equities of a partnership, like those of any other business, are measured on a *going-concern* basis, not a *liquidating* basis. When a partnership *does terminate*, the steps in the accounting process are

(1) Record the disposal of assets by crediting the assets for their book values, debiting Cash for the amount received, and debiting Loss on Realization or crediting Gain on Realization for the difference.

(2) Divide the net gain or loss on realization between the partners according to their income-sharing arrangement, and record it in their capital accounts.

(3) Close each partner's drawing account to his capital account.

(4) Record the payment of the liabilities in the order of their legal priority.

(5) Record the payment to the partners of the *balances in their individual capital accounts* resulting after entries (2) and (3) have been recorded.

The equity remaining after the liabilities of the business are paid off is not a *gain* or *loss*; it is an amount of *capital*, consisting of each partner's original investment, minus his withdrawals, and plus or minus his share of partnership gains or losses. *The balance remaining in each partner's capital account is the amount that he should be paid in liquidation.*

The following order of priority is used in settling the equities of *corporations* in liquidation:

(1) creditors,

(2) preferred stockholders whose stock is preferred as to assets on liquidation, and

(3) common stockholders.

Summary The owners' equity accounts of a corporation should identify the major components of *capital paid in* by stockholders and by others. Although the *source* of the amount paid in by stockholders in exchange for shares is owners' investment, state laws and variations in types of stock contracts may dictate that the components of the investment be recorded in two or more accounts.

Acquisitions of shares of *treasury stock* represent a reduction of the corporation's owners' equity. *Restrictions* on the availability of retained income for dividends which result from legal or contractual requirements or from management policy may be disclosed by footnotes, unless a formal transfer to a restricted retained income account is required. A *stock dividend* is accounted for as a transfer of owners' equity from retained income to paid-in capital.

All components of stockholders' equity should be considered when measuring past business performance by the rate of return on stockholders' equity.

The *partnership agreement* should spell out the partners' wishes on important financial matters, such as the nature of each partner's capital contribution and the manner of determining his compensation. Invested capital, labor, and risk bearing should be considered in arriving at a formula for dividing partnership income among the partners.

Discussion Questions and Problems

14-1

a. Distinguish clearly between the following forms of business ownership:
   (1) Proprietorship.
   (2) Partnership.
   (3) Corporation.
b. In view of the red tape and expense involved, is it worth-while for the owners of a small business to incorporate? Explain.

14-2   The owners' equity of a corporation is represented by shares of capital stock, of which common stock is the most important. What are the principal differences between common stock and other forms of capital stock?

14-3   Assume that a business corporation has only one class of capital stock. Define carefully what is meant by the following:

a. Authorized shares.
b. Unissued shares.
c. Issued shares.
d. Treasury shares.
e. Outstanding shares.

14-4   Explain how the following terms differ in meaning when used to describe capital stock:

a. Market value.   c. Par value.   e. Stated value.
b. Book value.   d. No-par value.   f. Liquidating value.

14-5   Distinguish clearly between the *paid-in-capital* and the *retained income* of a corporation. Why is it important to make this distinction in the accounting records?

14-6   Distinguish between the major sources of *paid-in capital*. Which are the more important sources?

14-7   Mrs. Abner was planning to invest in one of several stocks which had been recommended to her. Included in this group were Ken Corp. Common Stock and Ray Company Preferred Stock. Asking the meaning of "preferred," she was told that the preferred stockholder was entitled to receive dividends before any were paid to common stockholders, and that preferred stockholders had a right to be paid before common stockholders in case the company liquidated. "Obviously, then, I should buy the Ray Company Preferred Stock rather than the Ken Common," remarked Mrs. Abner.

Was Mrs. Abner correct in her conclusion? Explain.

14-8   Define "stated (or legal) capital." How does the distinction between *stated capital* and other paid-in capital affect the rights of stockholders?

14-9   How does the issuance of a *stock dividend* affect a corporation's paid-in capital and retained income? How does such a dividend affect individual stockholders' interests in the corporation?

14-10   How does a *stock splitup* affect a corporation's paid-in capital and retained income? How, if at all, does a stock splitup affect individual stockholders' interests in the corporation?

14-11   State the purposes for which each of the following might be used, and point out the main differences in accounting required for each:

a. High par value stock.
b. Stock with nominal par value.
c. Stock with no par value.

14-12   The word "par" is often used in describing both stocks and bonds.

a. Does it mean the same thing in both cases? Explain.
b. How is the par value treated in accounting for each of these security classes?

14-13

a. What is meant by a *subscription* to capital stock?
b. What is the nature of the account credited for an unpaid subscription?
c. How should Subscriptions Receivable to Capital Stock be reported in the financial statements if (1) subscriptions are to be collected in the near future, (2) subscriptions are to be collected in the distant future, and (3) the board of directors does not intend to demand payment of the subscriptions, and the related shares of stock have not been issued?

14-14   The 1973 annual report of Anclote Corporation showed the following under Stockholders' Equity:

Income retained in the business	
Appropriated for increased replacement	
cost of facilities.....................	$ 42,000,000
Unappropriated............................	386,540,000
	428,540,000

a. What is the purpose of the appropriation? By what accounting entry was it established? Does it represent specific assets set aside for replacement of facilities? Explain.
b. What does the total, $428,540,000, represent?

14-15

a. What is the purpose of a stock dividend?
b. How does a stock dividend differ in effect from a cash dividend from the point of view of the corporation? From the point of view of the stockholder?
c. How should a stock dividend be recorded by the issuing company?

14-16

a. What is the purpose of a stock splitup?
b. What is the effect of a stock splitup on the corporation? On the stockholder?
c. How should a stock splitup be recorded on the books of the corporation?
d. How does a stock splitup differ in purpose and effect from a stock dividend?

14-17   A corporation was organized in January 1972 to purchase an automobile dealership. Its charter authorized the issuance of 20,000 shares of a single class of capital stock. Six thousand shares were issued for cash to a group headed by an attorney, and another 5,000 shares were issued to the dealer in exchange for the assets of the automobile agency. The attorney's group later donated 1,000 of their shares to the corporation. It was expected that these shares would be reissued later under a management compensation plan.

Required   a. Show the status of the capital stock shares after the above transactions were completed.
b. Compute the dealer's percentage of the total owners' equity.

14-18   A corporation was authorized to issue 10,000 shares of capital stock with a par value of $25 per share. Early in its life 4,000 shares were issued for cash at par, and somewhat later 3,000 additional shares were issued for cash at $55 a share.

a. Show how you would present these facts in a statement of financial position.
b. Carver owns 50 shares which he bought at the time of the corporation's formation, and Douglas owns 50 shares for which he paid $55 a share. Which stockholder has the greater interest in the company? Explain.
c. How can you explain Douglas's willingness to pay more for the stock than did Carver?

14-19   The Baden Corporation had been in business for some years and had 20,000 shares of $100-par value capital stock outstanding. On May 5, 1974, the corporation issued 5,000 additional shares through an investment banker. The banker sold these shares to the public at $132 per share and remitted the proceeds, less $12 a share commission, to the Baden Corporation. The corporation also received a bill for legal services of $2,000 in connection with the issue.

a. How should these facts be accounted for on the books of the Baden Corporation?
b. When, and to what extent, do they affect the corporation's income? Explain.

14-20   A corporation originally issued all its 45,000 shares of authorized capital stock for the par value of $5.00 share. Some years later the corporation reacquired 2,000 shares for $4.70 a share and in the same accounting period reissued them for $5.50 a share.

a. What valid business reason might the corporation have had for trading in its own stock?
b. How much income did the corporation make on trading in its stock? Explain.
c. How would your answer to part b differ if the stock had been reissued for $4.50 a share?
d. Show how these facts would appear in the financial statements (1) after the stock had been repurchased but before it had been reissued and (2) after it had been reissued. Prepare answers for both parts b and c.
e. How does "treasury stock" differ legally from "unissued stock"?

14-21   A corporation originally issued 4,500 shares of its no-par common stock (stated value, $50 a share) for $80 each. Later, when shares were trading on the market for $100 a share, 1,000 shares were issued in exchange for copyrights related to the production of computerized instructional materials. The copyrights had a fair market value of $8,000.

a. Present journal entries to record the two stock issues.
b. A group of stockholders contended that the shares related to acquiring the copyrights were issued at a discount. Do you agree? Explain.

14-22 The Sunset Corporation presents the following information regarding its capital stock on December 31, 1973:

	Number of Shares		
	Authorized	Issued	In Treasury
6% cumulative preferred stock, par $100 per share	4,000	3,000	0
Common stock without par value, stated value $1 per share	250,000	150,000	10,000

Preferred stock dividends have been paid in full to December 31, 1971.

Required
a. How many shares of each class of stock are unissued? Outstanding?
b. The board of directors would like to declare a dividend so that the common stockholders will receive 20 cents a share, and asks you how much cash would be required. Prepare a table, with supporting computations, showing the total amount of dividend that would be necessary for each class of stockholders.
c. If the board of directors declares the dividend on December 31, 1973, payable on January 15, 1974, to stockholders of record on January 6, 1974, what entries should it make: (1) On December 31? (2) On January 6? (3) On January 15?
d. How should the dividend be reported in the 1973 financial statements?

14-23 The Arctic Corporation charter was approved on January 2, 1974, authorizing the issuance of 80,000 shares of capital stock of $5 par value. The following events occurred during January:
Jan. 8—8,000 shares were issued for cash at $6 per share.
12—Subscriptions were received for 4,000 shares at $7.50 per share. Nothing was collected at this time. The stock was to be issued when individual subscribers paid their subscriptions in full.
15—The corporation's attorneys submitted a bill for $5,000 for their services in organizing the corporation and getting its charter approved. They agreed to accept 800 shares of stock in full settlement.
25—Subscribers to 1,000 shares (see Jan. 12) paid their subscriptions in full. Their stock was issued.
28—Three thousand shares were issued for land which had cost the new stockholders $7,500. The board of directors agreed that its present fair value was was about $18,000.

Required
a. Journalize the foregoing transactions.
b. Show how the resulting balances would appear in the classified financial position statement of January 31.

14-24 The charter of the Doke Corporation, approved on February 9, 1973, authorized the corporation to issue 60,000 shares of stock without par value. On March 2, 1973, the corporation issued 20,000 shares for cash at $80 a share. The board of directors assigned a stated value of $50 to each share. On April 27 the corporation issued 10,000 shares for cash at $90 a share. On the same day it exchanged 2,000 shares for patents for which the owners had previously been asking a price of $200,000.

Required
    a. Record the foregoing transactions in journal form.

    b. Present the stockholders' equity section of the financial position statement on April 30. If the corporation aquires 200 shares of its own stock from a stockholder on May 1, how many shares would then be outstanding? Unissued? How much money would be required to pay a cash dividend of $5 a share on that date, after the reacquisition?

14-25   On January 3, 1973, the Wren Corporation was authorized to issue 4,000 shares of 6 per cent cumulative preferred stock of $50-par value and 200,000 shares of common stock without par value. The preferred stock conveyed no voting rights, but was preferred as to assets on liquidation in the amount of $40 per share.

    The following events occurred in 1973:

Jan.   9—One thousand shares of preferred stock were sold for $52,000 cash.

Mar. 11—Subscriptions were received for 300 shares of preferred stock at $54 per share, but nothing was paid on the subscriptions and the stock was not issued.

April 14—Cash was received for 25,000 shares of common stock sold for $8 per share. No stated value was assigned to this stock.

Dec. 31—Net income for the year was $35,000, as shown by a credit balance in Income Summary. Show the closing entry.

Dec. 31—The board of directors declared a cash dividend of 6 per cent on the preferred stock, payable on January 15, 1974, to stockholders of record on December 31, 1973.

Dec. 31—The board of directors declared a 10 per cent stock dividend on common stock, to be issued immediately. The stock was issued.

Required
    a. Journalize the foregoing transactions.

    b. Show how the resulting balances would appear in the December 31, 1973, financial position statement.

14-26   Refer to the data in Problem 14-25. The following additional transactions occurred in 1974:

Jan.   4—The preferred stock subscriptions of March 11, 1973, were collected in full.
        15—The cash dividend on preferred stock was paid.

Mar. 17—Reacquired 2,000 shares of common stock in full settlement of a customer's delinquent account of $16,200.

June 30—The stockholders approved a two-for-one stock splitup for the preferred stock. The number of shares authorized was increased to 8,000, the par value of each share was reduced to $25, and the old stock was called in and exchanged for twice as many new shares.

Dec. 31—The net loss for the year, including all foregoing transactions, was $13,500. Close the Income Summary account.

Required
    a. Journalize the 1974 transactions.

    b. Present the December 31, 1974, Stockholders' Equity section of the financial position statement in good form, with complete disclosure of important information.

14-27   The Lunar Company has acquired 500 shares of treasury stock for $48,000. The laws of the state in which the company is incorporated limit total distributions to stockholders, whether in the form of dividends or treasury stock acquisitions, to the amount of retained income. The Stockholders' Equity section is reported as follows:

Capital stock, $100 par value: 10,000 shares authorized, of which 6,000 shares have been issued and 500 are in the treasury.......................................		$600,000
Paid-in capital in excess of par		12,000
Retained income:		
Restricted because of the purchase of treasury stock...	$48,000	
Unrestricted..	33,000	81,000
		$693,000
Deduct cost of 500 shares of treasury stock		48,000
Total stockholder's equity		$645,000

Required

a. Why does treasury stock appear *three times* in the Stockholders' Equity section?

b. Prepare the Stockholders' Equity section if an acceptable alternative method had been used to record the acquisition of the treasury stock.

c. Record the entry for the reissuance of 300 of the treasury shares for $110 cash per share, using the cost method of accounting for treasury stock.

d. Restate the Stockholders' Equity section to include the results of part c.

14-28   The Forster Corp. had the following account balances on February 28, 1973, the end of its accounting year:

Capital stock, $100 par (authorized, 4,000 shares).........	$250,000
Retained income reserved for new plant	105,000
Retained income, unrestricted	50,000

The state law provides that total distributions to stockholders cannot exceed retained income.

On January 2, 1974, the company reacquired 100 of its own shares, paying cash. On January 8 the company reissued 20 of these shares.

Required

a. Record the treasury stock transactions under the cost (incomplete-transaction) method if the shares were (1) reacquired for $104 a share and reissued for $98 a share, and (2) reacquired for $97 a share and reissued for $102 a share.

b. Record the treasury stock transactions under the par-value (retirement) method, using the facts in part a.

14-29   On December 31, 1974, the Lowell Company presented its Stockholders' Equity as follows:

Capital stock (5,000 shares of $100 par value authorized, of which 500 are unissued and 300 are in the treasury)...	$450,000
Premium on common stock......................................	22,500
Retained income..	110,000
	$582,500
Deduct treasury stock (cost)....................................	32,000
Total stockholders' equity......................................	$550,500

Required

a. At what average price was each share of the capital stock issued?

b. At what average price was each share of the treasury stock purchased?

c. Present the Stockholders' Equity section in better form and explain any changes you make.

d. Assuming that the Lowell Company later reissued 100 shares of the treasury stock for $97 a share cash, draft the journal entries to record the reissuance.

e. Assume that, instead of the facts in part d, the 100 shares were reissued for $112 a share cash. Journalize the entry for reissuance.

14-30

a. If you were planning to form a partnership with two other people, what are some of the types of provisions you would wish to include in the partnership agreement?

b. Must the partnership agreement be in writing to be valid? Explain.

c. If there is no formal partnership agreement and the partners disagree as to how to divide partnership income, what position does the law take if the disagreement is taken to court?

14-31   "As long as a partnership is limited to a few partners it is a desirable form of business organization. When the business has many owners it is better to incorporate." Is this a reasonable statement? Why?

14-32   Roy Barnes and Sam Durgan are planning to organize a business to manufacture a new consumer product. Barnes is furnishing $50,000 cash to finance operations, but is not planning to participate in the management of the business. Durgan will devote full time to supervising the operations of the business. Barnes has extensive property holdings other than the proposed interest in the new business, but Durgan's other assets are negligible. The two men have decided to form a partnership and wish to provide a fair and practical method for distributing the partnership net income or net loss.

a. What provisions for sharing the partnership income would you suggest? Why? How would you go about determining specific amounts or percentages for each part of your partnership income-sharing plan?

b. Present the prospective partners a series of illustrations showing the results of your suggested plan if the partnership operating results are (1) moderately good, (2) very good, (3) moderately bad, and (4) very bad.

14-33   Mr. Wilkins is general manager of the Semi-Fini Wood Products Company. He draws a salary of $15,000 a year and owns one-third of the net assets of the business.

a. How would the salary of Mr. Wilkins be treated on the income statement if Semi-Fini were incorporated?

b. How would the salary be treated on the income statement if the business were a partnership?

c. Is a difference between the answers to parts a and b justified? Why?

14-34   Miller and Lee formed a partnership by written agreement effective on July 1, 1973, to carry on a retail business. Miller invested merchandise worth $30,000 and Lee invested cash of $10,000, which was deposited in a partnership bank account. The business was to be carried on in a rented building. The doors were to be opened to the public on July 10. Profits and losses were to be shared equally.

On the night of July 1 the building and all its contents were totally destroyed by fire. The partners had neglected to take out any insurance. As a result of the catastrophe the partnership was dissolved by agreement on July 2.

How would the partnership cash be distributed?

14-35   Prior to distributing the income of the partnership of Black and Brown for 1973, the Income Summary account had a debit balance of $18,000. The partnership agreement provided that the partners would receive salaries of $15,000 and $12,000, respectively, and that any remaining balance would be shared equally. Each partner was permitted to draw cash up to the amount of his salary yearly. Undrawn balances of salary were to be added to capital. Black had withdrawn his full salary, $15,000, but Brown had not withdrawn anything during the year.

The partners' capital balances on December 31, 1973 were

Black.................... $60,000   Brown.................... $40,000

Brown had made an additional investment of $8,000 in cash on March 7, 1973.

Required   a. Set up T-account to reflect the 1973 events prior to closing entries.
b. Journalize and post entries necessary to distribute partnership income and to close the books.
c. Prepare a statement showing the changes in the partners' capitals for the year.

14-36   The capital accounts of Walker Bros. at December 31, 1974, were as follows: Will, $80,000; Larry, $40,000; and Edward, $120,000. The net income of the business for the year ended December 31, 1974, was $99,000.

Required   Prepare a tabulation of the income shares going to each partner and journalize the entries necessary to close Income Summary under each of the following agreements:

a. Net income is to be distributed in proportion to the partners' capital balances.
b. There is no partnership agreement.
c. Each partner is to be allowed 10 per cent interest on his capital balance, and the remainder is to be divided equally.
d. Will is to be allowed a salary of $16,000; Larry, a salary of $14,000; and Edward, a salary of $12,000. Each partner is also to be allowed a 10 per cent interest on his capital balance, and the remainder is to be divided equally.

14-37

Required   a. What would your answer have been in each of the situations in Problem 14-36 if the net income for 1974 had been $33,000?
b. Under what circumstances would you recommend each of the four methods of distributing the partnership income?
c. What more specific provisions are needed if compensation is to be given for capital investment? Why? What provisions would you recommend?

14-38   Alexander and Cyrus are in a partnership, sharing income equally. Their account balances on December 31, 1973, were as follows:

Cash...........................	$20,000	Notes payable..............	?
Accounts receivable.......	21,000	Alexander, drawings......	$ 4,000
Merchandise inventory...	50,000	Cyrus, drawings...........	7,000
Prepaid expenses..........	1,000	Alexander, capital.........	24,500
Accounts payable..........	10,500	Cyrus, capital..............	16,000

Required   a. Set up T-accounts showing these balances and the amount of Notes Payable.
b. Journalize and post any necessary closing entries.
c. Record the following liquidating transactions:

(1) The accounts receivable were sold without recourse for $17,000.

(2) The inventory was sold for $45,000.

(3) An insurance refund of $400 was received on cancellation of the unexpired part of the policy.

d. Journalize and post the entries for the payment of all claims in the legal order of priority.

14-39

Required   Complete the same requirements as in Problem 14-38, parts c and d, assuming the following facts in part c:

(1) The accounts receivable were sold without recourse for $10,500.

(2) The inventory was sold for $30,000.

(3) The prepaid expenses, consisting of supplies, were sold for $1,500.

Cases   14-1   Chemetron Corporation. The following stockholders' equity section appeared in the 1969 Annual Report of the Chemetron Corporation.

	December 31	
STOCKHOLDERS' EQUITY	1969	1968
Capital stock (Note 6):		
Preference, no par. Authorized 1,000,000 shares; issued:		
$4.50 series A: 12,400 shares (liquidating value $1,240,000)	17,714	17,714
$3.50 series B: 75,000 shares (liquidating value $7,500,000)	125,000	—
Cumulative preferred, $4\frac{1}{4}\%$ series, $100 par. Authorized and issued: 1969, none; 1968, 9,800 shares	—	980,000
Common, $1 par. Authorized 10,000,000 shares; issued: 1969, 3,695,861 shares; 1968, 3,623,294 shares		
(Note 5)	3,695,861	3,623,294
Total capital stock	3,838,575	4,621,008
Additional paid-in capital	49,163,832	40,561,594
Retained earnings (Note 4)	99,474,984	94,056,399
Total	152,477,391	139,239,001
Less treasury stock, at cost (Note 6)	9,968	167,555
Total stockholders' equity	152,467,423	139,071,446

The report also included the accompanying Statement of Consolidated Capital Stock and Additional Paid-In Capital.

Footnote 6, dealing with capital stock and treasury stock, is presented below. Footnote 5, not given here, dealt with stock options.

6) Capital Stock and Treasury Stock

During 1968 the shareholders authorized the creation of a new class of stock, having no par value and designated as preference stock.

The preference stock may be issued in one or more series with such terms as voting rights, rate of dividend, redemption prices, liquidation rights, convertibility and such other special rights, qualifications and limitations as shall be fixed by

STATEMENT OF CONSOLIDATED CAPITAL STOCK
AND ADDITIONAL PAID-IN CAPITAL
Year Ended December 31, 1969

	Capital Stock					Additional Paid-in Capital	Treasury Stock
	Preference		Cumulative				
	$4.50 Series A	$3.50 Series B	Preferred 4¼%	Common			
Balance December 31, 1968..............	$17,714	$ —	$ 980,000	$3,623,294		$40,561,594	$ 167,555
Acquisition of P & H Welding Products—75,000 shares (Note 1).............	—	125,000	—	—		6,552,070	—
Exercise of stock options—100 shares.............	—	—	—	100		2,000	—
Issuance of 2% stock dividend—72,467 shares, including 8 treasury shares.............	—	—	—	72,467		2,032,265	—
Redemption (7,904 shares) and retirement (9,800 shares) of 4¼% preferred stock.............	—	—	(980,000)	—		15,903	(157,889)
Purchase of treasury stock—10 shares—common..	—	—	—	—		—	(302)
Balance December 31, 1969.............	$17,714	$125,000	$ —	$3,695,861		$49,163,832	$ 9,968

437

the board of directors with respect to any series that the board shall authorize and issue.

The series A preference stock issued during 1968 has voting rights and a cumulative dividend of $4.50 per annum, is redeemable commencing July 1, 1973, and is convertible into 17,714 shares of common stock at an initial conversion price of $70 per share.

The series B preference stock issued during 1969 (Note 1) has voting rights and a cumulative dividend of $3.50 per annum, is redeemable commencing January 1, 1971, and is convertible into 125,000 shares of common stock at an initial conversion price of $60 per share.

At December 31, 1969, 254,414 shares of common stock were reserved for conversion of the series A and B preference stocks and the exercise of stock options. Capital stock held in the treasury was as follows:

	December 31, 1969	1968
Shares:		
Cumulative preferred $100 par, $4\frac{1}{4}\%$ series.........	—	1,896
Common, $1 par	439	421

Required

a. What is the purpose of the Statement of Consolidated Capital Stock and Additional Paid-in Capital? How does it relate to the other financial statements?

b. Why do you suppose the cumulative preferred stock was retired in 1969? Present the entry for retirement in journal form.

c. At what price were the stock options exercised in 1969? Journalize the entry for the exercise.

d. Record the issuance of the 2 per cent stock dividend.

e. Prepare a table showing how much cash would be required to pay dividends on the preference shares plus a $1.40 per share dividend on common stock, using stock data as of the end of 1969.

14-2   Jones, Simpson, and Thompson. At the end of 1972 Amos Jones, Thomas Simpson, and Durward Thompson were considering forming a partnership to carry on a retail business. Jones, who was already in business alone, offered to invest his net assets other than cash as his share of the partnership capital. He suggested that each of the other two invest cash equal to the agreed value of Jones's investment. The cash would be used to increase the working capital of the business and expand its facilities. Each would have a one-third interest in partnership assets and income. Jones' accountant had prepared the accompanying statement.

Shortly before the end of the year Mr. Jones had been offered $50,000 for his equity in the business.

Jones, Simpson, and Thompson met to discuss the proper treatment of Jones' assets and equities if the partnership were formed. They agreed that the accounts receivable were 95 per cent collectible, that the prepaid expenses would be of no value to the new business, and that it would cost $14,000 to replace the inventory. They also agreed that the equipment would have to be replaced in the very near future. An equipment company offered a trade-in allowance of $3,000 if all the equipment were traded in now on new items of a similar nature.

To determine the value of the land and building, the three decided to have them appraised by three local real estate dealers and to use the average appraised value.

AMOS JONES
Statement of Financial Position
December 31, 1972

ASSETS			LIABILITIES		
Current assets:			Current liabilities:		
Cash..................	$ 6,000		Accounts payable	$12,500	
Accounts receivable	10,000		Notes payable......	10,000	
Inventory	15,000		Total.........................		$22,500
Prepaid expenses...	500				
Total current assets.........		$31,500			
			OWNER'S EQUITY		
			Amos Jones, capital..............		36,000
Fixed assets:					
Land.............................	$ 5,000				
Building.............. $30,000					
—Accumulated					
depreciation...... 12,000	18,000				
Equipment.......... $10,000					
—Accumulated					
depreciation...... 6,000	4,000				
Total fixed assets............	$27,000				
Total assets	$58,500		Total equities................		$58,500

There was considerable variation in the estimates of the dealers. Dealer *A* appraised the real estate at $58,000; Dealer *B*, at $55,000; and Dealer *C*, at $49,000. Both of the latter dealers, however, were of the opinion that the real estate was located in a rapidly growing area and that future prospects for an increase in the real estate value were good. It was estimated that one-fourth of the total value applied to the land.

It was understood that the partnership would assume the liabilities of Mr. Jones' business.

Having concluded that Mr. Jones' proposal was reasonable, the three men signed a partnership agreement, to take effect on January 1, 1973. Each made the required investment. Actual business operations of the partnership were to begin on January 2, because January 1 was a holiday.

On the way to work on January 2 Mr. Jones died of a heart attack. His lawyer immediately informed Simpson and Thompson that it would be necessary to liquidate the business to provide funds to support Mrs. Jones. During the next two months the business assets other than cash were sold or collected, bringing in a total of $68,000 in cash. The only cash payments consisted of $3,000 for the costs of liquidation. No liabilities had been paid.

On February 26, Mr. Simpson and Mr. Thompson met with their lawyers and the lawyer representing the late Mr. Jones to discuss the final settlement of the business.

Required   a. Prepare a statement of financial position as of the date of Mr. Jones' death.

b. Record in summary form the events of January and February.

c. Prepare a statement of financial position as of February 26.

d. How should the business cash be divided on February 26, and in what order of priority?

e. How, in general, would the outcome have differed if the business had been organized as a corporation?

chapter 15

Accounting for Entities with Multiple Units

Purpose of Chapter

Often when top management delegates responsibility to division managers it is useful to treat parts of a single business as *separate accounting entities.* Financial reports should be prepared for each of these entities, and in addition *integrated financial statements* are needed to show the financial position and operating results of the business as a whole.

The integrated financial statements of the major divisions of a single corporation are called *combined financial statements.* The unified statements of several corporations related through common ownership are called *consolidated financial statements.*

This chapter outlines some of the major considerations involved in preparing and interpreting combined and consolidated financial statements. It also deals with the problems of combining the results of *foreign* operations with those of the domestic parent, and of reporting the financial results of *diversified companies,* or *conglomerates.*

COMBINATION OF BUSINESS ENTITIES

Purchase Versus Pooling of Interests

Two or more business entities which were formerly owned by separate individuals or groups are often *combined* under common ownership and control. When this happens, should the assets and equities *transferred to* the surviving entity continue to be measured on a *historical basis*, or should a *new basis* of measurement be established? To answer this question, accountants classify business combinations as either a *purchase* of one company by another, or a *pooling* of the interests in the separate companies into interests in the surviving company.

Accounting for the Purchase of a Business Entity

When separate businesses are combined in such a way that there is a *significant change in ownership*, with one or more of the former groups of owners retiring, the combination is considered to be a *purchase*. The prices paid by the new owners for the assets which are transferred to the surviving entity are set by arm's-length bargaining. Except by sheer coincidence they will *not be the same* as the valuations carried on the books of the selling entity.

One business often buys another by giving cash or other assets, or notes payable or bonds payable, in exchange for the net assets of the business being purchased. The *former owners* of the purchased business *have no ownership interest* in the combined entity.

Example 1   Corporation A has net assets with a book value of $100,000. Corporation B acquires all its stock in exchange for $120,000 cash and dissolves Corporation A. Corporation B has *purchased* Corporation A. The former stockholders of A have no interest in the combined entity.

There is a combination by purchase even if the acquired company is not dissolved, as long as the other facts in Example 1 remain unchanged.

When an entity is *purchased*, the historical values of its assets and liabilities should be replaced by the *values agreed on at the time of purchase*. A new basis of accountability is thus established for the assets and liabilities of the purchased entity, in terms of values that are meaningful to the *new owners*.

Example 2   The book values of Corporation A's assets (see Example 1) were $150,000 and the book values of its liabilities were $50,000. Corporation B agreed to assume the liabilities at their face value. At what value should B record the assets acquired from A?

Solution B should record the assets at $170,000, the price established in the purchase transaction.

In a combination by *purchase*, none of the owners' equity accounts of the seller are carried forward on the buyer's books.

Example 3   The owners' equity of Corporation *A* (see Example 2) consisted of $75,000 of Capital Stock and $25,000 of Retained Income. Neither balance will be carried over to the books of Corporation *B*, the purchaser.

If the selling entity is to be dissolved, the following accounting procedure is necessary:

(1) The individual assets on the seller's books are credited to show their transfer to the purchaser.

(2) The assets received from the purchaser in exchange for the business are debited on the seller's books.

(3) The assets received are later credited on the seller's books to record their distribution to the former owners of the selling company. The seller's owners' equity accounts are debited, and all the seller's accounts then will have zero balances.

Accounting for a Pooling of Interests

If two or more separately owned businesses are combined in such a way that substantially all the *ownership interests continue* in the surviving entity or entities, the combination may be treated as a *pooling of interests* for accounting purposes, rather than as a purchase if certain conditions are met.

Example 4   Corporation *D* combines with Corporation *C*. The former stockholders of *C* receive shares of the capital stock of *D* in proportion to their former interests in the owners' equity of *C*. Corporation *C* is dissolved. The combination is a *pooling of interests*.

In a pooling of interests the assets and equities of the combining companies are measured on the books of the combined entity at their *historical values*.

Example 5   Corporations *C* and *D* have the following condensed financial position statements before a pooling of interests:

	Corporation C	Corporation D
Assets	$250,000	$325,000
Liabilities	50,000	75,000
Owners' equity:		
Capital stock	125,000	200,000
Retained income	75,000	50,000

How should the assets and equities of surviving Corporation *D* be measured?

Solution

	Corporation D (combined)
Assets	$575,000
Liabilities	125,000
Owners' equity:	
Capital stock	325,000
Retained income	125,000

In the solution to Example 5 it is assumed that the former stockholders of

C who owned capital stock of $125,000 stated value received capital stock of *D* of equal stated value. It is then necessary only to add the historical values of all accounts of the combining companies.

In the exchange of capital stock it may be necessary to transfer some retained income to paid-in capital. If so, the *retained income* of the combined company is correspondingly *less*, and combined *paid-in capital* is correspondingly *more*, than the total retained income and paid-in capital of the combining companies.

Most business combinations are *purchases* rather than poolings of interest because of special conditions (beyond the scope of this text) which must be met to qualify the combination as a pooling of interests.

COMBINED FINANCIAL STATEMENTS

Preparation of Combined Financial Statements

A *single corporation*, partnership, or proprietorship may have operating divisions for which separate sets of accounting records are kept in order to report on the performance of decentralized management. Financial reports of the subdivisions should be prepared to permit evaluation of management effectiveness. In addition, *combined financial statements* are needed to show the results of the entire legal and economic entity. (Here the term *"combined"* is being used in a different sense than in the purchase of one entity by another or the pooling of two entities.)

The basic principle in preparing combined statements of the subdivisions is that their accounts are *added together* so as to give asset, liability, and owners' equity accounts from the point of view of a single entity. If the subdivisions deal with each other, they may have *mutual* asset-liability and revenue-expense pairs of accounts. To avoid double-counting in measuring the assets and equities of the economic entity, such mutual accounts must be *eliminated*.

The mutual accounts of subdivisions of an entity are called *reciprocal accounts*. After recording items in transit from one subdivision to another, and after correcting any errors in their mutual dealings, these accounts should be *equal in amount but opposite in sign*.

Example 6　The home office of Caro Company sold merchandise to a branch for $5,000 on credit. The home office should have an *Account Receivable from Branch* with a *debit* balance of $5,000, and the branch should have an *Account Payable to Home Office* with a *credit* balance of $5,000. These are *reciprocal accounts* with balances that are equal in amount but opposite in sign.

Two pairs of reciprocal accounts are needed to record interdivisional purchases and sales. One pair is the *Account Receivable* of the selling division and the reciprocal *Account Payable* of the buying division as shown in Example 6. The other pair includes reciprocal *inventory change accounts* to record the inventory shipments made by the selling division and the inventory shipments received by the buying division.

Example 7   To record the inventory shipments, the home office of Caro Company in Example 6 should have an account called *Inventory Shipments to Branch* with a *credit* balance of $5,000, and the branch should have an *Inventory Shipments from Home Office* account with a $5,000 *debit* balance. These also are *reciprocal accounts* which should have balances that are equal but opposite in sign after all shipments in transit have been recorded.

The balances of all *reciprocal accounts* should be offset against one another—that is, *eliminated*—when combined financial statements are made for the business as a unit. Although the reciprocal accounts of a divisionalized business may show that one division owes money to another, there is neither an asset nor a liability from the standpoint of the business as a whole. It means nothing to stockholders, creditors, or other outsiders to say that the business owes itself money. Moreover, an exchange of products or services between divisions is neither a purchase nor a sale of the business as a whole. It is just as though merchandise had been moved from one part of the warehouse to another.

There may be frequent transfers of money, goods, or other assets between divisions of a decentralized entity, moving in either direction or both directions. The net balance may be either a receivable or a payable from the viewpoint of a particular division. In such circumstances the accounting is simplified by using accounts such as "Branch Current" or "Division A Current" and "Home Office Current" for the reciprocal accounts which express the interdivisional *receivable-payable* relationship.

Inventory Markups Between Divisions

Merchandise shipped from one division of a business to another is sometimes priced *above its historical cost* to the selling division. The purpose may be to simulate competitive market prices to aid in evaluating the performance of divisional management. Whatever the reason, none of the markup on *unsold goods* should be included in the asset for ending inventory. The total business entity does not realize any income from the interdivisional sale until the goods have been sold to customers *outside* of the entity.

Example 8   Assume that the home office of the Caro Company in Example 6 sells goods to the branch at 25 per cent above original cost. How should the $5,000 shipment be valued in the ending inventory of the branch, if all is still on hand?

Solution   Of the billed price to the branch, $\frac{25}{125}$ or $1,000 represents an *unrealized markup*. This should be eliminated from the value of the branch inventory, and only $4,000 should be included in reporting the inventory of the combined entity.

CONSOLIDATED FINANCIAL STATEMENTS

The several divisions of an incorporated entity may be organized as *different corporations*, with the same ownership and top management. Although related in economic function, these corporations are distinct legal entities. Divisional managers and the creditors of the separate companies need separate sets of financial statements for each corporation. It is also usually desirable to prepare unified *consolidated financial statements* of the economic organization as a whole, disregarding the lines between the legal entities.

Criteria for Preparing Consolidated Statements

Consolidated financial statements are needed to evaluate the overall financial condition and operating results of two or more corporate entities with a *dominant central financial interest* which is accompanied by administrative control.

Ownership by one company of a substantial percentage of the voting shares of stock of another company is a necessary, but not a sufficient, condition to establish the existence of a *dominant central financial interest*. As a minimum, one company must own more than 50 per cent of the outstanding stock of the other to justify preparation of consolidated statements. The company which owns a majority of the other's stock is called the *parent*, and the company a majority of whose stock is owned by another company is called a *subsidiary*.

Administrative control of the activities and resources of the subsidiaries must accompany the parent-subsidiary relationship in order to justify the preparation of consolidated statements. Such control implies that each company is operated as if it were a department or branch of a larger entity. The statements of affiliated companies which are engaged in production and distribution should be consolidated if the conditions of ownership and control are met. Real estate companies or equipment-leasing companies which own property used by the parent should be consolidated with the parent and its other production and commercial affiliates. However, subsidiaries which perform finance or insurance functions should ordinarily not be in consolidated statements of production and distribution companies. To do so would result in adding together dissimilar assets and sources of income.

Consolidated statements should probably *not* be prepared when

(1) The parent's control is likely to be temporary, or when it does not rest with the majority owners because the subsidiary is in bankruptcy.

(2) A relatively large amount of nonvoting common stock or preferred stock is held by the minority interest, so that there is no dominant central financial interest.

(3) The ending dates of the affiliates' fiscal periods do not fall within a reasonably short span of time.

(4) Disturbed conditions in the form of exchange restrictions or unstable political of economic conditions exist in the foreign countries in which a subsidiary is located. Such subsidiaries should not be consolidated with the parent, but appropriate disclosure of their results and status should be made.

The parent-subsidiary relationship may be *direct* or *indirect*. For example, if Company *P* owns 100 per cent of the capital stock of Company *S* and Company *S* owns 75 per cent of the stock of Company *T*, Company *P* owns a majority interest in Company *S* directly and in Company *T* (75 per cent) indirectly.

Reciprocal Elements of Investment and Stockholders' Equity at Acquisition

The basic set of reciprocal accounts between parent and subsidiary corporations are the parent's asset, Investment in Stock of Subsidiary, and the corresponding portions of the subsidiary's stockholders' equity accounts.

In the simplest case, the parent acquires 100 per cent of the subsidiary's stock when the subsidiary is formed. On the date of acquisition the parent's investment account and the subsidiary's stockholders' equity accounts are *exactly reciprocal* to each other; neither will appear in the consolidated statements. The subsidiary's asset and liability accounts will be added to those of the parent (*excluding the investment account*). The resulting balances are the *consolidated* assets and equities. Consolidated capital stock is equal to the parent's capital stock. Consolidated retained income is equal to the parent's retained income.

Illustration 15-1 shows how the account balances of the parent and subsidiary would be consolidated at date of acquisition in this simple case.

Illustration 15-1

CONSOLIDATION OF 100 PER CENT OWNED SUBSIDIARY AT DATE OF ACQUISITION

	Financial Position, January 1, 1973			
ASSETS	Company P	Company S	Eliminations	Consolidated
Investment in stock of S.............	$105,000		$105,000	
All other assets........................	600,000	$200,000		$800,000
Total assets.........................	$705,000	$200,000	$105,000	$800,000
EQUITIES				
Liabilities.............................	$300,000	$ 95,000		$395,000
Paid-in capital.......................	200,000	105,000	$105,000	200,000
Retained income....................	205,000	0		205,000
Total equities.....................	$705,000	$200,000	$105,000	$800,000

Consolidation Procedure After Acquisition

On dates after the acquisition date, *consolidated retained income* includes the *parent's share of the net change in the subsidiary's retained income since the investment was acquired.*

Example 9   On December 31, 1973, the retained income of Company P (see Illustration 15-1) is $250,000 and the retained income of Company S is $40,000. What is the consolidated retained income?

Solution   Consolidated retained income is $290,000, the retained income of P, $250,000, plus 100 per cent of the change of S's retained income since acquisition ($40,000 − 0).

Consolidated *net income* includes the parent's net income, plus the parent's share of the subsidiary's net income (after any double counting has been eliminated).

Example 10 Assume that in Example 9 Company *P* paid a dividend of $30,000 in 1973 and Company *S* paid no dividend. Consolidated net income is computed as follows:

Parent's net income..	$ 75,000
Plus parent's 100% of subsidiary's net income.....................	40,000
Consolidated net income...	$115,000

Minority Interest in Consolidated Stockholders' Equity

When a parent owns a major part, but not all, of the stock of a subsidiary, there is a *minority interest* in the stockholders' equity of the subsidiary. This minority interest is reported as a separate item of stockholders' equity in the consolidated financial position statement.

Example 11 Company *P* acquired 80 per cent of the stock of Company *S* for $84,000 when it was formed. Company *S* paid no dividends during 1973. How would the reciprocal elements and remaining balances be accounted for at the end of 1973?

Solution

	Company P's Books	*Company S's Books*	
	Investment in Stock of S	*Paid-in Capital*	*Retained Income*
Separate company balances..........	$ 84,000 Dr.	$105,000 Cr.	$ 40,000 Cr.
Eliminate 80% of *S*'s stockholders' equity accounts at acquisition	(84,000)	(84,000)	
Balances:			
Minority interest in *S*, 20%.......		$ 21,000	$ 8,000
Parent's share of *S*'s retained income change since acquisition, 80%.....................			32,000

Nonreciprocal Remainder in Investment and Subsidiary Equity Accounts

A parent will usually pay more or less than book value for the capital stock of a subsidiary, particularly if it buys the subsidiary's stock from stockholders rather than directly from the subsidiary. Rarely does the market value of the stock of an established corporation coincide with the stock's book value.

After eliminating the parent's share of the subsidiary's stockholders' equity accounts at the date of acquisition there will be a *nonreciprocal remainder* in the *investment* account. This remainder is a *debit* if the parent paid *more than its proportion of book value* for the stock, and a *credit* if it paid *less*. The remainder should be assigned to specific accounts if possible.

An investment's cost may be *more than the book value* of the subsidiary's stock because certain assets are *undervalued* on the subsidiary's books. It may be more because the parent is recognizing *goodwill* of the subsidiary. If the cause of the excess can be identified, in preparing consolidated statements it should be transferred from the Investment in Stock of Subsidiary account to the appropriate account. If the cause cannot be identified, the remainder should be reported in the consolidated financial position statement as an asset, Goodwill.

Similarly, if the parent pays *less than book value* for the stock of the subsidiary, it may be in recognition of the fact that some of the subsidiary's specific assets are *overvalued*. If so, those assets should be reduced in the consolidated financial position statement. If they cannot be identified, the credit should be reported as Excess of Book Value at Acquisition of Investment in Subsidiary over Cost. This account is, in effect, a contra-account to assets as a whole.

Other Types of Eliminating Entries

Any reciprocal pairs of accounts on the books of the parent and subsidiary that result from intercompany dealings should be eliminated in the consolidated work sheet. Examples of such reciprocal accounts are

Accounts Receivable and Accounts Payable
Notes Receivable and Notes Payable
Bond Investment and Bonds Payable
Dividends Receivable and Dividends Payable
Sales Revenue and Merchandise Purchases (or Cost of Goods Sold)
Interest Revenue and Interest Expense
Dividend Revenue and Dividends Paid

After elimination of these reciprocal accounts the consolidated balances reflect the totals of assets and liabilities from the point of view of those outside the consolidated group, and total revenue realized and expense incurred from dealings with outsiders.

A profit made by one company on a sale to an affiliated company should be *eliminated from consolidated income*, to the extent that it is reflected in the assets of the separate companies on the date of the consolidated statements.

Example 12 *Elimination of intercompany markup in inventory.* During 1973 Company *P* sold merchandise for $20,000 to Company *S*, its wholly owned subsidiary. These goods had cost *P* $14,000. *S*'s ending inventory included some of this merchandise for which *S* had paid *P* $5,000. At what value should this inventory be included in the consolidated financial position statement?

Solution The *unrealized intercompany profit* included in *S*'s ending inventory is $1,500, which is 30 per cent of $5,000. *S*'s inventory should be included in consolidated inventory at $3,500, its cost to the consolidated entity. The unrealized profit should be eliminated from consolidated net income.

In addition, Sales Revenue and Cost of Goods Sold Expense accounts should be reduced by the amount of the intercompany sale, $20,000, to avoid double counting.

In Example 12 the intercompany markup of $1,500 will not be realized until the goods are sold outside of the consolidated group of companies.

The amount of the elimination for intercompany profit in inventory should be based on the *gross margin* of the selling company. The entire gross margin which pertains to the ending inventory should be eliminated whether the goods were sold by the parent to a subsidiary or vice versa. Moreover, the entire amount should be eliminated even if the sale were made by a subsidiary in which there is a minority interest.

Computing Consolidated Net Income

Consolidated net income equals the sum of

(1) *The separate company net income of the parent* (after adjustments for unrealized intercompany markups on sales made by the parent), and

(2) *The parent's share of the separate company net income of the subsidiary* (after adjustments for unrealized intercompany markups on sales made by the subsidiary).

A revenue or expense which has been adjusted for unrealized intercompany markups is stated on a *consolidated basis.* The consolidated income statement reports each revenue and expense item on a consolidated basis, without reduction for the minority interest. Total expense is then subtracted from total revenue on a consolidated basis. The *minority interest in the subsidiary's income* (adjusted to a consolidated basis) is deducted as the final item in the consolidated income statement.

Example 13   Company P owns 80 per cent of the stock of Company S. Unrealized intercompany markup included in S's ending inventory, resulting from sales made by P to S during the year, amounts to $4,000. Company P's net income on a separate company basis is $50,000; S's is $10,000. What is the amount of consolidated net income, and what is the minority interest in net income?

Solution   *Consolidated net income* is $54,000, which is the sum of P's $46,000 net income on a consolidated basis (after eliminating the $4,000 unrealized intercompany profit) and 80 per cent of S's $10,000 net income. The minority interest in Company S's net income is $2,000.

Consolidated Financial Statements

Illustrations 15-2, 15-3, and 15-4 present condensed consolidated financial statements, using the facts of Example 13 and other assumed facts.

Illustration 15-2

COMPANY P AND SUBSIDIARY S
Consolidated Income Statement
For the Year Ended December 31, 1974

Sales revenue.	$470,000
Deduct cost of goods sold expense.	324,000
Gross margin on sales.	146,000
Deduct other expenses.	90,000
Net income on a consolidated basis.	56,000
Deduct minority interest in net income of Subsidiary S.	2,000
Consolidated net income (to Retained Income Statement).	54,000

Illustration
15-3

COMPANY *P* AND SUBSIDIARY *S*
Consolidated Retained Income Statement
For the Year Ended December 31, 1974

Consolidated retained income balance, January 1, 1974	$ 86,000
Add consolidated net income for the year (from Income Statement)	54,000
Total	140,000
Deduct dividends	15,000
Consolidated retained income balance, December 31, 1974 ...	125,000

The consolidated retained income balance for January 1, 1974, is the sum of the retained income of Company *P* on that date, $70,000, and the parent's 80 per cent share of Company *S*'s $20,000 increase in retained income from the date the investment was acquired to the beginning of the current year.

Illustration
15-4

COMPANY *P* AND SUBSIDIARY *S*
Consolidated Financial Position Statement
December 31, 1974

ASSETS

Current assets:		
Cash	$ 29,800	
Accounts receivable...................................	75,000	
Merchandise inventory	116,000	
Total current assets..		$220,800
Property, plant, and equipment:		
Property, plant, and equipment (cost)...........	180,000	
Deduct accumulated depreciation..............	26,000	
Unexpired cost..		154,000
Intangible assets:		
Goodwill..		8,000
Total assets...		$382,800

LIABILITIES

Current liabilities:		
Accounts payable..		32,000

STOCKHOLDERS' EQUITY

Minority interest in stock of Company *S*..........................		25,800
Capital stock, $100 par: authorized, issued, and outstanding, 2,000 shares.....................	$200,000	
Add consolidated retained income (from Retained Income Statement).............................	125,000	
Controlling interest in consolidated stockholders' equity..		325,000
Total equities...		$382,800

The dividends paid are those paid by the parent to its stockholders—the *controlling interest* for whom the consolidated statements are primarily prepared.

This discussion of the principles and procedures of consolidated financial statements has necessarily been condensed and highly simplified. The objective has been to give the reader a basic understanding sufficient to interpret published financial statements.

ACCOUNTING FOR FOREIGN BRANCHES AND SUBSIDIARIES

Two major problems of accounting for foreign branches and subsidiaries are

(1) Whether the circumstances justify including the assets and results of the foreign operations in the combined or consolidated financial statements.

(2) How to express the accounts of the foreign and domestic entities in terms of a *common monetary unit* (usually dollars) in preparing combined or consolidated statements.

Criteria for Combining or Consolidating Accounts of Foreign Entities

The *values* and the *availability* of the assets and net income of branches and subsidiaries in some foreign countries may be *uncertain* because of internal political upheavals, wars, and restrictions on the exchange of funds between those countries and the domestic company. Where such uncertainty is great it may be undesirable to present combined or consolidated statements which include the foreign branches or subsidiaries. If such foreign balances are not included in the unified statements, supplementary reports should be prepared to show the assets and equities of the foreign entities, their income for the year, and the parent company's equity in them.

Earnings from foreign operations should be included in domestic accounts only to the extent that funds have been received in the United States, or that unrestricted funds are available to be sent. Provision should be made for known losses or probable losses in realizing foreign earnings in dollars.

A loss from a major devaluation of a foreign currency is reported in the income statement as an *extraordinary item*.

Exchange of Currencies

When funds are to be sent between countries, they are exchanged from one currency to another at the current rate of exchange between the two currencies. For example, if the Swiss subsidiary of a U.S. company wishes to remit 10,000 Swiss francs to the United States and the current rate of exchange is one Swiss franc equals $0.25, the remittance will be converted into 2,500 dollars. The computation is

$$\text{Sfr } 10,000 \times 0.25 \text{ dollar equivalent of Sfr } 1 = \$2,500.$$

If $1,200 U.S. dollars are to be remitted to Switzerland when the current exchange rate is Sfr 1 = $0.24, the remittance will be converted as follows:

$$\$1,200 \div 0.24 \text{ dollar equivalent of Sfr } 1 = \text{Sfr } 5,000.$$

If a monetary claim receivable or payable in a foreign currency is settled at a later date, there may be an *exchange gain or loss* resulting from the change in value of the foreign currency in the domestic currency.

Example 14   Suppose that a U.S. merchant bought merchandise from a Swiss manufacturer for 1,000 Swiss francs on June 1, when the exchange rate was Sfr 1 = $0.25. The debt was paid on July 2, when the exchange rate was Sfr 1 = $0.24. On June 1 the account payable was equivalent to $250, but it was settled for $240. There is an *exchange gain* of $10.

Exchange gains and losses are a normal risk of the business, and are reported as a component of *income before extraordinary items.*

Translating Foreign Accounts into Domestic Currency

If the accounts of a foreign branch or subsidiary are stated in the foreign currency, they must be *translated*, or expressed in the equivalent amount of domestic currency, in order to prepare combined or consolidated statements. The general principles for translating foreign accounts are

(1) *Financial items* should be translated by using the *current* exchange rate prevailing on the date of the financial position statement.

(2) *All other accounts* should be translated at the *historical* rates of exchange in effect when the items in the accounts originated.[1]

Financial items consist of the foreign currency and both long- and short-term *claims* to receive or pay a *fixed number* of foreign currency units. Examples are

Cash	Accounts Payable
Accounts Receivable	Notes Payable
Notes Receivable	Bonds Payable

The dollar equivalent of such financial assets and liabilities is *affected immediately* by changes in the rate of exchange. If the local currency declines in relation to the U.S. dollar, financial assets in local currency will provide fewer dollars on conversion. Furthermore, debts payable in the local currency can be satisfied with fewer dollars.

Physical assets of the foreign entity, consisting of inventories and fixed assets, are usually not affected by fluctuations in the rate of exchange. A substantial decline in the value of a foreign currency unit in relation to the dollar usually results from inflation in the foreign country. Consequently, prices in the foreign country may be expected to rise, including the prices of the inventories and the services of the fixed assets. For this reason such physical assets should be translated at the historical rate when the foreign entity acquired them.

If a *nonfinancial account* contains only one or a few items, each component can be translated at the rate of exchange that existed at the date of the transaction.

---

[1] Some accounting authorities advocate translating *current accounts* at the current rate of exchange, and *noncurrent accounts* at the *historical rate*. The method stated above seems preferable.

Example 15　　A foreign subsidiary's Equipment account consisted of the following debits:

July 5, 1963............... 1,000 pounds (exchange rate, 1 pound = $2.00)
March 1, 1970.......... 1,000 pounds (exchange rate, 1 pound = $1.80)
　　Balance................ 2,000 pounds

At what value should the Equipment be shown in a consolidated statement expressed in U.S. dollars?

Solution　　　　　　　　　　$2,000 + $1,800 = $3,800.

If there are many components of a nonfinancial account, an *average of the exchange rates* during the period when the transactions originated can be used in translating the account balance.

Example 16　　The Sales Revenue balance of the foreign subsidiary was 400,000 pounds, consisting of 250 entries for daily sales totals. The average exchange rate during the year was 1 pound = $1.84. Sales should be translated at $1.84 × 400,000, or $736,000.

Special Problems in Translating Accounts

Reciprocal account balances between the domestic and the foreign entity can be translated by *substituting* the domestic account balance for its foreign reciprocal. Thus the domestic currency balance of Merchandise Shipments to Branch should be substituted for the foreign currency balance of Merchandise Shipments from Home Office.

Retained income of the foreign subsidiary should be translated by using the rates which apply to each of its components. The domestic currency balance of retained income used in the preceding year's financial statements is substituted for the foreign subsidiary's beginning retained income balance. Dividends, revenue, and expense for the current year are translated at the historical rates which apply to each.

Depreciation and *accumulated depreciation* on fixed assets are translated by multiplying the appropriate depreciation percentages by the cost of the fixed assets, translated at the historical rates of exchange existing when each component was acquired.

Capital stock of the foreign subsidiary is translated at the rate of exchange prevailing when the parent acquired the stock.

When the trial balance of the foreign branch or subsidiary has been translated into domestic currency by using the various recommended rates of exchange, it is unlikely that the debits will equal the credits. The difference is an Exchange Adjustment. If a debit is needed to balance the translated trial balance, there is an Exchange Loss. If a credit is required, it is an Exchange Gain.

Conservative accounting practice has been to treat the *exchange losses* as *realized* by reporting them as deductions in the current income statement, but to treat the *exchange gains* as *unrealized*. Exchange gains under this practice are carried forward as a financial position statement item. It seems more defensible to consider both exchange gains and losses to be unrealized, and to report neither in the income statement under ordinary circumstances.

FINANCIAL REPORTING FOR DIVERSIFIED COMPANIES

Diversified Companies, or Conglomerates

In the past businesses have often expanded by *horizontal* or *vertical* acquisitions, but in recent years an increasing number of businesses have grown by *diversification*, or *conglomerate merger*.

Growth through horizontal or vertical acquisition results in an entity whose activities are highly integrated and concentrated in the production and distribution of a relatively narrow range of products. By contrast, a conglomerate merger results in an entity whose production and distribution activities may be unrelated and spread over many diverse products and services.

Example 17   A textile manufacturer may expand *horizontally* by acquiring the facilities of competing textile manufacturers. It may expand *vertically* by acquiring facilities for manufacturing cellulose as a source of synthetic fibers, or by acquiring facilities for manufacturing, wholesaling, and retailing finished garments. The same textile manufacturer may expand through *conglomerate merger* by acquiring affiliates in diverse markets such as the manufacture of office equipment, soft drinks, cosmetics, and fabricated steel.

Two Definitions of Accounting Objectives

There are two different views as to the appropriate methods of preparing financial statements for conglomerate businesses:

(1) The *total system reporting* view is that the conglomerate organization should be considered in its entirety. By tradition, the accounting entity includes all economic activity in which the investment of a dominant central ownership interest is used. According to this view, only combined or consolidated financial statements for the *entity as a whole* present fairly the pertinent information of its financial position and operating results.

(2) The *segmental reporting* view is that traditional methods of preparing combined or consolidated financial statements for the entity as a whole do not provide information vitally needed for business decision making. Effective decisions require information for evaluating business results by *operating segments*, such as industry grouping, product line, geographical market, or functional division of the entity. The aim is to disclose the extent to which each business segment contributes to the total revenues and income of the entity. Gross margins and the amounts of capital and overhead charges assigned to each segment may be disclosed.

Should Segment Reporting Be Required?

The main issue in reporting on conglomerate companies to outside financial statement users is whether it is necessary or desirable to disclose business results by entity segments. *Arguments in favor* of such disclosure are

(1) When an entity diversifies its operations into unrelated markets it loses identification with a particular industry. The combined or consolidated financial statements can no longer be meaningfully compared with statements of other firms in the industry, or with financial statistics of the total industry.

(2) The combined or consolidated statements of a highly diversified firm may offset unfavorable trends in some important segments of the firm with favorable results from uncertain and less important segments. The statements may therefore be misleading in efforts to evaluate management effectiveness.

Example 18   The Dome Corporation had diversified sales of $1 billion and net income of $300 million in 1972. In 1973, sales increased to $1.1 billion and net income increased to $350 million. Not disclosed was the fact that a division which specializes in industrial construction for foreign corporations had an unusually good performance in 1973, accounting for an increase of $200 million in consolidated sales and an increase of $80 million in consolidated net income. If this fact were disclosed, it would be clear that both sales and net income from the traditional operations of the business had declined significantly from 1972 to 1973.

(3) From the standpoint of antitrust policy, the combined or consolidated statements of a highly diversified business do not disclose the extent to which profits from markets in which the business has a dominant position might be used to subsidize unfair trade practices in other markets.

Arguments opposing reporting by segments are

(1) Disclosure of financial data by business segments could lead to adverse exploitation of the reporting company by its competitors.

(2) Segmental reporting would require complex and subjective allocations of common overhead costs and capital investments. These allocations could cause the statements to be misleading to persons who are not informed on the nature of the firm's internal operations.

(3) No generally accepted standards exist for making the required accounting allocations.

The issue of whether segmental reports should be required is likely to be settled by publishing more detailed information, although final resolution of the problem has not yet occurred.

Summary   For management purposes it may be desirable to maintain separate sets of accounts and reports for a home office and a branch, even though they are legally one entity. *Reciprocal accounts* showing receivable-payable relationships, interdivisional operating transactions, and interdivisional markups in ending inventory should be *eliminated* in preparing *combined statements* of the home office and the branch.

Consolidated statements may be desirable when a unified economic organization is operated through the legal form of more than one corporation. Where a dominant central financial interest exists, accompanied by administrative control, consolidated financial statements of the economic entity are ordinarily useful. In preparing consolidated statements the reciprocal elements in the stockholders' equity accounts of the subsidiary and the parent's Investment in Stock of Subsidiary should be eliminated. Eliminations should also be made of other reciprocal pairs of accounts in the financial statements of the separate entities and of unrealized intercompany markups.

Combined and consolidated statements involving a domestic entity and a foreign branch or subsidiary may be desirable in the absence of exchange restrictions or political upheavals in the foreign country. The trial balance of the foreign entity must be translated into domestic currency by the use of appropriate exchange rates.

A business combination may be effected as a purchase or a pooling of interests. If it is a purchase, a new basis of accountability for assets arises. If it is a pooling, the assets and retained income of the pooled companies are added together and the existing basis of accountability is continued.

Financial reporting for diversified companies is in a state of flux. Some authorities advocate reporting to outside users on the results of business segments, while others maintain that such reporting would be detrimental.

Discussion Questions and Problems

15-1

a. The terms "combined" and "consolidated" have different meanings when used in reference to financial statements. Explain the difference.

b. Do *combined statements* or *consolidated statements* take the place of the financial statements of the separate organizational units? Why?

15-2

a. Under what conditions should the combination of two business entities be accounted for as the *purchase* of one by the other?

b. Under what conditions should the combination of two business entities be accounted for as a *pooling of interests?*

c. Are there any circumstances under which *consolidated* financial statements would be used to account for a *pooling of interests?* Explain.

15-3

a. What is the effect of the type of consideration given for acquired stock in determining whether a business combination is a purchase or a pooling?

b. How are the assets acquired measured by the resulting entity if the combination is a purchase? A pooling?

c. How is the retained income of the resulting entity at the date of combination measured if the combination is a purchase? A pooling?

15-4   In January 1973 the Axil Company was formed to acquire the net assets of Onel Company and Arnold Company. At the time of acquisition Onel Company had net assets of $250,000 (book value), sales of $1.5 million a year, and net income of $22,000 a year, while Arnold Company had net assets of $280,000 (book value), annual sales of $1.3 million, and net income of $30,000. Cash of $100,000 and $300,000 of Axil Company's 8 per cent first mortgage bonds were given in exchange for the net assets of Arnold Company. Ten thousand shares of Axil Company's $20-par value common stock were issued in exchange for the net assets of Onel Company. No other stock of Axil Company was issued.

a. Should this combination be accounted for as a *purchase* or a *pooling of interests?* Explain.

b. What differences would appear in Axil Company's subsequent financial statements under the purchase and the pooling methods of accounting?

15-5   On December 31, 1973, Rola, Inc. had net assets with book value of $480,000 and common stock of 20,000 shares issued and outstanding. On January 1, 1974, 5,000 additional common stock shares were issued for all the outstanding stock of Alto, Inc., whose books showed net assets of $96,000.

May this combination be accounted for as a *pooling of interests?* Explain, listing the most important assumptions required for your answer.

15-6

a. What is meant by *reciprocal* accounts?

b. Give three examples of reciprocal pairs of financial position accounts and three examples of reciprocal pairs of income statement accounts as related to divisions of a decentralized business.

c. Give an example of a reciprocal pair of accounts particularly related to accounting for a home office and its branch.

d. Give an example of a set of reciprocal accounts which are particularly related to accounting for a parent and its subsidiary.

15-7

a. Why must *reciprocal accounts* be eliminated in preparing *combined* or *consolidated* financial statements?

b. Give an example of a situation in home office-branch accounting which requires an eliminating entry, and show the eliminating entry.

c. Give an example of a situation in parent-subsidiary accounting which requires an eliminating entry, and show the eliminating entry.

d. Give examples of two situations in parent-subsidiary accounting in which a non-reciprocal element remains in certain accounts after eliminating entries have been applied. What is the nature of the nonreciprocal elements?

15-8

a. On December 30, 1973, Company *A* mailed a check for $500 to unrelated Company *B* in settlement of an account payable. Company *B* received the check on January 2, 1974. Both companies use the calendar year as their accounting period. How would these facts be shown in the financial statements of each company for 1973?

b. On December 30, 1973, Home Office *C* mailed a check for $500 to Branch *B* in settlement of an account payable. The branch received the check on January 2, 1974. Both companies use the calendar year as their accounting period. How would these facts be shown in the combined financial statements for 1973?

15-9

a. Why might a home office wish to add a markup to the cost of goods which it ships to its branch for sale?

b. What adjustment is needed in preparing combined financial statements if some of the goods shipped by the home office to the branch at a markup are on hand in the branch's ending inventory? What is the purpose of this adjustment?

c. Does this same type of situation apply to the dealings of a parent and its subsidiary company? Explain.

15-10   Home Office E reported a net income of $24,000 in its separate financial statements for 1973, and Branch F reported a net income of $10,000. Combined financial statements for the home office and branch reported a net income of $18,000 for the year. Was an error made? Explain.

15-11

a. What two basic conditions must be met before it is appropriate to prepare consolidated financial statements?

b. Would it be proper to prepare consolidated statements of Companies P, S, and T if Company P owned 75 per cent of the common stock of Company S and Company S owned 90 per cent of the stock of Company T? Explain.

c. Would it be proper to prepare consolidated statements of Companies U, V, and W if Company U owned 80 per cent of Company V and 20 per cent of Company W, and Company V also owned 60 per cent of Company W? Explain.

d. Would it be proper to prepare consolidated financial statements of Companies A and B if A owns 100 per cent of the outstanding bonds of B and 40 per cent of its common stock? Explain.

e. Would it be proper to prepare consolidated statements of Companies C and D if C owns 90 per cent of the common stock of D, but C's fiscal year ends on June 30 and D's on December 31?

15-12

a. Would it be proper to prepare consolidated statements of Companies E and F if E manufactures steel and F mines iron ore for sale to E? Company E owns 80 per cent of company F's stock.

b. Investment Company I owns 60 per cent of the common stock of Industrial Company J, which it acquired over the years as a good source of dividend income and growth in value. Company I's management does not participate actively in the management of Company J. Should consolidated statements be prepared? Explain.

c. Manufacturing Company M owns 100 per cent of the common stock of Finance Company N that was organized to finance retail sales of Company M's product. Should consolidated statements be prepared? Explain.

15-13   Why may the parent's cost of an investment in the stock of a subsidiary (1) exceed and (2) be less than the corresponding stockholders' equity of the subsidiary at the date of acquisition? What procedures should be followed, and how should the excess or deficiency be reported in the consolidated financial statements?

15-14

a. Why do you suppose the minority interest in the net income of a subsidiary is deducted as a single sum on the consolidated income statement, rather than being deducted from each consolidated revenue and expense amount?

b. Why do you suppose the minority interest in a subsidiary is shown as a single amount in the consolidated financial position statement, rather than being allocated as reductions of each consolidated asset and liability account?

15-15

a. Under what types of circumstances is a domestic home office not justified in preparing combined statements including its foreign branch?

b. When a foreign subsidiary company is excluded from the consolidation, what types of information must be presented in the consolidated statements?

15-16   What exchange rate should be used in translating each of the following accounts of a foreign branch into its domestic currency equivalent?

(1) Cash
(2) Accounts Receivable
(3) Merchandise Inventory, End of Year
(4) Home Office Current
(5) Sales Revenue
(6) Equipment
(7) Long-Term Notes Payable
(8) Merchandise Shipments from Home Office
(9) Purchases (in foreign country)
(10) Equipment—Accumulated Depreciation

15-17

a. How do exchange gains or losses occur when a domestic company has a subsidiary in a foreign country?
b. How should exchange gains and losses be shown in consolidated financial statements?

15-18

a. What are the characteristics of a *conglomerate merger*?
b. How does a conglomerate merger differ from expansion by *vertical* or *horizontal* acquisition?

15-19

a. Distinguish between the *segmental* and *total system reporting* approaches to conglomerate reporting.
b. List the major arguments for and against segmental reporting.

15-20   Colley Corp. acquired all the stock of Founder, Inc. at a time when their condensed financial position statements were as follows:

	Colley Corp.	Founder, Inc.
Current assets..	$ 68,000	$ 42,000
Property, plant, and equipment (net).............	186,000	172,000
Total assets...	254,000	214,000
Current liabilities......................................	$ 39,000	$ 31,000
Long-term liabilities..................................	66,000	54,000
Capital stock...	100,000	75,000
Retained income.......................................	49,000	54,000
Total equities.......................................	254,000	214,000

Colley paid cash to settle all Founder, Inc.'s current liabilities and issued 96,000 shares of its own capital stock (60 per cent of the amount previously outstanding) in exchange for Founder's capital stock. The stock issued had a fair market value of $2 a share.

Required   a. Assume that the combination is a *purchase* and present a condensed financial position statement of the surviving company.
b. Assume that the combination is a *pooling of interests* and present a condensed financial position statement of the surviving company.
c. List the major assumptions required to justify the treatments in parts a and b.

15-21   Walsh Mfg. Co. has a warehouse and sales office at its home office and a branch sales office in another city. Merchandise for sale is shipped to the branch from the home office warehouse, and the branch is billed at 20 per cent above the total of manufacturing cost. The markup is to place the branch purchase costs on a par with those of its competition.

Trial balances on December 31, 1973, the close of the first year of branch operations, are given below. On this date merchandise inventory of the home office had a cost of $60,000, and the inventory at the branch had a cost to the branch of $30,000.

	Trial Balances, Dec. 31, 1973			
	Home Office		Branch	
	Debits	Credits	Debits	Credits
Cash...	$ 20,000		$ 5,000	
Accounts receivable.........................	25,000		15,000	
Merchandise inventory, Dec. 31, 1972.....	70,000			
Property, plant, and equipment............	120,000			
—Accumulated depreciation................		$ 60,000		
Branch current...............................	57,000			
Inventory shipments from home office.....				90,000
Purchases....................................	200,000			
Other expenses...............................	35,000		17,000	
Sales revenue.................................		220,000		$ 70,000
Inventory shipments to branch—cost......		75,000		
Inventory shipments to branch—unrealized markup.........................		15,000		
Capital stock.................................		125,000		
Retained income, December 31, 1972.....		32,000		
Home office current..........................				57,000
Totals......................................	$527,000	$527,000	$127,000	$127,000

Required   Prepare a combined trial balance, giving effect to all adjustments and eliminations that are necessary.

15-22   Panco, Inc. owned 80 per cent of the common stock of the Schultz Corporation. Condensed income statement data of the two companies for 1973 were

	Panco, Inc.	Schultz Corp.
Sales revenue..	$500,000	$200,000
Cost of goods sold expense...........................	300,000	140,000
Gross margin.......................................	200,000	60,000
Other expenses......................................	150,000	40,000
Net income..	50,000	20,000

During 1973 Panco sold goods to Schultz for $100,000, priced at its regular rate of markup. One-fourth of these goods were on hand in Schultz's ending inventory. On December 31, 1973, Schultz sold surplus equipment to Panco for $30,000. It was carried on Schultz's books before the sale at cost, $50,000, less accumulated depreciation of $35,000. Its estimated remaining useful life on the date of sale was five years.

Required   a. Compute the net income of each company on a consolidated basis.

b. How much of the total net income on a consolidated basis applies to the controlling interest? To the minority interest?

15-23   The Pitt Company bought 800 of the shares of $100-par value capital stock of the Anton Company for $120,000 on the date of the Anton Company's formation, January 1, 1973. The remaining 200 shares were issued to the public at a price of $150 a share. During 1973 Pitt earned a net income of $60,000 on its own operations (excluding investment income) which increased its Retained Income balance to $220,000 on December 31, 1973. Anton Company earned a net income of $15,000 and paid a cash dividend of $8,000 on December 18, 1973.

Required   Compute the following:

a. The nonreciprocal element in Investment in Stock of Anton Company on the parent's books.

b. The nonreciprocal amount in Anton's stockholders' equity accounts on January 1, 1973, immediately after the capital stock had been issued. What was the nature of this nonreciprocal element?

c. The net income of Pitt for 1973 as shown on its separate company books.

d. The consolidated net income (controlling interest) for 1973.

e. The minority interest on December 31, 1973.

15-24   Alto, Inc. acquired 90 per cent of the common stock of Stan Corp. from the public on January 1, 1973, paying $210,000. On that date Stan Corp. had the following stockholders' equity balances:

Capital stock, $10 par value.....................................	$200,000
Paid-in capital in excess of par value........................	20,000
Retained income...	40,000

During the next three years the two companies earned income and paid dividends as follows:

	1973	1974	1975
Net income (loss):			
Alto, Inc..................................	$80,000	$60,000	($20,000)
Stan Corp.	30,000	(20,000)	40,000
Dividends paid:			
Alto, Inc..................................	20,000	20,000	0
Stan Corp.	0	0	16,000

Required   a. What is the nature of the nonreciprocal element in Investment in Stock of Stan Corp.? The amount? What further information is needed?

b. What is the nature of the nonreciprocal element in the stockholders' equity accounts of Stan Corp. on January 1, 1973? What are the amounts?

c. Compute consolidated net income (controlling interest) for 1973, 1974, and 1975.

d. If Alto's retained income was $100,000 on January 1, 1973, compute its amount at the ends of 1973, 1974, and 1975.

e. Compute the minority interest on December 31, 1975. Explain the reason for the change.

15-25   The Pictorial Corp. purchased 18,000 common shares of the Scenic Company on the market for $150,000 on January 1, 1973. The excess of the price paid over the related book value of the subsidiary's common stock equity was in recognition of the fact that the land owned by the subsidiary was undervalued.

The following accounts are taken from the trial balances of the two companies at December 31, 1973:

	Pictorial Corp.	*Scenic Corp.*
Investment in stock of subsidiary.....................	$150,000	
Property, plant, and equipment.....................	180,000	$120,000
Property, plant, and equipment—accumulated depreciation.......................................	60,000	30,000
Capital stock, no-par value, Scenic (20,000 shares outstanding).....................................		100,000
Retained income, Jan. 1, 1973........................	40,000	10,000

Required   Explain how the excess of the price paid over the related book value would be treated in the consolidated financial statements on January 1, 1973.

15-26   The Potomac Corp. acquired 80 per cent of the outstanding stock of Susquehanna, Inc. from the public on January 1, 1970, paying $220,000 cash. The stockholders' equity of the subsidiary company on that date included Capital Stock of $150,000 and Retained Income of $100,000. The accompanying balances are taken from the trial balances at the end of 1973. Both companies use perpetual inventory systems.

During 1973 Susquehanna sold merchandise which had cost $80,000 to Potomac for $120,000. The ending inventory of Potomac included some of these goods at $36,000, the cost to Potomac. Potomac also sold merchandise costing $40,000 to Susquehanna for $65,000 during 1973, but none of this merchandise was included in the ending inventory. However, Susquehanna had paid in cash only $50,000 of the invoice price. Potomac had paid for all of its purchases from Susquehanna.

	Trial Balances	
Debits	*Potomac Corp.*	*Susquehanna, Inc.*
Accounts receivable.............................	$ 50,000	$ 55,000
Merchandise inventory.........................	80,000	90,000
Investment in stock of subsidiary............	220,000	
Cost of goods sold expense....................	210,000	120,000
Accounts payable...............................	40,000	30,000
Capital stock....................................	200,000	150,000
Retained income, Jan. 1, 1973..............	87,000	140,000
Sales revenue...................................	300,000	180,000

Required   a. At what amount should inventory be reported in the year-end consolidated statement?

        b. What is the nonreciprocal component of the Investment in Stock account, and how would you dispose of it?

        c. What other eliminating entries are needed on the basis of the information given?

Cases   **15-1**   **Gulf Oil Corporation.** The following items appeared in the footnotes to the Gulf Oil Corporation 1970 Annual Report:

Note 1—Principles of Consolidation

The accounts of Gulf Oil Corporation and all subsidiary companies more than 50% owned are included in the consolidated financial statements except for those engaged in real estate activities. Investments in 50% owned companies and in real estate subsidiaries are stated on an equity basis. The change to the equity basis in 1970 for real estate subsidiaries had no effect on either net income or net assets. Investments in less than 50% owned companies and other investments are stated at cost.

Balances and transactions in foreign currencies have been translated to United States dollars as follows: long-term investments and properties—at rates current on dates of acquisition; accumulated depreciation, depletion and amortization and related provisions against income—on basis of dollar value of the related assets; all other assets and liabilities—at rates current at end of period; and operating income and other expenses—at average monthly rates.

At December 31, 1970 and 1969, consolidated net assets related to operations in the Western Hemisphere amount to $4,123 million and $4,021 million, respectively, and in the Eastern Hemisphere to $1,155 million and $1,019 million, respectively. Consolidated net income for 1970 and 1969 includes amounts attributable to operations in the Western Hemisphere of $433 million and $469 million, respectively, and in the Eastern Hemisphere of $117 million and $142 million, respectively."

Note 13—Bolivia

On October 17, 1969 Gulf's business and assets in Bolivia were seized by the Bolivian government.

In September, 1970 the corporation reached agreement with the Bolivian government with respect to compensating Gulf for its properties in Bolivia seized by that government. The amount of indemnification was established by Supreme Decree on September 10, 1970 and is to be paid without interest over a period of not more than twenty years and is contingent upon exportation of sufficient hydrocarbons from certain fields within that period.

The amounts receivable under the terms of the indemnification decree and other arrangements have been recorded in the 1970 accounts, the effect of which was the recovery of the consolidated net book value of the Bolivian assets plus certain other assets which had been previously written off in the consolidated accounts. The effect of the settlement on net income was not material.

Required
a. What justification can you see for not including subsidiaries engaged in real estate activities in the consolidated statements?
b. Under the "equity basis" the investment account is increased to reflect the parent's share of the subsidiary's net increase in retained income since the stock was acquired, and decreased to show its share of losses. The corresponding credit for share of increase and debit for share of loss are reflected in consolidated net income. Compare, using summary journal entries, the method used in accounting for 50%-owned companies with that used for less-than-50%-owned companies. What justification can you see for the different accounting treatment?
c. Do you agree with the corporation's method of translating foreign accounts? Explain.
d. How would you recommend recording the seizure of Gulf's business assets by Bolivia in 1969? Where should this information appear in the 1969 financial statements?

15-2   Marshall Field & Company. Early in 1970 The Halle Brothers Company was merged into a subsidiary of Marshall Field & Company. Halle had nine stores and 1969 sales of about $70,000,000.

The following two items appeared in Notes to Financial Statements in Marshall Field's 1970 Annual Report:

(1) On November 30, 1970, the Company, through a subsidiary, acquired all of the outstanding common and preferred shares of The Halle Brothers Company in exchange for the following shares of Marshall Field & Company:

> 397,133 common shares
> 21,719 Series A preferred shares
> 21,000 Series B preferred shares

This merger has been accounted for as a purchase. The shares issued have been recorded at their fair market value of $9,045,690 on June 24, 1970, the date that an agreement in principle was reached. The par value of $1 per share has been credited to the respective capital stock accounts and the balance of the $9,045,690 purchase price to paid-in surplus. Assets and liabilities of Halle are reflected at their fair value as determined by the purchase price. The accompanying consolidated financial statements include the results of operations of Halle for the two months ended January 31, 1971 and its assets and liabilities as of that date.

(5) On May 15, 1970, in accordance with the Agreement and Plan of Merger changing the Company's state of incorporation from Illinois to Delaware as approved by stockholders on May 6, 1970, all of the 8,757,838 issued common shares were converted from no par value to a par value of $1 per share and the excess of stated value over par value in the amount of $13,735,920 was transferred from the common stock account to paid-in surplus.

The report contained the following statement of paid-in surplus.

	Fiscal Year Ended	
	January 31, 1971	January 31, 1970
PAID-IN SURPLUS		
Balance at beginning of year.	$ 8,904,669	$ 8,947,594
Excess of fair market value over par value of stock issued in acquisition	8,605,838	—
Excess of stated value over par value of common stock converted from no par value to par value	13,735,920	—
Excess of cost over par value of Series A and B preferred stock purchased and retired	(30,991)	—
Expenses of poolings of interests	—	(42,925)
Balance at end of year	$31,215,436	$ 8,904,669

The following is an excerpt from the Consolidated Balance Sheet.

STOCKHOLDERS' EQUITY

Preferred Stock—
    Authorized 1,000,000 shares of $1 par value, issuable
        in series; issued at par value:
        Series A, $2.40 cumulative; $52 per share
            redemption and liquidation value (aggregate $1,128,712); 21,706 shares (Note 1) $ 21,706 $ —

Series B, $3.00 cumulative; $52 per share redemption and liquidation value (aggregate $1,060,800); 20,400 shares (Note 1)	20,400	—
Common Stock— Authorized 20,000,000 shares of $1 par value; 9,154,971 shares issued at January 31, 1971, at par value (Notes 1 and 5)......................	9,154,971	22,493,758
Paid-in surplus..	31,215,436	8,904,669

Required

a. Debiting "Assets," reconstruct the entry from the consolidation's standpoint for the purchase of Halle.

b. How was the total credit to paid-in capital accounts probably determined in part a?

c. What became of the retained income of Halle in the combination, from the point of view of the consolidated company?

d. Would the assets acquired from Halle be reported on the consolidated statements at their historical values to Halle or on another basis? Explain.

15-3   Eastman Kodak Company. The following is an excerpt from the note on "Principles of Consolidation" in the 1969 Annual Report of Eastman Kodak Company:

> The financial statements of subsidiaries operating outside the U.S. are translated into U.S. dollar equivalents generally at official exchange rates applied as follows:
>
> 1. Net current assets, except inventories, and long-term debt at fiscal year-end rates.
>
> 2. Inventories, properties and accumulated depreciation, and deferred income taxes at rates applicable to the time of acquisition or deferment. (In prior years, inventories were translated at fiscal year-end rates; this change did not affect 1969 net earnings significantly.)
>
> 3. Net earnings at average rates with dollar equivalents adjusted for exchange differences resulting from the foregoing procedures.

Required

a. Do you think the change in the method of translating inventories was justified? Why?

b. Do you agree with translating deferred income taxes at exchange rates applicable to the time of deferment? Why? Does this imply that deferred income taxes is a monetary or a nonmonetary account?

c. Assume that a significant amount of depreciation is deducted in the income statement other than as a component of inventories. Would you then agree with the method used for translating net earnings? Why?

chapter 16

Accounting for the Effects of Changing Prices

Purpose of Chapter

In determining the *income* of a business for a time period, accounting measures the period's *revenues* and matches the related expenses against them. In a desire for *objective* measurement, *exchange prices* established in *completed transactions* are used as the *basis of accounting* for the period's revenues and expenses. The purpose of making these measurements is to report operating results of past periods to aid in evaluating management effectiveness and in predicting the results of future periods.

By using exchange prices of completed transactions in measuring and reporting business income accounting implicitly *assumes that the monetary unit has an unchanged significance* as a unit of exchange value from one time to another. To the extent that this assumption is not true, comparison of income measurements made in different accounting periods may not yield reliable results.

This chapter examines some of the problems in interpreting accounting data which result from changes of prices in general, as well as from changes in the prices of specific elements reflected in the financial statements. It also considers some widely advocated solutions to these problems.

Impact of Changing Price Levels on the Significance of Accounting Measurements

In times of relatively *stable* economic conditions, market price data are likely to have approximately the same significance from one period to another. Accounting measurements at different times can then be compared with reasonably reliable results. In modern history there have been *few* periods of such stable conditions, and *many* periods in which major adjustments in economic conditions have caused significant changes in *general price levels*, and thus in the comparative significance of price data of different times.

The *general price level* refers to the *total of the prices of a given quantity of goods and services* at a given time. Price totals of this collection of goods and services at different times are compared by computing their percentage relationship, or *price index*, in comparison with the price total of a base year. The price index of the *base year* equals 100; total prices of other years are stated as a percentage of this base.

More often than not in recent history the price levels have *increased*, although there have been some instances of major price-level declines—notably the depression of the early 1930s. The following are selected indexes from the Consumer Price Index, prepared by the U.S. Bureau of Labor Statistics. In this series the index for 1967, the base year, is 100.

Year	Consumer Price Index
1933	38.8
1945	53.9
1967	100.0
1969	109.8

This index shows that prices increased about 10 per cent from 1967 to 1969, and that prices in general more than doubled from 1945 to 1969. To express it another way, a dollar in 1969 would buy less than half as much as would a dollar in 1945.

In many other countries, notably France, Germany, Italy, and Brazil, the change in the general price level in modern times has been much more extensive.

The basis of accounting for a firm's assets is *not usually changed* when general price levels change, unless the change is of major proportions. Thus, the costs of long-lived assets are expressed in dollars of *mixed purchasing power*. Assets acquired in one year and recorded in terms of the then current dollars are shown in the same accounts, and added to the purchase prices, of similar assets acquired at other times in exchange for dollars of different monetary significance. Then in computing business income these costs, which are stated in terms of *mixed* purchasing power per dollar, are deducted from revenues expressed in monetary units of relatively *current* purchasing power. When this happens income becomes an ambiguous and less useful measure of business progress, unless the amount of *gain or loss* that results from purchasing power changes is reported.

Under changing price levels, when goods bought in one year are sold in the following year their money costs are often matched with revenues expressed in terms of a different price level. The lack of comparability is especially great when expenses include cost expirations from *long-lived assets*, such as plant and equipment. Example 1 illustrates this situation.

Example 1   In 1971 a business paid $5,000 for a machine which was expected to have a useful life of five years. In 1973, when the general price level and the prices of similar machines had both doubled, the business rented the machine to a customer for one year for $2,200 cash. What is the 1973 income as measured by conventional accounting methods, and what is the income in terms of dollars of the same purchasing power?

Solution   (a) A *conventional income statement* would summarize the 1973 results as follows:

Revenue	$2,200
Deduct depreciation ($\frac{1}{5}$ of original cost)	1,000
Net income	$1,200

Revenue is expressed in 1973 dollars, depreciation in 1971 dollars, and net income in a mixture of the two.

(b) An income statement expressed in dollars of the *same general purchasing power (common dollars)* would show

Revenue	$2,200
Deduct common-dollar depreciation ($\frac{1}{5}$ of 200% of original cost)	2,000
Common-dollar net income	$ 200

The original cost of the machine in terms of 1971 dollars is restated in the 1973 dollar cost equivalent by multiplying it by 200/100, the ratio of the general price index of 1973 to that of 1971.

The analysis in Example 1 shows that the $1,200 net income reported by conventional accounting procedures includes an *illusory gain* of $1,000, resulting from the rise in the general price level since the machine was acquired. The business is parting with one-fifth of the machine's stock of service benefits, which had a cost of $2,000 in terms of 1973 purchasing power. Revenue in 1973 must be $2,000 in order to recover the purchasing power originally expended for one year's services of the machine.

The lack of comparability of financial statements which results from changing price levels is not a new phenomenon, nor is it confined to rising prices alone. Equally serious misrepresentation of business results may occur during periods of price *decline*.

In view of the frequent and sometimes serious instability in the purchasing power of the monetary unit, those who prepare and those who use accounting reports have been concerned with two questions:

(1) Is the magnitude of the change in the value of the monetary unit great enough to justify *recognizing the change* in the accounts?

(2) If so, *how* can the accounting recognition best be accomplished?

Specific Price Movements Versus General
Price Movements

Before attempting to answer these questions, it is well to distinguish between two types of price movements: *general and specific*. *General price-level changes*, as previously explained, are price movements of an aggregate quantity of various types of goods and services. *Specific price changes* are movements in the price of particular commodities or services. For example, the price level as reflected by the Consumers' Price Index may increase during a given month even though the price of beef (a specific price which is included in the aggregate) declines. The specific prices of other commodities which are included in the total must increase more than enough to offset the reduced price of beef.

Movements in the specific prices of business assets are quite common.

Example 2   A retail business purchased 100 units of Article X for $20 each on November 1, 1973, expecting to sell them for $30 each. On December 31, 1973, the articles were still in the inventory. It was then expected that they could be sold for $36 each. The replacement cost of each unit was $24 on December 31. At what amount should the inventory be reported in the December 31, 1973, financial position statement? (There has been no change in the general price level.)

Solution   Under the realization concept, the inventory would continue to be measured at $20 a unit (a total of $2,000) on December 31. The apparent increase in value is not included in the accounts until it is confirmed by sale.

In Example 2 there has been a specific price increase of $4 a unit, or $400 in total, while the inventory items have been owned. The business is apparently better off as a result, but the evidence is not considered to be convincing enough to warrant recording the gain in the accounts. Instead, the *gain* will be reported when it is *realized* by sale.

Example 3   Continuing Example 2, assume that the inventory is sold early in January, 1974 for $36 a unit. How is the sale reported?

Solution
Sales revenue... $3,600
Deduct cost of goods sold expense................................ 2,000
Gross margin... $1,600

Operating Versus Holding Gains

The $1,600 reported as gross margin in Example 3 under conventional accounting procedures may be analyzed into two parts:

(1) An *operating gain* of $1,200. This is the amount by which current sales revenue of $3,600 exceeds the current replacement cost of the inventory, $2,400 (computed by multiplying 100 units by $24).

(2) A *holding gain* of $400 which results from the increased value of these inventory items, in terms of purchase prices, while they have been owned. The holding

gain is computed by subtracting the $2,000 historical cost of the inventory from its current replacement cost of $2,400. Both have been *realized* by sale.

Both the *operating* and the *holding gain* in Example 3 are *real*. Since there was no change in the general price level in this illustration, both are gains in value in terms of common dollars.

Illusory Gains

To the extent that there has been an increase in the *general price level* while an asset has been owned, there has been an *illusory gain*. An *illusory loss* occurs when the general price level declines. Example 4 shows how gross margin might be analyzed if the general price level has increased since the item sold was purchased.

Example 4

The 100 inventory items were bought for $20 each when the general price index was 100. Later they were sold for $36 each when their replacement cost was $24 per unit and the general price index was 105. Of what elements does the $1,600 gross margin, reported by conventional accounting, consist?

Solution

Gross margin consists of three components:

(1) An *illusory gain* of.. $ 100
   (This is the amount necessary to adjust the historical cost of the inventory for the change in the price level—that is, 5% of $2,000.)

(2) A *holding gain* of 300
   (This is the amount by which the specific price increase in the replacement cost of inventory exceeds the adjustment for the change in the general price level: that is, $400 — 5% of $2,000.)

(3) An *operating gain* of... 1,200
   (This is the amount by which revenue exceeds the current replacement cost of the inventory—that is, $3,600 — $2,400.)

Total, the *gross margin* reported by accounting.................... $1,600

Formulas for analyzing the components of accounting income may be stated as follows:

Accounting income = Revenue — Expense, both stated in historical dollars.

Illusory gain or loss = Expense adjusted for general price-level change — Expense stated in historical dollars.

Holding gain or loss = Expense adjusted for specific price change — Expense adjusted for general price-level change.

Operating gain or loss = Revenue — Expense adjusted for specific price change.

Income as reported by *accounting* may consist of several combinations of gains and losses, as Example 5 illustrates.

Example 5   Inventory was acquired for $10,000 in 1972 when the general price index was 120. It was sold in 1973 for $12,000. At that time the replacement cost of the inventory was $13,500 and the general price index was 105. Compute the components of accounting income.

Solution   Accounting income $= \$12,000 - \$10,000$.................. $= \underline{\underline{\$2,000}}$

Illusory gain or loss:
      Expense adjusted for general price change
      — expense in historical dollars
      $= (\frac{105}{120} \times \$10,000) - \$10,000$
      $= \$8,750 - \$10,000$.............................. $= (\ 1,250)$ (loss)

Holding gain or loss:
      Expense adjusted for specific price change
      — expense adjusted for general price change
      $= \$13,500 - \$8,750$ .... 4,750 gain

Operating gain or loss:
      Revenue — expense adjusted for specific price change
      $= \$12,000 - \$13,500$ .... $(\ 1,500)$ (loss)
     Total .... $\underline{2,000}$ gain

Should Accounts Reflect the Changing Value of the Dollar?

In determining whether the accounting records kept in terms of historical costs should be adjusted for changes in price levels, one should make a careful distinction between changes in *general price levels* and changes in *specific prices*. Those who advocate adjusting the accounts for general price changes argue that doing so *does not involve a departure from historical cost*, on which most accounting measurements are based. Use of general price indexes to adjust the historical cost data merely results in shift to *adjusted cost*, they maintain. Such an adjustment is needed to reflect *changes in the scale of the measuring stick*, the monetary unit which is used in making accounting measurements.

Making adjustments for changes in *specific* prices, on the other hand, would result in a *departure from the historical cost basis* of accounting. It would involve recording both *unrealized gains and losses* in connection with increases or decreases in the replacement cost of assets still on hand. Accountants are generally willing to record reasonably foreseeable losses before they are confirmed by sale, but they balk at recognizing unrealized gains.

The extent to which changing general price levels reduce the comparability of financial statements depends partly on the *rapidity of changes* in price levels, partly on the *quantities of assets* of each age group which a given business owns, and partly on the *rate of turnover* of those assets for the given business. The *materiality* of the price-level effect can be judged by comparing (1) the amount of price-level change pertaining to assets and equities with *total assets and equities*, and (2) the amount of the effect of price-level change on income components with *income before income tax*.

Even in times of rapid changes in the purchasing power of money, conventional accounting does not materially misstate the results of businesses with relatively small amounts of long-lived assets and a rapid rate of turnover of current assets. The problem is more significant for businesses with large amounts of long-term assets and long-term liabilities, and it tends to increase as the lives of those assets and liabilities increase.

In the recent history of some countries, the rate of price-level change has been so rapid that it has been necessary to adjust the values of long-lived assets in the accounts. In the United States changing price levels have affected some businesses more acutely than others.

Comprehensive General Price-Level Adjustments

In 1969 the Accounting Principles Board issued a statement in which it voiced the opinion that financial statements adjusted for general price-level changes present useful information not available from basic historical-dollar financial statements. The Board felt that such adjusted information might be presented *in addition to* the basic historical-dollar financial statements, but that financial data adjusted for general price levels should not be presented as the basic financial statements.[1]

The Board[2] recommended that

1. A *distinction* be made *between monetary* and *nonmonetary* items in preparing general price-level statements. Assets and liabilities are "monetary" for this purpose if their amounts are fixed—by contract or otherwise—in numbers of dollars, regardless of general or specific price changes.

2. *Nonmonetary items should be restated* in dollars of current general purchasing power at the end of the current period. This restatement does not result in gains or losses, but merely adjusts the historical values of these items to their current purchasing-power equivalents.

3. *Monetary assets and liabilities are already stated in dollars of current general purchasing power.*

4. *Gains and losses on monetary items* resulting from general price-level changes should be *reported as a separate item* in income statements adjusted for general price-level changes.

5. *Income statement items should be restated in dollars of general purchasing power at the end of the period.*

Comprehensive adjustments of all accounts to reflect general price-level changes, reported in supplementary statements, have some rather surprising results. They show increases in the stated values of nonmonetary assets and equities. They also reveal purchasing-power gains and losses of the following kinds, which are not shown by conventional accounting statements:

(1) Gains or losses from holding monetary assets.

(2) Losses or gains from owing monetary liabilities.

In times of *price-level increase* there are *losses from holding monetary assets* and

---

[1] American Institute of Certified Public Accountants, *APB Statement No. 3*, "Financial Statements Restated for General Price-Level Changes," June 1969, Paragraph 25.

[2] *Ibid.*, Paragraphs 33, 18, 35, 38, 43, 39.

gains from owing monetary liabilities. In times of price decrease, monetary-asset holdings result in gains and monetary liabilities result in losses to the business. These gains and losses help to emphasize the desirability of maintaining just the right amount of working capital needed to conduct business. Excess holdings result in a needless speculative gain or loss.

Example 6   Assume for simplicity that a firm owned $10,000 of cash on December 31, 1972, when the general price index was 100, and the same sum on December 31, 1973, at a time when the general price index was 105. There were no cash collections or payments during the year. How should these facts be shown in the financial position and income statements for 1973?

Solution   Cash should be reported as $10,000 in the year-end financial position statement.
    The $10,000 Cash balance at the beginning of the year was equivalent to $10,500 in terms of the end-of-year purchasing power ($10,000 × $\frac{105}{100}$). The firm would have had to own $10,500 of Cash at year end in order to maintain the same purchasing power as at the beginning of the year. It had only $10,000; therefore the 1973 supplementary income statement should report a $500 loss from holding monetary items during a period of price-level increase.

Example 7   The same firm owed $5,000 of Notes Payable at the beginning and end of the year. No payments were made during the year. How would these facts be reported?

Solution   Notes Payable will be reported at face value, $5,000, in the year-end financial position statement.
    For the debt to have remained unchanged in terms of constant purchasing power, it would have had to be $5,250 at year end (computed by multiplying the beginning balance of $5,000 by $\frac{105}{100}$). The actual ending debt balance was $5,000, a decline of $250 in *real terms*. The firm is $250 *better off* in terms of *purchasing power.*

Example 8   Assume that the Cash balance was unchanged during 1973 at $10,000, but that the beginning general price index was 100 and the ending index was 93. How would this be reported?

Solution   The ending Cash balance would again be reported at its face amount of $10,000 in the financial position statement.
    The year-end equivalent of the beginning Cash balance is $9,300, or $\frac{93}{100}$ × $10,000. The business actually has $10,000 year-end dollars; therefore it has had a $700 *purchasing-power gain* from holding Cash during a year of falling prices.

Partial Price Adjustments Within the Historical-Cost Framework

Two proposals which are commonly advocated for giving effect to price changes in the financial statements, while continuing to adhere to historical costs, are

(1) Rapid write down of fixed assets.

(2) Use of the LIFO inventory method.

Rapid write-down of fixed assets. Some businesses have attempted to combat the effect of rising price levels on their financial reports by using accelerated depreciation and similar methods which result in the rapid write-off of assets. Even in the absence of increasing prices, these methods would seem to be appropriate when the asset yields greater service benefits during its earlier years. Where the pattern of periodic service benefits is not greatest in the early years of an asset's life, accelerated depreciation and similar methods provide only a *temporary solution* to the problem of reporting in times of price-level increases. Rapid depreciation may, mostly by coincidence, give a more realistic income figure than straight-line depreciation during the earlier years of fixed assets' lives. As a result, however, the income distortion in later years when the overdepreciated assets are still in use is compounded. Depreciation over the life of a fixed asset cannot exceed its historical cost; therefore, recording *extra depreciation in early years* can only be accomplished by recording *less depreciation in later years*. As a result, the later years are not charged with the full cost of the services received from the assets, thus overstating income. Moreover, the proper unexpired cost of the assets is not shown in the statement of financial position. With income overstated and assets understated during the latter part of their lives, the overstatement of rate of return on assets is compounded.

Use of the LIFO inventory method. Sometimes the use of the LIFO inventory method is advocated as a means of coping with the effect of changing price levels on financial statements. As a sole method of making such adjustments, it could be successful only if the only business accounts which were affected by price-level changes were the inventory accounts. Even for the inventory accounts and the cost of goods sold, however, LIFO has serious limitations as a means of adjusting for price-level changes. The method results in charging most recent costs incurred to cost of goods sold. These costs are those of a specific type of asset, and only by coincidence will they reflect the movements of the general price level. Moreover, the inventory asset balance which results under the LIFO inventory method is likely to be wholly out of line with the current cost of inventories, either on the basis of historical costs adjusted for general price-level changes or on the basis of the current replacement costs of inventory components.

The most satisfactory method of adjusting the accounts to reflect general price-level changes is to adjust *all* the accounts, not just the inventory or the long-term accounts. The effect of the adjustments should be reported in *supplementary*, not *primary*, financial statements.

Price Adjustments Which Depart from Historical Costs

Earlier chapters have devoted some attention to the propriety of departing from accounting based on historical exchange prices in order to report current values. (See, for example, "Realized Versus Unrealized Changes in Asset Values" on p. 68 of Chapter 4.)

Three general methods which have been advocated for adjusting the accounts to current values are

(1) *Appraisal* of properties and adjustment of the accounts.
(2) Computation of depreciation on the basis of *current replacement costs*.
(3) Conversion of the historical costs of certain assets to current values by using *specific price index numbers*.

Adjustment of properties on the basis of appraisal. It is acceptable to adjust the accounts to show current market values which have been estimated by appraisal when

(1) The original cost cannot be determined.
(2) A significant interest, or all, of a business is purchased.
(3) A corporation is reorganized under legal proceedings.

A large element of *subjectivity* often enters into the process of estimating value by appraisal. Appraised values may be based on the replacement cost of an asset in similar condition. Where similar assets have a ready market such values may be easy to determine, but this is not the case for highly specialized assets. In addition, *technological change* since the existing asset was acquired complicates the appraisal process. Should the estimated replacement cost be for an identical asset or for a new asset which will perform the same function?

Appraisals are also often quite expensive. In addition, unless the price level remains stable for a long period, the revised figures will soon be out of line with current values and the appraisal process will have to be repeated.

Depreciation on replacement cost. This method is similar to a comprehensive adjustment of asset values, the main difference being that it is advocated for specific fixed assets rather than for the enterprise as a whole. It is supported by the argument that the amount of income available for distribution to owners cannot be determined until there has been a provision for maintaining the productive capacity of the business. Current market values provide the best measure of the value of service benefits received currently.

Because of technological change, it is difficult to estimate current replacement costs for some types of assets.

The *funds for the replacement* of an asset are not provided by *any* depreciation or valuation method. They come instead from revenue, from borrowings, from the sale of other assets, or from investments by the owners.

Conversion of cost to a current basis by using specific price indexes. Specific price indexes have been advocated as a means of expressing accounting data in current dollars, on the ground that the average change in all prices may not reflect accurately the impact of price-level changes on a particular enterprise. Plausible as this argument may seem, the philosophy behind specific price adjustments is quite different from that supporting general price-level adjustments. The use of specific price indexes for adjusting asset and other accounts would have the effect of recognizing both *unrealized holding gains* and *unrealized holding losses* on individual assets. This is contrary to the realization concept of accounting.

As was explained earlier, the use of general price-level adjustments is intended merely to correct for the illusion that the business is better off when the general price level has increased (or worse off when it has declined). It is defended as a *correction of a defect in the unit of measure* rather than as a recognition of real gains and losses from owning assets.

Acceptability of Using Current Values in the Accounts

Some accountants favor using current prices, rather than historical exchange prices, as a basis for accounting when there is adequate evidence of the current prices. They argue that a *price,* or *holding, gain,* whether or not it is *realized* is just as much a part of *business income* as a gain realized when an asset is sold They favor reporting *unrealized holding gains as a part of income* when they are supported by reliable evidence, as well as reporting *unrealized holding losses* as deductions from income. For example, they would consider increases in the quoted prices of highly salable assets, such as marketable securities, to be proper components of business income.

Although there appears to be growing support for using current values in the accounts on a selective basis, particularly in the case of highly marketable securities, the weight of accounting opinion is still in favor of retaining historical exchange prices in the accounts. Where the effects of general price-level changes have been significant, reports based on historical prices can be supplemented by statements adjusted for general price-level changes.

Summary   The measurement procedures of accounting implicitly assume that the monetary unit has the same significance as a unit of exchange value from one time to another. Under the rapidly changing price levels of modern history, this assumption has often been untrue to a major extent. The result is to reduce or destroy the comparability of a firm's financial statements from one period to another.

Various devices have been suggested to ensure statement comparability in the face of seriously changing prices. It may be useful to prepare supplementary statements, reflecting adjustments for general price-level changes on a comprehensive basis. In addition to stating all accounts in terms of their *current purchasing-power equivalent,* such statements show the *gains and losses* which have resulted from *holding monetary assets* and *owing monetary liabilities.*

While general price-level adjustments adhere to the principles of historical accounting measurements, the use of *current values* as a basis for accounting is a departure from historical exchange prices. Such values may be determined by appraisal, by estimate of replacement cost, or by use of specific price indexes for selected groups of accounts. Their use in the accounts introduces elements of *unrealized holding gains and losses,* as well as the realized holding gains and losses which are included in income under historical-based accounting. The dominant view of accounting authorities opposes the use of current values in the accounts as a substitute for historical values.

Discussion
Questions
and
Problems **16-1**   "In using exchange prices of completed transactions as a basis of measuring and reporting business income, accounting *implicitly* assumes that the monetary unit has the same significance as a unit of exchange from one time to another." Do you agree with this statement? Explain, using specific examples.

16-2   Define the following:

a. Purchasing power.
b. General price level changes.
c. Specific price changes.
d. General price index.

16-3   Distinguish between the following bases of accounting measurement:

a. Historical dollars.
b. Dollars adjusted for general price changes.
c. Dollars adjusted for specific price changes.

16-4   The financial position statement usually expresses the assets and equities of a business in terms of *mixed purchasing power*. Explain this fact and show what the resulting effects are on periodic income measurement.

16-5   Some items in accounting statements are expressed in current dollars, whereas other items are normally expressed in dollars of a prior year or years.

a. Name the principal financial position statement items which might not be expressed in current dollars. If any part of your answer depends on the accounting procedures employed by the particular company, explain fully.
b. Name the principal items in the income statement which might not be expressed in current dollars. If any part of your answer depends on the accounting procedures employed, explain fully.

(Adapted from AICPA Examination in Theory of Accounts.)

16-6

a. In what specific sense do appraisals, replacement costs, and specific price-index adjustments serve a common accounting purpose?
b. In what specific sense do accelerated depreciation, LIFO inventory, and general price-index adjustments serve a common accounting purpose?
c. Does the common purpose in part a differ from that in part b? Explain.
d. How effectively does each method in part a serve the common purpose? How effectively does each method in part b?

16-7   The general manager of the Cumberland Manufacturing Company received an income statement covering the calendar year 1973 from his controller. "Joe," he said to the controller, "this statement indicates that a net income of two million dollars was earned last year. You know the value of the company is not that much more than it was this time last year."

"You're probably right," replied the controller. "You see, there are factors in accounting which sometimes keep reported operating results from reflecting the change in the value of the company."

Prepare a detailed explanation of the accounting conventions to which the controller referred. Include justification, to the extent possible, for the generally used accounting methods.

(Adapted from AICPA Examination in Theory of Accounts.)

16-8   What gains or losses appear in the income statement when general price-level adjustments are made that do not appear when the income statement is based on historical valuations?

16-9   On January 1, 1968, when the price index was 100, Kuler Company paid $16,000 for a machine which had a ten-year expected life and no salvage value. On December 31, 1973, when the price index was 143, the machine had a net disposal value of $8,500 and an estimated replacement cost new (minus depreciation) of $12,000. The price index was 130 on December 31, 1972.

a. At what amount would the machine ordinarily be shown in Kuler Company's December 31, 1973, financial position statement? How much depreciation would ordinarily be deducted in the 1973 income statement?
b. Using the additional cost and price data, illustrate how the machine might be more realistically represented in the December 31, 1973, financial position statement.

16-10   On March 17, 1974, when the general price index was 100, a business acquired for resale merchandise at a cost of $8,000. One-fourth of the merchandise was in the December 31, 1974, inventory, at which time the general price index was 110. The replacement cost of the goods in the inventory on that date was $2,400.

a. How much of the change in the value of the inventory was due to movements in the general price level? To changes in specific prices?
b. List the most important assumptions required to answer the questions in part a.
c. How would you recommend that these changes be shown in the accounts?
d. How would your answers to parts a and b differ if the replacement cost of the inventory on December 31 had been $1,800?

16-11   On January 1, 1974, the Campus Car Co. paid $12,000 for three new convertibles to be rented to student organizations. The cars had a two-year expected useful life with a salvage value of $1,500 each. For the year ending December 31, 1974, the company reported net income of $3,200 after deducting straight-line depreciation. On December 31, 1974, the cars had an appraisal value of $2,250 each, while new cars of the same model were priced at $4,200 each. During the year the general price index rose by 8 per cent.

a. How much of the 1974 income would you consider to be an *illusory* gain?
b. List the important assumptions on which your answer to part a is based.
c. How relevant are the appraisal value and replacement cost in this problem?
d. How would you recommend that the results of your analysis be shown in the accounting reports?

16-12

Required   In each of the following situations compute the accounting net income or net loss and analyze it into (1) illusory gain or loss, (2) holding gain or loss, and (3) operating gain or loss.

a. Sales in 1974 were $400,000. Merchandise sold, having an acquisition cost of $240,000, was acquired in 1973 when the average general price index was 120. The average general price index in 1974 was 130, and the estimated replacement cost of goods at the time of sale was $275,000.

b. Sales in 1974 were $900,000. Cost of goods sold of $630,000 represented the cost of inventory acquired when the general price index was 80 and the specific price index applying to this class of merchandise was 90. The average general price index in 1974 was 70 and the average specific price index was 100. Other expenses, all stated in terms of the 1974 general price level, amounted to $200,000.

16-13   In 1974 Crane Co. reported sales of $1,200,000. Cost of goods sold included the following:

(1) *Materials* of an original cost of $300,000, acquired when the general price index was 100 and the specific price index of materials was 120. These indexes were 110 and 115, respectively, at the time the goods were sold.
(2) Depreciation of $100,000 on factory machinery. The machines were acquired when both the general price index and the specific price index of machinery were 60. The specific price index of machinery at the time the goods were sold was 150.
(3) Direct labor of $400,000, expressed in terms of the price levels current at the time the goods were sold. All other expenses totaled $200,000 in terms of the price levels current when the goods were sold.

Required   a. Compute net income according to generally accepted accounting principles.
b. Analyze the accounting net income into (1) operating gain or loss, (2) holding gain or loss, and (3) illusory gain or loss.

16-14   A fixed asset was acquired in 1972 for $24,000 when the general price index was 130 and the specific price index was 110. The machine had an estimated useful life of four years with no salvage value. In 1974 net earnings before depreciation were $10,000, the general price index was 117, and the specific price index was 121.

Required   a. Compute the major components of accounting income.
b. Explain how the effects of this analysis might be shown in the financial position statement and the income statement.

16-15   Below are comparative financial position statements of a securities dealer at the beginning and end of 1973:

	December, 31	
	1973	1972
Cash......................................	$15,000	$10,000
Marketable securities.................	60,000	40,000
Total assets..........................	$75,000	$50,000
Bank notes payable	$55,000	$45,000
Owners' equity.......................	20,000	5,000
Total equities......................	$75,000	$50,000

No distributions were made to owners during the year. The general price index was 110 on December 31, 1972, and 121 on December 31, 1973.

Required   a. Compute the gain or loss from holding monetary assets.
b. Compute the gain or loss from owing monetary liabilities.
c. Show the amount of the change in owners' equity that is due to illusory gains or losses and the amount that is due to operating gain or loss.

16-16   The accounts of the Inflated Company, based on historical dollar amounts, have the following balances on December 31, 1973:

	Debit	Credit
Cash..	$ 5,000	
Accounts receivable	25,000	
Inventories (LIFO)	20,000	
Property, plant, and equipment.....................	275,000	
—Accumulated depreciation.........................		$175,000
Accounts payable..		18,000
Income tax payable		10,000
Capital stock...		50,000
Retained income..		57,000
Sales		150,000
Cost of goods sold......................................	90,000	
Depreciation	25,000	
Other expenses..	10,000	
Income tax expense (40%)..........................	10,000	
	$460,000	$460,000

The property, plant, and equipment were acquired on January 1, 1968, when the general price index was 100. The LIFO inventory is stated in terms of the same price level. Cost of goods sold and other expenses reasonably reflect 1973 price levels. The general price index on December 31, 1973, was 160.

Required

a. Show in parallel columns condensed financial statements (1) as prepared by the company and (2) reflecting changes in the general price level. Assume that the net loss on monetary accounts in 1973, expressed in year-end dollars, was $1,000.

b. Compute the rate of return before tax on total assets under each method, assuming that total assets did not change during the year.

c. What causes the differences between the rate of return computed on the historical financial statements and the rate shown by statements which have been adjusted for the effects of general price-level changes?

d. How, if at all, would you recommend that the Inflated Company report the effects of general price-level changes?

Cases   **16-1   Newport News Shipbuilding and Dry Dock Company.** The following item appeared in an Associated Press release:

LATHE PURCHASED
AFTER FIGURING

Newport News, Va. (AP)—Back in 1936 the Newport News Shipbuilding and Dry Dock Company purchased a huge heavy-duty engine lathe for $6,600. In 20 years it was depreciated on the books in the amount of $6,300 and this amount set aside for replacement.
It was sold for $3,700, making $10,000 available for replacement. The new lathe cost $36,000 and $26,000 had to be taken from profits after taxes. Taxes amounted to 54 per cent of earned profit and, therefore, $57,000 had to be earned in profits. The company figures it required $807,000 in new business to make enough to buy the new lathe.

Required

a. In what way did the company probably "set aside the amount for replacement"?

b. Is the problem of this company an unusual one?

c. Record the entries for the sale of the old lathe and the purchase of the new one.

d. What factors contributed to the reported "gain" on the disposal of the old lathe? Was this probably a gain in terms of common dollars?

e. What method of depreciation would you recommend that the company use on similar assets in its tax return? Why?

16-2   French Price-Level Adjustments. The following item appeared in "Notes to Financial Statements" in an April 17, 1959, prospectus for Simca, a French company. The financial statements were for the year ended December 31, 1958.

> Note 4. Property, Plant and Equipment and Reserves for Depreciation. Under French tax laws, companies may recognize the loss in purchasing power of the French franc by revaluing their fixed assets. The revaluation of physical properties may be based on estimates of current useful value with the limitation that the value thus found may not exceed the amount that would have been obtained by applying approved co-efficients to the original cost of the properties and to the recorded provisions for depreciation. These co-efficients which are published by the French Government are intended to give expression to the change in price level each year beginning with the year 1914. Upon recording such a revaluation, companies may subsequently deduct from taxable income depreciation computed on the basis of the higher amounts. The surplus resulting from revaluation is maintained in a special reserve for revaluation and may be used to increase the stated value of capital stock upon payment of a relatively small tax.
>
> The Company has revalued its properties on three separate occasions, at the end of 1945, 1949, and 1951, on the basis of co-efficients of revaluation authorized by the French Government as of those dates. See Note 9 to Financial Statements. Thereftter, the Company has charged against earnings depreciation on the higher amounts, as permitted by French tax law.

Required   a. Explain how the French system for adjusting for higher prices operates. Is it a comprehensive or a partial adjustment for price changes?

b. How are the price-level adjustments in France related to income taxation? In what way does this relationship relieve the taxpayer in times of increasing prices? What problem of matching does it create in the financial statements?

16-3   N. V. Philips' Gloeilampenfabrieken. N. V. Philips' Gloeilampenfabrieken (Philips Incandescent Lamp Works Co.) of the Netherlands has been using replacement costs in its financial reports for a number of years. As Mr. A. Goudeket,[3] chief internal auditor of the company, states:

> At Philips we hold to the view that there can be no recognition of income for a period unless the capital employed in the business at the beginning of the period has been maintained, that is to say, after it has been established that the purchasing power of that capital at the end of the period is equal to that at the beginning of the period.

The accounting system of Philips is decentralized; each section has its own financial statements. Mr. Goudeket explains:

> In accordance with the principles of "accounting for management," the responsible managers of all levels must know periodically the income and the capital employed, both in total and in detail. For this purpose the replacement value is applied. In other words, the application of the replacement value theory is not

---

[3] "An Application of Replacement Value Theory," *Journal of Accountancy,* July 1960, p. 38. This article gives the reasoning behind Philips' accounting practice and explains the methodology used in making price-level adjustments.

merely a calculation technique used in preparing the annual statements of the concern. It is integrated in the accounting system of all sections of the concern at every stage. In this way it is ensured that all information for management is compiled in accordance with this principle, and thus the replacement value automatically enters into all management considerations and decisions.

The following excerpts from Mr. Goudeket's article explain briefly the methods that are used in adjusting individual accounts for price-level changes:

Fixed Assets

The replacement value is determined on the basis of the trend of the specific price levels and not of the general price level: that is to say, the trend of prices is followed separately for buildings, dwelling houses, machinery, etc. Each group of assets is regularly revalued by means of index numbers. (Page 38)

Inventories

. . . standard prices are in operation for all groups of inventories, that is to say for goods purchased, for semi-finished products and for finished goods. For the establishment of the replacement value the starting point is the price level which formed the basis for the calculation of the standard prices. The trends in the price levels of the various elements of the standard prices are followed and their effect on the standard prices is calculated. Whenever the fluctuation in price levels is material enough to cause an inventory adjustment, the standard prices are adjusted to replacement value by means of index numbers. (Page 39)

If a price increase occurs, the accounts of fixed assets at replacement value are increased to the current price level with a credit to revaluation surplus for fixed assets, which is an owners' equity account. Depreciation is based upon replacement value. Declines in price levels are charged to the revaluation account until it is exhausted, and thereafter to income. Care is taken to determine that such decreases result from changes in price and not from economic or technical causes. Declines of the last two types are charged to income.

A similar revaluation surplus account is used for inventories.

Mr. Goudeket explains the accounting policy with respect to intangible assets and monetary accounts (assets other than inventories, fixed assets, investments, and intangibles) as follows:

In its external reports Philips includes intangible assets at no value, so that revaluation problems do not occur. As regards the treatment of these accounts internally, particular mention should be made of initial costs. These represent expenditures made in connection with the starting up of production of new products, which expenditures are recovered in a certain period out of a precalculated volume of production. The revaluation of this asset is similar to that of inventories.

. . . The details of the procedure are given below on the basis of a classification of the balance sheet directed at this problem.

Balance Sheet
as at the Beginning of the Period

Inventories, fixed and intangible assets, and investments...	a	Stockholders' equity...............	c	
"Monetary" assets (as previously defined)	$\frac{b}{x}$	Liabilities	$\frac{d}{x}$	

Inventories, fixed and intangible assets, and investments are revalued according to the procedure set forth above. Since part of the stockholders' equity is invested in other (monetary) assets, the purchasing power of that part will diminish in case of a decrease in value of currency of the country. For this reason we calculate, on the basis of the cost-of-living index, how many currency units represent the same purchasing power as the part of capital which at the beginning of the period was invested in "monetary" assets. In the example given, this amount equals $b - d$. This balance, multiplied by the inflation-factor based on the cost-of-living index, leads to the entry:

Dr. Cost of inflation .... (income account)
Cr. Reserve for diminishing purchasing power of capital
        invested in monetary assets .... (capital account)

Thus the income statement shows a result after the purchasing power of stockholders' equity has been maintained. (Page 41)

Philips' consolidated statement of financial position for 1964 contained the following items (among others):

	Millions of Guilders	
Property, plant, and equipment:		
Replacement value..................................	5,012	
Depreciation...	2,112	2,900
Intangible assets..		—
Interests in nonconsolidated subsidaries and		
associated companies..........................		390
Sundry noncurrent assets.............................		158
Stocks:		
Factory stocks...	1,317	
Advance payments by customers.................	− 147	
	1,170	
Commercial stocks....................................	1,311	2,481
Debtors (details omitted)..............................		2,147
Liquid assets (details omitted).......................		729
		8,805
Share capital and reserves:		
Ordinary share capital..............................	968	
6% cum. part. pref. share capital................	144	
Share premium account...........................	506	
Retained profit	1,954	
Revaluation...	621	
		4,193
Minority shareholders' interests		145
Sundry provisions (details omitted).................		886
Long-term liabilities (details omitted)..............		1,065
Current liabilities (details omitted).................		2,316
Profit for distribution..................................		200
		8,805

The replacement value of property, plant, and equipment increased 223 million guilders owing to changes in replacement value in 1964, with a corresponding increase of 96 million guilders in accumulated depreciation.

Stocks (inventories) rose in 1964 by 93 million guilders as a result of revaluation, which was credited to the Revaluation Account.

The Revaluation Account balance ranged from 292 million guilders in 1955 to 621 million in 1964.

Required a. Comment on the reasons Philips gives to support replacement cost accounting. Does the method used for adjustments seem to accomplish the company's objectives?

b. Are the price indexes used in the adjustments specific or general? Explain.

c. Compare Philips' method of price-level adjustment with that used in the United States (see Problem 16-16) and in France (see Case 16-2).

d. Comment on the company's practice of accounting for intangibles. (Sums paid for goodwill are charged to Profit and Loss, and the method of accounting for research, development, and patents is explained in the case.)

chapter 17

Planning and Accounting
for Income Taxes

Purpose of Chapter

Earlier chapters have discussed the underlying principles and the methods used by a business in measuring its financial status at any given time and its progress toward its income objectives. The income tax on corporations has been described as a *business expense* which must be deducted in computing the net income of the corporation, and the unpaid balance of income taxes is a *liability* which must be reported in the corporation's statement of financial position.

When questions of differences between the methods of determining the components of *taxable income* and *business income* have arisen, the reader has been referred to this chapter for a fuller explanation. This has been done because the objectives of measuring taxable income and business income are significantly different, and so are the forces which help to develop their rules of measurement.

The purpose of this chapter is to acquaint the reader with some of the basic considerations involved in *tax planning* for a business, as well as to indicate some of the key differences between reporting *taxable income* and reporting *business income* for general purposes.

Different Objectives of Business Accounting and Income Taxation

Chapter 1 stated that the objectives of accounting are to provide information for

(1) Making decisions concerning the alternative uses of limited resources.

(2) Planning and controlling the effectiveness with which an economic entity's human and material resources are used.

(3) Assisting in, and reporting on, the custodianship of economic resources.

(4) Aiding the accomplishment of social goals through government and other social organizations.

The principal purpose of income taxation is to *raise revenue* to finance the activities of the government. Taxing authorities think of income as a measure of the taxpayer's *ability to pay* for the support of those activities. This purpose significantly influences Congress when it is enacting laws to define the components of taxable income and the progressive rates of federal income tax. It also has a significant effect on the Treasury Department in formulating regulations to aid in interpreting the laws and on the Internal Revenue Service in enforcing the tax laws and regulations. It is equally important to the legislators and the tax enforcement officials of those states which have state income tax laws.

Other purposes of income taxation also help to shape the specific provisions of income tax laws and regulations. Congress occasionally grants special tax benefits to groups or industries in order to *promote the national welfare*. One example is the special tax benefits given to the petroleum and other extractive industries to encourage the development of productive wells and mines.

Income taxation has also been used consciously in recent decades in attempts to *stimulate national economic activity* in times of recessions and to brake runaway booms. This has been done chiefly by varying tax rates and the amounts of certain deductions from taxable income. In the last few years the government has used such tax provisions as accelerated depreciation, additional first-year depreciation allowances, the investment tax credit, and guideline tax-depreciation lives as means of stimulating capital investment and thereby stimulating economic activity.

It is to be expected that the *business income before tax and the taxable income of a given business will often be materially different* because of the different objectives of measuring each.

Importance of Income Taxes in Business Decisions

Even though the income before tax reported in the general financial statements of a corporation may differ from that reported in its income tax return, income taxes can by no means be ignored in making business decisions.

If the business is organized as a *corporation*, it is considered to be a separate legal person subject to income tax. Currently the income tax rates on most types of business corporations are 22 per cent of the first $25,000 of taxable income and 48 per cent of all taxable income over $25,000.

A business which is organized as an individual proprietorship or a partnership is not subject to income tax as an entity. Instead, the shares of income *earned* by the owners of such businesses, whether distributed to them or not, are taxable to them as *individuals*. Income tax rates for individuals have changed frequently. The current rates range from 14 per cent of income in the lowest bracket to 70 per cent of income in the highest bracket. Beginning in 1972 *earned income* (including most forms of current compensation for personal services) is subject to a maximum tax rate of 50 per cent.

The major part of corporate income which is distributed to stockholders is subject to *double taxation*: once as taxable income of the business corporation which earns it, and a second time as taxable *dividend income* of the stockholder. Certain deductions and exclusions which apply to stockholders help to reduce the amount of dividends subject to the second tax.

Even though a particular business is not now earning a large taxable income, its potential income tax expense in the future may be substantial. Some decisions relating to the *form of business organization*, the *types of transactions* in which it engages, the *form of its transactions*, and the *manner in which it reports them for tax purposes* will have a significant influence on the *amount of its income tax burden* in the future as well as in the current year. They also have an important bearing on the *timing* of the payment of taxes as between years, even in cases where the total dollar income tax effect of alternatives is the same over a series of years. If a taxpayer has a choice of paying a given amount of income tax currently or in a later year, it is *advantageous for him to postpone the payment*. He can earn a return in the meantime on the funds not currently required to pay the tax. In reality, of course, the decision is more complicated, because the taxpayer does not know for certain that the tax rates will not be higher in the year to which the payment is postponed.

Good management requires that the responsible persons plan the transactions of a business and the manner of reporting them for tax purposes in such a way as to *maximize* the amount and rate of *income after income taxes*. If revenue and all other expense items are unchanged by the amount of current income taxes, decisions should be made so as to minimize the burden of taxes on the business in the long run, considering both the total amount and the timing of taxes. The businessman and his tax adviser should use every legal means at their disposal to accomplish these objectives.

Effect of Taxation on Business Form

The *corporation* is subject to income tax as a *taxable entity*, whereas the income of a business organized as a proprietorship or partnership is considered to be the taxable income of the individual owners, whether it is distributed to them or not.

Reasonable amounts of salaries of stockholders who are also corporation officers are treated as expenses of the corporation before arriving at its net income subject to income tax. In a partnership or proprietorship, on the other hand, the tax law makes no distinction between the parts of income which the owner earns as salary, as payment for the use of capital, and as compensation for risk.

The following partial table of current tax rates for married persons who file joint tax returns will be used in Example 1 and in some of the problems at the end of the chapter.

Taxable Income	Tax (before credits)
$ 0 to $ 1,000	14%
1,000 to 2,000	$ 140 plus 15% of amount over $ 1,000
2,000 to 3,000	290 plus 16% of amount over 2,000
3,000 to 4,000	450 plus 17% of amount over 3,000
4,000 to 8,000	620 plus 19% of amount over 4,000
8,000 to 12,000	1,380 plus 22% of amount over 8,000
12,000 to 16,000	2,260 plus 25% of amount over 12,000
16,000 to 20,000	3,260 plus 28% of amount over 16,000

An individual may exclude from his gross income the first $100 of dividends received from qualified domestic corporations. The dividend exclusion may be doubled if a husband and wife file a joint return and each receives the full amount of dividends an individual may exclude.

Example 1 illustrates in a hypothetical situation the effects of differences in corporation and individual tax, differences in the tax status of management salaries, double taxation, and the dividend-income exclusion.

Example 1   *A* and *B* are trying to decide whether to organize their business as a partnership or as a corporation. Each plans to invest $25,000, and each feels that $8,000 a year is reasonable compensation for his services. They expect that the revenue of the business will be $100,000 and that operating expenses other than owners' salaries will be $69,000. All net income will be distributed to the individual owners in cash. A comparison of the income tax status of the two forms of organization appears on p. 489.

Caution should be used in interpreting Example 1. It does *not* prove that the partnership form always has an income advantage over the corporate form, or even that it has an advantage in this case. It merely illustrates the procedure for making the comparison. The results will be different if the business is expected to suffer losses during its early years, or if it is expected to earn income which will be taxed at the 48 per cent rate. The income tax of each of the individual owners will depend on the amount of his income from other sources, the number of his personal exemptions, and the amount of his personal deductions. If they have large amounts of taxable income from other sources, the owners may find that their taxable income from a partnership would be taxed at rates higher than the 48 per cent maximum rate applicable to corporations.

In the example it was also assumed that the business did not grow, but that all earnings were distributed. The relative desirability of the two forms of organization changes when the growth of a business is to be financed by retained income. In the corporate form, earnings retained in the business are not taxed to the individual stockholders as dividend income. However, the tax laws limit the extent to which corporations can retain income by providing that a penalty can be assessed on "unreasonable accumulations" of retained income. The total income of a partnership is taxable to the partners whether they reinvest it in the business or not. If their income is subject to high tax rates and they

COMPARISON OF INCOME TAX STATUS OF CORPORATION
AND PARTNERSHIP

Financial results of the business:	*Corporation*		*Partnership*	
Sales		$100,000		$100,000
Deduct expenses:				
Officers' salaries........................	$16,000		$ 0	
Other expenses.........................	69,000	85,000	69,000	69,000
Net income before income tax............		$ 15,000		
Deduct corporate income tax at 22%...		3,300		
Net income....................................		$ 11,700		$ 31,000
Deduct income distributed to owners...		11,700		31,000
Increase in owners' equity of the business...................................		$ 0		$ 0

Income and tax payments of each owner:	*Corporation*		*Partnership*	
Officer's salary...............................	$ 8,000			
Dividends.....................................	5,850			
Share of partnership income:				
Salary....................................			$ 8,000	
Remainder, shared equally..........			7,500	
Total income of each owner.........		$ 13,850		$ 15,500
Individual income tax computation, under corporation:				
Exclude dividends of....................		200		
Deduct personal exemptions and deductions (assumed)...........		3,650		
Taxable income...........................		$ 10,000		
Tax on first $8,000......................		$ 1,380		
Tax on remaining $2,000 at 22%		440		
Total tax of each owner.............		1,820		
Individual income tax computation, under partnership:				
Deduct personal exemptions and deductions (assumed)..........				3,650
Taxable income...........................				$ 11,850
Tax on first $8,000......................				$ 1,380
Tax on remaining $3,850 at 22%.....				847
Total tax of each owner...........				$ 2,227
Disposable income of each owner.....		$ 12,030		$ 13,273
Disposable income of both owners..........		24,060		26,546

must withdraw from the partnership the cash needed to pay their taxes, the business organized as a partnership may not be able to grow as rapidly as if organized as a corporation.

There are many more complicated features of the income tax law which the owners of a business should consider in deciding on its form of organization. Also, under certain conditions corporations may elect to be taxed as partnerships.

In addition to the income tax status, in deciding on the form of organization the owners should consider advantages and disadvantages not related to taxation, such as the duration of the life of the business, the extent to which owners are personally liable for business debts, the ease with which ownership interests may be transferred, the ease and flexibility with which the business can be managed, and the legal and other costs involved.

Tax Saving by Means of Long-Term Capital Gains

Where there is a choice, it is generally better for a business to receive income in the form of *long-term capital gains* than in the form of *ordinary income*. Capital gains result from the *sale of capital assets*, or from the *exchange* of one capital asset for another of a different type. *Capital assets* include all business property, with the following major exceptions:

(1) Inventory items and other property which are held primarily for sale to customers in the ordinary course of business.

(2) Real estate and depreciable business property which are used in the business.

(3) Copyrights; literary, musical, or artistic compositions; and similar property, under certain circumstances.

(4) Accounts or notes receivable acquired in the course of business in exchange for goods or services sold.

(5) Certain short-term government obligations issued on a discount basis.

A *long-term capital gain or loss* results from the sale of a capital asset which the business has held for more than six months. A *short-term capital gain or loss* results from the sale of a capital asset held for six months or less.

All of a taxpayer's capital gains and losses must be considered together in computing his tax. The excess of *net long-term capital gains* from all transactions combined over *net short-term capital losses* is taxed as though it were a single long-term capital gain. Such excesses are subject to the following maximum tax rates:

(1) For corporations the maximum tax rate on the gain is 30 per cent.

(2) On capital gains of individuals up to $50,000 the tax rate is limited to 25 per cent of the gain. The maximum tax rate on additional gains is gradually being increased to 35 per cent.

Net short-term capital gains are taxed at the same rates as ordinary income. Special rules apply to the deduction of capital losses against ordinary income.

Although real estate and depreciable property used in the business are not capital assets under the definition of the tax law, some *gains* on the sale of such property may be treated as long-term capital gains. Others are treated as ordinary income. If net losses from the sale or exchange of such property exceed net gains, the loss is considered to be an *ordinary loss* and is deductible in full in the tax return. When the net gain associated with property of these types which has been held for more than six months exceeds the losses, the difference may be treated as a long-term capital gain in some cases and as ordinary income in others.

Example 2   During 1973 a business had the following transactions:

(1) Stock of the Worth Corp. which had been acquired for $3,000 on December 31, 1972, was sold on July 1, 1973, for $8,000.

(2) Stock of the Poor Company which had been purchased for $10,000 on August 1, 1973, was sold on December 5, 1973, for $8,000.

What was the taxable status of these transactions?

Solution   Both transactions are capital asset transactions; therefore

Net long-term capital gain from sale of Worth Corp. stock.........	$5,000
Minus net short-term capital loss from sale of Poor Co. stock......	2,000
Equals excess of net long-term capital gains over net short-term capital losses...	$3,000

If the transactions are those of an individual, only $1,500 (half of the $3,000) is included in the tax return of 1973, and the tax may not exceed 50 per cent of this amount. If the transactions are those of a corporation, the tax is limited to 30 per cent of $3,000. If the corporation's income exceeds $25,000, the ordinary income rate would be 48 per cent.

In planning a *single* sale or exchange of a capital asset, management should generally try to have a gain qualify as a *long-term capital gain,* which is taxable at a reduced rate. To minimize the *total burden* of taxes, however, the tax effect of ordinary income and ordinary losses for the current period and other periods must also be considered.

Planning the timing of a number of capital asset transactions is more complicated. If a capital gain and loss occur in the same year, they partially or wholly offset each other. It may be advantageous to time a long-term capital gain transaction so that it will occur in one year and will be taxed at a reduced rate, and to time a capital loss so that it will occur in a different year and can be partially or wholly offset against ordinary income subject to tax.

Business owners as individuals may be able to reduce their taxes by arranging for their income from the business to be taxed as a long-term capital gain rather than as ordinary income. For example, it may be desirable and feasible for a stockholder to receive his gain from the growth of a corporation as a long-term capital gain when he sells the stock rather than as annual dividends.

Example 3   An individual is planning to invest $100,000 in a corporation for five years. He thinks that, if he receives his compensation in the form of dividends of $10,000 a year, the stock can be sold for $100,000 at the end of five years. On the other hand, if the corporation uses its income to finance growth for the five-year period, the stock will probably sell for $150,000 at the end of five years. What will be the tax effect of each alternative if the individual's other income is such that additional annual income will be taxed at about 50 per cent?

Solution   This individual's tax on his annual dividends will be approximately 50 per cent of $10,000, or $5,000 a year. After paying income tax, his net receipts from the corporation will be $5,000 a year for five years. The tax on the long-term capital gain will be 25 per cent of $50,000, or $12,500, paid at the end of five years.

Under this alternative, his net receipts will be $37,500 at the end of the fifth year. This solution does not evaluate the effect of differences in the timing of receipts and payments from the point of view of either the individual or the corporation.

Tax Saving in Choice of Financing Methods

The principal outside sources of funds for long-term investment in the business are the issuance of bonds, preferred stock, and common stock.

Interest paid to bondholders is a *deductible expense* in computing business income subject to tax, but dividends paid to preferred and common stockholders are not deductible. The use of bonds as a source of financing reduces the net interest cost on borrowed capital by the amount of the tax reduction which the borrower receives for the interest expense.

Example 4   A corporation wishes to raise $1,000,000 of additional capital by issuing either five per cent bonds or five per cent preferred stock. Future income before deducting interest and income tax is expected to be about $175,000 a year. What are the comparative after-tax costs of each method of financing?

Solution

	5% Bonds	*5% Preferred Stock*
Income before interest and income tax......	$175,000	$175,000
Deduct bond interest expense.................	50,000	
Income subject to income tax.................	$125,000	$175,000
Deduct federal income tax (22% of the first $25,000 plus 48% of income over $25,000)............................	53,500	77,500
Net income..	$ 71,500	$ 97,500
Deduct dividends on preferred stock.........		50,000
Net income to common stock equity.........	$ 71,500	$ 47,500

The net cost of funds obtained by borrowing is 2.6 per cent (5 per cent of the sum borrowed, minus income tax at 48 per cent of 5 per cent of the sum borrowed). The net cost of obtaining funds by preferred stock is 5 per cent.

The tax deductibility of interest has sometimes caused businesses to ignore considerations of financial safety in choosing between bonds and stocks. The *business risk associated with bonds is greater* because they require *fixed payments* of interest and principal. If earnings decline, these fixed requirements may cause the business financial difficulty. At the same time, the tax advantage also declines. If there is no income before interest and tax, there is no tax reduction associated with the interest. In such a case, the net interest cost in Example 4 would be 5 per cent, not 2.6 per cent. Tax loss carryovers partly or wholly alleviate this condition.

TAX SAVING BY CHOICE OF ACCOUNTING METHODS

In addition to opportunities which most businesses have for reducing their income tax burden by planning the form and nature of business transactions, there are also a number of *choices of accounting methods* by which businesses may attempt to *minimize* or *postpone* their taxes. The corporate or individual taxpayer should choose very carefully its methods of reporting transactions for tax purposes. In many cases, changes of method are permitted only if the Treasury Department gives permission, and taxpayers are not permitted to change back and forth in such a way as to "have their cake and eat it, too."

Circumstances in Which Tax Postponement Is Desirable

Many of the elections which a taxpayer is permitted to make in reporting taxable income deal largely with the *timing* of taxable revenue or deductible expenses. A given method of reporting taxable income results in a *postponement of taxable income* if it permits the taxpayer to *report revenue later* or to *deduct expenses earlier* than does an alternative method.

Example 5 A taxpayer is trying to decide which of two methods to use in reporting a tax deduction: method *X*, which will result in a tax deduction of $10,000 in 1973 and zero in 1974, or method *Y*, which will result in a tax deduction of zero in 1973 and $10,000 in 1974. Other taxable income for each of the two years is expected to be $40,000. What effect will each method have on taxable income?

Solution

	1973	1974	Total for Two Years
Method *X*:			
Other taxable income.........	$40,000	$40,000	$80,000
Deduction in question.........	10,000	0	10,000
Taxable income..............	$30,000	$40,000	$70,000
Method *Y*:			
Other taxable income.........	$40,000	$40,000	$80,000
Deduction in question.........	0	10,000	10,000
Taxable income..............	$40,000	$30,000	$70,000

Method *X* will postpone $10,000 of taxable income from the first year to the second.

Postponement of taxable income to a later year lessens the burden of income taxes on the business

(1) If the *tax rate* on the income in question is *lower in the second year* than in the first; or

(2) If the applicable tax rate is expected to be the same for both years, and the business can in the meantime *earn a return* on the funds not paid out in taxes until later; or

(3) Even though the tax rate on the postponed taxable income increases, the business can *earn more* on the funds temporarily retained than the amount of the tax increase.

Example 6 If the taxpayer in Example 5 would have to pay income tax of 48 per cent on the $10,000 in question in 1973 but expects the applicable tax rate in 1974 to be

22 per cent, method X would result in a total tax saving of $2,600 for the two-year period.

Example 7   If the taxpayer in Example 5 expects the applicable tax rate to be 48 per cent in both 1973 and 1974, method X will not reduce the total income tax. However, if the taxpayer can earn 6 per cent on the $4,800 *not* paid out in taxes at the end of the first year under method X as compared with method Y, it will have $288 more before taxes and $149.76 more after taxes at the end of 1974 by using method X.

Example 8   The taxpayer in Example 5 will be better off if it postpones the item of taxable income to 1974 if it can earn 6 per cent on its money during 1974, unless the applicable tax rate increases to about 50.94 per cent.[1]

The following sections describe some of the alternative methods which a taxpayer may choose to change the *timing* of taxable income.

Cash Versus Accrual Basis of Accounting

This textbook has presented the basic principles and chief uses of the *accrual basis* of accounting, under which *income* is defined as the difference between *revenue earned* and *expenses and losses incurred*. Income tax law permits a business to use the *cash basis* of measuring taxable income unless inventories are a significant factor in its operations. Under the cash basis, items of revenue are included in taxable income in the period in which they are *collected*, and expenses are deducted in the period in which they are *paid for*. The taxpayer must amortize long-term unexpired costs, such as depreciable assets, over the tax periods during which the assets are used.

The cash-basis taxpayer can influence the amount of its periodic taxable income to some extent by changing the timing of revenue collections or expense payments.

Even if the taxpayer uses the *accrual basis* of reporting *taxable income*, the tax rules generally provide that revenue items collected in advance, such as rentals, are taxable when the taxpayer collects them. This provision is in conflict with the requirements of the accrual basis of accounting for *business income*, which treat only *earned* amounts as revenue.

The business which uses the accrual basis of income tax reporting is usually not permitted to deduct expenses until all factors which affect their amounts have become definite. Most of the "estimated expenses" for product warranties and similar items, which are proper deductions in computing business income, cannot be deducted in the tax return until the period in which liabilities to specific individuals are incurred.

---

[1]   Let x = the increase in the tax rate which will cause the increase in future taxes to be equal to the interest (after taxes) earned on funds temporarily retained

$$\$4,800x = \text{the resulting increase in the 1974 tax bill}$$
$$\$288(0.52 - x) = \text{the after-tax earnings on the funds temporarily invested}$$
$$\$288(0.52 - x) = \$4,800x$$
$$x = 0.02943.$$

The present rate, 48 per cent, plus the computed increase, 2.94 per cent, equals 50.94 per cent.

Installment Sales Method

A taxpayer may elect to report as taxable income only the part of the gross margin on installment sales which is reflected in *cash collections* on the installment accounts receivable during the current accounting period. Under the rules of financial accounting, on the other hand, the entire sales price is generally considered to be realized revenue at the time of the sale, and the entire cost of goods sold is deducted as an expense in the same period.

Example 9 A business sold merchandise on installment accounts for a total of $200,000 in 1973, collecting $80,000 in cash in that year. Cost of goods sold totaled $120,000 and other operating expenses were $20,000. Uncollectible accounts were expected to be 3 per cent of sales, and collection costs in future years were expected to be $6,000. During 1973 the unrecovered cost of goods repossessed was $1,000.

What would be the comparative results of using the installment sales method for tax reporting and the accrual basis in the financial statements?

Solution

	1973 Income	
	Income Statement	Tax Return
Sales revenue.............................	$200,000	$200,000
Deduct loss from uncollectibles (estimated).......................	6,000	
Net sales revenue.....................	$194,000	
Deduct cost of goods sold..............	120,000	120,000
Gross margin..........................	$ 74,000	$ 80,000
Deduct uncollected gross margin, 120/200		48,000
Collected gross margin..............		$ 32,000
Deduct operating expenses:		
Collection costs (estimated)........ $ 6,000		
Loss on unrecovered cost of repossessions		$ 1,000
Other operating expenses........... 20,000		20,000
Total operating expenses........	26,000	21,000
Income before income tax............	$ 48,000	
Taxable income.........................		$ 11,000

When the entire gross margin is considered to be realized under *accrual accounting*, proper matching requires that estimated future uncollectibles and collection costs be deducted from the gross margin. Tax rules permit only the deduction of collection costs actually incurred and the unrecovered cost of the merchandise when installment customers default in their payments.

Percentage-of-Completion and Completed-Contract Methods

In reporting income from long-term contracts, the taxpayer is permitted to use either the *percentage-of-completion method* or the *completed-contract method*. Under the *percentage-of-completion method* income is reported in each period in the same proportion as costs incurred on the contract during the period bear to the estimated total cost of the entire contract.

Example 10   Early in 1973 a contractor signed a contract promising to complete the construction of a building for a price of $500,000. At the end of 1973 the construction costs incurred to date totaled $150,000, and it was estimated that $250,000 more would be required to complete construction. What was the 1973 income under the percentage-of-completion method?

Solution   Estimated total income on the contract is $100,000 (contract price of $500,000 minus estimated total costs of $400,000). Costs to date are $150,000/$400,000 of total costs; therefore income earned to date is 150/400 of the total estimated income on the contract, or $37,500.

The taxpayer may *postpone reporting taxable income* to the period in which the *contract is completed*. If the contract extends over several years, reporting the entire amount of income in a single year may result in higher total taxes than spreading it over several years, particularly if the taxpayer is an individual. His income in the year of completion of the contract may be taxed at much higher rates than would apply to smaller amounts of income reported in several different years.

Inventory Method

As a general rule, the tax law permits a taxpayer to use any inventory method which is acceptable for financial accounting. The taxpayer must use an inventory method consistently, and must usually obtain the permission of the Internal Revenue Service to change methods. This permission is not given freely.

There is a considerable difference of opinion as to what components should be included in determining the cost of an inventory item, particularly an item which has been manufactured. The status of direct costing as an acceptable method for income tax purposes is very doubtful.

The lower-of-cost-or-market method may be used as a tax inventory method unless the LIFO cost method is in use.

LIFO has received attention chiefly as a method for postponing income taxes indefinitely. The time at which it is adopted, the expected movement of acquisition costs of goods in the future, and the extent to which ending inventory balances are likely to decline or increase are important factors in estimating whether LIFO will result in tax benefits. If future costs are expected to rise substantially and future inventory balances are expected to remain constant or to increase, LIFO will probably *postpone income taxes* indefinitely. In times of declining prices, however, LIFO will result in higher income taxes than the FIFO or the average-cost methods of measuring inventory. Furthermore, if a part of inventory which has been assigned a low unit cost on a LIFO basis is liquidated during a period of high income, the method may result in higher taxes than another method would.

If a business uses LIFO in its income tax returns, it must also use LIFO in reporting to its stockholders and creditors.

Depreciation Method

The Internal Revenue Code of 1954 permitted taxpayers to use any one of several *accelerated depreciation* methods for new property with an estimated useful life of three years or more acquired after 1953. Tax regulations differentiate between real estate and other types of depreciable property. The best known of these methods, the *uniform-rate-on-declining-balance method* and the *sum-of-years'-digits method*, were described and illustrated in Chapter 12. In addition, the taxpayer can use any other consistent method of depreciation which does not accumulate a greater amount of depreciation during the first two-thirds of the property's life than would be accumulated under the declining-balance method at twice the straight-line rate.[2]

The taxpayer may elect to use an accelerated depreciation method for one asset or group of assets and not for others. He may use one method for assets acquired in one year and another method for those acquired in later years.

Example 11 shows how the sum-of-the-years'-digits depreciation method postpones the payment of income taxes as compared with the straight-line method.

Example 11   A taxpayer has just acquired a new machine with a cost of $3,000, an estimated useful life of five years, and an estimated salvage value of zero. It expects the taxable income during the next few years to be subject to corporate income tax at 48 per cent. What are the comparative effects of the straight-line and sum-of-the-years'-digits methods of depreciation on its net income and net cash receipts, if the taxpayer uses the same method in both its general-purpose financial statements and its income tax returns?

Solution

	Year 1	Year 2	Year 3	Year 4	Year 5
Straight-line depreciation	$ 600	$600	$600	$600	$600
Sum-of-the-years'-digits depreciation ...	1,000	800	600	400	200
Difference in taxable income under SYD method.........................	−$ 400	−$200	$ 0	+$200	+$400
Difference in income tax, at 48%	− 192	+ 96	0	+ 96	+ 192
Difference in net income after tax......	−$ 208	−$104	$ 0	+$104	+$208
Difference in net cash receipts by years (equaling tax postponed)	+ 192	+ 96	0	− 96	− 192
Cumulative difference in net cash receipts under SYD method ...	+ 192	+ 288	+ 288	+ 192	0

As a result of the postponement of income tax under the sum-of-the-years'-digits depreciation method, the taxpayer has the use of $192 more money in year 2 than it would have under the straight-line method, $288 more in the third year, $288 in the fourth, $192 in the fifth, and none thereafter. If any return at all can be earned on those funds, the taxpayer will be better off by using the sum-of-the-years'-digits method in this case, where the income tax rate on the business does not increase.

In addition to the use of accelerated depreciation methods, the taxpayer can postpone the payment of income tax by electing to deduct *additional first-year*

---

[2] *Internal Revenue Code of 1954*, Sec. 167(b).

depreciation on property with a useful life of six years or more. Taxpayers may elect, in addition to the ordinary first-year depreciation, to deduct an initial amount of 20 per cent of the cost of tangible personal property acquired. This special deduction applies to only $10,000 of investment for each taxpayer, except that on joint returns the limit is $20,000.

Taxpayers may use the Asset Depreciation Range (ADR) system in determining the lives of property for tax purposes. Under this system the life for depreciation purposes may vary as much as 20 per cent either way from the guideline lives established by the Internal Revenue Service. For example, if the IRS guideline life is 10 years, the taxpayer may use any life from 8 to 12 years.

Other Important Choices of Accounting Method

Certain expenditures incurred for the purpose of exploring a mineral deposit may be deducted in the year in which they are incurred, or they may be treated as deductions in the periods in which the mineral is sold.

If a corporation wishes, it may deduct organization costs over a period of not less than 60 months. From the standpoint of financial accounting, such costs are considered to be an asset with a benefit for the life of the corporation.

The taxpayer also has a choice of deferring or not deferring the deduction of research and experimental costs whose nature is current expenses rather than capital expenditures.

A method for determining the effects of differences in the timing of tax payments on the after-tax rate of return of the business is presented in Chapter 26.

OTHER DIFFERENCES BETWEEN FINANCIAL AND TAXABLE INCOME

In addition to the differences caused by election of accounting methods, the income of businesses as reported in their general-purpose financial statements may differ from that reported in their income tax returns because of (1) the nontaxability of some exchanges, (2) gains on the involuntary conversion of property, (3) the special deductions allowed for percentage depletion, and (4) the carrying back and forward to other years of business casualty losses and operating losses.

Nontaxable Exchanges

When a taxpayer exchanges property (other than inventory), which it holds for productive use in its business or for investment, for property of a like kind to be held for the same purpose, it has neither a taxable gain nor a deductible loss. According to recognized accounting principles, there may be a gain or loss on such an exchange, measured by the difference between the unexpired book cost of the asset parted with and its fair market value at the date of the exchange.

Example 12   A taxpayer traded a machine with an original cost of $10,000 and accumulated depreciation of $4,000 for a smaller machine. On the date of the trade the old machine could have been sold for $5,000. What is the amount of the gain or loss for tax purposes?

Solution   Because property held for productive use in the business is being traded for like property to be held for the same purpose, there is neither a taxable gain nor a deductible loss. The exchange has the following effect for tax purposes:

INCOME TAX METHOD

A, Machine (new)...	6,000	
A, Machine—Accumulated Depreciation (old)............	4,000	
A, Machine (old)...		10,000
To record the trade of an old machine for a new one, with no effect on taxable income.		

The tax cost of the new machine, which is used for computing depreciation on future tax returns, is $6,000.

FINANCIAL ACCOUNTING METHOD

A, Machine (new)...	5,000	
A, Machine—Accumulated Depreciation (old)............	4,000	
OE, Loss on Exchange of Machine..........................	1,000	
A, Machine (old)...		10,000
To record the trade of an old machine for a new one at a loss of $1,000.		

The cost of the new machine to be used in computing depreciation for financial accounting purposes in the future is $5,000.

Under the income tax method of recording tax-free exchanges, the gain or loss on an asset which is no longer owned is carried forward to future periods as an addition to or reduction from the cost of the new asset.

Gains on Involuntary Conversions

When a taxpayer receives cash for an asset which has been condemned for public use, or when he receives the insurance proceeds for an asset which has been destroyed by a casualty, in effect he has sold the asset against his will. Tax rules provide that he may *elect not to report the gain at the time of the involuntary conversion* if he uses all the cash received to replace the asset. His cost of the new asset for tax purposes is its cost, minus the gain that was not recognized. Losses on such involuntary conversions must be deducted in full at the time they are incurred.

Percentage Depletion

A taxpayer may elect to compute the depletion on a natural resource by the *production method*. To do so he divides the *cost* of the resource by the estimated total number of units to be extracted, and then multiplies this unit rate of depletion by the number of units extracted during each period. Taxable income is reduced by depletion applicable to the number of units *sold* during the period.

The taxpayer may elect to deduct, in lieu of depletion based on cost, an allowed percentage of the gross income obtained from the property. This *percentage depletion* may be deducted for income tax purposes even when the total previous deductions for depletion have exceeded the original cost of the asset.

Loss Carrybacks and Carryforwards

An undue hardship would often be worked on businesses if their net income of one year were taxed at a high rate, with no offsetting refund in succeeding loss years. To prevent this, the income tax provisions permit a business which incurs a loss to combine its periodic taxable income over a series of years. This is especially beneficial to new businesses, which often operate at a loss during their early years. It also helps to stabilize the results of businesses over cyclical economic swings.

Under current law a taxpayer may carry a net tax loss back for three years and forward for five, to be offset against any taxable income in those years.

Example 13   A taxpayer had a net tax loss of $50,000 in 1974. To what years may it be carried as an offset to taxable income?

Solution   The 1974 loss may be carried to the following years, in sequence, until it is exhausted: back to 1971, 1972, and 1973, and forward to 1975, 1976, 1977, 1978, and 1979.

The taxpayer may be entitled to refunds of taxes paid in earlier years. The loss carryforwards will reduce the amount of income tax that it would otherwise pay on the basis of net income earned in later years.

Tax-averaging procedures are also available to individuals whose taxable income fluctuates significantly from year to year.

Summary   The objectives of income taxation are to provide revenue for the support of governmental activities and to promote or discourage particular business activities, according to the judgment of the legislative body. General-purpose accounting is designed to report the financial progress and status of a business to managers, stockholders, creditors, and others who have a direct interest in its affairs. Because of these differences in purpose, there are many differences between the determinants of *taxable income* and those of *business income*.

A business should strive to maximize its rate and amount of income in the long run. Income tax is a significant factor to be considered in planning alternative courses of action to achieve this objective. Income tax provisions may have an important effect on the way in which the business is organized; on the types, form, and timing of the transactions in which it engages; and on the manner in which it accounts for these transactions in its income tax returns.

Income tax rules do not follow a completely unified theory of income measurement. For this reason they should not be permitted to dictate the methods which the business uses in its general-purpose financial reports. However, where there are substantial differences between the income reported for income tax purposes and that reported in the financial statements, the effects of such differences on periodic income tax expense, income, and related assets and liabilities should be disclosed. The section "Matching Income Tax Expense with Business Income" on p. 385 of Chapter 13 describes the appropriate methods of reporting these effects.

Discussion Questions and Problems

17-1 "Both the income tax return and the financial statements are designed to report the *income* of a business for a period of time. Since they are designed to accomplish the same purpose, they should follow the same method. Uniformity of method can best be achieved by law; therefore, accounting methods of reporting should follow the requirements of the income tax laws." Discuss the validity of this statement, giving reasons if you disagree with any part of it.

17-2 For income tax purposes rent collected in advance is fully taxable in the period in which it is received. For general accounting purposes, however, it is treated as additions to income only to the extent earned.

a. How can the income tax treatment be justified?
b. How can the financial accounting treatment be justified?
c. How would you reconcile these opposing viewpoints in the financial statements?

17-3 "A corporation is subject to double taxation; therefore, it will pay the owners of a business to organize it as a partnership."

a. Illustrate what is meant by "double taxation."
b. If double taxation cannot be avoided in a given case, will the partnership form result in lower income tax than the corporate form? Explain.
c. If the partnership form of organization seems likely to minimize the income tax burden on the business and the individual owners combined, would you recommend that it be used for the business? Why?

17-4

a. What are some of the important income tax considerations in organizing a business? In raising its capital?
b. How significant is income tax in the planning of accounting methods for a small partnership? A large partnership? A small corporation? A large corporation? How would its effect on the four differ?

17-5

a. What is meant by a *capital expenditure* in accounting?
b. What is meant by a *capital asset* under the income tax law? How does it differ from a capital expenditure?
c. Suppose that the income tax rate on ordinary income of a corporation is 50 per cent. If it has one capital transaction for the year, resulting in a gain of $10,000, and other income of $25,000, what is the difference in income tax if the gain is considered to be a long-term rather than a short-term capital gain?

17-6 "The tax burden of a business can be minimized by proper timing of its taxable revenue and deductible expenses."

a. Should the deduction of expenses be postponed if the income tax rates are expected to be the same in the future? If they are expected to be higher? If they are expected to be lower? Explain each answer.

b. Would it be advantageous for a business to switch to the use of the installment sales method of reporting in its tax return if the collection period of its installment sales averages 36 months, the current tax rate is 40 per cent, and the effective rate for the next five years is expected to be 44 per cent? Explain. (Ignore any penalty on change of method.)

17-7

a. Under what circumstances may a business use the cash basis of reporting in its income tax return?
b. What factors might lead a business to select this tax-reporting method?
c. Under what circumstances would it be proper for a business to use the cash basis in its financial reporting?

17-8

a. Explain what is meant by the installment sales method of reporting taxable income.
b. Under what circumstances might a taxpayer wish to use this method in its tax return?
c. Under what circumstances would it be acceptable for it to use this method in its financial statements?
d. Assume that a business finds it advantageous to use the installment sales method in its tax return, but that generally accepted accounting principles require it to use the accrual sales basis of reporting revenue in its financial statements. What special procedures are needed in its financial statements under these circumstances?

17-9

a. Under what circumstances is a business justified in using the LIFO inventory method in its income tax return?
b. Under what circumstances should it use LIFO in its financial statements?
c. May the business use LIFO in its tax return and not in the financial statements?
d. What circumstances might cause a business which had previously adopted LIFO for tax purposes to regret its decision?

17-10

a. Under what circumstances would it be best for a business to use accelerated rather than straight-line depreciation in its income tax return?
b. Under what circumstances would accelerated depreciation be appropriate in the financial statements?
c. Assuming that accelerated depreciation is best for tax purposes and straight-line depreciation for general reporting, what special accounting procedures are required?
d. What circumstances might cause a business to regret its decision to use accelerated depreciation?

17-11   In January, 1963, the Farrar Co. purchased a building for $100,000. Depreciation has been recorded on the basis of an estimated life of 40 years and zero salvage value. Because of rapid increases in construction costs, the insurable value of the building on December 1, 1973, was $90,000. On that date the building was totally destroyed by fire. Shortly thereafter the insurance company paid the Farrar Cc. $90,000 in compensation for the loss. The Farrar Company used this money and $20,000 additional to buy a new building on December 30, 1974.

a. What was the effect of these events on the financial statements of the Farrar Co. in 1974? Depreciation is recorded to the nearest whole year.

b. What special election might the company make in its 1974 tax return? Under what circumstances would this election seem wise?

c. Assuming that the election in part b was made, what would be the effects on the company's 1975 tax returns and financial statements?

17-12

a. What is meant by *percentage depletion?*
b. How does it differ from depletion in the financial statements?
c. What is the principal objective of percentage depletion?

17-13   Hargrett and Isell are trying to decide whether to organize their business as a partnership or as a corporation. They expect annual sales to average $200,000 and operating expenses, other than management compensation, to average $150,000. Each feels that he must receive a salary of $18,000 from the business. If the business is incorporated, all income is expected to be distributed as dividends. Hargrett and Isell would own equal amounts of capital stock, or share equally in partnership net income after salaries. Personal tax exemptions and deductions of each are expected to be $5,000. Each is entitled to exclude dividends of $200 from taxable income.

Applicable tax rates for corporate income are 22 per cent for the first $25,000 and 48 per cent for any remainder. Personal tax rates are given on p. 488.

Required   Compare the effects of the corporate and partnership forms on the disposable income of Hargrett and Isell. Operating income from other sources is $50,000.

17-14   During 1973 the Sanders Corp. had the following sales of property:

(1) Common stock of Jasper Co. acquired on July 7, 1972, for $3,500 was sold on February 2 for $6,000.
(2) A lot of special sale merchandise which had been acquired in December, 1972, for $4,000 was sold in July 1973 for $7,000.
(3) A vacant lot which the Sanders Corp. had purchased in 1955 for $1,000 was sold in May, 1973, for $7,000. It had been originally purchased for speculative gain rather than use.
(4) Preferred stock of the Karen Corp. acquired on January 19, 1973, for $3,000 was sold on June 26 for $1,800.
(5) A lot had been acquired for $8,000 on December 19, 1964, for use as a parking lot for employees. It was so used, and was sold on November 17, 1973, for $12,000.
(6) Common stock of the Alpha Co. which had been acquired on February 20, 1973, for $4,000 was sold on July 3, 1973, for $7,000.

Required   a. List the long-term capital gains and losses.
b. List the short-term capital gains and losses.
c. Compute the excess of net long-term capital gains over net short-term capital losses for the year.
d. Compute the amount of ordinary income from the preceding transactions.
e. Which transactions might have been timed more advantageously? Explain.

17-15   A corporation is trying to decide whether to raise $400,000 of additional capital by issuing 6 per cent bonds payable due in ten years or $4\frac{1}{2}$ per cent cumulative preferred stock. Its annual net income available for the payment of a return to the bondholders or preferred stockholders, before deduction of income tax, is expected to be $80,000.

Required   a. Prepare a table comparing the effects of the issuance of bonds and preferred stock on the amount of return available to common stockholders:

      (1) If the expected income materializes.

      (2) If the net income before interest, dividends, and income tax is only $25,000.

    b. What other factors should the corporation consider before making a decision?

17-16   The Jiffy Appliance Co., Inc., began business in 1973. During the year it made the following sales:

	Sales Price	Cost of Goods Sold
Cash sales...................................	$ 50,000	$40,000
Sales on regular account....................	100,000	70,000
Sales on installment account..............	150,000	90,000

Collections on regular charge accounts during 1973 were $60,000 and collections on installment accounts were $45,000. Salaries and other operating expenses were $50,000.

Required   a. Compute the company's income tax for 1973 if it elects to use the installment sales method in its tax return. Assume a tax rate of 40 per cent.

    b. Compute the amount of tax postponed in 1973.

    c. Present the necessary journal entries and the relevant parts of the financial statements if the company, in addition to part a, uses the full accrual basis in its financial statements.

17-17   Refer to Problem 17-16. The facts are the same except that a two-year warranty is given on products sold. Total costs of servicing products sold under warranty are expected to be 5 per cent of sales. Such costs specifically incurred in 1973 were $2,000. The tax rate is assumed to be 40 per cent in all years.

Required   a. Compute the company's income tax for 1973 under the installment sales method.

    b. Present the necessary journal entries and the relevant parts of the financial statements if the company, in addition to a, uses the full accrual basis in its financial statements.

17-18   The Cherokee Construction Company, Inc., is engaged in constructing bridges. Its activities have been as follows during the past three years:

	1971	1972	1973
Contract let on Bridge No. 1, Coosa River, contract price.............................	$500,000		
Costs incurred on Bridge No. 1..............	50,000	$200,000	$150,000
Contract let on Bridge No. 2, Etowah River, contract price.............................	306,000		
Costs incurred on Bridge No. 2..............	60,000	120,000	75,000
Contract let on Bridge No. 3, Oostanaula River, contract price.....................		770,000	
Costs incurred on Bridge No. 3..............		450,000	50,000

Bridge Nos. 1 and 2 were completed in 1973. It is anticipated that Bridge No. 3 will be completed in 1974, and that it will require additional costs of $150,000.

Required   a. Compute the taxable income and the annual income tax of the company for 1971, 1972, and 1973 under the completed-contract method.

    b. Compute the taxable income and the annual income tax of the company for the three years under the percentage-of-completion method.

c. Which method seems to be preferable for tax purposes in this situation? Why? Under what circumstances might the other method be better?

17-19 The Equipage Company bought a machine for $210,000 early in January 1973, paying $210,000. The machine was expected to have a useful life of six years and no salvage value. Equipage elected to use the sum-of-the-years'-digits method of depreciation for tax purposes.

Required

a. Assume that the income tax rate is 40 per cent in all years. Compute the amount of income tax payment postponed each year and cumulatively in comparison with straight-line depreciation.
b. Assume that funds not currently required to pay taxes can be invested at the end of each year at a return of 6 per cent per year, after taxes. Compute how much better off Equipage will be at the end of six years by using SYD depreciation.

17-20 Refer to Problem 12-30 p. 362.

Required

a. Journalize the entry for the trade under the income tax method.
b. Compute the depreciation for 1973 under the income tax and financial accounting methods.
c. What will be the difference in income before tax under the two methods in 1973? In 1974?

17-21 The Monaghan Corp. acquired an automobile three years ago at a cost of $6,000 and has deducted depreciation of 20 per cent a year in its financial statements and in its income tax returns. In 1973 it is planning to trade the old automobile for a new one which has a list price of $8,000. A new car dealer has offered a trade-in allowance of $2,700 on the old car. Another dealer has offered to pay $2,200 cash for it.

Required

a. Show the necessary journal entries for the trade:
   (1) Under the income tax method.
   (2) Under the financial accounting method.
b. Show the necessary journal entries under both methods if the automobile had been sold for cash and the proceeds applied toward the cash purchase of the new automobile.

17-22 The Sizemore Corporation reported the following amounts of taxable income and net income before tax:

1969......$12,000   1970......$20,000   1971......$30,000   1972......$25,000

Applicable tax rates were 22 per cent of the first $25,000 and 48 per cent of income in excess of $25,000 for each year. In 1973 the corporation suffered a net loss of $100,000.

Required

a. Compute the amount of the tax-refund claim at the end of 1973.
b. Journalize all entries relating to income tax in 1973.
c. Journalize all necessary entries if net income for 1974 is $50,000, before deducting income tax.

17-23 The O'Keeffe Corporation's reported taxable income for the past four years was as follows:

1970........$20,000 net income   1972........$50,000 net income
1971......... 15,000 net income   1973........(60,000) net loss

Required   a. Compute the amount of tax liability originally owed by the corporation at the time its tax returns were filed for each of the four years. Assume that current rates were in effect.

b. Compute the amount of income tax as finally determined for each year.

c. How do the carryback and carryforward provisions benefit businesses?

d. How do they help to stabilize economic activity?

e. How do they encourage the formation of new businesses and the making of additional capital investments by existing businesses?

Cases   **17-1**   **A Contrast in Depreciation Policies:** *A. Youngstown Sheet and Tube Company.* The 1962 annual report of the Youngstown Sheet and Tube Company contained the following statement:

Depreciation

Our provision for depreciation and depletion in 1962 was $39,917,892, compared with $31,061,180 in 1961.

In previous annual reports we have commented on the inadequacy of allowances for depreciation for Federal income tax purposes. During 1962, the Treasury Department issued Revenue Ruling 62-21 permitting the use of shorter economic useful lives in computing depreciation of production facilities for Federal income tax purposes. Because of the prospective rapid technological changes facing the steel industry, we believe that some downward revision in the economic useful life estimates used in computing depreciation of production facilities is appropriate. Consequently, the shorter lives permitted by the Treasury Department have been used in computing depreciation for both book and income tax purposes on assets acquired subsequent to 1954, using the sum-of-the-years'-digits method. Likewise, we intend to apply these shorter lives to future asset acquisitions.

With respect to assets acquired in 1954 and prior years, the shorter lives permitted under this revenue ruling were used in computing depreciation for Federal income tax purposes. However, it was not considered necessary to shorten the estimated life of this group of properties for book purposes because under the Company's present accounting practice these assets will become fully depreciated in approximately ten years. The tax reduction ($4,350,000) resulting from the increased depreciation allowable for tax purposes, but not recorded on the books, has been charged to income and credited to a reserve for future income taxes. This reserve will be available to absorb the increase in future Federal income taxes that will occur, in a relatively few years, when depreciation charges on these assets for book purposes exceed those allowable for tax purposes. In this way, net income is not distorted.

As a result of past accounting practice, the undepreciated balance remaining in our fixed asset account is less than the amount remaining to be depreciated for tax purposes. As part of an extended program to adjust this difference, our provision for depreciation for book purposes was approximately $1,600,000 lower in 1962 than it otherwise would have been.

Changes in depreciation, after the effect of Federal income taxes, had the result of reducing 1962 net income by approximately $2,100,000, or about 60¢ per share.

Youngstown's Consolidated Balance Sheet showed a Reserve for Future Federal Income Taxes of $41,760,000 on December 31, 1961, and $50,660,000 on December 31, 1962.

B. The Colorado Fuel and Iron Corporation. The 1962 annual report of The Colorado Fuel and Iron Corporation contained the following comments in the President's letter to the shareholders:

Depreciation

After careful consideration of its long-range financial and tax position, the Corporation elected for financial purposes to change, as of January 1, 1962, to the straight-line method of depreciation on assets previously depreciated on the sum-of-the-years'-digits method. This change resulted in a reduction of $3,820,142 in depreciation for the year. As permitted by the Revenue Act of 1962, assets previously depreciated on the sum-of-the-years'-digits method will be depreciated for tax purposes on the straight-line method beginning January 1, 1963.

Taxes

The Internal Revenue Service has examined the Corporation's income tax returns through the year 1961 and no additional assessments are anticipated. Accordingly, the Corporation restored to income Federal income taxes previously provided and no longer required in the amount of $2,196,712. The loss in 1962, together with a loss carry-forward at the beginning of the year, is available to offset future taxable income.

The Revenue Act of 1962 provided for an investment credit against Federal income taxes up to 7% of the cost of certain depreciable property acquired and placed in service after 1961. The credit applicable to such acquisitions during 1962 amounted to $165,000 which will be available to offset future taxes of the Corporation.

The following data are from the company's Earnings Statements:

	1962	1961
Earnings (loss)...	$(5,226,792)	$2,005,759
Special Items:		
Loss in connection with closing of plants......	3,881,990	1,450,023
Provision in prior years for federal income taxes no longer required..................	(2,196,712)	—
	1,685,278	1,450,023
Earnings (Loss) after Special Items...............	$(6,912,070)	$ 555,736

Under Current Liabilities, Federal Income Taxes of $1,585,223 were reported on December 31, 1961, and none on December 31, 1962. Deferred Federal Income Taxes of $1,266,300 at the end of 1961 and none at the end of 1962 were reported under Other Liabilities and Reserves.

Required   a. Why did Youngstown Sheet and Tube Company use the sum-of-the-years'-digits method in its tax return? In its financial statements?

b. Why did Colorado Fuel and Iron change from using sum-of-the-years'-digits method to the straight-line method for tax purposes? For book purposes? Compare the reasons for its depreciation policies with those of Youngstown. Which company's policies seem to be more justifiable? Why?

c. Why did Youngstown adopt shorter useful lives for some assets but not for others?

d. Do you think that the stockholders would react unfavorably to Youngstown's reduction in income of $2,100,000 after taxes as a result of the change in depreciation methods? Explain.

e. How should Colorado Fuel and Iron show its tax-loss carryforward in the body of its financial statements?

17-2   Sears, Roebuck & Co. In 1961 Sears, Roebuck & Co. changed its method of reporting taxable income from the sales accrual method to the installment sales method. Sears continued to report the profit on installment sales in its income statements of the year of sale. In the year ended January 31, 1962, Sears reported income tax expense not currently payable of $178.5 million on installment sales of that year. It reported corresponding items of $96.4 million in fiscal year 1963 and $67.7 million in fiscal 1964.

The following data were taken from the company's consolidated income statements.

	Fiscal Year Ended January 31		
	1964	*1963*	*1962*
	(in millions of dollars)		
Income (before tax)	$484.3	$448.4	$414.4
Provision for federal income taxes	223.3	215.2	194.3
Net income	$261.0	$233.2	$220.1

Required

a. Why did the company change its tax-reporting method? Was the change beneficial? Explain.

b. What accounts on the company's financial statements were affected by the change to the installment sales method of reporting in the tax returns? How were they affected?

c. Reconstruct the entries necessary to reflect in the financial statements the effect of using the installment sales method in the tax returns.

d. Assuming that Sears could earn a rate of return of 13 per cent a year, before taxes, how much better off would it be as a result of the change at the end of 1964? Show your computations.

part III

ACCOUNTING IN MANAGEMENT PLANNING AND CONTROL

chapter 18

Cost Concepts and Managerial Decisions

Introduction: Financial Versus Managerial Accounting

One hears frequent references to "financial accounting" and "managerial accounting." The distinction between the two rests primarily on the *use* to which accounting information is put. *Managerial accounting* provides information for *internal use* by managers to aid them in planning and controlling the activities of the firm. *Financial accounting*, on the other hand, provides information to *outsiders* such as investors, creditors, and governmental agencies, who make decisions that affect external relationships of the firm.

In planning and controlling a firm's operating activities, *management needs more detailed information* than is usually provided to outsiders. A medium-sized firm, for example, may provide separate financial reports to management for each operating department or division of the firm, but only one set of general financial statements to outsiders. Moreover, to be useful in planning and controlling operations, managerial accounting reports often include *budgetary figures and estimated future values of assets and income* to meet special needs of management, while financial accounting reports are limited to *historical valuations* based on *generally accepted accounting principles*.

This chapter and the remainder of this text are chiefly concerned with principles and applications of managerial accounting and the use of accounting data in making managerial decisions.

In making decisions, managers evaluate the alternatives open to them by comparing their expected consequences. Accounting reports and analyses specify these expected consequences in monetary terms and indicate their probable impact on the firm's income and financial position.

Example 1   One of the objectives of the management of a motel chain might be to diversify geographically. Accountants prepare analyses of the investments required, together with the expected revenues and expenses, for the various locations being considered by management. *Managers* can use these analyses in choosing between the available alternatives. On the other hand, the motel chain's *stockholders* need financial information in comparing the past and expected future performance of the chain with those of alternative investment opportunities in other businesses which they might be considering, such as utility shares, an apartment building, or a restaurant venture.

INFORMATION FOR PLANNING AND CONTROL

Accounting information for internal use is tailored to the decisions to be made by managers. Accounting data can help managers (1) to *develop plans* for accomplishing the firm's objectives, (2) to *organize* the firm's personnel and other resources for carrying out the plans, and (3) to *measure and control* performance—that is, to keep it in line with plans.

Information for Planning

Planning is probably the most creative aspect of managerial responsibility. In planning, managers first conceive of the long-range *goals* of the firm; they then make them specific in terms of *operational objectives*. The process of specifying business objectives requires information about past events that will aid in *predicting* future events and that can be used to judge whether the objectives can be achieved and are economically sound.

Example 2   Mr. Phillip Crowe, an employee of Acme Car Rentals, decided that he could use his knowledge and experience most effectively by establishing his own business. His ultimate *goal* was to have an automobile rental agency. His first *objective* was to lease some type of equipment other than automobiles to individual customers. Mr. Crowe examined data on the profitability of leasing household tools and equipment, trucks, trailers, and chinaware. He found that all these alternatives were feasible, but his best potential profit at minimum risk pointed toward leasing trailers. After evaluating the further alternatives of operating independently or acting as the agent of a national trailer-leasing agency, he decided to operate independently. He then began working on the details of organizing his business.

Business plans can be classified as either *short-*, *medium-*, or *long-range* in scope. Accountants are mainly concerned with short- and medium-range planning problems, for these problems lend themselves most effectively to *financial analysis*. Long-range plans are likely to cover decades and to be more concerned with nonquantitative considerations, such as the firm's public image, the nature of its work force, and the development of its organizational structure. Short- and medium-range plans are typically made for one or a few accounting *periods*, and they may cover the entire life of a special project which is being evaluated. A *project* is any business action which is important enough to justify separate planning.

Period Plans

The *period plan* most frequently used is the annual *budget*. This type of plan may include revenues and expenses for either the organization as a whole or for any of its parts. For some organizational units it includes only estimated expenses. The periodic budget shows the effects of *projects* that are expected to begin and end within the budget period. It may also include *portions* of a project whose life extends for more than one accounting period, but only a part of which falls within the current planning period.

Example 3   The Paradox Corporation has the following *period plans* for 1973: a sales budget, a budget of cash flows, a manufacturing cost budget, and a general and administrative expense budget.

The company also has two *project plans* which will begin in 1973: (1) a plan to construct a new office building and (2) a plan to purchase a new power generator. The building is expected to last 50 years; its construction will be begun and completed in 1973. The power generator will be purchased in 1973 but is expected to last for 20 years. The cash expenditures for these new facilities will take place in 1973 and will be reflected in the 1973 *cash budget*. The related depreciation and operating expenses will affect *income* in *period budgets* throughout the total lives of the assets. Prior to deciding favorably on the building and generator projects, management evaluated each by using a project budget to determine whether the expenditures would be sufficiently profitable.

Project Plans

Project plans differ from *period plans* in several respects:

(1) They are not related exclusively to any particular accounting period, but may extend over one or more periods.

(2) They do not necessarily pertain to any one subdivision of the organization, or to the whole organization, as period plans usually do.

(3) Project plans usually include information about alternative possibilities and, if the project life is long, some adjustment to recognize the time value of money and the risk involved.[1]

(4) They are limited to an evaluation of the *incremental* consequences of the particular alternatives. They do not consider *total* costs and revenues, as

---

[1] Chapter 25 shows how the time value of money is considered through present value computations.

period budgets usually do. The term *incremental* refers to *differences*—to changes in revenues and costs, or to changes in cash receipts and payments, which specifically result from choosing a given course of action.

Example 4   In evaluating the purchase of the new power generator in Example 3, the Paradox Corporation considered three alternatives: (1) purchasing electricity from the local power company, (2) constructing a nuclear power plant, and (3) constructing a conventional power plant. The accountant prepared a schedule of estimated power requirements over the expected life of the power plants, and then compared the costs of acquiring the power from each of the three sources. Finally, because of the long period of time involved and the need for a substantial outlay of funds if the company decided to invest in its own power plant, the accountant included in the calculations for the second and third alternatives appropriate present-value computations to provide for the recovery of the required investment.

Relevance of Future Costs and Revenues in Planning

Historical costs and revenues are relevant in evaluating alternative courses of action only to the extent that they provide a basis for estimating future costs and revenues. In selecting the best alternative it is convenient to consider only the *difference* (increase or decrease) in future costs and revenues, or receipts and payments, that will result from each alternative.

Example 5   Assume that you own a 1961 Chevrolet in good running condition, which you bought two years ago for $200 and which you can now sell for $150. One day a tire blows out, causing you to drive into a ditch. As a result the wheels are thrown out of alignment and a hole is punched in the oil pan. You learn that to repair the car you will have to spend $65. If you do not repair it, you can sell it to a junk dealer for $30. What should you do?

Solution   Your alternatives are (1) to sell the car for $30 "as is," or (2) to spend $65 and be able to drive the car or sell it for $150. Spending the $65 will increase your total historical investment in the car to $265. The only relevant data for this decision, however, are the resulting *future selling prices* of $30 and $150, which result from the alternative courses of action, and the *additional future outlay* of $65 which would be required under the second alternative. Alternative 2 will result in an incremental net receipt of $85 (the $150 selling price minus the $65 additional outlay). This is a $55 advantage over the $30 net receipt which can be expected from Alternative 1.

The original $200 investment in the car is *not relevant* to the present decision *because it cannot be changed* under either alternative. Similarly, once you repair the car, the $65 expenditure becomes irrelevant to any future decision.

After decisions have been made concerning the projects to be carried out in future periods, the period plans can be completed. In completing these period plans business managers can establish *objectives* for revenues and costs in terms of *budgetary estimates*. Period plans should take into account all significant information concerning future costs and revenues which can be obtained with reasonable effort and reasonable accuracy.

Accomplishing Plans with the Aid of Accounting Systems

After management has developed plans of action for the organization and its subdivisions, a *system* for implementing the plans must be developed. The implementation of a plan requires

(1) The collection and allocation of the *resources* needed to accomplish the desired results.

(2) An *information network* to report periodically on the progress of the undertaking and to signal *deviations* between planned and actual results. The *accounting system* aids management in meeting these organizational requirements.

The accounting system is designed with many purposes in mind, but most important to the organizing process are (1) *identifying the information* needed by management to measure and control performance in accordance with the plan and (2) *installing the controls* necessary to ensure the efficient and effective use of resources.

Both of these purposes are achieved by means of *budgets*. A budget expresses in *monetary terms* the revenue, expense, and cash flow objectives which management expects to achieve during the planning period. The plan is most effective when managers at all levels are given some responsibility in developing it. The completed budget communicates these objectives to the managers who are responsible for taking action to produce the desired results. The budgetary objectives also provide *standards* against which the actual results can be evaluated.

In *organizing* to carry out the business plans, the accounting information system is designed as part of the overall organization of the firm. Procedures are established to collect, process, summarize, and report the data needed by management. A written *accounting manual* outlines these procedures, and includes charts of accounts and instructions for recording both routine and unusual transactions. The accounting system is built around the organization of the business in such a way as to identify and protect the assets of the firm and to encourage their efficient use. A key element of the accounting system is the identification of *responsibility centers*. The activities of each center fall under the responsibility of a particular manager. Accounting reports are designed to show clearly how each manager has discharged his responsibility.

Controlling Operations with the Aid of Accounting Information

Organizing is the means by which business plans are put into action. After the plans are put into effect, actual results are periodically measured to determine whether they correspond with the plan. *Significant differences* between planned and actual outcomes are reported to management. This procedure of focusing attention only on significant departures of actual results from planned results is called *management by exception*. Techniques for analyzing and reporting the *causes* of these significant differences are usually built into the accounting system.

Two basic ideas underlie the principle of management by exception:

(1) Important changes in operating conditions which might require corrective action are brought to light quickly.

(2) The time and effort of managers are not wasted in the needless review of minor differences, but are more effectively directed toward corrective action in areas where substantial gains can be made or substantial losses can be avoided.

COST AND REVENUE BEHAVIOR

It cannot be emphasized too strongly that the data which are relevant to business decisions pertain to the *future* and not merely to the past. Budgetary reports and standards for evaluating performance of actual business results reflect the *expected future values* of revenues, expenses, assets, and equities.

Although predicting future values is subject to much uncertainty, two general methods of prediction are often used with reasonably reliable results: *judgmental association* and *statistical inference*.

Prediction by Association

Knowledge of *cause-and-effect relationships* which exist between elements of business income—revenues and expenses—is of great assistance in estimating the future values of the events which are reflected in the financial budget. Some of these cause-and-effect relationships can be reliably estimated on the basis of law, or of contracts and agreements for the purchase or sale of goods or services.

Example 6 The Ajax Company pays its salesmen a commission of 3 per cent of sales and its manager 1 per cent. If the sales for 1973 are estimated to be $190,000, the commission expense will be 0.04($190,000), or $7,600. Assuming that the same commission agreement holds for future sales, this relationship between sales and commission expense will remain unchanged.

In Example 6 the amount of commission expense *depends* on the amount of sales revenue; therefore commission expense is the *dependent variable* in this relationship and sales revenue is the *independent variable*. The *degree* of relationship between the two, or *correlation*, is perfect. Assuming that the commission agreement remains unchanged, the company would be 100 per cent accurate in predicting that commission expense would be 0.04 of sales revenue at any volume of sales.

Example 7 The Ajax Company has signed a ten-year lease providing for the payment of $6,000 annual rental. The lease expires December 31, 1978. If sales are expected to increase from $150,000 in 1972 to $175,000 in 1973, what will be the change in rental expense?

Solution   None. Rent expense, as set by the contract, will be $6,000 in 1973 and in each
of the succeeding years while the present contract remains in effect.

In Example 7 the amount of rent expense is *independent* of the volume of sales,
and does not vary at all with changes in sales revenue. However, it does accrue
in equal periodic amounts, and therefore varies in direct proportion to time.
Assuming that the rental contract remains unchanged, the company could
accurately predict rent expense in a lump-sum amount of $6,000 for each year.

Variable expenses. Expenses which change in the same direction as, and in
proportion to, changes in revenue or sales volume are called *variable* expenses.
The commission expense in Example 6 fits this definition; Illustration 18-1

Illustration 18-1

An Expense Perfectly Variable with Revenue.

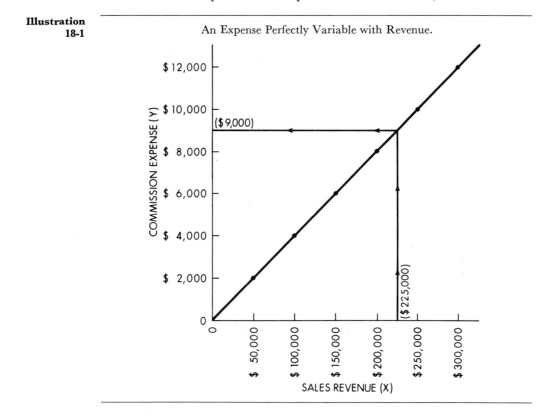

shows this relationship graphically. In such a graph it is customary to show the
values of the *independent variable* along the *horizontal,* or *X,* axis, and those of
the *dependent variable* along the *vertical,* or *Y,* axis. The diagonal line shows the
relationship of commission expense to sales. Its location was determined by
plotting points for the amount of sales commissions for each amount of sales,
at $50,000 intervals, and then drawing a line to connect these points. The
graph can also be used to *predict* the amount of commission expense at any volume of sales.

Example 8   If the sales of Ajax Company for next year are expected to be $225,000, deter-
mine from the graph how much commission expense will be.

Solution   From the point on the X axis representing sales of $225,000, follow a vertical line to the diagonal line of relationship; then follow a horizontal line to the Y axis. The reading at that point, $9,000, is the estimated amount of commission expense if sales are expected to be $225,000.

The graph in Illustration 18-1 is used to show the general relationship of variable expenses to sales and is, of course, not needed to predict the amount of commission expense in this instance. It is a simple matter to estimate commission expense by multiplying any expected amount of sales revenue by 0.04. The specific formula is

$$Y = 0.04X.$$

Fixed expenses. Expenses that are relatively independent of revenue or sales volume and do not vary, or vary only slightly, with changes in revenue are called *fixed* (or *nonvariable*) *expenses.* The rent expense in Example 7 fits this definition, and is shown graphically in Illustration 18-2.

**Illustration
18-2**

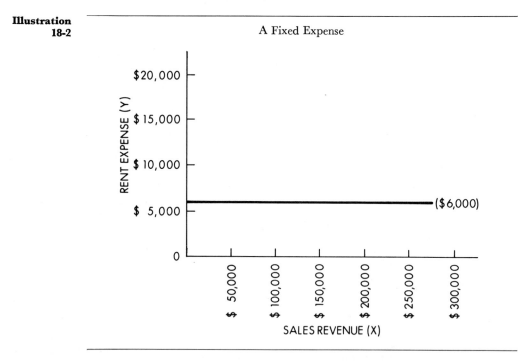

A Fixed Expense

In this graph the amount of rent expense is plotted for each amount of sales at $50,000 intervals. The graph illustrates that fixed expenses remain unchanged as sales revenue increases or decreases.

Total expenses. Total expenses for any given volume of sales can be estimated by combining fixed expenses with variable expenses, as shown by the graph in Illustration 18-3. At revenue volume A, total expenses will be equal to the dollar amount corresponding to the lower arrow on the Y axis. At the higher revenue B, total expenses will be equal to the point shown by the upper arrow. The increase in sales revenue measured by the horizontal distance from A to B

Illustration
18-3
Changes in Total Expenses Resulting from an Increase in Revenues

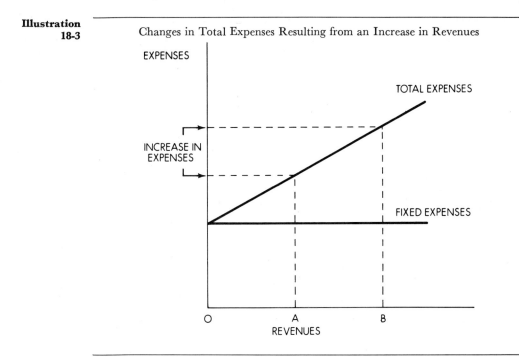

results in the increase in expenses measured by the difference between the two arrows on the Y axis.

Example 9 Assume that total fixed expenses for the Ajax Company amount to $60,000 and that variable expenses amount to $75,000 for a sales level of $150,000. If sales revenues are expected to rise to $180,000, what will be the total of estimated expenses?

Solution The fixed expenses will remain at $60,000 while the variable expenses will amount to $75,000/$150,000 times $180,000, or 50 per cent of $180,000. Therefore, the expected expenses at the new sales level of $180,000 are $60,000 + $90,000, or $150,000.

As long as the variable expenses remain in the same proportion to sales, and as long as the fixed expenses do not change because of a change in level of activity, total expenses can be estimated for any level of sales in the manner illustrated in Example 9.

Prediction by Statistical Inference

The behavior of some expense items can be estimated accurately by reasoning or by the use of relationships which are set by law (for example, property tax rates) or by contract (for example, commissions). Expense items whose components and behavior are more complex can often be predicted by means of graphs or formulas derived by statistical analysis of historical accounting information.

Example 10   In planning for 1973 the controller of Ajax Company wished to know whether Other Salaries and Sales Revenue were closely related in behavior. The following data were taken from the general ledger accounts for 1972:

| | Actual Results for 1972 | |
Month	Sales (X)	Other Salaries (Y)
January......................................	$ 13,000	$ 1,200
February	11,000	1,050
March	12,000	1,100
April...	10,000	1,040
May	10,000	1,030
June	9,000	1,000
July..	8,000	930
August	7,000	900
September..................................	10,000	1,040
October.....................................	15,000	1,270
November..................................	20,000	1,530
December	25,000	1,700
Totals	$150,000	$13,790

A *statistical scattergraph* can be used to determine visually whether there seems to be any consistent relationship between two variables. This is done in Illustration 18-4 for the monthly Sales and Other Salaries presented in Example 10. Each dot represents the Sales Revenue and the corresponding Other Salaries

Illustration 18-4   Scattergraph Showing Relationship of Other Salaries to Sales Revenues

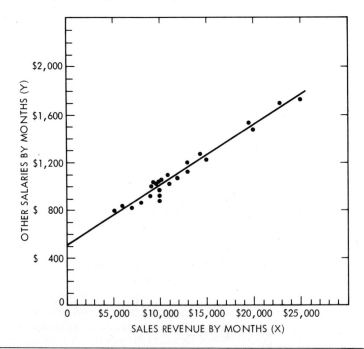

Expense for a month. A line connecting the dots would be almost straight, indicating that there was a close relationship in 1972 between changes in the amount of Other Salaries and changes in the amount of Sales. Assuming that the same pattern of relationship can be expected to continue in 1973, the straight line which was fitted visually to the dots in the scattergraph can be used to predict the amount of Other Salaries. If estimated Sales Revenue is given for the year or for any month, the amount of Other Salaries for the same period can be estimated by the same method illustrated in Example 8. In this case, however, there is a *mixed expense* rather than a perfectly variable expense.

Mixed Expenses

An expense which varies in the same direction as, but less than proportionately with, the volume of sales is called a *mixed expense*. Mixed expenses have both a fixed and a variable component.

The fixed and variable portions of a mixed expense, such as Other Salaries in Example 10, can be estimated in the following manner:

(1) Determine the amount of change in Other Salaries that occurs between any two different sales levels. For example, take sales levels of $10,000 and $20,000:

	Sales Level	Other Salaries
	$20,000	$1,530
	− 10,000	− 1,030
Change	+$10,000	+$ 500

(2) Divide the increase in expenses by the increase in sales in order to determine the percentage of variable costs per dollar of sales:

$$\$500/\$10,000 = 0.05 \text{ or } 5 \text{ per cent.}$$

(3) To determine the amount of the variable component of Other Salaries for any given sales level, multiply the percentage calculated in (2) by the amount of Sales:

	(a)	(b)	(c)
Sales volume...	$20,000	$10,000	$15,000
Variable Other Salaries (0.05 × sales)................	1,000	500	750

(4) To estimate the amount of the fixed component of Other Salaries at any given sales level, subtract the amount of variable Other Salaries expense from total Other Salaries expense at that sales level:

	(a)	(b)	(c)*
Sales volume...	$20,000	$10,000	$15,000
Total Other Salaries per accounting records..........	1,530	1,030	1,270
Deduct variable amount..................................	1,000	500	750
Fixed amount of Other Salaries.........................	$ 530	$ 530	$ 520

The computation illustrates the fact that this method of calculation simply approximates costs. It is equally possible that fixed salaries may amount to $530 and variable cost to $740.

(5) To estimate the total amount of Other Salaries at any given level of sales, multiply the per cent of variable Other Salaries by the amount of sales and add the amount of nonvariable Other Salaries:

	(e)	(f)
Sales revenue	$22,500	$18,000
Variable Other Salaries (0.05 × Sales)	$ 1,125	$ 900
Nonvariable Other Salaries	530	530
Total expected Other Salaries	$ 1,655	$ 1,430

This method of computing the nonvariable and variable components of a mixed expense account is identical with using the formula for a straight line to determine total expected costs. The formula for a straight line is

$$Y = a + bX,$$

where a is a constant representing the fixed component of the expense, b is the ratio of the variable component to sales, and X is the volume of sales. Taking Example (f) above to estimate Other Salaries for a sales volume of $18,000, the formula would be stated as follows:

$$Y = a + bX$$
$$Y = \$530 + (0.05)\$18,000$$
$$Y = \$1,430.$$

This method of estimating the components of fixed and variable costs has some limitations. Only two points on the line (two levels of volume) were chosen in making the computations. Cost behavior at volumes above and below the two points may not reflect that relationship which exists within the two points. There might even be slight fluctuations between the two points, as seen for Example (c) above, which computed fixed costs of $520 for a sales volume of $15,000. However, if the deviations of costs from the line which describes their behavior are small or predictable, this method produces results which are sufficiently accurate for planning purposes.

A more accurate method of locating the line of relationship between a cost and revenue is the *method of least squares*. Although it is beyond the scope of this text, its formula is presented in elementary statistics books.

Limitations of Cost and Revenue Relationships

Even though an analysis of past results shows a high degree of relationship between the amounts of two variables, such as an expense and sales revenue, the relationship may not be one of cause and effect. The close association of the two amounts may result from *coincidence*. This is especially true when the relationship is estimated on the basis of a small number of observations of past data. Sometimes judgment is sufficient to determine whether such a relationship is *causal* or merely *coincidental*.

The underlying conditions affecting either the independent variable or the dependent variable may change in such a way that the relationship between them changes. To illustrate, the 4 per cent commission rate in Example 6 will not remain unchanged indefinitely. The lease contract in Example 7 will terminate in a few years, when a new annual rental is likely to come into effect. Furthermore, the business might eliminate many employees by automating clerical procedures, thus significantly reducing the amount of Other Salaries in Example 10 without greatly changing the sales volume. When the underlying conditions change, the established variable and fixed expense relationships may not give reliable estimates of future expenses without some modification.

Example 11   A business which has formerly paid a sales commission at a uniform rate on all products changes to a policy of paying a different rate on each class of product. The relationship of sales commissions to total sales in the future will depend on the proportions of sales of each class of product to total sales, as well as on the individual commission rates.

The behavior of some expense items may be highly predictable (either completely variable or completely nonvariable) when changes in sales revenue are small, but unpredictable when the changes in sales revenue are relatively large. Sometimes these expense items can be predicted with reasonable reliability by using an independent variable other than sales revenue—such as number of units sold, number of employees, or amount of floor space occupied.

Example 12   Employer's payroll tax expense tends to vary closely with changes in total salary expense. Because salary expense includes some components which are variable and others which do not vary with sales revenue, it is difficult to predict the relationship of payroll tax expense to sales. It is easier to estimate its amount in relation to estimated salaries. The amounts of some expense items are closely related to the dollar amounts of assets or liabilities.

Example 13   The amount of depreciation expense depends directly on the total cost of depreciable assets. The amount of interest expense depends on the face amount of liabilities owed.

Relevant range. Fixed costs typically remain unchanged in amount until a certain limit of *capacity* is reached, whereas costs which tend to be variable often decline per unit as economies of larger-scale operations are attained. For example, a retail store may have to buy additional display counters if sales volume increases beyond a given point. The depreciation of the counters will increase the amount of fixed expenses. On the other hand, perhaps the additional supplies which will have to be used may be purchased at a lower unit cost when larger orders are placed. The effects of such changes are shown in the three graphs in Illustration 18-5. The range of capacity within which fixed costs remain constant and variable costs remain directly proportional to sales volume is called the *relevant range.*

Note in Graph (a) that the nonvariable expenses increase in *steps* as additional expenses are incurred at certain levels of capacity.

The variable expenses in Graph (b) increase at a decreasing rate beyond a given level of capacity. When nonvariable and variable expenses are added together, a disjointed, or discontinuous, total expense line may result. Although costs may behave in this manner, it does not invalidate attempts to estimate

**Illustration
18-5**

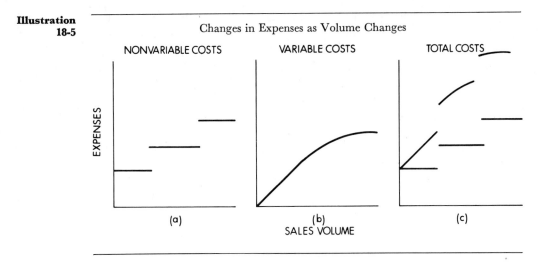

Changes in Expenses as Volume Changes

future expenses; it simply makes estimation more difficult. It is still possible to estimate total expenses for any given level of sales volume from Graph (c) in Illustration 18-5, just as it was possible to do so in the graph shown in Illustration 18-4.

Because some costs actually behave as shown in Illustration 18-5, it is ordinarily useful to recognize *four types of cost and expense behavior*:

(1) *Fixed in amount* by contract, management policy, or operating conditions and *not subject to change* during the planning period. (*Example:* A ten-year lease at a fixed annual rental.)

(2) *Fixed in amount* by contract, management policy, or operating conditions, but *subject to change* during the planning period. (*Examples:* The planned amount of advertising, or the planned amount of charitable contributions, both of which are usually set by management policy but are subject to change.)

(3) *Variable directly or indirectly with sales revenue or with some other financial element.* (*Example:* A business borrows on short-term notes to finance seasonal additions to its inventories. The inventory balance should vary with expected future sales, and the amount of interest expense should vary with the amount of inventory financed by notes.)

(4) *Mixed,* consisting of both a fixed and a variable component. (*Example:* Other Salaries of Ajax Company. This item consists partly of compensation for general office work, which may be expected to remain relatively constant without regard to the volume of sales; partly of the salaries of veteran salesclerks, whom management might feel obligated to retain even if sales declined drastically; and partly of compensation to additional salesclerks who are hired during periods of peak activity.)

Summary   *Accounting for management* purposes differs in use, emphasis, and methodology from accounting to persons outside of the firm. The measurements made for reporting to outsiders are constrained by generally accepted accounting principles, but management is entitled to receive any information that is needed, provided it is relevant and dependable. Management accounting tends to be more oriented to the *future* than is financial accounting, and it deals more frequently with *subdivisions* of the organization rather than with the organization as a whole.

Accounting helps management to perform the processes of planning, organizing, and controlling the resources of an organization to accomplish specific objectives. Accounting serves as an internal communication device to *motivate* people to perform in accordance with the organization's plans.

Management *plans* are usually for specific *projects* or particular accounting *periods*. In these plans accounting expresses expectations in financial terms, so that management can choose from feasible alternatives, communicate objectives to responsible individuals, and then organize and control the business resources needed to accomplish the objectives. The organization process is partially implemented by designing accounting procedures, reports, and internal controls to help accomplish the plans.

Management's ability to forecast events and formulate objectives that are feasible and economically sound is based on the principles of *cost and revenue behavior*. Some cause-and-effect relationships between financial elements can be estimated by judgmental association based on established custom, policy, law, or contracts. Other more complex relationships require statistical analysis of historical accounting data.

Costs and expenses that tend to vary directly in proportion to changes in sales are described as *variable*; those whose amounts are independent of sales changes are described as *fixed*, or *nonvariable*. Total expenses can often be budgeted with reasonable reliability by using a simple linear formula which combines fixed and variable elements.

Discussion Questions and Problems

18-1   *Managerial* accounting and *financial* accounting serve different but related purposes. Explain the difference.

18-2   In what sense might financial accounting involve greater legal and ethical responsibility than managerial accounting? How might managerial accounting have a greater impact on those interested in the results of the business?

18-3   Managers are concerned with planning the future activities of a business and controlling their effectiveness. Stockholders, with an ownership interest in the business, are also concerned with the effectiveness of business activities. Explain the difference in the information needed by these two parties.

18-4   "Financial accounting focuses primarily on *past* events and transactions."

a. How does this focus of attention differ from that of managerial accounting?
b. If financial accounting deals largely with past events, why do difficulties arise in choosing among alternative measurement rules in financial accounting?
c. It has been contended that every single measurement which appears in a statement of financial position is based on some assumption about the future. Using specific examples, explain whether or not this is true.

18-5

a. How does accounting information about the past aid management in *planning* the activities of a business?

b. How would you recommend that the need for accounting information for planning affect the design of the classification of accounts of a business with several subdivisions?

18-6   Budgets may reflect plans for profits as well as plans for the resources needed to accomplish objectives and the means of financing them.

a. What type of information about the past is needed in planning for future profits?
b. What type of information about the past is needed in planning for resources and how to finance them?

18-7

a. Give an example of a *period plan* and a *project plan*.
b. Can a period plan include more than one project plan? Illustrate.
c. Can a project affect more than one period plan? Illustrate.
d. When do you think project plans should be prepared? When should period plans be prepared?

18-8   Why do *period plans* usually include *total* anticipated revenues and expenses, while *project plans* include only *incremental* revenues and expenses?

18-9   Define *management by exception*. How does accounting assist in this process? Should all exceptions be reported for managerial consideration? What criteria should be used in selecting which exceptions to report, if not all are to be reported?

18-10   Because *future* costs and revenues are used in analyzing alternative courses of action available to management, it follows that all historical costs and revenues are irrelevant.
       Do you agree with this statement? Why?

18-11   Give an example of each of the following:

a. An expense which varies closely with the number of products sold.
b. An expense which varies closely with sales revenue.
c. An expense which varies closely with another expense.
d. An expense which varies with the length of time involved.
e. An expense which varies with revenue, but in a step fashion.
f. A revenue which varies to some extent with an expense.
g. An expense which varies closely with the value of an asset.
h. An expense which varies closely with the value of a liability.

18-12   "In the very short run, all expenses are fixed; in the long run, all are variable."

a. Explain whether or not this statement is correct.
b. If it is correct, of what use is this fact in preparing a budget for the next year?

18-13   Most expenses are neither perfectly variable nor perfectly fixed, but behave as *mixed expenses*. Explain this statement and give three examples of a mixed expense.

18-14   The controller of the Reno Company has noted that several items of expense move in the same direction as sales but do not change in direct proportion to sales.

Required   a. Using the monthly planning data below, determine (1) the fixed component of each expense account and (2) the percentage of the variable component to net sales.
       b. Estimate the amount of each expense for April, if net sales are expected to be $35,000.

	1973 Plan		
	January	*February*	*March*
Sales	$25,000	$30,000	$32,000
Sales salaries............................	5,500	6,000	6,200
Delivery expense........................	750	800	820
Insurance.................................	700	800	840

18-15   Below is Video, Inc.'s period plan for income in January 1973. The plan is based on three possible sales volumes.

VIDEO, INC.
Planned Income Statement
For the Month of January 1973

Unit volume..............................	800	1,000	1,200
Revenues	$80,000	$100,000	$120,000
Expenses:			
Cost of goods sold....................	$48,000	$60,000	$72,000
Commissions	3,200	4,000	4,800
Rent	3,600	4,000	4,400
Salaries................................	10,000	10,000	10,000
Other....................................	5,200	6,000	6,800
Total expenses....................	$70,000	$84,000	$98,000
Income before taxes...................	$10,000	$16,000	$22,000

Required   a. Which of the planned expenses are variable, fixed, or mixed?
b. Compute the fixed and variable portions of each mixed expense and of total expenses.
c. What amount would be budgeted for each expense and for total expenses at sales of 900 units?
d. Compute the relationship between revenue changes and income changes. Can this relationship be used in business planning? Explain.

18-16   The financial position statements of two similar companies in the same industry, as of December 31, 1973, are as follows:

ASSETS	*Company A*	*Company B*
Cash	$ 50,000	$175,000
Accounts receivable..................................	75,000	250,000
Inventories..	150,000	250,000
Land	100,000	
Plant and equipment............... $1,000,000		
Less accumulated depreciation... 300,000	700,000	
Prepaid expenses.....................................	5,000	5,000
	$1,080,000	$680,000

LIABILITIES AND OWNERS' EQUITY	*Company A*	*Company B*
Accounts payable......................................	$ 60,000	$ 90,000
6% notes payable	20,000	100,000
30-year, 6% first-mortgage bonds payable......	750,000	
Owners' investment...................................	100,000	100,000
Retained income.......................................	150,000	390,000
	$1,080,000	$680,000

The annual sales for each company are approximately the same. The net income of each, before deducting interest and income taxes, was 20 per cent of sales in 1973.

Required a. Explain in detail in what way you would expect the fixed expenses of the two companies to differ.

b. In what way would their net incomes as a percentage of revenues probably differ?

c. What differences in the policies of the two companies can you detect from the illustrated statements?

18-17 Graphic Sales Company had the following sales and expenses in 1971 and 1972 (by quarters):

| | Actual Results for 1971–1972 | |
Calendar Quarter	Units Sold	Total Expense
1971—1st	360	$33,500
2nd	290	30,700
3rd	250	28,700
4th	600	45,000
1972—1st	410	34,900
2nd	350	28,800
3rd	320	27,100
4th	700	51,500

Required a. Prepare a statistical scattergraph and draw a line to show the relationship between total expense and units sold.

b. Using the line in the scattergraph, compute total fixed expense and total variable expense per unit.

c. What is the *relevant range* of the trend in these data?

d. Explain the principal weaknesses of the relationships computed from the scattergraph.

Cases **18-1 Centro Corporation.** Centro Corporation manufactures and sells a broad line of products to consumers, doing business primarily in three western states. It was organized ten years ago and now has about 2,000 employees and 300 stockholders.

The top management of Centro, consisting primarily of the founders, has prided itself on its annual financial reports. These have been widely recognized for reflecting sound accounting principles for general-purpose financial statements. The annual reports have been distributed widely among the corporate management, stockholders, potential stockholders, and major creditors. Quarterly financial statements have been prepared for the use of management, reporting the income of the business as a whole and its financial position at the end of each calendar quarter. The rate of return on stockholders' investments has compared rather favorably with that of similar firms.

Recently Centro employed a new controller, a college graduate with a major in accounting and ten years of experience in corporate accounting. The new controller, Mr. Dumont, has proposed several major changes in the firm's accounting and reporting, including the following:

(1) The preparation of annual operating budgets, with supporting budgets for the manufacturing, selling, and administrative functions. Mr. Dumont suggests that top management establish its objectives for the next few years in a general way and for the next year specifically, in consultation with the production manager,

the sales manager, and himself. Guidelines for budget preparation would then be given to the managers of major divisions and departments. Their tentative budgets would be reviewed by the controller, and conferences would be held to reconcile any major disagreements.

(2) The annual budgets would be supported by more detailed budgets for each month.

(3) Monthly reports would be prepared for each department and division, reporting both the budgeted figures and the actual results for the month.

(4) Major expenditures (generally involving an outlay of $5,000 or more) would required a detailed analysis of expected profitability. These analyses would be reviewed by the controller, who would then make a recommendation to top management as to whether or not the expenditure should be made.

(5) Follow-up reports of major expenditures would be made, showing summaries of actual results as compared with the estimates made in advance.

Mr. Carlan, the production manager, and Mr. Weiss, the sales manager, are somewhat concerned about the proposals. In private discussions with Mr. Marquis, the president of the firm, they have expressed the view that they will be spending a lot of time in unnecessary paper work. As they point out, profits have been satisfactory in the past, so why should such earth-shaking changes be made in the accounting and reporting system?

Required
a. As Mr. Marquis, what information would you seek about the probable results of the new system and the problems involved in establishing it? Outline a series of questions that you would ask Mr. Dumont, the controller, in this connection.

b. As Mr. Dumont, the controller, present the strongest arguments you can for the proposed changes, and reply to Mr. Marquis' questions concerning the disadvantages of the system.

c. Identify examples of costs of the production, selling, and administrative functions that are likely to be fixed for purposes of the annual budget.

d. Identify examples of costs of the production, selling, and administrative functions that are likely to be variable for purposes of the annual budget.

e. Identify several types of mixed costs that are likely to cause Mr. Dumont difficulty in implementing his proposed changes in accounting and reporting.

chapter 19

Profit Planning

Purpose of Chapter

The proper aim of *planning*, a vital function of management, is to improve the effectiveness of managerial action. In the absence of definite plans the future of a business enterprise is highly uncertain. Without concrete goals to strive for and specific measures with which to gauge its progress, the entity is likely to drift unprofitably. But when management crystallizes its goals in terms of *attainable objectives*, the activities of the enterprise can be systematized, the future can be made clearer, and the entity is more likely to prosper financially.

Business managers usually *specify their objectives* in one or more of the following terms:

(1) Earning a given amount of net income.
(2) Earning a particular percentage of income on the assets invested.
(3) Earning a particular percentage of net income to sales.
(4) Attaining a certain share of the market.
(5) Meeting specific delivery schedules.
(6) Meeting specific cost standards.

Of the criteria currently in use, *net income is the most important measure of the effectiveness of business performance.*

The activities of a business entity are related to the entity's overall objectives by means of the *budgeted income statement.* This statement projects the various elements of income for a year or a longer time span. Underlying the expression of these elements in terms of money and the preparation of the income budget are the concepts of revenue and cost behavior that were considered in Chapter 18. This chapter focuses on the use of these concepts in developing the *income plan* of an entity in advance, and then in reporting on the effectiveness of the entity's *actual performance.*

COST-PROFIT-VOLUME (OR BREAK-EVEN) ANALYSIS

The major aim of business planning is to relate all activities of the firm to the firm's overall profit objective. This is done through the comprehensive budget, or profit plan, for a year or longer time period. The budget projects income elements on the basis of expected patterns of cost and revenue behavior. A method of analysis often used in this type of planning is called *cost-profit-volume analysis,* or *break-even analysis.*

Break-even analysis focuses on the net income that is likely to result at various sales volumes, after deducting both variable and fixed expenses from revenue. This method is especially useful in evaluating the potential effects on income of various courses of action which involve changes in the volume of sales, in cost and selling prices, and in fixed or variable cost relationships.

Break-even Point

The volume of sales at which total sales revenue equals total expenses is called the *break-even point.* At this volume there is neither a net income nor a net loss; the business merely breaks even. The formula for computing the break-even point is

$$S\text{(sales revenue)} = V\text{ (variable expense)} + F\text{ (fixed expense)}.$$

Variable expense (V) can be expressed as a constant percentage (vS) of sales (S). Thus at the break-even point,

$$S - vS = F.$$

Although the break-even point is expressed here in terms of sales revenue, it can also be stated in terms of physical units sold if just one type of unit is involved.

The difference between sales revenue and variable expense ($S - vS$ in the above equation) is called the *contribution margin,* or simply the *contribution.* At the break-even point contribution is equal to total fixed expenses. At other sales volumes contribution is equal to the algebraic sum of fixed expenses and income (it is equal to fixed expense plus net income, or fixed expense minus net loss).

Since variable expenses can be expressed as a constant percentage of sales revenue, and since contribution is the difference between sales revenue and variable expenses, contribution can also be expressed as a constant percentage of sales revenue. This *contribution percentage* is the complement of (100 minus) the variable expense percentage, as shown by the following:

$$\text{Contribution percentage} = \frac{S - vS}{S}$$

$$= 100 - v.$$

Example 1   The Recca Mfg. Co. manufactures and sells a single product at a price of $10 per unit. In 1972 the company had sales revenue of $300,000, variable expenses of $225,000, and fixed expenses of $50,000. Calculate the total contribution, the percentage of variable expense to sales, and the contribution percentage.

Solution   The total contribution ($300,000 minus $225,000) is $75,000. The variable expense percentage is 75 per cent. The contribution percentage (100 minus 75) is 25. Note that the contribution per unit of product is $2.50 ($10.00 minus $7.50).

The objective of a business enterprise is to earn an income, not merely to break even. Still, knowledge of the break-even point may be useful to management in situations such as the following:

(1) It may help in estimating *how large an increase in sales volume, or increase in contribution percentage, or decrease in fixed expenses, is needed to convert operations at a loss to profitable operations.* Also, even though the business is currently earning a net income, management may wish to know the *margin of safety*—that is, how great an unfavorable change can be withstood before operations become unprofitable.

Example 2   In evaluating the risk of the business, the management of Recca Mfg. Co. wishes to know how much sales could decline before operations would result in a net loss. The existing percentage of variable expenses to sales is assumed to remain unchanged, and fixed expenses are assumed to remain constant within the relevant range.

Solution   If the variable expenses of Recca Mfg. Co. are 75 per cent of sales and fixed expenses are $50,000 as shown in Example 1, the break-even point is calculated as follows:

$$S - 0.75S = \$\ 50,000$$
$$0.25S = \$\ 50,000$$
$$S = \frac{\$\ 50,000}{0.25}$$
$$S = \$200,000.$$

Proof of computation

RESULTING INCOME STATEMENT

Sales..	$200,000
Deduct variable expenses, 75% of sales..............................	150,000
Contribution to fixed expense and income.......................	$ 50,000
Deduct fixed expenses...	50,000
Net income..	$ 0

Conclusion   A decline in the sales of Recca Mfg. Co. from $300,000 to $200,000 would result in zero income. This would be a decline of $33\frac{1}{3}$ per cent of sales. The margin of safety is thus $100,000 of sales in absolute terms, or $33\frac{1}{3}$ per cent in relative terms.

From Example 2 it can be seen that the *break-even point in sales revenue* can be computed quickly by *dividing total fixed expenses by the contribution percentage*. Moreover, *break-even volume in physical units* (if only one type of unit is sold) can be calculated by *dividing total fixed expenses by the contribution per unit* ($50,000 ÷ $2.50 = $20,000).

(2) A second use of the break-even calculation is to *aid management in estimating the degree of risk associated with a proposed change in* either (a) the amount of *fixed expenses* or (b) the *percentage of variable expenses* (and therefore the percentage of contribution) to sales.

Example 3   Recca Mfg. Co. is considering whether to add $6,000 to advertising expense in an effort to increase sales volume. If this change is made, what volume of sales will be needed to break even?

Solution
$$0.25S = (\$50,000 + \$6,000)$$
$$S = \$224,000.$$

The break-even point would be increased from $200,000 to $224,000 if the additional advertising expenditure is made. Sales needed to break even would be $76,000 below present sales of $300,000.

Example 4   What would be the break-even point of Recca Mfg. Co. if the contribution percentage were reduced from 25 per cent of sales to 20 per cent, assuming that fixed expenses remained at $50,000?

Solution
$$0.20S = \$\ 50,000$$
$$S = \frac{\$\ 50,000}{0.20}$$
$$S = \$250,000.$$

Conclusion   The break-even sales revenue would be increased from $200,000 to $250,000.

If it is desired to find how much of a change would be needed to produce a desired amount of net income before income tax, the basic approach is the same.

Example 5   If the desired net income before taxes of Recca Mfg. Co. for 1973 is $30,000 and all other factors are expected to behave as they did in 1972, what sales volume will be needed?

Solution
$$0.25S = \$50,000 + \$30,000$$
$$S = \frac{\$80,000}{0.25}$$
$$S = \$320,000.$$

The Break-even Chart

The relationships between revenues, expenses, and income are often portrayed graphically by a *break-even chart*. Such a chart includes a total expense line and a revenue line. Two common forms of the break-even chart are shown in Illustration 19-1. Form II used in this illustration is usually preferable because it emphasizes the *contribution* from various volumes of sales. It shows how much of fixed expenses is covered by revenues at volumes below the break-even point, and how much revenues exceed the total of variable and fixed expenses at sales above break-even volume.

Illustration 19-1

Two Forms of the Break-even Chart

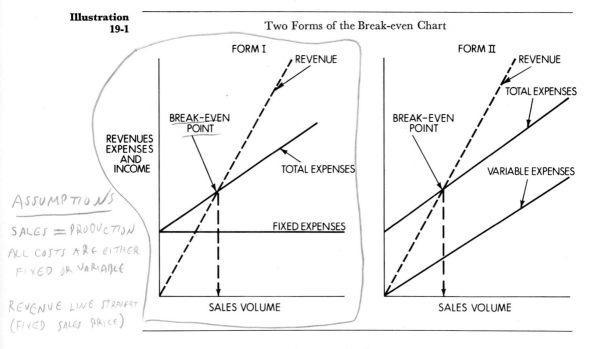

A break-even chart for Recca Mfg. Co. appears in Illustration 19-2. The vertical line labeled "Break-even Sales" shows that this point is reached for Recca when dollar sales are $200,000. If sales volume is greater than $200,000, there will be a net income, represented by the vertical distance between the revenue and the total expense lines.

The break-even chart can also be used to estimate the amount of income or loss which will result from a given volume of sales, or the amount of sales revenue required to produce a given amount of net income or net loss. The vertical line labeled "$300,000 sales" shows that when sales are $300,000 there is expected to be a $25,000 net income before income tax. The vertical line labeled "$150,000 Sales" shows that a net loss of $12,500 can be expected if sales fall to $150,000. (Computation by the formula shows that at this volume of sales variable expenses would be 0.75 of sales, or $112,500; fixed expenses would be $50,000; and total expenses, $162,500. This would result in a net loss of $12,500 when compared with total revenue of $150,000.)

The break-even chart can be used to give a quick approximation of the income effects of various possible levels of sales. Computation by formula would require more time, and the results are often not as easy to visualize as in the graphs. The graphic relationships of costs, volume, and profit are somewhat rough approximations, but they are sufficiently accurate for most purposes.

**Illustration
19-2**

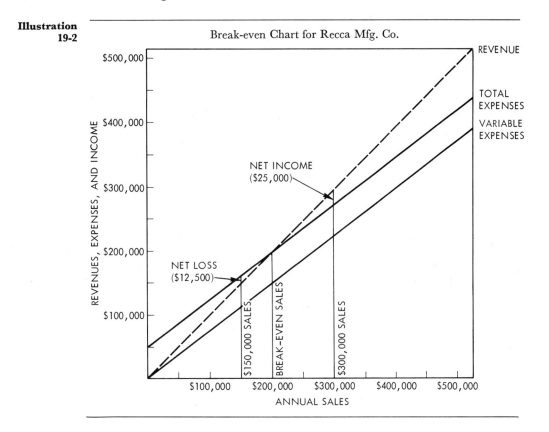

Break-even Chart for Recca Mfg. Co.

Complications in Break-even Analysis

The assumptions which underlie the usual break-even calculations should be clearly understood. They are

(1) That expenses can be accurately classified as fixed or variable, or that the fixed and variable components of mixed expenses can be identified.

(2) That the fixed expense and the variable expense relationships are linear over the relevant range.

(3) That selling prices per unit remain constant as volume changes.

(4) That the sales mix remains constant. The *sales mix* is the combination of various types of products or services sold. Sales mix can change as a result of selling *more* or *less* of one product in relation to other products, including the addition or elimination of individual types of products in the line of goods sold.

(5) That production volume equals sales volume for a manufacturing enterprise.

If variable and fixed expense relationships do change, more than one break-even point may exist for the same firm. This does not invalidate break-even analysis, but several computations may have to be made. Illustration 19-3 shows this type of situation.

**Illustration
19-3**

A Break-even Chart When Expense Behavior Changes

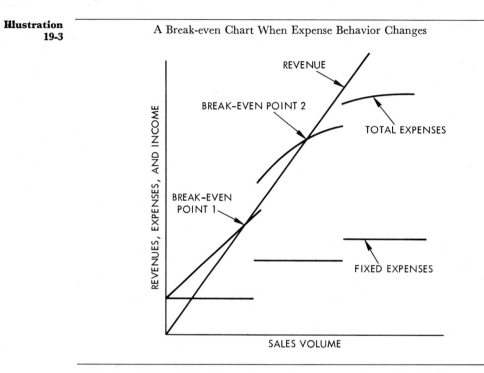

If *sales mix is altered,* changes occur in revenue, in total variable expenses, or in both. If total revenues decrease as a result of the sales mix change, the revenue line on the break-even chart will drop (or move clockwise). If variable expenses increase, the total expense line will rise (or move counterclockwise). The effect in both instances would be to raise the break-even point. Because the change in sales mix will affect either revenues or variable costs or both, a change will take place in *contribution.* This change in contribution can be calculated and new break-even points computed for the change in mix by (1) calculating the contribution as a per cent of sales for the pertinent mix and (2) dividing this per cent into the total fixed costs.

Example 6   Audio Corporation, with fixed expenses of $30,000, has four major product lines with a sales mix as shown below. (a) What is the break-even point for the current sales mix? (b) What will the break-even point be if the company can sell $5,000 more of tape recorders (50 at $100) at the sacrifice of being able to sell $5,000 less of phonographs (100 at $50)?

	Phonograph Records	Tape Recorders	Phonographs	Needles and Supplies
Unit sales	10,000	100	200	Mixed
Average selling prices	$ 4	$ 100	$ 50	$ 2
Average variable expenses	$ 3	$ 50	$ 30	$ 1
Total sales	$40,000	$10,000	$10,000	$ 2,000
Total contribution	10,000	5,000	4,000	1,000

Summary: Total sales $62,000
         Total contribution 20,000
         Weighted contribution percentage............ 32.3% ($20,000/$62,000)

Solution (a) The break-even point for the current sales mix can be found by dividing total fixed expenses of $30,000 by the weighted contribution percentage of 32.3 percent. The break-even point is $92,879.

(b) If $5,000 of sales of tape recorders is substituted for $5,000 of sales of phonographs, the break-even point will fall, because recorders make a larger contribution per unit and per dollar of sales. To compute the break-even point for the new sales mix, the new weighted contribution percentage must be calculated as follows:

	Phonograph Records	Tape Recorders	Phonographs	Needles and Supplies
Unit sales	10,000	150	100	Mixed
Total sales	$40,000	$15,000	$ 5,000	$ 2,000
Total contribution	10,000	7,500	2,000	1,000

Summary: Total sales $62,000
Total contribution............................ 20,500
Weighted contribution percentage .... 33.1% ($20,500/$62,000)
The new break-even point is $30,000/0.331 = $90,634.

Example 7 Assume that the management of Audio Corporation wishes to know the sales level needed to earn net income of $10,000, given the new sales mix of 10,000 phonograph records, 150 tape recorders, 100 phonographs, and the same relative volume of needle and supply sales. The relative mix is expected to remain the same at any sales volume.

Solution
$$0.331S = \$30,000 + \$10,000$$
$$S = \$120,846.$$

Conclusion Sales of $120,846 would have to be made in order to earn a net income of $10,000.

INCREMENTAL ANALYSIS

Basic Method

The principal aim in business decisions is to select courses of action that will increase the firm's total income and rate of return. In cases where the required investment in assets and the business risk are the same for competing alternatives, the choice is made by *comparing the amounts of additional income* that are expected to result from each alternative. The alternative which is expected to make the largest addition to income should be selected. If all available courses of action will reduce income, the alternative which will cause the smallest reduction should be chosen.

The potential effects of alternative courses of action on business income may be compared by using *incremental analysis*. This involves a comparison of the *differences in additional revenues and additional expenses*, and then of the *differences in additional income*, that are expected to result from each course of action. Examples 8 and 9 illustrate incremental analysis.

Example 8

| | Alternative | | Income Difference, A vs. B |
	A	B	Greater or (Less)
Expected additional:			
Revenue...............................	$5,000	$4,000	$1,000
Expense	3,000	2,600	(400)
Contribution	$2,000	$1,400	$ 600

Conclusion   Investment and risk being equal, *A* is the better course of action because it will result in a contribution $600 greater than will *B*.

"Incremental" should be interpreted broadly to include both the *increases* and the *decreases* which are expected to result from a given plan of action.

Example 9   *C* and *D*, the only alternatives open to the business, will both result in revenue reductions.

| | Alternative | | Income Difference, C vs. D |
	C	D	Greater or (Less)
Expected reduction in:			
Revenue...............................	($3,500)	($4,000)	$ 500
Expense...............................	0	0	0
Contribution.........................	($3,500)	($4,000)	$ 500

Conclusion   *C* is the better alternative because it will result in a $500 *smaller reduction in income.*

Alternative courses of action can often be undertaken without increasing or decreasing some items of revenue or expense. An item whose amount is the *same for all alternatives* being considered is *irrelevant in making the decision.* It can be ignored for this purpose.

Causes of Differences in Incremental Contributions

The incremental contributions of alternative courses of action may differ from each other because of differences in any of three major factors:

(1) *Volume* of goods or services sold.
(2) *Unit selling prices* or *unit costs.*
(3) *Sales mix.*

Incremental analysis can determine the effect of differences in any of these factors as between decision alternatives, or of differences in any combination of factors. The relative desirability of the alternative courses of action can then be evaluated by comparing their expected differences in contribution, and thus in income.

The following sections illustrate how each of these factors affects incremental contribution.

Differences in Volume Sold

If the *volume* of products or services sold *differs* as between alternatives, but sales mix, sales prices, and unit costs are the same, the contribution of the alternatives differs in *direct proportion* to differences in volume.

Example 10   A popular rock-and-roll singing group was photographed on the beach at Nassau with a new model of portable phonographs sold by Ajax Company. The photographs were widely publicized and the demand of Ajax customers for this item doubled from 10 to 20 per week. If the increased demand continues for six months, what will be the effect on income?

Solution   This is an example of a change in *sales volume*.

Incremental revenue will be $80 for each of the additional 260 units expected to be sold (10 additional units a week for 26 weeks), or $20,800.

The *incremental expense* of obtaining these sales will be simply the additional cost of goods sold, because no extra selling effort will be necessary. If each phonograph costs Ajax $55, the incremental costs will be $55 for 260 units, or $14,300.

The *incremental contribution* resulting from this increase in volume will be

Incremental revenue...	$20,800
Deduct incremental expense......................................	14,300
Incremental contribution.......................................	$ 6,500

In Example 10 the income of Ajax Company will increase by the incremental contribution of $6,500.

Differences in Sales Price

Changes in the *selling prices* of products or services cause greater than proportional changes in contribution when volume of sales, sales mix, and unit costs are unchanged.

Example 11 illustrates how incremental anaysis is used to show the effects of a change in sales price.

Example 11   Ajax Company carries in its inventory some nationally advertised stereo diamond needles, which formerly sold for $10 each. The manufacturer's representative has informed Ajax that the new suggested selling price is $13, and that the manufacturer is undertaking a substantial advertising campaign to keep sales volume from declining as a result of the price increase. Ajax Company usually sells about 100 of these needles per month, and now has one month's supply on hand which could be sold at the new price of $13. Each needle costs Ajax $4. How much will the price increase change next month's income?

Solution   This is an example of a change in *sales price*. The expected results are

Incremental revenue = ($13 − $10) = $3 × 100 =	$300
Deduct incremental cost..................................	None
Incremental contribution...............................	$300

If the needles were sold at their former price of $10, the contribution would be $600 (100 units at $6). The contribution expected at the selling price of $13 is $900 (100 units at $9). Thus, while the selling price increases by $\frac{3}{10}$, or 30 per cent, the contribution increases by 50 per cent.

Differences in Volume, Sales Price, and Unit Cost

Example 12 shows the effects of differences in three factors—*volume, sales price,* and *unit cost*—on incremental contribution.

Example 12   The manufacturer's representative informed Ajax Company that the Super Sound cartridge, which was designed to hold the diamond needle, would cost Ajax $11 per unit in the future rather than $8 as formerly. The suggested retail price would be raised from $25 to $30. The representative stated that he anticipated a volume decrease of 10 per cent as a result of the higher retail price, but that the effect of the decrease in volume on income would be offset by the higher selling price.

Was the manufacturer's representative correct?

Solution   This is an example of a change in *volume* accompanied by a change in *unit prices* and *costs.* Ajax usually sold about 40 Super Sound cartridges each month; thus the change in income would be

	Income Increase or (Decrease)
Incremental revenue:	
Increase in price ($30 − $25) = $5 × 36 new units........... $180	
Decrease in volume (40 − 36) = 4 × $25 old price........... (100)	
Incremental revenue	$ 80
Incremental cost:	
Increase in unit cost ($11 − $8) = $3 × 36 new units........ ($108)	
Decrease in volume (40 − 36) = 4 × $8 old cost.............. 32	
Incremental cost..	(76)
Incremental contribution	$ 4

Another way of computing the change in contribution is to compare the contribution expected at each volume of sales; thus

$$\text{Present contribution} = 40 \text{ units} \times (\$25 - \$\ 8) = \$680$$
$$\text{Planned contribution} = 36 \text{ units} \times (\$30 - \$11) = \underline{\ \ 684}$$
$$\text{Expected increase in contribution} .... = \ \ \ \ 4$$

Conclusion   The manufacturer's representative was correct. Even if next month's sales should drop to 36 units and costs should increase to $11 per unit, Ajax would make slightly more profit on the cartridges than at present.

Differences in Sales Mix

If the dollar total of sales remains unchanged but there is a *shift in sales mix* from products with a lower contribution percentage to products with a higher contribution percentage, there will be an increase in contribution. Conversely, a shift to products with a lower contribution percentage, with total dollar sales remaining constant, will decrease total contribution.

Example 13 shows how incremental analysis would be applied to a *change in sales mix.*

Example 13   The manager of Ajax Company is considering changing the manner in which two different tape recorders are displayed, and asking his salesmen to push the Tony Model instead of the Recco Model. He feels that instead of continuing to sell equal numbers of each tape recorder (five of each per month), the change will permit the sale of four Tonys for every Recco sold, even though the total number of recorders sold will not be increased. The Tony sells for $140 and costs Ajax $90, while the Recco sells for $140 and costs $100. Should Ajax make the change?

Solution   This is an example of a change in *sales mix.* The following analysis is based on monthly sales of ten units. Five units of each recorder are now sold per month; the change will increase sales of the Tony by three and decrease the sales of the Recco by three:

Contribution per Tony ($140 — $90)............................. $ 50
Contribution per Recco ($140 — $100) 40
  Difference per unit in favor of Tony........................... $ 10
Increase in contribution if three units are shifted from
    Recco to Tony... $ 30

Conclusion   The change should be made. Even though no more tape recorders are sold, a higher contribution will result from substituting sales of Tonys for sales of Reccos.

Examples 10 through 13 have shown how changes in volume, price, cost, and mix will affect incremental contribution and income. To estimate the change in income that will result from a given change in one of these factors, only the *incremental* revenues and expenses should be considered. *Incremental revenue minus incremental cost equals incremental contribution—the change in income.*

Unfortunately, most actual situations are more complicated than the examples given. One reason is that changes occur in costs other than the cost of products sold. For example, additional sales commissions are likely to be incurred when total revenue increases. This does not change the method of analysis; it makes it more complex. In Example 10 the incremental commission expense would have to be added to the incremental cost of goods sold to determine the incremental cost. The incremental contribution would be the incremental gross margin minus the incremental commissions.

Summary   *Cost-profit-volume* (or *break-even*) *analysis* assists in evaluating the potential effects on income of courses of action which will change the volume of sales, the cost and selling prices, and the fixed or variable cost relationships. It does so by estimating the *contribution*—the difference between sales revenue and variable expense—and comparing the contribution with fixed expenses and planned income. The effects of various alternatives on income can be estimated by using the *formula* for a straight line which expresses these relationships, or by a *chart.*

Incremental analysis aids business management in selecting the most profitable course of action from among alternatives. It involves a comparison of the differences in additional revenues and additional expenses, and the related differences in additional income, that are expected to result from each course of action.

The incremental contributions of alternatives may differ because of differences in *volume*, in *unit selling prices or unit costs*, or in *sales mix*. The effects of each type of difference, or of combinations of differences, can be estimated by incremental analysis.

Discussion Questions and Problems

19-1   Business objectives are often stated in terms of (1) earning a given amount of net income, (2) earning a given rate of return on investment, and (3) earning a given percentage of net income to sales.

a. If you were planning to invest a large sum in a business, which of these objectives would be most important to you? Why?
b. In what way would accomplishment of the other two objectives be important to you as an investor?

19-2   It has often been said that accounting is a useful device for communicating between levels of management.

a. How can accounting assist top management in communicating its *objectives* downward through the organization?
b. To what extent would you recommend two-way communication in using accounting for *planning* purposes?
c. How can accounting communicate information for *control* purposes?

19-3   In what specific ways does accounting relate the operating activities of a business to the overall profit objective of the business?

19-4   "Break-even analysis has limited usefulness as a planning tool, for no business is interested in breaking even. It is interested instead in making as much income as it can."
Comment on this statement.

19-5   Illustrate each of the following and explain how it is related to planning.

a. Contribution margin
b. Break-even point
c. Margin of safety
d. Sales mix
e. Incremental revenue
f. Incremental expense

19-6   Distinguish between *incremental analysis* and cost-volume-profit (or break-even) analysis.

19-7   In project planning, does *incremental income* have the same meaning as *contribution margin*? Explain your answer. Would your answer be the same for *period planning*? Explain.

19-8   What are some of the assumptions which underlie the preparation of the traditional break-even chart? For each of these assumptions, indicate how the analysis could be changed in order to be useful and realistic.

19-9   Illustrate how the following could occur:

a. A company's sales revenue increased but its net income decreased.
b. A company's sales revenue increased and its variable expenses also increased.
c. A company's sales revenue increased and its variable expenses decreased.

19-10   A company sells its only product for $250 per unit. Variable expenses are $150 per unit and fixed expenses are $100,000 a year.

a. Compute the variable cost percentage.
b. Compute the contribution percentage.
c. Compute the break-even point expressed in terms of sales revenue.

19-11   A company has fixed expenses of $40,000 a year, variable expenses of $60 per unit of product, and a selling price of $100.

a. If the company planned to break even, what would be the desired contribution?
b. If the company planned to earn income of $30,000, what would be the desired contribution?
c. What contribution would result in a net loss of $10,000?
d. If the company is currently realizing a net loss of $7,000, what additional contribution would be required to earn income of $9,000?
e. How many units of product would have to be sold in order to break even?

19-12   Alden Company has variable expenses of 80 per cent of sales and fixed expenses of $40,000.

a. What is the company's break-even point in sales revenue?
b. If the selling price is $20 per unit, how many units must be sold in order to break even?
c. What amount of sales revenue would be required to realize income of $20,000?
d. If fixed expenses are increased by $8,000, how much sales revenue would be required to break even?
e. What would the break-even point be if the variable expense percentage were reduced to 60 per cent?

19-13   Olid Sales Company realized income of $10,000 in 1973 with sales revenue of $280,000. Fixed expenses are $158,000 per year.

a. What is the company's variable cost percentage?
b. By how much would sales revenue have to be changed to show net income of $20,000?
c. By how much would the contribution margin have to be changed in order to double the margin of safety?
d. By how much could the contribution percentage be reduced before sales of $280,000 would yield a net loss?

19-14   In 1973, Cecala Company had a $100,000 margin of safety. Total revenues were $450,000 and the variable expense ratio was 60 per cent.

a. What was the company's net income in 1973?

b. What were total fixed expenses in 1973?

c. What is the company's break-even point expressed in sales revenue?

d. By how much could fixed expenses be increased before the company would have a net loss?

e. By how much would sales revenues have to be changed to show net income of $28,000?

f. By how much would sales revenue have to be changed to show net income of $20,000 if fixed expenses were increased by 10 per cent?

19-15   Mavis, Inc. realized income of $2.8 million in 1972 on sales of 100,000 units. Sales volume increased by 20 per cent in 1973, giving an income of $3.6 million.

Required   a. Compute

1. Contribution per unit.

2. Total fixed costs.

3. Break-even volume in units.

b. List the most important assumptions which you made in order to make these computations.

c. Assume that the 1973 volume increase resulted from a $10 per unit reduction in selling price as compared with 1972. Recompute your answers to part a for 1973.

d. Assume that the 1973 volume increase resulted from a 10 per cent increase in fixed costs as compared with 1972. Recompute your answers to part a for 1973.

19-16   Yukon Company sells two products, X and Y. In 1973 it bought 6,000 units of X for $12 a unit and resold them for $20 a unit, and bought 2,000 units of Y for $8 a unit and sold them for $10 each. Product X requires packaging at a cost of $1 a unit, and salesmen are paid a commission of 20 per cent of sales price for selling it. Product Y requires no packaging and the sales commission is 10 per cent. Fixed expenses are $9,000. Income taxes are not to be considered in this problem.

Required   a. Prepare a statement showing the 1973 contribution for each product and for the company as a whole.

b. Compute the weighted average contribution percentage.

19-17   Assume that the Specialty Products Company, with fixed expenses of $30,000, has two products which it now sells at the following prices and volumes:

	Tahitian Surprise	Jamaican Limbo
Revenue per unit.............................	$10.00	$ 4.00
Cost per unit.................................	4.00	2.00
Volume sold.................................	10,000 units	20,000 units

Required   a. Which product is the more profitable?

b. Assuming that the same sales mix would exist at any sales volume, what is the break-even point in dollars?

c. What level of sales is necessary to attain an income of $100,000 before taxes?

d. Assume that the company has developed a new product, the Oriental Dream, which could be manufactured with present facilities and has a potential selling price of $7.00 and a variable cost of $2.00. If the company could sell an equal number of Tahitian Surprises and Oriental Dreams, and if the ratio of Tahitian Surprise sales to Jamaican Limbo sales should remain the same, what would be the new break-even point?

19-18   Killebrew Corporation sells two products, K and L. Its gross-margin components for the past two years were as follows:

	1973	1972
Sales revenue:		
Product K	$132,000	$ 60,000
Product L	60,000	90,000
Totals	$192,000	$150,000
Deduct cost of goods sold:		
Product K	$110,000	$ 48,000
Product L	39,000	54,000
Totals	$149,000	$102,000
Gross margin	$ 43,000	$ 48,000

In 1972 the selling price of K was $10 a unit, while in 1973 it was $12. Product L sold for $100 a unit in each year. Management was shocked to see that a 28 per cent increase in sales resulted in a $5,000 decrease in gross margin.

Required   Prepare a detailed explanation of the causes of the decline in gross margin, showing the effect of changes in quantities, prices, costs, and product mix.

19-19   The income statement of an unincorporated retail store for 1973 was as follows:

Sales (5,000 identical units)		$200,000
Expenses:		
Store rent	$ 30,000	
Salesmen's commissions	40,000	
Cost of goods sold	120,000	$190,000
Net income		$ 10,000

Salesmen's commissions are a constant percentage of sales price. The store lease has five more years to run at the same annual rental.

Required   a. Compute the contribution per unit.
b. Compute the sales volume below which the company would operate at a net loss (the break-even volume).
c. Compute the break-even sales volume for 1974 if the company rented additional space for $15,000 a year and other operating conditions remained unchanged.
d. Prepare an income statement for 1974 if the number of units is expected to remain unchanged but the sales price per unit is expected to decline $2. No other changes in operating conditions are anticipated.
e. If the number of units sold in 1974 doubles and all other factors behave as they did in 1973, prepare the resulting income statement.
f. Compute the volume of sales that would be needed under 1973 conditions to double the amount of net income.

19-20   Refer to Video, Inc.'s period plan in problem 18-15 and compute the following:

a. Contribution per unit.
b. Contribution in total for sales of 1,400 units.
c. Incremental contribution for a planned increase in sales of 400 units (from 1,200 to 1,600).

d. Break-even point in units.

e. Break-even point in dollars. Prepare a break-even chart.

f. Unit sales necessary to attain a net income of $30,000 (ignore taxes).

g. Unit sales to attain a net income of $20,000 assuming that fixed expenses increase by 10 per cent and variable expenses per unit increase by $10 (ignore taxes).

h. Unit sales (and dollar sales) necessary to attain a return of 10 per cent on shareholders' investment of $540,000 *after* paying taxes of 40 per cent but before a dividend of $50,000.

Cases   **19-1   The Cary Corporation.** The Cary Corporation pays its salesmen a commission of 10 per cent of sales and its manager a salary of $15,000. With 1972 sales revenue of $130,000, cost of goods sold was $78,000; depreciation of building, $7,000; and property taxes and insurance on the building, $4,000. There were no other expenses.

The management is considering two plans for increasing 1973 sales to $160,000. Plan 1 will change the variable expenses to 75 per cent of sales; plan 2 will increase fixed expenses by $7,000 instead. Present computations to show

a. Which plan will be more profitable if the expectations materialize.

b. Which plan will be better if sales remain unchanged.

c. Which plan requires the higher volume of sales to avoid an operating loss.

What other information do you need in order to recommend one of the plans to management?

If only the information in your analysis in parts a, b, and c is available, which plan would you advise management to adopt? Why?

19-2   The Zeroid Company. The Zeroid Company, which sells a single product, has kept the following records of its operating results for the past three years:

	1973	1972	1971
Sales.....................................	$2,200,000	$1,800,000	$2,400,000
Cost of goods sold.....................	1,320,000	1,080,000	1,440,000
Officers' salaries.......................	50,000	50,000	50,000
Salesmen's commissions..............	110,000	90,000	120,000
Heat.....................................	30,000	38,000	25,000
Depreciation of equipment...........	24,000	22,000	22,000
Other fixed expenses	250,000	250,000	250,000
Other variable expenses..............	308,000	252,000	336,000

Required   a. Prepare an estimated income statement if sales for 1974 are expected to be 20 per cent more than in 1973.

b. Prepare an estimated income statement for 1974 if sales are expected to be $1,800,000 and cost of goods sold is expected to become 57 per cent of sales.

c. Prepare an estimated income statement for 1974 if the company sold its building, thereby reducing fixed expenses $100,000 a year, and signed a lease at an annual rental of $90,000 a year. No gain or loss would be made on the sale of the building.

d. Would you recommend that the company take the action in part c on the basis of the information given? What other information is needed?

Cases   **19-3   Jack Ronsom.** Jack Ronsom, supervisor of a state park, has been watching for the right opportunity to have his own business. Mr. Ronsom's present home town, with a population of approximately 3,000, is 75 miles from a large city. It is located near several other state-owned and privately-owned parks and a number of large lakes and resorts which are fast becoming national tourist attractions. During the spring and summer months thousands of people visit the area, some staying for several weeks.

Many tourists neglect to bring adequate clothes and sports equipment for their visit. Several merchants in the town carry a few items of sportswear, and some of the hardware stores have a limited selection of sports equipment and fishing supplies. However, there is no sporting goods store with an adequate selection within a 50-mile radius. Mr. Ronsom thinks that a store which sells sporting equipment, summer play-clothes and informal clothing, and picnic supplies would be successful.

For several months he has gathered information relevant to planning his proposed business. During the spring and summer months the principal attractions for tourists are swimming, boating, fishing, and picnicking. During the fall months, fishing, hunting, and mountain climbing are preferred. Throughout the year thousands of people stop by just to enjoy the scenery and the delightful climate of the area. Mr. Ronsom estimates that average attendance for the spring and summer months of 1972 was 200,000 people per month, and average attendance during the fall and winter months was 50,000 per month. During the past five years the average annual growth in attendance has ranged from 10 per cent to 15 per cent.

Mr. Ronsom plans to finance the business principally by using $35,000 of personal savings. He has found a desirable, centrally located plot of land which the owner is willing to sell for $5,000. A local contractor estimates that the type of building suggested by Mr. Ronsom will cost $27,000. Mr. Ronsom plans to finance two-thirds of the cost of the building by a five-year mortgage loan. He estimates that the cost of furniture and equipment will be $4,000. He anticipates that most of the remainder of his initial investment will be needed to finance the purchase of merchandise.

Mr. Ronsom and his wife plan to devote full time to the business, and he thinks that one full-time salesclerk will be sufficient. During the peak season of the busy summer months, he will be able to hire high school students from the local area. He plans to use his own automobile for routine business operations, including buying trips.

Mr. Ronsom expects the principal expense of the business to be the cost of merchandise, which he estimates will be 60 per cent of selling price. The cost of utilities in the area is relatively small, and Mr. Ronsom predicts that advertising, supplies, summer salaries for clerks, and other miscellaneous expenses will not exceed 15 per cent of sales. His major worry is the drop in attendance which takes place during the winter months.

Mr. Ronsom has prepared an estimate of his expenses for the first year, grouped into two categories—those which will be more or less fixed throughout the year, and those which will vary with sales. He realizes that his figures are not absolutely accurate, but he thinks that they will be a satisfactory guide to enable him to decide whether the venture will be profitable. His estimates are as follows:

Fixed expenses:

Depreciation of building (estimated useful life 30 years, estimated salvage value zero)	?
Depreciation of equipment (estimated life 10 years, no salvage value)	?
Interest at 7% of the unpaid balance of the loan	?
Insurance	$ 500
Full-time clerk's salary	4,800
Taxes (other than income tax)	400
Utilities (based on a $30-per-month average)	360

Mr. Ronsom will be giving up a job which pays him an annual salary of $9,000 in order to operate the business. He thinks that he should earn at least a 20 per cent return (before income tax) on the capital which he is investing.

Required
a. Using Mr. Ronsom's estimates, what is his break-even point?
b. What are the chief uses of this calculation? The shortcomings?
c. How much must the sales of the sporting goods store be in order to fulfill Mr. Ronsom's requirement of a 20 per cent return on his investment?
d. Has Mr. Ronsom omitted any major expenses in his estimate?
e. Point out any other important factors which Mr. Ronsom should consider in deciding whether or not to make the proposed investment.
f. What types of accounting analyses and reports should be prepared for the sporting goods store, and how often?

19-4   General Motors Corporation. The January 29, 1971, issue of *The Wall Street Journal* reported on efforts of General Motors Corporation to overcome a drastic downslide in 1970 sales revenues and profits. Gross revenues declined by $5.4 billion in 1970 from a total of $24.3 billion in 1969. Net income in 1970 dropped 65 per cent to $609 million from $1,707 million a year earlier.

According to the report, GM executives attributed the decline in revenues and income to lower unit volume caused by "the general slowdown in the U.S. and Canadian economies and more importantly, to the (U.A.W.) strike against General Motors." GM sales in 1970 totaled 5.4 million units, significantly below the 7.2 million autos and trucks sold the previous year. Shortly before year end, however, the strike was settled, and GM hoped to earn at least $640 million of net income from accelerated volume in the first quarter of 1971 to partially offset the $135 million deficit realized in the 1970 fourth quarter.

Required
a. Explain clearly how a decrease in unit sales volume can cause a drastic decline in net income.
b. Analyze GM's volume-profit data given above and compute relationships for variable costs, contribution margin, and fixed costs. Also compute GM's expected break-even volume in units.
c. List and evaluate the major assumptions which you made in order to answer part b.
d. On the basis of your analysis and evaluation in parts b and c, explain how GM's management might reasonably expect to offset the 1970 fourth quarter losses early in 1971.

chapter 20

Budgeting and Performance Reporting

Purpose of Chapter

Chapter 19 showed how break-even and incremental analysis may be used to aid management in selecting the most profitable from a group of alternative courses of action under consideration.

The present chapter shows how the specific plans, or alternative courses of action chosen by management, can be reflected in financial terms in the form of a *budget*. It points out how parts of the budget, as well as of reports on actual results, are identified with the *responsibility center* which has the authority and responsibility for carrying out that part of the entity's activities. It illustrates how to prepare budgets and how to analyze differences of actual results from planned results.

REPORTING FOR RESPONSIBILITY CENTERS

Accounting and Decentralized Management

A budgetary control system is primarily concerned with the effectiveness of managerial action. Budgets alone are meaningless unless they are used to *motivate* responsible action and to *direct* operations toward accomplishing objectives that have been established as desirable.

Responsibility for making decisions in many modern business enterprises is *decentralized* to a large extent. Specific tasks are assigned to particular individuals who are capable of performing them, and sufficient authority is delegated to enable these individuals to carry out their decisions.

If an entity is to decentralize its decision-making responsibility effectively, it must have an *information system* for *communicating objectives* and *coordinating action* between its decision centers. If the entity plan is to be fulfilled, each person who is assigned responsibility for directing the action of others must understand clearly what specific tasks he is expected to accomplish, and how the accomplishment of these tasks relates to the periodic progress of the business as a whole. The accounting information system for managerial decisions therefore requires a system of accounts which focuses on specific *responsibility centers*, and which highlights the strong and weak points of the performance over which each responsible manager has *direct control*.

Responsibility Center Accounts

A *responsibility center* is any subdivision of business activity—a division, department, or other segment—that is under the direction of a responsible manager. The accounts are tailored to report the particular revenue, expense, asset, and equity elements which are assigned to the responsibility center and for which the manager of the center is directly accountable. To permit *comparison of actual results with planned results* for each responsibility center, the operating accounts are classified along the same lines as the activities covered by the budget.

Direct Versus Common and Controllable Versus Noncontrollable Financial Elements

To facilitate effective coordination and control, the budgets, accounts, and performance reports of each responsibility center should emphasize the financial items which are *directly traceable* to that center of activity. Only secondary emphasis, if any, should be given to *common* elements that relate to several responsibility centers or to the firm as a whole.

Example 1   The asset, equipment, and its periodic depreciation expense are both *directly traceable* to a given department if the equipment is used solely in that department.

The expenses of the top executive office of a manufacturing company which has three plants in different locations apply to all the plants in *common*. The top executive expenses applicable to each plant cannot be traced in a direct and convincing way. Likewise, the assets used in the top executive office are common to all the plants of the company.

It is an established principle of management that an individual who is to be held *responsible* for accomplishing a particular objective must be given *sufficient authority* to control the resources required to accomplish it. Accounting reports prepared for each level of management follow this principle by classifying the financial elements directly traceable to the responsibility center—the revenues, expenses, assets, and equities—into two groups: those which are *controllable* and those which are *noncontrollable* by the manager of the responsibility center.

A financial element is *controllable* by a manager if he has the responsibility and authority to take action which will change its amount significantly. It is *noncontrollable* if he cannot change it significantly, even if someone higher in the organization can.

Example 2   The buyer for a merchandising department in a department store can control payroll expense to some extent if he has authority to hire or discharge part-time salesclerks. He can control advertising expense if he has authority to decide the number, frequency, size, and types of advertisements of the goods for sale by his department. He cannot control payroll expense if he is not consulted about the number of employees assigned to his department, or advertising expense if he has nothing to do with determining the number and types of advertisements. Both expenses are then controllable by the manager who decides the quantities and types of each service to buy.

The buyer *can control* the amount of the investment in inventory, within the limits set by company policy, by the manner in which he directs the functions of buying and selling within the department.

The *effectiveness* with which a responsibility center manager performs his responsbility is evaluated from reports of the *controllable* items.

Degrees of Controllability

Whether or not a given financial element is controllable by a given manager depends partly on the *division of authority and responsibility* in the particular firm, partly on the *length of time* in question, and partly on the *nature of the element*. Rarely are the amounts of financial elements completely controllable by any one person.

All financial elements are controllable to some extent if a long enough time period is considered, but for very short periods the amounts of many items cannot be changed by anyone within the business.

Example 3   The *departmental buyer* in Example 2 cannot control the amount invested in equipment, or the amount of periodic depreciation expense, if he does not have the authority to make decisions regarding equipment acquisitions and disposals. If such decisions are made by the *president*, the asset equipment and the related depreciation expense are controllable by the president *in the long run*. However, for short periods even he may be powerless to control their amounts.

Distinction Between Controllable and Variable Expenses

Classification of expenses as controllable or noncontrollable is not the same as classifying them as variable or fixed, although the two bases of classification are closely related. The latter basis distinguishes *variable expenses, which change in proportion to changes in sales volume,* from *fixed expenses, whose behavior is not related to changes in sales volume.* An expense item may be *variable* from the point of view of the business as a whole, but *noncontrollable* by a given department manager because he cannot change its amount. An example would be a bonus to the president based on sales volume. On the other hand, equipment depreciation, a *fixed* expense, can be *controlled* in the long run by the action of the manager who has authority to buy or dispose of equipment.

Allocation of Common Financial Elements to Responsibility Centers

For many purposes, managerial effectiveness is best evaluated on the basis of the financial elements *directly traceable to,* and *controllable by,* the responsible manager. For other purposes it is useful to evaluate the performance of a subdivision of the business from the viewpoint of the organization as a whole. In such cases appropriate parts of the *common,* or *indirect,* elements which pertain to more than one responsibility center are assigned to individual responsibility centers.

Apportionment of common expenses, revenues, and assets to subdivisions of a business should be made in a way that will reasonably reflect how much of the common financial element is attributable to the individual responsibility centers. Reasonable *bases of allocation* are sought by associating the behavior of the common element with some other factor which seems to *cause* changes in its amount. The common element is then allocated to each organizational unit in proportion to the *unit's use of the causal factor.*

Example 4   A department store occupies a single building, for which it pays an annual rent of $12,000. Each of the four department heads has shown tendencies to spread the merchandise of his department over a wide area, with resulting inefficient space utilization. The president thinks that it will soon be necessary to acquire a larger building at a higher rent unless the wasteful tendency is corrected. He feels that the present volume of merchandise handled could, through efficient planning, be accommodated in less space. To make the department managers conscious of the cost of occupying building space, he instructs the accountant to develop a fair basis for charging rent to each department. How should the allocation be made?

Solution   An obvious basis for allocating rent expense would be in proportion to the floor space occupied by each department. If Department A occupies $\frac{1}{4}$ of the total floor space, it would seem reasonable to charge $\frac{1}{4}$ of the rent expense, or $3,000, to Department A. For more complex figures, an alternate approach can be used:

a. $\dfrac{\text{Total rent expense}}{\text{Total square feet of floor space}} = \text{Rent per square foot}$

b. Square feet in department $\times$ Rent per square foot
$$= \text{Rent expense of department.}$$

The fairness as well as the usefulness of such more or less arbitrary bases of cost allocation is often limited.

Example 5 The manager of Department A objected to the charging of rent to departments on the basis of square feet of floor space. He contended that his department, being in a relatively inaccessible location near the rear of the store, should pay a lower rate of rent than departments in better locations.

The manager of Department C thought that the charge should be based on cubic feet of space, rather than square feet. The ceilings were somewhat lower in his department than elsewhere in the store, with the result that his available space for wall displays and shelf storage was less.

Distinction between common expenses and fixed expenses. Common expenses are those items of expense which cannot be identified convincingly with the operations of any particular unit of the business, whereas *fixed* expenses are items which do not change in proportion to changes in revenue. A common expense may be either variable or fixed, and a fixed expense may be either direct or common.

Example 6 A company has a national sales office but ships goods sold directly from each of three branch manufacturing plants. If it pays its national sales manager a commission based on sales, the commission expense *varies* with total sales revenue but is *common* to all three plants.

Allocations of common expenses and other common financial elements are useful if they help management accomplish its objectives more than would the alternatives of *not allocating*, or of reporting the common elements in some other fashion. Businesses usually plan and report their operations in a way which emphasizes the *direct* revenues, expenses, and assets of each responsibility center (those which are directly traceable to each center). The plans and reports focus attention on the *net contribution* of each responsibility center—the excess of its direct revenues over its direct expenses—to the expenses which are *common* to the business as a whole. This approach helps to avoid arbitrary allocations of common elements in the budgets and reports to managers of subdivisions —allocations which are sometimes meaningless to the subdivision manager.

Principles related to this type of planning and performance reporting are considered in the remainder of this chapter.

PREPARATION OF THE BUDGET

In modern budgeting practice, it is customary to ask each individual responsible for managing a segment of business operations to prepare his own tentative budget for the items under his control. The theory is that the individuals who are to execute the business plans will exert greater effort to accomplish goals which they have *participated* in setting. There are, of course, limits to this approach. The budget supervisor should examine the details of departmental estimates for evidence of overoptimism, overpessimism, or wasteful planning. He should review the parts of the plan to see that they are coordinated with each other where necessary and are reasonable in view of the availability of labor, merchandise, facilities, and funds. He should determine whether the planned contribution margin of revenue over direct expenses, the percentage of this margin to assets used by the department, and the budgeted rate of return for the business as a whole are consistent with the objectives. If he thinks they are not, he should recommend action to bring the departmental and over-all plans into line with the firm's goals or, if necessary, to revise the goals. It is important that the department manager understand the reasons for any changes in his budget and that he continue to feel that the plan is his own, not one *imposed* on him from above.

The Sales Budget

The logical starting point in preparing the operating budget is the *sales budget*. Revenue is a critical element in projecting income, because it is the independent variable which influences the behavior of many important expenses. Variations in sales revenue from one period to another are often influenced markedly by external factors such as booms, recessions, and wars. Many businesses, especially those whose sales seem to be causally related to national income, base their estimates largely on the estimated total national income, or on total expected sales of the industry. The probable effect on sales of changes within the business organization must also be carefully considered.

The Planning Budget and the Flexible Budget

It is useful to distinguish between two forms of the budget: the *planning budget* and the *flexible budget*.

Planning budget. In making plans for the future management considers many important alternatives which will have varied effects on revenues, expenses, assets, and equities. The tentative decisions regarding some of the more important alternatives are often reflected in the form of a preliminary budget. After several partial or complete revisions, the preliminary budget is modified and accepted as the plan of action of the business for the coming period. In this final form, the *planning budget* expresses in detail the operating results which management initially wishes to accomplish during the coming period.

Flexible budget. It is not satisfactory to prepare a budget at the beginning of the period and then leave it as a rigid plan of action. Important unforeseen changes in internal or external conditions may require budget revisions during the budget period.

It is essential that management receive timely information on its actual results in comparison with the plan. A comparison of actual operating performance with the *planning budget* would show management *what the business did* in comparison with *what it initially planned to do*. It may not reveal, however, how well the business performed with regard to how it *should have performed* under the conditions which actually existed.

Example 7   In its planning budget for 1972, Fox Company had forecast cost of goods sold for January of $120,000, or 60 per cent of sales. Actual sales for January were $180,000 and actual cost of goods sold amounted to $111,000. Was the performance on this expense item $9,000 better than expected?

Solution No, because cost of goods sold should usually bear an approximately constant relationship to sales, 60 per cent in this illustration. If sales were less than the forecast, cost of goods sold should also have been less than the forecast, maintaining the 60 per cent relationship. Considering that sales for the month were actually $180,000, cost of goods sold should have been $108,000 (60 per cent of $180,000). The cost of goods sold was actually $3,000 too much, considering the level of sales volume actually attained.

A form of the budget which compares what the business actually did with what it should have done under the circumstances which prevailed is called the *flexible budget*. Although the *planning* budget contains the amounts of revenue and expense at the planned level of activity, the *flexible* budget permits comparisons of actual expenses with standards of what expenses should have been at the level of operations actually achieved.

Illustration of Flexible Budget

Examples 8 and 9 show how a flexible budget is prepared.

Example 8 The Zany Products Company was attempting to provide a means for measuring performance of its Toy Division for the month of December 1972. Because forecasting sales was a very difficult job, owing to the unusual nature of the market, the manager of Zany Products felt that a flexible budget should be prepared so that the expenses of attaining the actual sales for the month could be compared with some standard of performance.

ZANY PRODUCTS COMPANY—TOY DIVISION
Flexible Budget for Product and Selling Costs
Month of December 1972

Unit sales	10,000	12,000	14,000	16,000	18,000
Product costs	$20,000	$24,000	$28,000	$32,000	$36,000
Sales commissions	5,000	6,000	7,000	8,000	9,000
Delivery costs	10,000	10,500	10,500	11,000	11,000
Advertising	8,000	8,000	8,000	8,000	8,000
Budgeted expenses	$43,000	$48,500	$53,500	$59,000	$64,000

Assuming that the unit sales for Zany Products for December amounted to 16,000 items, the budgeted costs for this level of operations would be $59,000. The individual costs of products and selling effort should correspond to the specific items listed in the flexible budget.

The budgeted expense at any level of operations for a given organization, or division thereof, may be calculated by the following formula:

Budgeted expense =
Fixed expense + Variable expense per unit (times number of units).

Example 9 Assume that in a particular production process experience has shown that materials and labor are $12 per unit, fixed costs (depreciation, supervision, and so forth) are $40,000, and mixed costs amount to $2 per unit, plus a constant amount of $10,000, regardless of the level of production. Given this information, the flexible budget for a production level of 10,000 units can be calculated as follows:

Budgeted costs = $40,000 + $10,000 + 10,000 units ($12 + $2)
Budgeted costs = $190,000.

Budgeted costs could be similarly computed for any level of operations where variable costs remain the same per unit, and where fixed costs do not increase or decrease.

MEASURING AND REPORTING PERFORMANCE

Timely information is essential to the control of business operations. Frequent *feedback* of actual results of controllable financial elements as compared with their budgeted amounts aids management in taking corrective action when operating performance is off target. The effort expended in developing budgets is of little value if many months pass before operating figures are compared with them.

Content of Budgetary Reports

The budgets and the performance evaluation reports for each responsibility center should focus management's attention on the *contribution* to income that is directly attributable to, and controllable by, the responsible manager. This is done by

(1) Deducting the center's direct and controllable variable expenses from its revenue to highlight its *total contribution*.

(2) Deducting the center's direct and controllable fixed expenses from its total contribution to emphasize its *net contribution* to expenses which are not controllable by the center manager, and to income of the firm as a whole.

The analysis of differences between the planned and actual revenues and expenses should be made on the basis of flexible budget figures.

Illustration of a Planning Budget

Illustration 20-1 shows the March 1972 *planning budget* for Contact Corporation's Marketing Division organized in a manner which will facilitate later performance evaluation. The budget shows an expected *total contribution* of $37,500 from the division's operations for the month. The responsibility center's *net contribution* is expected to be $12,500, after deducting its controllable fixed expenses from its total expected contribution.

The budget also shows that the Marketing Division's planned *net income before tax* is $4,500 for March, after allocating $8,000 of noncontrollable General Administrative Expense to the division.

Illustration
20-1

CONTACT CORPORATION
Marketing Division
Planning Budget of Operations
For the Month Ending March 31, 1972

	Amount		*Per Cent of* *Net Sales*
Net sales revenue.................................		$150,000	100.0%
Deduct direct, controllable expenses:			
Variable divisional expenses:			
Cost of goods sold.........................	$90,000		60.0%
Sales commissions.........................	6,000		4.0
Salaries (variable part)	7,500		5.0
Other variable expense..................	9,000		6.0
Total variable expenses............		112,500	75.0
Total contribution to controllable fixed expenses, noncontrollable expenses, and income.............................		37,500	25.0
Fixed divisional expenses:			
Depreciation.................................	$ 1,000		
Rent..	6,000		
Salaries (fixed part).........................	14,000		
Advertising	4,000		
Total direct, fixed expenses......		25,000	
Net contribution to noncontrollable expenses and income.................................		12,500	
Deduct noncontrollable and common expense:			
General administrative expense........		8,000	
Net income before income tax..............		$ 4,500	

Illustration of a Performance Report

Illustration 20-2 reports the actual results of the Marketing Division for March in comparison with the budget. The report shows the *variances* (increases or decreases of actual results from planned results) of expenses, total contribution, net contribution, and net income before tax. This report gives management an indication of the operating effectiveness of the Marketing Division. An analysis of the causes of the variances can lead the divisional management to take corrective action where necessary.

The Marketing Division's *net loss* of $1,600 for March, shown in the second column, was $6,100 less than the planned *net income* of $4,500, shown in the planning budget (Illustration 20-1). The actual total contribution of $31,150 was $6,350 less than the planned contribution of $37,500. To aid in interpreting these unfavorable variances in net income and contribution and to provide useful information about the Division's operating effectiveness, the budgeted expenses in column 1 have been adjusted to reflect the *flexible budget allowances* for the actual volume of sales achieved.

The flexible budget allowances were based on the assumption that the

Illustration
20-2

CONTACT CORPORATION
Marketing Division
Report of Budgeted and Actual Operations
For the Month of March, 1972

	(1) Flexible Budget Allowance at Actual Volume	(2) Actual Results	(3) Increase (Decrease) from Planned Income Due to — Usage, Price, or Spending (Col. 1–2)	(4) Increase (Decrease) from Planned Income Due to — Volume Change
Net sales revenue............................	$135,000	$135,000	$ 0	Not applicable
Deduct direct, controllable expenses:				
Variable expenses:				
Cost of goods sold......................	81,000	83,500	(2,500)	
Sales commissions......................	5,400	5,400	0	
Salaries (variable part)...............	6,750	7,000	(250)	
Other variable expense...............	8,100	7,950	150	
Total variable expense........	101,250	103,850	(2,600)	Not applicable
Total contribution...........................	33,750	31,150	(2,600)	($ 3,750)
Fixed expenses:				
Depreciation	1,000	1,000	0	
Rent	6,000	6,000	0	
Salaries (fixed part)	14,000	14,500	(500)	
Advertising	4,000	3,250	750	
Total fixed expense............	25,000	24,750	250	Not applicable
Net contribution to noncontrollable expenses and income......................	8,750	6,400	(2,350)	(3,750)
Deduct noncontrollable and common expense:				
General administrative expense	8,000	8,000	0	Not applicable
Net income (loss) before income tax.....	$ 750	($ 1,600)	($ 2,350)	($ 3,750)

expenses of the division should have followed the normal behavior of fixed and variable expenses. Thus the *fixed expenses* should have been the *same as in the planning budget,* even though actual sales volume was $15,000 less than planned. *Variable expenses* should have remained a *constant percentage* of actual sales volume. The flexible budget allowances for variable expenses were computed as follows:

Variable Expense	Allowed Percentage of Sales	Actual Sales	Allowed Amount
Cost of goods sold	60	$135,000	$ 81,000
Sales commissions	4		5,400
Salaries (variable part)	5		6,750
Other variable expense	6		8,100

According to the flexible budget allowance in column (1) of Illustration 20-2, the Marketing Division's total contribution for March should have been $33,750 at the actual volume of sales reached, $135,000. The net income before tax should have been $750. In the flexible budget both total contribution and net income are $3,750 less than in the planning budget. This difference is the *volume variance*, shown in column (*4*) of the performance report and explained in the next section.

Analysis of Variances from Budget

Volume variance. The volume variance shows the difference between planned and actual contribution, and between planned and actual net income, that is *attributed to differences of actual sales from planned sales.* It is based on the assumption that the planned volume of sales was a desirable and reasonably attainable objective of the current period. Since expenses which vary in direct proportion to sales volume are expected to be proportionately higher or lower than their planned amounts when sales are higher or lower, these differences in actual variable expenses from planned variable expenses are *not relevant* in evaluating management's performance effectiveness. What *is relevant* in performance evaluation is the difference between planned contribution and actual contribution that results from actual sales volume being different from planned sales. This *volume variance* can be computed by multiplying the difference of actual sales from planned sales (in this case, a decrease of $15,000) by the contribution percentage (here, 25 per cent). The result for the Marketing Division for March 1972 is an *unfavorable volume variance* of $3,750.

Price variance. A price variance occurs when a product or service is sold at a unit price which is more or less than the planned price. If Contact Corporation (in Illustrations 20-1 and 20-2) sold the same number of physical units in March as had been planned, the $15,000 decrease of actual sales revenue from planned sales revenue would have resulted from a decrease in the *selling price* of each unit. For example, if it had been planned to sell 75,000 units at $2 a unit and 75,000 units were sold for a total of $135,000, the unit selling price was $1.80, or 10 per cent lower than the planned selling price.

Spending variance. A spending variance occurs when the unit cost of a productive resource, such as materials, labor, or insurance, is more or less than the planned unit cost. For example, the $250 unfavorable variance of Salaries (variable part) from the planned amount could be attributed to an increase in salary rates if the number of persons employed in March was the same as the planned number.

Usage variance. A usage variance (sometimes called an *efficiency variance*) occurs when the physical quantity of a productive resource actually used is more or less than the quantity allowed in the flexible budget for the actual sales volume. For example, the favorable variance of $150 in Other Expenses in column (3) of Illustration 20-2 could be attributed to using a smaller quantity of supplies than normally required for $135,000 in sales, if the price of supplies per unit was the same as budgeted.

Summary Accounting reports to management follow the pattern of authority and responsibility assigned to various managers within the organization. Internal reports for the use of management identify the *responsibility center* for which the report was prepared.

A key concept in internal reporting is to identify with each manager those financial elements—revenues, expenses, and assets—which are *directly traceable* to his responsibility center and *controllable* by him. Items which are *common* to several responsibility centers, and which are *noncontrollable* by the particular manager, may be reported to him as supplementary information. Assignment of common expenses to individual responsibility centers requires *allocation*, sometimes arbitrary, on the basis of causal factors.

The *planning budget* expresses the operating results which management expects to accomplish during the budget period. Interpretation of actual results in comparison with the plan is facilitated by the use of a *flexible budget*. This is an estimate of what various expenses *should have been* at the actual level of activity— even if different from the planned level of activity. The differences of actual expenses and revenues from the plan are designated as *volume*, *price*, *spending*, or *usage variances*. They are reported to management for investigation and whatever corrective action seems appropriate.

Discussion Questions and Problems

20-1   What is a *budgetary control system*? What is its purpose? How does it function?

20-2   It is a truism of management that *authority* must be commensurate with *responsibility* in all phases of business activity. What part does this play in accounting reports?

20-3   What is a *responsibility center*? How does this concept influence an entity's system of accounting?

20-4   Give an example of each of the following:

a. An asset that can be directly traced to the production department of a manufacturer.
b. An asset that cannot be traced directly to either the production or the sales department of a manufacturer.
c. A cost that can be directly traced to the production department of a manufacturer.
d. A revenue and an expense that cannot be identified with any specific subdivision of a business.

20-5   What are the purposes of allocating expenses to a business subdivision? What are the major difficulties involved in making such allocations? What are the principal limitations of the usefulness of such allocations in reports to the management of subdivisions?

20-6   Whether an expense or revenue item is controllable by a particular manager depends partly on the period of time involved, and partly on the assignment of responsibility. Explain.

20-7   Give an example of each of the following:

a. A fixed manufacturing cost that is controllable by the production manager.
b. A fixed manufacturing cost that is not controllable by the production manager.
c. A variable expense that is controllable by the sales manager of a retail store.
d. A variable expense that is not controllable by the sales manager of a retail store.

20-8   The manager of a small manufacturing company made the following remark: "Budgets are a waste of time, because nobody can predict accurately what is going to happen in the future. And besides, budgets tie management's hands if changes need to be made because of unexpected operating conditions."

How would you respond to this manager?

20-9 How does a planning budget differ from a flexible budget? How are the two related?

20-10 "If a planning budget is too optimistic, this is automatically corrected in the flexible budget." Is this true? Is there any adverse consequence of overoptimistic planning?

20-11 The X Retail Store has the six following operating departments, each headed by a manager: Sales Department A, Sales Department B, Sales Department C, Finance, Maintenance, and Personnel. The department heads are responsible directly to the president, who is interested in evaluating the effectiveness of each department manager in contributing to the store's income.

a. How would you suggest that the performance of the three selling department managers be evaluated?
b. Prepare an outline form of statement which might be used to report the monthly results of Sales Department A.

20-12 The accounting department of a large manufacturing company prepared monthly operating reports for each department foreman. Copies of these reports, together with a summary of them, were submitted to the division manager. The president received a summary of operations for the company as a whole, supported by copies of all division managers' and foremen's reports.

a. What is the reason for such a plan?
b. What are the weaknesses?

20-13 A nationwide company with manufacturing plants and sales offices in many cities has decided to prepare financial reports for the manager in charge of each office, showing allocated common expenses as well as directly traceable items.

a. On what basis would you recommend that each of the following be allocated?
   (1) President's salary.
   (2) Total fire and theft insurance premiums.
   (3) Cost of nationwide advertising.
   (4) Income tax.
   (5) Cost of installing the entire accounting system.
   (6) Interest expense.
   (7) Cost of training understudies for key executives.
   (8) Cost of a company park in Kentucky available for the use of any employee.
   (9) Rent of the central office in Pittsburgh.
b. What are the advantages and disadvantages of such allocations in reports to subdivisions?

20-14 The Mariposa Company has three principal divisions, Manufacturing, Sales, and Administration, all housed in the same building. The space occupied by these three divisions is as follows:

> Manufacturing............................35,000 square feet
> Sales...10,000 square feet
> Administration........................... 5,000 square feet

Required a. Indicate by a check mark the nature of each of the Mariposa Company's costs from the viewpoint of the Sales Division.

	Amount	Direct	Common	Control-lable	Noncon-trollable
President's salary...........	$45,000	( )	( )	( )	( )
Depreciation of building	10,000	( )	( )	( )	( )
Taxes on building..........	2,000	( )	( )	( )	( )
Heat..........................	1,500	( )	( )	( )	( )
Electricity....................	1,000	( )	( )	( )	( )
Sales manager's salary.....	15,000	( )	( )	( )	( )
Shipping supplies used.....	3,000	( )	( )	( )	( )

b. State how you would allocate the common costs to the three divisions. Where sufficient information is available, make the actual allocations.

c. What are the chief limitations of each method of allocation used in part b?

20-15   The Tarey Company is preparing its planning budget for the coming fiscal year. How should it plan the amounts for each of the following?

(1) Advertising expense.
(2) Transportation out expense.
(3) Depreciation expense.
(4) Interest expense.
(5) Losses from uncollectibles.
(6) Cost of goods sold expense.
(7) Sales.

20-16   The accountant of a company presented an income statement showing the contribution of each division to common expenses and income. The president remarked that the contributions of the divisions totaled more than the net income of the business, and asked for an explanation.

What explanation could the accountant have given?

20-17   Department *A* has stayed within its planning budget on every single item, while Department *B* has exceeded its budgeted figures for more than half of the items. Should the manager of Department *A* be commended because his department has operated more effectively than Department *B*? Explain.

20-18   The manager of a department of a retail store learned that cost of goods sold expense was 1 per cent larger than the figure in the planning budget for a certain month, while supplies expense was 5 per cent larger.

a. On which of the two should he focus primary attention? Why?

b. What possible explanations could he find for the two variations from the budgeted amounts?

20-19   Refer to Example 8 for the Zany Products Company in this chapter and answer the following questions:

a. Can this flexible budget also be used as a planning budget? Explain.

b. Assume that the company sold 18,000 units and incurred total costs of $65,400. Was performance better or worse than it should have been? What would you do to determine the cause of the difference?

c. Assume that December sales were 15,000 units. How would you use the flexible budget to measure cost performance? Calculate the total costs which might be expected at this level of operations, and the costs of each type.

d. How can this flexible budget improve performance measurement as compared with the planning budget?

20-20

Required Assume that the flexible budget formula for a certain company was

$$\text{Budgeted costs} = \$50,000 + \$5 \text{ per unit.}$$

a. What would the budgeted costs be for a volume of 10,000 units?

b. Assume that at volumes in excess of 10,000 units fixed costs increase 10 per cent and per unit variable costs decrease by 5 per cent. What would be the budgeted costs for a volume of 15,000 units?

c. Assume that included in the $50,000 and $5 costs shown in the formula are mixed costs which amount to $1 per unit plus $3,000 for each daily work shift. If 10,000 units are all that can be produced on one shift of work, what would be the budgeted costs for 12,000 units?

20-21 Ratan Corporation's flexible budget is based on the following specifications:

	Variable Per Unit	Variable Per Cent	Fixed
Sales price..	$90	100%	
Cost of goods sold..................................	54	60%	
Salaries and commissions.........................	9	10%	$12,000
Supplies...	9	10%	
Other expenses.......................................			16,000
Total expenses.....................................	$72	80%	$28,000

The planning budget for 1973 was based on an expected sales volume of 1,400 units. Actual sales revenues were $119,600 on 1,300 units. Cost of goods sold expense was $71,500, salaries and commissions totaled $23,460, supplies expense was $12,000, and other expenses totaled $16,000.

Required a. Prepare a performance report and identify all variances of actual from budget.

b. Identify the possible causes of each variance.

20-22 Gammon Sales Company prepared the following budget for 1973:

	Total	Product 1	Product 2	Product 3
Sales	$100,000	$ 50,000	$ 30,000	$ 20,000
Cost of goods sold.............	67,000	30,000	21,000	16,000
Gross margin....................	$ 33,000	$ 20,000	$ 9,000	$ 4,000
Variable operating expenses	16,000	8,000	4,800	3,200
Contribution to nonvariable expenses.................	$ 17,000	$ 12,000	$ 4,200	$ 800
Nonvariable expenses	$ 13,000			
Net income before income tax........................	$ 4,000			

Actual sales for the year were $120,000, but there was a net loss of $2,200. Sales of Product 1 were $20,000; of Product 2, $20,000; and of Product 3, $80,000. Variable and nonvariable expenses behaved exactly as they were expected to.

Required Prepare an analysis of the reason or reasons for the disappointing results.

20-23   The Perdu Company prepares monthly reports to help department managers control their costs. Just before the end of 1972 the following budget for Department *A* was prepared for January 1973:

Sales..		$8,000
Cost of goods sold...		4,800
Gross margin...		$3,200
Direct operating expense:		
Variable...	$1,200	
Nonvariable	700	1,900
Contribution to common expense......................................		$1,300

The actual results for January were

Sales..	$8,500
Cost of goods sold...	5,300
Gross margin...	$3,200
Direct operating expense (including $700 nonvariable)...............	2,700
Contribution to common expense......................................	$ 500

Required   a. Prepare a report to the manager of Department *A* analyzing the effectiveness of his operations for the month.

b. Comment on any significant phases of the operating results.

20-24   The Taylor Wholesale Grocery Company operates three branches in neighboring cities. At the end of the fiscal year the chief accountant prepared financial statements for each branch. The summary statement presented to the president of the company is shown below:

TAYLOR WHOLESALE GROCERY COMPANY
Income Statement
For the Year Ended December 31, 1973

	Branch A	Branch B	Branch C
Sales revenue..	$150,000	$100,000	$200,000
Deduct direct expenses:			
Cost of goods sold.......................................	$ 90,000	$ 62,000	$110,000
Payroll..	17,000	13,000	19,000
Supplies...	200	150	225
Utilities...	550	450	600
Transportation out and delivery......................	2,500	1,900	3,100
Depreciation of plant and equipment..............	10,000	9,600	11,250
	$120,250	$ 87,100	$144,175
Branch contribution to common expenses and income...	$ 29,750	$ 12,900	$ 55,825
Deduct expenses common to all branches:			
Advertising expense......................................	$ 6,000	$ 4,000	$ 8,000
General and administrative salaries (allocated equally)...	15,000	15,000	15,000
Other administrative expenses........................	1,000	1,000	1,000
Total common expenses....................................	$ 22,000	$ 20,000	$ 24,000
Net income (loss) before income tax...................	$ 7,750	($ 7,100)	$ 31,825

Required   a. What are the advantages of the type of statement illustrated from the point of view of (1) the branch managers and (2) the president?

b. What are the disadvantages of the illustrated statement form?

c. Explain how expenses common to all branches have been allocated. Do you agree with this basis of allocation? If not, what would you have done?

d. Select examples of the following types of expenses, from the point of view of the branch managers:

(1) Direct and controllable.

(2) Direct and noncontrollable.

(3) Common and noncontrollable.

(4) Variable and noncontrollable.

(5) Variable and direct.

(6) Nonvariable and controllable.

20-25   Bancroft Manufacturing Company occupies a single one-story building. It has a Production Division, a Sales Division, and a Treasury and Accounts Division, each under a division manager.

The company wishes to assign all expired costs to the appropriate divisions in order to measure periodic income and the cost of its product inventories, as well as to evaluate the performance of the division managers.

Required   a. Using the following information, prepare a schedule showing the amount of each expired cost which you would charge to each division for the year ended December 31, 1973. Show your computations.

b. Point out any weaknesses of the results in part a.

c. In view of these weaknesses, what method of presentation do you recommend in the divisional operating statements?

	Production	*Sales*	*Treasury and Accounts*
Area occupied (sq. ft.)	14,000	7,000	4,000
Number of employees	150	25	15
Number of electrical outlets	200	60	40
Kilowatt-hours used	60,000	8,000	12,000

	Expired Cost
Building depreciation	$10,000
First aid salaries and supplies	500
Electricity	4,000
Heat	3,000
President's salary	25,000
Repair of roof over factory wing	800

20-26   The Naylor Company prepared the following comparison of actual results with the planning budget for one of its sales divisions for the month of July 1973:

	Planning Budget	*Actual*
Sales revenue	$50,000	$42,000
Cost of goods sold	30,000	27,000
Controllable expenses:		
Supplies	2,000	1,800
Travel expense	4,000	3,500
Sales commissions	3,000	2,520
Manager's salary	1,000	1,000
Depreciation	2,500	2,500

Required   Assuming that the company uses a flexible budget, prepare a report showing

    a. The difference between actual and planning budget.
    b. The flexible budget amounts as a percentage of sales.
    c. The flexible budget amounts for the actual volume.
    d. The volume variances.
    e. The price or spending variances.

20-27   Oregon Products Company's top management has budgeted total sales for 1973 at $2 million. The sales quotas of the various regional sales managers and their staffs are

Region 1	$ 400,000
Region 2	600,000
Region 3	1,000,000

    The budget director, after analyzing past results and consulting with each regional manager as to plans, has developed the following data for planning operating expense allowances:

Variable expenses as per cent of sales:	*Region 1*	*Region 2*	*Region 3*
Cost of goods sold	65%	67%	70%
Salesmen's commissions	5	5	4
Shipping costs.............................	3	2	2
Other......................................	5	6	6
Nonvariable expenses:			
Automobile depreciation................	$ 5,000	$ 8,000	$15,000
Supervisory salaries......................	30,000	35,000	50,000
Other......................................	28,000	28,000	29,000

Required   a. Prepare a planning budget for each of the regions and for the company as a whole.
    b. Explain the major limitations of the planning budget in this situation.
    c. In view of these limitations, would you recommend the use of a planning budget? Why?

Cases   **20-1**   **Bonanza Stores Corporation.** Bonanza Stores Corporation operates ten supermarkets in a large metropolitan area. As a result of expert management and excellent reputation in the area, the corporation has prospered in recent years and now has over 5,000 stockholders.

    In addition to groceries, meat, and produce, the company's stores sell a line of high-markup, nonfood items.

    On January 1, 1973, Bonanza Stores Corporation purchased its eleventh store. This store had formerly been operated as a supermarket, but its income was far below the average of similar grocery stores. The former owners decided that they no longer wished to compete with the chain stores and agreed to sell the assets of their business to Bonanza for $220,000.

    The accompanying income statement of Store No. 11 for the year ended December 31, 1972, as prepared by the former owners, is compared with percentage performance standards based on the average past performance of Bonanza Stores Corporation's other ten stores.

STORE NO. 11
BONANZA STORES CORPORATION
Income Statement
For the Year Ended December 31, 1972

	Actual Results of Store #11	Standard Company Percentages
Net sales...	$1,341,700	100.00%
Deduct cost of goods sold...........................	1,151,900	81.50
Gross margin on sales (Schedule 1)................	189,800	18.50
Deduct operating expenses:		
Advertising...	$ 10,400	1.00
Depreciation.......................................	16,800	1.37
Miscellaneous......................................	9,535	0.60
Repairs and maintenance........................	1,900	0.13
Salaries...	94,400	6.00
Supplies...	37,835	2.90
Utilities...	8,200	0.60
Total operating expenses...........................	179,070	12.60
Income from operations.............................	10,730	5.90
Deduct financial expense:		
Interest expense...................................	5,200	0.40
Income before income tax..........................	5,530	5.50%

With the addition of an extensive line of nonfood items, the operations of Store No. 11 will be accounted for on a four-department basis. Sales mix is of crucial importance to a supermarket of this type, since the gross margins for the various sales categories differ widely. Comparisons of the sales mix and gross margins achieved by Store No. 11 during 1972 and the standard goals of the Bonanza Stores Corporation are included in the accompanying information:

STORE NO. 11
BONANZA STORES CORPORATION
Gross Margin on Sales
For the Year Ended December 31, 1972

Schedule 1

	Departments			
	Grocery	*Meat*	*Produce*	*Total*
Net sales........................	$756,800	$460,600	$124,300	$1,341,700
Cost of goods sold............	658,000	397,500	96,400	1,151,900
Gross margin on sales.......	$ 98,800	$ 63,100	$ 27,900	$ 189,800

Sales Mix

Department	1972 Actual Per Cent of Total Sales	Standard Per Cent of Total Sales
Grocery..	56.4%	60%
Meat..	34.3	25
Produce..	9.3	10
Nonfood items...	—	5
	100.0%	100%

Gross Margins to Net Sales

Department	1972 Actual	Company Standard
Grocery	13.1%	15%
Meat	13.7	20
Produce	22.4	25
Nonfood items	—	40%

Sales goals of $1,500,000 for 1973 and $1,600,000 for 1974 were set for Store No. 11 by the management of Bonanza. Departmental sales goals are based on the company's standard sales mix.

Operating expenses are classified as variable or fixed according to the predominant nature of the expense. It is company policy to spend 1 per cent of the budgeted sales amount for advertising. Salary expense includes salaries and year-end bonuses paid to the store manager and department managers based on a percentage of actual sales in excess of established annual quotas.

Actual results for Store No. 11 for 1973 were as follows:

Net sales:	
Grocery	$860,000
Meat	350,000
Produce	165,000
Nonfood items	70,000
Cost of sales:	
Grocery	730,000
Meat	270,000
Produce	123,750
Nonfood items	34,000
Advertising expense	14,700
Depreciation	20,000
Miscellaneous	9,400
Repairs and maintenance	6,500
Salaries	94,000
Supplies	38,000
Utilities	9,000
Interest expense	3,200

Required

a. Compare the operating results of Store No. 11 for 1972, under the former ownership and management, with Bonanza Stores Corporation's standards. What areas apparently should receive greatest management attention?

b. Compare the actual results of Store No. 11 for 1973 with its operating budget and a flexible budget. Identify volume and price or spending variances.

c. Comment on the causes of the major variances of actual results from planned results.

d. What segments of operations should receive special attention in 1974? What general type of action would you recommend?

e. What additional income statement information is needed by management?

20-2   Fairfax Motors, Inc.   The accountant of Fairfax Motors, Inc. prepared the following operating budget for 1974. The budget provided for a sales increase of 5 per cent and an operating income increase of 20 per cent as compared with 1973 results. The planned sales mix and gross-margin percentages were the same as those of the preceding year.

FAIRFAX MOTORS, INC.

Planned Sales, Gross Margin, and Net Income

For the Year Ending December 31, 1974

Gross Margin:	Units	Sales Revenue	Cost of Sales	Gross Margin
New cars.........................	150	$450,000	$420,000	$ 30,000
Used cars........................	250	185,000	122,500	62,500
Total..........................	400	635,000	542,500	92,500
Deduct operating expenses...				75,400
Operating income...				17,100
Add other income..				6,600
Income before income tax				23,700
Estimated income tax..				5,200
Net income...				18,500

Fairfax Motors, Inc. finances most of its car sales through the CFG Credit Corporation. Customers' time payment contracts are discounted with full recourse to Fairfax Motors, Inc. in exchange for which Fairfax shares generously in the finance charges earned. This participation is represented by "other income" in the 1974 budget.

Fairfax Motors' 1974 operating summary, presented below, showed total revenues of $653,000, significantly greater than expected. However, net income was only $6,620, far below the $18,500 initially expected.

To evaluate the cost effectiveness of Fairfax Motors, Inc. in 1974, the accountant prepared the accompanying comparison of planned and actual operating expenses.

FAIRFAX MOTORS, INC.

Income Statement

For the Year Ended December 31, 1974

Gross Margin:	Units	Sales Revenue	Cost of Sales	Gross Margin
New cars.........................	160	$466,900	$448,000	$ 18,900
Used cars........................	246	186,100	127,920	58,180
Total..........................	406	653,000	575,920	77,080
Deduct operating expenses...				75,380
Operating income...				1,700
Add other income..				6,790
Income before income tax				8,490
Income tax expense...				1,870
Net income...				6,620

FAIRFAX MOTORS, INC.
Comparison of Budgeted and Actual Operating Expenses
For the Year ended December 31, 1974

Operating Expenses	Planned Cost	Actual Cost
Officers' salaries	$14,000	$14,250
Other salaries and wages	26,000	26,470
Rent	4,800	4,800
Repairs	1,000	790
Taxes (property and payroll)	3,600	3,750
Interest	4,500	4,590
Advertising	4,500	4,420
Utilities	2,000	1,930
Supplies	1,700	1,750
Transportation expense	6,000	5,490
Telephone	2,000	2,050
Insurance	3,500	3,530
Other expenses	1,800	1,560
Total operating expenses	75,400	75,380

Required   a. Compare the planned and actual sales, cost of goods sold, and gross margin of Fairfax Motors, Inc. and explain the variances.

b. As far as the data permit, apply flexible budgeting principles and evaluate Fairfax Motors' cost effectiveness in 1974.

c. What improvements would you recommend in the reporting of financial information for Fairfax?

chapter 21

Measuring the Flow
of Working Capital
and Cash

Purpose of Chapter

Chapter 8 identified some income and financial position measurements that are widely used to evaluate the effectiveness of business performance. Ratios of *liquidity* and *solvency* were suggested as indicators of management's efficiency in administering business assets and of how future results might be improved. However, typical ratios such as the *current ratio*, the *quick ratio*, and *asset turnover* alone often do not reveal important movements in elements of the working capital of a business.

The short-run and long-run effectiveness of business activity vitally depend on continuous inflows and outflows of cash and other components of working capital. Analyses of the flow of working capital show in detail the *sources* from which working capital flows into the business during a period and the *uses to which it is put*, and reveal changes in important trends of financial position from one date to another. This chapter considers the measurement of past working capital flows and the projection of future working capital and cash flows as means of planning and controlling the firm's financial affairs.

FUNDS FLOW ANALYSIS

Working Capital and Its Sources

The financial position statement separates the resources of a business into *current assets* and *long-lived assets.* The current assets, which include cash, accounts receivable, inventories, and prepaid expenses, comprise the firm's *total working capital.* Total working capital should be distinguished from *fixed capital* (sometimes called *sunk capital*), which is composed of the firm's long-lived assets.

The financial position statement also shows the firm's equities, which represent the *sources* from which the business obtained *the capital* that is invested in its assets. The equities, or *capital sources,* consist of *current liabilities* and *noncurrent equities.* The latter includes *long-term liabilities* and *owner's equity.*

What proportion of the total working capital of a business is provided from current liability sources, and what proportion is from noncurrent sources? This question involves a distinction between *total working capital* and *net working capital.* The *net working capital* of a firm can be computed in two ways:

(1) *The excess of total noncurrent equities over total long-lived assets.* This indicates the amount of the total working capital that is provided by long-term sources of financing.

(2) *The excess of total working capital over current liabilities.* This indicates *liquidity,* the margin by which the business is capable of currently satisfying its short-term financial obligations. This aspect of working capital was considered in Chapter 8.

Example 1   The Tricote Company began business on January 1, 1972, with the following assets and equities:

ASSETS		EQUITIES	
Cash	$ 5,000	Accounts payable	$10,000
Merchandise inventory	10,000	Bank note due in 1977	4,000
Equipment	10,000	Owner's investment	11,000
Total assets	25,000	Total equities	25,000

What amounts of working capital were provided from current and noncurrent sources?

Solution   The total working capital is $15,000, of which $10,000 is from current liabilities and $5,000 is from long-term financing. This can be shown as follows:

Working Capital		*Working Capital Sources*	
Cash	$ 5,000	Current liabilities	$10,000
Merchandise inventory	10,000	Noncurrent sources (net working capital)	5,000
Total	15,000	Total	15,000

The solution in Example 1 shows net working capital as a *combined equity* (long-term source) which reflects the liquidity margin above current liabilities. Alternatively, the *net working capital* provided from long-term sources can be treated as a *combined asset.*

Example 2 The net working capital of the Tricote Company can be shown as a single asset in the following manner:

ASSETS		EQUITIES	
Net working capital......	$ 5,000	Bank note due in 1977...	$ 4,000
Long-lived assets..........	10,000	Owner's equity............	11,000
Total....................	15,000	Total....................	15,000

The Flow of Funds

The preceding section emphasized the *sources* of a firm's working capital at a given time and the amount of *net working capital* that is provided *from noncurrent sources*. In evaluating financial trends it is often useful to emphasize a more dynamic concept: that of the *flow of funds*. A typical statement of the flow of funds shows the *changes* in net working capital that occurred in the period, the *sources of the additions* to net working capital, and the *uses* which resulted in any net working capital decreases.

Total working capital is increased whenever additional current assets are financed through an increase in current liabilities. In Example 1 the Tricote Company purchased its inital $10,000 of merchandise inventory on trade credit, creating a current liability of $10,000 in accounts payable. Since such increases in current assets are offset by related increases in current liabilities, there are no resulting changes in *net working capital*. Moreover, when current assets are used to pay current liabilities, total working capital decreases, but net working capital is unchanged. *The flow of funds is concerned only with changes which result in increases or decreases in net working capital.* These changes may come from either *operating* or *nonoperating sources*.

Importance of Measuring Funds Flows

Investors and creditors are interested in knowing how effectively the managers of a business plan and control the quantity and types of its resources and the means by which they are financed. Poor managerial action will result in unnecessarily low profits, and sometimes in the inability of the business to pay its debts as they come due. Good managerial planning will provide for payment of maturing liabilities and for the investment of excess monies in profit-producing assets.

The income and financial position statements do not give an adequate picture of the firm's funds flows. The stream of funds is not the same as the income stream. *Outflows* of funds represent *investments made* by the firm in various assets—investments which may or may not prove to be profitable. The fate of these investments is reported in the income statement. *Inflows* of funds represent *disinvestments* made by the firm by disposing of assets, or new funds obtained by long-term financing. The funds statement reports the sources and amounts of the inflows, but it remains for the income statement to show whether the use of the inflowing funds was profitable.

The main purposes of reporting funds flows to stockholders are (1) to help them understand changes in assets and asset sources which are not readily evident in the income statement or the financial position statement; (2) to explain how the additional resources derived from profitable operations of the business have been used; and (3) to point out the financial strengths and weaknesses of the business.[1] This additional information assists the stockholder in evaluating managerial performance and in making his investment decision. It also assists another major type of outside financial statement user, the creditor, in determining how the business has used the funds he has loaned it and in judging whether the business can probably repay an existing or prospective loan.

Managers rely upon funds statements for help in the following:

(1) Estimating the amount of funds needed for growth.
(2) Improving the rate of income on assets.
(3) Planning the temporary investment of idle funds.
(4) Securing additional working capital when needed.
(5) Securing economies in the centralized management of cash in organizations whose management is decentralized.
(6) Planning the payment of dividends to stockholders and interest to creditors.
(7) Easing the effects of an insufficient cash balance.[2]

Funds from Operations

The *operations* of a business are a main source of additional working capital. When products from merchandise inventory are sold for more than their inventory cost plus other *expenses which require a current expenditure*, current assets are increased without an offsetting increase in current liabilities. A word of caution is in order on this point, because not all expenses require a *current expenditure. Depreciation expense, and the amortization of other noncurrent asset balances, do not involve the use or expenditure of current assets.* Therefore, these expenses are not deducted from operating revenues in computing the amount of additional working capital provided by operations.

The additional working capital provided by the operations of a period comes primarily from the period's operating revenues, after deducting all expenses of the period which require an expenditure of working capital (giving up a current asset or incurring a current liability). However, it is often convenient to compute the amount of additional funds provided from operations by *adding back to the period's net income* all the period's expenses, losses, or other income deductions *which do not involve a working capital expenditure*, and deducting any nonoperating revenues or gains which *do not involve an actual receipt of working capital.*

Example 3 The Tricote Company began and ended its first year of operations with the following assets and equities. No dividends were paid, and there were no extraordinary gains or losses during the year. What amount of additional working capital was provided from operations?

---

[1] Hector R. Anton, *Accounting for the Flow of Funds* (Boston: Houghton Mifflin Company, 1962), p. 84.

[2] National Association of Accountants, *N.A.A. Research Report No. 38*, "Cash Flow Analysis for Managerial Control" (New York: N.A.A., 1961), pp. 6–10.

ASSETS			EQUITIES		
	12/31/73	*1/1/73*		*12/31/73*	*1/1/73*
Cash.....................	$ 7,000	$ 5,000	Accounts payable.....	$12,000	$10,000
Merchandise			Bank note due		
inventory......	14,000	10,000	in 1977.........	5,000	5,000
Equipment	10,000	10,000	Owner's investment..	10,000	10,000
Accumulated					
depreciation ..	(1,000)	0	Retained earnings....	3,000	0
Total assets	30,000	25,000	Total equities.......	30,000	25,000

Solution Total working capital (current assets) increased by $6,000 ($21,000 minus $15,000) from January 1 to December 31. Of this increase, $2,000 came from an increase in current liabilities and $4,000 came from operations. Long-term liabilities and owner's investment were unchanged and provided no new funds for the period. The amount of funds provided from operations is computed as follows:

Net income of the period	$3,000
Add *depreciation expense* (which does not require	
a current expenditure)	1,000
Additional funds provided by operations	4,000

In Example 3 the change of $3,000 in Retained Income is equal to the net income of the period. This is because no dividends were paid and no prior period adjustments were made during the period. Changes in Retained Income which result from prior period adjustments and extraordinary gains and losses must be excluded in order to determine the change due to operations.

The only change in the balance of net long-lived assets in Example 3 is a reduction due to the $1,000 increase in accumulated depreciation. Frequently long-lived asset accounts show increases and decreases which result from acquisitions and disposals. These must also be considered in analyzing changes in net working capital.

This section has treated the operations of a business as a *source* of additional net working capital. *Operations* is a *source* if the net current assets derived from revenue exceed the net current assets applied to expenses.[3] However, it is a *use* of net working capital if the net current assets applied to expenses are greater than net current assets derived from revenue.

Nonoperating Sources and Uses of Funds

In addition to the operations of a business, typical *sources* of additional net working capital are

(1) Sale of long-lived assets, such as plant and equipment or securities held for long-term investment.

(2) Borrowing from long-term lenders.

(3) Issuance of capital stock.

---

[3] The term "net current assets" refers to current assets minus current liabilities. An expense may be accompanied by a *reduction* of (credit to) a *current asset,* or an *increase of* (credit to) a current liability. In both cases net current assets have been applied to expenses.

Typical *uses* of funds which may reduce net working capital are

(1) Purchase of long-lived assets.
(2) Payment of long-term liabilities.
(3) Repurchase of capital stock.
(4) Payment of dividends.

Method of Determining Sources and Uses of Net Working Capital

The major sources and uses of working capital may be analyzed by the following steps:

(1) Summarize the period's *changes in working capital* accounts.
(2) Summarize the period's *changes in noncurrent accounts*.
(3) Reconstruct accounting entries which will show the changes in net working capital.

Needed for these steps are a comparative statement of financial position at the beginning and end of the period, an income statement for the period, and a retained income statement.

The following statements of Sound Center, Inc. (presented in more detail on pp. 173–74) will be used to illustrate the procedure. Supporting schedules of fixed asset additions and retirements and of new issues and retirements of long-term liabilities and capital stock would permit a more refined analysis.

SOUND CENTER, INC.
Condensed Income Statement
For the Year Ended December 31, 1973

Net sales revenue		$300,000
Deduct cost of goods sold		210,000
Gross margin on sales		90,000
Deduct operating expenses:		
Expenses requiring current expenditure	$80,000	
Depreciation	2,500	82,500
Income before federal income taxes		7,500
Corporate federal income tax		1,650
Net income (to Retained Income Statement)		5,850

SOUND CENTER, INC.
Retained Income Statement
For the Year Ended December 31, 1973

Retained income at beginning of year	$43,700
Add net income (from Income Statement)	5,850
	49,550
Deduct dividends	2,000
Retained income, end of year (to Financial Position Statement)	$47,550

SOUND CENTER, INC.
Financial Position Statement

	December 31	
ASSETS	1973	1972
Current assets:		
Cash..	$ 7,000	$ 11,000
Accounts receivable.......................................	73,000	70,000
Deduct estimated uncollectibles....................	(4,000)	(3,000)
Merchandise inventory	92,000	64,400
Prepaid expenses..	7,000	5,600
Total current assets.................................	175,000	148,000
Property, plant, and equipment:		
Equipment (cost)	47,500	21,000
Deduct accumulated depreciation....................	(9,500)	(7,000)
Total property, plant, and equipment...........	38,000	14,000
Total assets...	213,000	162,000
LIABILITIES		
Current liabilities:		
Notes payable to banks..................................	28,000	18,000
Accounts payable...	55,550	41,700
Corporate federal income tax payable.................	450	300
Total current liabilities.................................	84,000	60,000
Long-term liabilities:		
Long-term notes payable.................................	31,450	8,300
Total liabilities...	115,450	68,300
STOCKHOLDERS' EQUITY		
Capital stock, $50 par, 1,000 shares.......................	50,000	50,000
Retained income (from Retained Income Statement)...	47,550	43,700
Total stockholders' equity	97,550	93,700
Total equities...	213,000	162,000

Summarizing Changes in Working Capital Accounts

Illustration 21-1 shows changes in the current assets, current liabilities, and net working capital of Sound Center, Inc. from December 31, 1972, to December 31, 1973. In the illustration total working capital (current assets) increased by $24,000 through additions to current liabilities, and $3,000 of additional net working capital came from noncurrent sources. The decrease in the *current ratio* from 2.47 to 2.08 and the *quick ratio* from 1.30 to 0.90 indicate that the increase in total working capital is not entirely favorable. The liquidity of the business is lower because a large amount of the available working capital is tied up in additions to merchandise inventory. If further analysis were to reveal a definite trend in this direction, a reevaluation of policies relating to purchasing, inventory control, and sales promotion might be signaled.

Illustration 21-1

SOUND CENTER, INC.
Analysis of Changes in Composition of Working Capital
For the Year Ended December 31, 1973

	Working Capital Increase (Decrease)	December 31, 1973	December 31, 1972
Current assets:			
Cash	($ 4,000)	$ 7,000	$ 11,000
Accounts receivable, net.............	2,000	69,000	67,000
Merchandise inventory..............	27,600	92,000	64,400
Prepaid expenses......................	1,400	7,000	5,600
Total current assets................	$27,000	$175,000	$148,000
Current liabilities:			
Notes payable to banks..............	($10,000)	$ 28,000	$ 18,000
Accounts payable	(13,850)	55,550	41,700
Taxes payable.........................	(150)	450	300
Total current liabilities...........	($24,000)	$ 84,000	$ 60,000
Net working capital	$3,000	$ 91,000	$ 88,000
Current ratio		2.08	2.47
Quick ratio.............................		0.90	1.30

Summarizing Changes in Noncurrent Accounts

T-accounts or a transaction work sheet may be used to reconstruct entries which explain the cause of changes in net working capital. T-accounts are used here, but the method of analysis in the work sheet is the same. The following steps are required in preparing for the analysis:

(1) Open a T-account for Net Working Capital and for each noncurrent asset and noncurrent equity. Also open a T-account for *Change in Net Working Capital from Operations*. The purpose of the last account is to explain one of the important causes of change in net working capital.

(2) On the proper side of each noncurrent account and of *Net Working Capital* enter the *net change* in the account from the beginning to the end of the period, as shown by the comparative statement of financial position. Draw a line across the account below the amounts of change. These are the amounts which are to be explained as sources or uses of working capital.
 (a) An *increase in an asset*, a debit change, is shown on the *debit* side of the asset account, and a *decrease* is shown on the *credit* side.
 (b) An *increase in an equity* is a *credit*, and a *decrease* is a *debit*.

(3) Add the changes recorded in the T-accounts to be sure that total debits equal total credits.

The T-accounts which summarize the net changes in Sound Center's noncurrent accounts in Illustration 21-1 are as follows:

A, Net Working Capital

Increases		Decreases
Net change	3,000	

A, Equipment (cost)

Net change	26,500		

A, Equipment—Accumulated Depreciation

		Net change	2,500

L, Long-Term Notes Payable

		Net change	23,150

OE, Capital Stock, $50 Par

(Net change, 0)

OE, Retained Income

		Net change	3,850

A, Change in Net Working Capital from Operations

Increases	*Decreases*

Addition shows that the total *net debit changes* in the T-account balances, $29,500, is equal to the total of the *net credit changes*.

Reconstructing Entries To Explain Net Working Capital Changes

After preparing the T-accounts as shown in the preceding section, the following additional steps are useful in analyzing the period's changes in net working capital:

(4) Record a *summary entry* for each type of transaction which caused a change in noncurrent accounts. Identify the parts of each entry by letters or numbers. A debit to a noncurrent account may be offset by a credit (and a credit to a noncurrent account may be offset by a debit) to one of the following accounts:

(a) *Another noncurrent account.* Such a transaction has no effect on net working capital, but the entry should be made so that all changes in noncurrent accounts will be explained.

(b) *Change in Net Working Capital from Operations.* This account is debited or credited to offset a noncurrent account change which also affects *income* for the period. Its balance is later transferred to Net Working Capital. A brief explanation of the reason for the change should be entered in the account.

(c) *Net Working Capital.* This account is debited or credited to offset a change in a noncurrent account which also affects a *current* account, but which is *not used in determining income* for the period. A brief explanation of the reason for the change should be entered in the account.

(5) Compare the net changes in accounts *explained* by the summary entries in step (4) with the *changes to be explained* which were recorded in the T-accounts in step (2). The analysis is not complete until all changes have been explained.

(6) Prepare a formal statement from the information recorded in the *Change in Net Working Capital from Operations* and the *Net Working Capital accounts*.

In performing step (4), the summary entries are recorded here first in journal form for clearer explanation, and then are posted to the T-accounts. The journal entries may be omitted in actual practice.

(a)

A, Change in Net Working Capital from Operations......	5,850	
OE, Retained Income		5,850

To record the tentative increase in net working capital equal to reported net income for the period, and to explain part of the change in Retained Income.

(b)

A, Equipment..	26,500	
A, Net Working Capital.....................................		26,500

To record the decrease in net working capital resulting from the purchase of equipment.

In analyzing the flow of net working capital, it is customary to show an acquisition of a long-lived asset as though it reduced net working capital, and an increase of a long-term liability as though it increased net working capital, even though the liability was increased directly as a result of the purchase of the long-lived asset.

(c)

A, Change in Net Working Capital from Operations......	2,500	
A, Equipment—Accumulated Depreciation		2,500

To adjust the tentative amount of increase in net working capital resulting from operations, recorded in entry (a). Depreciation expense of $2,500 was deducted in arriving at the reported net income, $5,850, and yet it did not require the use of net working capital. Instead, it is merely a cost expiration of a noncurrent asset.

(d)

A, Net Working Capital	23,150	
L, Long-Term Notes Payable.............................		23,150

To record the increase in net working capital resulting from borrowing on long-term notes.

(e)

OE, Retained Income	2,000	
A, Net Working Capital		2,000

To record the decrease in net working capital resulting from payment of dividends.

(f)

A, Net Working Capital   8,350
    A, Change in Net Working Capital from Operations...   8,350
    To transfer the total amount of net working capital
    derived from operations to the Net Working Capital
    account.

The T-accounts resulting from these entries are as follows:

A, Net Working Capital

Increases		*Decreases*	
Net change	3,000		

Explanation of Increases		*Explanation of Decreases*	
Borrowing on long-term		Purchase of equipment	(b) 26,500
notes	(d) 23,150	Payment of dividends	(e) 2,000
Operations	(f) 8,350		28,500
	31,500		
Net increase, 3,000			

A, Equipment (cost)

Net change	26,500		
(b) 26,500			

A, Equipment—Accumulated Depreciation

		Net change	2,500
		(c) 2,500	

L, Long-Term Notes Payable

		Net change	23,150
		(d) 23,150	

OE, Capital Stock, $50 Par

(Net change, 0)

OE, Retained Income

		Net change	3,850
(e) 2,000		(a) 5,850	
		Net increase, 3,850	

A, Change in Net Working Capital from Operations

Increases			Decreases		
Net income	(a)	5,850	Transferred to Net		
Add depreciation (which			Working Capital	(f)	8,350
does not affect net					
working capital)	(c)	2,500			
Total increase in net					
working capital					
from operations		8,350			8,350

Statement of Changes in Net Working Capital

The preparation of the following Statement of Changes in Net Working Capital from the preceding analysis is merely a formality. The necessary information can be found in the Net Working Capital and the Change in Net Working Capital from Operations accounts.

SOUND CENTER, INC.
Statement of Changes in Net Working Capital
For the Year Ended December 31, 1973

Sources of net working capital:		
Operations:		
Net income for the period.....................................	$5,850	
Add depreciation expense, which does not affect net working capital but which was deducted in computing net income......................................	2,500	
Total increase in net working capital from operations		$ 8,350
Borrowing on long-term notes payable.....................................		23,150
Total increases in net working capital...............................		31,500
Uses of net working capital:		
Purchase of equipment	$26,500	
Payment of dividends on capital stock	2,000	
Total decreases in net working capital.................................		28,500
Net increase in net working capital.......................................		$ 3,000

Alternative Forms and Titles

Statements of the changes in net working capital often show the amount of net working capital at the *beginning* of the year, the *change* during the year, and the net working capital at the *end* of the year. They should be supported by detailed statements of the beginning and ending balances of the individual current assets and current liabilities, which together comprise net working capital. These details are particularly important when there have been important shifts in the composition of current assets or current liabilities during the period.

The term "funds" is often used as a synonym of net working capital. Alternative statement titles in common use are *Statement of Sources and Uses of Funds*, *Statement of Sources and Application of Funds*, and *Statement of Changes in Financial Position*.

The external analyst who does not have access to the detailed information contained in the company's ledger accounts often uses a similar method for explaining the major changes in the *cash* of the business during the year. He tries to reconstruct in summary from the net effect of transactions between cash and all other accounts, and reports the results in a *Statement of Cash Flow*.

PROJECTING FUTURE CASH FLOWS

The preceding discussion and illustrations dealt with the reasons for *past* changes in the working capital of a business. Probably most analysts are interested in this information as a means of projecting the working capital changes that are likely to occur in the *future*, preliminary to deciding what action they are going to take as managers, stockholders, or creditors.

The same general approach may be used in summarizing *expected future changes* in working capital. Often the information given consists of the present balances of accounts and expected future *transactions*, rather than the present and expected future account *balances*. It is easier to project the changes in cash and other working capital elements by recording these expected transactions directly than by computing the differences between beginning and ending balances.

The Cash Budget

One of the most important parts of any company's financial plan is the *cash budget*. Its purpose is to show the probable amount of cash receipts and payments expected during future time periods and the expected cash balance at the end of each period. The cash budget usually includes a cash forecast for the next year and for each quarter of the year. Monthly forecasts are desirable for at least the next quarter, and if a business finds itself in a tight cash position, it may wish to prepare weekly cash forecasts for the next month.

Although the *expected sales* for the period covered by the budget is a key figure in planning, good historical records of cash flow are also essential. Such records provide information about past relationships of receipts and expenditures that is helpful in forecasting the effect of the expected volume of activity on future cash receipts and payments.

Forecasting Cash Receipts

The *cash receipts* of a business come from five main sources:

(1) *Operating revenues*, which are primarily from sales. There is a time lag after sales on credit before collections are made. The extent of the lag is determined by the company's credit terms, its collection efforts, habits of customers, and economic conditions.

(2) *Nonoperating revenues*, such as interest and refunds of payments made in earlier periods.

(3) *Sales of assets other than merchandise*, such as investment securities and fixed assets.

(4) *Borrowings from short-term or long-term lenders*, such as bank loans or proceeds from the sale of bonds.

(5) *Additional investments by owners*, which come primarily from selling additional shares of capital stock.

The amounts and timing of cash receipts from selling long-lived assets and from issuing bonds or capital stock are often irregular. Funds flow records of past periods, analyses of the company's net working capital needs, and plans for future asset replacement or expansion will often aid in estimating the nature and probable amounts of such receipts expected in the budget period.

Cash receipts from *operating revenues, nonoperating revenues, and working capital loans (such as bank borrowings)* occur with considerable regularity. Their timing and amounts can be estimated with reasonable accuracy from past records by taking into account the nature of the business, the type of its product, seasonal fluctuations, and conditions of the economy.

Sales budget. Expected sales volume is the starting point for estimating the cash receipts likely to result from operating revenues during the budget period. An analysis of past records will show what proportions of a month's operating revenues are for cash sales and for credit sales, and what percentages of the credit sales have typically been collected in the month of sale and in each following month. With proper allowances for important changes in the company's credit terms, collection procedures, habits of its customers, and economic conditions, these percentages can be used to estimate the cash receipts expected on collections from customers in each month of the budget period.

Example 4 Records of the Tranton Company show that sales in the past have consistently been about 40 per cent for cash and 60 per cent on account. Budgeted sales for the first four months of 1973 are:

	Total	40% Cash	60% Credit
January	$ 70,000	$28,000	$42,000
February	50,000	20,000	30,000
March	80,000	32,000	48,000
April	110,000	44,000	66,000

The company sends a monthly statement of account to its customers on the last day of the month. An analysis of cash receipts and sales by months indicates that 70 per cent of the credit sales of a given month are usually collected in the following month, 29 per cent are collected in the second following month, and 1 per cent are never collected. The balance of Accounts Receivable on December 31, 1972, consists of the following items:

100% of December charge sales of $90,000	$ 90,000
30% of November charge sales of $60,000	18,000
1% of January–October charge sales of $450,000	4,500
Balance, December 31, 1972	$112,500

What amount of cash receipts from sales should be collected in January 1973?

Solution Cash receipts from sales in January 1973 should include $28,000 for cash sales and $80,400 from collections on accounts receivable, computed as follows:

70% of December charge sales of $90,000	$63,000
29% of November charge sales of $60,000	17,400
Total January collections on account	$80,400

Collections for later months are computed in the same manner.

Forecasting Cash Disbursements

A business usually makes *cash disbursements* for a variety of important purposes. In estimating expected cash payments for the budget period it is useful to classify them as *required* or *discretionary*.

Discretionary cash payments are those for which management has some leeway in deciding *how much* the payment is to be, *when* it is to be made, or even *whether* it is to be made at all.

Example 5   Management has discretion as to the timing of early payment of liabilities. It has considerable discretion in both the timing and the amount of dividends, purchases of securities for investment, and purchases of fixed assets.

Required payments depend mainly on the volume of sales; the credit terms and other contractual provisions which apply to purchases of goods, services, and facilities; the methods used by the business in financing its net working capital needs; and special provisions of the law.

Example 6   Payments for rent and interest, and principal payments on loans with definite due dates, are *required by contract* to be made at specific times. Payments for taxes are governed by law.

Example 7   Payments for utilities and salaries must be made periodically *according to contract*, but their amounts vary to some extent *according to the quantity of the service used*, which depends to some extent on operating activity.

Merchandise inventory budget. The largest single type of required payments of a merchandising company is usually that for goods bought for resale. The amount of merchandise purchased depends on the expected sales of the budget period, the desired level of the ending inventory, and the amount of merchandise on hand at the beginning of the period. The timing of cash disbursements for merchandise purchases depends on the applicable credit terms and the policy of the business as to prompt payment.

Example 8   The Tranton Company buys its merchandise on terms of 2/10, n/30. The bills are paid, subject to the cash discount, on the last day of the discount period. Purchases are made evenly throughout each month. At the end of any month the company plans to have an inventory of goods on hand sufficient to fill the expected sales of the following three months. The invoice cost (before discount) of goods purchased averages 60 per cent of selling price.

Sales for the first four months of 1973 are expected to be

January	$70,000	March	$ 80,000
February	$50,000	April	$110,000

The balance of accounts payable on December 31, 1972, included $14,000 (before discount) for merchandise purchases in December, and the merchandise inventory balance was $120,000 at invoice price (before discount). What are the required cash payments in January relating to merchandise purchases?

Solution   The total *merchandise purchases* required in January will be $66,000, computed as follows:

	Selling Price	*Cost, 60%*

Merchandise required:
Desired ending inventory, January 31, equal to
expected sales of

February.................................	$ 50,000	
March...................................	80,000	
April	110,000	
Total............................	$240,000	$144,000
Add expected January sales.....................	70,000	42,000
Total merchandise required in January..............		$186,000
Deduct merchandise available in beginning inventory...		120,000
Required purchases in January..............................		$ 66,000

In Example 8 purchases are made evenly throughout the month. Payments for purchases during the last ten days of January will not be made until February because the discount period will not have expired. Required cash payments in January will be $56,840, after the 2 per cent discount. This can be computed as follows:

$98\% \times \frac{1}{3}$ of December, 1972 purchases of $42,000..........	$13,720
$98\% \times \frac{2}{3}$ of January, 1973 purchases of $66,000.............	43,120
Total required payments.......................................	$56,840

Controlling Cash Balances

The *cash budget* serves management in several ways in controlling the working capital needs of the business. It enables management

(1) To anticipate times when the available cash will be high or low in comparison with current cash needs.

(2) To make profitable uses of excess cash balances temporarily not needed for current payments.

(3) To arrange for temporary loans from banks or other lenders when the amount of available cash will not be sufficient for required current payments.

Illustration 21-2 shows the cash budget of Tranton Company for January 1973. The budget shows the amount of cash that is available for required payments in the budget period and emphasizes the *excess cash available for discretionary payments* (or, if the reverse circumstances occur, the amount of additional cash that must be provided).

The cash budget in Illustration 21-2 indicates that cash available in January is expected to be $16,850 more than the amount needed for required current payments. The proper use of this excess depends on how long it likely will be before required cash payments exceed the amount of cash available. Monthly cash forecasts for the coming year should be prepared in the same manner as the January forecast.

Illustration
21-2

TRANTON COMPANY
Cash Budget
For the Month Ending January 31, 1973

Estimated cash available:
  From operations:

Cash sales...	$28,000	
Collections for charge sales of prior months...............	80,400	
Total estimated receipts from operations.........................		$108,400
Add beginning cash balance..		60,700
Estimated total cash available...		$169,100

Estimated cash required:
  Required payments:
    Liabilities of preceding month:

Accounts payable...	$50,880	
Taxes payable, other......................................	3,700	
Dividends payable...	2,000	

    Liabilities of current month:

Merchandise purchases....................................	43,120	
Payroll..	12,800	
Rent...	800	

    Irregular payments:

Accrued interest payable.................................	1,350	
Insurance premiums paid.................................	12,600	
Total required payments..		$127,250
Add desired ending cash balance for future operations...............		25,000
Estimated total cash required..		$152,250

Difference:

Cash available for discretionary payments (if cash available is greater than cash required).......................................		$ 16,850
or		
Additional cash required (if cash required is greater than cash available)..		0

Illustration 21-3 shows the expected monthly *increases* and *decreases in available cash*, and adds these changes to the beginning cash balance to give a *cumulative balance*. This illustration indicates that, if no discretionary payments are made and no cash is received from additional sources, the Tranton Company will probably need to borrow $11,150 ($25,000 desired balance minus $13,850 expected balance) at the end of March in order to maintain its cash balance at the desired level. It will need to borrow even more in April and May. Thus the $16,850 which the cash budget shows will probably be available at the end of January as excess cash ($41,850 expected balance minus $25,000 desired balance) should be used only for temporary investments. If it is used for other purposes, that much additional cash must be borrowed in March, April, and May.

The bar chart in Illustration 21-4 shows at a glance the amount of cash that will probably be available for temporary investments, and the amount of

**Illustration
21-3**

TRANTON COMPANY
Estimated Cash Balance by Months
For the Year Ending December 31, 1973

Month	Estimated Receipts from Operations	Estimated Payments Required	Monthly Cash Increase (+) or Decrease (−)	Cumulative Cash Balance
January 1 balance......				+ $60,700
January...................	$108,400	$127,250	− $18,850	+ 41,850
February.................	90,000	98,000	− 8,000	+ 33,850
March....................	80,000	100,000	− 20,000	+ 13,850
April......................	70,000	85,000	− 15,000	− 1,150
May.......................	90,000	100,000	− 10,000	− 11,150
June......................	70,000	55,000	+ 15,000	+ 3,850
July	80,000	60,000	+ 20,000	+ 23,850
August...................	60,000	50,000	+ 10,000	+ 33,850
September...............	55,000	47,000	+ 8,000	+ 41,850
October.................	65,000	56,000	+ 9,000	+ 50,850
November	75,000	70,000	+ 5,000	+ 55,850
December................	100,000	90,000	+ 10,000	+ 65,850
Total for year.........	$943,400	$938,250	+ $ 5,150	

additional cash that will be required from sources other than operations, at the
end of each month of the coming year. It also shows the approximate length
of time which the respective sums will be available or required. The chart
reveals that the peak requirement for additional cash will be $36,150 at the end
of May, and that the peak seasonal excess of cash will be $40,850 at the end of
December. Both the requirement of additional cash and the later availability
of excess cash are temporary.

Dotted line (*A*) in the chart points out that $8,850 of the January 1 cash
balance of $60,700 will not be needed for two months, and can be invested
temporarily at least until February 28. The right-hand scale, which allows for
the desired minimum cash balance of $25,000, is used in finding this amount.
Similarly, dotted line (*B*) shows that the company will need to borrow $11,150
at the end of March for at least $3\frac{1}{2}$ months. Additional borrowings will be required in April and May.

To be useful in anticipating working capital needs, the cash budget should
be continuously updated as actual cash balances become known. Analysis of
actual collection and payment experience facilitates more accurate estimates
of future cash changes. The projected cash balances should reflect the latest
information. As each month passes a cash budget for an additional future month
can be prepared so that there will always be a cash budget for a year in advance.

Monthly reports comparing actual receipts, payments, and balances with
the corresponding budget estimates are useful in estimating cash needs and
improving efficiency in making collections and payments.

Illustration
21-4
Analysis of Estimated Cash Balances by Months for the Year Ended December 31, 1973.

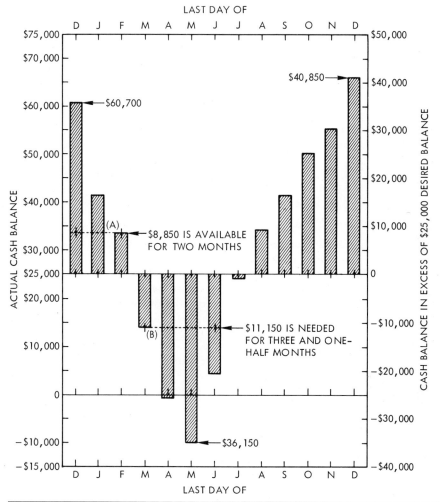

Summary   Analyses of *past working capital flows,* including the *sources* of increases in total working capital and the *uses* to which these short-term resources are put, are useful to management and other statement users. They give valuable information about the firm's past commitments of resources to long-term uses and the methods it has used in financing these investments. Projections of *expected working capital flows* in the future are also of great importance to management and outside statement users in their planning.

The *cash budget* is an indispensable tool in managing the finances of a business. Forecasts of cash receipts, cash disbursements, and cash balances indicate when needs for cash will occur, how the needs may be met, and when excess cash balances will be available for *discretionary payments.*

Discussion
Questions
and
Problems

21-1

a. Distinguish between *working capital* and *fixed capital* and give two examples of assets that are components of each.
b. What are the major *sources* of the working capital and the fixed capital of a business?

21-2

a. Distinguish clearly between the *total working capital* and the *net working capital* of a business.
b. Explain two different methods of computing net working capital. What is the significance of each method?
c. List three ways of *increasing* and three ways of *decreasing* net working capital.

21-3

a. Explain what is meant by the "flow of funds."
b. What is the relationship between working capital flows, cash flows, and funds flows?

21-4   "The *operations* of a business are a main source of additional working capital."

a. Explain how the income statement of a business may be used in computing the amount of working capital derived from operations.
b. What income statement components are omitted in computing the working capital obtained from operations? Why are they omitted?
c. Explain the difference between the two ways of computing the working capital obtained from operations. How do their results differ?

21-5

a. Explain fully how a *cash flow* statement would be similar to a *working capital flow* statement.
b. How would the uses of each statement be similar? How would they differ?

21-6   A banker has been asked to approve a 90-day loan for a small business. In support of this loan application, the manager of the business submitted projected statements of income, financial position, and cash flow. The banker remarked that he would prefer to have the comparative financial statements for the last three years.

   If the loan is to be paid out of cash generated by future operations, why would the banker wish historical statements?

21-7   The net change in Retained Income is usually a composite of sources and uses of net working capital. What are the most common sources and uses that are usually reflected in the change in this account?

21-8

a. What is usually the best estimate with which to begin preparation of a cash budget?
b. Given an estimate of sales for the coming period, how would you translate this into estimated cash collections? Where would you get the necessary information?

21-9

a. If the sales budget for a period has been prepared, how would you use this information in preparing a budget of merchandise purchases?

b. Given a solution in part a, how would you estimate the cash payments required for merchandise for the coming period? Illustrate with an example.

21-10

a. Give two examples of *required* payments for a manufacturing company.
b. Give three examples of *discretionary* payments for a manufacturing company.
c. Explain why it is useful in cash budgeting to distinguish between required and discretionary payments.

21-11 Indicate whether each of the following transactions would be a source (increase) or use (decrease) of working capital:

a. Sale of merchandise on account.
b. Sale of merchandise for cash.
c. Borrowing cash on a short-term note payable.
d. Collection of accounts receivable.
e. Purchase of merchandise on account.
f. Purchase of equipment on account.
g. Purchase of equipment in exchange for long-term notes payable.
h. Declaration of dividend payable in cash.
i. Payment of dividend declared earlier.
j. Payment of accounts payable.
k. Return of merchandise to supplier for credit.
l. Issuance of capital stock for cash.
m. Issuance of a dividend in the form of capital stock.
n. Recording periodic depreciation.
o. Sale of used equipment for cash.

21-12 During February 1973 the Moody Company had the following unrelated transactions:

a. Purchased equipment for $5,000. One-half was paid in cash and the balance was due in one year.
b. Paid accounts payable of $2,000 in cash.
c. Sold for $100 a truck which was completely depreciated and not in use.
d. Purchased for $4,000 some stock of another company as a temporary investment of excess funds.
e. Purchased merchandise inventory of $500 on account.
f. Issued a 90-day note in payment of an account payable of $850.
g. Paid interest on a note payable in the amount of $24, and paid off the note principal of $400.
h. Purchased a three-year insurance policy for $120.
i. The owners invested an additional $5,000 in the business.
j. The company discovered a cash shortage of $10 in the petty cash fund.

Required Considering each of the above transactions separately, how would each affect a statement of working capital flows?

21-13 At January 1, 1973 and December 31, 1973, the Flaky Donut Shoppe had statements of financial position as follows:

	1/1/73	12/31/73
Cash..	$ 250	$ 400
Accounts receivable.......................................	150	300
Supplies...	50	10
Equipment (net of accumulated depreciation).......	900	850
Building (net of accumulated depreciation)..........	5,000	4,800
Total assets	6,350	6,360
Accounts payable...	85	140
Owners' equity..	6,265	6,220
Total equities	6,350	6,360

Required   a. What is the net working capital at the beginning and end of the year, and the amount of the change therein?

b. Assume that the Donut Shoppe had sales of $22,000 during the year, that no withdrawals were made by the owners, and that no changes took place affecting equipment and building except for depreciation. Prepare a funds statement for changes in net working capital.

21-14   The following are condensed statements of the Lawrence Company:

Income Statement
For the Year Ended

	Dec. 31, 1973	Dec. 31, 1972
Sales...	$425,000	$350,000
Operating expenses (including depreciation of $10,000)	340,000	280,800
	85,000	69,200
Bond interest expense............................	3,000	4,200
Net income before tax	82,000	65,000
Income tax expense..............................	36,000	27,500
Net income..	46,000	37,500

Statement of Retained Income
For the Year Ended

	Dec. 31, 1973	Dec. 31, 1972
Retained income, beginning of year..........	$ 27,500	$ 25,000
Net income for the year.........................	46,000	37,500
	73,500	62,500
Dividends...	35,000	35,000
Retained income, end of year.................	38,500	27,500

Statement of Financial Position

	Dec. 31, 1973	Dec. 31, 1972
ASSETS		
Cash..	$ 9,000	$ 15,000
Accounts receivable	35,000	31,000
Inventories..	160,000	145,000
Plant and equipment............................	120,000	105,000
—Accumulated depreciation	(37,000)	(27,000)
Total assets......................................	$287,000	$269,000

LIABILITIES

Accounts payable	$ 20,000	$ 12,500
Income tax payable	36,000	27,500
6% bonds payable due 12/31/78..............	50,000	70,000
Total liabilities	$106,000	$110,000

STOCKHOLDERS' EQUITY

Capital stock	$142,500	$131,500
Retained income.................................	38,500	27,500
Total stockholders' equity...................	181,000	159,000
Total equities....................................	$287,000	$269,000

Required

a. You have received a letter from a bondholder asking about the liquidity position of the company. Prepare a statement of changes in net working capital in the form of a funds statement and comment upon the results.

b. In addition to the letter from the bondholder, several stockholders have asked for an explanation of why their dividends were not increased in 1973 in view of the increase in earnings. What light does the statement of changes in net working capital shed on the answer to this question?

21-15   The accompanying condensed financial statements are taken from the annual report of the Forseman Corporation for the year ended December 31, 1973.

Required

a. Calculate the change in net working capital during 1973.

b. Prepare a statement of working capital flow for the year.

c. What changes in working capital do you think were most significant during the year?

FORSEMAN CORPORATION
Comparative Statement of Financial Position

	Years Ended December 31			
ASSETS	1973		1972	
Current assets:				
Cash..	$20,000		$18,000	
Accounts receivable......................	30,000		20,000	
Inventories...............................	55,000		29,000	
Total current assets..............		$105,000		$67,000
Fixed assets:				
Equipment (cost).........................	50,000		40,000	
Deduct accumulated depreciation....	22,000		15,000	
Total fixed assets.................		28,000		25,000
Total assets......................		133,000		92,000
LIABILITIES				
Current liabilities:				
Accounts payable	12,000		10,000	
Notes payable............................	20,000		15,000	
Corporate income tax payable........	6,000		4,000	
Total current liabilities		38,000		29,000
Long-term liabilities:				
6% bonds payable in 1979.........................		0		15,000
Total liabilities		38,000		44,000

STOCKHOLDERS' EQUITY

Capital stock	68,000		40,000	
Retained income	27,000		8,000	
Total stockholders' equity		95,000		48,000
Total equities		133,000		92,000

Combined Statement of Income and Retained Income
For the Year Ended December 31, 1973

Sales		$210,000
Deduct expenses:		
Depreciation	$ 7,000	
Income tax	6,000	
Interest	900	
All other expenses	171,100	
Total expense		185,000
Net income		25,000
Deduct dividends		6,000
Addition to retained income		19,000
Add retained income, December 31, 1972		8,000
Retained income, December 31, 1973		27,000

21-16   The Warren Company makes 40 per cent of its sales for cash and the remainder on account. In the past, losses from uncollectible accounts have averaged 1 per cent of sales on account. The company finds that usually about 60 per cent of charge sales are collected in the month following sale, 25 per cent in the second following month, and 14 per cent in the third following month.

Total actual sales in the preceding three months have been

October 1972, $40,000; November, $50,000; December, $100,000. January sales are expected to be $70,000.

Required   a. Determine the expected net revenue from sales for January 1973.

b. Prepare a schedule of the expected cash collections from customers during January 1973.

21-17   The Parma Products Company sells goods at a gross margin of 40 per cent of sales price. The company pays for all its merchandise on the tenth of the month following purchase and likes to maintain an inventory balance at the end of each month sufficient for the expected sales of the two following months. Because of an unexpected slump in sales for December 1972, excessive inventory has accumulated. The statement of financial position on December 31, 1972, shows inventory of $55,000 and accounts payable for merchandise totaling $12,000. Budgeted sales for the first few months of 1973 are

January	$30,000	March	$30,000	May	$32,000
February	25,000	April	36,000	June	30,000

Required   Prepare a schedule to estimate the following for each of the first three months of 1973:

(1) Cost of goods sold expense:

(2) Required purchases of merchandise.

(3) Required cash payments for merchandise.

21-18   Tankersley Mfg. Co. has projected its estimated cash receipts from operations and its estimated cash payments required for the next six months as follows:

	Estimated Receipts	Estimated Required Payments
July, 1973	$63,000	$59,000
August	72,000	81,000
September.............................	80,000	84,000
October................................	60,000	70,000
November.............................	78,000	67,000
December	80,000	61,000

Its cash balance on June 30, 1973, was $10,000, which is the minimum balance considered safe by the management. The company finds that its typical operating cycle is six months, and anticipates a slight rate of growth in 1973.

Required a. Prepare a statement of estimated cash balances by months for the period from July through December.

b. What type of action, if any, would you recommend that the company plan at the end of each month? Explain.

21-19   The Faulkner Company is preparing a cash forecast for the month of January 1974. Its ending cash balance on December 31, 1973, was $8,000. The company's bank requires that it maintain a minimum balance of $4,000 on deposit as a condition for a loan recently made.

The company makes all its sales on account. An analysis of past records shows that typically 40 per cent of the accounts are collected in the month of sale, 59 per cent are collected in the following month, and 1 per cent are uncollectible. Sales for November 1973 were $60,000 and for December, $80,000. Expected sales for January and February 1974 are $40,000 and $80,000, respectively.

The company purchases all its merchandise for cash. Cost of goods sold is 60 per cent of sales. Management plans to have an inventory balance of $45,000, at cost, on hand at the end of January. The actual inventory balance on December 31, 1973, was $35,000.

Other required cash payments for January are expected to be $20,000.

Required a. Compute the amount of expected cash receipts for January 1974. Show your computations in orderly form.

b. Compute the amount of purchases required in January. Show your computations.

c. Prepare a cash budget for January.

d. Explain how the results in part c may be used by management.

21-20   The Mergatroid Company makes all its sales on account on terms which require payment within 10 days from the end of the month of sale. Each unit is sold for $100, and each unit is purchased for $75. The company finds that it usually collects 60 per cent of the accounts resulting from the sales of a given month in the month following sale, 30 per cent in the second following month, and 5 per cent in the third following month. The remainder result in uncollectible accounts. Sales for the preceding September totaled $12,000; for October, $16,000; for November, $20,000; and for December, $30,000. An estimate of uncollectible accounts is provided at the end of the month of sale. Accounts not collected by the end of the third month after sale are written off as uncollectible at that time.

In January 1973 the company expects to sell 300 units; in February, 150 units; and in March, 200 units. The company likes to have on hand at the end of each month an inventory sufficient to fill the sales expected in the two following months. It pays for $\frac{3}{4}$ of its purchases in the month of purchase and for $\frac{1}{4}$ in the following month. In December 1972 the company bought 200 units for a total cost of $15,000. It paid for $\frac{3}{4}$ of these purchases in December. The inventory of merchandise on December 31, 1972, consisted of 400 units. The sales of December had varied substantially from the expected sales.

The company expects its income for 1973 to fall within the 40 per cent tax rate bracket. Its December 31, 1972, balances, other than those referred to above, were

Cash	$ 6,000
Equipment (estimated total life, 10 years)	24,000
Equipment—accumulated depreciation	7,200
6% note payable due October 1, 1973	10,000
Accrued interest payable (due Oct. 1, 1973)	150
Accrued income taxes payable (for 1972, due March 15, 1973)	6,000
Capital stock	40,000
Retained earnings	?

Monthly variable expenses, other than those mentioned, are expected to be 10 per cent of sales. Monthly fixed expenses, other than those mentioned, are expected to be $4,000. Both of these expense items will be paid in the month in which they are incurred.

a. Prepare the December 31, 1972, statement of financial position.
b. Prepare a cash budget for January 1973.
c. Prepare a budgeted income statement for January 1973.

Cases   **21-1   Hale Manufacturing Company.** The chief lending officer of the City Insurance Company is considering a ten-year, 6 per cent loan to the Hale Manufacturing Company to finance the expansion of its manufacturing facilities. The lending officer has Hale's most recent income and retained income statements. An assistant has prepared a summary of changes in financial position accounts from December 31, 1972, to December 31, 1973.

HALE MANUFACTURING COMPANY
Income Statement
For the Year Ended December 31, 1973

Net sales		$160,000
Cost of goods sold		95,000
Gross margin		65,000
Operating expenses:		
Salaries	$15,000	
Rent	7,200	
Depreciation	3,800	
Advertising	1,100	
Repairs and maintenance	2,400	
Miscellaneous	2,500	
Total operating expenses		32,000
Income from operations		33,000
Deduct financial expense:		
Interest expense		2,000
Income before federal income tax		31,000
Corporate federal income taxes		8,380
Net income		22,620

HALE MANUFACTURING COMPANY
Retained Income Statement
For the Year Ended December 31, 1973

Retained income, December 31, 1972...................	$57,000
Add net income for 1973	22,620
	79,620
Deduct dividends...	12,000
Retained income, December 31, 1973..................	67,620

HALE MANUFACTURING COMPANY
Financial Position Changes
From December 31, 1972, to December 31, 1973

ASSETS	*Increase*	*Decrease*
Current assets:		
Cash	$19,220	
Temporary investments...................		$ 5,000
Notes receivable...........................	3,000	
Accounts receivable.......................	12,000	
Inventories	1,900	
Prepayments................................		900
Property, plant, and equipment:		
Land...	—	—
Buildings and equipment (cost)	15,000	
Deduct accumulated depreciation	3,800	
EQUITIES		
Current liabilities:		
Notes payable..............................		6,200
Accounts payable..........................		9,000
Corporate income tax payable	1,000	
Long-term liabilities:		
Notes payable to banks...................	20,000	
Stockholders' equity:		
Capital stock, $50 par....................	25,000	
Retained income...........................	10,620	
Totals.....................................	111,540	21,100

The loan officer suggests that it would be useful to project the net working capital position to the end of 1974, assuming that the loan is to be granted and that all funds will be expended by the end of that year. Hale's management objects, stating that such a statement would be merely guesswork.

Required

a. Do you agree with the management of Hale, or do you think that a projected funds statement for 1974 would be useful in evaluating the loan request?

b. Prepare a statement of working capital flows for 1973.

c. Assuming the following additional information, prepare a projected statement of working capital flows for 1974:

  (1) The $30,000 loan is granted.

  (2) Buildings and equipment are purchased for $35,000 cash.

  (3) Net income is $25,000, dividends are $12,000, and the net asset increase is used to pay off long-term notes payable.

(4) All other account balances in the financial position statement remain unchanged from the end of 1973.

21-2   Holly Sugar Corporation. The Consolidated Balance Sheet and the Consolidated Source and Use of Funds statements of Holly Sugar Corporation and its subsidiaries are presented in the accompanying information.

Required   Comment on noteworthy changes in the sources from which working capital was derived and the uses to which it was put in 1970 and 1971.

HOLLY SUGAR CORPORATION AND SUBSIDIARIES
Consolidated Balance Sheet
March 31, 1971 and 1970

ASSETS	1971	1970
Current assets:		
Cash	$ 2,838,342	$ 3,186,799
Marketable securities—at market, not in excess of cost	181,763	714,887
Receivables	10,201,440	11,557,084
Inventories—at cost, not in excess of market (Note 2)	18,425,648	25,843,659
Prepaid expenses	2,788,029	2,602,052
Total current assets	34,435,222	43,904,481
Property, plant, and equipment (Note 3):	90,342,502	94,140,508
Less accumulated depreciation	37,099,745	38,319,835
Net property, plant, and equipment	53,242,757	55,820,673
Other assets (Note 4)	1,575,366	1,791,179
Total assets	$89,253,345	$101,516,333

LIABILITIES AND EQUITY		
Current liabilities:		
Notes payable and current portion of long-term debt	$ 9,200,000	$ 22,100,000
Accounts payable and accruals	8,392,722	5,997,788
Taxes	2,206,699	2,713,728
Total current liabilities	19,799,421	30,811,516
Long-term debt—excluding current portion (Note 5)	20,195,000	20,395,000
Deferred federal income taxes (Note 6)	6,622,000	6,032,000
Self-insurance reserves (Note 7)	458,580	1,986,221
Stockholders' equity (Notes 8 and 9):		
Common stock	8,377,045	8,377,045
Additional paid-in capital	5,490,471	5,490,471
Retained earnings (Note 5)	32,408,164	32,521,416
Total	46,275,680	46,388,932
Less treasury stock—at cost	4,097,336	4,097,336
Total stockholders' equity	42,178,344	42,291,596
Total liabilities and equity	$89,253,345	$101,516,333

HOLLY SUGAR CORPORATION AND SUBSIDIARIES
Consolidated Source and Use of Funds
Years Ended March 31, 1971 and 1970

	1971	1970
Funds were provided by:		
Net income (loss)	$1,286,113	($2,464,785)
Depreciation	3,082,870	3,334,274
Deferred income taxes	590,000	604,000
Funds provided from operations	4,958,983	1,473,489
Proceeds from bank financing	—	4,500,000
Total funds provided	4,958,983	5,973,489
Funds were used for:		
Capital expenditures for modernization	1,744,028	8,012,640
Cash dividends	1,399,365	1,856,582
Reduction of long-term debt	200,000	600,000
Other	72,754	(1,428,930)
Total funds used	3,416,147	9,040,292
Increase (decrease) in working capital	$1,542,836	($3,066,803)

Manufacturing
Cost Analysis

Purpose of Chapter

Earlier chapters have explained how the accountant seeks to measure the periodic income of a business by matching its expired costs with the related revenues. It has been shown how the accounts of a firm are tailored to correspond with its responsibility centers in order to facilitate the planning and control of operating revenues and expenses.

Most of the illustrations previously used have dealt with accounting for *trading concerns* (wholesalers and retailers). The principles which underlie accounting for *manufacturing concerns* are the same, although there are some important differences in application. This chapter considers some of these differences in applying basic accounting principles to planning and controlling manufacturing *operations*, and to the valuation of manufacturing *inventories*.

Production Costs and Distribution Costs

The activities of a business entity are usually classified according to functional responsibility. For example, it is customary to classify the operating activities of a manufacturer as either *production* or *distribution*. All activities associated with the *manufacture* of physical units of product are classified as responsibilities of production management. Activities related to *selling* the product (including advertising, sales promotion, and delivery) are included in distribution.

Recognition of the functional distinction between production and distribution, or other nonmanufacturing activities, underlies the different accounting treatment of *product costs* and *period costs*. Accounting attempts to associate *all costs* incurred in the manufacturing process with *units of product*. The theory is that the manufacturing process merely combines and transforms productive factors—materials, labor, and various other resources—into a more desirable form, the finished product. The costs of the factors used in producing a unit of finished product are accumulated in the accounting records as the cost to be identified with the product. Until the product is sold, it is considered to be an *asset* of the entity, an *inventory* item, and is valued at the unit cost of production. In the accounting period in which a unit of product is sold its future service potential to the entity expires, and the related unit cost of production is transferred from the *asset, inventory*, to the *expense, cost of goods sold*.

In contrast to production costs, accounting makes no attempt to relate the costs of distribution activity, such as salesmen's salaries, advertising, and delivery, to particular units of product. Since it is very difficult to determine objectively to what extent distribution activities produce *future benefits* extending beyond the current accounting period, their costs are assigned directly to expense accounts in the period in which the activity takes place.

Basic Elements of Production Cost

The accounts of most manufacturers recognize three main elements of product cost:

(1) *Direct materials*. Every manufactured product contains raw materials (such as steel, lumber, and cement) or prefabricated parts or components. These materials and parts are used directly in the manufacturing process as the substance from which finished products are derived. The term *direct materials* reflects the close physical relationship between the basic materials resource and the final product. Because of this close physical connection, the costs of materials can ordinarily be *objectively identified* with units of completed product without undue clerical expense, and are therefore treated as *direct costs of the units of product*.

(2) *Direct labor*. In many kinds of manufacturing, workers (such as metalsmiths or lathe operators) are directly involved in the task of converting direct materials into final product. As a result of this direct physical involvement, the wages and other compensation of such workers can be objectively associated with finished or partially finished units of product. They are therefore treated as *direct costs of the units of product*.

(3) *Manufacturing overhead*. This is a general category which includes all costs incurred in the manufacturing process except the costs of direct materials and direct labor. A few of the many types of manufacturing costs included in manufacturing overhead are

(a) Indirect labor—Factory wages which it is not possible or practical to trace directly to units of product. An example is factory maintenance labor.

(b) Indirect materials—Items of material used in manufacturing which it is not possible or practical to trace directly to units of product. An example is oil used in lubricating factory machines.

(c) Factory maintenance.

(d) Factory insurance.

(e) Factory property taxes.

(f) Factory heat, light, and power.

(g) Depreciation of factory machinery.

(h) Depreciation of factory building.

Manufacturing overhead costs are of many different types and can be associated only *indirectly* with product units. The allocation of factory overhead costs to units of product is one of the most challenging problems of accounting, and is the subject of the next chapter.

The sum of direct materials and direct labor costs is often referred to as *prime cost;* the sum of direct labor and manufacturing overhead costs is frequently called *conversion cost.*

Production Cost Centers

The production function of a manufacturing firm does not include responsibility for generating revenue. Consequently, the effectiveness of the manufacturing process cannot be measured directly by the revenue stream. The production manager's responsibilities are usually stated in terms of a required physical volume of production. The *production objective* is to achieve the desired volume of output at *minimum cost*, consistent with acceptable product quality. The *average unit cost of goods manufactured* is therefore the most pertinent measure of production performance.

Because of the focus on unit product cost as the major gauge of manufacturing effectiveness, production departments are usually designated in accounting as *cost centers* rather than profit centers. The *profit center* concept relates to the activities of the entity as a whole, or to segments of the entity which have responsibility for both revenue and costs. The *cost center* concept applies to any unit of activity within an organization which is the responsibility of a single individual, and for which cost data (but no revenue data) can be collected directly. While one person may be responsible for more than one cost center, the responsibility for a single cost center should not be divided among two or more persons.

Example 1   In a given factory all costs of operating a single large machine are accumulated in the accounting records. The *foreman* in charge of the group of employees who operate the machine is assigned responsibility for controlling the machine's operating costs. The *machine operation* is a *cost center.*

Example 2   In the same factory the costs of operating the factory Personnel Department are collected in the accounts. The *personnel manager* is responsible for controlling these costs, therefore the *personnel department* is a *cost center.*

Since a primary objective of a cost center is to *minimize costs,* the effectiveness of manufacturing operations depends largely on the following *controllable* elements:

(1) *Volume* of output.
(2) *Efficiency in usage* of resource factors.
(3) *Cost prices* of resource factors.

The way in which each of these elements influences the cost effectiveness of a manufacturing cost center is shown by the product unit cost computation, which is as follows:

$$\text{Product unit cost} = \frac{\text{Total manufacturing cost for the period}}{\text{Number of units produced, or Volume}}$$

$$= \frac{\text{Sum of (Price} \times \text{Quantity of all resources used)}}{\text{Number of units produced}}.$$

From the formula it can be seen that product *unit cost decreases* as production *volume increases,* provided that total production cost remains the same. If the output of a manufacturing cost center is less than the required volume, unit cost is too high and cost effectiveness is too low.

Product *unit cost increases* as the *quantity* of a resource used *increases* or as the *price* paid for a given productive factor *increases.* Thus inefficient usage of productive factors—using a larger quantity of a given factor than is ordinarily required to produce a unit of product—decreases cost effectiveness. Likewise, paying a higher price than is ordinarily required to obtain productive resources increases the unit cost and reduces the cost effectiveness of a production cost center.

Example 3   Suppose that the machine cost center in Example 1 incurred total costs of $1,800 each week for two weeks. During the first week 100 units of product were completed, but only 90 units were completed during the second week. The average cost of processing a unit of product through the machine cost center increased from $18 the first week to $20 the second. This reflects a decrease in the cost effectiveness of the cost center and its manager, the foreman, due to a decrease in units completed during the second week.

Direct and Indirect Production Costs

In computing the unit cost of manufacturing it is customary to assign all factory costs to units of product. The accountant must often trace some manufacturing costs through many different cost centers in arriving at the final result, the *unit cost of a completed manufactured product.* The routes by which costs flow through the accounts to the units of product may be both *direct* and *indirect.*

Little difficulty arises in the accounting treatment of *direct materials* and *direct labor.* These items can be directly associated with the units of physical product. *Manufacturing overhead,* however, cannot be physically traced to units of output. The problem of assigning manufacturing overhead to units of product is solved in two steps:

(1) Overhead is first assigned to departmental cost centers in the factory.

(2) The costs thus assigned to factory cost centers are then reassigned to the units of product which are processed by the cost centers.

All manufacturing overhead is *indirect* with respect to units of product. Overhead may be either *direct or indirect* from the point of view of a *factory cost center*.

Direct cost center overhead includes those overhead costs which are traceable without question to the activities of a particular factory cost center. In the accounting records these costs are first charged directly to the cost center and its responsible manager; they are then allocated indirectly to the units of product processed by the cost center.

Example 4   The machine in Example 1 is used in manufacturing a single type of product. Each month an equal share of the cost of operating the machine cost center is assigned to each complete unit of product on which the machine was used during the month. Proportionate costs are allocated to units partly completed during the month.

Indirect cost center overhead includes those overhead costs which are allocated indirectly to a cost center from other cost centers. These indirect costs are combined with the direct overhead of the cost center, and then allocated to units of product.

Example 5   The costs of the Personnel Department in Example 2 are reassigned to the production departments, including the machine cost center in Example 1, on some reasonable basis. This might be in proportion to the number of full-time employees in each department. The cost of each unit of manufactured product thus includes a part of the cost of operating the factory Personnel Department. The costs of other factory service departments, such as maintenance and dispensary, are treated in a similar manner.

Whether an item of overhead cost is *direct* or *indirect* depends on the costing unit in question. If the costing unit is the Personnel Department, costs which can be traced without question to that department are direct. If the costing unit is a *unit of product*, all costs of the Personnel Department are *indirect*.

The Relationship of Production Cost to Income

Net income measures the effectiveness of the operating performance of the entity as a whole. In businesses which sell a product the largest operating expense—and thus one of the most important factors in determining net income —is *cost of goods sold*. This expense measures the expiration of the service potential of product inventories.

In a merchandising business finished products are purchased from other businesses for resale. Until they are sold they are treated as an asset, *Merchandise Inventory*, and are valued at their acquisition prices. The cost of goods sold expense for a merchandising business is measured by relating the purchase cost prices to the units sold by some systematic method, such as weighted average, FIFO, LIFO, or specific identification.

Unlike a merchandising business, a manufacturer produces the products which it sells rather than buying them already completed. *Like* the merchandiser, however, the manufacturer treats the inventories of productive factors as assets at their acquisition cost until the units of finished product to which they relate are finally sold. Three inventory accounts are used for this purpose:

(1) *Materials and supplies.* This account includes costs incurred in the purchase of raw materials and factory supplies which are awaiting use in production.

(2) *Goods in process inventory.* This account includes the costs of direct materials, direct labor, and manufacturing overhead already used in production, awaiting completion of the product.

(3) *Finished goods inventory.* This account includes the costs of direct materials, direct labor, and manufacturing overhead which have been transferred from Goods in Process Inventory when the product was completed. These unit costs of Finished Goods will be reassigned to *Cost of Goods Sold Expense* when the articles are sold.

Reporting Cost of Goods Sold of a Manufacturer

After the costs of manufacturing each unit have been determined, the procedure for accounting for *Finished Goods Inventory* is much the same as that for *Merchandise Inventory.* The only difference is that *unit production cost,* rather than purchase price, is used as the basis for valuing the items in inventory or in cost of goods sold expense.

Manufacturing businesses often prepare a separate statement or schedule which shows the components of cost of goods sold. An example of this report appears in Illustration 22-1. To emphasize the similarity of the manufacturer's

Illustration 22-1

Schedule of Cost of Goods Sold
For the Month Ended January 31, 1972

A Manufacturer

Direct materials	$17,000
Direct labor	14,000
Manufacturing overhead (see supporting schedule)	7,000
Total manufacturing cost added this period	$38,000
Add beginning goods in process inventory	8,000
Total	$46,000
Deduct ending goods in process inventory	12,750
Cost of goods completed this period	$33,250
Add beginning finished goods inventory	0
Cost of goods available for sale	$33,250
Deduct ending finished goods inventory	13,250
Cost of goods sold (to Income Statement)	$20,000

A Merchandiser

Net cost of purchases	$33,250
Add beginning merchandise inventory	0
Cost of goods available for sale	$33,250
Deduct ending merchandise inventory	13,250
Cost of goods sold (to Income Statement)	$20,000

cost of goods completed this period and the merchandiser's *net cost of purchases*, the cost of goods sold schedules of a manufacturer and a merchandiser are presented in parallel columns.

The information in the manufacturer's schedule was obtained by analyzing the general ledger accounts related to manufacturing, using the Calla Machine Company illustration which appears later in this chapter. (One would expect, of course, that a manufacturer would ordinarily be able to produce goods at a lower cost than he could buy them from outside.)

Periodic and Perpetual Inventory Methods

The inventories of manufacturers may be measured by either the *periodic* or the *perpetual* inventory method, although the latter is usually preferable. The periodic inventory method is most appropriate when the inventory amounts are relatively small and the inventory components are simple.

In most manufacturing processes, the relationship of many important types of production costs to specific items of product is indirect and complex. As a result, it is frequently quite difficult to use the *periodic inventory* method to determine the costs of units in various stages of completion (goods in process inventory) and the costs of unit manufactured (finished goods) at various times under changing conditions. If a periodic inventory system is used, the cost per unit is the average cost of all units completed since the last periodic inventory was taken. It is necessary to estimate the stage of completion of work in process in order to compute an average unit cost, and the results so obtained are sometimes subject to a wide margin of error.

Under the conditions just described, it is preferable to use a *perpetual inventory* record to accumulate the costs of units in the process of manufacture, unless the cost of doing so outweighs the benefits. A perpetual inventory system permits the computation of average unit costs more frequently and provides more current information relating to the trends of unit costs for the use of production, accounting, and other management groups.

In most cases the perpetual inventory method permits better control over the inventories through safeguards in the receiving, storing, and issuing functions.

Systems for Assigning Production Costs to Product Units

Production costs are assigned to specific product units through the goods in process inventory accounts of individual production *cost centers*. The two basic systems of setting up the cost center inventory accounts for this purpose are (1) *job order* (or *production order*) cost systems and (2) *process* cost systems.

In a *job order cost system*, a separate costing record is established for each job (or production) order worked on in the cost center (or group of cost centers). These job costing records form a *subsidiary ledger*, containing the supporting detail for the general ledger account, *Goods in Process Inventory*. The subsidiary cost record for each physical job is identified by the number of the job. Production costs which are directly traceable to each job order, such as direct materials and direct labor, are accumulated in the corresponding job account. At intervals a share of manufacturing overhead which is considered to apply to the job is recorded on the related job cost record.

The job order system is appropriate when production is performed on *dissimilar* units or lots of product, rather than on a continuous flow of a homo-

LARGE EXPENSIVE CUSTOM UNIQUE

geneous product. Job order costing is well suited to the construction industry, to the manufacture of specialized machinery, and to other situations where items are being manufactured according to the specifications of a customer. Job order costing is also sometimes used when a product is being manufactured for stock in identifiable batches, lots, or units.

A *process cost system* is more suitable when *production is largely continuous* and the *product is homogeneous*—that is, one unit of product cannot be distinguished from other units. It is well adapted to the needs of refineries and chemical plants. In a process cost system a separate goods in process inventory account is used for the entire production of each *production cost center*. All costs of direct material, direct labor, and manufacturing overhead attributable to the cost center's activity during a time period are accumulated in the center's work in process account. They are then apportioned to the center's entire quantity of production for the same period. The process cost system thus develops an *average cost* of all units produced in the cost center *during the costing period*, which may be a day, a week, or a month.

Although many of their accounting procedures are different, the job order system and the process cost system have in common the objectives of providing information concerning the unit costs of production for purposes of *inventory valuation* and *cost control*. In computing unit costs both systems have two important tasks:

(1) *Accumulating the total production costs* attributable to each particular segment of production for a given time period. These segments are the units produced for each particular job under a job system, or total units produced by a process under a process system.

(2) *Measuring the physical units produced* during the same period, to be divided into total production cost in computing unit costs. This divisor, under both cost systems, must express the volume of production for the period—both completed and partially completed units—in the common denominator of *equivalent whole units produced*.

Example 6

The Calla Machine Company processed a customer's order for three machines, using 15,000 pounds of steel purchased for $0.50 per pound and 1,500 hours of direct labor costing $4.00 per hour. Manufacturing overhead was assigned to the job on the basis of 50 per cent of direct labor cost. At the end of the month two machines were completed and ready for shipment, and it was estimated that the third machine was one-half complete. Compute the average unit cost.

Solution

The total cost to date of the job order, which is still in the process of being manufactured, is $16,500. The average unit cost *per equivalent completed machine* is $6,600, computed as follows:

$$\text{Average unit cost} = \frac{\text{Sum of (Price} \times \text{Quantity of all factors used)}}{\text{Number of units produced}}$$

$$= \frac{\$0.50(15,000\,\text{lb}) + \$4.00(1,500\,\text{hr}) + 0.5(\$4.00)(1,500\,\text{hr})}{2.5\ \text{Equivalent no. of machines completed}}$$

$$= \frac{\$7,500 + \$6,000 + \$3,000}{2.5}$$

$$= \frac{\$16,500}{2.5}$$

$$= \$6,600.$$

Illustration of Job Order Cost Accounting Procedure

The Calla Machine Company builds machines according to the specifications of its customers. On December 31, 1971, the balances of its factory inventory accounts were as follows:

A, Materials Inventory...	$24,000
A, Goods in Process Inventory..	8,000
A, Finished Goods Inventory..	0

The company uses a job cost system to accumulate the cost of each machine manufactured. The balance in the Goods in Process Inventory consisted of the following costs incurred in November and December 1971 on Job No. 115, which was not yet complete:

Direct materials...	$3,500	
Direct labor..	3,000	
Manufacturing overhead.......................................	1,500	
Total cost to date..		$8,000

The following journal entries record the transactions of January 1972 which are closely related to manufacturing operations. Other entries are omitted.

(1)

A, Materials Inventory...	15,000	
L, Accounts Payable..		15,000
Total materials purchased during the month.		

(2)

A, Goods in Process Inventory......................................	17,000	
A, Materials Inventory		17,000
Total materials used on jobs, as follows:		
Job No. 115	$3,000	
Job No. 116 (new).....................................	8,000	
Job No. 117 (new).....................................	6,000	

(3)

A, Goods in Process Inventory.......................................	14,000	
A, Manufacturing Overhead Clearing Account....................	3,000	
OE, Sales Salaries Expense...	2,000	
OE, Administrative Salaries Expense...............................	1,000	
L, Accrued Salaries Payable.....................................		20,000
To record total pay earned by employees during January.		
Details of the factory payroll were as follows:		
Directly traceable to jobs:		
Job No. 115...	$ 1,500	
Job No. 116...	8,000	
Job No. 117...	4,500	
Total debit to Goods in Process..................	$14,000	
Not directly traceable to jobs:		
Factory supervision.................................	$ 1,200	
Factory maintenance salaries......................	1,800	
Total debit to Manufacturing Overhead Clearing Account........................	$ 3,000	

In entry (3) the amounts of sales and administrative salaries, which are classified as *period costs*, are debited immediately to expense accounts. Factory costs which can be traced *directly to jobs* are recorded on the job cost sheets for each job. Their total is debited to Goods in Process Inventory, a general ledger controlling account whose balance is equal to the sum of the subsidiary job cost records. Factory costs which cannot be traced directly to specific jobs are collected in a *Manufacturing Overhead Clearing Account*. An example is the use of indirect materials, recorded in entry (4).

(4)

A, Manufacturing Overhead Clearing Account	500	
A, Materials Inventory		500

Indirect materials used (those not traceable to specific jobs) for lubrication, cleaning, and maintenance.

(5)

A, Manufacturing Overhead Clearing Account	200	
A, Unexpired Insurance...		200

Expiration of insurance premiums applicable to the factory.

(6)

A, Manufacturing Overhead Clearing Account	3,300	
L, Accounts Payable		3,300

Amounts owed for January factory overhead costs such as rent, repair services, and utilities.

The total costs show by the individual job cost sheets for jobs which have not been finished must equal the balance of the Goods in Process controlling account in the general ledger.

At regular intervals, usually once a month, total manufacturing overhead is reassigned to individual jobs.

When the total of actual factory overhead is allocated to the individual job cost records, an entry is made in the general ledger debiting Goods in Process Inventory for the total overhead allocated. This is shown in entry (7). After this entry is posted the balance of the Manufacturing Overhead Clearing Account will be zero (will be *cleared*).

(7)

A, Goods in Process Inventory..	7,000	
A, Manufacturing Overhead Clearing Account.............		7,000

The indirect manufacturing costs were reassigned to individual job cost sheets in proportion to the direct labor costs of each job. It was assumed that each job caused overhead costs to be incurred in about the same proportion as it caused direct labor costs to be incurred. Total manufacturing overhead was 50% of direct labor cost for January ($7,000/$14,000); therefore the January overhead of each job was considered to be 50% of its direct labor cost. The results are

Job No. 115...................... 50% of $1,500 = $ 750
Job No. 116...................... 50% of 8,000 = 4,000
Job No. 117...................... 50% of 4,500 = 2,250

(8)

A, Finished Goods Inventory..	33,250	
A, Goods in Process Inventory.................................		33,250

Job Nos. 115 and 116 were completed, with total costs as follows:

	Job No. 115	Job No. 116
Direct materials....................	$ 6,500	$ 8,000
Direct labor........................	4,500	8,000
Manufacturing overhead........	2,250	4,000
Totals............................	$13,250	$20,000

(9a)

A, Accounts Receivable...	30,000	
OE, Sales Revenue...		30,000
Job No. 116 was shipped to the customer.		

(9b)

OE, Cost of Goods Sold Expense...................................	20,000	
A, Finished Goods Inventory...................................		20,000
The cost of producing Job No. 116 was matched with the revenue from its sale.		

Posting the transactions of the Calla Machine Company to the general ledger accounts related to factory operations produces the results shown in Illustration 22-2.

The detailed job order cost records in the Goods in Process subsidiary ledger would contain the following information:

Goods in Process—Job No. 115

Date	Reference	Materials	Labor	Overhead	Credits	Debit Balance
1971						
Dec. 31	Balance	3,500	3,000	1,500		8,000
1972						
Jan.	(2)	3,000				11,000
	(3)		1,500			12,500
	(7)			750		13,250
	(8)				13,250	0

Goods in Process—Job No. 116

Date	Reference	Materials	Labor	Overhead	Credits	Debit Balance
1972						
Jan.	(2)	8,000				8,000
	(3)		8,000			16,000
	(7)			4,000		20,000
	(8)				20,000	0

Goods in Process—Job No. 117

Date	Reference	Materials	Labor	Overhead	Credits	Debit Balance
1972						
Jan.	(2)	6,000				6,000
	(3)		4,500			10,500
	(7)			2,250		12,750

Illustration 22-2   Flow of Costs in a Manufacturing Enterprise Using a Job Order Cost System.

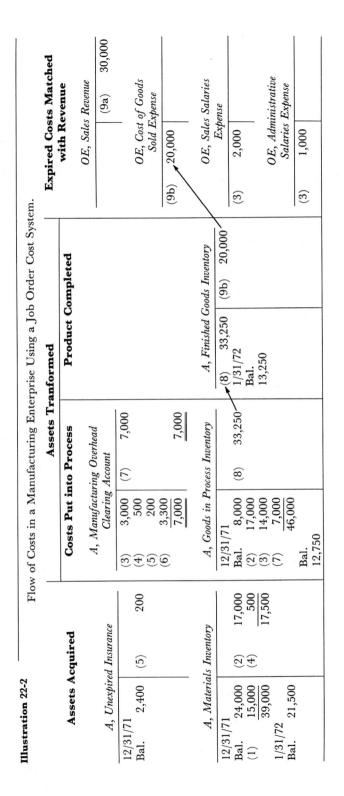

Note that the total effect on the subsidiary job order cost sheets for each numbered entry is the same as the effect on the Goods in Process Inventory general ledger account in Illustration 22-2. The total of the ending balances of the job cost sheets, $12,750, also agrees with the ending balance of Goods in Process Inventory.

Limitations of the Job Order Cost System

The foregoing illustration was intentionally simple, and for that reason it failed to show some of the shortcomings of the job order system of assigning production costs to units of product. The following are some of job order costing's major limitations:

(1) It requires detailed records of the materials issued and the labor cost of each job. If there are many jobs in process at a given time, the clerical effort required to collect this information can be extensive.

(2) It combines in a single total the costs incurred on a job during several periods. Unless care is taken, it may hide important trends in production efficiency.

(3) It presents difficulties in allocating factory overhead to individual jobs.

Accounts Required in a Process Cost Accounting System

A manufacturing company which uses a *process cost* accounting system, like one which uses a job order system, maintains inventory accounts for finished goods, goods in process, and materials and supplies. Of the general ledger accounts of the two systems, only *goods in process inventory* accounts are likely to be different. The following variations are common under process cost systems:

(1) A *single goods in process inventory* account is used. This is appropriate when there is only one production process.

(2) Or, a separate goods in process inventory account is used for *each element of cost*: *Goods in Process—Materials*, *Goods in Process—Labor*, and *Goods in Process—Manufacturing Overhead*. This variation is useful when there is one production process but separate unit costs are desired for each element of cost.

(3) Or, a goods in process inventory account is used for *each process* of a factory with more than one process. Each account parallels the responsibility of the manager in charge of the process.

(4) Or, a separate goods in process account is used for *each element of each process*.

At the end of each time period for which unit costs are to be computed, a *cost of production report* is prepared. It summarizes the total manufacturing costs incurred according to elements, the physical number of units produced, and the cost of each element for each unit of manufactured product.

The divisor used in computing the cost of each type of input (such as materials, labor, and manufacturing overhead) in a unit of output should be the *number of equivalent whole units completed as to that input*.

Example 7 In a given cost center a labor cost of $100 was incurred in manufacturing four units which were complete as to labor and three units which were one-third complete. What was the labor cost of a complete unit?

Solution The partially finished units have a labor input equivalent to one-third of the labor in a completed unit. The *number of equivalent whole units completed as to labor* is computed as follows:

$$4 + \tfrac{1}{3}(3) = 5.$$

The cost of labor in a complete unit is $100/5, or $20.

Illustration of Process Cost Accounting Procedure

The Burson Chemical Company manufactures a single product, *Burmical*, by using one productive process. Liquid and solid raw materials are mixed together, cooked in vats for four days, and then transferred to bulk storage tanks awaiting shipment to customers. The company computes the average cost of manufacturing a gallon of Burmical once a month.

At the beginning of April 1972 the vats were empty. During April 24,000 gallons of Burmical were completed and transferred to the storage tanks. On April 30 the vats contained 4,000 gallons of mixture, including all of the necessary raw materials, which had been placed in the vats at the beginning of April 29. No further loss from evaporation was expected. Labor is incurred evenly throughout the productive process.

The balances in the relevant general ledger accounts on April 30, representing costs incurred during the month, were

	Debit
Goods in Process Inventory—Materials	$56,000
Goods in Process Inventory—Labor.......................................	10,400
Goods in Process Inventory—Manufacturing Overhead...............	13,000

Illustration 22-3 shows the computation of unit costs for the Burson Chemical Company for April 1972.

Illustration 22-3

BURSON CHEMICAL COMPANY
Cost of Production Report
For the Month Ended April 30, 1972

		Units				
			In Process at End			
Type of Input	Complete	Number	Fraction Completed	Equivalent Whole Units	Total Cost	Unit Cost
Materials..........	24,000	4,000	All	28,000	$56,000	$2.00
Labor	24,000	4,000	1/2	26,000	10,400	0.40
Manufacturing overhead	24,000	4,000	1/2	26,000	13,000	0.50
Totals					$79,400	$2.90

The average cost of manufacturing a gallon of Burmical, $2.90, could *not* have been computed by dividing the total cost, $79,400, by the 28,000 gallons on which work was performed during the period. A unit in process should not be assigned the same amount of cost as a unit finished and transferred to the storage tanks. Although it has had all the necessary material added to it, it has had only half of the necessary amount of labor and manufacturing overhead.

The only journal entry needed on April 30 is one to record the transfer of costs from goods in process to finished goods, as follows:

(10)

A, Finished Goods Inventory......................................	69,600	
A, Goods in Process Inventory—Materials.............		48,000
A, Goods in Process Inventory—Labor..................		9,600
A, Goods in Process Inventory—Mfg. Overhead......		12,000
To transfer the cost of 24,000 gallons completed at $2.90 each to Finished Goods Inventory.		

After this entry has been posted, the balances remaining in the Goods in Process Inventory accounts will be

Goods in Process—Materials.................	$8,000	(4,000 units × $2.00)
Goods in Process—Labor	800	(4,000 units × ½ × $0.40)
Goods in Process—Mfg. Overhead..........	1,000	(4,000 units × ½ × $0.50)

Summary

The accounts of most manufacturers recognize three main elements of product costs: *direct materials*, *direct labor*, and *manufacturing overhead*. These costs are assigned to the units of product being manufactured, flowing from Materials and Supplies Inventory to Goods in Process Inventory, and then to Finished Goods Inventory when the product is completed. In the period when the product is sold its cost is transferred from Finished Goods Inventory to Cost of Goods Sold Expense, and is matched with the related Sales Revenue.

Manufacturing performance is the responsibility of *production cost centers*, whose objective is to achieve the desired volume of output at minimum cost. The effectiveness of these cost centers in manufacturing operations depends largely on the controllable elements: *volume of output, efficiency of resource usage*, and *cost prices of resources used*. Unit product costs are a gauge of production management's effectiveness.

The two basic systems of determining unit costs for financial reporting and for management control are *job order* and *process*. The job order cost system is appropriate when production is performed on dissimilar units or lots of product. The process cost system is more suitable when production is largely continuous and the product is homogeneous. Although the methods used under these two types of systems differ, they have two main tasks in common:

(1) *Accumulating the total production costs* incurred by each segment of production for a given time period.

(2) *Measuring the physical units produced* during the same period, to be divided into total production cost in computing unit costs.

22-1   Classify the following costs of a manufacturer as *production* costs or *distribution* costs:

a. Inward transportation of raw materials.
b. Salary of sales manager.
c. Cost of telephone in purchasing department office.
d. Salary of bookkeeper who keeps raw materials perpetual inventory records.
e. Cost of manufacturing goods which are spoiled in process.
f. Depreciation on warehouse in which are stored raw materials and finished goods.
g. Cost of heating plant building which includes factory, sales warehouse, and general administrative offices.
h. Cost of bandages used in factory first-aid room.

22-2   In the accounting records of a manufacturer, production costs are *transformed* and later they *expire*. Explain briefly the difference between a *cost transformation* and a *cost expiration*.

22-3   It has been said that the manufacturer's *cost of goods completed* is parallel to the merchandiser's net *cost of purchases*.

a. To what extent is this comparison valid?
b. What are the major differences between the two?

22-4   A large retailer buys some merchandise in bulk and packages it in smaller quantities for resale.

a. Using assumed amounts, show how you would account for the acquisition, packaging, and sale of the merchandise.
b. How does this situation resemble the inventory accounting of a manufacturer? How does it differ?

22-5   A manufacturer incurred $40,000 in production costs to manufacture 800 units of product, and another $40,000 in distribution costs to sell 600 of the completed units.

a. How much of the $40,000 production costs *expired* during the period?
b. How much of the the $40,000 of distribution costs expired during the period?
c. Explain briefly why accounting treats the two types of costs differently.

22-6   Give an example of each of the following in determining the unit costs of manufacturing dining-room tables:

a. Direct materials.   d. Indirect labor.
b. Indirect materials.   e. Manufacturing overhead.
c. Direct labor.

22-7

a. Give three examples of factory production departments.
b. Give three examples of factory service departments.
c. Give three examples of departments of a manufacturing business which are neither factory production nor factory service.
d. Explain how cost information can be used to evaluate the performance of each of the three types of departments (production, service, and other).

22-8   Explain briefly the difference between a *cost center* and a *profit center*. Under what circumstances might it be useful to establish profit centers for a manufacturing business? Give an example of a situation in which such a practice might be useful.

22-9   The Oporto Manufacturing Company has three divisions: Production, Marketing, and General Administration. The Production Division has a factory personnel department and two production departments, all located in the same building. Oporto seeks to determine the full cost of each unit of product by means of a historical cost accounting system. It incurred the following types of costs in a given month:

 (1) Advertising
 (2) Depreciation—delivery trucks
 (3) Depreciation—factory machinery
 (4) Depreciation—personnel office equipment
 (5) Materials used on product
 (6) Wages of machine operators in the factory
 (7) Janitor's cleaning supplies
 (8) Power for factory machinery
 (9) Electricity for lighting production building
(10) Salary—president
(11) Salaries—sales manager
(12) Salaries—personnel officer of factory
(13) Salaries—factory foremen
(14) Cost of storing finished product

Required   a. Indicate by the letter *P* those costs which become a part of the unit cost of manufactured products, either directly or indirectly. Indicate by the letter *E* those costs which are treated as expired costs of the period in which they are incurred.

b. For each product cost selected in part a, use letters as appropriate from the following:

DS—Direct charge to factory service department.
DP—Direct charge to factory production department.
DU—Direct charge to units of product.

Use the letters *IS*, *IP*, and *IU* to denote *indirect* service, production, and unit charges, respectively. *Caution:* Some product costs are direct charges to one activity and indirect charges to other(s).

22-10

a. Which is likely to have more general ledger inventory accounts, a job order system or a process cost system? Explain.
b. What is the nature of the subsidiary accounts under each system? Which system is likely to require more subsidiary accounts? Why?
c. Which system is likely to require more clerical effort? Why?

22-11   Describe carefully how production costs are associated with individual physical units of product under (1) a job order cost system and (2) a process cost system.

22-12   Which method of accumulating costs of product, job order or process, do you think would be more appropriate for the following?

a. A paper manufacturer
b. A driveway construction company
c. An oil refinery
d. A manufacturer of special-order machine tools

e. A cannery
f. A chemical plant
g. A book publisher
h. A manufacturer of military airplanes

22-13   "The job order cost system merges dissimilar costs and hides important trends in unit costs."

a. Why is this true?

b. How would you suggest that this limitation be overcome?

22-14

a. In what ways does the job order method resemble the specific-identification method of accounting for merchandise inventory?

b. How do the two methods differ?

22-15   The assembly department of a manufacturer has *prime costs* (costs of direct materials and direct labor) of $8 per unit of product, variable manufacturing overhead costs of $4 per unit, and fixed manufacturing overhead costs of $12,000 per month.

a. What would be the average unit cost if 300 units of product were produced? If 400 units were produced? If 200 units were produced?

b. Explain what would happen to the average unit costs (1) if prices of direct materials were decreased 10 per cent and (2) if direct labor rates were increased by 5 per cent.

c. Explain what would happen to the average unit costs if output per direct labor hour were increased by 2 per cent.

d. Explain what would happen to the average unit costs if fixed manufacturing overhead costs were increased by $600 per month with a resulting decrease of $1 per unit in variable manufacturing overhead costs. Give examples.

22-16   The records of the Croix Mfg. Co. contained the following data at the end of its accounting period, December 31, 1973 (thousands of dollars):

Sales	$2,500
Raw material purchases	300
Direct labor	700
Factory depreciation	100
Indirect labor	70
Indirect materials	120
Power	60
Selling expense	300
Administrative expense	250
Beginning inventories:	
Raw materials	700
Goods in process	300
Finished goods	800
Ending inventories:	
Raw materials	250
Goods in process	340
Finished goods	760

Required   a. Prepare a schedule of cost of goods sold expense for 1973.

b. Prepare an income statement for 1973.

22-17   The Millsap Mfg. Co. reported the following results for the year ended December 31, 1973 (thousands):

Product units sold		100
Sales revenue		$4,800
Cost of goods sold:		
Prime costs	$1,600	
Manufacturing overhead	600	2,200
Gross margin on sales		$2,600

There were no changes in inventories of raw materials or goods in process during the period. However, the inventory of finished goods increased by 25,000 units from January 1 to December 31, 1973.

a. What was the total cost of goods manufactured during 1973?
b. What change would have occurred in the gross margin if the manufacturing overhead costs had been $150,000 higher?
c. List the most important assumptions that you had to make in order to answer parts a and b.

22-18   The business of the Johann Co., a manufacturer, is subject to sharp seasonal swings in the level of production. The company maintains a sizable inventory, which fluctuates significantly as sales orders fluctuate. The company has been calculating average unit costs of production once a month. The unit costs of its principal product were computed as follows for March and April:

	Unit Costs of Manufacture	
	March	April
Direct materials	$17.75	$17.30
Direct labor	11.25	10.70
Manufacturing overhead	12.00	30.00
Totals	$41.00	$58.00

In March 24,000 units were manufactured, whereas only 10,000 were manufactured in April. The largest elements of the overhead are facility costs, such as depreciation, insurance, and property taxes on plant and equipment.

a. Explain the probable reason for the large change in the total unit costs of production.
b. At the end of April there were 17,000 finished units on hand, of which 7,000 were manufactured in March and the remainder in April. At what amount should these finished units be reported in inventory in the April 30 financial position statement?
c. What alternative measure of the ending inventory for April might be appropriate?

22-19   Pelsink Mfg. Co. incurred total manufacturing costs of $240,000 in January. During the month 1,600 units were completed and transferred to finished goods inventory. On January 31, 800 units remained in process and averaged 50 per cent complete.

a. Compute the average unit cost of production for January.
b. At what amount should the units remaining in goods in process inventory be shown on the January 31 financial position statement?
c. What major assumptions about the production cycle are required to answer part a?

22-20   Spevac Mfg. Co., Inc. incurred total manufacturing costs of $640,000 in 1973. The total cost of production averaged $80 per unit. Seven thousand units of product were completed and transferred to finished goods inventory during the year. The units remaining in goods-in-process inventory on December 31, 1973, averaged one-half complete.

a. How many equivalent units of product were manufactured in 1973?
b. How many units of product remained in goods in process inventory at the end of 1973?

22-21   A brick manufacturer makes his product in three stages: (1) *forming*, in which the clay is crushed, ground, and shaped into bricks; (2) *drying*, in which the bricks are dried slowly at temperatures between 100° and 300°F; and (3) *burning*, in which the bricks are placed in a kiln and subjected to temperatures up to 2000°F to make them strong. The manufacturer makes three standard types of bricks, usually in consecutive periods of about one week for each type.

    a. What general ledger accounts and subsidiary records would you suggest that the manufacturer use for his operations?

    b. How often would you recommend that he compute the unit costs of bricks? What are the advantages and disadvantages of your recommendation?

22-22   Spelunk Manufacturing Co., which uses a job order cost accounting system, had the following balances on December 31, 1972:

Materials Inventory...	$55,000
Goods in Process Inventory......................................	33,000
Finished Goods Inventory..	70,000

A summary of 1973 transactions is

  (1) Purchased raw materials on account for $180,000.

  (2) Issued material costing $193,000 for use on jobs, and material costing $8,000 for miscellaneous factory work which could not be identified with specific jobs.

  (3) Returned excess material costing $4,000, not needed on current jobs, to the storeroom for future use.

  (4) Pay earned by employees was as follows:

Directly traceable to jobs..	$81,000
General administrative salaries................................	22,000
Factory supervision and maintenance........................	24,000
Sales salaries...	27,000

  (5) Factory depreciation was $8,000.

  (6) Expired insurance on factory machinery and raw materials inventories was $2,000.

  (7) Liabilities incurred for other expired factory overhead items amounted to $5,000.

  (8) Reassigned the actual indirect manufacturing costs to specific jobs in proportion to the direct labor cost incurred on each job during this period. (There is insufficient information to permit keeping the Goods in Process Inventory subsidiary ledger.)

  (9) Completed goods costing a total of $293,000.

  (10) Sold goods costing $305,000 on account for $440,000.

Required   a. Record the foregoing transactions in journal form.

    b. Post the entries in part a to T-accounts.

    c. Prepare an income statement for 1973, assuming for simplicity that no other costs were incurred.

22-23   The following information was taken from the job order cost sheets of the Entrecote Mfg. Co., which uses a job order costing system, at the end of December. Work was done on only three jobs during December. Of these, Job No. 87 was completed on December 22 and the other two were still in process on December 31.

	Job No. 87 Costs		*Job No. 88 Costs*		*Job No. 89 Costs*	
	November	*December*	*November*	*December*	*November*	*December*
Direct materials....	$2,500	$1,800	$6,000	$2,000	$1,500	$1,200
Direct labor.........	4,000	2,000	3,000	6,000	6,000	8,000
Factory overhead ..	2,800		2,100		4,200	

Actual overhead was assigned to jobs at the end of November in proportion to the November direct labor cost on each job. No overhead allocation has been made for December. Actual overhead cost for December was $10,000.

Required a. What overhead rate was used in November?
b. Using the same basis of allocation, compute the December overhead charge for each job and make the necessary journal entry.
c. What would the overhead assigned to each job for November and December have been if the allocation were on the basis of direct materials cost?
d. Under what circumstances would the direct materials basis of allocating factory overhead to jobs seem more appropriate? The direct labor basis?
e. What method of allocating overhead might be superior to both the direct materials and the direct labor basis? Why?

22-24   The Airco Mfg. Co. uses a process costing system to account for the production of its single product. Material is added at the beginning of the production cycle. Direct labor and manufacturing overhead costs are incurred evenly over the production process.

During May, 60,000 units of product were completed. On May 31 there were 30,000 units in process, two-thirds completed. On May 1 there were no units in process. Manufacturing costs for the month were

Direct materials..	$63,000
Direct labor...	$96,000
Manufacturing overhead 50% of direct labor cost	

Required a. Prepare a cost of production report for May, showing detailed computations of equivalent units of production and unit costs by elements.
b. Present journal entries to record the costs of production and the transfer of completed units to Finished Goods Inventory.

22-25   The Alta Chemical Company manufactures its products in one continuous productive process. Raw material is added at the beginning of the process. A careful record is kept of all material withdrawn from the storeroom each month, all labor costs incurred, and all manufacturing overhead. The quantity of finished product transferred to stock, measured in pounds, is weighed on a large scale.

The following data relate to production for the month of June 1973:

(1) There were no units in process at the beginning of the month.
(2) During June 21,500 pounds of raw material were issued to the production department from the storeroom. At the end of the month 500 pounds of material were unused and in good condition on the production floor. Each pound of material had cost $5.
(3) Direct labor cost for June was $23,100, sales salaries were $3,500, and general salaries were $2,400.
(4) Factory overhead costs amounted to $13,200, selling overhead to $2,500, and general overhead to $6,000.
(5) During June 10,000 pounds of product were transferred to finished stock.
(6) At the end of June 4,000 pounds of semifinished product were still in the process of production. All necessary material had been added and all of the shrinkage which normally occurs during the production process had already taken place. One-

fourth of the necessary labor and factory overhead cost had been incurred on the goods in process.

Required
a. Prepare a unit cost of production report for June.
b. Journalize entries necessary to record the foregoing data for June.
c. How can the unit cost figures computed in part a be used by the Alta Chemical Company?
d. What are the shortcomings of the unit cost figures in part a and how would you recommend that they be improved?

22-26 The Ligusto Mfg. Co. completed 8,400 units of product in January which were transferred to Finished Goods Inventory at a cost of $117,600. At the end of January 1,600 units of product remained in process at an assigned cost of $14,400, and were three-eighths complete with respect to direct labor and manufacturing overhead costs. (Materials are added at the beginning of the production cycle.) Manufacturing overhead costs are charged to production at 50 per cent of direct labor cost.

Required
a. Compute the average total cost per unit produced in January.
b. Compute the equivalent units of production by elements.
c. Compute the direct materials, direct labor, and manufacturing overhead costs incurred in January.
d. List the most important assumptions, if any, that you made in order to answer parts a, b, and c.

Cases

22-1   Lyle Company. Lyle Company, a medium-sized manufacturing company, maintains its own power plant, a cafeteria, and a central office to service its two production departments, *Machining* and *Assembly*. Actual costs of the three service departments are allocated to the production departments at the end of each month as follows:

Service Department	Basis of Allocating Costs to Production
Power plant..	In proportion to number of kilowatt-hours used
Cafeteria	In proportion to number of employees
Central office.......................................	In proportion to number of product units completed

In March 1973 the company's controller is considering the reasonableness of the established procedures for allocating indirect overhead costs and has compiled the following data:

	Total	Machining Department	Assembly Department
January results:			
Floor space (sq. ft.)............................	40,000	20,000	20,000
Number of employees..........................	150	100	50
Machine hours used............................	12,000	2,400	9,600
Direct labor hours used.......................	4,200	3,000	1,200
Kilowatt-hours used............................	250,000	100,000	150,000
Product units completed......................	4,800	2,400	2,400
Power cost assigned............................	$ 5,000	$ 2,000	$ 3,000
Cafeteria cost assigned........................	$ 12,000	$ 8,000	$ 4,000
Central office cost assigned..................	$ 14,000	$ 7,000	$ 7,000
Total.......................................	$ 31,000	$ 17,000	$ 14,000

	Total	Machining Department	Assembly Department
February results:			
Floor space (sq. ft.).............................	40,000	20,000	20,000
Number of employees..........................	140	98	42
Machine hours used	8,800	2,200	6,600
Direct labor hours used.......................	3,600	2,700	900
Kilowatt-hours used	150,000	75,000	75,000
Product units completed......................	4,000	2,400	1,600
Power cost assigned...........................	$ 4,400	$ 2,200	$ 2,200
Cafeteria cost assigned	$ 11,000	$ 7,700	$ 3,300
Central office cost assigned...................	$ 14,000	$ 8,400	$ 5,600
Total.......................................	$ 29,400	$ 18,300	$ 11,100

Because of labor unrest and an unauthorized slowdown, February production in the Assembly Department was unseasonably low. The Machining Department manager has complained that, although he met his production quota with fewer labor hours and machine hours in February than in January, he was charged with a much greater share of central office overhead costs. Moreover, he objected that while he used fewer kilowatt-hours in February, he was charged a larger amount for power costs.

The controller pointed out that the company has a large amount of fixed costs which continue regardless of production levels and that all costs must be charged to some department and assigned to product units completed. He said that since the Machining Department completed a larger proportion of total units in April, it was logical that Machining should bear a larger proportion of indirect overhead costs.

The Machining Department manager contended that he should be charged a fixed amount each month for the central office overhead costs and a set price per kilowatt-hour used for power costs.

Required

a. What criteria should be used in assigning indirect overhead costs to production departments?

b. Explain and evaluate the reasoning of the controller for assigning total overhead costs to products.

c. Is there any merit to the argument of the Machining Department manager? Explain.

d. Outline a system for assigning the service department costs to the production departments which will be fair and reasonable.

chapter 23

Reporting
Manufacturing
Overhead Costs

Purpose of Chapter

Chapter 22 dealt with two basic methods—*job order* and *process costing*—of determining the unit costs of manufactured product for purposes of financial reporting and management control. Both methods identify the costs of direct materials, direct labor, and manufacturing overhead with distinct *production cost centers* and then assign these costs to units of product. Information on unit costs of products is used in *appraising the performance* of production responsibility centers, as well as in *valuing manufacturing inventories* for purposes of preparing the income and financial position statements.

The present chapter examines in more detail the problems involved in assigning manufacturing overhead costs to units of product. It considers the accounting procedure for assigning overhead costs to products at a *predetermined rate*, and for reporting *variances* between actual overhead and the overhead thus assigned. It also compares the effects on net income of two widely used reporting methods, one which includes and another which excludes *fixed factory overhead* in assigning costs to product units.

Manufacturing Cost Behavior

In most manufacturing enterprises, the *quantities* of direct materials and direct labor used in manufacturing products tend to vary in direct proportion to the number of product units manufactured. Thus, when *materials prices* and *wage rates* are unchanged, direct materials cost and direct labor cost behave as *variable costs*.

Example 1   When 1,000 units of product are produced by Kemmel Co., 2,000 pounds of direct materials and 1,500 direct labor hours are used. When 2,000 units are produced, 4,000 pounds of direct materials and 3,000 hours of direct labor are used. If the materials price is unchanged at $2 per pound and direct labor rates are unchanged at $4 per hour, the volume change causes total direct materials cost to increase from $4,000 to $8,000, and total direct labor cost to increase from $6,000 to $12,000.

The total cost of each factor changes in direct proportion to changes in the quantity of production; that is, both are *variable costs*. The average cost for direct materials is $4 per unit produced, regardless of the total quantity of production. The cost of direct labor is similarly $6 per unit produced.

On the other hand, *Manufacturing overhead costs* often behave differently from the costs of direct materials and direct labor. Manufacturing overhead is a heterogeneous group of costs which includes some fixed and some variable elements. Variable costs include indirect materials and electric power, which tend to vary closely with the number of units produced. Other manufacturing costs, such as rent, property taxes, insurance, and depreciation, are relatively independent of changes in production volume. Manufacturing overhead is thus a *mixed cost* which contains components of both variable and fixed cost.

Example 2   When Kemmel Co. manufactures 1,000 units of product, total manufacturing overhead costs are $24,000; when 2,000 units are produced, total manufacturing overhead costs are $28,000. Since the volume increase of 1,000 units causes a $4,000 increase in total manufacturing overhead, the *variable manufacturing overhead* is calculated to average $4 per unit of product. Fixed manufacturing overhead is calculated to be $20,000, regardless of the number of units produced.

In many manufacturing concerns, manufacturing overhead is *predominantly* a fixed cost and tends to change more in proportion to the passage of time than in proportion to changes in the volume of production. The average overhead cost per unit of product therefore usually fluctuates *inversely* with changes in volume of production. That is, the *fixed* overhead component of manufacturing cost assigned to each unit of product will be relatively *high* in periods of *low* production and *low* in periods of *high* production.

Example 3   The Kemmel Co. manufactured 1,000 units in January and 2,000 in February. What were the total and unit costs by elements for each month?

Solution	Total Costs	Units Produced	Cost Per Unit
January:			
Direct materials...............................	$ 4,000	1,000	$ 4
Direct labor......................................	6,000	1,000	6
Variable mfg. overhead......................	4,000	1,000	4
Fixed mfg. overhcad..........................	20,000	1,000	20
Totals	$34,000	1,000	$34
February:			
Direct materials...............................	$ 8,000	2,000	$ 4
Direct labor......................................	12,000	2,000	6
Variable mfg. overhead......................	8,000	2,000	4
Fixed mfg. overhead..........................	20,000	2,000	10
Totals	$48,000	2,000	$24

The difference between the average total cost per unit in January, $34, and the average total unit cost in February, $24, is due solely to the fact that the same total fixed cost of manufacturing overhead was distributed over fewer units in January. Production was not less efficient in January, since variable costs per unit remained unchanged. It is not reasonable to assume that the product is more valuable to customers in January than in February simply because it has a higher overhead cost per unit. Thus unit cost data are of limited usefulness when manufacturing overhead costs are allocated to units of product without allowing for the fluctuations caused by *seasonal increases and decreases in the volume of production.*

Predetermined Manufacturing Overhead Rate

One way to smooth out the effects of seasonal fluctuations on the average amount of fixed manufacturing overhead per unit of manufactured product is to divide the *total amount of actual overhead cost for the year* by the *number of units produced* during the year. If this procedure is followed, however, total unit costs cannot be calculated until after the end of the accounting period, when total costs and production data are available. This is ordinarily too late to be useful in making operating decisions. More timely information can be obtained by using a *predetermined overhead rate* based on estimates made in advance for overhead costs and production volume for the year.

Example 4   The Kemmel Co. decided to use a predetermined rate to smooth out seasonal fluctuations in unit overhead costs and to provide timely information on total unit production costs. The rate was computed as follows:

$$\frac{\text{Estimated manufacturing overhead for the year, } \$240,000}{\text{Estimated units to be produced during the year, } 80,000}$$

$$= \text{Estimated average overhead per unit, } \$3.$$

The predetermined overhead rate is used in computing the cost of units manufactured during the year and in making journal entries transferring costs from

Manufacturing Overhead Clearing Account to Goods in Process Inventory. The following is an example.

(1)

A, Goods in Process Inventory..............................	3,000	
A, Manufacturing Overhead Clearing Account...		3,000

To record the estimated overhead costs for 1,000 units actually manufactured in January, at a predetermined rate of $3 per unit.

During the month actual overhead costs are accumulated in the clearing account by entries such as the following:

(2)

A, Manufacturing Overhead Clearing Account.........	19,700	
L, Accounts Payable.....................................		15,000
A, Prepaid Expense		1,000
A, Materials and Supplies Inventory.................		3,700

To record actual overhead for January.

After posting these entries the items in the clearing account would be

A, Manufacturing Overhead Clearing Account

1973			*1973*		
Jan.	(Actual overhead)		Jan.	(Overhead transferred	
	(2)	19,700		to Goods in Process at	
				predetermined rate)	
				(1)	3,000
	Balance, 16,700				

Bases for Allocating Predetermined Overhead to Products

In the preceding illustration the business manufactured a single product, and it was feasible to assign manufacturing overhead in equal amounts to each unit of product by using a predetermined overhead application rate. Most manufacturers produce a number of different products, however. There is usually no practical means by which the quantities of different types of product can be totaled and divided into total overhead costs to arrive at an average cost per unit. Some *factor other than units produced* must therefore be used as a basis for overhead apportionment.

The factor selected should be one with which overhead costs show a cause-and-effect relationship. It should also be a factor which can be directly identified with the physical units of product. The most widely used factors for assigning overhead to units of product are:

(1) The number of direct labor hours worked,
(2) The amount of total direct labor cost, or
(3) The number of direct machine hours spent in producing each unit of product.

Example 5   The management of a manufacturing company thought that the job orders produced were responsible for manufacturing overhead approximately in proportion to the number of labor hours worked on each job. The budget estimate for

1973 was as follows:

$$\frac{\text{Estimated manufacturing overhead, \$500,000}}{\text{Estimated direct labor hours, 100,000}}$$
= Manufacturing overhead per direct labor hour, \$5.

During 1973, 12 direct labor hours were worked on Job No. 401, and the job was assigned manufacturing overhead of \$60 (12 hours times the predetermined rate of \$5 per hour).

Overhead allocated to Job No. 402 was \$80, determined by multiplying the 16 actual hours spent on the job by \$5.

When substantial parts of manufacturing overhead are thought to vary in proportion to different factors, more than one basis may be used for assigning parts of the overhead to units of product.

Example 6   The estimated factory overhead of the Moloch Mfg. Co. for 1973 is expected to be \$180,000, composed of the following:

Costs of purchasing, storing, issuing, and accounting for materials...	\$30,000
Costs of the personnel office, the dispensary for employees, hospitalization insurance, vacations, and over-time premiums...	60,000
Depreciation, insurance, repairs, and maintenance of factory machinery	40,000
Other factory overhead costs....................................	50,000

How should these costs be assigned to units of product?

Solution   The following are four of the many different bases that might be used for assigning factory overhead to products manufactured in this situation:

(1) Costs related to materials usage might be assigned to jobs produced on the basis of the cost of materials used on each job.

(2) Costs related to direct labor might be assigned to jobs produced on the basis of the cost of direct labor used on each job.

(3) Costs related to factory machinery might be assigned in proportion to the number of machine hours used on each job.

(4) The remaining overhead costs might be assigned to jobs on some arbitrary basis, such as an equal amount per unit produced (if there is one product) or the number of labor hours spent on each job (if there are several products).

Using *multiple rates* for assigning factory overhead to units of product might produce a more reliable result than using a single basis for allocating all factory overhead to products. It is quite possible, however, that the added reliability of the more refined allocation *may not be worth the cost* of making it. In Example 6 it would be necessary to keep a record of the costs of direct materials and direct labor, as well as the number of labor and machine hours used on each batch of product. While the results might appear to be more accurate, they would still be based on arbitrary assumptions about the relationship of overhead costs to certain factors.

Factory Overhead Variances

When predetermined rates are used for assigning overhead to units of product, it is unusual for the amount of overhead assigned in a given period to be exactly equal to the total amount actually incurred. Differences between the actual overhead and the amount assigned to products by using the predetermined rate are called *underapplied* or *overapplied* overhead.

An *underapplied* overhead appears in the accounting records as a *debit* balance in the Manufacturing Overhead Clearing Account, while an *overapplied* overhead is a *credit* balance in this account.

Under- and overapplied overhead balances at the ends of months during an accounting year may be the result of *seasonal fluctuations* in the rate of production activity. Such variances can be expected to cancel out, and approach zero, by the end of the accounting year.

Example 7 For 1973 Lidell Company estimated a production volume of 40,000 units of product and total factory overhead costs of $240,000, including $80,000 of variable costs and $160,000 of fixed costs. The predetermined rate for assigning overhead to products is $6 per unit—$2 variable and $4 fixed.

Actual overhead costs, and overhead costs assigned to products for each quarter of 1973, were

Time Period	Actual Overhead	Applied Overhead	Under- or (Over-)Applied
Quarter 1	$ 50,000	$ 36,000	$ 14,000
Quarter 2	72,000	96,000	(24,000)
Quarter 3	68,000	84,000	(16,000)
Quarter 4	50,000	24,000	26,000
Total	$240,000	$240,000	0

In Example 7, production was *seasonally low* in Quarters 1 and 4, and large amounts of *underapplied* overhead resulted. In Quarters 2 and 3, however, when production was *seasonally high*, there were large amounts of *overapplied* overhead. By the end of the year the over- and underapplied balances canceled out and the *net overhead variance* for the year was zero.

A word of caution is in order: Overhead variances often result from other than seasonal factors, and in real life the seasonal fluctuations are not usually as perfect as in Example 7.

Other Causes of Overhead Variances

When there is a significantly large net overhead variance that is not the result of seasonal fluctuations, it is ordinarily useful to investigate the causes of the variance so that management may take whatever corrective action is appropriate. The following may be the reasons for the nonseasonal variances:

(1) The number of units actually produced was significantly higher or lower than the number anticipated in setting the predetermined overhead rate. This results in a *volume variance*.

(2) The total amount actually spent for manufacturing overhead costs was more or less than the amount anticipated. This is a *budget variance*, which may be due to changes in spending or in production efficiency.

Example 8   Assume that the Lidell Company in Example 7 produced 30,000 units of product in 1973 and that actual overhead costs were $230,000, including $70,000 variable elements and $160,000 fixed. Overhead applied for 30,000 units at $6 per unit is $180,000. Thus overhead is *underapplied* by $50,000 ($10,000 of underapplied variable overhead and $40,000 of underapplied fixed overhead).

The $40,000 fixed overhead variance in Example 8 occurred because the $160,000 of fixed overhead anticipated in the budget was assigned to only 30,000 units of product, at the rate of $4 a unit, instead of to 40,000 as expected. This *volume variance* shows the amount by which the budgeted fixed overhead costs are over- or underapplied because the *actual volume* of production activity is greater or less than the *planned volume*. The amount of the volume variance may be computed by multiplying the difference between units of actual activity and units of planned activity by the predetermined fixed overhead rate per unit. (In this case, 10,000 fewer units produced multiplied by $4 equals the volume variance of $40,000.)

The $10,000 of underapplied *variable* overhead in Example 8 is a *budget variance*. Such a variance is the combined result of the following factors:

(1) The price paid for units of overhead factors may be greater or less than the *budgeted price*.

(2) The quantity of overhead factors used per unit of finished product may be either greater or less than the *quantity budgeted* per unit.

(3) The *mix* of overhead factors used may have changed so that the average cost of overhead per unit of product is more or less than the amount budgeted.

The *volume variance* includes only under- or overapplied *fixed* overhead, but the *budget variance* can include both *variable* and *fixed* overhead components.

Disposing of Overhead Variances

The existence of substantial amounts of overhead variances indicates that manufacturing operations have not gone according to plan. These variances should be reported to the appropriate responsibility centers for information, and for such corrective action as seems appropriate. In general, the causes of such variances may be faulty planning, faulty operations, or changes in external conditions beyond the control of production management.

Underapplied manufacturing overhead exists as a *debit* balance in the Manufacturing Overhead Clearing Account at the end of the year; *overapplied* overhead is a *credit* balance. These balances must be reported in the financial statements. The proper reporting of overhead variances depends on the *cause* of the variance.

If the cause of the variance is grossly *inefficient operating performance*, the variance should be treated as a *loss* in the income statement of the year in which the inefficiency occurred. It would be improper to assign it to the asset inventory. To do so would imply that the greater the inefficiency of production, the more valuable is the product.

In most cases it is appropriate to assign the amount of the over- or under-applied overhead to the *units produced* during the period. If *all, or most, of the units produced in the period have been sold*, it is appropriate to transfer the balance of the Overhead Clearing Account to Cost of Goods Sold Expense. If a significant number of units produced during the period have not been sold, the overhead variance should be apportioned between inventories and cost of goods sold.

To illustrate the allocation method, assume that there is a debit balance of $10,000 in the Manufacturing Overhead Clearing Account at the end of 1973. Of the year's production, 70 per cent has been sold, 20 per cent is in Finished Goods Inventory at the end of the year, and 10 per cent is in year-end Goods in Process Inventory. The following entry shows how this variance might be allocated:

1973

Dec. 31	OE, Cost of Goods Sold Expense	7,000	
	A, Finished Goods Inventory.................	2,000	
	A, Goods in Process Inventory...............	1,000	
	A, Manufacturing Overhead Clearing Account		10,000

To allocate the manufacturing overhead variance in proportion to the year's production reflected in each account.

INCOME MEASUREMENT UNDER DIRECT COSTING

Chapter 22 and the earlier part of this chapter dealt with methods of accounting for production costs under *full costing* (also called *absorption costing*). Under full costing, all elements of manufacturing costs—direct materials, direct labor, and both variable and fixed manufacturing overhead—are added to the asset, "inventory," as *product costs*.

Effects of Full Costing Illustrated

In measuring the income of a business, *product costs* are deemed to *expire* and are charged to expense in the period in which the products are *sold* rather than when they are manufactured. If the number of units produced is greater than the number of units sold in a given accounting period, the costs assigned to the unsold units are carried forward in inventory to future periods. If the number of units sold exceeds the number of units produced in a later period, the cost of goods sold expense will be greater than the production costs of that period.

Example 9   In 1973 the Beige Company manufactured 10,000 units of product at an average cost of $200 per unit and sold only 5,000 units. In 1974 production volume again was 10,000 units, while sales increased to 15,000 units. What was the cost of goods sold expense in 1974?

Solution   Cost of goods sold expense in 1974 was as follows:

Production costs of 5,000 units brought forward from 1973...	$1,000,000
+ Production costs of 10,000 units manufactured in 1974	2,000,000
Total cost of goods sold in 1974.........................	$3,000,000

Fixed manufacturing overhead is often a large part of total production costs. Since *fixed cost tends not to change in total* with changes in production volume, the amount of fixed costs assigned to each unit of product is greater when production volume is low than when it is high. The total unit cost of production is correspondingly greater.

The fluctuations in unit costs caused by changes in production volume can have misleading results. For example, high unit production costs of goods produced in periods of slack activity may be carried forward and charged to cost of goods sold expense in later periods when the average unit costs of production are lower. This is especially true under the FIFO and weighted-average methods of computing inventory.

Another cause of misleading results in the income statement is a change of volume of production in an opposite direction from a change in operating efficiency. *Decreases in volume* of production may thus cause *fixed manufacturing costs per unit to increase* more than the reductions in unit variable manufacturing costs which result from greater efficiency. Conversely, *increased production volume* may cause *unit fixed costs to decline* more than unit variable costs increase as a result of decreased operating efficiency.

Opposite changes of volume of production and production efficiency may lead to the confusing phenomenon of the *net income of a period being higher than that of the preceding period, while production efficiency and the volume of sales are lower.* Example 10 shows how this can happen.

Example 10

	1974	1973
Units sold...	900	1,000
Unit selling price..	$ 600	$ 600
Units manufactured.....................................	1,500	1,000
Fixed manufacturing overhead.......................	$240,000	$240,000
Fixed overhead per unit................................	$ 160	$ 240
Variable manufacturing costs per unit..............	$ 210	$ 170

Compute the gross margin for each year.

Solution

	1974		1973	
Unit selling price..............................		$600		$600
Unit manufacturing cost:				
Variable.......................................	$210		$170	
Fixed...	160	370	240	410
Unit gross margin..............................		230		190
Total gross margin for:				
900 units sold..............................		$207,000		
1,000 units sold..............................				$190,000

In Example 10 *operating efficiency* decreased from 1973 to 1974, as shown by the increase in unit variable manufacturing costs from $170 to $210. This decrease in efficiency was obscured in the gross margin per unit, which *increased* from $190 in 1973 to $230 in 1974. The increase in unit gross margin occurred because the increase in volume produced caused unit fixed manufacturing costs to decline by $80.

Total gross margin in the example rose from $190,000 to $207,000, even though sales volume declined by 100 units. The decrease in unit fixed manufacturing costs which resulted from spreading fixed costs over more units produced *more than offset* the effects of lower efficiency and lower sales volume.

Opposite changes in these factors can cause net income to decline even though efficiency and sales volume improve.

Direct Costing Defined

The preceding section showed that under *full costing*, where fixed manufacturing overhead is treated as a product cost, the reported net income of a business may fluctuate between periods because of differences in production volume, and that this fluctuation may have misleading effects on net income. To cope with this problem, many accountants advocate using the *direct costing* method of measuring income.

Direct costing is a procedure by which only *variable manufacturing costs*—direct materials, direct labor, and variable factory overhead—are treated as *product costs*, and *fixed manufacturing costs* are treated as *expenses of the period* in which they are incurred. Under direct costing, fixed factory overhead is not assigned to product units. Thus no fixed factory overhead is carried forward from one period to another in inventories.

Example 11   The Beige Company in Example 9 had fixed manufacturing costs of $1,000,000 per year in 1973 and 1974, and variable manufacturing costs were $100 per unit. What would the cost of goods sold expense be in 1974 under direct costing?

Solution   Under *direct costing* the 1974 cost of goods sold expense would include

1973 variable production costs of $100 a unit for the 5,000 units brought forward in finished goods inventory......	$ 500,000
1974 variable production costs of $100 a unit for the 10,000 units produced in 1974	1,000,000
Total..	$1,500,000

This is in contrast to total cost of goods sold under full costing, which was $3,000,000.

The term "direct costs" usually refers to those elements of cost that can be traced clearly to specific product units or to a specific segment of operations. Some fixed costs are directly traceable to specific productive departments, and are therefore *direct* costs in this sense. It would thus be more accurate to use the term "variable costing" to describe the accounting method whereby fixed manufacturing overhead is excluded from unit product costs, and only variable manufacturing overhead is included.

Income Effects of Direct Costing Illustrated

Income computed under the direct costing method differs from income computed under full costing only by the amount of *fixed factory overhead* that is *included in the increases or decreases in manufacturing inventories* during the period. Fixed selling and administrative costs are treated as period costs under both methods, and are deducted from income as incurred.

Example 12
The Chartreuse Company manufactured 10,000 units each in 1973, 1974, and 1975. The fixed manufacturing overhead for each year was $50,000, or $5 per unit. Units sold were as follows:

1973.........8,000   1974.........12,000   1975.........10,000

How much would income for the three years differ under the direct costing and full costing methods?

Solution
In 1973 there were 2,000 *more units produced* than sold; therefore fixed overhead was added to finished goods inventory at the rate of $5 a unit under the full costing method. *Full costing* will show a $10,000 *higher profit* than direct costing (2,000 units × $5 fixed overhead per unit).

In 1974 there were 2,000 *fewer units produced* than sold. Fixed overhead was subtracted from finished goods inventory at the rate of $5 a unit under full costing. *Full costing* will therefore show a $10,000 *lower profit* than direct costing.

In 1975 the inventory remained unchanged because *production and sales were equal*. Full costing and direct costing will therefore present the same net income.

Under direct costing increases and decreases in production volume alone do not cause fluctuations in the unit cost of production, and do not obscure trends in sales volume or in the effectiveness with which cost factors are used.

Illustrations 23-1 and 23-2 compare the effects of the full costing and direct costing methods on the income of Cavendish Manufacturing Company for 1973 and 1974.

In Illustration 23-1 the sales price per unit was $500 in both years. Direct materials cost per unit was $60 in both years, and variable factory overhead remained unchanged at $40. The *direct labor* per unit decreased from $120 to $110, reflecting an *increase in efficiency*. Fixed factory overhead increased from $160 to $240 per unit produced because of the decline in production volume from 1,500 units to 1,000 units. Under *full costing, income* before income tax *declined* from $40,000 in 1973 to $5,000 in 1974, in spite of an increase of 200 in the number of units sold and a decrease of $10 in the unit cost of direct labor.

Illustration 23-2 shows the same facts for the Cavendish Manufacturing Company under the *direct costing* method. Under this method *income increased* $53,000 from 1973 to 1974 (from a loss before tax of $40,000 to an income before tax of $13,000). One would expect an increase in sales volume and an improvement in production efficiency to result in a higher income.

The direct costing income statements emphasize the *manufacturing margin* (revenues minus variable production costs) and the *total contribution* (the excess of revenue over all variable costs). From this contribution are deducted the *period costs: fixed* production costs and *fixed* distribution costs.

The differences between income reported under full costing and direct costing may be explained as follows:

(1) Income under full costing was $80,000 *more* than under direct costing for 1973 (the difference between a loss of $40,000 and an income of $40,000).

Illustration
23-1

CAVENDISH MANUFACTURING COMPANY
Income Statement (Full Costing)
For the Years Ended December 31

	1974		1973	
	(1,000 Units Produced; 1,200 Units Sold)		*(1,500 Units Produced; 1,000 Units Sold)*	
Sales...		$600,000		$500,000
Deduct cost of goods sold expense:				
Production cost incurred:				
Direct materials...........................	$ 60,000		$ 90,000	
Direct labor..............................	110,000		180,000	
Factory overhead:				
Variable..............................	40,000		60,000	
Fixed..................................	240,000		240,000	
Total................................	450,000		570,000	
Add beginning finished goods inventory	190,000		0	
Cost of goods available for sale	640,000		570,000	
Deduct ending finished goods inventory	135,000		190,000	
Cost of goods sold expense...............		505,000		380,000
Gross margin......................................		95,000		120,000
Deduct distribution costs:				
Variable.....................................	60,000		50,000	
Fixed..	30,000	90,000	30,000	80,000
Income before income tax		5,000		40,000

In this year 500 more units were produced than were sold, and therefore *fixed factory overhead* of $80,000 was *added* to inventory of finished goods in 1973 (500 units times $160 fixed overhead per unit). Fixed overhead added to inventory under full costing therefore explains the difference in income reported under the two methods.

(2) Income under full costing was $8,000 *less* than under direct costing for 1974 (the difference between an income of $13,000 and an income of $5,000). In 1974 there were 200 more units sold than produced; therefore *fixed factory overhead* of $8,000 was *subtracted* from inventory of finished goods in 1974. This was computed as follows:

Overhead at $160 per unit included in 500 units made in 1973 and sold in 1974	$80,000
Less overhead at $240 per unit for 300 units made in 1974 and included in 1974 ending inventory..............	72,000
Decrease in factory overhead included in inventory........	$ 8,000

(3) Income for 1973 and 1974 combined, a loss of $27,000, is $72,000 less under direct costing than net income under full costing, a total of $45,000. This is exactly equal to the amount of fixed manufacturing overhead that the full costing method assigns to the inventory increase during the two years.

Illustration
23-2

CAVENDISH MANUFACTURING COMPANY
Income Statement (Direct Costing)
For the Years Ended December 31

	1974		1973	
	(1,000 Units *1,200 Units Sold)*		*(1,500 Units* *1,000 Units Sold)*	
Sales		$600,000		$500,000
Deduct direct cost of goods sold:				
Production costs incurred:				
Direct materials.......................	$ 60,000		$ 90,000	
Direct labor............................	110,000		180,000	
Variable factory overhead.........	40,000		60,000	
Total..........................	210,000		330,000	
Add beginning finished goods inventory	110,000		0	
Cost of goods available for sale	320,000		330,000	
Deduct ending finished goods inventory	63,000		110,000	
Cost of goods sold expense..............		257,000		220,000
Manufacturing margin.........................		343,000		280,000
Deduct variable distribution costs.........		60,000		50,000
Contribution to fixed expenses and income		283,000		230,000
Deduct period costs:				
Fixed production costs....................	240,000		240,000	
Fixed distribution costs..................	30,000	270,000	30,000	270,000
Income (loss) before income tax................		13,000		(40,000)

The computation is

Fixed overhead in inventory at end of 1974..................	$72,000
Deduct fixed overhead in inventory at beginning of 1973	0
Increase during 1973 and 1974................................	$72,000

In summary, general rules for comparing the income effects of direct costing and full costing are

(1) Fixed production costs are *not added to inventory* under direct costing but are treated as *expenses of the period* in which they are incurred.

(2) When *more* units are *produced than sold* during a period, *full costing will give a higher income.* This is true because there is an increase in the fixed manufacturing overhead component of inventory.

(3) When *more* units are *sold than produced* during a period, *direct costing will give a higher income* because there is a decrease in the fixed manufacturing overhead included in inventory.

Management Uses of Direct Costing

The main issue in direct costing is whether fixed manufacturing overhead should be assigned to products or treated as a period cost. How fixed costs are treated in inventories is not relevant in controlling the activities of individual manufacturing cost centers, but it is important in planning and evaluating the performance of the firm as a whole. From the viewpoint of the firm as a whole direct costing has the following advantages:

(1) It distinguishes between those elements of cost which are directly related to the entity's *operating activities* (variable costs) and those which are related to the entity's *capacity to produce and sell products* (fixed costs).

(2) It emphasizes the *contribution* to fixed overhead and income as a means of measuring the entity's operating efficiency and its effectiveness in using productive capacity.

(3) It *facilitates planning and control decisions* in that the reported periodic net income tends to change in the same direction as sales, and is not affected by changes in the amount of fixed production costs included in inventory when production volume and inventory levels change.

To apply direct costing, total costs must be carefully separated between *variable costs* (relating to *operating activities*) and *fixed costs* (relating to *capacity*). Mixed costs must be split into their variable and fixed components. Direct-costing analysis may then be expressed graphically, as in Illustration 23-3. The graph shows interrelationships of cost, sales price, volume, and income, assuming that the behavior of all costs are related to sales revenue in a linear (straight-line) fashion over the *relevant range* of sales volume (the range in which the actual volume of activity is likely to fall).

Direct-costing analysis can help managers answer such questions as

(1) How many more units must be sold to offset a selling price reduction of a given amount?

(2) How much must unit selling prices be increased to neutralize the effect of a given wage increase on profits?

(3) Should management accept a given order at a selling price below the full cost per unit?

In Illustration 23-3 the "income path" line crosses the vertical axis at minus $270,000 (point *A*). This indicates that at zero volume of sales there would be a loss of $270,000, equal to the total fixed costs.

Point *B* shows that there is a loss of $40,000 when sales are $500,000.

Point *C* shows that when sales are $600,000 net income is $13,000.

Point *D* denotes the break-even sales volume.

Dividing the total fixed cost of $270,000 by the *contribution percentage* of 46 per cent indicates that the break-even sales volume is approximately $587,000. The contribution percentage shows that 46 cents out of each dollar is available to cover fixed expenses and income. It is determined by subtracting the percentage of variable expenses to sales from 100 per cent (100 per cent — 44 per cent variable cost of goods sold — 10 per cent variable distribution costs).

Although direct costing has some distinct advantages for managerial decision making, it is not acceptable for external financial reporting or for income tax purposes. From the standpoint of the general accounting system, a desirable compromise is one under which

**Illustration
23-3**

Cavendish Manufacturing Company Income Graph for the Year Ended December 31, 1973.

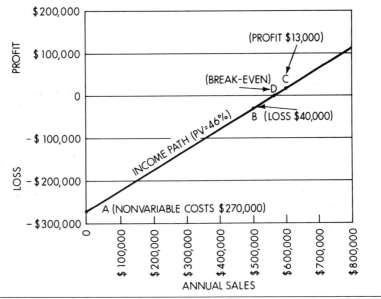

(1) *Direct-costing* statements are prepared for *internal use* for monthly or other short reporting periods.

(2) The year-end financial statements prepared for *outsiders* are adjusted to a *full-costing* basis by assigning an appropriate share of fixed factory overhead to inventory.

Summary   Production costs include *variable costs,* which tend to change in direct proportion to changes in production volume, and *fixed costs,* which tend to be incurred in proportion to the passage of time, regardless of volume changes. Fixed production costs cause the product's total unit cost to be higher in periods of slack activity and lower when production is high.

Predetermined overhead rates are used in assigning factory overhead costs to products so as to provide more timely information and to smooth seasonal fluctuations in the amount of fixed cost assigned to each product unit. Direct labor hours, direct labor cost, or direct machine hours are the usual bases on which predetermined overhead rates are applied to units of product.

Factory overhead variances—overapplied and underapplied overhead—usually occur when factory overhead is assigned to products by a predetermined rate. A *volume variance* results when actual production is more or less than the planned volume. A *budget variance* occurs when the amount spent for variable or fixed overhead items is greater or less than the amount budgeted. Overhead variances are reported to the appropriate responsibility centers for attention and appropriate action. They are then disposed of in the accounting records at the end of the period by assigning them to product costs or to losses, depending on the cause of the variance.

Under the *full costing* method, both variable and fixed factory overhead costs are included in unit product costs. *Direct*—or variable—*costing* treats *fixed manufacturing costs as an expense* of the period in which they are incurred, and assigns only variable manufacturing costs to units of product.

Direct costing distinguishes between those costs directly involved in operating activities (*variable costs*) and those costs related to *capacity to produce and sell* (*fixed costs*). Direct costing reports aid the evaluation of performance by emphasizing the *contribution* of the operating segment being reported on to fixed costs and income. Under direct costing, periodic net income is not affected by changes in the amount of fixed manufacturing overhead included in inventory.

Discussion Questions and Problems

23-1   The management of the Montagne Mfg. Co. is preparing an operating budget for 1973. In the past the company has operated on a single shift, but because of the increased demand for the product it appears that it will be necessary to work two eight-hour shifts for a part of 1973. The company has available a cost analysis separating manufacturing costs into fixed and variable components for 1973.

Give an example of a manufacturing cost that (a) is fixed and will remain fixed under two shifts, (b) is variable and will remain variable under two shifts, and (c) will behave differently under two shifts than it did under one.

23-2   Give an example of a "step" cost of manufacturing. What problems do such costs create in using predetermined manufacturing overhead rates? What solution would you suggest?

23-3   List three types of manufacturing costs that decrease per unit as the volume of production increases. How should these costs be handled when the volume of production activity is subject to large seasonal fluctuations?

23-4

a. What is the purpose of the Manufacturing Overhead Clearing Account?
b. What type of account is it? Explain fully.

23-5

a. What is meant by a manufacturing overhead variance?
b. What is meant by a manufacturing overhead volume variance?
c. How might a volume variance originate?
d. How would you recommend that it be disposed of in the accounting records at the end of a monthly reporting period? At the end of an annual accounting period? Explain.

23-6

a. What is meant by a manufacturing overhead spending variance?
b. How does such a variance originate?
c. Give an example of an overhead spending variance. Who is responsible for its incurrence? What disposition would you recommend for it at the end of the annual accounting period? Why?

23-7   Under what circumstances should each of the following bases be used for allocating manufacturing overhead to jobs in a factory which makes machines to the specifications of customers?

(1) Direct material cost
(2) Direct labor hours
(3) Direct labor cost

(4) Machine hours
(5) A combination of two or more of the above

23-8   Listed below are several overhead costs commonly incurred by manufacturing companies. You are to list appropriate bases for assigning these costs to production.

a. Costs of ordering, receiving, storing, and issuing materials.
b. Costs of cafeteria, health service, and personnel counseling.
c. Costs of electrical power generated by company plant.
d. Costs of general administrative functions of top management.

23-9   Define "full costing" and "direct costing." Explain briefly how reported income differs under these two methods.

23-10   "Fluctuations in unit costs caused by changes in production volume can have misleading results." Illustrate how this can happen.

23-11   Tonague Company uses a *predetermined overhead rate* to assign manufacturing overhead costs to products. Estimated production volume for 1973 is 18,000 units. Total manufacturing overhead costs for the year are expected to be $420,000, including $240,000 of variable costs.

Required   a. What is the predetermined overhead rate?
b. How much overhead costs will be assigned to products if 22,000 units are manufactured?
c. How would you treat the over- or underapplied overhead?
d. How would your answer to part c differ if there were no fixed manufacturing overhead costs?

23-12   Peak Mfg. Company, which has sharp seasonal swings in its production volume, uses a predetermined manufacturing overhead rate established at the beginning of each year. The budget for 1973 showed expected production of 60,000 units and expected manufacturing overhead costs of $420,000, of which $150,000 was nonvariable.

During January 1973 the company produced 9,000 units. The estimate of total units to be produced during the year was unchanged. Total actual overhead cost incurred in January was $54,300.

Required   a. Journalize the entry to transfer overhead costs to Goods in Process at the predetermined rate.
b. Analyze the overhead variance into its components.
c. What disposition of the variance would you recommend? Why?

23-13   Marzo Mfg. Co.'s monthly budget includes $24,000 for fixed manufacturing overhead costs and $3 per unit of product for variable manufacturing overhead. Fixed manufacturing overhead costs are applied to products at a predetermined rate of $2 per unit, based on an expected annual volume of 144,000 units. In July 15,000 units of product were manufactured. Actual manufacturing overhead costs totaled $72,500, of which $70,000 was for variable elements.

Required   a. Journalize the entries to record the actual overhead costs and to transfer overhead costs to Goods in Process at a single predetermined rate.
b. Compute the amount of the overhead variance that is due to (1) volume variance,

(2) budget variance for variable overhead elements, and (3) budget variance for fixed overhead elements.

23-14   Late in December 1972 the controller established the rate for assigning manufacturing overhead to production for 1973. He estimated that total manufacturing overhead would be $700,000, and that 350,000 direct labor hours would be worked.

The report of actual manufacturing overhead incurred in 1973 in comparison with the budgeted figures, as reported on January 8, 1973, was as follows:

	Budgeted	Actual
Supervision...	$ 50,000	$ 52,000
Vacation pay..	40,000	44,000
Overtime premium.......................................	33,000	30,000
Heat and light..	37,000	34,500
Building rent..	127,000	127,000
Property taxes..	45,000	48,100
Insurance on equipment and materials.............	20,000	21,000
Depreciation on machinery............................	160,000	170,000
Personnel office expense...............................	80,000	84,000
Factory cost accounting expense......................	50,000	48,000
Building and machinery maintenance...............	58,000	47,000
Totals...	$700,000	$705,600

Records showed that the actual number of direct labor hours worked in 1973 was 275,000.

Required   a. Compute the total manufacturing overhead variance for 1973.

b. Prepare a report analyzing the variance into its causes, giving as much detail as possible.

c. What action do you think management should take as a result of the variance? Why?

d. What accounting disposition do you think should be made of the variance? Why?

23-15   The Vanzant Mfg. Co. uses a job order system for assigning manufacturing costs to individual units of product. It has decided to change from a system of allocating actual factory overhead costs to jobs at the end of each month to a predetermined system of allocating overhead. Most of the factory overhead varies with the passage of time rather than with the volume of production. At the beginning of 1973 estimated production costs for 1973 are

Direct materials..	$600,000
Direct labor...	800,000
Factory overhead..	500,000

The jobs manufactured vary considerably in their relative requirements for direct materials and direct labor.

During January 1973 direct materials actually used were $33,000 and direct labor was $40,000. Actual factory overhead for the month, computed during the first week of February when all January bills had been received, amounted to $42,000. The production volume for 1973 is still expected to equal the budgeted figure.

Required   a. What basis would you recommend for assigning predetermined overhead to jobs produced during the year? Why?

b. Compute the predetermined overhead rate.

c. Record in journal form the assignment of factory overhead to Job No. 101, which was begun on January 5 and completed on January 14 with a direct labor cost of $4,000 and a direct materials cost of $3,000.

d. Make summary journal entries for the total January manufacturing costs.

e. Prepare an analysis to explain the balance in the Factory Overhead Clearing Account at the end of January. What disposition would you make of the balance?

23-16   The Sisco Company manufactured 4,000 units of product each year in 1973, 1974, and 1975. Manufacturing costs each year were $6 per unit for all variable components and $40,000, or $10 per unit, for fixed overhead. Units sold were 2,000 in 1973, 4,000 in 1974, and 6,000 in 1975.

Required

a. How much does income differ for each of the three years and in total under the direct costing and full costing methods?

b. By what dollar value did manufacturing inventories change each year and in total under the direct costing and the full costing methods?

23-17   The Anton Mfg. Co. assigns actual manufacturing overhead costs to products. Manufacturing overhead costs for production of 10,000 units are $80,000, including $50,000 of fixed manufacturing overhead.

Required

a. Compute and compare the cost of goods sold expense for 1973 under both direct and absorption costing if 10,000 units of product were manufactured and sold.

b. Assume that 10,000 units were manufactured and 8,000 units were sold, and repeat the requirements of part a.

c. Assume that 8,000 units were manufactured and 10,000 units were sold, and repeat the requirements of part a.

d. Would the results in part a, b, or c be different if the company used a predetermined rate for assigning manufacturing overhead costs to products? Explain.

23-18   The Nontab Mfg. Co. uses a predetermined overhead rate to assign manufacturing overhead costs to products. This rate is based on a normal production volume of 20,000 units per year, fixed manufacturing overhead costs of $80,000 a year, and variable manufacturing overhead costs of $2 per unit of product.

Required

a. Compute and compare the cost of goods sold expense for 1973 under both direct and absorption costing if 20,000 units of product were manufactured and 16,000 units were sold.

b. Assume that 16,000 units were manufactured and 20,000 units were sold and repeat the requirements of part a.

c. Assume that 22,000 units were manufactured and 18,000 units were sold and repeat the requirements of part a.

d. Write a brief explanation of why the cost of goods sold expense differs under direct and absorption costing.

23-19   Mathis Mfg. Co. uses a full costing system based on actual historical costs in accounting for product inventories. The company reported operating results as follows:

	1974	1973
Units sold	2,000	1,800
Sales revenue	$600,000	$540,000
Cost of goods sold	282,000	253,800
Gross margin	$318,000	$286,200

Production volume in 1974 was 2,000 units of product, down from 2,600 units in 1973. Fixed manufacturing overhead costs were $182,000 in each year.

Required

a. Analyze the reported results for changes in production efficiency and the effectiveness with which unit costs were controlled.

b. Reconstruct the reported results on a direct costing basis and point out how the revised statement might be more useful in revealing underlying trends.

23-20   Aimes Fabricating Corp. manufactures and sells a single product. Manufacturing costs are budgeted at $8 per unit for direct materials, direct labor, and variable overhead combined, plus $40,000 for fixed overhead. Selling and administrative costs are budgeted at $20,000 plus 30 per cent of sales revenues at a selling price of $40 per unit. Accordingly, the company would normally require $120,000 in sales revenue (sales of 3,000 units) in order to break even, and $140,000 in sales revenue (sales of 3,500 units) in order to realize income of $10,000. However, in its 1973 financial statement Aimes Fabricating Corp. reported income of $10,000 on sales revenue of only $120,000, having sold 3,000 units at the budgeted price of $40 per unit. Four thousand units of product were manufactured, and actual costs behaved exactly according to the budget.

Required

a. Construct Aimes Fabricating Corp.'s 1973 income statement on a *full costing* basis.

b. Reconstruct Aimes Fabricating Corp.'s income statement on a *direct costing* basis.

c. Analyze the results reported in the 1973 income statement and explain why the company reported a $10,000 income rather than a break-even situation.

23-21   The Varicot Company's income graph for the year ended December 31, 1973, appears below:

Illustration 23-21

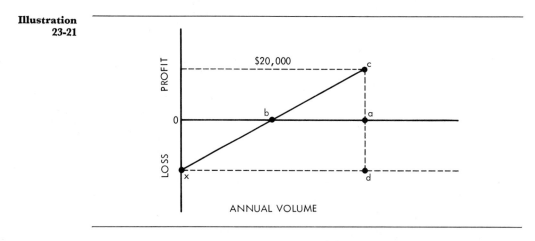

This graph is based on $40,000 a year in budgeted fixed costs, $8 per unit in variable costs, and a selling price of $20 per unit. Income in 1973 was $40,000.

Required   For each of the listed elements, name the concept and compute its amount.

a. *oa*   e. *ba*   h. *cd/xd*

b. *ox*   f. *cd*   i. *ac/ba*

c. *ac*   g. *ac/oa*   j. *ox/ob*

d. *ob*

Cases   **23-1**   **Ryle Company Power Plant.** Ryle Company, a medium-sized manufacturer, maintains its own power plant to serve its three production departments, *A*, *B*, and *C*. It has been assigning actual power costs to the departments at the end of each month in proportion to the number of kilowatt hours used by each during the month.

In April 1973 Mr. Walker, manager of Production Department *A*, has called upon the company's controller to explain why, although his department used fewer kilowatt-hours in April than in March, it has been charged a larger amount for power cost for April. During the course of the discussion the following information is examined:

	Total	Department A	Department B	Department C
March results:				
Kilowatt-hours used.....	250,000	100,000	30,000	120,000
Per cent of total hours...	100%	40%	12%	48%
Power cost assigned......	$8,000	$3,200	$ 960	$3,840
April results:				
Kilowatt-hours used.....	150,000	75,000	45,000	30,000
Per cent of total hours...	100%	50%	30%	20%
Power cost assigned......	$7,040	$3,520	$2,112	$1,408

Mr. Barnum, the controller, points out that the power department has a large amount of fixed costs which continue regardless of the level of output. "All power costs must be charged to some department," he says. "We have to have enough capacity to serve your peak requirements, and that costs each department something. Your department used a greater share of the output of the power plant for April than for March, and therefore it must bear a higher amount of power costs."

"It just doesn't make sense to me," replies Mr. Walker, "that we have to pay more for using less. We ought to be charged at a flat rate of so much per kilowatt-hour every month."

Required   a. Is there any merit in Mr. Walker's point of view? Explain.
b. Estimate the amount of the power department costs which are fixed.
c. Outline a system which can be used to measure the efficiency of the power department, and at the same time to charge the production departments fairly for the use of power.

23-2   **Dunrite Machining Co.** The Dunrite Machining Co. is expanding operations and plans to use a job order cost accounting system with a predetermined rate for assigning factory overhead costs to individual jobs. Estimated activity and factory overhead costs for 1973 are as follows:

Direct labor time	200,000 hours
Direct machine time	800,000 hours
Direct materials used...	50,000 tons
Factory overhead costs:	
Indirect labor.................................... $180,000	
Overtime premium............................ 60,000	
Indirect materials.............................. 150,000	
Supervision....................................... 72,000	
Depreciation 300,000	
Rent 120,000	
Property taxes................................... 48,000	
Insurance... 60,000	
Utilities... 96,000	
Total.......................................	$1,086,000

Approximately 20 jobs are in process at any given time and about 200 jobs are completed each year. The proportion of labor time of highly paid hourly workers to all workers is about the same for all jobs. In the past indirect labor and overtime premium have varied closely with direct labor costs, and indirect materials and utilities have varied with machine time. Direct labor rates are expected to average $4 per hour. All other costs have tended to be constant over time.

The month of lowest activity usually accounts for about 6 per cent of the year's production, whereas the peak month accounts for about 20 per cent.

Required a. Describe three possible ways in which the Dunrite Machining Company might use predetermined rates for assigning overhead costs to jobs.

b. If a single predetermined overhead rate is used, what should it be? Why?

c. Using a single predetermined rate, prepare T-accounts to illustrate debits and credits to the overhead clearing account in the months of lowest and highest activity.

d. What rates would you recommend if dual rates are used? Why?

e. Using dual rates, prepare new T-accounts to illustrate debits and credits to the overhead clearing account in the months of lowest and highest activity.

f. What other factor(s) should be considered in deciding what rate to use?

23-3   Lowhring Corp. The Lowhring Corp., which uses a process cost accounting system, manufactures a single product which sells for $140 a unit. The company began business on January 1, 1973, and experienced a dramatic upsurge in sales in 1974. However, management has been highly disappointed with the profit performance. Although sales zoomed from $1,120,000 in 1973 to $1,680,000 in 1974, net income plunged from $30,000 the first year to a loss of $30,000 the second year. The results were reported as follows:

	1973	*1974*
Revenues..	$1,120,000	$1,680,000
Expenses:		
Prime costs...	$ 400,000	$ 600,000
Variable mfg. overhead	160,000	240,000
Fixed mfg. overhead..............................	300,000	600,000
Selling expense	180,000	220,000
Administrative expense..........................	50,000	50,000
Total expenses	$1,090,000	$1,710,000
Net income (loss)	$ 30,000	($ 30,000)

The reported results were especially confusing to Lowhring Corp.'s president because his earlier computations had indicated that the company would break even with sales of 10,000 units and $1,400,000 in revenues.

Required a. Analyze Lowhring Corp.'s reported results for 1973 and 1974 and explain the decline in net income. Support your analysis and explanation with computations.

b. Describe the accounting procedures followed in making the corporation's income statements.

c. Evaluate the results of Lowhring Corp.'s process cost accounting system in the light of the major objectives of managerial accounting.

23-4   Tailored Products, Inc. Tailored Products, Inc., manufactured two products: the "Standard," which sold for $20 a unit, and the "DeLuxe," which sold for $40 a unit. The Standard model required much less expensive material than the

DeLuxe model, but considerably more hand and machine work. Selling costs were much greater per dollar of sales for the DeLuxe model because of its higher unit price. The company allocated fixed manufacturing overhead to the two classes of products in proportion to the direct labor cost of each. It allocated fixed administrative expense more heavily to the Standard model (in proportion to sales price) than to the DeLuxe model because of the greater time spent on the former. The ratio used allocated twice as much fixed administrative overhead to the Standard model per dollar of sales as to the DeLuxe model.

In 1973 total sales of each model were $800,000. The manufacturing plant operated at capacity, and Tailored Products earned a net income of $260,000 before income tax. The chief accountant prepared the following analysis of results in terms of a unit of each class of product:

	Standard			DeLuxe	
Selling price per unit...........		$20	100%	$40	100.0%
Cost of manufacturing..........	$12		60%	$22	55.0%
Cost of selling and administration..................	5		25%	11	27.5%
Total costs		17	85%	33	82.5%
Income before income tax...		$ 3	15%	$ 7	17.5%

Contribution to 1973 income
Standard model........................... 40,000 units @ $3 = $120,000
DeLuxe model............................ 20,000 units @ $7 = 140,000
    Total... $260,000

Observing that the profit margin on the DeLuxe model was 17.5 per cent as compared with 15 per cent for the Standard model, management decided to assign three-fourths of its 1974 sales budget to the DeLuxe model and only one-fourth to the Standard model. This it could easily do because of a large potential demand for the DeLuxe model. Budgeted profits for 1974 were

Standard model............................. 20,000 units @ $3 = $ 60,000
DeLuxe model.............................. 30,000 units @ $7 = 210,000
    Total.. $270,000

Sales for 1974 were as budgeted by the management of Tailored Products, Inc., but the actual income before tax was bitterly disappointing. It was only $180,000, $80,000 less than 1973 in spite of the fact that the company was concentrating more of its sales on its more profitable product.

A business consultant who was called in to help explain the results made the following analysis of cost behavior:

	Standard	DeLuxe
	(Per Unit)	
Variable costs:		
Material..	$ 3.00	$18.00
Direct labor	4.80	2.40
Selling costs..	2.20	7.60
Totals	$10.00	$28.00
Fixed costs:	(Totals)	
Manufacturing overhead................................	$200,000	
Administrative expense....................................	180,000	

The chief accountant had allocated manufacturing overhead to the two classes of products in proportion to their direct labor costs in 1973. In the same year, two-thirds of administrative cost was assigned to the Standard model and one-third to the DeLuxe.

Required
a. Prepare income statements for 1973 and 1974 for each class of product and for their total, using the company's procedures.
b. Prepare income statements for 1973 and 1974 as the consultant might have prepared them, emphasizing the cost behavior.
c. Why were profits lower in 1974?
d. What changes in the company's accounting methods would you recommend?

chapter 24

Standard Costing for
Production Control

Purpose of Chapter

The two preceding chapters dealt with methods of analyzing and reporting *historical costs* of manufacturing operations. Attention was focused on *responsibility centers* for which costs are accumulated and reported. Information on actual unit costs was emphasized as a useful means of gauging the performance of each responsibility center.

This chapter is concerned with the use of *standard costs* as goals of the production process and as benchmarks for evaluating performance.

Standard Costs Defined

Standard costs are scientifically determined benchmarks which are used in planning and controlling manufacturing operations. In *planning* activities for each period, management must make clear the nature of each task to be performed and give attention to how its performance will be measured. Standard costs make specific the cost objectives of each task. When compared with actual costs, they provide measures of operating effectiveness.

When operating effectiveness is improved, standard costs may exceed actual costs. When actual costs exceed standard costs, a less than desirable level of operating effectiveness is signaled. The differences between actual costs and standard costs are called *variances*. An analysis of significant *unfavorable variances* (which show that operating effectiveness is less than desired) should lead to an investigation into possible ways to eliminate unnecessary and excessive costs. An analysis of significant *favorable variances* (which indicate that operating effectiveness is better than planned) may disclose sources of cost savings that can be made permanent and extended into other areas of activity.

Bases of Setting Cost Standards

Standard costing is an essential part of budgeting. The *flexible budget* expresses a firm's cost and revenue objectives for a particular period. These objectives include the results expected of each production cost center, stated in terms of standard costs.

The starting point of a standard cost system is a scientific study of the amount of direct materials, direct labor, and manufacturing overhead that is required to produce *one unit* of manufactured product at reasonable cost and efficiency.

Standards for the *quantity* of each component of the product are set by carefully observing manufacturing operations and taking into consideration any changes in manufacturing conditions that are expected to occur during the period for which the standards are being set. Standard quantities of labor are often set on the basis of motion and time studies, which carefully time each step of the labor operations needed to manufacture the product. Quantity standards for materials usage are based on similar scientific studies.

Standards for the *prices* of each productive factor are usually set by observing existing market conditions and by considering the probable results of future negotiations for purchase and wage contracts.

Cost standards for a production activity can be based on any of several different levels of attainment:

(1) *Ideal results*, which express a desirable goal to be sought, but one which can be attained only in the long run (if at all).

(2) *Expected actual results*, which reflect merely a natural extension of the usual method of action.

(3) *Attainable effective results*, which require some improvement over past results, but are less demanding than the long-run ideal.

The third level, *attainable effective results* (sometimes called *currently attainable performance*), is the best standard to use in most practical situations. It seeks a disciplined approach which will upgrade production effectiveness, while avoiding employee frustration and giving the satisfaction of a significant accomplishment.

Illustration of Standard Cost Specifications

Chapter 22 explained the accounting objective of assigning all production costs to units of product. Standard costing adheres to this objective, but emphasizes the distinction between assigning costs to *inputs* and *outputs*.

The major purpose of standard costing is to help management control the effectiveness of production activity. The keynote of manufacturing effectiveness is *productivity*, which expresses a relationship between the units produced (*output*) and the factors used (*input*). When the cost of factors used increases relative to the value of the product, productivity decreases (and vice versa). Phrased differently, when the costs of the factors actually used in producing a unit of product exceed the *standard cost allowed* for the product, productivity—or cost effectiveness—is below the desired level.

The standard specifications for a unit of product show the *standard costs allowed per unit of product (output)* for each of the input factors. These cost allowances are used in assigning a money valuation to the units produced by a manufacturing cost center. The standard specifications also include detailed *price* and *quantity* components for each input factor. These represent the specific cost objectives sought in controlling the acquisition cost (price) and usage (quantity) of each input factor. Illustration 24-1 is an example of a detailed standard cost specification sheet.

Illustration 24-1

SOUTHILL CHEMICAL CORP.
Standard Cost Sheet for One Gallon of Product KM

	Input		Output
	(2)	(3)	(4)
(1)	Factor	Factor	Product
Factor	Quantity	Price	Unit Cost
Direct Material Y..................	1.5 gal	$2.00	$ 3.00
Direct labor........................	2.0 hr	2.50	5.00
Variable mfg. overhead...........	2.0 hr	2.00	4.00
Fixed mfg. overhead*.............	2.0 hr	1.00	2.00
Total.............................			$14.00

*Note on production capacity: Normal volume is 300,000 gallons, or 600,000 direct labor hours, per year. Annual fixed manufacturing overhead is $600,000 ($50,000 per month).

In Illustration 24-1 *standard unit costs* are derived from the detailed *cost standards* for each resource input. These inputs are measured first in physical terms—gallons of direct materials, hours of direct labor—and then in terms of money cost. *Predetermined rates based on input quantity* are used to assign factory overhead *to operations of the cost center.* The *standard unit costs* are used to assign costs to completed product units.

In Illustration 24-1 each gallon of Product KM manufactured in a period is assigned a cost of $14. To evaluate the period's performance, the total of such costs assigned to *products manufactured* in the period may be compared with the total costs of the *factors actually used* in the period. An analysis of the specific causes of any *variance*, or difference, which occurs between these two measures may bring to light opportunities for management to improve production and cost effectiveness.

CONTROLLING VARIABLE MANUFACTURING COSTS

Distinction Between Direct Costs and Capacity Costs

It is often useful to separate manufacturing costs into two categories based on the nature of the resources and activities involved. These are

(1) *Direct (variable) costs*, sometimes called *activity costs*, which include the costs of all activities that are directly involved in the process of manufacturing physical units of product.

(2) *Capacity costs*, which include the costs involved in developing the capability of performing manufacturing activities and producing products. Capacity costs will be considered further in a later section of this chapter.

In controlling *direct (variable) manufacturing costs*, responsibility for specific cost elements is identified with particular cost centers under the direction of a manager who is capable of influencing their amounts. The manager's main responsibilities are

(1) To control the *costs of resources*—direct material, direct labor, and variable factory overhead—*acquired* for use in manufacturing products.

(2) To control the *efficiency* of converting these resources into finished manufactured products.

The *cost standards* for allowable resource *prices* and *quantities* are used as criteria for evaluating the performance of these responsibilities.

Spending (Price) Variances

The prices paid for resource factors are controllable to some extent. For example, *prices paid for direct materials* can be influenced by purchasing in large quantities, or by making long-term purchase commitments and scheduling deliveries well enough in advance to avoid rush orders. *Direct labor rates* can be influenced somewhat in negotiations with employees or union representatives, and by carefully matching labor skills with job requirements. Prices paid for variable overhead items may be controlled to some extent through careful bargaining in purchasing.

The accounting system can aid in controlling prices paid for productive resources by pinpointing responsibilities and establishing *variance accounts* to show deviations between actual and standard prices. This can be done by recording the resource acquisitions at standard prices and the liabilities for paying for them at actual prices. The differences are debited or credited to variance accounts, which measure the effectiveness of managerial performance.

Direct materials price (or spending) variance

Example 1   In January 1974 the purchasing officer of Southill Chemical Corp. (see Illustration 24-1) contracted to buy 44,000 gallons of material Y at a total cost of

$79,200. What accounting entries should be made to record this transaction and show the *direct materials price (or spending) variance*?

Solution   The average price of this purchase is $1.80 per gallon ($79,200 ÷ 44,000 gallons), which represents a cost saving of $0.20 compared to the $2.00 per gallon *cost standard* in Illustration 24-1.

The entry should be:

A, Raw Materials Inventory (44,000 gal at standard price of $2)..	88,000	
L, Accounts Payable (44,000 gal at actual price of $1.80)...		79,200
Materials Price Variance (44,000 gal at cost saving of $0.20)...................................		8,800

The *Materials Price Variance* in Example 1 represents the cost saving that might be attributed to effective performance of the purchasing responsibility.

Direct labor rate variance

Example 2   The Southill Chemical Corp.'s production in March 1974 required 63,000 hours of direct labor at a cost of $163,800. What accounting entries should be made to record this transaction and show the *direct labor rate variance*?

Solution   The average wage rate for March was $2.60 per hour ($163,800 ÷ 63,000 hours), which was above standard. The entry should be

A, Goods in Process Inventory (63,000 hr at standard rate of $2.50).....................................	157,500	
Direct Labor Rate Variance (63,000 hr at excess rate of $0.10)..	6,300	
L, Wages Payable (63,000 hr at actual rate of $2.60)...		163,800

The labor rate variance in Example 2 might be the result of ineffective performance in negotiating wages or making work assignments.

Variable overhead spending variance

Example 3   Assume the same facts as in Example 2 and that the actual cost of variable factory overhead in March 1974 was $125,000. What entry should be made to show the *variable overhead spending variance*?

Solution   The quantity of variable overhead used in the Southill Chemical Corp.'s March production is measured indirectly, in proportion to direct labor hours. That is, 63,000 hours' worth of variable overhead elements were used in manufacturing products in March. The standard cost assignable to this quantity of variable overhead elements is $126,000 (63,000 hours' worth of overhead elements at $2 per hour). The entry should be

A, Goods in Process Inventory (63,000 hr at standard rate of $2 per hr).....................................	126,000	
A, Factory Overhead Clearing Account (actual variable overhead)............................		125,000
Variable Overhead Spending Variance..........		1,000

The credit balance in Variable Overhead Spending Variance in Example 3 implies a cost saving resulting from improved effectiveness in spending for overhead elements.

Any variable factory overhead spending variance that results from using a predetermined rate should be interpreted cautiously. Effective control is attained only when the amounts of specific cost elements are in close alignment with their respective standard costs. A predetermined rate such as that in Example 3 is a substitute measure for the actual quantity of a conglomeration of overhead elements. The standard cost assigned by using the variable overhead rate ($2.00 per direct labor hour in the example) will at best represent only a rough approximation of the amount that would result from separate measurement of standard costs of the individual overhead components.

Efficiency (or Usage) Variances

Manufacturing efficiency is expressed by the ratio at which productive factors are converted into finished manufactured product. In Illustration 24-1, the standard of efficiency for usage of material Y in Southill Chemical Corp.'s Product KM is one unit of product for 1.5 gallons of material. Usage of more than 1.5 gallons per unit of product represents inefficient production. Similarly, the standard labor efficiency is one unit of product for two hours of direct labor. If an average of two hours of labor per unit of product is actually used, as allowed by standard specifications, production is efficient.

In monetary terms, *manufacturing efficiency* is measured by comparing the *actual factor quantities used valued at standard prices* (or rates) with the *number of units manufactured valued at the standard unit cost.*

Example 4   In September 1974 Southill Chemical Corp. used 30,000 gallons of material Y and 45,000 hours of direct labor to manufacture 22,000 completed units of product. Calculate the *efficiency* (or *usage*) *variances for direct materials, direct labor, and variable overhead.*

Solution   *Efficiency variance computation:*

Input Factor	(1) Input Factor Quantity × Standard Price	(2) Units Produced at Standard Unit Cost	(3) Efficiency Variance Col. 2 − Col. 1
Direct materials	$ 60,000 (30,000 gal @ $2)	$ 66,000 (22,000 units @ $3)	$6,000 F* (3,000 gal @ $2)
Direct labor	$112,500 (45,000 hr @ $2.50)	$110,000 (22,000 units @ $5)	$2,500 U* (1,000 hr @ $2.50)
Variable overhead	$ 90,000 (45,000 hr @ $2)	$ 88,000 (22,000 units @ $4)	$2,000 U* (1,000 hr @ $2)
Totals	$262,500	$264,000	$6,000 F 4,500 U

*"F" denotes favorable and "U" denotes unfavorable variances.

Recording Efficiency Variances

The efficient conversion of productive resources into completed manufactured products, production management's main responsibility, is reflected in the *Goods in Process Inventory* account.

In a *historical-cost accounting system*, Goods in Process Inventory is debited for the *actual costs* of productive factors used in a period, and credited for the actual costs apportioned to the product units completed during the period.

In *standard costing*, manufacturing efficiency can be measured by *debiting* Goods in Process for the *quantities of factors used valued at standard prices*, and *crediting* Goods in Process for the *number of equivalent units produced multiplied by the standard unit cost*. The difference between these debits and credits to Goods in Process Inventory is a *variance*. It should be transferred from Goods in Process by appropriate debits or credits to individual accounts for *materials usage variance*, *labor efficiency variance*, and *variable overhead efficiency variance*.

The journal entries to record the facts of Example 4 are as follows:

A, Goods in Process Inventory..............................	262,500	
A, Raw Materials Inventory.............................		60,000
A, Payroll Clearing Account............................		112,500
A, Manufacturing Overhead Clearing Account.....		90,000
To record actual costs of input factors put into process.		
A, Finished Goods Inventory.................................	264,000	
A, Goods in Process Inventory..........................		264,000
To transfer goods completed to Finished Goods at standard prices of input factors.		
A, Goods in Process Inventory..............................	1,500	
Labor Efficiency Variance...................................	2,500	
Variable Overhead Efficiency Variance...................	2,000	
Materials Usage Variance.............................		6,000
To transfer the efficiency variances from Goods in Process Inventory to separate accounts.		

The *Materials Usage Variance* in Example 4 indicates that the actual efficiency of materials usage for the period was better than the planned level. The *Labor Efficiency Variance* and the *Variable Overhead Efficiency Variance* show that performance was below the planned levels. Whenever variable overhead usage is measured in terms of direct labor hours, the variable overhead efficiency variance is determined by labor efficiency.

Standard Quantities Allowed as a Measure of Completed Units

In evaluating manufacturing efficiency, the output of a production cost center is appropriately measured by valuing the product units it completes at the *standard unit cost*. The phrases "standard hours allowed" or "standard quantity allowed" translate the number of units produced into *equivalent input terms*. They express the quantity of each productive factor that is allowed, under standard specifications, for the quantity of output which was actually produced. Thus in the solution to Example 4 the $66,000 of materials cost assigned to the 22,000 units of output could be stated in equivalent terms as 33,000 standard gallons allowed at $2 per gallon.

The important point to remember is that any expression of "standard quantity allowed" is a measure of *output* (units completed), and not a measure of the quantities of input factors.

Emerging Theory of Managerial Cost Accounting

In *financial accounting theory*, costs incurred in manufacturing a product represent unexpired service potentials until the product is sold. When the product is sold, the service potentials expire and become expenses (or cost sacrifices). These are matched with the revenues from the sale—the value of the product—to compute the income, or profit.

According to the *theory of pure competition* in economics, each factor of production tends to receive its marginal value-product. Under ideal conditions, so the theory goes, the sum of all cost sacrifices made in producing and selling a product is equal to the total revenues (value-product) received for the product, and no profit exists.

In *managerial accounting*, costs incurred in manufacturing a product are compared with a standard which anticipates a desired or optimal result. Under optimal conditions actual costs of the productive factors are equal to the standard costs assigned to the product units manufactured, and no favorable variance (gain) or unfavorable variance (loss) exists.

In emphasizing the use of standard unit costs as a means of assigning money valuations to product units, the preceding sections of this chapter strongly imply that standard unit costs reflect in at least a rudimentary way the value-product (or marginal contribution) of the manufacturing cost factors. The theory is incomplete, but it is useful in conceptualizing the objectives of standard costing and in understanding cost accounting methodology.

The concept of *cost absorption* has strongly influenced accounting thought. According to this concept, the accounting objective is reached when all production costs are assigned to products. This fosters the misleading notion that the test of an effective cost accounting system is the absence of under- or over-applied manufacturing costs at the end of the period. Such thinking tends to crowd out serious consideration of the critical role that frequently is—and more often should be—performed by accounting in developing and implementing effective management information and control systems.

The emerging theory of managerial cost accounting seeks *independent measures of input activity and output achievement*. It discourages the frustrating idea that the accounting aim is merely to "spread" production costs over a given volume of product units.

CONTROLLING FIXED MANUFACTURING COSTS

Usefulness of Fixed Cost Variances

Chapter 21 distinguished between *fixed costs* and *controllable costs*. Given enough time, however, the amount of almost any cost can be influenced in some degree by management, and to that extent is a controllable cost. Thus information about fixed overhead variances should be useful at some level of management in evaluating performance.

Top management frequently must consider whether to expand or contract the firm's productive capacity. *Capacity*, or capability to manufacture and sell a product, depends on having an organization staffed with competent personnel and adequately endowed with plant and equipment. In obtaining these resources relatively high levels of fixed costs are incurred. In making high-level fixed cost commitments, management makes decisions concerning expected future demand and optimal volume levels of production. In acquiring fixed assets and other capacity resources, management must also bargain for satisfactory costs and prices for these resources. Variance information based on standards of attainable performance should aid in evaluating the effectiveness of these long-run decisions.

Fixed Overhead Spending Variance

Fixed costs—the costs of using productive capacity for a period—are *not expected to change* as a result of changes in the period's volume of production. This does not imply, however, that the actual fixed costs are always exactly equal to the lump-sum amount that is budgeted for a period. Budgeted or standard fixed costs are estimates of what these costs *should be*, or *are expected to be*, in a period, although the final commitments made in the period might result in larger or smaller expenditures than were expected. These differences are called *fixed overhead spending variances*. Examples are increased salaries of management personnel, increased tax rates on productive factors, reduced insurance premiums, and additions to plant and equipment which cause increased depreciation.

Fixed Overhead Volume Variance

Budgeted fixed manufacturing cost is a money measurement of the input of productive capacity for a period. It is the price, as well as the cost, of using the organizational resources and plant facilities for the period's production. The utilization of the aggregate of the capacity resources is the physical concept of the input.

The effectiveness of a firm's capacity utilization depends on production volume over a relatively long time span. A standard unit cost of product that is calculated by dividing a period's standard or budgeted fixed manufacturing cost by a *standard normal volume* may be useful in reflecting this long-run production effectiveness. When production volume is lower than the standard normal volume, the actual fixed cost per unit of product is higher than the standard cost. The resulting unfavorable *volume variance*, if it persists, may signal a need to investigate ways of improving long-run production effectiveness.

Example 5   In September 1973 actual fixed manufacturing costs of Southill Chemical Corp. were $52,000. Production was 22,000 completed units of product. Calculate the *fixed overhead spending and volume variances*.

Solution   The variance analysis follows.

Input Factor	(1) Input Quantity × Actual Price	(2) Spending Variance (Col. 3 — Col. 1)	(3) Input Factor Quantity × Standard Price	(4) Volume Variance (Col. 5 — Col. 3)	(5) Units Manufactured × Standard Unit Cost
Fixed mfg. overhead	$52,000	2,000 U*	$50,000	6,000 U*	$44,000
	(Actual fixed cost)		(Budgeted fixed cost)		(22,000 units at $2)

*"F" denotes favorable and "U" denotes unfavorable variances.

The actual fixed factory overhead of $52,000 (the total of actual costs of the individual fixed overhead elements for the period) exceeds the amount budgeted for the period, $50,000, giving a $2,000 unfavorable *spending variance.*

The $44,000 of standard costs *allowed for units produced* (22,000 units × $2 per unit) is less than the $50,000 of *budgeted fixed cost for the period's capacity utilization*, giving a $6,000 unfavorable *volume variance.*

Accounting for Fixed Manufacturing Overhead Costs

The appropriate accounting procedure for fixed manufacturing overhead costs depends on the nature of the costs and how production is organized. Ideally, *each production department* should have an *overhead clearing account.* All *direct* factory overhead costs of the department should be debited to this account, as should all *indirect* costs periodically allocated from other departments. These debits to the factory overhead clearing account have corresponding credits to appropriate liability or asset accounts.

To show performance effectiveness, the factory overhead clearing account should be credited for the period's *budgeted* amount of fixed factory overhead costs, with a corresponding debit to the departmental Goods in Process Inventory account. Any resulting differences between the *actual fixed costs debited* and the *budgeted fixed costs credited* to the factory overhead clearing account would be caused by *spending* more or less than the amount that management planned to spend for fixed resources during the period. After being reported to the appropriate responsibility centers, these differences should be transferred from the *factory overhead clearing* account to an account called *Fixed Overhead Spending Variance.*

As products are completed, the departmental *Goods in Process Inventory* should be *credited for the standard costs allowed* for the completed units of product (completed units times the standard unit cost), with corresponding *debits to the Finished Goods Inventory* account. Any resulting differences between the budgeted fixed costs debited and the standard costs of completed product units credited to the Goods in Process Inventory account would be caused by production volume being above or below the *normal volume.* These differences should be transferred by appropriate debits and credits to an account called *Fixed Overhead Volume Variance.*

The *volume variance* can always be calculated as the difference between the number of product units completed at standard normal volume and the number of units actually completed in the period, multiplied by the standard unit cost for fixed factory overhead.

Example 6   Assume the same facts as in Example 5. What entries should be made to record the fixed manufacturing costs and show the *fixed overhead spending and volume variances?*

Solution   The journal entries are

A, Factory Overhead Clearing Account....................	52,000	
A, L, Appropriate Assets or Liabilities...............		52,000
To record *actual departmental fixed costs* incurred in the period.		

A, Goods in Process Inventory..............................	50,000	
A, Factory Overhead Clearing Account.............		50,000
To charge *budgeted fixed costs* to production of the period.		

Fixed Overhead Spending Variance........................	2,000	
A, Factory Overhead Clearing Account.............		2,000
To close Overhead Clearing and record the unfavorable *spending variance*.		

A, Finished Goods Inventory (22,000 units at $2)......	44,000	
A, Goods in Process Inventory (22,000 units at $2)..		44,000
To transfer product units *completed* at standard unit cost.		

Fixed Overhead Volume Variance (3,000 units at $2)...	6,000	
A, Goods in Process Inventory (3,000 units at $2)...		6,000
To transfer the *volume variance* (25,000 units normal volume minus 22,000 units actual volume times $2) from Goods in Process Inventory.		

Reporting and Using Variance Information

The variances which have been developed in the accounts by the use of the standard cost accounting system, as well as their supporting details (price and quantity variances for each principal type of material and for each major labor operation, and manufacturing overhead spending variances for each major class of manufacturing overhead), should be *reported to the individual managers who are responsible* for those phases of production.

The next step in the management control process consists of *determining the cause of each significant variance.* The cost accountant may be able to explain some of the variances, especially those caused by budgeting errors. The manager who is responsible for the activity which resulted in the variance should be asked to explain the reasons for variances of significant amount. The purchasing manager, for example, should be called upon to explain materials price variances. It may be that they were caused by hand-to-mouth buying, or that a price change was unavoidable, or that the production department caused the excess price by setting unnecessarily tight material specifications.

The variances should be divided into *controllable* and *noncontrollable* groups. The responsible manager should take proper steps to prevent the recurrence of controllable unfavorable variances, and to extend elsewhere the opportunities for cost savings brought to light by favorable variances.

Disposing of Standard Cost Variances

The *accounting disposition* of variances from standard cost should be *governed by the cause of* each variance. If the standard is considered to have been properly set and the variance is due to performance that is *controllable*, the variance should be reported in the *income statement* of the period in which it occurs. A favorable variance is an addition to income; an unfavorable variance, a deduction. The *proper value of the asset, inventory, is standard cost* in this case—the cost under efficient operating conditions. This is the cost that is expected to benefit future operations.

Example 7   A debit labor efficiency variance of $25,000 was caused by a stoppage of work due to a shortage of materials. How should this variance be disposed of in the accounting records?

Solution   It should be deducted from the current year's income statement, preferably as a separate item. None of it should be included in the ending inventories of Goods in Process and Finished Goods.

Variances due to such unusual occurrences as strikes, presumably noncontrollable, are *losses*. They should be deducted from income in the period in which they occur.

If standards are set on a basis other than currently attainable levels of performance, such as *ideal results*, significant variances from standard should be *apportioned to product units* so as to have a sound basis of inventory valuation. If variances are due to noncontrollable external conditions which reflect new operating conditions, such as changes in material prices and labor rates, the same treatment should be followed.

Example 8   A labor efficiency variance of $40,000 was reported in 1973 under a cost system which used ideal standards. How should it be disposed of in the accounts?

Solution   It should be treated as an *adjustment of the standard costs* actually charged to production during 1973. Assume that the standard cost of direct labor charged to Goods in Process during the year was $400,000, and at the end of the year $50,000 is in Goods in Process Inventory, $100,000 is in Finished Goods Inventory, and $250,000 is in Cost of Goods Sold Expense. The adjustment, which is 10 per cent of the standard cost ($40,000/$400,000), should be allocated as follows:

	Standard Cost	Adjustment (10%)	Adjusted Cost
Goods in Process	$ 50,000	$ 5,000	$ 55,000
Finished Goods	100,000	10,000	110,000
Cost of Goods Sold	250,000	25,000	275,000
Totals	$400,000	$40,000	$440,000

The standard cost specifications should be revised if the condition that caused the variance is expected to continue into the future and is beyond the control of management.

Summary   *Standard costs* are scientifically determined benchmarks used in planning and controlling manufacturing operations. When compared with actual costs they measure operating effectiveness. Usually standards are set on the basis of currently attainable performance.

Variances are calculated and reported as the difference between *standard costs allowed* for actual production and *actual costs* incurred. Standards are established for the price and quantity of direct material and direct labor. Comparison of standard costs with actual costs yields information on *price* (or rate) and *efficiency* (or usage) variances. Other variances resulting from comparisons with standard are the *variable overhead spending variance*, the *fixed overhead spending variance*, and the *fixed overhead volume variance*.

After being reported to the responsible managers, variances that represent *controllable differences* from standard are disposed of as deductions or additions in computing *income* of the period in which they occur. If standards are based on ideal performance, their apportionment to product units is justified.

Discussion Questions and Problems

24-1

a. What are the main purposes of a standard cost system?
b. How are standards established for each of the elements of manufacturing cost?

24-2   What are the advantages and disadvantages of a standard cost system as compared with a historical cost system in terms of the following?

a. Control of costs.
b. Keeping perpetual inventory records.
c. Measuring periodic income.

24-3

a. Explain how the use of standard costs facilitates *management by exception.*
b. Would you recommend that only *unfavorable* variances from standard costs be reported to management? Explain.

24-4   How are standard costs related to budgeted costs? How do the two differ?

24-5   A manufacturer is planning to establish a standard cost accounting system. The factory manager has recommended that the cost standard be the same as the average results of the past 12 months.

a. What merit is there to the factory manager's recommendation?
b. List and explain three alternative bases that may be used for setting cost standards.
c. What problems can arise from standard costs that are too "loose"? From standards that are too "tight"?

24-6

a. How does the use of a predetermined rate for assigning manufacturing overhead costs to units of product resemble the operation of a standard cost system?

b. How do the two differ?

24-7

a. Explain how *activity costs* differ from *capacity costs*.
b. How are standard costs used in controlling activity costs?
c. How are standard costs used in controlling capacity costs?

24-8

a. Explain and give an example of a *price (spending) variance* and an *efficiency (usage) variance*.
b. Explain how these variances are computed for controlling the costs of *direct materials, direct labor,* and *variable manufacturing overhead*.

24-9   It is difficult to set standards which can be useful in measuring performance.

a. Do you think that performance standards can be set more easily for production workers than for sales personnel? Why?
b. Do you think that performance standards can be set more easily for a factory production worker than for the factory manager? Why?

24-10   Explain how the concept of *standard hours allowed* is used in evaluating the efficiency of manufacturing activity.

24-11   "Fixed costs are constant for a given time period and are not expected to change as a result of changes in the volume of production. This implies that total actual fixed costs for a period will exactly equal the budgeted fixed costs, with no variance." Do you agree? Explain.

24-12

a. Explain what is meant by each of the following and give an example, using amounts of your own choice:
    (1) Fixed overhead spending variance.
    (2) Fixed overhead volume variance.
b. Is information about fixed overhead cost variances useful to management? Explain.

24-13

a. Give an example of a *profit center* and a *cost center*.
b. What types of cost standards might be set for each of these centers?

24-14   Perhaps the most important aspect of a standard cost accounting system is the investigation and action taken by management as a result of reported variances. For each of the variances listed below, state

a. What manager would be responsible.
b. What management action, if any, should be taken.
c. What disposition of the variance should be made in the accounting records.
All the variances are significantly large.
(1) A credit materials quantity variance caused by unrealistic product specifications.
(2) A debit materials price variance caused by unexpected price changes which seem likely to continue.
(3) A labor quantity variance caused by the use of inexperienced labor.
(4) A labor quantity variance caused by a shortage of materials.
(5) A labor price variance caused by signing a new labor contract at higher rates.

(6) A credit balance in the factory overhead volume variance at the end of the year resulting from operations considerably above the normal rate.

(7) A credit balance in the factory overhead spending variance account due to careless budgeting.

24-15   For each of the variances listed below, state

a. What manager would be responsible.

b. What management action, if any, should be taken.

c. What disposition of the variance should be made in the accounting records.

All the variances are significantly large.

(1) A debit materials quantity variance caused by the use of inferior material.

(2) A credit materials price variance caused by the use of the cheaper grade of material in situation (1) for a trial period.

(3) A debit materials quantity variance caused by defective machinery.

(4) A debit labor quantity variance caused by defective machinery.

(5) A labor price variance caused by using employees of a higher than standard pay grade and rate (who would otherwise have been idle) to perform a given task.

(6) A debit variance in the factory overhead volume variance caused by a bottleneck in Production Department 3.

(7) A credit balance in the factory overhead spending variance caused by a price reduction for electricity.

24-16   Hill Plastics, Inc. manufactured 2,200 units of a new product in 1974. The company assigns no fixed factory costs to new products during the introductory period. The following costs standards apply:

Direct material X............2 gal @ $4 per gal......	$ 8
Direct labor...................4 hr @ $3 per hr........	12
Variable factory overhead. 4 hr @ $2 per hr........	8
Total..	$28

During 1974 the company purchased and sold 4,500 gallons of material X at $4.20 per gallon. Direct labor consisted of 9,000 hours at $3.20 per hour. Variable manufacturing overhead costs totaled $17,200.

Required   a. Compute the standard costs allowed for the 1974 output and compare them with the actual costs incurred for each cost element.

b. Analyze the standard cost variances into their major components.

c. Assume that 5,000 gallons of material X had been purchased and 4,500 gallons used in 1974. How would this change your analysis in part b?

d. Assume that 10,000 direct labor hours had been used in 1974. How would this change your analysis in part b?

24-17   Automatic Products Company budgets $2,400,000 of fixed manufacturing overhead costs for one of its manufacturing divisions. The division has a practical capacity of 180,000 direct labor hours and 60,000 units of completed product a year. In 1974 the division's employees worked 172,000 direct labor hours in producing 54,000 units of completed product. Actual fixed manufacturing overhead costs totaled $2,491,000 for the division.

Required   a. Prepare standard cost specifications for the division's fixed manufacturing overhead.

b. Compute standard costs allowed for the 1974 output and compare this with the actual cost incurred.

c. Analyze the fixed factory overhead variance from standard into its main components.

d. Assume that 190,000 direct labor hours had been worked and that 66,000 units of product had been completed in 1974. How would this change your analysis in part c?

24-18   Northrup, Inc. uses the following standard costs in controlling its manufacturing operations:

Factor	Quantity	Price	Standard Unit Cost
Direct materials..................	6 lb	$3	$18
Direct labor.......................	3 hr	5	15
Variable overhead...............	3 hr	3	9
Fixed overhead...................	3 hr	2	6
Total............................			$48

Production in 1974 consisted of 15,000 units of product. The ending inventory was the same as the beginning inventory. Purchases totaled $275,280, and the direct materials usage variance was a credit of $3,600. Direct labor used consisted of 44,000 hours at a cost of $241,000. Actual factory overhead was $137,000 variable and $95,000 fixed. The volume variance was a $3,000 debit.

Required

a. Compute the quantity of materials used, the average purchase price, and the materials price variance.

b. Compute the direct labor quantity and price variances.

c. Compute the variable overhead spending and efficiency variances.

d. Compute the budgeted fixed overhead cost, the normal volume, and the fixed overhead spending variance.

24-19   At the end of December 1973 you find the following accounts, together with total debit and credit changes during December, in the general ledger of a manufacturing company which uses a standard cost system:

	Debits	Credits
Materials and supplies inventory.........................	$18,000	$14,000
Goods in process inventory...............................	60,000	45,000
Factory overhead clearing account......................	17,000	17,000
Finished goods inventory...................................	45,000	37,000
Materials price variance....................................	800	
Materials quantity variance...............................		1,000
Labor price variance..	2,000	
Labor quantity variance....................................		None
Overhead spending variance..............................	1,500	
Overhead volume variance.................................	None	None

Required

a. Reconstruct summary journal entries to record December production costs.

b. Analyze the cost elements in the Finished Goods Inventory balance on December 31.

c. How should management use the information on variances?

24-20   The Novel Gadget Co. has been manufacturing the Thingamajig for several years. On the basis of its past experience, together with a careful study by production engineers, it estimates that the cost per Thingamajig under efficient operating conditions should be as follows:

Standard Cost Per Thingamajig

5 feet of material at $3 per foot..	$15
1.5 hours of direct labor at $8 per hr	12
1.5 hours of factory overhead at $4 per hr.........................	6
Total...	33

The factory overhead rate was based on the assumption that 15,000 hours would be worked during a normal month and that fixed overhead would be $2 per unit. Actual production figures for November 1974 were as follows:

Number of Thingamajigs produced	10,000 units
Quantity of materials used...............................	50,400 feet
Direct labor hours worked................................	16,000 hours
Cost per pound of materials..............................	$ 2.90
Cost per hour of labor	$ 8.40
Actual factory overhead ($\frac{1}{3}$ for fixed elements)	$63,000

Required   a. Prepare a table showing for each element of cost (1) the total actual cost of production for November, (2) the total standard cost for November, and (3) the total variance for the month, identified as a debit or a credit.

b. Analyze the total variance for each cost element into its main components.

c. Who should explain the cause for each variance in part b?

d. List a possible cause of each variance and explain what disposition you would make of the matter.

24-21   Pad Products Corp. uses a standard cost accounting system and applies manufacturing overhead on the basis of direct labor hours used. The following cost standards have been set for one carton of Whiff, a new product, at a normal volume of 1,800 cartons per month:

24 oz of material P.........................	@	$0.50 an oz
1 container.....................................	@	0.50
1 hr of direct labor..........................	@	5.00 an hr
1 hr of variable overhead.................	@	2.00 an hr
Fixed overhead..............................	@	3.00 a carton

During October 1973 the company purchased 50,000 ounces of material P at $0.47 an ounce and 2,000 containers at $0.50 each. Direct labor costs consisted of 1,850 hours at $5.25 an hour. Actual manufacturing overhead was $4,300 for variable elements and $6,000 for fixed elements. Completed production consisted of 1,600 cartons. There was no ending Goods in Process Inventory, but there were 11,000 ounces of material P and 390 unused containers on hand on October 31.

Required   Record journal entries to summarize the results for October, setting up price and quantity variances where possible for each element of cost.

Cases   **24-1**   **Jackson Company.** Jackson Company manufactures a single product for distribution through wholesalers. The company has used a system of currently attainable cost standards for many years to aid in profit planning and to control manufacturing operations.

The following cost standards were reviewed and put into effect at the beginning of 1973:

JACKSON COMPANY
Standard Cost Specifications

Factor	Quantity	Price	Unit Cost
Direct material..............................	10 lbs.	$1.50	$15
Direct labor..................................	2 hrs.	2.50	5
Variable factory overhead................	2 hrs.	3.00	6
Fixed factory overhead*..................	2 hrs.	2.00	4
Total			$30

*$39,000 budgeted for 1973.

In 1973 Jackson Company had sales of $450,000, up 25 per cent from a year earlier. Although the company was under considerable inflationary pressure during the year (prices of materials and services purchased advanced approximately 6 per cent), manufacturing costs per unit of product were held down by an improved processing technique. Operating results for 1973 are reported in the following income statement.

JACKSON COMPANY
Income Statement
For the Year Ended December 31, 1973

Sales revenue......................................		$450,000
Cost of goods sold (at standard cost):		
Direct material...............................	$150,000	
Direct labor	50,000	
Manufacturing overhead....................	100,000	
Total	$300,000	
Add: Net variance (Schedule A).........	1,300	301,300
Gross margin.....................................		$148,700
Selling and administrative expenses:		
Commissions..................................	$36,000	
Shipping.......................................	7,000	
Salaries	38,000	
Other expenses...............................	21,800	102,800
Income before income taxes...................		$ 45,900

JACKSON COMPANY
Schedule A
Variances of Manufacturing Costs from Standard
For the Year Ended December 31, 1973

	Debit (Credit)	
Direct materials variances:		
Price..	$11,800	
Usage...	(7,500)	
Net...		$4,300
Direct labor variances:		
Wage rate......................................	$ 3,000	
Efficiency	(2,500)	
Net...		500
Overhead variances:		
Budget..	(500)	
Volume..	(3,000)	
Net...		(3,500)
Net variance from standard costs.............		$1,300

The 1973 opening and closing inventories at standard cost were as follows:

Inventory	January 1, 1973	December 31, 1973
Raw materials	$ 0	$27,000
Goods in process*	30,000	30,000
Finished goods	25,000	40,000
Total	$55,000	$99,000

*Goods in process averaged one-half complete as to the usage of all factors of production.

Required

a. How many units of product were sold in 1973? How many were manufactured?

b. How many units would be produced at normal capacity?

c. Compute the following:

(1) Quantity of materials purchased.

(2) Quantity of materials actually used.

(3) Quantity of labor actually used.

(4) Actual price of raw materials.

(5) Actual labor rate.

d. Analyze the overhead budget variance into spending and efficiency components.

e. In view of the company's use of "currently attainable standards," how should the 1973 variances be interpreted?

f. What changes would you recommend in the standard cost specifications? Explain.

chapter 25

Fundamentals of
Present Value Analysis

Purpose of Chapter

Part III of this book has dealt with a twofold emphasis in managerial accounting which highlights (1) the *period plan*, or budget, as a means of making specific the operating objectives of an enterprise, and (2) *periodic information feedback* as a means of evaluating progress toward the period's objectives.

To develop the period plan, managerial accounting provides information for estimating the *income elements that are expected to be realized in a particular future time period*. After the plan has been put into action, the *income elements actually realized in the period* are measured and reported as feedback for evaluating how effectively the planned objectives were accomplished.

Business decisions frequently involve comprehensive plans for *projects which extend over many time periods*, rather than merely plans for a single period. Projects which deserve comprehensive planning may involve new methods of performing existing activities, adding new activities, abandoning old ones, or substituting new ones for old. To aid these decisions, managerial accounting provides information for estimating and comparing the *potential or expected future profitability* of the alternatives being considered. This chapter deals with methods of making these profitability estimates.

Importance of Cash Flow

The *incremental, or net, cash flow that a project is expected to produce* is the sole basis of the project's value or potential benefit to a business. This is true whether the project involves an investment in a bond, a machine, a manufacturing plant, or an entire business. The cash inflow is the only source from which the capital invested in a project can be recovered and from which a net income can be derived.

In deciding which projects to undertake, which projects to continue in operation, and when to discontinue them, management *compares the additions to the net cash inflow* of the business which might be derived from each alternative that is being considered. The alternatives which promise the *most profitable* additions to the net cash inflow of the business are usually accepted for investment.

The net cash inflows expected from different projects are seldom identical. The main differences which influence their comparative profitability are

(1) Differences in the *total amount* of net cash inflow.

(2) Differences in the *life* or duration of the cash inflow.

(3) Differences in the *timing* of specific payments.

(4) Differences in the *degree of uncertainty* that the net inflow will in fact be realized, or that its actual amount will coincide with the amount expected.

Example 1   Mizell, Inc. is considering two projects, each of which requires a $10,000 initial investment. The projects are *mutually exclusive*; that is, if one is selected, the other will not be. The expected net cash inflows are as follows:

Year	Project A	Project B
0	Investment ($10,000)	($10,000)
1	6,000	0
2	4,000	1,000
3	2,000	3,000
4	1,000	4,000
5	0	6,000
Total	$3,000	$4,000

Which project is likely to be the more profitable?

Solution   The total net cash inflows of $4,000 for Project B are $1,000 greater than those of Project A. Project B has a longer life than A. The timing of the specific cash flows is quite different, as indicated by comparing the annual receipts of the two projects. The uncertainty of the net inflows is not explicitly measured, although the earlier recovery of the $10,000 invested in Project A (2 years compared with $4\frac{1}{3}$ years for B) implies a lower degree of risk for A.

Importance of Timing of Cash Flows

Many projects, such as special sales of merchandise, are often begun and completed in the same accounting period. For such short-lived projects, the differences in the timing of cash receipts and disbursements are usually of relatively minor importance and may be ignored. In projects which extend over many accounting periods, differences in the timing of cash receipts and disbursements may have a controlling influence on the projects' relative profitability.

Example 2   Both Project C and Project D involve rendering a service to business customers, and only one can be undertaken. Each is expected to result in a net cash inflow of $2,000 over a two-year period, timed as follows:

	Project C	Project D
Collection at end of year 1	$1,500	$ 500
Collection at end of year 2	500	1,500
Total collections	$2,000	$2,000

Which project has the more profitable net cash inflow if differences in timing are considered?

Solution   Project C is the more profitable. Although the total net cash inflow from the two projects is expected to be the same for the two-year period, Project C is expected to make $1,000 more cash available for business use at the end of year 1. This $1,000 can be reinvested in other profitable projects, and the additional earnings during year 2 would cause the total earnings of the firm, if it invests in Project C, to be greater than if it invests in Project D.

If the net cash inflows from alternative plans are equal, the plan which promises the earlier cash receipts or the later cash disbursements has an advantage from the *time value of money*. This reflects the fact that in a modern economy money commands a definite interest return.

The Payback-Period Method

One criterion often used in comparing alternative projects is the *payback period*. This is the number of periods, usually years, required for the expected *cash inflow* of a project to equal the initial investment, or *cash outflow*. Presumably, the shorter the payback period, the more desirable is the investment. This method assumes that the early receipts are considered to be the recovery of the invested capital, and that no income results until the entire investment is recovered. In Example 1 the payback period for Project A is 2 years and for B it is $4\frac{1}{3}$ years. Thus, according to the payback-period criterion, Project A is preferable to Project B.

The payback-period method is often a reliable guide when the net cash inflows are highly uncertain. This is in keeping with the principle that the quicker the capital investment is recovered, the lower is the risk. The method is also useful when highly profitable alternatives are in abundance and there is little need to make refined analyses of their relative profitability. However, the payback-period method has several weaknesses. It ignores the net cash inflows in periods beyond the payback time, makes no explicit measure of profitability, and does not consider the effect of the time value of money.

Average Rate of Return (ROR) Method

Another method often used in comparing alternative investments is the average annual *rate of return (ROR)* on the capital investment. The formula for this calculation is

$$\frac{\text{Average additional annual income}}{\text{Average additional investment}} = \text{Average rate of return.}$$

The additional annual income may be computed before or after considering *income tax*, although an after-tax computation is usually preferable. The average additional annual income is computed by *subtracting from the average annual net operating receipts* (net cash inflow) an *annual allowance for the recovery of the additional investment* (amortization). The average additional investment is computed by adding the project's initial incremental investment to its expected salvage value at the end of the project, and dividing the sum by 2.

Example 3   The before-tax cash inflows expected from a proposed new machine of Company X are as follows:

Time Periods	Initial Incremental Investment	Expected Salvage Value	Expected Net Operating Receipts (Net Inflows)
0	$7,000		
1			($1,750)
2			($1,750)
3			($1,750)
4			($1,750)
5		0	($1,750)
Total.............	$7,000	0	($8,750)

Solution   What is the machine's expected average rate of return?

Average additional net operating receipts ($8,750 ÷ 5)..............	$1,750
Average annual allowance for investment recovery ($7,000 ÷ 5)	1,400
Average additional annual income.......................................	$ 350
Average additional investment ($7,000 + 0) ÷ 2	$3,500

Average rate of return (ROR) $= \dfrac{\$350}{\$3,500} = 10\%$

The *average rate of return method,* unlike the payback-period method, assumes that the initial investment is recovered systematically over the entire life of the project. It explicitly recognizes the timing of income in measuring the project's relative profitability. It is often called the *unadjusted rate of return method* because it ignores differences in the timing of the project's expected cash flows. It treats a dollar of cash receipts expected to be realized 10 or 15 years in the future as having significance equal to a dollar expected next year. For this reason, the average rate of return method has limited usefulness when refined measures of the relative profitability of investment alternatives are needed.

Methods of Adjusting for Differences in Timing of Cash Flows

The expected cash flows of alternative projects available for business investment should usually be compared on a basis which takes into account *differences in the timing* of their respective cash receipts and payments. This kind of comparison can be made by stating the expected net cash flow of each project as one of the following.

(1) Its *future value* (the net amount to which the cash flows will accumulate at compound interest at a given time in the future).

(2) Its *present value* (the net amount to which the cash flows would be discounted at compound interest to the present time).

(3) Its *time-adjusted rate of return* (*TAROR*) (the compound rate of earnings which will discount the *net cash inflow* to an amount equal to the initial incremental investment).

A knowledge of the *mathematics of compound interest* is needed to make calculations for these comparisons.

The Future Value of an Investment

The *future value* of an investment is measured by the amount to which the cash flows of the project will accumulate at compound interest at a given future date. To illustrate, if $100 is deposited in a savings account to earn 4 per cent interest per annum compounded annually, its *future value* one year from the date of the deposit is $104 (the $100 repayment of the initial sum invested plus the earnings of $4). If this investment is to be compared with an alternative investment, the comparison should be based on an equal lapse of time.

When the interest earned on an investment for a given period is computed at the end of the period and added to the investment instead of being paid to the investor, it is said to be *compounded*. Usually a quoted interest rate is an *annual rate* unless some other period is specified; and annual compoundings are usually implied unless there is a statement to the contrary. The shorter the compounding period, the more important is the effect of the time value of money.

Example 4   Should a company deposit $100,000 of idle cash in a savings account in Bank *A*, which pays interest once a year at the rate of 4 per cent of the beginning balance, or in Bank *B*, which pays 2 per cent interest every six months? The banks are equally sound; therefore, the risk that each bank will fail to pay principal or interest is the same.

Solution   Compare the future values of the two plans after one year.

	Deposit in Bank A	*Deposit in Bank B*
Original deposit to be repaid at end of year.......	$100,000	$100,000
Interest credited at end of first six months	0	2,000
Deposit balance during second six months	$100,000	$102,000
Interest credited at end of year	4,000	2,040
Deposit balance at end of year.......................	$104,000	$104,040

The future value of a deposit in Bank B is $40 greater than a deposit in Bank A at the end of one year; therefore it is the better alternative. This advantage results from a difference in the timing of the interest receipts: The $2,000 interest received in Bank B at the end of the first six months is reinvested to earn interest of $40 (2 per cent of $2,000) during the second six months.

Determining Future Value by Formula

In Example 4 Bank A's interest rate is 4 per cent a year, *compounded annually;* Bank B's rate is 4 per cent a year, compounded semiannually, *or 2 per cent a half-year, compounded semiannually.* The balance on deposit in Bank B at the end of the first six months was 102 per cent of the initial amount deposited (100 per cent of the $100,000 initial investment plus 2 per cent, or $2,000, for the interest compounded at six months). The balance in Bank B at the end of the second six months was 102 per cent of the $102,000 compounded balance at the end of the first six months. The future amount of the deposit in Bank B at the end of any number of future time periods can be visualized as follows:

Time Periods	Initial Investment	$\times$	Ratio of Future Value to Investment	$=$	Future Amount
0	$100,000		1.00		$100,000
1	100,000		1.02		102,000
2	100,000		(1.02)(1.02)		104,040
3	100,000		(1.02)(1.02)(1.02)		106,120
4	100,000		$(1.02)^4$		108,240
.	.		.		.
.	.		.		.
.	.		.		.
n	100,000		$(1.02)^n$		$100,000(1.02)^n$

where n refers to the total number of time periods involved.

Generalizing, the future amount to which any initial capital investment will accumulate at a compound rate of earnings after the lapse of a given number of time periods can be computed by the formula

$$S_n = S(1 + i)^n,$$

where S_n is the *future value* of the accumulation
S is the *original sum* of money invested
i is the *rate* at which earnings are compounded each period
n is the *number of periods*

Determining Future Value by Tables

Because compound-interest calculations are used frequently in business, printed tables are available which show the *ratios* of the future value of an investment to the original sum invested for various rates of compound interest and various numbers of compounding time periods. An example of these tables appears in Appendix I on p. 724. The ratios are called the *amount of $1 at compound interest.* The tables would show in Example 4 that the ratio of the accumulated balance in Bank B to the original sum after one year would be 1.0404, which is equal to the amount of $1 plus interest compounded at 2 per cent for two periods. Multiplying the sum originally deposited, S, by this ratio of future dollars to present dollars gives the amount to which the deposit will accumulate at the end of a year. The formula for using the tables to compute the *future value* is

$$S_n = S(a)$$
$$= \$100,000(1.0404)$$
$$= \$104,040,$$

where a is the ratio shown in the table for the future amount of $1 at compound interest.

Future Value of a Series of Equal Payments or Receipts

Preceding sections have shown how to find the future amount to which a lump-sum investment will accumulate when the initial sum, the elapsed time, and the rate of interest are known. This method may also be used for a *series of payments* instead of a single lump-sum payment. It would involve computing the accumulation on each sum from the date of its payment to a common future date, and then adding the individual accumulations. This procedure becomes tedious, however, when there are many periodic payments. If the periodic *payments are equal*, a short-cut formula or a table may be used to compute the future value of the entire series.

A series of such equal periodic payments is called an *annuity*, and each of the periodic payments is called a *rent*. The ratio of the future accumulation to the amount of the periodic rent is called the *amount of an annuity of $1*, frequently designated as A. It is the amount of future accumulation *per dollar* of periodic rent for the appropriate interest rate and number of time periods. This ratio is multiplied by the amount of the periodic rent, R, to give the total future accumulation, S_n. That is,

$$S_n = R(A).$$

Example 5 A business is planning to build a plant addition in two years. It expects to accumulate the needed funds by depositing $10,000 at the end of each year in a savings bank which pays 5 per cent interest compounded annually. How much will be available for the plant expansion at the end of two years?

Solution $$S_n = R(A) = \$10,000(2.05) = \$20,500.$$

The ratio 2.05 is obtained from Appendix IV, on p. 727, which shows the amount of an annuity of $1 for various periods at various rates of interest. It is the A ratio for two periods at 5 per cent.

A variation of this formula can be used to compute the amount of the equal periodic payments if the future sum, the number of periods, and the interest rate per period are known. The formula is

$$R = \frac{S_n}{A}.$$

Example 6 A business wishes to accumulate a fund of $20,000 by making equal periodic payments into a savings account at the end of each year for four years. Balances on deposit will earn 4 per cent interest per year, compounded annually. What amount of equal periodic payment is required?

Solution
$$R = \frac{S_n}{A} = \frac{\$20,000}{4.24646} = \$4,709.81.$$

The Present Value of a Sum of Money

The preceding sections have shown how alternative investment plans may be compared on the basis of their *future values*—the amounts to which their expected cash flows will accumulate at compound interest at the end of a given number of periods. It is customary, however, to compare investment proposals in terms of *present values*—the amounts to which their expected cash flows would be discounted at compound interest to the present time.

Example 7 How much can a business afford to pay today for a savings certificate which can be redeemed for $100,000 a year from now, if the best alternative use of money at equal risk will earn 4 per cent a year, compounded annually?

In this illustration the future value, S_n, of the investment at the end of one year is known; it is the present value, S, which is to be computed. This may be done either by formula or by tables, as explained in the following sections.

Determining Present Value by Formula

The relationship between a future value and a present sum can be expressed as the ratio of the future value to the present sum. Thus

$$a = \frac{S_n}{S}.$$

Conversely, this relationship can be expressed as the ratio of a present value to a future sum. Thus

$$p = \frac{S}{S_n}.$$

The latter ratio, designated by p, is referred to as the *present value of $1 at compound interest*.

The ratios for a and p are reciprocals of (1 divided by) each other. That is, $p = 1/a$, and $a = 1/p$. If p is known, a can be determined, and vice versa.

Example 8 If a, the amount of $1 at compound interest, for three periods at 6 per cent per period is 1.19102, what is p, the present value of $1 due three periods hence at 6 per cent per period?

Solution
$$p = \frac{1}{a} = \frac{1}{1.19102} = 0.83962.$$

Example 9   If p for four periods at 5 per cent per period is 0.82270, what is a for four periods at 5 per cent period?

Solution

$$a = \frac{1}{p} = \frac{1}{0.82270} = 1.21551.$$

The present value of a sum to be received or paid at a future time is computed by the formula

$$S = S_n\left(\frac{1}{1+i}\right)^n,$$

where S is the present value of the cash flow
S_n is the future sum of money
i is the earnings rate for each compounding period
n is the number of compounding periods

Example 10   The following illustration shows how this formula may be applied to the facts in Example 7:

Solution

$$S = S_n\left(\frac{1}{1+i}\right)^n$$

$$S = \$100,000\left(\frac{1}{1.04}\right)$$

$$S = \$100,000(0.96154)$$

$$S = \$96,154, \text{ the present value of } \$100,000$$
$$\text{to be received one period later.}$$

Conclusion   If the savings certificate is now for sale for less than $96,154, the business would be better off to buy it. If its price is higher, the business should invest in the best alternative, which will pay $100,000 at the end of the year for $96,154 invested now.

Proof of Computation

Present value of certificate.....................................	$ 96,154
Interest received at the end of the year, 4% of $96,154	3,846
Future value at the end of one year.........................	$100,000

Present value computations are just as appropriate for the seller of an asset as for the buyer, and just as appropriate for the borrower of money as for the lender. The *seller* would wish to select that plan which promised to yield a *cash inflow* of the *greatest present value*. The *buyer* would wish to select that plan which promised to require a *cash outflow* of the *smallest present value*.

Determining Present Value from Tables

A table which shows today's value, p, of each dollar to be received or paid in the future for various rates of interest and time periods appears in Appendix II on p. 725. The total present value, S, of a future sum of money, S_n, is computed by multiplying S_n by p for the appropriate interest rate and number of time periods. That is,

$$S = S_n(p).$$

Example 11   A business is considering making an investment in a non-interest-bearing bond which promises to pay the face amount of $100,000 at the end of two years. Alternative investments of equal risk yield an annual rate of return of 4 per cent. How much is the bond worth now?

Solution   1. Find the number of periods for which interest is compounded (2) and the rate for each compounding period (4 per cent).
2. Find the column for the applicable interest rate (4 per cent) in Appendix II.
3. Find the figure in this column on the line for the proper number of periods (2).

Periods	4% *Interest Rate*
1	0.96154
2	**0.92456** ←
3	0.88900

4. Multiply the ratio at this point (0.92456), p, by S_n, the sum to be received in the future ($100,000). The product, S, is $92,456, the amount that the bond is worth at present at a rate of 4 per cent.

Proof of Computation

Present value of bond...	$ 92,456
Interest for first year, 4%.....................................	3,698*
Future value at the end of one year.........................	$ 96,154
Interest for second year, 4%.................................	3,846*
Future value at the end of two years.......................	$100,000

Note: Amounts are rounded to the nearest dollar.

Present Value of a Series of Equal Payments or Receipts

A plan which involves a series of payments, like one with a single payment, can be evaluated in terms of its present value. This could be done by multiplying each payment by the ratio of the present value of $1, p, for the appropriate period, and adding the products. However, tables of the *present value* of an annuity of $1, often called P, give a single ratio which expresses the current equivalent of each dollar of the future *series* of equal periodic payments. Appendix III on p. 726 contains a table of P ratios. The P ratio, multiplied by the amount of the periodic payment, R, gives S, the present value of the series of payments. That is,

$$S = R(P).$$

Example 12   A business is considering investing in a savings bond due in two years. The bond contract promises to pay the lender $40 at the end of the first year, $40 at the end of the second, and the face amount, or *par*, of $1,000 at the end of the second year. How much can the business afford to pay for the bond today if its best alternative use of money at equal risk will earn 5 per cent a year, compounded annually?

First solution

1. The periodic payments of $40, the nominal interest on the bond, constitute an annuity. Multiply $40 by the present value of an annuity of $1 for two periods at 5 per cent, determined from Appendix III.
2. Multiply the face amount by *p*, the present value of $1 due at the end of two periods at 5 per cent, determined from Appendix II.
3. Add the products.

Computation

Present value of rents .... $ 40 × 1.85941 = $ 74.38
Present value of face amount......... $1,000 × 0.90703 =   907.03
Present value of savings bond $981.41

Conclusion

If the price of the bond is less than $981.41, the business would gain by buying it. If it is more, the business should select the alternative investment, which pays a 5 per cent return.

**Proof of
Computation**

Initial investment .... $ 981.41
Earnings first year at 5%...................................   49.07
Total accumulation at end of first year.................... $1,030.48
Cash collected at end of first year........................ −   40.00
Balance invested during second year...................... $ 990.48
Earnings second year at 5%...............................   49.52
Total accumulation at end of second year................ $1,040.00
Cash collected at end of second year:
    Face $1,000.00
    Nominal interest ....   40.00   − 1,040.00
Investment balance at end of second year............... $ .00

Second solution

Use a table of bond values, which expresses as a single ratio the relationship of the present value of all receipts on the bond—interest coupons as well as face— to each $1,000 of the bond's face amount.

A variation of this formula may be used to compute the amount of the equal periodic payments if the present sum, the number of periods, and the interest rate per period are known. The formula is

$$R = \frac{S}{P}.$$

Example 13

A business is buying on the installment plan a machine which has a cash price of $5,000. Equal payments are to be made at the end of each year for five years. Interest accumulates on the unpaid balance at the rate of 6 per cent per year. What is the amount of each annual payment?

Solution

$$R = \frac{S}{P} = \frac{\$5,000}{4.21236} = \$1,186.98.$$

The Time-Adjusted Rate of Return Method (TAROR)

The *time-adjusted rate of return method* (*TAROR*) is becoming widely accepted as the most reliable means of comparing alternative investment proposals. The time-adjusted rate of return is the compound rate of earnings that will discount the net cash inflows of a project to a present value which equals the amount of the initial investment.

Present value tables can be used to calculate the time-adjusted rate of retun of an investment proposal if the following are known: (1) the initial net cost of the investment, (2) the amount of net cash receipts for each future period, and (3) the estimated useful life of the investment. The procedure is to find the compound rate of earnings which will discount the estimated future receipts of the investment to an amount that is equal to the known initial cost of the investment.

Example 14 If a business invests $675.56 in a non-interest-bearing bond now, it will receive $1,000 at the end of ten years. What is the time-adjusted rate of return?

Solution 1. Compute the ratio for p by dividing the initial investment, S, by the expected future payment S_n:

$$\frac{\$675.56}{\$1,000} = 0.67556 = p.$$

2. Follow the line in the present value of $1 table for the given number of periods, n, to the interest rate column in which the ratio for p is located. On the line for ten years in Appendix II, the p ratio of 0.67556 is located in the 4 per cent column. Therefore, the expected time-adjusted rate of return is 4 per cent.

Example 15 A machine which costs $7,360 is expected to reduce operating costs $1,000 a year for ten years. What time-adjusted rate of return will it yield?

Solution
$$P = \frac{S}{R} = \frac{\$7,360}{\$1,000}$$
$$P = 7.360.$$

In the table for the present value of an annuity of $1 in Appendix III, this exact ratio is on the line for ten years and in the 6 per cent column. The time-adjusted rate of return expected on the investment is therefore 6 per cent.

It is unlikely that the exact p or P ratio for a given investment proposal will appear in the present value table as it did in Examples 14 and 15. A reasonable approximation of the ratio will be satisfactory for most business purposes. If greater accuracy is desired, an interpolation can be made between the two nearest ratios in the table and between their corresponding interest rates.

TAROR and the Payback-Period Reciprocal

If an investment has a very long useful life and a relatively short payback period, the *reciprocal* of (1 divided by) the payback period is often an accurate approximation of the investment's time-adjusted rate of return.

Example 16   A company invested $100,000 in a perpetual bond (that is, a bond whose principal amount never becomes due), and receives $10,000 a year in interest payments. The *time-adjusted rate of return* (which is also equal to the average rate of return because of the infinite investment life) is 10 per cent ($10,000 ÷ $100,000). The *payback period* is ten years ($100,000 investment divided by $10,000 annual net cash receipts), and the payback period reciprocal is $\frac{1}{10}$ or 10 per cent.

Example 17   The incremental cost of an investment is $10,000 and its expected incremental annual receipts are $2,000. The payback period is therefore five years and the reciprocal of the payback period, $\frac{1}{5}$, indicates an expected rate of return of 20 per cent. Reference to Appendix III shows that a P ratio of 5 is consistent with the following estimated lives and rates of return:

Estimated Life	Rate of Return with $P = 5$
10 years	15%
15 years	18+
20 years	19+

In Example 17, the payback-period reciprocal overstates the time-adjusted rate of return only slightly when the estimated life of the investment is three or more times as great as the payback period. The return estimated by the payback-reciprocal method is 20 per cent, as compared with 18+ per cent TAROR for a 15-year life and 19+ per cent TAROR for a 20-year life. The payback-reciprocal method is often used under such conditions as a quick way to estimate the time-adjusted rate of return.

Summary of the Use of Tables

Compound-interest tables have many business applications. The purpose of the present chapter has been to explain their derivation and basic uses, which may be summarized as follows:
1. Amount of $1, a (Appendix I):

Problem   To what future sum, S_n, will a given amount invested or owed now, S, accumulate at compound interest?

Solution $$S_n = S(a).$$

2. Amount of an annuity of $1, A (Appendix IV):

Problem (a)   To what future sum, S_n, will a series of equal periodic investments, R, accumulate at compound interest; or to what future sum, S_n, will a debt owed in a given series of equal periodic payments, R, accumulate?

Solution (a) $$S_n = R(A).$$

Problem (b)   What equal periodic installment, R, should be invested to accumulate a given future sum, S_n, at compound interest; or what equal installment, R, should be paid to settle a future debt of a given amount, S_n?

Solution (b)
$$R = \frac{S_n}{A}.$$

3. Present value of $1, p (Appendix II):

Problem   What sum, S, should be invested now to accumulate a given fund, S_n, in the future; or what sum, S, should be paid now to settle a given debt, S_n, due in the future?

Solution
$$S = S_n(p).$$

4. Present value of an annuity of $1, P (Appendix III):

Problem (a)   What sum, S, should be paid now in exchange for a right to receive a series of equal periodic payments of a given amount, R, in the future; or what sum, S, paid now would settle a debt due in a series of equal future periodic payments, R?

Solution (a)
$$S = R(P).$$

Problem (b)   What equal periodic receipt, R, is necessary to justify the investment of a given sum now, S, at compound interest; or what periodic payment, R, should be made to settle a debt of a given amount now due?

Solution (b)
$$R = \frac{S}{P}.$$

Summary   This chapter has illustrated several methods of comparing plans which are expected to result in definite, regular amounts of future cash receipts and disbursements.

(1) The *payback-period method* is most useful when uncertainty of expected cash flows is the controlling factor, or when highly profitable alternatives are in abundance. However, it ignores long-term profitability and the time-value of money.

(2) The *average rate of return method* emphasizes profitability over the life of a project, but ignores the time-value of money.

(3) The *time-adjusted rate of return* and its variations of *future value* and *present value*, based on compound interest formulas, is the most reliable index of the relative profitability of alternative investment proposals.

(4) The *payback-period reciprocal* is used under some circumstances as a quick way to estimate the time-adjusted rate of return.

The certainty of the results of the plans illustrated in this chapter, such as the bond investments, is more apparent than real. Although the sums to be paid are definite amounts fixed by contract, there is a chance that the borrower may be unable or unwilling to live up to the terms of the contract. Chapter 26 deals with project planning when the amounts of expected receipts and payments for alternative plans are irregular or uncertain.

Discussion Questions and Problems   **25-1**   This chapter has illustrated some business situations in which a knowledge of the basic mathematics of compound interest is useful. Actually, the application of these computations in business is much broader.

List several types of business problems in which each of the following compound interest tables would help in arriving at a solution:

a. Amount of $1 at compound interest.

b. Amount of an annuity of $1 at compound interest.

c. Present value of $1 at compound interest.

d. Present value of an annuity of $1 at compound interest.

25-2   A business manager is trying to decide which of two business assets to purchase. He has estimated the net annual cash inflows over the useful life of each asset. The assets are expected to have equal useful lives. The manager is wondering whether to compute the present value of the net receipts from each, or to compute their future values, on the assumption that all receipts will be reinvested to earn a return.

a. Which method of comparison should he use? Why?

b. Should he select the asset with the higher or lower S? The higher or lower S_n? Why?

25-3

a. Under what types of circumstances would you recommend that the cash payback-period method be used in determining the desirability of an investment? What are its limitations?

b. Under what circumstances would you recommend the use of the payback-reciprocal method? What are its shortcomings?

25-4   Unadjusted rate of return is described as having "limited usefulness." What is the major weakness of this method?

25-5   As used in this chapter, what does the term "discounted" mean?

25-6

a. The ratio of the future value of an accumulation to each dollar invested now is 6.7114. How much must be invested now for each dollar accumulated at the end of the investment's term? If $n = 20$, what is i?

b. Each $0.50 invested now will accumulate to $1.00 at the end of nine years. What is the assumed i (earnings) rate?

25-7

a. Which of the following alternatives is likely to be more profitable for a business to undertake? Why? List the most important assumptions you have to make in order to answer this question.

Estimated Net Annual Cash Receipts	Alternative I	Alternative II
Year 1	$5,000	$3,000
Year 2	4,000	3,500
Year 3	3,000	5,500

b. If the estimated net annual cash receipts of Alternative II were $6,000 in year 3 and all other estimated receipts were the same as in part a, which alternative is likely to be more profitable? What further information do you need in order to give a conclusive answer, and how would you use it?

25-8   Which of the following business plans is likely to be relatively more profitable? Why? List the most important assumptions that you have to make in order to answer this question.

	Plan A	Plan B
Cash investment at beginning of Year 1....................	$15,000	$ 5,000
Estimated net annual cash receipts:		
Year 1...	1,500	1,500
Year 2...	1,500	1,500
Year 3...	1,500	1,500
Recovery of cash investment at end of year 3	15,000	5,000

25-9   A business is considering adopting one of the following two plans:

	Plan C	Plan D
Cash investment required at beginning of year 1	$25,000	$20,000
Estimated net annual cash receipts:		
Year 1...	6,000	4,500
Year 2...	7,000	5,500
Year 3...	8,000	6,500
Year 4...	9,000	7,500
Partial cash recovery of investment at end of year 4 ...	5,000	4,000

Required   a. Compare the income from the plans for each year and for the four-year period as a whole.

b. Compare the annual rates of return on investment for the two plans.

c. Which plan would probably be relatively more profitable for the business to adopt? Why? What further information would you need in order to give a more definite answer, and how would you use it?

25-10   The Johnson Company wishes you to measure the expected profitability of the two following equally risky projects:

	Project 1	Project 2
Initial cash investment required	$15,000	$15,000
Net cash inflows:		
Year 1...	8,000	6,000
Year 2...	8,000	6,000
Year 3...	1,500	6,000

Required   a. Which will be the more profitable when an i (earnings) rate of (1) 25 per cent is used? (2) 6 per cent?

b. Explain the results of part a.

25-11

Required   For each of the following situations, state:

(1) Which compound interest table should be used.

(2) (n) the number of time periods.

(3) (i) the earnings rate.

(4) The result.

a. A credit union pays its depositors an 8 per cent annual interest rate, compounded quarterly. At the end of three years what will be the total accumulation on an initial deposit of $2,000?

b. Using the facts in part a, how much must be deposited now to accumulate a balance of $2,000 in four years?

c. A man owes a $900 non-interest-bearing note which is due in three years. How much must he pay now to settle the debt if the lender requires an annual rate of return of 6 per cent, compounded semiannually?

d. An individual expects to be able to deposit $500 in a savings account at the end of each three months. Interest at the rate of 4 per cent per annum is credited to the account quarterly. How much will be accumulated in the account at the end of five years?

e. On March 31, 1973, a business issues bonds of a face amount of $1,000 each, which includes interest to the maturity date, March 31, 1981. Other businesses of equal risk are able to issue at par eight-year bonds which pay interest every six months, at an annual rate of 6 per cent. What price should the business expect to receive for each bond?

f. A widow wishes to purchase an annuity contract under which she will receive cash payments of $5,000 a year at the end of each of the next 20 years. If the current rate of interest for such investments is 5 per cent, how much will the contract cost?

25-12

Required   Using Appendices I, II, III, and IV as needed, compute the following:

a. The total amount on deposit in a savings account at the end of four years if $3,000 is deposited now at 6 per cent interest per annum, compounded semiannually.

b. The amount to be deposited in a savings account now in order to accumulate $10,000 at the end of two years. Annual interest at 8 per cent is credited quarterly.

c. The total amount on deposit in a savings account at the end of five years if $1,500 is deposited at the end of each year. Interest at the rate of 6 per cent per annum is credited annually.

d. The equal quarterly installments necessary to pay within three years for a machine with a cash price of $8,000. The seller charges interest of 8 per cent per annum, compounded quarterly.

e. The equal annual deposit that must be made in a savings account to accumulate $6,000 at the end of five years. Deposits are made at the end of each year and interest of 5 per cent is credited annually.

f. The cash price of a contract which promises the holder annual payments of $2,000 at the end of each of the next 15 years. The applicable interest rate is 6 per cent per annum.

25-13   The Cooper Company has been paying for equipment in annual installments of $2,500 on each December 31. The last installment, plus interest for one year at 6 per cent, is due on December 31, 1974.

Required   How much would Cooper Company have to pay on December 31, 1973, to settle the last installment if the lender allows a discount rate of 6 per cent for early payments?

25-14   On January 1, 1973, Frank Thompson paid $840.72 for a bond with a face value of $1,000. This bond has a 4 per cent nominal interest rate, paying interest yearly on December 31. The bond matures on December 31, 1977.

Required   a. What will be his time-adjusted rate of return if he holds this bond to maturity?
b. What will be his average unadjusted rate of return?

25-15   The Madigan Shop holds a note receivable which provides for payments of $200 on December 31 of each year from 1972 through 1978, each payment including principal and interest. Rapid Discount Corp. purchases the note on January 1, 1973, at a discount rate of 8 per cent compounded annually.

Required   Compute the amount the Madigan Shop will receive on discounting the note.

25-16   Under a bond contract, the lender usually has the right to receive equal periodic payments at the nominal interest rate as well as the face amount of the bond at maturity. For example, the investor in a 20-year, 6 per cent, $1,000 bond with annual interest payments will receive $60 at the end of each year and an additional $1,000 at the end of the twentieth year.

Required   If the best comparable alternative investment pays a 6 per cent return, compute at the date of purchase of the bond:

a. The value of each dollar of the first year's interest.
b. The value of each dollar of the seventh year's interest.
c. The value of each dollar of the twentieth year's interest.
d. The value of each dollar of the face amount.
e. The total value of the face amount.
f. The total value of the interest payments.
g. The total value of the bond contract.

25-17   The facts are the same as in Problem 25-16, except that the best comparable alternative investment pays a 5 per cent return.

Required   Compute at the date of purchase of the bond:

a. The value of each dollar of the face amount.
b. The total value of the face amount.
c. The total value of the interest payments.
d. The total value of the bond contract.

25-18   Federal government financing makes wide use of discount bonds, by which the lender collects all his interest at maturity. Assume that Series Z bonds will pay the lender a face amount of $100 at the end of five years for each $74.41 invested now.

Required   Using the compound interest tables in the Appendices, determine to what semiannual rate this is equivalent.

25-19   A manufacturer offers a purchaser of a machine his choice of paying $12,600 cash or making five payments of $2,800 each, the first due immediately and the remainder at six-month intervals.

Required   If the purchaser can borrow the money needed to buy the machine at an interest rate of 8 per cent a year, compounded semiannually, should he do so?

25-20   Several years ago a man paid $10,000 for a perpetual bond which pays interest of $800 yearly. The bond is transferable to others.

Required   If the interest rate which can now be earned on very long-term investments of comparable risk is 5 per cent, what is the bond worth?

25-21   An investor wishes to buy a business whose annual income he estimates will be $20,000 for a long time in the future. Comparable business ventures earn an average rate of return of 8 per cent.

Required   a. Estimate the value of the business as an annuity for 15 years.
b. Estimate the value as an annuity for 20 years.
c. Estimate its value as a perpetuity.
d. How significant are the differences between these estimates?

25-22   The Walters Co. purchased a $10,000 bond of Loquat Corp. on January 1, 1972, at an effective annual rate of 5 per cent. The bond matures on January 1, 1976, and pays nominal interest of 4 per cent annually on January 1.

Required   Compute the price paid for the investment.

25-23   Ultimo Company issued $300,000 face amount of three-year, 5 per cent bonds on July 1, 1972, the first day of its fiscal year. Interest-payment dates were July 1 and January 1. The bonds were issued to yield an effective interest rate of 6 per cent per annum, compounded semiannually.

Required   Compute the issue price of the bonds.

25-24   It is common practice for banks to lend money on notes which include in their face interest to maturity. Interest is then computed on the face amount. For example, Bank *A* takes a note of $1,000 in exchange for a one-year loan, deducts interest at 5 per cent of the face amount, and gives the borrower the proceeds of $950 in cash.

Required   What interest rate is Bank *A* actually charging by using this "bank-discount" method?

25-25   On March 1, 1972, an investor is considering buying a $10,000 bond of the Viburnum Company. The bond was originally issued for a 20-year period on March 1, 1964. Nominal interest is paid each March 1 at the rate of 6 per cent of par. Newly issued bonds of similar quality and term yield a return of 4 per cent per annum.

Required   What is the maximum amount which the investor should be willing to pay for the Viburnum bond?

25-26   The owner of a business is trying to decide how to finance the purchase of a store building. The Certain Insurance Company will take a ten-year mortgage note which requires annual interest payments of 5 per cent of the face amount of the note, $9,500. The Central Savings and Loan Association quotes a $4\frac{1}{2}$ per cent interest rate on a ten-year note for $10,000 face amount, from which it will deduct a discount of $500.

Required   Present computations to compare these two proposals.

25-27   A bride and bridegroom of a few months have found the house of their dreams. Its cost is $33,000, and it can be financed by a $3,000 down payment and a 25-year mortgage loan bearing interest at 8 per cent. The bridegroom has been advised not to spend more than 20 per cent of his annual income, after income tax, for housing, and he would like to know whether his salary is large enough to justify purchasing this house. For simplicity assume in your computation that salary receipts and mortgage payments both occur at the end of each year.

Required a. Compute the annual salary, after taxes, which the bridegroom must earn in order to afford this house on 20 per cent of his salary.

b. What must his income before tax be, assuming that the average effective income tax rate on his salary is 18 per cent?

25-28   The Jingle Realty Company has leased a building to a tenant for ten years under an agreement which requires the payment of an annual rental of $3,000 at the end of each year. At the beginning of the fourth year the Jingle Realty Company offers the tenant an opportunity to make an immediate payment of $14,000 in lieu of the remaining rentals. The tenant's treasurer estimates that his company can earn 10 per cent a year, compounded annually, on its funds if it does not make the advance payment.

Required a. Should the tenant accept the offer? Give computations to support your conclusion.

b. What condition probably induced Jingle Realty to make the offer?

25-29   The St. Joseph Co. borrowed $1,000,000 on 20-year, 6 per cent sinking fund bonds payable, issuing them on January 1, 1972, at par. The sinking fund provisions require that on December 31 of each year of the life of the bonds equal payments be made to a trustee, sufficient to accumulate a fund which will be used to retire the bonds at their maturity. The trustee estimates that the sinking fund balance will earn a return of 5 per cent per annum, compounded annually.

Required a. What equal periodic payments must be made into the sinking fund?

b. If the actual rate of earnings on the fund is only 4 per cent per annum, how much will be in the fund at the maturity of the bonds?

c. If the balance in the fund on January 1, 1982, is $400,000 and if the trustee estimates that this balance and all additional earnings can be invested at 6 per cent per annum for the remainder of the life of the bonds, what will be the revised amount of the annual payments into the fund for the remaining ten years?

25-30   The New London Corporation planned late in 1972 to issue 20-year bonds to finance some capital additions. In December arrangements were made to issue bonds of $400,000 face amount paying coupon interest of 7 per cent annually on December 31. Late in December 1972 the market interest rates took a sharp turn downward and the New London Corporation decided to delay the issue, scheduled for December 31, to take advantage of possible still lower interest rates. Accordingly, the bonds were issued on December 31, 1973, at a price which resulted in an interest cost of 6 per cent. The maturity date still remained December 31, 1992.

Required   Compute the amount New London received on issuance of the bonds.

Cases   **25-1   Downstate Utility Company.** On July 1, 1963, the Downstate Utility Company issued $500,000 of 20-year, 7 per cent, First Mortgage Bonds Payable. On June 30, 1973, the balance in Bonds Payable—Unamortized Discount was $12,000 after all adjusting entries had been made. The credit of Downstate Utility had improved significantly during the past decade, and this fact, coupled with a general decline in utility interest rates, caused the management to consider refunding the bonds. The First Mortgage Bond indenture contained a provision permitting early retirement of the bonds upon payment of a premium. Redemption prices were

Before July 1, 1968......................No redemption permitted
July 1, 1968–June 30, 1973............107% of par
July 1, 1973–June 30, 1978............105% of par
July 1, 1978–June 30, 1981............103% of par
July 1, 1981–June 30, 1983............101% of par
July 1, 1983 ....100% of par

Management had been advised by its investment bankers that a new ten-year issue sufficient to retire the old bonds and to pay all related costs could probably be floated on July 1, 1973, at an effective interest cost of 6 per cent per annum, payable annually. Legal and other costs in connection with refunding would be $10,000, payable immediately.

Required a. Would it be advantageous for the Downstate Utility Company to refund its bonds? Show present value computations to support your answer, ignoring the impact of income taxes.

b. Under income tax rules any loss on the retirement of bonds is deductible in full in the year in which the bonds are retired. Discount on bonds outstanding is deductible over the life of the bonds in computing taxable income. What effect does this situation have on the desirability of refunding the bonds?

chapter 26

Planning and Controlling Long-Lived Asset Additions

Purpose of Chapter

The preceding chapter illustrated several methods of comparing the relative profitability of alternative investment proposals. It emphasized how compound-interest mathematics can be used to compare investment alternatives when the *amounts and timing* of their expected future receipts and payments are *known*. If the *present value* of a proposed investment's expected future net cash inflows (when discounted at an interest rate equal to the company's best alternative use of funds involving equal risk) is greater than its initial outlay cost, the investment proposal can be profitably accepted. Similarly, if a proposal's *time-adjusted* rate of return is greater than the company's average cost of capital, the proposal can be profitably accepted.

Although bonds and similar *financial* contracts which *promise* specific sums of money at definite future times were used in earlier illustrations, most investments made by businesses are in *real* assets rather than in *financial* assets. Business investments usually involve the acquisition of productive resources such as land, buildings, equipment, and permanent working capital instead of securities and stocks. They involve *expected* rather than *promised* future receipts. The *amounts, timing, and degree of uncertainty* associated with the cash flow from such investments are all *indefinite.*

This chapter outlines appropriate methods of selecting long-range investments in view of these uncertainties. It also proposes a general approach to planning and administering a budget of the capital additions of the enterprise for the next year and for the longer term.

Purpose of a Capital Additions Budget

The *capital budget* is a plan for acquiring and financing additions to the long-lived assets of a business. Such a plan is required when management desires

(1) To replace old assets which are worn out or obsolete.
(2) To expand capacity to produce a greater volume of existing products or services.
(3) To begin producing new products or services.
(4) To decide whether to eliminate various activities, products, or services.

For several reasons the capital budget should be developed carefully and systematically before the asset additions are to be acquired.

First, long-lived assets require the expenditure of *large sums* of money, and management must know the amount of funds needed in time to make arrangements for their financing.

Second, the funds invested in long-lived assets are tied up in specialized items of plant and equipment and can usually be recovered only through operating revenues over a *long period of time.*

Third, these investments are subject to *high risks of loss* because of the long-term commitment of funds and the likelihood that significant changes will occur in the economy and in the internal operations of the enterprise.

Responsibility for Evaluating Investment Profitability

In most businesses the responsibility for coordinating the capital additions budget rests with top management. Specific investment proposals are often initiated by intermediate and lower levels of management which have a special interest in the projects and will be responsible for executing them. When the proposals are accepted by top management, the capital additions budget becomes a means of carrying out the necessary action.

The following two sections show how top management might choose between alternatives, given information on their expected profitability.

Types of Plans With and Without Capital Investment Requirements

When the alternative plans being compared require *no additional capital investment,* the plan chosen should be the one with the *greatest present value.* The present value of each plan may be estimated by discounting its expected future stream of net cash receipts at a rate which reflects the relative risks associated with the project. Examples of such alternatives are whether to change selling prices, whether to change marketing channels, whether to purchase a component part of the finished product or continue making it with facilities already owned which have no resale value, and whether to rearrange the flow of work. Often there are capital costs associated with such plans, but they are difficult to measure.

Examples of alternative solutions to a business problem, only one of which requires an additional capital investment, are decisions as to whether to replace equipment or plant prior to the ends of their useful lives or to continue to use the existing ones, and whether to lease or buy equipment or real estate.

Examples of alternatives, all of which *require additional capital*, are choices between several possible new machines or new plant locations.

There may be many possible alternative courses of action to supply a given business need; the decision may be not merely *whether* to replace an asset at all, but also *which* of several possible replacements to select. Usually some of the possibilities may be quickly eliminated from serious consideration. The detailed analysis can then be confined to the few best contenders.

Rationing Capital to Specific Projects

Often the favorable opportunities for capital additions which confront a business are greater than the funds available to finance them. It is then necessary to *ration funds* to investment projects on the basis of their *relative desirability*. One of the most important determinants of the desirability of investment plans is the comparative effect of each on the rate of return which the company earns on its assets. *Intangible*, or qualitative, considerations, such as the effect of a course of action on company prestige or on employee morale, also often have an important influence on capital investment decisions. It is usually advisable to make a careful, objective appraisal of alternatives by outlining the advantages and disadvantages of each, expressing them, where possible, in terms of dollars of expected cost and revenue. Then if the final choice is dictated by an intangible factor, at least management can see the cost of such a decision.

In some cases a business has *no choice* but to make a capital outlay, regardless of its expected rate of return. The capital investment may be necessitated by law or by a catastrophe, where the losses from the alternative of not making the outlay would be prohibitive. On the other hand, some proposed uses of capital may be rejected immediately because they will *never pay* for themselves in increased income. Between these two clear-cut extremes are a variety of possible capital expenditures which promise a wide range of profitability and where the right decision is not so clear. Some are optional or postponable; some are merely different ways of filling an important current need. It is to this wide band of borderline cases that the methods of analysis in this chapter apply.

Ranking Projects as to Rate of Return

To the extent that proposed capital additions may be compared on the basis of quantitative factors, it is useful to *rank each* according to the *expected rate of return* on the incremental investment it requires. This ranking often follows a preliminary comparison in which the best of several ways to accomplish each given purpose has been selected, also largely on the basis of rate of return on the investment. Assume that computations give the following results:

Project	Expected Cost	Expected Annual Return
A	$20,000	22%
B	30,000	20%
C	50,000	18%
D	50,000	17%

If the company's cash forecast plus an estimate of funds available from outside sources indicates that only $50,000 can be spent for capital outlay in the coming year, Projects A and B should be selected (assuming that profitable reinvestment opportunities will be available at their termination). Their combined $50,000 investment will probably increase the annual income of the business by $10,400 ($4,400 plus $6,000), while the next best. alternative, Project C, would bring in only $9,000.

There is a lower limit beyond which the ranking process should not be carried. One suggested minimum, below which projects will be rejected, is the *expected average cost of capital* to the business in the future. This is estimated by considering the net return which creditors and stockholders will probably require in order to continue supplying funds to the business. Another minimum is the *desired future rate of return* of the business. However, there is no substitute for judgment in evaluating the risks associated with alternative courses of action. Some projects involving a high degree of uncertainty should be rejected even though their expected rates of return are well above these minimum rates. Other projects whose profitability is practically assured may be accepted even though their rates of return are below these limits. The total capital budget of a business will thus consist of a combination of investments, some with a possible high return coupled with great uncertainty, and others with lower expected returns but greater certainty that they will be realized.

If in management's judgment the expected rates of return on all alternative projects are very low, management should consider (1) postponing all capital expenditures until a later time, when prospects may appear better; or (2) using the available funds for dividends to stockholders so that they may put them to more profitable use elsewhere.

Factors in Evaluating Investment Profitability

The profitability of an investment proposal depends on four factors:

(1) The expected *additional investment*.

(2) The expected additional *net cash inflows*, or *net reductions* (savings) *in cash outflows*.

(3) The *life* of the project.

(4) The degree of *uncertianty* that the expected net cash inflows or cash savings will actually materialize.

The reliability of the capital budget in guiding management decisions is influenced by systematic treatment of each of these factors. Suggested methods of analysis are discussed in the following sections.

Estimating Initial Incremental Investment

The first step in determining the relative profitability of an investment proposal is to *estimate the expected incremental investment*—the additional cash payment, S, which is required at the beginning of the project. This incremental expenditure consists of the total cost of the asset to be acquired, including the purchase price and any additional outlays for transportation, installation, and preparation for first use, as well as required additions to net working capital. If the new asset is a replacement, the net cash received as the salvage value of the old asset is subtracted from the cost of the new asset in determining the incremental investment.

Example 1(a)   At the end of 1973 Company X is trying to decide whether to continue to use an old machine for its estimated remaining useful life of five years or to replace it immediately with a new one. The facts about the two machines are as follows:

	Old Machine	New Machine
Original cost	$9,000	$10,000
Accumulated depreciation	4,000	0
Salvage value, 12/31/73	3,000	
Expected salvage value, 12/31/78	0	0
The productive capacity of the two machines is equal.		

What is the incremental cost, (S), of the new machine?

Solution   If the business purchases the new machine, it will sell the old one for $3,000 cash, and then pay a total of $10,000 for the new one. The net cash payment will be only the difference, $7,000; this is the *incremental cost* of the new machine.

A word of caution is in order. The $5,000 unexpired cost, or *book value*, of the old machine (its original cost of $9,000 minus accumulated depreciation of $4,000) should be ignored in computing the difference in the capital cost of the decision alternatives.[1] It is a *sunk cost*, representing a cash payment made at some time in the past. This historical fact has no relevance to the future action being considered in this decision. As one alternative, the old machine can be *used* without any additional investment. The other alternative is to *sell* the old machine for $3,000 and acquire the new machine for $10,000, an additional capital outlay of $7,000.

Only *future cash flows*, which *can* be affected by the choice now being made, are relevant in comparing the effects of alternative courses of action on the future income of the business. If the old machine is disposed of immediately, its

---

[1] Except for its effect on income taxes, which is discussed later in this chapter.

book value (minus any salvage value) is charged as a loss on disposal in the current year. If it is retained, its remaining book value (minus salvage value) will be charged to periodic depreciation expense. *Total income* under the two alternatives, therefore, *will be affected equally* by the book value of the old machine.

Estimating Incremental Future Receipts

The second step in determining the relative profitability of an investment proposal is to *estimate the differences in future periodic net receipts (R)* which can be expected under the alternatives being considered. Differences in expected net receipts may result from

(1) *Cost savings* of one plan as compared with other plans.

(2) *Additions to net revenues.*

(3) A combination of both additional net revenues and cost savings.

Records of past payments and receipts often provide valuable clues in estimating probable future payments and receipts, especially when the alternatives being considered merely consist of a continuation or an extension of existing activities. However, estimates of results expected in the future must allow for anticipated changes in prices and other conditions, both internal and external to the enterprise.

Only the operating receipts and payments which are *expected to be changed* under any of the plans need be listed in making a comparison of the estimated net receipts from alternative investments. The objective is to determine whether *differences in receipts* resulting from each alternative justify their respective *differences in investment.*

Example 1(b)   The expected annual operating costs of the two machines described in Example 1(a) are shown below. Expected revenues are omitted, because the two machines have equal productive capacity.

	Expected Annual Operating Costs	
	Old Machine	New Machine
Operator's wages	$4,000	$2,600
Waste materials...............................	1,000	400
Repairs..	200	50
Maintenance...................................	400	300
Property tax	120	320
Insurance.......................................	100	400
Totals	$5,820	$4,070

It is assumed that these operating costs are expected to be the same for each future year, and that differences in the time between the receipt of the various services and payment for them are negligible.

What will be the annual differential net receipts, *R*, if the old machine is replaced?

Solution

	New Machine's Expected Incremental Annual Net Receipts	
	Costs Saved	*Costs Added*
Operator's wages..	$1,400	
Waste materials...	600	
Repairs	150	
Maintenance	100	
Property tax...		$200
Insurance...		300
Totals	$2,250	$500
Deduct costs added.......................................	500	
Net annual operating saving of new machine, before income tax	$1,750	

Some analysts prefer to list all the costs of each alternative, whether or not they are different, as a reminder to consider all possible points of difference between the plans.

Evaluating Project Profitability

The relative profitability of alternative investment proposals can be estimated by several methods. Chapter 25 described the *payback-period method*, the *average rate of return method* (*ROR*), and the *time-adjusted rate of return* (*TAROR*) *method*. The preferable method is the TAROR, which is the compound rate of interest that will discount the expected net cash inflows (or cost savings) of an investment to a present value equal to the initial incremental investment.

Example 1(c)   The asset replacement problem illustrated in Examples 1(a) and 1(b) may be summarized as follows: The new machine will require an additional initial cash outlay of $7,000; it is expected to reduce cash payments for operating costs by $1,750 a year for the next five years, a total of $8,750. Does the expected future saving justify the additional asset investment?

Solution

$$P = \frac{S}{R} = \frac{\$7,000}{\$1,750}$$

$$P = \$4.000.$$

The table of the present value of an annuity of $1 in Appendix III shows the following:

Years	*6%*	*8%*	*10%*
5..	4.212	3.993	3.791

The expected rate of return on the investment in the new machine is slightly less than 8 per cent.

Conclusion   If the average cost of capital for the company is less than 8 per cent and the risk associated with this type of investment is not considered to be unusual, the company should replace the machine.

The *net present value method,* a close cousin of the time-adjusted rate of return method, also has strong support for estimating the relative profitability of investment alternatives. The *net present value* of a project is the *difference* between the *present value* of the expected cash inflows from the investment (discounted at a rate equal to the average cost of capital for the company) and the *initial incremental investment.* An investment which has a positive net present value will be more profitable than an equivalent sum invested at a rate equal to the company's cost of capital.

Example 1(d) Using the same data as in Example 1(c), compute the net present value of the new machine. Assume that the company's average cost of capital is 6 per cent.

Solution
$$S = R(P) = \$1,750(4.212)$$
$$S = \$7,371.$$

Present value of expected cost savings...........................	$7,371
Less: Initial incremental investment............................	7,000
Net present value...	$ 371

Conclusion The old machine should be replaced because the present value of new machine's expected incremental receipts is greater than the present value of the incremental investment.

Special Problems in Estimating the Rate of Return

Examples 1(c) and (d) illustrated the computation of an investment's estimated rate of return and net present value under simple assumptions. They were designed merely to show how to apply the basic mechanics of the methods. The following paragraphs explain briefly how to deal with some more complicated factors which are encountered in actual practice.

(a) *Unequal annual incremental receipts.* If the variations in the annual incremental receipts expected from a capital investment are relatively small, a satisfactory approximation of the rate of return may be calculated by using the *average annual incremental receipts.* If the annual variations are significant, the following *trial-and-error method* should be used:

(1) Multiply the incremental receipts of each year by the present value of $1 for the number of time periods from the present to that particular year, using a trial interest rate.

(2) The products in (1) represent the present value of each annual incremental receipt. When added together they should equal the incremental investment. If their total is greater than the incremental investment, the trial interest rate is too low, and a higher rate should be tried. If the sum of the present values is less than the incremental investment, the trial rate is too high. The trial process should be repeated until the correct interest rate can be approximated to the nearest whole per cent.

The trial-and-error procedure is illustrated in Example 2.

Example 2   A business is considering the purchase of a patent for $20,000. Its use is expected to result in operating cost savings of $5,000 the first year, $6,000 the second, $7,000 the third, and $8,000 the fourth. What is the expected rate of return on the investment?

Solution   A trial interest rate of 12 per cent is first used, as in the following tabulation.

	12% Trial Rate			10% Trial Rate		
Year	Estimated Incremental Receipts	Present Value Factor	Product	Estimated Incremental Receipts	Present Value Factor	Product
1	$5,000 ×	0.893 =	$ 4,465	$5,000 ×	0.909 =	$ 4,545
2	6,000 ×	0.797 =	4,782	6,000 ×	0.826 =	4,956
3	7,000 ×	0.712 =	4,984	7,000 ×	0.751 =	5,257
4	8,000 ×	0.636 =	5,088	8,000 ×	0.683 =	5,464
Total present values			$19,319	....		$20,222
Minus incremental investment			20,000	....		20,000
Remainders			−$ 681	............................+$ 222		

The total present value using a trial rate of 12 per cent is less than the incremental investment, indicating that the trial rate is too high. The present value using a 10 per cent trial rate is more than the investment, denoting that the trial rate is too low. The remainder is much less when the 10 per cent rate is used; therefore the expected rate of return is nearer 10 per cent than 12 per cent.

(b) *Substantial salvage value at end of life.* A substantial salvage value expected to be realized at the end of an asset's life may be treated as a cash receipt of the last year. This will probably cause the expected annual receipts to be unequal, in which case the trial-and-error method outlined in (a) is appropriate.

(c) *Investments with lives of different length.* The rates of return on capital investments which are mutually exclusive should be compared for the same time period. If it is a question of buying Machine A, which has an estimated useful life of 10 years, or Machine B, with an estimated life of 12 years, the comparison should be made for a 10-year period. The expected salvage value of Machine B at the end of 10 years, if substantial, can be treated as a receipt of the tenth year.

(d) *Investments with varying degrees of uncertainty.* When there is a wide range in an investment's expected annual receipts for a given year, an estimated amount may be determined by using *subjective probability* factors. Each possible value of a year's receipts is multiplied by a factor which reflects the estimated probability of that value's being the correct amount of receipts. The products of this multiplication are added, and the sum is the figure that should be used as the expected receipts for the year in computing the estimated rate of return on investment.

Example 3   Management feels that the year 1 incremental receipts from an investment may be any amount from $3,000 to $6,000. The expected receipts for the year, weighted by their probability of occurrence, are as follows:

Possible Amount of Receipts	Probability of Occurrence	Receipts Weighted by Probability
$3,000	0.1	$ 300
4,000	0.3	1,200
5,000	0.5	2,500
6,000	0.1	600
Totals	1.0	$4,600

The sum of $4,600 should be used as the estimated incremental receipts for the year in computing the expected rate of return.

The sum of the probability factors must always equal 1, because there will be only one outcome. The total receipts for the year will be one sum.

Sometimes the *possible loss* associated with a particular investment is *so great* that its occurrence would be seriously damaging or even fatal to the business. Even though the probability of such an outcome is relatively slight, management may reject the project because of its potential danger to the business.

Another approach in comparing the expected profitability of investments with varying degrees of uncertainty is to group together for consideration those projects which are thought to have a *similar degree of uncertainty*. A different minimum acceptable rate of return is then set for investments in each group. For example, the investments whose outcomes are most uncertain might be rejected unless their estimated rates of return were more than 40 per cent, while investments in the most certain group might be accepted if their estimated rates of return were more than 10 per cent.

Rate of Return After Income Tax

When the alternatives being compared *do not* require any incremental capital investment, the most profitable can be determined just as well by using expected net annual incremental receipts *before income tax* as by using receipts after tax. Although the after-tax receipts from each alternative will be reduced by income tax at the rate which the particular business must pay, the receipts from each alternative will be reduced by tax in approximately the same proportion.

When the alternatives *do* require an initial capital investment which is subject to amortization for income tax purposes (for example, depreciable equipment), the *timing of taxable income* by periods will differ from the *timing of net cash receipts* by periods. This is true because periodic *cost amortization* does not require a cash payment; rather, it is the *payment* for the depreciable asset that requires cash. Amortization of an asset's cost does affect cash flow *indirectly*, however, through its effect on the amount of periodic *income tax*. Because the tax rates applicable to a business are often quite high, investments which are subject to amortization should be compared for desirability on the basis of their *after-tax rates of return*.

When the incremental capital investment is subject to amortization for income tax purposes, the periodic incremental net receipts from the investment differ from the income subject to tax which it produces. The tax paid, in turn, is deducted in computing the periodic net receipts. Example 4 shows the method for computing the *rate of return after tax* on an investment, using the same basic data as those in Examples 1(a), 1(b), and 1(c) earlier in this chapter.

Example 4   Company X is trying to decide whether to use an old machine for its estimated remaining life of five years or to replace it with a new one which has an incremental cost of $7,000, an expected net annual operating saving before income tax of $1,750, and therefore an estimated before-tax rate of return of slightly less than 8 per cent. (Refer to Example 1(c) on p. 693.) For simplicity, it is assumed that the new machine will also have a useful life of five years. What is the estimated rate of return on the incremental investment *after income tax*?

Solution

	New Machine's Expected Incremental	
	Taxable Income	Net Receipts
New machine's net annual operating saving before income tax.............................	+$1,750	+$1,750
Deduct *incremental* annual depreciation on new machine for tax purposes, using straight-line method:		
Depreciation on new machine ($\frac{1}{5}$ of tax cost, $12,000,* minus salvage, 0)......................... $2,400		
Depreciation on old machine ($\frac{1}{5}$ of remaining cost, $5,000, minus salvage, 0)......................... 1,000	− 1,400	
Incremental taxable income........................	+$ 350	
Deduct income tax at 48%..........................	+ 168	− 168
Incremental income after tax.......................	+$ 182	
Incremental net receipts..............................		+$1,582

Income tax law does not recognize a gain or a loss when similar productive assets are exchanged. Hence, the cost of the new machine for tax purposes will be the unexpired cost of the old machine, $5,000, plus the $7,000 additional outlay for the new.

$$P = \frac{S}{R} = \frac{\$7,000}{\$1,582} = 4.425.$$

Appendix III shows that the approximate after-tax rate of return is slightly more than 4 per cent.

The use of *accelerated depreciation* for income tax purposes usually *increases the rate of return* which a business can earn on a new investment, especially if accelerated depreciation is permissible for the new asset but not for the old. The effect of the accelerated depreciation methods, which are described in Chapter 12, is to increase the net cash receipts of the early years by decreasing tax payments, and to decrease the receipts of the later years. A stream of declining annual receipts has a greater present value (and yields a greater rate of return) than a uniform stream which totals the same amount for a given period of years.

USING THE CAPITAL BUDGET

The Annual Capital Additions Budget

The capital additions budget for the next year should include the proposed outlays for the *specific* long-lived assets which the business plans to acquire during that period, classified by areas of responsiblity, together with the means of financing them. Example 5 shows a part of such a budget which applies to a single department of the business.

Example 5

MODERN PRODUCTS COMPANY
Shipping Department
Capital Additions Budget
For the Year Ending December 31, 1973

L. Watt, Manager

Item	Total Cost	Expected Starting Date	Expected Completion Date	Expected Monthly Payments January	Expected Monthly Payments February
Plant:					
Platform..........	$ 4,000	1/15/73	4/1/73	$1,500	$1,800
Rail siding.......	7,000	2/1	5/1		2,500
	$11,000				
Equipment:					
Scales	$ 500		6/1		
Truck	3,500		1/5	3,500	
	$ 4,000				
Grand total...	$15,000			$5,000	$4,300

The form should be extended to include cash requirements for each month of the year.

Some assets in next year's budget will be acquired to replace others which have worn out or become outmoded. Others will be needed to facilitate expected additional sales or to reduce operating costs. Still others will be needed to carry out new activities. Many of these investments will be selected on the basis of an evaluation of their potential rates of return, together with qualitative considerations. All of them should be *consistent* with the *long-range capital budget*.

The *cash budget* for the coming year should include an estimate of the outlay for each capital addition which is large enough to justify individual planning. It should also contain lump-sum provisions for estimated minor capital expenditures which individually are too small to warrant separate planning.

Administering the Capital Budget

Responsibility for originating a request to purchase a long-lived asset in most cases rests with the department head who will be responsible for its use. He may have permission to authorize small capital additions without futher approval, but larger projects require careful screening at higher levels of management.

Mere inclusion of a capital-addition item in the annual budget is not an authorization to purchase it. Careful control requires that specific approval be obtained before each order is placed, based on a consideration of the current availability of funds and of changes in asset requirements. The desirability of major projects is thus examined three times: first, in a broad way in the long-range budget; second, in the annual budget; and third, at the time the order is placed.

Frequent reports on the *status of spending* in comparison with the capital budget should be made to those who are in a position to control the amount of expenditures, particularly for projects which require a long time to complete. Where possible each budget allowance should be based on a cost standard for the acquisition. The following is an illustration of such a report.

Example 6

MODERN PRODUCTS COMPANY
Shipping Department
Capital Additions Report
For the Month Ended February 28, 1972

L. Watt, Manager

Item	Actual Cost		Esti-mated Total Cost	Budget Allowance	Estimated Under (Over) Budget	Explanation
	This Month	*To Date*				
Plant:						
Platform................	$1,602	$2,105	$ 3,900	$ 4,000	$100	
Rail siding.............	2,880	2,880	7,400	7,000	(400)	Increased
Total.................				$11,000		rail costs
Equipment:						
Scales...................	0	0	500	$ 500	—	
Truck...................	3,490	3,490*	3,490*	3,500	10	
Grand total.........	$7,972	$8,475	$15,290	$15,000	($290)	

*Completed project.

Supplementary data should include the expected completion date of projects and comments on factors which have caused delays or major changes in costs. The user of the report should require further investigation, when needed, of the causes of departures from budget allowances. He should then initiate steps to bring the costs into line.

A further means of focusing attention on deviations from the plan is to require special approval for each expenditure in excess of the original authorization.

Appraising the Performance of Investments

If management is to apply the lessons of past experience in improving income, it must *evaluate the performance of capital additions* after they have been acquired. Even if capital investments have been selected on the basis of a rigorous analysis of their expected profitability, follow-through is needed to assure that the expectations are fulfilled. Periodic comparisons, at least on a test basis, should be made to determine how well the actual performance of an asset measures up to expectations. If actual results are below the estimates, action should be initiated to improve them. When the fault lies in *inaccurate estimating*, efforts should be made to improve future estimates of acquisition costs, useful lives, and operating savings.

Summary   In comparing the relative profitability of alternative proposals for acquiring long-lived assets, it is often desirable to express each in terms of the *present value* of expected future net receipts and to select the project with the greatest present value. When one or both of the projects requires an initial incremental capital investment, it is also appropriate to compute the estimated *time-adjusted rate of return* on the incremental investment.

Both the *present value* and the *time-adjusted rate of return* computations require estimates of the *initial costs* of each alternative, the expected periodic *additions to net cash receipts* (or *net cost savings*), a *uniform life* for all alternatives to be compared, and the *probabilities* that the uncertain expected future cash inflows will *actually be realized*. The present chapter has considered methods of making these estimates.

In spite of the apparent precision of the methods used in estimating the relative future profitability of alternatives, the reader must remember that the comparisons are *merely estimates*. Moreover, the many factors bearing on a decision which cannot be expressed in terms of dollar costs must not be overlooked. Finally, planning alone will not bring about the expected income. *Action* must be taken to bring performance into line with the plans when the plans are sound, and to improve planning when they are not.

Discussion Questions and Problems

26-1   How does the capital budget help managers in the two vital functions of planning and control?

26-2   "Most investments made by businesses are in *real* assets rather than in *financial* assets." Explain the meaning of this quotation. What complications does this add in comparing investment alternatives of a business?

26-3   The process of comparing alternative long-lived asset acquisitions is very complex and time-consuming. For example, a business may have several alternative ways of performing a given job, and there may be hundreds of jobs within the business for which capital expenditures should be considered.

a. To what extent would you recommend the use of incremental comparisons, of the types illustrated in this chapter, in analyzing these alternatives?
b. In situations for which you do not think such incremental comparisons are appropriate, how should the business make capital expenditure decisions?

26-4   What is meant by a company's "average cost of capital"? How might this be measured for a particular business?

26-5   "The specific long-lived assets selected have a far-reaching effect on the productive capacity of a business and the amount of its operating expenses." Give an example of costs that will be largely fixed as a result of a decision to purchase a particular type of electronic data processing equipment.

26-6 How might the method of evaluating long-range plans which do not require additional capital investments differ from the evaluation of those which do require additional capital investments? In what ways might the two types of evaluations be similar?

26-7

a. When a business has more attractive investment possibilities than it has funds for investment, how would you recommend that the choices be made?
b. What conditions might cause a business to have fewer profitable investment opportunities than it had funds to invest? What solutions might be suggested in this case?

26-8 The president of a company was presented with plans for a highly profitable replacement of existing obsolete, yet still functioning, machinery. He wanted the replacement to be deferred for several years because the existing machinery was not yet fully depreciated on the books. He said, "We cannot afford the loss that would result from the sale. When the equipment is fully depreciated we will replace it—then we will not have this loss." Was the president's reasoning sound? Explain.

26-9 In preparing your company's capital budget for the coming year you find that some projects will apparently yield very stable and highly predictable results, others will be more irregular and uncertain, and still others will be characterized by a high degree of uncertainty.

State how you would allow for these differences in uncertainty in presenting comparisons of the projects to the board of directors for final decision.

26-10

a. Why might the prospective rate of return on a given investment be different for a company at different times?
b. Why might it be different for different companies at the same time?
c. Why might one company select a machine and another reject it, both on the basis of its estimated time-adjusted rate of return?

26-11 The Moheli Company's accounts show total assets of $196,500. A would-be buyer of the business makes a firm offer of $225,000 for the total assets.

a. Why might the value of the assets to the buyer be different from the amount at which they are stated on the seller's books?
b. What circumstances might lead the seller to decline the offer?

26-12 A manufacturing company is contemplating adding a newly developed product which will require an investment that is substantial in relation to its present assets. According to all indications the new product will be well received; however, if it is not, little of the capital can be recovered from the project.

Outline the type of analysis that you would present to management to take these factors into consideration.

26-13 Using tables where needed, make the following computations:

a. An additional investment of $6,000 is expected to result in annual operating savings of $800 for 15 years. What is its time-adjusted rate of return?
b. The payback period of an investment of $12,000, which has an estimated useful life of 18 years, is expected to be 8 years.
   1. What is the expected annual operating savings?

2. What is the expected time-adjusted rate of return?

3. What is the net present value if the discount rate is 10 per cent?

c. What maximum price should a company pay for an asset which is expected to yield an annual net additional revenue of $600 for six years, if the company's best alternative use of capital will pay a rate of return of 8 per cent?

d. If a company's alternative investments of similar risk are yielding a return of 8 per cent, how much can it afford to pay for each dollar of annual savings expected from an investment estimated to have a useful life of 14 years?

e. A capital outlay which is expected to yield a rate of return of 10 per cent has a cash payback period of 7.1 years. What is the estimated life of the investment?

f. The payback reciprocal of an investment which is expected to have a life of 14 years is $\frac{1}{6}$. What is the estimated time-adjusted rate of return? How accurate would the use of the payback reciprocal be in selecting or rejecting this investment?

26-14   Compute the following:

a. The time-adjusted rate of return of an investment with an initial net cost of $50,000 and expected incremental net cash receipts of $12,500 a year for six years.

b. The rate of return in part a, unadjusted for time differences.

c. The net present value of the investment in part a. The discount rate is 8 per cent.

d. The maximum capital investment warranted if the expected incremental annual net cash receipts is $10,000 and the minimum acceptable time-adjusted rate of return before tax is 20 per cent. Useful life is eight years.

e. The expected annual incremental cash receipts on an investment with an incremental cost of $25,000, a time-adjusted rate of return of 10 per cent, and an estimated useful life of 17 years.

26-15   Frank Doyle is trying to decide between two possible projects to help reverse the decline in profits which has recently occurred in his wholesale electronics company.

Plan I is a 6 per cent increase in product prices with continued use of existing marketing channels. This change requires no incremental capital investment and will yield an estimated $17,000 a year in incremental cash receipts.

Plan II is a change in marketing channels without changing the present price structure. This change will save $8,000 a year by releasing one salesman and provide $10,000 a year in additional sales receipts. Plan II requires an incremental investment of $3,500.

Required a. How can these plans be best evaluated if their benefits are expected to last indefinitely? Which would be the more profitable, assuming equal uncertainty?

b. How would you evaluate these plans, and which would you choose, assuming that the incremental cash flows are expected to last 8 years?

26-16   J. T. Tolleson, a young lawyer, is thinking of buying the legal practice of A. T. Mitchell, who wishes to retire. Mr. Mitchell lists the following assets devoted to his practice:

Cash...	$2,600
Office supplies..	300
Law library..	1,000
Office furniture and equipment.............................	3,000

Mr. Mitchell reports fees earned averaging $30,000 for the past few years, out of which he paid operating expenses of $7,000.

Required   a. To what extent should Mr. Tolleson consider the rate of return on assets in estimating the value of the property?

b. How would you recommend that he determine the amount he might be willing to pay for the practice?

26-17   Two projects, A and B, each require an initial investment of $1,000. Project A has an expected life of eight years, no salvage value, and expected net receipts of $245 annually. Project B has a five-year expected life, a salvage value of $1,000 at the end of the five years, and a 20 per cent expected time-adjusted rate of return (TAROR).

Required   a. Compute the time-adjusted rate of return for Project A.

b. Compute the expected net annual receipts for Project B.

c. Which project would you recommend and why?

d. Would your answer to part c be different if the net receipts of each project were to be reinvested at a return equal to the company's 8 per cent average cost of capital?

26-18   In considering the desirability of investing in Project X or Project Y, a company's controller proposes the following analysis:

	Project X	Project Y
Additional capital outlay	$25,000	$28,000
Estimated useful life......................................	7 years	10 years
Estimated salvage value..................................	0	0
Estimated net annual operating receipts (excluding depreciation)......................................	$ 5,000	$ 4,000

Required   a. Compute the time-adjusted rate of return on each project.

b. The company has noted a decline in the prospective and actual rates of return on its capital additions during the past few years. In view of this fact, which project would you advise the company to select? Explain.

26-19   Refer to Problem 26-18. Assume that both projects involve investments in depreciable assets, and that the company pays income taxes at a 50 per cent rate.

Required   a. Determine the after-tax time-adjusted rate of return for each project.

b. How does the income tax effect influence the decision reached in Problem 26-18?

26-20   A manufacturer is considering whether to invest $1,000 in a patented device that is expected to speed up its production process. The expected incremental yearly cost savings and their related probabilities are

Expected Cost Savings	Probability
$ 0	0.1
200	0.3
500	0.4
1,000	0.2

This device has an expected life of five years.

Required   a. What is the expected TAROR for this project?

b. Find the project's net present value assuming a discount rate of 10 per cent.

26-21   The Ricardo Corporation is considering a new plant in Brunnen. The plant is expected to have an initial cost of $80,000, a useful life of ten years, and no salvage value. Estimates of average annual revenues and operating costs (exclusive of deprecia-tion) and their probabilities of occurrence are

Estimated Revenues		Estimated Operating
Amount	Probability	Costs
$50,000	0.1	$42,000
60,000	0.2	50,000
70,000	0.4	56,000
80,000	0.2	65,000
90,000	0.1	70,000

Required
a. Compute the estimated time-adjusted rate of return, using the weighted average of the probabilities.
b. Compute the time-adjusted rate of return, assuming the most pessimistic results predicted.
c. How should the results in parts a and b be used in reaching a decision?

26-22   The following are examples of general problems that are often encountered in comparing the desirability of alternative uses of capital.

Required   Explain how you would handle each item in making such a comparison.

a. Machine A is expected to have a useful life of five more years; Machine B, an alter-native candidate to replace A, has an expected life of ten years.
b. Machine C is expected to result in greatest additional annual receipts in the early years of its life; Machine D, its competitor, is expected to result in greatest additional annual receipts in the late years of its life.
c. Machine E is expected to result in additional receipts of a stable annual amount throughout its life; Machine F, being considered as an alternative to it, may result in very high additional receipts or no additional receipts at all.
d. Machine G has an unamortized cost of $8,000. If it is replaced by Machine H, it can be sold for only $3,000. Machine H can be purchased outright for $20,000.
e. Machine I has an operating capacity of 9,000 units of product a year; Machine J, a proposed replacement, has a capacity of 25,000 units a year.
f. If Machine K is purchased to do work that is now done chiefly by hand, it will replace five men who now earn $7,000 a year each. The company's policy is to assign men displaced by technological improvements to other jobs in the business.

26-23   A real estate company owns two identical business buildings, each of which is leased for the next five years. The terms of each lease are as follows:

(1) The tenant of Building No. 1 has agreed to pay annual rent of $3,000 at the end of each year.
(2) The tenant of Building No. 2 has agreed to pay a minimum annual rental of $2,000 at the end of each year, and an additional amount equal to 1 per cent of the sum by which its net sales exceed $100,000. During the last three years the tenant has paid rentals of $1,480, $1,800, and $1,700, respectively.
Each building has annual operating costs (excluding depreciation) of about $400. Each has a resale value of $8,000 now, and is expected to have no salvage value at the end of five years.

Required   a. Compare the expected rates of return on the two buildings.

b. What other factors should be considered before deciding which asset is likely to provide the better return?

26-24   The Vital Distributing Company is considering changing its marketing system in one of two ways in order to improve its rate of return on total assets. In recent years its rate of net income before tax to total assets has been about 12 per cent per year. The estimated results of the two proposed plans, which are expected to have a life of three years, are

	Method 1	*Method 2*
Additional annual sales...	$60,000	$25,000
Additional annual operating expenses......................	51,000	18,000
Additional investment required in depreciable assets....	20,000	12,000

Capital for the expansion is readily available, partly from creditors and partly from stockholders.

Required   Evaluate the two methods.

26-25   "The unexpired cost of the asset to be replaced should be ignored in computing the difference in the capital cost of the old and new assets."

Early in 1973 management is considering replacing Machine 1, which was ten years old at the time. It had an original cost of $10,000 and an accumulated depreciation balance of $7,000. Machine 2, the possible replacement, has a cash cost of $12,000 without trade-in, or $7,000 if Machine 1 is traded. Machine 2 has an expected life of ten years while Machine 1 could conceivably be used for five more years.

Required   a. Present comparative condensed income statements for the five-year period affected by the decision, and state whether you think this comparison supports or disproves the quotation.
b. Show how another method of evaluating long-lived assets additions might help prove or disprove the quotation.

26-26   Lasser Corporation is considering installing one of two machines to handle additional business which is expected to last for the next six years. Estimated data for each machine are

	Machine A	*Machine B*
Cost...	$12,000	$14,000
Maximum output per year (units)..........................	2,000	2,500
Variable costs per unit of output...........................	3	3.50
Annual operating costs of machine........................	3,300	3,100
Annual depreciation...	2,000	2,500
Selling price per unit	6	6

All units produced can be sold. No additional working capital will be required.

Required   a. Compute the expected time-adjusted rate of return (before taxes) for each machine.
b. Compute the net present value for each (before taxes), assuming that an 8 per cent discount rate is considered appropriate.
c. Compute the unadjusted rate of return (before taxes) for each machine.

26-27   The Walker Company is considering acquiring one of the two labor-saving devices to which the following information pertains:

	Device No. 1	Device No. 2
Initial net cost..................................	$20,000	$18,000
Estimated annual operating savings.......	4,000	4,500
Estimated salvage value.....................	2,000	0
Estimated useful life.........................	7 years	5 years

Required

a. For each device compute the following (ignore income taxes):
   (1) The payback period.
   (2) The unadjusted rate of return.
   (3) The time-adjusted rate of return.
   (4) The net present value at a discount rate of 8 per cent.
b. Which device should the company buy? Why?

26-28   Refer to Problem 26-27.

Required

a. Compute the time-adjusted rate of return expected on each device, after allowing for federal income tax at 22 per cent on the first $25,000 and 48 per cent on the remainder. Other taxable income averages $20,000.
b. Explain how the use of the sum-of-the-years'-digits method for tax purposes would affect your answer.

26-29   The Martin Company is considering replacing existing Machine A with either new Machine B or C. Machine A was purchased three years ago at a cost of $20,000 and has been depreciated at the straight-line rate of 20 per cent.

Machine B has a list price of $33,000; a trade-in allowance of $4,500 will be given for Machine A. Machine C has a list price of $31,000, from which a trade-in allowance of $3,800 on Machine A will be deducted. Installation costs on either B or C will be $500.

As compared with Machine A, the new machines are expected to result in annual savings in operating costs as follows:

Year		Machine B	Machine C
1	....	$12,000	$ 7,000
2	....	9,000	7,000
3	....	7,000	7,000
4	....	5,000	7,000
5	....	2,000	7,000
Totals	....	$35,000	$35,000

Both machines B and C have an estimated life of five years and no expected salvage value.

Required

a. Using a rate of return of 8 per cent, compute the present value of the proposed investments in Machine B and Machine C.
b. If alternative investments of equal risk yield an 8 per cent return, what action would you recommend?
c. Would your answer in part c change if alternative investments of equal risk were yielding a 9 per cent return?

26-30   The Yarmouth Company estimates that $50,000 will be available for capital expenditures during 1973. Of this amount, $20,000 is to be reserved for emergency and nonpostponable projects. The company uses the payback period method to determine the most desirable capital expenditures. The following additions are being considered for 1973:

Project Number	Additional Capital Investment	Expected Annual Net Receipts	Estimated Life in Years
201	$10,000	$ 2,000	6
202	10,000	2,800	5
203	8,000	1,600	6
204	8,000	2,000	5
205	4,000	550	15
206	2,000	500	5
207	2,000	1,000	3
208	5,000	500	18
209	5,000	1,400	4
210	10,000	1,250	14

Required

a. Rank the projects in the order of their desirability under the payback-period method.

b. Compute the time-adjusted rate of return for each project (to the nearest per cent) assuming no expected salvage value of any of the above projects.

c. Explain any significant inconsistencies between your results in parts a and b.

d. Submit your recommended capital additions budget for 1973.

26-31 In a meeting on March 15, 1972, the board of directors of Zed Company authorized the construction of a new warehouse for the company at a total cost of $500,000. The project was expected to be started on May 1, 1972 and completed by April 30, 1974. Construction work was to be done by the company's own employees.

Construction began on May 22, 1972. On December 31, 1973, the following information was collected:

Costs incurred through Dec. 31, 1972......................................	$150,600
Costs incurred in 1973	$195,100
Unfilled orders for materials on Dec. 31, 1973.........................	15,000
Estimated percentage of total cost incurred through Dec. 31, 1973	65%
Estimated percentage of total construction time elapsed through Dec. 31, 1973..	60%

Required

a. Arranging the information in orderly form, prepare a Capital Additions Report for the board of directors as of December 31, 1973.

b. What additional information do you think might usefully be included in the report?

Cases

26-1 Carolina Equipment Company. In deciding on capital investment proposals which are expected to cost more than $5,000 and to last more than two years, the Carolina Equipment Company uses the time-adjusted rate of return method. The company reviews each such accepted investment shortly after installation and again at the end of one year of operation in order to find out whether the asset is operating according to plan.

In 1973 the company was considering whether to install a group of labor-saving machines which were expected to cost $20,000, to have a useful life of six years, and to reduce labor requirements by 3,000 man-hours a year at an average cost of $2.25 an hour. The machines were expected to require power at a cost of $450 a year, insurance and property taxes at $300 a year, and maintenance costs increasing gradually from $300 in the first year to $800 in the sixth. The machines were expected to have no net salvage value at the end of their lives and were to be depreciated by the straight-line method.

Estimating that the rate of return on this investment would be 2 per cent above its required minimum for outlays of this type, the company purchased the equipment early in 1974.

At the end of 1974, subsidiary records for equipment showed the following regarding these machines:

1/17/74	Invoice cost..	$20,000
	Transportation in	420
	Installation	480

The company had an unusually difficult time putting the machines into operating condition and charged $600, which it considered to be excessive installation cost, to 1974 expense. Maintenance for the year was $370, insurance $170, and power $435. No property taxes were assessed on the machines, because the company did not own them on January 1. It was estimated that the machines had actually saved 2,600 man-hours, but a new union contract went into effect on July 1, 1974, increasing the wage rate to $2.50 per hour. The deficiency in man-hours saved resulted largely from the excessive break-in period.

Required

a. Compute the rate of return which the company *expected* on this investment in 1973.
b. Compare the actual results for 1974 with the expected results.
c. By explanatory comments, evaluate the actual results of this investment.
d. Make, and justify, a revised estimate of the rate of return on the investment on the basis of all information which you have at the end of 1974.

26-2   Morgan Manufacturing Company. At the end of 1973 Morgan Manufacturing Company is trying to evaluate the relative desirability of acquiring Machine B or Machine C to replace Machine A, which is worn out. The machine selected will be used to make the company's entire output of Product No. XX-3, a staple article which the company sells for $1.20 a unit. The following information was taken from the accounting records for 1973:

Sales, 4,000 units at $1.20
Units produced, 4,000
Material cost, 13,200 lb at 15 cents
Operator's labor cost, 500 hr at $2
Depreciation on Machine A, $1,000
Property taxes and insurance, $100
Other variable costs, $0.05 per unit of product

Machine A had an original cost of $10,000 and its accumulated depreciation at the end of 1973 is $8,250. It could be sold outright for $1,000 cash, or traded in on either Machine B for $1,500 or Machine C for $2,000.

The following estimated data relate to Machines B and C:

	Machine B	*Machine C*
List price..	$10,000	$12,000
Estimated useful life...	10 years	10 years
Productive capacity, in units per year......................	6,000	10,000
Estimated salvage value...	0	0
Material usage per unit of product...........................	3 lb	3.4 lb
Cost of material per pound.....................................	0.14	0.14
Operator's labor time in hours per unit of product	0.10 hr	0.05 hr

	Machine B	Machine C
Operator's wage rate per hour..............................	$ 2.20	$ 2.50
Other variable costs per unit of product....................	$ 0.05	$ 0.05
Shipping cost of machine	$ 400	$ 600
Installation cost of machine	$ 200	$ 200
Machine insurance and property taxes per year	$ 300	$ 360
Fringe labor costs as a percentage of labor cost..........	20%	20%

The machine chosen will be operated by an employee who tends a group of similar machines. Machine C is semiautomatic, and although it will require the attention of a more skilled operator than will Machine B, it will require less of the operator's time. Machine C will cause a higher rate of scrap material, indicated by its greater usage of material per unit of product.

The sales manager expects that sales of Product No. XX-3 will average 5,000 units per year for the next few years.

Required

a. Prepare condensed estimated income statements for 1973, (1) assuming that Machine B is purchased and (2) assuming that Machine C is purchased. (Ignore income tax.)

b. Compute the unadjusted rate of return on each machine, before tax.

c. Compare the two machines on the basis of their time-adjusted rates of return, before tax.

d. List and evaluate the nonquantitative factors which you think are important in reaching a decision.

e. What is your recommendation, based on the information given? Support your decision with appropriate justification.

26-3 **The Investor Corporation.** The Investor Corporation is a diversified company with separate divisions operating in several different industries. The West Division was organized on January 1, 1973, to produce and sell a new product. The Investor Corporation's decision to invest in this new venture was based on an expected payback period of four years and a 24 per cent time-adjusted rate of return for the project. The actual rate of return for all divisions together has averaged 20 per cent. The West Division had net income of $80,000 in 1973, which gave ? 20 per cent rate of return on the divisional investment.

Required

a. Identify the important managerial accounting concepts referred to in the preceding paragraph and comment on their interrelationships.

b. Comment on the apparent effectiveness of the West Division's 1973 performance.

c. Compute the expected life of the project from the information given. List the main assumptions required to make your analysis.

part IV

ACCOUNTING
IN EVOLUTION

chapter 27

Accounting in Evolution

Purpose of Chapter

    The aim of earlier chapters of this book has been to present a balanced exposition of accounting as a useful source of financial information and as an analytical method for both management and other groups who are interested in the financial affairs of economic enterprises.

    As a means of analyzing and conveying information, accounting must evolve —and has evolved—in response to the changing knowledge, customs, and goals of society. The present chapter surveys some of the major forces which have influenced the historical development of accounting and examines some of the important trends which are influencing the current development of accounting.

The Origin of Double-Entry Accounting

    Frater Luca Paciolo, a Franciscan monk who lived in Italy, explained the operation of double-entry bookkeeping in his *Summa de Arithmetica, Geometria, Proportioni et Proportionalita*, which was published in Venice in 1494. The system, which had been developed during the preceding two centuries, was widely adopted and refined in the Italian commercial cities of the day. Soon it spread to other western countries, where it provided financial information which aided commercial expansion.

The developing tool of accounting was shaped primarily to serve the internal needs of each business unit. Early financial records kept by means of double-entry were concerned more with the quantities and types of business wealth (assets) and the claims against them than with the specific causes of changes in this wealth (revenue and expenses) which were related to business operations. Rarely were financial reports drawn from the financial records.

Increasing External Interest in Business Accounting

As businesses came increasingly to rely on the *credit* extended by their suppliers and bankers, the needs of creditors for financial information about their debtors were filled more frequently by the issuance of *financial statements.* This trend became pronounced in the United States in the latter part of the nineteenth century and the early part of the twentieth century. During this era the chief emphasis in financial statements was on financial position, and assets were commonly measured in terms of their *realizable values.* Many businesses did not even prepare income statements for the use of their stockholders and creditors, although such statements were becoming more widespread.

Ownership of large interests in American corporations by stockholders who took no active part in management grew during the early decades of the twentieth century. Trading in the ownership shares of corporations increased significantly. The stockholders and prospective stockholders came more and more to look upon their shares as *investments in going concerns of indefinite life.* As a result, the emphasis in financial reporting shifted from the realizable values of business assets to the *earning power* of a business which was expected to continue in operation. The income statement began to be considered more important than the financial position statement, with consequent emphasis on going-concern values rather than market values in accounting measurements.

The enactment of the federal income tax in 1913 and its revision in 1918 to recognize the *accrual basis* of measuring income spurred the interest of businesses in the careful measurement of income. As was pointed out in Chapter 17, however, the different objectives of income taxation and of general-purpose reporting of business income have led to significant divergences in the methods of measurement for the two purposes.

The stock market boom in the late 1920s brought with it an increasing interest in business-income measurement. The market crash of 1929 and its aftermath led to searching scrutiny of existing practices in selling and buying securities, as well as of financial reporting to stockholders. A special committee of the American Institute of Accountants (now the AICPA) on Cooperation with Stock Exchanges was organized to help educate the public as to the meaning and limitations of accounting reports and to take steps to make published reports more meaningful and reliable.

The Securities Act of 1933 and the Securities Exchange Act of 1934, both outgrowths of the stock market crash and the resulting investigations, have had an important influence on the requirements of accounting and on the quality of financial reporting. The latter act created the Securities and Exchange Commission, which has authority to specify the requirements for financial reports for those companies whose securities are listed on a national securities exchange or who wish to offer securities for sale to the public. As a representative of the interests of stockholders and of the public, the Securities and Exchange Commission has greatly helped the accounting profession to improve the quality of financial reporting. The SEC requires that financial statements submitted to it be accompanied by the audit report of the independent accountant who examined the statements.

The accounting profession has grown significantly both in number of members and in stature, rising to the challenge of the public clamor for more and better financial information. The American Institute of CPAs, through its research organizations, has issued bulletins to guide accountants in the application of accounting principles, in the use of terminology, and in conducting audits. The Accounting Principles Board, organized in 1959, has done much to improve accounting by sponsoring research studies dealing with current accounting problems and by issuing opinions to guide accounting practice.

There is by no means unanimity among accountants as to how to deal with all accounting and reporting problems. The remainder of this chapter explores some of these problem areas which are still largely unresolved.

Accounting Uniformity Versus Accounting Individuality

The increasing emphasis placed on the measurement of periodic business income as an aid in estimating the value of a continuing business entity has led to a demand for more uniformity in accounting. With repect to this demand, the Committee on Accounting Procedure of the AICPA[1] has said

> "*Uniformity* has usually connoted similar treatment of the same item occurring in many cases, in which sense it runs the risk of concealing important differences among cases. Another sense of the word would require that different authorities working independently on the same case should reach the same conclusions. Although uniformity is a worthwhile goal, it should not be pursued to the exclusion of other benefits. Changes of emphasis and objective as well as changes in conditions under which business operates have led, and doubtless will continue to lead, to the adoption of new accounting procedures. Consequently, diversity of practice may continue as new practices are adopted before old ones are completely discarded."

One of the objectives of the Accounting Principles Board of the AICPA, as stated in its Charter, was to exert a "continuing effort to determine appropriate practice and to narrow the areas of difference and inconsistency in practice."[2]

Again and again it has been stated in this book that accounting is a flexible

---

[1] *APB Accounting Principles*, Current Text as of Dec. 1, 1971, Par. 510.04 (New York: AICPA, 1971).

[2] "Report to Council of the Special Committee on Research Program," *Journal of Accountancy*, December 1958, p. 62.

tool whose specific features should be tailored to the needs of the individual business as much as conditions permit. Yet the greater the freedom that is permitted individual businesses in developing their accounting records and reports according to their own tastes, the greater is the likelihood that financial results will not be reported on a comparable basis from one business to another. In the absence of a reasonable degree of comparability of financial data between businesses, the stockholders, creditors, and other outside users of the financial statements will not be able to make *reliable comparative evaluations* of the financial progress and position of different businesses. Apparently the objectives of *uniformity and flexibility* in financial reporting are *in conflict* with each other. To what extent should each objective be pursued?

Many accountants are convinced that accounting principles are far too general, with the result that they allow too much latitude to businesses in the selection of accounting methods. Consequently, they feel financial statements lose much of their meaning to management, stockholders, creditors, and others. Some of the situations in which various acceptable accounting methods may result in significantly different measurements are summarized below.

There is wider agreement among businesses as to when revenue is realized than as to when costs expire. Still, the following major alternatives are found in business practice, and all are considered to comply with generally accepted accounting principles:

(1) Using the percentage-of-completion or the completed-contracts method of accounting for revenue under long-term construction contracts.

(2) Estimating in advance such revenue deductions as sales discounts, returns, and transportation cost, or waiting to deduct them in the future period in which their amounts are finally determined.

Many of the disagreements as to accounting method deal with the proper *allocation of costs* between accounting periods, past and future. Some important examples of alternative methods which are in wide use are the following:

(1) The FIFO, LIFO, average-cost, specific-identification, and lower-of-cost-or-market methods of measuring the unexpired cost of inventoriable items to be allocated to future periods. (By the same process, the remainder is assigned to the current period as an expired cost.)

(2) The straight-line, production, declining-balance, and sum-of-the-years'-digits methods of allocating the cost of depreciable assets to the periods of their useful life.

(3) Charging research and development costs directly to expense in the period in which they are incurred, or treating them as assets (unexpired costs) to be matched against the revenue from the resulting products in future periods.

(4) Charging exploration costs and intangible development costs (costs of drilling and developing wells exclusive of the cost of tangible equipment) of oil and gas properties to expense in the period in which they are incurred, or matching them against the revenue of future periods when the benefits are received.

(5) Allocating such intangible assets as goodwill and organization costs to an arbitrarily small number of years, in contrast to treating them as assets with a life of up to forty years.

Another major area of difference in the application of accounting principles is the question whether to use a broad or a narrow concept of *liabilities* in assigning to the current year's income statement costs which are *likely* (but not certain) to be paid in the future. In recent years there has been an increasing tendency in accounting practice to use a broad, rather than a narrow, concept of liabilities in order to provide a better matching of revenue and expense.

A further source of differences between the financial statements of various firms has resulted from different interpretations of *when a new accounting entity arises*. Under generally accepted accounting principles, a firm's assets should be accounted for on the basis of historical-cost prices until they are exchanged in market transactions for other assets—unless there is clear-cut evidence that their unexpired cost cannot be recovered through future sale. Equities are likewise accounted for on the basis of values established in past market transactions. Just what factors are necessary to determine that a new entity has resulted from a changes in ownership interests, and that a new basis of valuing assets and equities must be established? This has been a vexing problem for accountants.

Implicit in the procedures which accountants use in measuring and reporting business transactions is the *assumption that the monetary unit has the same significance* from one time to another. In times of relatively stable general price levels this assumption leads to reasonably dependable results. In recent history, however, there have been many more periods of price increases than of price decreases. As a result of the accountant's assumption of a stable monetary unit, assets which are acquired in one year and recorded in terms of that year's dollars are recorded in the same accounts, and added to, the costs of similar assets bought at other times in exchange for dollars of *unequal significance*. Likewise, in computing business income, costs which are stated in terms of money payments made at different times, and which represent different amounts of purchasing power per unit of money, are deducted from revenues which are expressed in monetary units of relatively current purchasing power. As a result of the changed significance of the money measuring unit from year to year, the items reported in the financial position statement and the income statement are not comparable to each other. The effect of this noncomparability is accentuated when computing the percentage of income to the assets invested in the firm.

Efforts of the Accounting Principles Board To Improve Comparability

Recent opinions of the Accounting Principles Board in the following areas have done a great deal to improve the comparability of financial statements between firms.

(1) In accentuating the trend toward a broader definition of liabilities, the APB has required that
    (a) Estimated costs of *pension plans*, though not certain, must be charged to expense of the current year and credited to a liability.
    (b) *Income tax allocation* procedures are required where there are material differences caused by reporting revenues and expenses at one time in the financial statements and at a different time in the income tax returns.
    (c) *Long-term leases* which are leases in name only must be treated as a

purchase of an asset and a creation of a liability. Treating them as *leases* would be indicated by the *form* of the contract without regard to its economic *substance.*

(2) The APB has developed guides for determining when a combination of corporations results in a *purchase* of one by the other, with a new basis of accountability being required of the company purchased, and when it is a *pooling* of interests, justifying a continuation of the historical basis of accounting for the assets and equities of both combining companies.

(3) The APB has established criteria for reporting extraordinary gains and losses in the income statement and correction of prior years' income in the retained income statement.

(4) The APB has established guidelines for reporting the effects of price-level changes on the accounts by means of reports supplementary to the primary income statement, financial position statement, and statement of retained income.

Unsettled Question of Reporting Current Values

Chapter 16 distinguished between the problem of reporting the effects of *general price-level changes* in the accounts and that of reporting *current prices of individual financial statement components.* The Accounting Principles Board has recognized the need of some firms to report the effects of general price-level changes on them by means of supplementary financial statements. Advocates of this reporting procedure contend that it is not a departure from the historical basis of accounting, but merely allows for the *changed significance of the measuring unit,* the dollar.

Reporting the effects of specific changes in the values of assets before the changes are confirmed by sale is quite a different concept. Such reporting would be contrary to established accounting principles, although *unrealized losses* are shown in the accounts as soon as they are supported by adequate evidence.

There are those who would like to see *unrealized gains,* as well as unrealized losses, reported in the financial statements when they are supported by reliable evidence. They argue that a *holding gain,* whether realized or not, is just as much a part of business income as a gain realized when an asset is sold. For example, they would consider increases in the quoted prices of highly salable assets, such as marketable securities, to be proper components of business income. The preponderance of current accounting thought, however, does not support taking unrealized gains into the accounts.

Current Developments in Management Accounting

Most of the issues discussed earlier in this chapter are important not only to the outside user of the financial statements of a business, but also to the management in its planning and control of business affairs. The following topics deal with recent developments in accounting that relate more particularly to management accounting.

The importance of psychology in management control. Earlier chapters have described the general framework of an internal management control system which can be employed to help keep the business moving toward accomplishing its objectives. It has been pointed out that business management is carried on through *people*, and that the best of management control systems and procedures will fail unless the people are motivated to operate these systems properly. It is difficult to overemphasize the importance of this point. In recent years there has been a growing body of knowledge of the forces which motivate the *behavior* of individuals and groups in the business environment. An understanding of these forces is essential to getting the best results from the system of management control. Future research seems likely to provide more useful knowledge in this area.

The increased use of statistical and mathematical methods. In recent years there has been an increasing use of statistical and mathematical methods in the solution of accounting and other business problems. The use of statistics in analyzing costs into their fixed and variable components is a relatively old application. Sampling is now widely used in both internal and independent auditing as a means of verifying the reliability of the accounting system without checking every transaction.

Statistical sampling techniques have been applied in determining which variances of cost from standard are significant enough to warrant investigation and which variances can be safely ignored. Statistical methods are also useful in some cases in estimating aggregate sums, such as total sales revenue, total cost of goods sold, and the like, without the necessity of measuring each individual transaction. These methods, referred to as *inductive accounting*, permit the reporting of important information currently and at relatively low cost by removing the necessity of summarizing every individual transaction before reporting totals.

The use of *subjective probabilities* in estimating the outcomes of alternative courses of business action has been very helpful in making operating and capital budgeting decisions. This methodology seems likely to be used more extensively in the future.

Mathematical methods have been particularly useful in solving such problems as determining the optimum quantity to carry in inventory or the optimum size of a production order so as to minimize total costs.

Electronic data processing. Technology in computers has changed rapidly in the last decade or two. At first accountants looked on computers chiefly as means of processing existing information more rapidly. Now it is being increasingly realized that computers can be used to furnish information that it was not feasible to obtain before. They can also be used to make routine decisions, such as reporting an out-of-stock condition for inventory, placing replenishing orders, and even making many of the calculations necessary in such decisions as those involved in capital budgeting.

Applicability of Accounting to Nonbusiness Entities

The foregoing exposition of accounting has highlighted its role in the decisions of business managers, stockholders, creditors, and others who have significant financial interests in the affairs of a business. This emphasis has perhaps obscured the essential part that accounting plays in the financial management of nonbusiness institutions, such as governments, schools, hospitals, clubs, and other organizations whose objectives are generally to provide service, rather than to maximize the income of the owners.

Most of the features of accounting are applicable to these organizations, except for income determination in the ordinary case. Even the accounting principles of income measurement apply to those functions of governments and institutions which parallel functions of private enterprise, such as the management of governmentally owned utilities and similar activities.

The Future of Accounting

The American Institute of Certified Public Accountants, the American Accounting Association, the Financial Executives Institute, the National Association of Accountants, the Securities and Exchange Commission, and other organizations have made noteworthy contributions to the development of accounting principles and the solution of current accounting problems. Undoubtedly the research effort of the AICPA which was inaugurated in 1959 will strengthen the principles on which modern accounting rests and increase the extent to which accepted accounting principles are applied in practice. In the future, however, accounting will most likely continue to evolve in response to the changing needs of business and of society in general. No doubt there will continue to be a lag between the best in theoretical principles and the majority of actual practice, although it is to be hoped that the lag will shortened.

It is still very important that accurate accounts be kept of the historical financial transactions of business. Although this chapter has emphasized some of the challenges to accounting based on historical measurements, these measurements still play a vitally important role in the management of a business and in the interpretation of its financial results by outside users of financial statements.

Discussion Questions and Problems

27-1   In the latter part of the nineteenth century and the early part of the twentieth century the outside users of business financial statements were chiefly bankers and other major creditors.

a. In what types of financial information were these creditors typically interested? How did their interest affect the methods which were used in measuring assets?
b. In many European countries today most business financing is derived from internal sources and from bankers, and the importance of markets for capital shares is rather limited. Under these circumstances, what do you suppose would be the most important financial statement? How would accounting measurements be affected?

27-2   Some people have contended that accounting principles should be precisely defined in detail so that the accounting profession and enterprise management can apply them to any situation which might arise, thus reducing the latitude within which the accountant must exercise his judgment.

a. What are the advantages and disadvantages of such an approach? Do you think it is desirable? Explain.
b. Do you think that it is feasible? Explain.

27-3   It has been suggested that accounting principles be given the force of law, and that there should be a high court of accounting which decides questions or disputes regarding the proper application of these principles. Are you in favor of this recommendation? Why?

27-4

a. What does the term "generally accepted" mean with relation to accounting principles?
b. If accounting principles must be generally accepted to be valid, what are the implications for progress in accounting?

27-5   "All the disagreement about when revenues are realized, and what specific costs should be matched against them, could be avoided if we reflected revenues in the accounts only as they were collected in cash and expenses as they were paid in cash. This method is both simple and objective." Do you agree with this statement? Why?

27-6   Accountants generally agree that when a new group of owners acquires a going business, the basis of accounting for the business assets should be changed.

a. How should the assets be measured after the sale of the business?
b. If stockholders who own 10 per cent of the stock of a business sell their shares to others, should the basis of measuring the business assets be changed? Why? What would your answers be if 60 per cent of the stock were sold?
c. How would your answers in part b be changed if the business were a partnership instead of a corporation?

27-7   Accounting describes and measures the forms, sources, and changes of economic factors and relationships in a business.

a. What are some of the important economic factors affecting the value of a business which a prospective buyer of a large interest in it should consider, but which are not in the accounting records? Why are they not in the accounts?
b. Are any of these items which are not usually reflected in the accounts ever properly included in the accounts of a business? Under what circumstances?

27-8   "We place too much emphasis on the market-place in accounting. Why should we wait until a product is sold to recognize revenue, and then treat the entire gain as though it occurred at the instant the product is sold? This denies the value of production, and it ignores the importance of such obvious physical changes as the growth of the timber in a forest, or the growth of cattle being fattened for sale."

a. Do you agree with the criticism expressed in this statement? If so, what exceptions to customary accounting practices would you recommend?
b. Describe a situation in which accounting does recognize income in proportion to production. Why is this justified under current accounting thought?

27-9   "Accountants do a pretty good job of matching the so-called *product* costs with revenue, but their matching of many *period* costs with revenue is often subject to question."

a. What is meant by "product" costs? Explain the accounting method used in matching them with revenue.
b. Give an example of a period cost which you consider to be properly matched with revenue under present accounting practices.

c. Give an example of a period cost which you consider to be improperly matched with revenue under present practices. How would you recommend that it be handled?

27-10

a. Is the process of assigning depreciation of long-lived assets to accounting periods based on amounts determined in market transactions?
b. Is the estimate made of the useful life of the depreciable asset based on objective evidence?
c. In view of your answers in parts a and b, is depreciation accounting justified under generally accepted accounting principles? Explain.

27-11   "We cannot base our financial accounting on predictions; it must be based on dependable, objective facts."

a. Do you agree with this statement? Explain.
b. What exceptions are there to this policy in customary accounting practice? How, if at all, can you justify each exception?

27-12   "When considering the problems of wide variations in accounting methods between businesses, coupled with rapidly changing price levels, the only financial ratio that has real meaning for the analyst is the quick ratio."

a. Do you agree with this statement? Explain.
b. If you agree, would you recommend that the financial analyst not compute any other ratios? Why?

27-13   Two of the important functions of a certain medium-sized city government are providing police protection and operating a city water works. The police department is financed from the general property taxes of the city, and the customers of the water works are charged in proportion to the metered quantity of water they use.

a. How can accounting be useful in each of these situations?
b. To what extent do you think that a modification of generally accepted accounting principles and customary practices would be needed for each?

27-14   The Conservative Company takes advantage of all opportunities for income tax postponement in its income tax return, and also uses the income tax-reporting methods in its financial statements. It uses the sum-of-the-years'-digits depreciation method and charges research and development costs to expense when they are incurred.

Its account balances at the end of 1973, after ordinary adjustments for the period, were

	Debit	Credit
Current assets	$ 70,000	
Accounts payable		$ 20,000
Federal income tax payable		24,000
Equipment	150,000	
—Accumulated depreciation		90,000
Capital stock		35,000
Retained income		15,000
Sales revenue		1,000,000
Depreciation	40,000	
Income tax expense	24,000	
Other expenses	900,000	
Totals	$1,184,000	$1,184,000

The company was organized on January 1, 1972, and purchased all its equipment at that time. No salvage value is anticipated. Research and development costs incurred in 1973 amounted to $60,000, of which 10 per cent is thought to have benefited 1973. The income tax rate is 40 per cent.

It is expected that equal benefits will be received from the equipment each year and that the business will continue indefinitely.

Required   Show in parallel columns condensed financial statements (1) as prepared by the company and (2) as they should be prepared under generally accepted accounting principles. Pay particular attention to proper matching of income tax with the income to which it relates.

Appendices

APPENDIX I

Future Value of $1 at Compound Interest (a)

Periods (n)	2%	3%	4%	5%	6%	8%	10%
1	1.0200	1.0300	1.0400	1.0500	1.0600	1.0800	1.1000
2	1.0404	1.0609	1.0816	1.1025	1.1236	1.1664	1.2100
3	1.0612	1.0927	1.1249	1.1576	1.1910	1.2597	1.3310
4	1.0824	1.1255	1.1699	1.2155	1.2625	1.3605	1.4641
5	1.1041	1.1593	1.2167	1.2763	1.3382	1.4693	1.6105
6	1.1262	1.1941	1.2653	1.3401	1.4185	1.5869	1.7716
7	1.1487	1.2299	1.3159	1.4071	1.5036	1.7138	1.9488
8	1.1717	1.2668	1.3686	1.4775	1.5938	1.8509	2.1436
9	1.1951	1.3048	1.4233	1.5513	1.6895	1.9990	2.3589
10	1.2190	1.3439	1.4802	1.6289	1.7908	2.1589	2.5938
11	1.2434	1.3842	1.5395	1.7103	1.8983	2.3316	2.8532
12	1.2682	1.4258	1.6010	1.7959	2.0122	2.5182	3.1385
13	1.2936	1.4685	1.6651	1.8856	2.1329	2.7196	3.4524
14	1.3195	1.5126	1.7317	1.9799	2.2609	2.9372	3.7976
15	1.3459	1.5580	1.8009	2.0709	2.3966	3.1722	4.1774
16	1.3728	1.6047	1.8730	2.1829	2.5404	3.4259	4.5951
17	1.4002	1.6528	1.9479	2.2920	2.6928	3.7000	5.0545
18	1.4282	1.7024	2.0258	2.4066	2.8543	3.9960	5.5600
19	1.4568	1.7535	2.1068	2.5270	3.0256	4.3157	6.1160
20	1.4859	1.8061	2.1911	2.6533	3.2071	4.6610	6.7276
30	1.8114	2.4273	3.2434	4.3219	5.7435	10.0627	17.4495
40	2.2080	3.2620	4.8010	7.0400	10.2857	21.7245	45.2597

APPENDIX II
Present Value of $1 at Compound Interest (p)

Periods (n)	1%	2%	3%	4%	5%	6%	8%	10%	12%	14%	16%	18%	20%	22%	24%	26%	28%	30%	40%
1	0.990	0.980	0.971	0.962	0.952	0.943	0.926	0.909	0.893	0.877	0.862	0.847	0.833	0.820	0.806	0.794	0.781	0.769	0.714
2	.980	.961	.943	.925	.907	.890	.857	.826	.797	.769	.743	.718	.694	.672	.650	.630	.610	.592	.510
3	.971	.942	.915	.889	.864	.840	.794	.751	.712	.675	.641	.609	.579	.551	.524	.500	.477	.455	.364
4	.961	.924	.888	.855	.823	.792	.735	.683	.636	.592	.552	.516	.482	.451	.423	.397	.373	.350	.260
5	.951	.906	.863	.822	.784	.747	.681	.621	.567	.519	.476	.437	.402	.370	.341	.315	.291	.269	.186
6	.942	.888	.837	.790	.746	.705	.630	.564	.507	.456	.410	.370	.335	.303	.275	.250	.227	.207	.133
7	.933	.871	.813	.760	.711	.665	.583	.513	.452	.400	.354	.314	.279	.249	.222	.198	.178	.159	.095
8	.923	.853	.789	.731	.677	.627	.540	.467	.404	.351	.305	.266	.233	.204	.179	.157	.139	.123	.068
9	.914	.837	.766	.703	.645	.592	.500	.424	.361	.308	.263	.225	.194	.167	.144	.125	.108	.094	.048
10	.905	.820	.744	.676	.614	.558	.463	.386	.322	.270	.227	.191	.162	.137	.116	.099	.085	.073	.035
11	.896	.804	.722	.650	.585	.527	.429	.350	.287	.237	.195	.162	.135	.112	.094	.079	.066	.056	.025
12	.887	.788	.701	.625	.557	.497	.397	.319	.257	.208	.168	.137	.112	.092	.076	.062	.052	.043	.018
13	.879	.773	.681	.601	.530	.469	.368	.290	.229	.182	.145	.116	.093	.075	.061	.050	.040	.033	.013
14	.870	.758	.661	.577	.505	.442	.340	.263	.205	.160	.125	.099	.078	.062	.049	.039	.032	.025	.009
15	.861	.743	.642	.555	.481	.417	.315	.239	.183	.140	.108	.084	.065	.051	.040	.031	.025	.020	.006
16	.853	.728	.623	.534	.458	.394	.292	.218	.163	.123	.093	.071	.054	.042	.032	.025	.019	.015	.005
17	.844	.714	.605	.513	.436	.371	.270	.198	.146	.108	.080	.060	.045	.034	.026	.020	.015	.012	.003
18	.836	.700	.587	.494	.416	.350	.250	.180	.130	.095	.069	.051	.038	.028	.021	.016	.012	.009	.002
19	.828	.686	.570	.475	.396	.331	.232	.164	.116	.083	.060	.043	.031	.023	.017	.012	.009	.007	.002
20	.820	.673	.554	.456	.377	.312	.215	.149	.104	.073	.051	.037	.026	.019	.014	.010	.007	.005	.001
21	.811	.660	.538	.439	.359	.294	.199	.135	.093	.064	.044	.031	.022	.015	.011	.008	.006	.004	.001
22	.803	.647	.522	.422	.342	.278	.184	.123	.083	.056	.038	.026	.018	.013	.009	.006	.004	.003	.001
23	.795	.634	.507	.406	.326	.262	.170	.112	.074	.049	.033	.022	.015	.010	.007	.005	.003	.002	
24	.788	.622	.492	.390	.310	.247	.158	.102	.066	.043	.028	.019	.013	.008	.006	.004	.003	.002	
25	.780	.610	.478	.375	.295	.233	.146	.092	.059	.038	.024	.016	.010	.007	.005	.003	.002	.001	
26	.772	.598	.464	.361	.281	.220	.135	.084	.053	.033	.021	.014	.009	.006	.004	.002	.002	.001	
27	.764	.586	.450	.347	.268	.207	.125	.076	.047	.029	.018	.011	.007	.005	.003	.002	.001	.001	
28	.757	.574	.437	.333	.255	.196	.116	.069	.042	.026	.016	.010	.006	.004	.002	.002	.001	.001	
29	.749	.563	.424	.321	.243	.185	.107	.063	.037	.022	.014	.008	.005	.003	.002	.001	.001	.001	
30	.742	.552	.412	.308	.231	.174	.099	.057	.033	.020	.012	.007	.004	.003	.002	.001	.001		
40	.672	.453	.307	.208	.142	.097	.046	.022	.011	.005	.003	.001	.001						

APPENDIX III

Present Value of an Annuity of $1 at Compound Interest ($P$)

Periods (n)	1%	2%	3%	4%	5%	6%	8%	10%	12%	14%	16%	18%	20%	22%	24%	25%	26%	28%	30%	40%
1	0.990	0.980	0.971	0.962	0.952	0.943	0.926	0.909	0.893	0.877	0.862	0.847	0.833	0.820	0.806	0.800	0.794	0.781	0.769	0.714
2	1.970	1.942	1.913	1.886	1.859	1.833	1.783	1.736	1.690	1.647	1.605	1.566	1.528	1.492	1.457	1.440	1.424	1.392	1.361	1.224
3	2.941	2.884	2.829	2.775	2.723	2.673	2.577	2.487	2.402	2.322	2.246	2.174	2.106	2.042	1.981	1.952	1.923	1.868	1.816	1.589
4	3.902	3.808	3.717	3.630	3.546	3.465	3.312	3.170	3.037	2.914	2.798	2.690	2.589	2.494	2.404	2.362	2.320	2.241	2.166	1.849
5	4.853	4.713	4.580	4.452	4.329	4.212	3.993	3.791	3.605	3.433	3.274	3.127	2.991	2.864	2.745	2.689	2.635	2.532	2.436	2.035
6	5.795	5.601	5.417	5.242	5.076	4.917	4.623	4.355	4.111	3.889	3.685	3.498	3.326	3.167	3.020	2.951	2.885	2.759	2.643	2.168
7	6.728	6.472	6.230	6.002	5.786	5.582	5.206	4.868	4.564	4.288	4.039	3.812	3.605	3.416	3.242	3.161	3.083	2.937	2.802	2.263
8	7.652	7.325	7.020	6.733	6.463	6.210	5.747	5.335	4.968	4.639	4.344	4.078	3.837	3.619	3.421	3.329	3.241	3.076	2.925	2.331
9	8.566	8.162	7.786	7.435	7.108	6.802	6.247	5.759	5.328	4.946	4.607	4.303	4.031	3.786	3.566	3.463	3.366	3.184	3.019	2.379
10	9.471	8.983	8.530	8.111	7.722	7.360	6.710	6.145	5.650	5.216	4.833	4.494	4.192	3.923	3.682	3.571	3.465	3.269	3.092	2.414
11	10.368	9.787	9.253	8.760	8.306	7.887	7.139	6.495	5.988	5.453	5.029	4.656	4.327	4.035	3.776	3.656	3.544	3.335	3.147	2.438
12	11.255	10.575	9.954	9.385	8.863	8.384	7.536	6.814	6.194	5.660	5.197	4.793	4.439	4.127	3.851	3.725	3.606	3.387	3.190	2.456
13	12.134	11.348	10.635	9.986	9.394	8.853	7.904	7.103	6.424	5.842	5.342	4.910	4.533	4.203	3.912	3.780	3.656	3.427	3.223	2.468
14	13.004	12.106	11.296	10.563	9.899	9.295	8.244	7.367	6.628	6.002	5.468	5.008	4.611	4.265	3.962	3.824	3.695	3.459	3.249	2.477
15	13.865	12.849	11.938	11.118	10.380	9.712	8.559	7.606	6.811	6.142	5.575	5.092	4.675	4.315	4.001	3.859	3.726	3.483	3.268	2.484
16	14.718	13.578	12.561	11.652	10.838	10.106	8.851	7.824	6.974	6.265	5.669	5.162	4.730	4.357	4.033	3.887	3.751	3.503	3.283	2.489
17	15.562	14.292	13.166	12.166	11.274	10.477	9.122	8.022	7.120	6.373	5.749	5.222	4.775	4.391	4.059	3.910	3.771	3.518	3.295	2.492
18	16.398	14.992	13.754	12.659	11.690	10.828	9.372	8.201	7.250	6.467	5.818	5.273	4.812	4.419	4.080	3.928	3.786	3.529	3.304	2.494
19	17.226	15.678	14.324	13.134	12.085	11.158	9.604	8.365	7.366	6.550	5.877	5.316	4.844	4.442	4.097	3.942	3.799	3.539	3.311	2.496
20	18.046	16.351	14.877	13.590	12.462	11.470	9.818	8.514	7.469	6.623	5.929	5.353	4.870	4.460	4.110	3.954	3.808	3.546	3.316	2.497
21	18.857	17.011	15.415	14.029	12.821	11.764	10.017	8.649	7.562	6.687	5.973	5.384	4.891	4.476	4.121	3.963	3.816	3.551	3.320	2.498
22	19.660	17.658	15.937	14.451	13.163	12.042	10.201	8.772	7.645	6.743	6.011	5.410	4.909	4.488	4.130	3.970	3.822	3.556	3.323	2.498
23	20.456	18.292	16.444	14.857	13.489	12.303	10.371	8.883	7.718	6.792	6.044	5.432	4.925	4.499	4.137	3.976	3.827	3.559	3.325	2.499
24	21.243	18.914	16.936	15.247	13.799	12.550	10.529	8.985	7.784	6.835	6.073	5.451	4.937	4.507	4.143	3.981	3.831	3.562	3.327	2.499
25	22.023	19.523	17.413	15.622	14.094	12.783	10.675	9.077	7.843	6.873	6.097	5.467	4.948	4.514	4.147	3.985	3.834	3.564	3.329	2.499
26	22.795	20.121	17.877	15.983	14.375	13.003	10.810	9.161	7.896	6.906	6.118	5.480	4.956	4.520	4.151	3.988	3.837	3.566	3.330	2.500
27	23.560	20.707	18.327	16.330	14.643	13.211	10.935	9.237	7.943	6.935	6.136	5.492	4.964	4.524	4.154	3.990	3.839	3.567	3.331	2.500
28	24.316	21.281	18.764	16.663	14.898	13.406	11.051	9.307	7.984	6.961	6.152	5.502	4.970	4.528	4.157	3.992	3.840	3.568	3.331	2.500
29	25.066	21.844	19.188	16.984	15.141	13.591	11.158	9.370	8.022	6.983	6.166	5.510	4.975	4.531	4.159	3.994	3.841	3.569	3.332	2.500
30	25.808	22.396	19.600	17.292	15.372	13.765	11.258	9.427	8.055	7.003	6.177	5.517	4.979	4.534	4.160	3.995	3.842	3.569	3.332	2.500
40	32.835	27.355	23.115	19.793	17.159	15.046	11.925	9.779	8.244	7.105	6.234	5.548	4.997	4.544	4.166	3.999	3.846	3.571	3.333	2.500

APPENDIX IV
Future Value of an Annuity of $1 at Compound Interest ($A$)

Periods (n)	1%	2%	3%	4%	5%	6%	8%	10%
1	1.0000	1.0000	1.0000	1.0000	1.0000	1.0000	1.0000	1.0000
2	2.0100	2.0200	2.0300	2.0400	2.0500	2.0600	2.0800	2.1000
3	3.0301	3.0604	3.0909	3.1216	3.1525	3.1836	3.2464	3.3100
4	4.0604	4.1216	4.1836	4.2465	4.3101	4.3746	4.5061	4.6410
5	5.1010	5.2040	5.3091	5.4163	5.5256	5.6371	5.8666	6.1051
6	6.1520	6.3081	6.4684	6.6330	6.8019	6.9753	7.3359	7.7156
7	7.2135	7.4343	7.6625	7.8983	8.1420	8.3938	8.9228	9.4872
8	8.2857	8.5830	8.8923	9.2142	9.5491	9.8975	10.6366	11.4360
9	9.3685	9.7546	10.1591	10.5828	11.0266	11.4913	12.4876	13.5796
10	10.4622	10.9497	11.4639	12.0061	12.5779	13.1808	14.4866	15.9376
11	11.5668	12.1687	12.8078	13.4864	14.2068	14.9716	16.6455	18.5314
12	12.6825	13.4121	14.1920	15.0258	15.9171	16.8699	18.9771	21.3846
13	13.8093	14.6803	15.6178	16.6268	17.7130	18.8821	21.4953	24.5231
14	14.9474	15.9739	17.0863	18.2919	19.5986	21.0151	24.2149	27.9755
15	16.0969	17.2934	18.5989	20.0236	21.5786	23.2760	27.1521	31.7731
16	17.2579	18.6393	20.1569	21.8245	23.6575	25.6725	30.3243	35.9503
17	18.4304	20.0121	21.7616	23.6975	25.8404	28.2129	33.7502	40.5456
18	19.6147	21.4123	23.4144	25.6454	28.1324	30.9057	37.4502	45.6001
19	20.8109	22.8406	25.1169	27.6712	30.5390	33.7600	41.4463	51.1601
20	22.0190	24.2974	26.8704	29.7781	33.0660	36.7856	45.7620	57.2761
30	34.7849	40.5681	47.5754	56.0849	66.4388	79.0582	113.2832	164.4962
40	48.8864	60.4020	75.4013	95.0255	120.7998	154.7620	259.0565	442.5974

Index

A